THIRD EDITION

CULTURAL PSYCHOLOGY

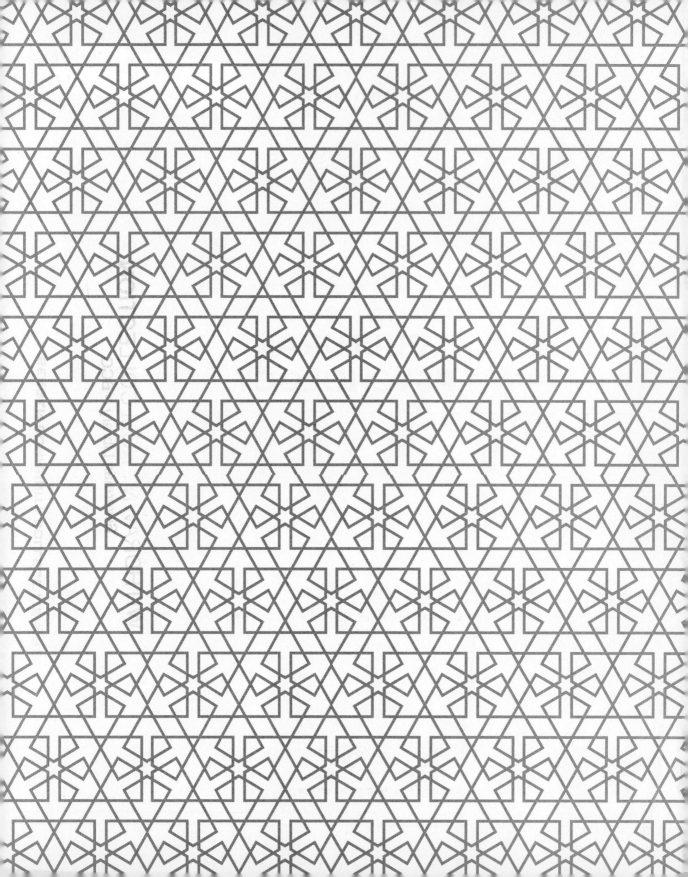

THIRD EDITION

CULTURAL PSYCHOLOGY

STEVEN J. HEINE

UNIVERSITY OF BRITISH COLUMBIA

W. W. NORTON
NEW YORK LONDON

W. W. Norton & Company has been independent since its founding in 1923, when William Warder Norton and Mary D. Herter Norton first published lectures delivered at the People's Institute, the adult education division of New York City's Cooper Union. The firm soon expanded its program beyond the Institute, publishing books by celebrated academics from America and abroad. By midcentury, the two major pillars of Norton's publishing program—trade books and college texts—were firmly established. In the 1950s, the Norton family transferred control of the company to its employees, and today—with a staff of four hundred and a comparable number of trade, college, and professional titles published each year—W. W. Norton & Company stands as the largest and oldest publishing house owned wholly by its employees.

EDITOR: Ken Barton
PROJECT EDITOR: Rachel Mayer
ASSISTANT EDITOR: Scott Sugarman
MANUSCRIPT EDITOR: Jackie Estrada
MANAGING EDITOR, COLLEGE: Marian Johnson
MANAGING EDITOR, COLLEGE DIGITAL MEDIA: Kim Yi
PRODUCTION MANAGER: Jane Searle
MEDIA EDITOR: Patrick Shriner
ASSOCIATE MEDIA EDITOR: Stefani Wallace
MARKETING MANAGER, PSYCHOLOGY: Lauren Winkler
DESIGN DIRECTOR: Rubina Yeh
DESIGNER: Jillian Burr
PHOTO EDITOR: Evan Luberger
PHOTO RESEARCHER: Julie Tesser
PERMISSIONS MANAGER: Megan Jackson
COMPOSITION/ILLUSTRATIONS: Graphic World
MANUFACTURING: Webcrafters, Inc.

Permission to use copyrighted material is included beginning on C-1.

Library of Congress Cataloging-in-Publication Data

Heine, Steven J.
    Cultural psychology / Steven J. Heine, University of British Columbia.—Third edition.
        pages cm
    Includes bibliographical references and index.
    ISBN 978-0-393-26398-5 (pbk.)
    1. Ethnopsychology.   I. Title.
    GN502.H45 2015
    155.8'2--dc23
    2015022957

W. W. Norton & Company, Inc., 500 Fifth Avenue, New York, NY 10110-0017
wwnorton.com

W. W. Norton & Company Ltd., Castle House, 75/76 Wells Street, London W1T 3QT

1 2 3 4 5 6 7 8 9 0

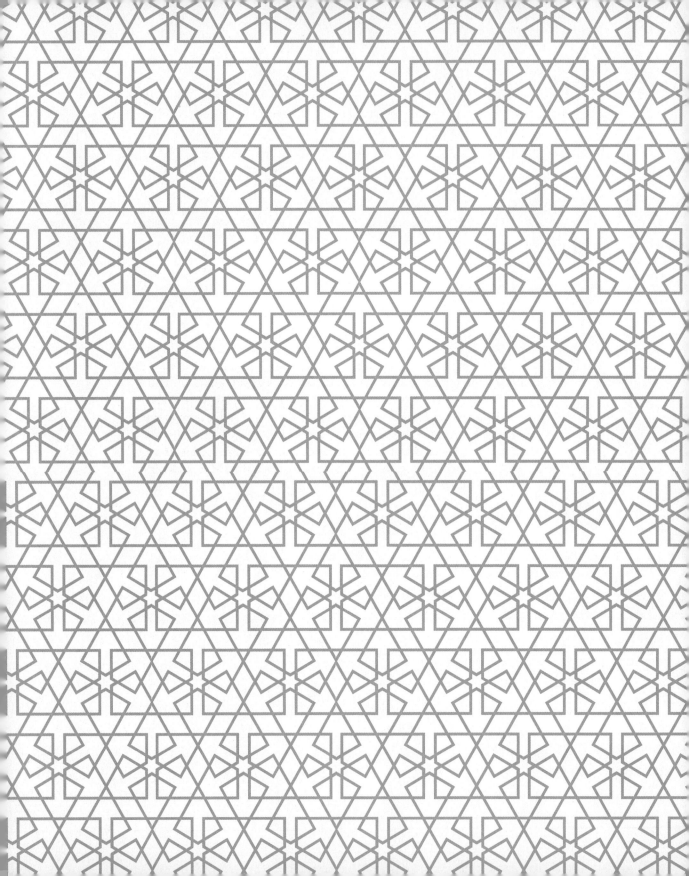

About the Author

Steven J. Heine is Professor of Social and Cultural Psychology and Distinguished University Scholar at the University of British Columbia. His research focuses on meaning, genetic essentialism, and cultural influences on motivations. He has published over seventy articles in such periodicals as *Science, Nature, Behavioral and Brain Sciences,* and *Psychological Review.* He received the Distinguished Scientist Early Career Award for Social Psychology from the American Psychological Association in 2003 and the Career Trajectory Award from the Society of Experimental Social Psychology in 2011. He lives with his family in Vancouver.

CONTENTS IN BRIEF

CONTENTS

xi

5 DEVELOPMENT AND SOCIALIZATION 159

6 SELF AND PERSONALITY 203

PREFACE

My own quest to become a cultural psychologist began upon graduating college. There I was with my BA degree in psychology, not knowing what to do with it. So, I moved to the small town of Obama in southwestern Japan (yes, it really was the town's name) to teach English and, hopefully, figure out what I wanted to do with my life. I thought I had been an attentive student in my psychology classes, and I had learned much about how people think. Imagine, then, my surprise upon moving to rural Japan and discovering that much of what I thought I understood about human nature didn't seem to explain how my new friends and colleagues thought and behaved. I went through a series of cross-cultural misunderstandings and gaffes before I came to realize that my ideas about human nature were just plain wrong—they may have explained the nature of North Americans, but they weren't so useful outside of that cultural context. This was interesting to me because from what I had learned in my psychology classes, people *should* think in the same ways everywhere. But in many ways they don't. That insight and those embarrassing cross-cultural misunderstandings led me down the path to becoming a cultural psychologist and eventually to writing this book.

Cultural psychology, as a field, is largely a new discipline, and it continues to produce striking evidence that challenge psychologists' understanding of human nature. In contrast to much conventional wisdom, this new field has been revealing that culture shapes how people's minds operate—sometimes in profound ways. The past couple of decades have been an exciting time, as an abundance of new research continues to demonstrate that culture is not just a thin veneer covering the universal human mind. Rather, this research has shown just how deeply cultural influences penetrate our psychology and shape the ways that people think. The research underscores how human thoughts occur within cultural contexts, and shows that different cultural contexts can lead to fundamentally different ways of thinking.

When I first started teaching cultural psychology, I greatly enjoyed teaching students about the exciting discoveries coming out of this new field. However, there wasn't really an undergraduate textbook that adopted a cultural psychological perspective. Without a textbook, teaching a course in cultural psychology usually meant having students read the original journal articles describing these new ideas. This made for stimulating classroom discussions, but it also meant that my courses on cultural psychology were typically limited to small seminars for senior students. I discussed this problem with cultural psychologists at other universities, and many said they were in the same situation. Cultural psychology had become a tremendously interesting and important discipline, and had rapidly developed a rich theoretical and empirical foundation unique from other approaches that considered the influences of culture. But at that point, the field lacked an undergraduate textbook that could be used in large lecture classes on cultural psychology, and consequently, very few students were learning about it. I reluctantly came to the realization that the quickest way that I could start teaching larger cultural psychology classes was to write a textbook myself. But it wasn't as easy as I thought it would be, as at first, I failed to appreciate just how much new and significant research was being conducted. In fact, the First Edition of this title took me four years to complete. And even now, as I send the Third Edition to the presses, there is much new and fascinating work that I unfortunately wasn't able to include in time for the deadline.

I tried to write a book focused on what I have found most interesting about the field of cultural psychology. Toward this end, I have written the chapters around some provocative key questions with which cultural psychologists are still struggling. For example, one theme that arises repeatedly throughout the book is the question, how similar are the psychologies of people from different cultures. Human brains are basically the same everywhere, yet people's experiences are vastly divergent, making this a difficult and important question to contemplate. Some other fundamental questions I address include: Where does culture come from? How are humans similar to and different from other animals? What are the many different ways to be human?

I also endeavored to integrate as much cultural diversity into the topics discussed as possible. The text considers research findings from every populated continent, including many investigations of subsistence cultures around the world, as well as explorations of the variance between ethnic groups within countries. I also wrote the chapters to provide a strong emphasis on experimental research throughout, while also paying particular attention to observation studies and ethnographies. I think it's important to gain a sense of the varieties of ways that we can go about studying culture. I also wanted to highlight how culture underlies all aspects of human psychology, so I have attempted to explore the role of culture across many disciplines both within psychology (e.g., clinical, cognitive, developmental, social, and personality psychology), and outside psychology (e.g., anthropology, evolutionary biology, linguistics, philosophy, sociology). Finally, students will find many detailed examples throughout the book that show how cultural psychologists' theories and research are relevant to their lives. Hopefully, the combination of these ingredients will yield an interesting and educational experience for the readers.

For Instructors

The instructor resources are outlined below.

Art PowerPoints

To aid instructors in quickly and easily creating their own visual aids linked directly to the student textbook, the art, tables, and charts from the book are available as JPEGs and in Art PowerPoints.

Lecture PowerPoints

Lecture PowerPoints, featuring many of the tables and charts from the book, as well as definitions of key terms and original figures, can be used as is or customized for each individual classroom.

Test Bank

The test bank features 490 questions, including 35 multiple-choice and 5 short answer questions in each chapter. All questions have been updated according to Norton's assessment guidelines to make it easy for instructors to construct quizzes and exams that are meaningful and diagnostic. All questions are classified according to educational objective, student text section, difficulty, and question type. The test bank is available in PDF and RTF formats.

Acknowledgments

I was very fortunate to receive an enormous amount of support in writing this book. First, this book would not exist without the sage guidance, clear-eyed vision, and unflagging encouragement on the part of my first editor, Jon Durbin, who worked very closely with me in the conceiving of and writing of the First Edition. Likewise, I am indebted to Sheri Snavely for her inspiration and keen judgment that led to the Second Edition. And I am especially grateful to the clever insights, persistent efforts, and creativity of my editor for this Third Edition, Ken Barton. I'm also very grateful to the rest of the terrific staff at W. W. Norton & Company: Jillian Burr, Evan Luberger, Rachel Mayer, Jane Searle, Patrick Shriner, Scott Sugarman, Julie Tesser, Stefani Wallace, and Lauren Winkler, who have endeavored behind the scenes and have made many important contributions to this book. I am also greatly appreciative of the extremely thoughtful and helpful comments I received from many reviewers, who I list below.

Previous Editions
Glenn Adams, *University of Kansas*
David Armor, *San Diego State University*
Mary Jo Carnot, *Chadron State College*
Jonathan Haidt, *New York University*
Stephan Mayer, *Oberlin College*
Ashleigh Merrit, *University of Texas*
Beth Morling, *University of Delaware*
Richard Nisbett, *University of Michigan*
Fernando Romero, *Glendale Community College*
Julie Spencer-Rodgers, *California Polytechnic State University, San Luis Obispo*

Third Edition
Michael Bender, *Tilburg University*
Thierry Devos, *San Diego State University*
Matt J. Goren, *University of California, Berkeley*
Igor Grossmann, *University of Waterloo*
Jeanne Marecek, *Swarthmore College*
Alex Mesoudi, *Durham University*
Karen Phalet, *Catholic University of Leuven*
Nick Rule, *University of Toronto*
Anre Venter, *University of Notre Dame*
Jennifer Wang, *University of Wisconsin–La Crosse*

This book benefited from several discussions over the years with my formal mentors, Darrin Lehman and Shinobu Kitayama, from whom I learned how to become a cultural psychologist, as well as from informal mentors who have educated me from afar, such as Dov Cohen, Hazel Markus, Dick Nisbett, and Paul Rozin. Also, hundreds of conversations over coffees or beers, or on ski lifts with the other members of the Human Evolution, Cognition, and Culture Centre at UBC—Mark Collard, Joe Henrich, Ara Norenzayan, Mark Schaller, and Ted Slingerland—have been instrumental for developing many of the ideas discussed in this book. I am deeply indebted to the daily conversations that I have with my wife, Nariko Takayanagi, on all matters cultural and Japanese, which have served to inform both the research I have conducted and the ideas that are in this book. I am especially grateful to Ben Cheung for his careful feedback of this Third Edition, and for his excellent work on the accompanying instructor's manual. I would also like to thank Andrew Ryder for his guidance in writing the mental health chapter. A number of my lab coordinators, including Matt Loewen, Louise Chim, Aiyana Willard, Eric Wong, Jenna Becker, and Hee Jin Kim played a key role in helping me conduct background research for the material in the book. Several chapters of this text also benefited from the feedback of many readers, including Emma Buchtel, Edith Chen, Ilan Dar-Nimrod, Takeshi Hamamura, Greg Miller, Janet Werker, and Katie Yoshida, as well as from the many undergraduates who sat as willing and patient guinea pigs as I tried out various drafts of the chapters with them in class. These readers all offered excellent advice, helping to make this a stronger text overall.

STEVEN J. HEINE
Vancouver, British Columbia
April, 2015

THIRD EDITION

CULTURAL PSYCHOLOGY

Unlike most readers of this textbook, this Kalahari San man does not see the Müller-Lyer illusion as an illusion. You need to grow up in an environment with carpentered corners to be susceptible to this key visual illusion.

1

WHAT IS CULTURAL PSYCHOLOGY?

Humans are an interesting bunch. If a team of alien biologists arrived at our planet and tried to catalog all the different species here, they would no doubt notice how peculiar we humans are. In many ways, we would seem to be ill adapted to survive. We're not particularly strong, we're not very fast, we don't have sharp teeth or claws, and we don't even have a furry coat to keep us warm. Furthermore, we don't ensure the survival of our species through rampant reproduction, like rabbits. The alien biologists would surely wonder what kind of strange beasts we are. The odds would certainly seem stacked against us. Yet despite the apparent disadvantages that humans have compared to other species, the alien biologists would notice that we've populated more parts of the world, in more diverse ecologies, using a broader range of subsistence systems and social arrangements, than any other species. And our numbers keep growing. How is it that humans have come to be so successful?

If these alien biologists were very keen, though, they might note that we humans do have one adaptation that compensates for all that we lack. Humans have culture. We rely on culture more than any other species, and it is our reliance on culture that has allowed us to succeed in such diverse environments. And this reliance on culture has important and profound implications for our thoughts and behaviors. Cultural psychology is the field that studies those implications.

A Psychology for a Cultural Species

One does not need to take a course on cultural psychology to recognize that humans are a cultural species. This fact is immediately evident whenever you travel to a different country or meet people from different cultural backgrounds. In many ways, people from different cultures live their lives differently; they speak different languages, have different customs, eat different foods, have different religious beliefs, have different child-rearing practices, and so on. Much about a person's lifestyle can be predicted just by knowing his or her culture.

Cultural psychology is not original in highlighting the many obvious ways that people's experiences differ around the planet. The unique contribution of cultural psychology, and the main thesis of this book, is that people from different cultures also differ in their psychology. One theme that will be returned to throughout this book is the notion that *psychological processes are shaped by experiences*. Because people in different cultures have many different experiences, we should then expect to find differences in many ways that they think. As you read through this book, I encourage you to examine the kinds of experiences that you have had and the ways that you think, and contrast them to the descriptions provided of people from other cultures.

Although experiences shape psychological processes, they clearly do not determine them. Psychological processes are constrained and afforded by the neurological structures that underlie them. And because the brains that people are born with are virtually identical around the world, people from all cultures share the same constraints and affordances of the universal human brain. Herein lies a challenge for making sense of virtually all cross-cultural studies in psychology: To what extent should ways of thinking look similar around the world because people share a universal brain, and to what extent should they look different because people have divergent experiences? Providing an answer to this question is not always straightforward, because some ways of thinking do appear to be highly similar around the world whereas others appear strikingly different. This tension between *universal and culturally variable psychologies* is another theme that will be addressed throughout this book. As you read through the various descriptions of psychological phenomena, I encourage you to ask yourself whether the evidence suggests that the phenomena are universal or culturally variable.

This chapter provides an overview of how culture is considered by psychologists. We explore questions such as how culture shapes the ways we think, how we can understand ways of thinking as being culturally universal or variable, why it can be important to understand cultural differences, and how the field of cultural psychology came to be.

What Is Culture?

This book investigates the relations between culture and the ways that people think and, as such, it's necessary to clearly define culture. The question of what culture is has been debated among anthropologists, sociologists, and psychologists for decades, and there is no single consensual answer that applies to all fields. Some people have focused on the symbolic aspects of culture, some have attended to the physical artifacts of culture, and some have emphasized the habits that are contained in culture.

In this book, I use the term "culture" to mean two different things. First, I use the term to indicate a particular kind of *information*. Specifically, I use culture to mean *any kind of information that is acquired from other members of one's species through social learning that is capable of affecting an individual's behaviors* (see Richerson & Boyd, 2005). In other words, *culture* is any kind of idea, belief, technology, habit, or practice that is acquired through learning from others. Humans are therefore a cultural species, as people have a great deal of "culture" that fits this definition.

Second, I use the term "culture" to indicate a particular *group of individuals*. Cultures are people *who are existing within some kind of shared context*. People within a given culture are exposed to many of the same cultural ideas. They might attend the same cultural institutions, engage in similar cultural practices, see the same advertisements, follow the same norms, and have conversations with each other on a day-to-day basis. At the most global level, sometimes I use the term "culture" to refer to broad swaths of the earth's population, which may even include people from a large number of different countries. For example, I often use the term "Western culture" in this book to refer to people participating in cultures that stem from countries clustered in northwestern Europe (e.g., the United Kingdom, the Netherlands, France, and Germany) and societies of British descent such as the United States, Canada, and Australia.

There are a few challenges with thinking about groups of people as constituting cultures. First, as you can see from the above definition, the boundaries of cultures are not always clear-cut. For example, individuals might be exposed to cultural ideas that emerge from distant locations, such as those from their immigrant parents, experiences that they have while traveling, advertisements that they see from multinational firms, or ideas that they learn from watching a foreign movie. Cultural boundaries are thus not distinct. Although we can never be certain that we have identified a clear cultural boundary that separates two or more samples, a shorthand practice used in many studies described in this book is to look at nationality as a rough indicator of culture. For example, Italians may be compared with Germans, even though we know that not every member of the Italian group was exposed to exclusively Italian cultural messages.

Adding to this complexity, there are other kinds of groups aside from countries that can be argued to have cultures. For example, you can hear people speak of Jewish culture, urban culture, gay and lesbian culture, high socioeconomic status culture, vegetarian culture, Millennial culture, Harvard culture, Mac-user culture, or Trekkie culture. What makes these groups arguably qualify as "cultures" is that their members exist within a shared context, communicate with each other, have some norms that distinguish them from other groups, and have some common practices and ideas. The more that people who belong to these groups share similar norms and communicate with each other, the more these groups warrant the label "culture." But, as you can imagine, there aren't always going to be firm boundaries that distinguish any of these groups. The fluid nature of cultural boundaries weakens researchers' abilities to find differences between cultures, but when such differences are found, they provide powerful evidence that cultures do differ in their psychological tendencies.

A second challenge, as will be described in Chapter 3, is that cultures also change over time, and some shared cultural information disappears as new habits replace the old (although much cultural information persists across time as well). Cultures are thus not static entities but are dynamic and ever changing.

Last, and perhaps the most important challenge in considering cultures as groups of people, is the variability among individuals who belong to the same culture. People inherit distinct temperaments (they are born with predispositions toward having certain kinds of personality traits, abilities, and attitudes), they each belong to a unique collection of various social groups with their own distinctive cultures (for example,

Jason grew up on Oak Street, attended King George Elementary School, often met with his extended family of several cousins, played on the Maple Grove junior soccer team, was in the band at Carnegie High School, and was a founding member of the *Perspectives* school newspaper that he worked on for three years), and they each have had a unique history of individual experiences that has shaped their views. Hence, all of these individual differences lead some people to reflexively embrace certain cultural messages, staunchly react against other cultural messages, and largely ignore some other cultural messages. Individuals are nothing if not variable, and the findings that are identified in the studies reported in this book do not apply equally to all members of cultures; the studies reflect average tendencies within cultural groups, and sometimes those cultural groups are extremely broad, such as contrasts between "Western" cultures and "East Asian" cultures (the latter encompassing cultures that have been exposed to Chinese Confucian cultural traditions, such as China, Japan, Korea, and Vietnam). So to say that Westerners are more emotionally expressive than East Asians would mean that, on average, people from Western cultures score higher on some measure of emotional expressiveness than people from East Asian cultures, yet there is also an enormous degree of individual variation that includes some extremely expressive East Asians and some quite unexpressive Westerners. Cultural membership does not determine individual responses.

In this latter sense, then, the term "culture" refers to dynamic groups of individuals that share a similar context, are exposed to many similar cultural messages, and contain a broad range of different individuals who are affected by those cultural messages in divergent ways.

Psychological Processes Can Vary Across Cultures

Much of this book focuses on numerous psychological processes that emerge in quite different ways across cultures. Some kinds of cultural variation in psychology may already be familiar to you, as you can observe the differences directly yourself. For example, one striking way that people's psychology differs between cultures is their sense of humor. What is funny in some cultures might not be seen as that funny in others. The American comedian Jerry Lewis was enormously popular in the 1950s in the United States, but his style of slapstick humor ultimately lost much of its appeal for American audiences. Despite the fact that Lewis had not starred in a successful comedy in the United States since his famous role in *The Nutty Professor* in 1963, his zany humor continued to be appreciated by the French for decades. He was regularly praised by French cinema critics, and in 2006 Lewis received the Légion d'honneur from the French minister of culture for being "French people's favorite clown." Likewise, although the American sitcom *Seinfeld* has enjoyed enormous success in the United States, being named by *TV Guide* in 2002 as the "greatest television show of all time," it flopped miserably in Germany because most Germans did not find it funny. Yet Germans continued to watch, and love, the 1960s-era American sitcom *Hogan's Heroes*. Cultures differ so much in their humor preferences that some Hollywood studios are apparently steering away from making comedy movies, because even if a comedy ends up being a big hit domestically, it usually won't be appreciated, in, say, China (unless, curiously, the film stars Adam Sandler) and typically won't bring in as much revenue from the international box office (Obst, 2011).

The observation that people's sense of humor differs is something you may have noticed yourself if you've watched foreign comedies or have friends from other countries. I think that these kinds of readily observable cultural differences in preferences are the ways that most people think about cultural variation: People from other cultures are different because they like different kinds of jokes, prefer different kinds of food, wear different clothes, worship different gods, vote for political parties with different concerns, and so on. Such differences in preferences are familiar to us because we see similar kinds of differences in preferences among people from our own culture. But as you'll learn from this book, cultural variation in psychological processes can extend much deeper than just preferences. Many basic psychological processes, such as the ways people perceive the world, their sense of right and wrong, and the things that motivate them, can emerge in starkly different ways across cultures. And the fact that basic psychological processes vary in important ways across cultures raises a difficult question: How can we understand the workings of the human mind when it apparently works in different ways in different contexts? Arguments for cultural variability in psychological processes are controversial, and this controversy reveals the differing underlying assumptions that are embraced by many psychological researchers.

Is the Mind Independent from, or Intertwined with, Culture?

Richard Shweder, who is viewed by many to be the father of the modern incarnation of cultural psychology, argues that much of the field of psychology (what he calls **general psychology**) inherently assumes that the mind operates under a set of natural and universal laws that are independent from content or context (Shweder, 1990). He argues that the guiding assumption of general psychology is one captured in the lyrics of a song by Paul McCartney and Stevie Wonder: "People are the same wherever you go." Surely, in many ways people really are the same wherever you go, and some researchers have attempted to document the many ways that people's thinking can be said to be the same across all cultures. For example, in all cultures people speak a language using between 10 and 70 phonemes, they all smile when they are happy, they all have a word for the color black, they are all disgusted at the idea of incest between parents and children, and they all understand the number 2. A list of all the human universals that have been documented can be found in a 12-page chapter in the fascinating book *Human Universals* (Brown, 1991). The study of human universals is a highly interesting, albeit enormously challenging, enterprise that tells us a great deal about human nature. We can learn much about how the mind works by identifying the universal and invariant ways that it operates.

However, in many important ways people are *not* the same wherever you go. For example, in some languages pronouns can be dropped while in others they cannot, people in some cultures bite their tongues when they are embarrassed whereas people in other cultures do not, some languages do not have a word for blue, people in some cultures are disgusted at the idea of incest between cousins whereas people in other cultures are not, and in some cultures people do not understand the number 5. The study of human variability is also a very interesting and challenging enterprise that greatly informs our understanding of human nature and of the ways that the mind operates.

If you have taken a course on introductory psychology before, think back to the questions that were investigated in that course. Was it a course primarily on what all humans share in common, or was it primarily a course on the ways that some people think differently from others? Shweder argues that general psychologists, perhaps as captured in your intro psychology course, tend to be more captivated by arguments about human universality than about cultural variability. This interest in universality, Shweder proposes, arises because general psychologists tend to conceive of the mind as a highly abstract central processing unit (CPU) that operates independently of the content that it is thinking about or of the context within which it is thinking. The underlying goal of general psychology, as Shweder sees it, is to provide glimpses of the CPU operating in the raw so that we can understand the set of universal and natural laws that govern human thought. Context and content are viewed as unwanted noise that cloud our ability to perceive the functioning of the CPU, and thus elaborate experiments are conducted in the highly controlled environment of the laboratory to provide the purest view of the CPU. The computer metaphor here is no accident; indeed, the CPUs in computers do largely function independently of content and context. The wiring between the different semiconductors is not affected by the context that they are in, nor of the content that they are processing. The mind as computer is a metaphor that has been embraced so strongly within general psychology that many of the theories could equally be applied to computers as to human brains.

According to this perspective of general psychology, important cultural variation in ways of thinking cannot exist because cultures merely provide variations in context and content that lie *outside* the operations of the underlying CPU. If cultural differences do appear in psychological studies, this universalist perspective would suggest that they must reflect the contamination of various sources of noise, such as translation errors, or the differences in familiarity that people have with being in psychological experiments. They could not reflect differences in the CPU because it is universally the same across all contexts. General psychology would argue, then, that virtually all of human psychology is universally experienced in similar ways.

In contrast, an assumption that tends to be embraced by cultural psychologists is that in many ways the mind does *not* operate independently of what it is thinking about. According to this view, thinking is not merely the operation of the universal CPU; thinking also involves interacting with the content that one is thinking about and participation in the context within which one is doing the thinking. Cultural psychologists would argue that to fully understand the mind it is important to consider, say, whether one is thinking about food, weapons, sexual partners, or sacred rituals. It is critical to consider whether one's behaviors increase one's status within the community, violate a law, demonstrate affection to one's child, or are consistent with religious doctrine. Furthermore, the ways that people think about these kinds of behaviors are influenced by the very specific and particular ways that cultural knowledge shapes their understanding of those behaviors. Because humans are cultural beings, their actions, thoughts, and feelings are immersed in cultural information, and this information renders these actions, thoughts, and feelings to be *meaningful* (see Bruner, 1990, for an in-depth discussion). That is, these actions, thoughts, and feelings come to relate to other things beyond them.

For example, the simple act of an American college student going out to have a cappuccino might mean for that student a chance to quench her thirst, a demonstration that she has quit her diet, an effort to wake herself up so she can study, or an opportunity to pursue a romantic partner. The identical action can come to take on different meanings, and the potential meanings that are available are influenced by the cultural context within which they occur. For example, in some other cultural contexts women going to coffee shops on their own is not seen as appropriate, people do not strive for ideal body weights that are less than what they currently have, it can be seen as sinful to seek artificial stimulants to obtain energy, and romantic relationships are typically arranged by family members rather than sought out by individuals themselves. That is, the same array of meanings that may be derived from the experience of an American college student going to a coffee shop are not available in all cultures; instead, other arrays of meaning are available there. Humans seek meaning in their actions, and the shared ideas that make up cultures provide the kinds of meanings that people can derive from their experiences. Cultural meanings are thus entangled with the ways that the mind operates, and we cannot consider the mind separate from its culture.

Cultural psychology's challenge to general psychology may strike you as somewhat heretical; is there any empirical evidence that mind is enmeshed with cultural influences? Much of the rest of this book will provide such evidence, but for now here is one pithy example. Take a look at the boxes in **Figure 1.1**. This kind of box with a line is used in what is known as the figure-line task (Kitayama, Duffy, Kawamura, & Larsen, 2003). In this task, participants are shown a box that has a line drawn inside

Look at the stimulus. Do not measure the length of the line in it.

Stimulus

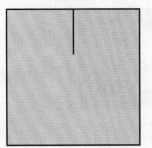

FIGURE 1.1

Try for yourself: Analytic versus holistic perception.

In the "absolute task" square, draw a line that is as close as possible to the absolute length of the line in the stimulus. Then, in the "relative task" square, draw a line that is as close as possible to the relative length of the line in the stimulus—that is, the line should be one-third the height of the "relative task" square. Measure each of your lines with a ruler.

Absolute Task

Relative Task

Result:
The "absolute" line should be 12 mm long. The "relative" line should be 6 mm long.

Explanation:
As we'll explore more in Chapter 9, people from Western cultures tend to perform better at the absolute task. People from non-Western cultures tend to perform better on the relative task. Which task were you more accurate in? Is this result consistent with what researchers would expect, given your cultural background?

of it. They are then shown two smaller boxes and are asked to (a) draw a line in the first box that is identical in length to the line shown in the top "stimulus" figure (this is termed an *absolute length task*), and then (b) in the second small box, to draw a line that is identical in proportion to its box as the original line is in proportion to the stimulus box (about 1/3—this is termed the *relative length task*).

In one study, university students who were either of European-American cultural background or who had recently moved to the United States from East Asia had their brains scanned using functional magnetic resonance imaging (fMRI) while making

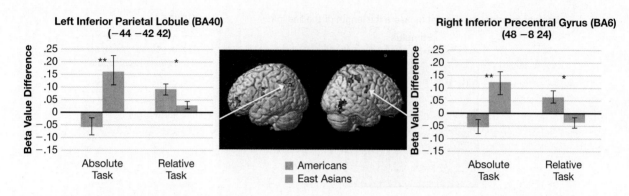

FIGURE 1.2 Americans show more activation of these regions (which are associated with intentional control) when engaged in the relative task. East Asians show more activation of these same regions when performing the absolute task (Hedden et al., 2008).

judgments with the figure-line task (Hedden, Ketay, Aron, Markus, & Gabrieli, 2008). The results are shown in **Figure 1.2**. When European-Americans completed the relative length task, they showed more activation in the left inferior parietal lobule and the right precentral gyrus than they did when they completed the absolute length task. These two regions of the brain are both associated with attentional control, indicating that the relative length judgment was more difficult for the European-Americans and required more concentration than the absolute length judgment. In contrast, when the East Asians made the same judgments, they showed more evidence of attentional control when they completed the absolute length task compared with the relative length one. That is, the East Asians found the absolute length judgment to be especially difficult, which is a finding that replicates much past research (e.g., Kitayama et al., 2003), and indicates cultural differences in analytic versus holistic reasoning, as we'll explore in more detail in Chapter 9. The same task, then, elicits different patterns of brain activation across cultures. The experiences that East Asians and European-Americans have had in their lives come to differentially shape how their brains respond to simple tasks involving estimating the lengths of lines. This is an example of how mind and culture cannot be disentangled; the mind is shaped by its experiences, and cultures differ in the kinds of experiences that they provide.

But how could the brain be shaped by cultural experiences? Here is where the utility of the brain as computer metaphor really starts to break down. Unlike computers, brains continue to change, grow, and rewire themselves in response to their experiences. Brains are highly plastic throughout our lives, especially when we are young. Our hardware changes in response to what we do. One famous example is a study that was done on taxi drivers in London. Cabbies in London are faced with daily challenges of navigating one of the busiest and most complex street grids in the world. As they gain experience over the years, they create detailed mental maps that aid them in figuring out what is the best way to get from point A to point B. And importantly, their experience in navigating through these mental maps actually changes the structure of their brains. The posterior region of the hippocampus facilitates spatial memory in navigation (O'Keefe & Nadel, 1978). In fact, small mammals and birds that depend on spatial memory for food storage have unusually large volumes in their hippocampi relative to other related species (Lee, Miyasato, & Clayton, 1998). Similarly, the taxi drivers in London develop larger volumes of the posterior region of their hippocampi relative to other humans. It's not the case that people with exceptional navigational skills (and large posterior hippocampi) become taxi drivers; rather, driving a cab leads to better navigational skills and a larger posterior hippocampus. The study found that the longer a London taxi driver has been driving a cab, the larger his posterior hippocampus had become (Maguire, Gadian, Johnsrude, Good, Ashburner, et al., 2000).

This study is not unique, and several other studies have found evidence that physical aspects of the brain change in response to experience, such as increasing amounts of gray matter in certain regions of the brain when people learn how to juggle (Draganski et al., 2004; **Figure 1.3**) or engage in mindfulness practice (Hölzel

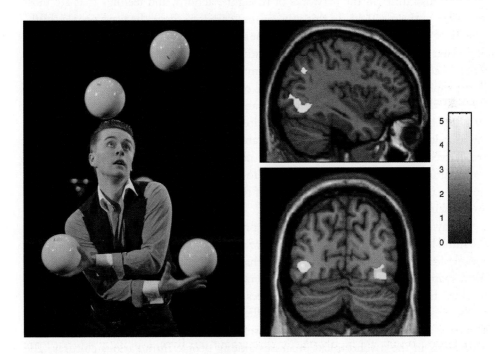

FIGURE 1.3 Experiences come to shape the brain. When people learn how to juggle they show an increase in volume of gray matter in the regions highlighted in the brain scan.

et al., 2011). Regularly encountered experiences can thus ultimately come to change the structure of the brain. The nature of the brain is not fixed from birth, but rather changes in the response to certain experiences. And because cultures provide people with particular sets of experiences on a daily basis, we can see how cultural influences could change their brains. Although people around the world are all born with relatively the same brains, with time, they come to have different brains by way of their different cultural experiences.

Cultural psychologists tend to explain cultural differences in psychological processes as follows: To the extent that people in one culture are faced with a particular cultural idea (e.g., the belief that it is good for children to become independent from their parents at a young age), they will think a great deal about that idea, creating a rich network of thoughts, behaviors, and feelings that surround it. These networks of information will be activated whenever people encounter something that reminds them of this idea, be it a conversation that they hear, a memory of what has happened in the past, the situation they are in, or their impressions that others around them are concerned with this idea. If people consider these networks of information often enough, the networks should become chronically activated, such that they come to mind and become prioritized ahead of other networks of information that are less likely to be activated. Because cultures differ in the ideas their members frequently encounter, they will also differ in the networks of thoughts, actions, and feelings that are most accessible to the members. In this way, culture comes to shape the ways people think.

Many cultural psychologists would thus view as ultimately misguided the goal of general psychology to understand the mind after it has been stripped clear of the noise of content and context. Because human thought is sustained by the meaning that people pursue, any efforts to bleach out this meaning to more clearly reveal the underlying CPU would only distort and misrepresent what the mind actually is. Humans are so embedded in their cultural worlds that they are always behaving as cultural actors, and their thoughts are always sustained by the meanings that are derived from their cultures. There are no occasions when people step outside of their cultural meaning systems and start to think instead like the universal human (see Geertz, 1973, for a rich elaboration of this); people's thoughts are forever bound up in their own cultural meaning systems.

Many cultural psychologists would argue that culture cannot be separated from the mind because *culture and mind make each other up.* Cultures emerge from the interaction of the various minds of the people that live within them, and cultures then, in turn, shape the ways that those minds operate. And because cultures often do differ in dramatic ways in terms of their practices, institutions, symbols, artifacts, beliefs, and values, the ways that people from different cultures think, act, and feel should also vary in important ways. Cultural psychologists thus expect to find significant differences in the psychological processes among people from various cultures. The remaining chapters in this book will elaborate on those differences.

Case Study: The Sambia

Discussions of cultural differences in psychological processes are often quite controversial. The controversy seems to rest on the contrasting views of the mind inherent in the perspectives of general psychology (i.e., the mind operates independently of content and context) and cultural psychology (i.e., the mind is shaped by content and context). I have had countless discussions and debates with other psychologists about various cultural differences in ways of thinking. In many instances we disagree about whether the observed cultural difference reflects a deep difference in the ways that people from different cultures think (which is usually the position that I take) or whether it represents a superficial difference of no significance or is the product of some kind of bias in the experimental design (which is often the position that my opponents take). In many of these instances, we can have a good debate because the evidence is such that there is room to interpret it in either way. People who have received psychological training are often rather resistant to accepting the idea of real cultural differences in ways of thinking, and I anticipate that many of the readers of this book will be similarly resistant. As an initial effort to demonstrate that psychological differences between cultures can run deep, I describe here a case study of the Sambia (for a more detailed exploration, see the ethnography by Herdt, 2006). It represents one of the more dramatic instances of a cultural difference that is covered in this book.

The Sambia live in an expansive valley perched high up a mountain range, over a mile above sea level, in the eastern highlands of Papua New Guinea. Their environment is one of the least accessible places on the planet. Until a few decades ago, they had been a ferocious warring people, engaged in constant battles with neighboring tribes in the valley. Today, they are largely peaceful, and they exist by hunting and by cultivating taro gardens and pandanus nut groves. However, one cultural practice has persisted since their warring days: their initiation practices to transform young boys into men (**Figure 1.4**).

The Sambia believe that femaleness is an innate natural essence, whereas maleness is a tenuous essence that must be explicitly cultivated. Boys are viewed as existing in the female world, hanging out with their mother, and doing what are viewed as female tasks, such as babysitting and weeding. Boys are believed to be contaminated from their mother's wombs, they are seen as too dependent on their mothers for protection and warmth, and their feminized position is highlighted as they wear the same type of grass apron as females. The men are often quite openly hostile to the boys, taunting them by saying, "Go back to your mother where you belong!"

As a former warrior tribe, the Sambia viewed as crucial a process for boys to become masculinized, and the Sambia had lengthy initiation procedures to rid boys of their feminine habits and transform them into brave and fighting men. Much of that initiation ritual involves painful practices, such as piercing the septum of the

FIGURE 1.4 A Sambian initiate is tested by sucking a flute in preparation for his transformation into manhood.

nose and thrashing the boys with sticks. The Sambia are not unique in having such initiation rituals—indeed, throughout history many warrior societies have had similar initiations to recruit and train male warriors. The goal of the initiation is to give boys a sense of power, which is termed *jerungdu*. *Jerungdu* is physical strength and is viewed as the supreme essence of maleness. However, boys are believed to be born without any *jerungdu*; they get it through semen. Semen is viewed as the physical basis of *jerungdu*. Without semen, a boy has no *jerungdu*, and he has no masculinity. However, the male body is believed to be incapable of manufacturing semen—it must be acquired. And it is acquired by the boys through years of ritualized homosexuality. From the age of around 7, boys regularly ingest semen by performing daily oral sex on adolescent boys and men. In their late teens they stop ingesting semen from others, switch roles, and start providing semen to younger boys, who perform fellatio on them. They usually get married after the age of 17 or so, and after a few years of marriage, men typically become fathers, and at that point their sexual practices become exclusively heterosexual (at least officially; apparently impromptu and private homosexual encounters may, for some, continue throughout their lives). Each time a man ejaculates he loses semen and *jerungdu*, but once he is a man he is capable of replacing it by ingesting some white tree sap. Hence, the publicly recognized sex life of Sambian men tracks an arc of exclusively homosexual behaviors from the age of 7 until they are married, a period of bisexual behaviors (sex with their wives, and oral sex with younger boys) from the time they are married until they enter fatherhood, and then exclusively heterosexual behaviors after that. In contrast, Sambian females do not have any similar practices of ritualized homosexuality—they are expected to be exclusively heterosexual.

These kinds of male initiation practices have been found in many societies in Melanesia. The nearby Etoro and Kaluli, for example, also believe that it is important for boys to acquire semen to get power; Etoro boys perform ritualistic oral sex like the Sambia, whereas Kaluli boys receive their regular doses of semen through the anus. The Etoro find the Kaluli initiation practices to be disgusting, and the feelings appear to be mutual (Kelly, 1980).

Sambian views of sexuality and sexual identity stand in sharp contrast to those of Western society. Sexual orientation tends to be viewed as a lifestyle among Westerners—a lifestyle that affects how people view themselves, shapes the activities that people pursue, and determines the others with whom they associate. Whereas Westerners might identify themselves as homosexual, bisexual, or heterosexual, every Sambian male proceeds through all of these stages in sequence. Homosexuality and bisexuality are minority types of sexuality among Westerners, yet among Sambian men, homosexuality, bisexuality, and heterosexuality are universal and natural stages in life. They serve as behaviors rather than as a basis of Sambian identity. Moreover, among Sambian men, it is heterosexuality that is held in disdain because contact with women is viewed as especially contaminating and draining of a man's *jerungdu*.

I include this rather dramatic contrast between Sambian and Western culture to make two points. First, the distinctiveness of the Sambian initiation rituals underscores how humans live in cultural worlds. Our actions are fraught with meaning, and this meaning is derived from particular cultural experiences. A Sambian father *desires* to rid his 7-year-old son of the contaminating feminine influence of his mother, and he *wants* his son to perform oral sex on a married man as a means to toughen him up. However startling and bizarre the Sambian initiation practices may be to us, they carry deep meaning for the Sambians, and Sambians have a rich set of thoughts and emotions associated with these practices that people who are not socialized in Sambian contexts do not. We cannot fully understand the psychological experiences of Sambians without considering the cultural contexts in which their actions occur.

Second, the Sambian sexual practices raise an important question: What aspects of sexuality are human universals? Sexual orientation serves as a key basis of identity in the West, and the rights of gay people remain among the most politically contentious topics, especially in the United States. The Sambia do not have the construct of sexual orientation. This suggests that as biologically grounded as our sexual motives are, they become shaped by specific cultural beliefs and practices.

Psychological Universals and Levels of Analysis

The American poet Mark Van Doren made this observation about human nature: "There are two statements about human beings that are true: that all human beings are alike, and that all are different. On those two facts all human wisdom is founded." With this profound statement Van Doren has identified the issue that underlies the enterprise of cultural psychology.

When we consider culture and psychology we have two contrasting views. One view is that psychological processes are essentially the same everywhere, and the other is that psychological processes emerge differently across cultural contexts. It would seem that it should be straightforward to demonstrate which view is better supported by the evidence; all you would need to do is measure some psychological variables across a number of different cultures, and if the results tend to look the same everywhere, the general psychologists would win, whereas if the results look substantially different, the cultural psychologists would claim victory. However, the controversy continues because it is difficult to agree upon what kinds of evidence would be best suited to test a question of universality.

For example, consider the question of marriage. Is it culturally universal? The answer depends on what you mean by marriage. If you mean the kind of marriage that is common in Western cultures in which a man and a woman fall in love and agree to share their lives exclusively with each other until either one of them dies or they get divorced, then marriage is *not* universal, as there are many cultures in which people do not form such relationships (Ford & Beach, 1951). On the other hand, you could instead consider marriage in a more abstract sense, as some kind of formal arrangement in which men and women stay together in an enduring relationship (whether there be multiple women per man or multiple men per woman, and whether or not there were feelings of love prior to the marriage), with public recognition of exclusive sexual access among those who are married, and centered on the rearing of children. A definition of marriage gets even more abstract when we include same-sex marriage, which recently has been recognized in more than a dozen countries around the world. With this kind of abstract definition, we could say that marriage is a cultural universal because there are relationships in almost all cultures that fit this more abstract definition (Goodenough, 1970; for an example of a culture that seems to not even fit with this more abstract definition, see the work on the Na of China, by Hua, 2001). One eternal source of controversy in discussing human universals, then, is whether the phenomena under question are posed in particular, concrete terms or in more general, abstract terms. The level of abstraction that one entertains influences the success that one has in identifying evidence for universality. At more abstract levels there is often more evidence for universals; however, at more abstract levels the phenomena under question are often too abstract to be of much utility. This tension between universal and culturally specific psychologies will be evident in many of the topics that we discuss in this book.

A second reason that it is not straightforward to settle controversies regarding whether certain psychological phenomena are universal is that there are a number of different levels by which we can consider evidence for universality. A hierarchical framework has been proposed for considering whether particular psychological phenomena or cognitive tools are universal (Norenzayan & Heine, 2005). **Figure 1.5** depicts a decision tree for determining the level of universality that best fits a given psychological process. Note that the appropriate level of universality for a given psychological phenomenon can often be debated because some evidence might point more to one level whereas other evidence might suggest a different level. The existence of this hierarchy of levels of universality underscores the complexity of discussions of whether a psychological process can be said to be universal.

We can think of different psychological phenomena as cognitive tools. Just as a hammer is used for pounding nails, specific cognitive tools, such as a quantity estimator, can be seen as having the purpose of estimating quantities. Let's go through the decision tree to see how we can identify the level of universality is most appropriate

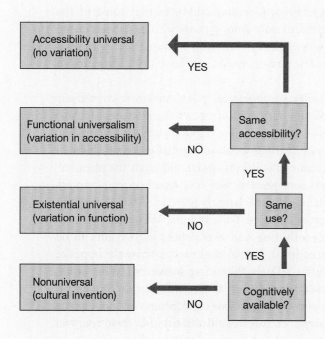

FIGURE 1.5

The decision tree for determining the degree of universality in a psychological process (Norenzayan & Heine, 2005).

FIGURE 1.6 People trained to use an abacus perform calculations differently from those who have not been trained.

for a given psychological phenomenon. If we find that a particular cognitive tool can be said to not exist in all cultures, this reflects an absence of universality and is termed, appropriately enough, a **nonuniversal**. Nonuniversals are cultural inventions. An example is abacus reasoning. An abacus is a calculation tool that is used in some parts of the Middle East and in Asia (**Figure 1.6**). People from cultures where they are trained to use the abacus think about numbers differently than those who are from cultures that do not use the abacus. Abacus users tend to favor the odd-even distinction, they think in base units of fives, and they make a particular pattern of errors not seen in non-abacus users (Miller & Paredes, 1996). The cognitive tools associated with abacus reasoning can be said to be non-existent in people who have not been trained in them. Much of numerical reasoning appears to be a nonuniversal (Carey, 2004; Gordon, 2004), in that some of the cognitive tools involved seem to be present only among those who have been raised in cultures that use them (we'll discuss cultural variation in numerical reasoning more in Chapter 9). There are rather few nonuniversals that have been identified in the cross-cultural literature.

If we can conclude that a particular psychological phenomenon is cognitively available in all cultures, then we move up our decision tree to the next step. At this step we must decide whether the phenomenon is used in the same way across cultures. If the answer is "no," the phenomenon qualifies as an **existential universal.** Here, a psychological phenomenon is said to *exist in multiple cultures,* although the phenomenon *is not necessarily used to solve the same problem, nor is it equally accessible* across cultures. That is, the psychological phenomenon is latently present, although it might be used to achieve different ends across cultures. For example, Westerners tend to find experiences with success to be motivating and experiences with failure to be demotivating (e.g., Feather, 1966). In contrast, East Asians tend to show the opposite pattern, whereby they work harder after failures than after successes (Heine et al., 2001b; Oishi & Diener, 2003). Intrinsic motivations to do one's best are present in both cultural groups; however, experiences with successes and failures are not equally likely to lead to such motivations across cultures (we'll discuss this topic more in

Chapter 8). Increased persistence in the face of failure thus fails the test of functional universals and can be said to be an example of an existential universal.

If we conclude that a psychological phenomenon is used to solve the same problems across cultures, then we move up to the next step in the decision tree. Here we must decide whether the phenomenon is equally accessible to people in all cultures. If the answer is "no," we can call the phenomenon a **functional universal**. Functional universals are psychological phenomena that *exist in multiple cultures*, are *used to solve the same problems* across cultures, yet are *more accessible to people from some cultures than others*. In the case of functional universals, the cognitive tool serves the same function everywhere, although it may not be used that much in some cultures. For example, one large-scale investigation explored whether people from a variety of subsistence societies around the world tended to punish those who acted unfairly, even if that punishment was costly for the individual to mete out (Henrich et al., 2006; we'll explore this topic more in Chapter 12). Such costly punishment was evident in all 15 societies that were investigated: apparently, costly punishment is meted out in response to unfair behavior universally—such punishment thus serves a similar function. However, considerable variation also occurred in the amount that each of the societies was willing to punish offenders. For example, among the Tsimane of Bolivia, participants spent up to 28% of their earnings to punish others who were unfair. In contrast, among the Gusii of Kenya, participants spent more than 90% of their earnings. The costly punishment of others is thus not accessible to the same degree across cultures. Some other examples of functional universals that will be discussed later in this book include certain kinds of categorization rules (e.g., Norenzayan, Smith, Kim, & Nisbett, 2002), an attraction to similarity (e.g., Heine & Renshaw, 2002), and the role of negative affect in depression (e.g., Kleinman, 1982). Many of the cross-cultural studies summarized in this textbook are testing whether a phenomenon meets the standards of functional universals.

Last, if we conclude that a psychological phenomenon is equally accessible in all cultures then we conclude that it is an **accessibility universal**. This is the strongest case for universality and indicates that a given psychological phenomenon *exists in all cultures, is used to solve the same problem* across cultures, and *is accessible to the same degree* across cultures. (By accessibility we mean the likelihood of a person using the particular psychological phenomenon.) There are likely many accessibility universals, although few have been documented thus far in psychological research. The best candidates would be those psychological phenomena that emerge very early in infancy or are shared across species. For example, social facilitation—the tendency for individuals to do better at well-learned tasks and worse at poorly learned ones when in the presence of others—has been shown to occur in both insects and humans (e.g., Zajonc, Heingartner, & Herman, 1969). It would be surprising if this tendency varied significantly across cultures, and indeed, there is thus far no evidence for any cultural variability. Likewise, a folk understanding of the laws of physics (e.g., an understanding that objects cannot just disappear), is evident among infants at a very early age, and thus also likely reflects accessibility universals (e.g., Baillargeon & DeVos, 1991). Much research is needed to confidently demonstrate that a phenomenon is an accessibility universal, and thus far we can only claim that it seems reasonable to anticipate that some phenomena are likely accessibility universals.

The Psychological Database Is Largely WEIRD

At this point, we know very little about the extent to which many psychological processes are universal. This is largely due to the inescapable fact that in many cases we don't yet have the data that would allow us to test the question of whether a phenomenon is universal. The vast majority of psychological studies have thus far been largely limited to explorations of the minds of people living in Western, Educated, Industrialized, Rich, and Democratic (**WEIRD**) **societies** (Henrich, Heine, & Norenzayan, 2010b). For example, a recent analysis of the top journals in six subdisciplines of psychology found that 68% of the participants were American and 96% came from Western industrialized countries (Arnett, 2008). Even more problematic, these samples are not representative of Westerners more generally, because the sampling method that has become standard in cognitive, social, personality, and some research in clinical psychology is to recruit participants from undergraduate psychology classes (Sears, 1986). Approximately 70% of all psychology study participants are undergraduate students (Arnett, 2008). This means that a randomly selected American undergraduate is more than 4,000 times more likely to be a research participant in a psychology study than is a randomly selected participant outside of the West. This itself reflects an interesting, and as of yet unexplained, cultural psychological finding: Why are Westerners, especially North Americans, so much more interested in psychology than the rest of the world? At many North American institutions the most popular major is psychology, whereas in many universities around the world psychology is not even offered as a topic of study. For some reason, North Americans appear to be more fascinated with psychological questions than are those from much of the rest of the world. Why do you think it is that you are taking a course on psychology? Can you identify any cultural reasons that have resulted in your sitting here and reading this book?

Thus, perhaps the strongest evidence for Shweder's contention that general psychology does not concern itself with content or context is the fact that psychology has adopted a sampling methodology that itself largely ignores questions about the generalizability of its findings. The extremely narrow samples used by most psychologists make good sense if the mind really does exclusively operate according to universal laws. To the extent that this is true, any person's mind is as good as anyone else's for revealing its universal nature. If minds are universally similar, you might as well study the most conveniently accessible ones. There is no need to be off trekking through the highlands of New Guinea to recruit study participants if their minds are functioning identically to those of Western college students, who can be enticed to participate with some extra course credit or a few dollars.

But the cost of this sampling method for psychology has become more and more evident as cross-cultural studies have been conducted. You see, it's not just that the typical psychological database represents a very narrow slice of the world's population; it also represents a very *unusual* slice. For many of the ways of thinking discussed in this book, the findings that come from WEIRD samples appear to be different from those obtained in other samples. For example, you have probably already seen the **Müller-Lyer illusion** shown in **Figure 1.7**. The line on the left looks longer than the line on the right. That people reliably see this illusion, and that you can't help but see the left line as longer than the right line, led some to argue that this illusion represents something about the innate structure of the human brain (e.g., Fodor, 1983). However, when a team of cross-cultural psychologists explored how people from a number of subsistence societies around the world perceived this illusion, together with samples of European-descent South Africans and American undergraduates (Segall, Campbell, & Herskovits, 1963), they found striking cultural differences, shown in **Figure 1.8**. The Y axis shows the point of subjective equality (PSE), which mea-

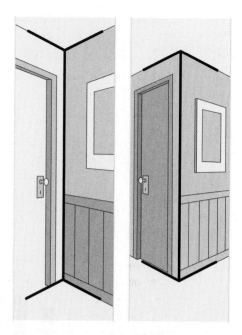

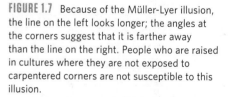

FIGURE 1.7 Because of the Müller-Lyer illusion, the line on the left looks longer; the angles at the corners suggest that it is farther away than the line on the right. People who are raised in cultures where they are not exposed to carpentered corners are not susceptible to this illusion.

sures the percentage that the line on the right must be longer than the line on the left before the two lines are judged to be equal in length, and the X axis lists the different cultures that were studied.

Two important points have been derived from these findings. First, not only is the Müller-Lyer illusion only an illusion in some cultures (the two lines are not perceived as different in length by the San and by South African miners), but it points to a psychological mechanism that underlies the illusion. People are susceptible to the Müller-Lyer illusion because the angles of the lines are similar to the angles that they see when they look at carpentered corners, which provide information about relative distance, as seen in Figure 1.6. If people are not exposed to carpentered corners (especially in childhood; McCauley & Henrich, 2006), they don't learn that the corners provide depth cues and they are not susceptible to the illusion. Hence, learning about the cultural variation in the illusion has helped psychologists understand why some people see this illusion—it's not an innate feature of the human brain, but something that is learned through having experiences with corners.

Second, the American sample is the outlier in this case; it represents the extreme end of the distribution. If you wanted to learn about the prevalence and the

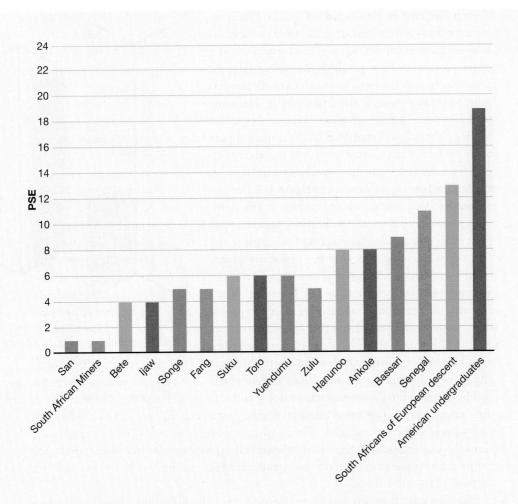

FIGURE 1.8 The larger the point of subjective equality (PSE), the more pronounced is the Müller-Lyer illusion. American undergraduates are more susceptible to this illusion than those from the other cultural groups that have been studied (Henrich et al., 2010b).

magnitude of the Müller-Lyer illusion throughout the world, you would get an exaggerated estimate if you focused on American samples. And this tendency for American student samples to show an extreme pattern of responses is not an exception. The available cross-cultural data reveal that, for many of the key findings in psychology (ranging from perceptions of fairness to moral reasoning, self-concepts, reasoning styles, desires for choice, and many others), (1) people from industrialized societies respond differently than those from small-scale societies; (2) people from

Western industrialized societies demonstrate more pronounced responses than those from non-Western societies; (3) Americans show yet more extreme responses than other Westerners; and (4) the responses of contemporary American college students are even further different than those of non-college-educated American adults (Henrich, Heine, & Norenzayan, 2010b). WEIRD samples really are quite weird in their ways of thinking, and building theories about the human mind exclusively from these samples is problematic.

Psychology has largely relied on narrow and unrepresentative samples, which weakens its ability to address questions about how well findings from any particular study generalize to other human samples. One key goal of cultural psychology is to gather findings from a broad enough array of cultures to be able to more confidently explore questions about human universals and human diversity. This goal is a challenging one, as there are some barriers for gaining access to a broad swath of cultures in that most psychologists don't receive training in other cultures, some cultures are harder to gain access to as they might not have local psychologists working there who can serve as collaborators, and it is far more costly and difficult for Western psychologists to collect data across the world than it is to collect data with convenient samples of students from their universities. Thus far, the most common non-Western samples to be studied are student samples from East Asia, as there are many psychologists there who collaborate with international teams. The samples are similar to Western samples in many other respects (e.g., they are students, from usually wealthy backgrounds, living in complex societies), which makes the cross-cultural comparisons more straightforward to interpret; and, as you'll see in the remaining chapters, there are many pronounced psychological differences between people from East Asian and Western cultural backgrounds. However, the field still has not done nearly enough research to explore other non-Western cultural regions. Perhaps you'll participate in some research on other understudied populations someday.

Why Should We Study Cultural Psychology?

Over the past couple of decades, many researchers from around the world have been exploring questions about how culture shapes people's psychology. Why might people be interested in such questions? What does cultural psychology offer to the field of psychology and to people more generally?

One good reason to learn about cultural psychology is that, for those interested in understanding how the human mind operates, it's important to understand the role cultural experiences play in terms of how people come to think and feel. As noted earlier, many psychological findings that have been obtained from American undergrads emerge somewhat differently in other samples, and our theories about human nature will be misguided if we don't consider the diverse ways that people can make sense of themselves and their worlds. Experiences are central to the development of psychological tendencies, and cultures provide people with certain kinds of experiences. One reason to learn about cultural psychology, then, is that we'll have a distorted and incomplete understanding of the human mind if we fail to consider the role of culture.

This first reason to study cultural psychology is the same kind of reason that one could offer for learning about any field—gaining knowledge in that field is important for developing one's understanding about related topics. However, given the nature of the questions explored in cultural psychology, one might raise an entirely different kind of question about its value as a field. How does learning about cultural psychology affect the ways that people think and lead their lives? This latter question is important to consider, given that cultural psychology's focus on differences between cultures can touch upon some sensitive issues that are highly relevant to our lives.

With the increase in globalization over the past several decades, people are coming into contact with others from diverse cultural backgrounds more than ever before. What is the best way to deal with group differences in a multicultural community? Should those differences be ignored so that people can focus on the similarities they share with those from other cultures, and perhaps attend to all that humans have in common? Or should such cultural differences be acknowledged and be viewed as a source of strength? This is a sensitive and controversial issue that divides society and psychologists.

As noted earlier, in some respects "people are the same wherever you go." Taking this perspective is called a "**color-blind**" (or "culture-blind") **approach**, and many people adopt this mind-set with the best of intentions. The hope underlying this approach is that people will interact with each other without giving much attention to anyone's ethnic background. In the words of some advocates for racial equality, "the way to stop discrimination on the basis of race is to stop discriminating on the basis of race" (*Parents Involved in Community Schools v. Seattle School District No. 1*, 2007, p. 2768). So perhaps the best way for people of different backgrounds to get along is to stop attending to cultural differences and focus instead on people's common human nature.

In support of this perspective, much research has shown that people can very easily be led to adopt an "us versus them" mind-set and favor their own group over other groups (Gaertner, Mann, Murrell, & Dovidio, 1989). Research in this tradition consistently finds that as soon as you tell people that there are two groups and that they belong to one of them, you quickly tend to get discrimination between the two groups, with people treating those in their own group better than those in the other group. This discrimination will occur even when those groups are based on the most trivial of distinctions, such as whether people are told they belong to a group of people who prefer art by the painter Wassily Kandinsky or a group who prefer art by the painter Paul Klee (Tajfel, 1974). Attention to differences between groups can lead to discrimination, so it follows that if people's attention is not drawn to the differences between cultures, they will be less likely to create boundaries between themselves and others, and they will all get along better.

In contrast to this color-blind strategy, attending to and respecting group differences is frequently called a **multicultural approach**. The rationale behind this approach is that people really *do* identify strongly with their groups, and most group identities are far more meaningful than the kind that can be artificially created in the lab. Furthermore, people are especially likely to identify with their groups if their groups are smaller than other groups or are disadvantaged in some way. Minority groups tend to greatly value their group identities, and they often respond quite negatively to efforts by majority group members to ignore what makes them distinctive (Verkuyten, 2005). Efforts to downplay group differences may come across as suggesting that minority members would be accepted as long as they shed their distinctive cultural identities and act like those in the majority group. This multicultural approach, then, suggests that people will fare better when the distinctive characteristics of their groups are attended to and appreciated.

So there are two conflicting perspectives about the best way for people from different cultures to deal with each other. What happens when you experimentally compare these two approaches? The findings from studies that make these comparisons are quite consistent (for a review see Apfelbaum, Norton, & Sommers, 2012): Groups that emphasize multicultural messages fare better in numerous respects than groups that emphasize color-blind messages. For example, one extensive study of a few thousand employees from various companies assessed the relationship between each company's attitude toward diversity and their employees' engagement with their work (Plaut, Thomas, & Goren, 2009). The more multicultural (and the less color-blind) the attitudes of the white employees, the more the minority employees were engaged with their work. Similarly, minority employees have more trust in, and comfort with, a company that offers multicultural messages than with one that offers color-blind messages, especially when the company has only a few minority members (Purdie-Vaughns, Steele, Davies, Ditlmann, & Crosby, 2008). Likewise, European-Canadian and First Nations (native Canadian) participants had more positive conversations with each other after being exposed to multicultural messages than after being exposed to color-blind messages; further, the multicultural messages increased the identity security of the First Nations participants while reducing the amount of negative emotions expressed by the European-Canadians (Vorauer, Gagnon, & Sasaki, 2009). Likewise, when White Americans were exposed to color-blind arguments they came to act in more prejudicial ways toward minorities than when they were exposed to multicultural arguments (Holoien & Shelton, 2012). In another study, young children were presented with either a multicultural or a color-blind story and then heard an account of a physical assault between a White and Black student (Apfelbaum, Pauker, Sommers, & Ambady, 2010). Those who had heard the color-blind story were less likely than those who heard the multicultural account to see racial discrimination as being involved in the assault, despite the fact that the assault was explicitly described to the students as being due to racism. The color-blind story apparently prevented students from seeing discrimination where it really existed. Moreover, White students also show more positive attitudes toward minority members when the environment presents multicultural messages than when it presents color-blind ones (Richeson & Nussbaum, 2004; Wolsko, Park, Judd, & Wittenbrink, 2000), although Whites often do not view efforts to emphasize multi-culturalism as positively as minority members do (Morrison, Plaut, & Ybarra, 2010; Plaut, Garnett, Buffardi, & Sanchez-Burks, 2011). That Whites are not as enthusi-astic about multicultural messages as minority members is perhaps not surprising; color-blind messages are more likely to be perceived as legitimizing any existing ethnic inequalities (Knowles, Lowery, Hogan, & Chow, 2009).

These findings thus suggest another good reason to learn about cultural psychol-ogy. An increased understanding and appreciation of cultural differences can lead people of different cultural backgrounds to get along better, be more engaged in their work, and be able to detect discrimination when it exists. Indeed, research has found that students who take a course on cultural psychology show an overall increase in cultural awareness and cultural intelligence, which improves intercultural under-standing (Buchtel, 2014). These studies suggest that people fare best when they try to understand how people from different cultures might be different rather than when they choose to not attend to those differences.

You Are a Product of Your Own Culture

When we read ethnographies or cross-cultural studies involving "exotic" people, it is not difficult to appreciate that culture affects other people. Somehow, though, it is far more difficult to appreciate how culture influences us. We don't speak with a dis-cernible accent—only people from other places do. Although we can't hear our own accents, they are plainly evident to people who speak other languages or dialects. This point holds more generally to culture: For the most part, our cultures remain invisible to us, although everyone else can see them. As the anthropologist Clyde Kluckhohn remarked, "It would hardly be fish who discovered the existence of water" (1949, p. 11). Our own thoughts and behaviors appear natural to us because we really don't know how we could think and behave otherwise. However, people from many other cultures around the world would be quite surprised to learn about the things we do. For example, when people from around the world learn about North American cul-tural practices, it is not uncommon to hear, "They put their babies in cages when they sleep!"; "They talk to young children as if they were psychotherapists, asking them to explore their feelings!"; "Couples feel oddly compelled to keep reassuring themselves that they love each other, even when they call their partners from the office!"; "They send their elderly parents off to institutions instead of caring for them themselves!"

In many ways we don't really come to understand our own culture until we see it in contrast to other cultures. As the political sociologist Seymour Martin Lipset (1996) used to say: "Those who only know one country know no country." One perspective that I hope you gain from reading this book is a greater appreciation for your own culture. As with people from the most exotic and remote cultures on the planet, the ways that you think and behave are guided by the particular cultural experiences you have had.

Furthermore, our values also are shaped by our cultural experiences. We are socialized to think that particular ways of doing things are good and

"Why is it so wet?"

moral—usually, the very ways that are common within our own culture. As such, culturally normative behavior comes to be seen as natural, and deviations from that natural path often tend to be viewed as less desirable or even immoral. This leads people to the error of **ethnocentrism**—that is, judging people from other cultures by the standards of one's own culture. Our cultures ultimately socialize us to be ethnocentric because we are socialized to value normative cultural behaviors. As you'll see, learning about other cultures can sometimes be provocative as people confront other ways of doing things that go against their own cultural values. These experiences should help you gain a new perspective on how your culture has influenced you.

Where Does Cultural Psychology Come From?

The study of culture in psychology is not new. Indeed, the person who is widely seen as the father of psychology as a discipline, and who created the world's first psychological laboratory in 1879, Wilhelm Wundt, was himself a cultural psychologist. Wundt became famous for introducing experimental methods into the study of psychology and launching the field as a science. What is less well known, however, is that he wrote a 10-volume tome titled *Volkerpsychologie*, or *Elements of Folk Psychology* (1921), which roughly captures much of the inquiry of modern-day cultural psychologists. Wundt's contributions to the study of experimental psychology were enormously influential to all fields of psychology; however, his ideas about cultural psychology were largely ignored by the field.

Since Wundt's early contributions, the study of culture in psychology has had a number of revivals, although it was never fully embraced by mainstream psychology until recently. One of the more enduring developments occurred in the former Soviet Union, where developmental psychologists Lev Vygotsky, Alexander Luria, and Aleksei Leontiev developed what became known as the **Russian cultural-historical school**. This school of thought argued that people interact with their environments through the "tools," or human-made ideas that have been passed to them across history, such as cultural inventions like the wheel, agriculture, or democracy. According to this view, all of human thought is sustained and expressed through accumulated human-made ideas as they are practiced in day-to-day activities (e.g., Luria, 1928; Vygotsky, 1929, 1978). These ideas have been developed and extended more recently by a number of researchers (e.g., Cole, 1996; Cole, Gay, Glick, & Sharp, 1971; Rogoff, 2003; Scribner & Cole, 1981; Wertsch, 1998) and have influenced much of cultural psychology.

Beginning just prior to World War II and continuing for a couple of decades was a period when a number of anthropologists and personality psychologists worked together in an interdisciplinary enterprise that was known as "culture and personality studies." Ruth Benedict wrote a book in 1934, *Patterns of Culture,* that is often seen as one of the prototypic exemplars of the enterprise. In this book, she argued that culture was for populations what personality was for individuals, and these ideas were elaborated and critiqued by subsequent scholars. This collaboration among psychologists and anthropologists attracted some of the most influential figures across the disciplines and led to a great outpouring of research. However, in the 1950s the enterprise ultimately met an ignoble demise as it was criticized for not attending sufficiently to individual variation within cultures and for being unable to develop a strong and coherent research program (Levine, 2001).

The field of social psychology started out very much in the same tradition as cultural psychology. A guiding tenet of the field, as espoused by one of the most influential social psychologists, Solomon Asch, was that social psychology "stood for the belief that no psychology can be complete that fails to look directly at man as a social being" (Asch, 1959, p. 364). However, the ascendancy of the experimental method in social psychology was often paralleled by an effort to exert greater experimental control over the study of social nature. For example, the study of the social relations that people have with members of other groups tends not to look at people's actual relationships but instead is usually investigated by creating random and artificial groups (e.g., Hamilton & Gifford, 1976; Tajfel, 1970), and the study of people's attraction toward each other is typically investigated by having people evaluate fictitious strangers whom they never meet (e.g., Byrne, Clore, & Worchel, 1966) or by being exposed to inanimate stimuli (e.g., Zajonc, 1968). Much of the recent growth in cultural psychology has occurred among social psychologists who want to more forcefully consider the influence of people's social relations on thought.

Psychology was dominated by the perspective of behaviorism in the early to mid-20th century, when the mind came to be viewed as largely irrelevant to psychological research. Rather, the concern then was with observable behaviors that could be influenced through conditioning of simple stimulus-response relations. In the 1950s psychology entered what became known as the "cognitive revolution," as researchers rejected the tenets of behaviorism and began to focus on the meaning that people created through their encounters with the world. One of the leading architects of the cognitive revolution, Jerome Bruner, however, argued that soon after the revolution began it became distracted from its initial vision by becoming more concerned with computer metaphors for understanding the functions of the mind (Bruner, 1990). Meaning became replaced with information, and meaning-making with information processing. Bruner argued that cultural psychology has picked up the torch that was originally carried by early proponents of the cognitive revolution and has again addressed how people derive meaning from their worlds.

In addition to the various subfields and trends that have explored the relations between culture and psychology over the past century, a number of individual researchers have persistently wrestled with this topic. Some of the key figures who delved into the psychological study of culture in the 1960s, 1970s, and 1980s include John Berry, Michael Bond, Michael Cole, Roy D'Andrade, Ken Gergen, Patricia Greenfield, Geert Hofstede, Walter Lonner, Sylvia Scribner, Marshall Segall, and Harold Stevenson. The tremendous research efforts of these people, along with those of many other cross-cultural psychologists, played a key role in setting the stage for cultural psychology to be reintroduced to mainstream psychology as a new and revolutionary way of thinking about the mind.

The most recent reincarnation of cultural psychology, and its most impactful, appeared when a number of seminal papers and books were published nearly simultaneously. In 1989 Harry Triandis, who had been conducting leading work in culture and psychology for decades, wrote a highly influential article in which he argued that there are a number of cultural dimensions and aspects of the self-concept by which much of the observed variation across cultures can be understood (Triandis, 1989b). In 1990 Jerome Bruner published a book arguing that human psychology can only be properly understood by considering the meaning that people derived from their encounters with their worlds. In that same year, an edited book by Stigler, Shweder, and Herdt contained a number of key articles that provided exemplars for how culture could be incorporated into psychological research. That same book also included an article by Richard Shweder that provided a theoretical foundation for the psychological study of culture. In that paper, Shweder made cogent arguments that mind and culture mutually constitute each other, and thus need to be studied together. One year later, in 1991, Hazel Markus and Shinobu Kitayama published a landmark article that has since become the most cited paper in cultural psychology. In that paper, they made the case that many psychological processes, such as cognitions, emotions, and motivations, can be viewed through the lens of the self-concept.

They then demonstrated that researchers can come to understand and predict cultural differences in many psychological processes by attending to the ways that the self-concept is shaped differently across cultures. These four seminal works, building on the groundwork provided by earlier forays into the study of psychology and culture, and buttressed by the many papers that emerged in subsequent years, have led to the foundation of a new field of psychology.

Hence, although people have been conducting cultural psychological research for some time, they have been relatively few in number and their contributions had managed to be largely ignored. It has been about a quarter century since cultural psychology began to be taken seriously by much of mainstream psychology. In that time, some of the more prestigious psychology departments have established programs in cultural psychology, leading to an explosion of research on the topic.

In doing the research for this book, I have consistently had two thoughts: First, that there has been a flood of excellent research in cultural psychology over the past quarter century. Indeed, so much has come out over this time that it has been hard for me to keep up. Second, despite this enormous amount of research, many key questions about the relation between culture and psychology have yet to be investigated. There are large gaps in our knowledge base waiting to be filled regarding how culture influences psychology. In particular, many of the world's cultures remain unexplored frontiers in terms of psychological testing. In all likelihood, psychologists will be grappling with cultural psychological research for many decades to come.

SUMMARY

Cultural psychology can be contrasted with much of "general psychology" in that it views the mind and culture to be ultimately inseparable. The guiding assumption is that psychological processes are influenced by the content that is being processed and by the context within which it is processed. With this view, people who participate in different contexts should be expected to think differently.

Controversy continues over whether given psychological processes are universal to all cultures or are specific to certain cultures. These arguments are controversial because the evidence for the universality of a process often depends on the level of abstraction by which that process is considered. Furthermore, there are four different levels of universality of psychological processes (listed in order of increasing universality): nonuniversals, existential universals, functional universals, and accessibility universals.

The extent of universality that exists for most psychological processes is still unclear. This is largely because the database for psychological research has generally been limited to North American undergraduates in psychology classes. Much recent research has shown that when other populations are investigated, the findings often look quite different across cultures.

When people adopt a multicultural approach and attend to cultural differences, people of different cultural groups get along better and are more engaged.

Cultural psychology is not new, as there have been a number of attempts to study culture's influences on ways of thinking throughout the history of psychology. The more recent incarnation of the field started in the early 1990s and has been the most influential. The past two decades have produced an enormous amount of research that at the same time has raised many more unanswered questions.

THINK ABOUT IT

1. What kinds of groups are cultures? Can you think of examples of some groups that would clearly deserve the label "culture," and other groups that would clearly not?
2. In what ways are other psychology courses that you may have taken similar to or different from Shweder's description of "general psychology"?
3. What does it mean to say that culture and mind make each other up?
4. The behaviors of Sambian initiation rituals would surely qualify as sexual crimes in most, if not all, modern industrialized cultures. Do you think the rituals are morally wrong because they violate laws and norms that are common throughout most of the rest of the world, or do you think they are acceptable because they are sustained by local cultural meanings?
5. Given the variation in kinds of marriages that are practiced around the world, in what ways can we say that marriage itself is a cultural universal?
6. What can psychologists do to ensure that they don't rely so much on WEIRD samples?
7. What do you think are the costs and benefits of maintaining a multicultural perspective? How about for maintaining a color-blind perspective?
8. What do you think are some of the distinctive norms and practices of the cultures that you belong to?

KEY TERMS

General Psychology, 8
Nonuniversal, 20
Existential Universal, 20
Functional Universal, 21

Accessibility Universal, 21
WEIRD Societies, 22
Müller-Lyer illusion, 23
Color-Blind Approach, 26

Multicultural Approach, 27
Ethnocentrism, 29
Russian Cultural-Historical
 School, 30

Truganini was the very last full blood Aboriginal Tasmanian to ever live. Her people were exterminated over the years by aggressive policies of the European settlers and by the diseases that they introduced throughout Australia. When Europeans first arrived in Tasmania they encountered a culture with the smallest collection of tools of any human society ever recorded. The Aboriginal Tasmanian appear to have lost many earlier cultural technologies when a small group of them first left mainland Australia to arrive in Tasmania more than 30,000 years ago.

TRUGANINI

THIS MEMORIAL
IS DEDICATED TO
THE MEMORY OF
TRUGANINI
1812 - 1876

2

CULTURE AND HUMAN NATURE

t must have been quite the spectacle. From the 1940s through the 1970s, at small towns up and down the eastern seaboard of the United States, Noell's Ark Gorilla Show provided a unique and immensely popular vaudeville experience with its traveling circus. The spectacle had juggling acts, animal shows, and a ventriloquist. But their star attraction was described in the posters put up around town: "Wanted, athletic men to earn $5 per second by holding 85-pound ape's shoulders to the floor." Many large and brawny men, in a valiant effort to impress their dates, took up this challenge to wrestle an adult chimpanzee in front of an audience (**Figure 2.1**). What happened in these matches? It was no contest—the men always lost. Always. Most matches were over in a few seconds. The chimps wore facemasks to protect opponents from their fierce teeth. Later, the chimps started wearing gloves after one chimp named Snookie rammed both thumbs up a man's nose and yanked them apart, tearing his nostrils. Ultimately, the authorities put an end to these matches, although it wasn't clear whether the primary concern was the well-being of the chimps or of their hapless challengers (Farley, 2004; Noell, 1979).

I describe this colorful tidbit of Americana to make an important point: Humans are real wimps. Frankly, it's rather embarrassing. The men in these wrestling matches were a self-selected group who were far larger than their opponents, often had much wrestling experience, and were strongly motivated both by cash and the desire not to look like a fool in front of a large audience, and yet they could not last more than a few seconds against their hairy rivals. This fact is perhaps surprising, given that humans and chimpanzees shared a common ancestor approximately 5 to 7 million years ago. Given how brawny other ape species are (orangutans and gorillas are far stronger than chimpanzees), that common ancestor was likely at least as

FIGURE 2.1 The chimpanzees of Noell's Ark Gorilla Show never lost a bout to their human challengers.

muscular as a chimpanzee. So what happened? Why did we end up becoming the scrawny ape species that could get trounced by all the others? Why couldn't we evolve all of our uniquely human characteristics and still keep the powerful muscles that our ancestors had? Just imagine how useful all that extra strength would have been. But as a species we don't have a lot of muscle mass, and this is informative in telling us how we got what we do have. In this chapter, we'll consider why humans lost their muscles, and related issues regarding the evolutionary trade-offs that our human ancestors confronted when they became a cultural species.

Is Culture Unique to Humans?

Before we consider how humans became a cultural species, let's consider whether other animals could also be said to have culture. This latter question is controversial, in part, because of the lack of consensus regarding a definition for culture. A different way of defining culture than what I provided in Chapter 1 is to say that it refers to some kind of symbolic coding—that is, of having a set of signals, icons, and words that refer to something else that most members of that culture recognize. If we accept this definition, then, yes, humans are the only species that have culture, because no other species appears to have symbolic coding (Deacon, 1997). But this is a rather unsatisfying and circular definition in that we are defining culture in terms of what is uniquely human (i.e., having symbolic coding) and then concluding that culture is therefore unique to humans.

The definition of culture that I provided in the previous chapter is much broader, and it avoids this problem of circularity. That is, are humans unique in being able to learn information from other members of their species through social transmission? If we accept this definition, then, no, humans are by no means the only species to have culture. There are many clear examples of cultural learning in the animal kingdom. Perhaps the most famous example is the case of a very clever female macaque named Imo who lived on a small island off Japan (Kawamura, 1959). One day Imo was given some pieces of sweet potato, and she went to some nearby water to wash the sand off before eating them. Within 3 months, Imo's mother and a couple of her playmates also started washing their potatoes. Three years later, 40% of the other macaques in Imo's troupe were washing their potatoes. It appears that potato washing was a strategy that was invented by Imo, was learned by those around her, and then subsequently became part of the cultural repertoire of a subgroup of macaques living in the same troupe.

Another example of cultural learning can be seen in chimpanzees. Chimps love to eat termites—these insects are very nutritious and apparently (to chimps, at least) delicious. The challenge, however, is to figure out a way to get these tiny snacks out of the large, rock-hard mounds they live in. Chimps from Mt. Assirik in Senegal have

FIGURE 2.2 An example of cultural learning among chimpanzees.

been shown to use tools to extract termites from the mounds (**Figure 2.2**). Specifically, the chimps take a twig, peel the bark from it, and then stick the twig into a termite mound to fish out the termites. Chimps from Gombe National Park in Tanzania also use tools to extract termites, but they do so in a different way. These chimps also peel bark from twigs, but unlike the Senegalese chimps, they use the bark to fish out the termites (Whiten et al., 1999). These appear to be learned behaviors that are culturally transmitted from one generation of chimps to another. At least two different cultures of chimps have thus formed—the twig-fishers versus the bark-fishers. Actually, at this point, 39 specific behaviors have been identified that distinguish some troupes of chimps from others, including the ways in which they clean their bodies with leaves, attract attention from others by slapping branches, and use objects to tickle themselves (Whiten et al., 1999). One can thus speak of different cultures of chimpanzees.

Culture is evident not only in primate species—some of the most impressive instances of complex cultural learning have been identified among dolphins and whales, both in feeding strategies and in vocalizations (for a review, see Rendell & Whitehead, 2001). For example, one population of bottlenose dolphins has been found to use marine sponges as foraging tools: They tear off a sponge, carry it over their beak, and then probe their beak into the sand and coral while protecting themselves from getting scratched. This is a behavior that dolphins in one particular region apparently learn from their mothers (Krutzen et al., 2005). Furthermore, different populations of killer whales have been found to speak different dialects, to the point that researchers can recognize a whale pod by the sounds they're making. And these dialects have been shown to change over time (Deecke, Ford, & Spong, 2000), just as human culture does.

Moreover, it is not just in the most intelligent species that we see evidence for cultural learning. For example, pigeons appear to learn specific food acquisition strategies from other pigeons (Lefebvre & Giraldeau, 1994). Various bird species learn specific calls from other birds, and these calls come to change across time and geography (e.g., Irwin, 2000). Even guppies (Lachlan, Crooks, & Laland, 1998) and different species of octopus (e.g., Fiorito & Scotto, 1992) have shown evidence of learning from others. Some forms of cultural learning are thus evident across a broad swath of the animal kingdom.

Cultural Learning

Humans, then, are not unique in being able to engage in cultural learning. However, humans do seem to stand out in contrast to other animals in the extent of their cultural learning skills. Although many species of animals have been shown to be able to learn cultural information, none of the nonhuman species seem to be very good at it. For example, although the Japanese macaques were able to learn Imo's technique of washing potatoes, they didn't learn it very well. It took years for the potato washing to get learned by others, and many of the macaques never figured it out. In contrast, humans frequently learn new information from each other, and often with only a single exposure to it. Many aspects of human cultures are shared by nearly every member of the culture; for example, dialects, some cultural practices, and specific tools are often so widespread in a particular culture that they are accessible to virtually everyone in that culture. So the cultural learning by the macaques and by other animals at least seems to be very slow compared to the kinds of cultural learning evidenced by humans.

Furthermore, humans seem to be unique among other species in *whom* they choose to imitate. There is no indication, for example, that macaques who are learning a new skill like potato washing choose which macaques to imitate. Any model that they regularly encounter appears to be equally likely to be imitated. In contrast, much evidence suggests that humans are quite particular about whom they choose to imitate. Humans are said to have a **prestige bias**: They are especially concerned with detecting who has prestige—that is, they seek others who have skills and are respected by others—and they try to imitate what these individuals are doing (Henrich & Gil-White, 2001).

A recent study tested whether 4-year-old children are indeed more likely to imitate the behavior of a prestigious model (Chudek, Heller, Birch, & Henrich, 2011). The children saw two adult models go through a number of binary decisions, such as choosing which of two toys to play with or choosing which of two kinds of food to eat, and each model made the opposite choice of the other. Prior to the models making their decisions, though, the children saw two bystanders who attended only to one of the models while ignoring the other—this is how "prestige" was operationalized in the study. Later, when the children had the

SIPRESS

"Which celebrities do this type of yoga?"

chance to make their own choices, they were more likely to imitate the choices that had been made by the prestigious model than the model who had been ignored by others. Humans thus seem to have a prestige bias that makes them especially likely to imitate those who are viewed by others as more prestigious.

Imitating prestigious others is a very efficient way of cultural learning. Rather than picking someone at random to imitate and perhaps learning from models who don't really know what they are doing, individuals are more likely to learn successfully if they target those people who are especially talented. If you want to learn how to be a successful basketball player, a good place to start would be to watch what LeBron James does, rather than watching someone like me, who couldn't play basketball to save his life.

Identifying signs of prestige and then imitating people who displayed those signs are skills that were likely selected for in the course of human evolution. Our ancestors who did this were more likely to acquire the highly useful cultural knowledge that gave them a survival advantage compared with those who did not. Moreover, when trying to learn a skill from others, it isn't always clear what particular behaviors are responsible for achieving success. For example, is LeBron James's phenomenal basketball success due to his workout routine, to the way he studied his childhood hero, Michael Jordan, to his yoga exercises, or to the advice he took from the coach that he lived with as a child?

Because it is not clear what the critical behaviors for success are, individuals would fare best by having a general imitating mechanism, by which they are attracted to prestigious individuals, whom they observe and try to imitate, regardless of what they are doing. Advertisers capitalize on this general imitating mechanism when they use prestigious people like LeBron James to sell us products that don't seem to have anything to do with the source of their prestige. For example, LeBron James appears in commercials for Coca-Cola, State Farm Insurance, Microsoft, McDonald's, and the lawnmower maker Cub Cadet—none of which would appear to be relevant to his basketball skills.

Our general imitating mechanism leads us to want to do everything that prestigious people do, even if we often end up copying the wrong behaviors. This strategy should increase the likelihood that we learn the skills that really do lead to success. A side effect of prestige biases is that humans tend to be fascinated with famous people and want to know everything about them, such as how much weight they have gained or who they are sleeping with (**Figure 2.3**). Indeed, the rise of the likes of Paris Hilton and Kim Kardashian shows that our prestige biases are so strong that they can sometimes become self-sustaining—people can become famous simply for being famous, and their legions of fans come to follow their every move. Prestige biases can also have a dark side, in that people may sometimes imitate a celebrity's destructive habits, such as the spate of copycat suicides that frequently occur after a celebrity takes his or her own life (Mesoudi, 2009). Hence, prestige biases may be responsible for humankind's adept cultural learning, but they have also contributed to the creation of tabloids.

Humans' unusually sophisticated cultural learning skills further rests on two key capacities: the ability to consider the perspective of others, and the ability to communicate with language. These are described later in the chapter.

THEORY OF MIND. Another feature of the ways that humans engage in cultural learning appears to be unique, or nearly unique, compared with other animal species. When humans learn from others, they are able to take on the perspectives of those others. Humans have what is known as a **theory of mind**. A theory of mind means that people understand that others have minds that are different from their own, and thus that other people have perspectives and intentions that are different from

FIGURE 2.3 Humans' prestige biases can help make sense of why so many people care about the minutiae of Kim Kardashian's life.

their own. For example, a 1-year-old child will point to a toy that he wants, indicating that he understands that his mother is not aware of where the toy is and that he is also motivated to share this information about the toy's location with his mother. The child understands that his mother has different thoughts in her head than he does. This understanding of others' intentional states is evident in humans across all cultures, and it appears to develop at a fairly similar rate across cultures (Callaghan et al., 2005).

Such a theory of mind is not evident in most other species, and even in our closest genetic relatives, chimpanzees, the evidence is somewhat mixed (Povinelli, Perilloux, Reaux, & Bierschwale, 1998; Tomasello, Kruger, & Ratner, 1993). Specifically, although chimpanzees that are trained by humans do appear to be able to take on the perspective of others (e.g., Savage-Rumbaugh, McDonald, Sevcik, Hopkins, & Rubert, 1986), especially when they are incentivized for doing so (Bräuer, Call, & Tomasello, 2007), chimpanzees in the wild show far less evidence. For example, chimpanzees in the wild do not point to outside objects, do not hold objects up to show them to others, do not bring others to locations so that they can observe things there, do not actively offer objects to other individuals by holding them out, and do not intentionally teach other individuals new behaviors (Tomasello, 1999). Furthermore, chimpanzees do not appear to strive to share their experiences and activities with others of their own kind (Tomasello, Carpenter, Call, Behne, & Moll, 2005).

The points about what specifically wild chimpanzees can and cannot do continue to be debated in the literature (de Waal, 2001; Tomasello et al., 1993; Whiten, 1998), and it is difficult to say conclusively what is the full extent of their capabilities. What we can say confidently, however, is that human abilities and motivations to imagine the perspectives and intentions of others and to share their own perspectives and intentions with others are far superior to those of chimps and other animals. And this difference in ability and motivation to consider the intentions of others has important consequences for cultural learning.

If individuals are able and motivated to understand the intentions of others, then this provides an important step in being able to fruitfully engage in cultural learning. For example, imagine seeing someone use a tool, such as using a stick, to knock some out-of-reach bananas off a shelf. If one is able to appreciate the intentions of the other, he or she is likely to think, "Oh, Bonzo over there wants to get those bananas. He's using that stick in his hand to reach up and knock them off the shelf." By appreciating what Bonzo is trying to do with the stick, the individual can internalize Bonzo's goals and be better able to reproduce them. When given the chance, the individual is likely to try to use the stick to get some out-of-reach bananas for himself, and use it in the same way that Bonzo did. This would be an example of one kind of cultural learning known as **imitative learning**. In imitative learning, the learner internalizes something of the model's goals and behavioral strategies (Tomasello, 1999; Tomasello et al., 1993). The learner is copying precisely what it thinks the model is trying to do. Imitation may be the sincerest form of flattery, but as we'll see, it's also the most reliable route for cultural learning.

Tomasello and colleagues argue that chimpanzees have such a difficult time taking on the perspective of others that instead of engaging in imitative learning, they tend to focus on the object itself. By watching Bonzo try to knock the bananas down with a stick, they come to learn that the stick can be used to knock down bananas. That is, they learn that the stick affords such banana-knocking strategies. When they then have the opportunity, they try to figure out for themselves how they could use the stick to knock down some bananas. This kind of learning is an example of a second kind of cultural learning known as **emulative learning**. In emulative learning, the learning is focused on the environmental events that are involved—how the use of one object could potentially effect changes in the state of the environment. The key difference between emulative learning and imitative learning is that emulative learning does not require imitating a model's behavioral strategies. An emulative learner is only focusing on the events that happen around the model, rather than what the model *intends* to accomplish. Emulative learners try to figure things out for themselves once they get an idea by observing others.

Emulative learning can be a very clever and creative form of learning. The individual has to use creative insight and problem-solving skills to imagine how an object could be used in a new way. Consider the following study: Chimpanzees and 2-year-old human children were compared to see how they learned a novel task

(Nagell, Olguin, & Tomasello, 1993). Researchers presented the chimpanzees and the children with a model using a rake-like tool to get a desired object (some food for the chimpanzees or a toy for the children) that was kept out of reach. The model used the rake to get access to the out-of-reach object in one of two ways. In one condition, the chimpanzees and children observed the model use the rake in the most effective way. That is, the rake was turned upside down with the teeth pointing up, which provided a wide tool that could easily be used to drag the object within reach. In a second condition, a different group of chimpanzees and children observed the model use the rake in a rather ineffective way—dragging it with the teeth down (see **Figure 2.4**). Although it was possible to drag the object toward them like this, it was less effective because the object sometimes slid between the teeth.

After watching the model, the chimpanzees and children had the chance to use the rake themselves to get the object. The children showed evidence of true imitative learning, in that they tried to do precisely what the model had done. They used the rake in the same way that the model had, even though this meant that in the "teeth-down" condition, they had a more difficult time getting the object. Chimpanzees, in contrast, showed evidence of emulative learning. Regardless of how the model had used the rake, the chimpanzees used the rake in the most effective "teeth-up" position. They thus seemed to notice that the rake could be used to get the object and then figured out for themselves, very creatively, that the rake would be most effective if it was used to drag the object with the teeth up. A number of other studies provide evidence that chimpanzees and other primates tend to solve problems with emulative learning rather than imitative learning (e.g., Custance, Whiten, & Fredman, 1999; Tomasello, 1996).

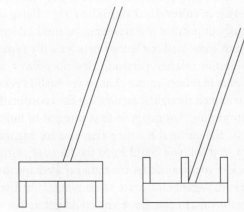

Teeth-Down Position   Teeth-Up Position

FIGURE 2.4

The two rake positions that were possible for the chimpanzee and 2-year-old participants (Nagell et al., 1993).

Other research similarly finds that when children imitate a model, they imitate all of the model's actions, including irrelevant actions. So, for example, if a model who is retrieving a toy from a plastic jar first taps the jar with a feather, 3- to 5-year-old children who want to retrieve the toy will also do the same irrelevant feather tapping (Lyons, Young, & Keil, 2007). Chimps in contrast are far more efficient—they copy only the behaviors that are directly relevant to achieving the goal while ignoring the irrelevant ones, as one would expect with emulative learning (Horner & Whiten, 2005). Children will even copy irrelevant behaviors when they are alone, after an experiment is finished, and when they were explicitly told not to copy any actions that are irrelevant (Lyons, Young, & Keil, 2007). Children's overimitation is not just a function of them being raised in an environment where they expect ordered and guided instruction from adults. Among the Kalahari Bushmen, adults do not provide much guided instruction, but their children show as much overimitation as in WEIRD settings (Nielsen & Tomaselli, 2010).

So in these kinds of studies, whose actions would appear to be smarter—the actions of the chimpanzees or those of the overimitating children? Well, if we looked at the effectiveness and efficiency of the behaviors, the chimpanzee's tendencies to only imitate the relevant behaviors would seem to win out. This is a critical point: Emulative learning can be a very effective and intelligent kind of learning. However, although emulative learning is often very effective, and in these studies it may entail more successful strategies for solving the problems than imitation learning, it has one critical drawback: Emulative learning does not allow for cultural information to accumulate, a point we'll return to later.

LANGUAGE FACILITATES CULTURAL LEARNING. Sophisticated cultural learning is possible, in part, because humans have a theory of mind. A second related adaptation that fostered humans' abilities to engage in cultural learning is language. Being able to communicate with others is enormously important for conveying cultural information. Language allows ideas to be communicated without having to be visually demonstrated. Through language people can question, clarify, persuade, describe, direct, and explain—they can manipulate the thoughts in others' minds. Language enables people to convey their beliefs, intentions, and complex thoughts, facilitating the coordination of behavior among individuals living in groups. Language is thus integral to human cultural learning. Consider, for example, the cultural learning that you are engaging in by reading this book. How well do you think you could learn the ideas of cultural psychology that are covered in this book if you did not have language? Perhaps there are some key pictures that might be able to vaguely illustrate some points. Or if your instructor was particularly skilled at gesturing, maybe he or she could get across the gist of some other points. But the vast majority of the material in this book would simply be impossible to communicate without language. Cultural ideas are most successfully transmitted through language.

Similar to the evidence for cultural learning in animals, contrasting the language abilities of other species with those of humans reveals that although some species have some features of language, none have the rich abilities of humans. Some animals have small vocabularies of specific calls; for example, vervet monkeys make different calls to alert other monkeys to threats such as eagles and snakes (Cheney & Seyfarth, 1990). Enculturated chimpanzees and gorillas have been taught a number of words of sign language (e.g., Savage-Rumbaugh et al., 1986); however, they do not use these signs to communicate in the ways that humans do (Pinker, 1994). Moreover, no species has shown clear evidence for grammar or syntax, although the full linguistic capabilities of whales, who likely possess the best nonhuman language skills, remains somewhat unknown. In contrast, humans from all cultures, even those from cultures that appear to be quite simple or "primitive," have remarkably complex grammar and syntax, and they all have rich vocabularies. Humans have far more sophisticated ways of communicating their ideas than any other primate species.

In sum, humans differ from their nearest primate relatives in their abilities to have a rich theory of mind and to have an extensive language. These two adaptations, which likely evolved in tandem, allow humans to learn from each other in ways that other species cannot. They allow for individuals to learn cultural information from each other in highly precise ways. And this high-precision cultural learning provided humans with a truly unique advantage over other species that has profound implications: Human cultural learning is *cumulative*.

Cumulative Cultural Evolution

The one way that human cultures stand head and shoulders above all other animal cultures is that the cultures of humans are cumulative. That is, after an initial idea is learned from others, it can then be modified and improved upon by other individuals. The cultural information thus grows in complexity, and often in utility, over time. This process is called the **ratchet effect** (Tomasello et al., 1993). Like a ratchet, which can go forward but does not slip backward, cultural information can continue to accumulate without losing the earlier information. A modified practice is learned by others, who then add their own modifications, and these modifications accumulate over time.

To have cumulative cultural evolution you need creative invention, which we often can observe among many species, such as when a clever chimpanzee first figured out how to fish termites out of their mounds with a twig. In addition, however, you need reliable and faithful social transmission. The newly invented tool or practice needs to be replicated accurately enough that others have a solid foundation upon which to build any future innovations. This kind of high-fidelity social transmission requires accurate imitative learning and sophisticated communication. No other species of animal has been shown to have any capacity for significant cumulative cultural evolution (Dean, Vale, Laland, Flynn, & Kendal, 2014). In other species, the learning and retention of cultural knowledge is so poor that they are unable to build on each other's discoveries. Individuals figure things out on their own through emulative learning; they are not able to build on innovations by their peers. New generations of chimps are not likely to be any better at fishing out termites than their ancestors were, millions of years ago. There is just too much slippage in their ratchets.

Here is an example of cumulative cultural evolution. Imagine that you need to pound something, and you have to create something that would help you with the pounding. It probably wouldn't be all that difficult for you to fashion yourself a rudimentary hammer. If you were to build yourself a hammer, you would probably think about how you could put a heavy object with a flat surface on the end of a stick, and would fashion something like the kinds of hammers that you see for sale at the hardware store. You would likely be able to create a fairly effective hammer—one that was surely more effective than the stones that chimpanzees use to crack open nuts, and that frequently bruise their fingers. However, you might not realize that your creation of this simple invention is possible only because of your reliance on millions of years of accumulated cultural information. **Figure 2.5** shows the history of hammers that has been obtained from the archaeological record. Our hominid ancestors were using simple stones and suffering the concomitant bruised fingers for millions of years before a Pleistocene Einstein figured out how to attach the stone to a stick. There were several iterations, spread out over many millennia, before people started to make the kind of hammer that you're probably most familiar with today. The hammer in your toolbox was thus not invented from scratch. It is the current end product of a very long series of inventions, adaptations, and modifications.

The idea of how to make a hammer might strike you as incredibly obvious. But this is because you have grown up in a world that included the cultural ideas of hammers, and you have been influenced by them through cultural learning. For millions of years our hominid ancestors were going about smashing rocks together and bruising their fingers because the idea of tying the rock to the end of a stick never occurred to them. And remember, this is just the simple hammer! Think about all the accumulated innovations and ideas that went into creating all the other tools around you, such as the technology used in computers, cell phones, or satellites.

The tools that we use are all the most recent product of many years, if not millennia, of accumulated cultural innovations. And the speed of these innovations has been growing at exponential rates (Price, 1963). For example, archaeologists estimate

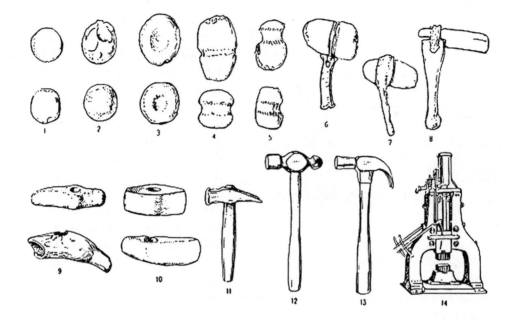

FIGURE 2.5 The evolution of the hammer, from the archaeological record to modern times (Hough, 1922). Number 14 is a gigantic steam hammer (1842).

that up until 100,000 years ago, major technological innovations appeared at the rate of approximately 0.0015 per thousand years. From that time until 40,000 years ago, the rate increased to about 0.05 innovations per thousand years. Then, from that time until 12,000 years ago, the rate of change increased to 0.55 innovations per thousand years. And from 12,000 years ago to 9,000 years ago, which coincided with the birth of agriculture, the rate of change increased sharply to about 5.2 innovations per thousand years (Lenski & Lenski, 1987). From that time on, cultural innovations have progressed at a dizzying pace that continues to increase. The U.S. Patent and Trademark Office now issues more than 500 patents each day! Take the example of the computer. The speed at which accumulated cultural innovations appear in the computer is captured in Moore's Law, which states that the data density (e.g., the number of transistors on integrated circuits) that can be built into computers doubles approximately every 18 months. This means that if you are about to buy a computer, you can get one that will be approximately twice as powerful if you wait for another 18 months. This also means that the computers sold today are approximately one million times more powerful than the ones that were sold 30 years ago. Each innovation in computer technology is built on accumulated cultural knowledge.

The reason that cultural accumulation has been increasing at a progressively rapid pace is that the human population continues to grow and people have been becoming more and more interconnected. Why is population size related to the speed

"When I was your age, things were exactly the way they are now."

of cultural evolution? Consider the following experiment (Derex, Beugin, Godelle, & Raymond, 2013). French university students played a computer game in which they had to design a fishing net. They were shown a rather intricate fishing net, which was later put away out of their view, and were asked to try to re-create it, and improve it if possible, using a computer program. They did this for 15 trials and earned points after each trial based on how well fashioned their nets were. The nets were complicated to make, so participants would often fail to re-produce some key steps in the process and would lose points. The participants were run in groups that ranged from 2 to 16 members; after each trial they could see the list of scores earned by their group-mates, and they were allowed to click on one of the nets of their group members to see precisely how it was made. Not surprisingly, the participants usually clicked on the group member's net that had earned the highest number of points—that is, they selected the best model and tried to copy from it. At the end of the 15 trials, their final products were compared to the initial net that they had been shown. The probability that participants were able to recreate the original fishing net at the end of the 15 trials is shown in **Figure 2.6**. Those who were run in groups of 2 were

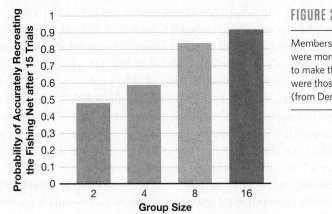

FIGURE 2.6

Members from larger groups were more likely to learn how to make the fishing nets than were those from smaller groups (from Derex et al., 2013).

unlikely to be able to reproduce the net—only about half of the people in groups of 2 could to do so by the end of the 15 trials—and they lost points because their nets were not very effective. In contrast, almost every person who had been run in groups of 16 was able to reproduce the nets after 15 trials. The presence of a larger number of models ensured that those in the large groups almost always had a talented model to copy from. Moreover, some of the members of the larger groups, but none of the members of the smaller groups, came up with innovations that made their fishing nets even more effective than the original nets they were shown.

This study reveals how the larger the group of people, the better cultural information can be maintained and improved upon. This is because you're more likely to encounter a successful model to copy from out of a larger group than out of a smaller group. Relatedly, there will be more innovations that come from a larger group than from a smaller group, so a larger group will be more likely to have at least one person stumble upon a good idea. Larger groups should lead to faster cultural evolution.

Another way that to see the relation between group size and cultural evolution is to look at the cultural complexity of people living in isolated environments, where there would be little exposure to people from other parts of the world. The South Pacific is a particularly good place to investigate, as the islands were colonized by Polynesians more than a thousand years ago, and they remain thousands of kilometers apart from each other. One investigation measured the population and the degree of cultural complexity in the existing technologies among the different islands at the time of their first contact with Westerners. A very straightforward relationship was revealed: The islands with the largest populations at the time of first contact (such as Hawaii) had far more different kinds of tools than the islands with the smallest populations (such as Malekula; Kline & Boyd, 2010). Bigger populations allowed for the more rapid spread of cultural innovations.

Moreover, it's not just the size of the group that matters—what is also crucial is how connected the members of the groups are. For example, if you live in a large city but never venture out of your house to talk to anyone, it doesn't matter how many great ideas there are around you—you wouldn't encounter them yourself. Another study explored the importance of the interconnectedness among group members for cultural learning by having groups of five people try to reproduce a complicated rock-climbing knot, which involved several distinct steps, across several trials, using a similar kind of design as the fishing net study. But the participants in one of those groups of five was allowed to interact only with one of their group members, whereas participants in the other groups were allowed to interact with all five of their group members. The results: The groups that had more interactions were more likely to reproduce the complicated knot (Muthukrishna, Shulman, Vasilescu, & Henrich, 2014). Culture thus evolves faster in larger groups that are well connected. One way that we can see this is that most innovations tend to come from cities or places where like-minded people are clustered (such as university towns, or industrial hubs such as

Silicon Valley); in these places, one is more likely to encounter successful models to imitate and build upon their ideas. Moreover, with the rise of the Internet people can now potentially connect with a large fraction of the whole world's population, which should further accelerate the rate of cultural change. This increasingly rapid cultural evolution that the world has experienced means that more and more cultural ideas are becoming available, and thus there is a growing foundation of ideas on which to build new ideas. Ideas beget other ideas, and culture accumulates.

The key role that cultural learning plays in the accumulation of cultural innovations can also be seen in the reverse situation: Why do cultures sometimes lose ideas? Despite the general trend toward an accumulation of cultural knowledge, there are a number of historical examples of cultures experiencing a loss of their accumulated knowledge—their ratchets have slipped. One famous case is with the first human settlers to Tasmania. Humans initially arrived in Tasmania from Australia approximately 34,000 years ago by crossing a land bridge that was later cut off from the rest of Australia by a 200-kilometer stretch of ocean that rose after the last Ice Age. When Europeans arrived in the 18th century, they found only scattered foraging bands that possessed the simplest technology known of any contemporary human group. Curiously, archaeological investigations show that the 18th-century Tasmanians had even simpler technologies than Tasmanians did thousands of years earlier, as judged by the archaeological record. Tasmanians appeared to have lost some key technological knowledge over that time, such as the ability to make bone tools, cold-weather clothing, fishhooks, and boomerangs (Bowdler, 1982; Jones, 1995). The entire toolkit of 18th-century Tasmanians consisted of only about 24 items, in contrast to the hundreds of items possessed by 18th-century aboriginal Australians just across the Bass Strait. Henrich (2004) argues that this loss of knowledge was the result of a shortage of models to copy from: There were only about 4,000 people living on Tasmania when the Europeans arrived, scattered over a fairly large territory, and they were completely isolated from other cultural groups.

Similar losses of technologies have occurred in other societies in which a small group of people was cut off from a larger population, either through physical isolation, such as among the Melanesians living in the Torres Islands (Rivers, 1926), or by cultures adopting reclusive habits, such as among the Siriono of Bolivia (Holmberg, 1969) or the Piraha of Brazil (Everett, 2005). Henrich has demonstrated with a simple mathematical model that complex cultural knowledge can deteriorate if the size of a population of interconnected minds shrinks, leaving learners with a shortage of skilled models to copy from. Behavioral experiments also show that small groups are more likely to lose the ability to make complex objects than larger and more connected groups are (Muthukrishna et al., 2014). This is because people typically try to copy from the most talented model available, although few will be able to learn the skill as well as the model. In an absence of talented models to copy from, the ratchets will slip, and cultural knowledge will deteriorate.

Thus far, I've only discussed cumulative cultural innovations in terms of technologies, but accumulation is not limited to physical tools. Cultural ideas such as democracy or interest-bearing loans also represent the accumulation of ideas and innovations spread out over human history. This book will make the argument that psychological mechanisms can undergo cumulative cultural evolution as well. One example is mathematical reasoning. You can likely easily engage in mathematical reasoning that involves addition, multiplication, and fractions. If you're especially talented, you might even be able to figure out problems involving quadratic equations, probability, calculus, irrational numbers, or matrix algebra. We were not born with the innate capacity to reason about numbers in these ways, which is evident by the fact that people from some cultures are incapable of even counting numbers past 3 or so, or of estimating the amount of rather small quantities (we'll explore this more in Chapter 9). Rather, these different kinds of mathematical reasoning strategies can be understood as cultural products that have become more and more complex as people have added innovations to earlier ways of thinking about numbers. Reflecting this, more recently discovered mathematical concepts are more complex than ones that were discovered earlier, and when children learn mathematical concepts in school they do so in roughly the same order that the mathematical concepts were discovered—you first need to understand the relatively simple principles of geometry before you can begin to make sense of the more complex principles of calculus (Mesoudi, 2011). This kind of cultural evolution is not possible unless cultural learning is of the highest fidelity, when individuals are able to understand a model's intentions, mimic them faithfully, and then, only when the model's behaviors are successfully imitated, build on them to allow for cultural evolution. We'll discuss more about how cultures change over time in the next chapter.

The fact that humans uniquely have cumulative culture is an important point. Unlike other species, we do not just live in physical worlds. In addition to the physical characteristics of our environment, humans are a cultural species that exists within worlds consisting of cultural information that has accumulated over history: **cultural worlds** (Luria, 1928). Think of all of the cultural ideas that make up your own world: notions such as children receiving an education at school, markets being the places to acquire most goods and services rather than producing them yourself, governments providing you with formal laws, militaries protecting you from foreign invaders, households consisting of monogamous nuclear-family arrangements, having access to distant places that can be reached via mechanized transportation, and being able to learn ideas from places even farther afield through books, television, or the Internet. You probably haven't given much thought to the role that notions such as these play in your life, because people tend to take such cultural practices as given, but they are all examples of cultural ideas that were not present throughout most of human history. And these cultural ideas greatly influence the ways that we live our lives, determining much of what we do on a daily basis. We are all born into rich cultural worlds, and we are constantly learning, and being influenced by, the shared ideas that make up our cultures. Hence, if we wish to understand why people behave and think in the ways that they do, we need to also consider the kinds of cultural information that people encounter in their daily lives.

Why Are Humans Adept at Cultural Learning?

The abilities to speak and have a theory of mind were key adaptations for cultural learning, and these have allowed humans to develop so much of what we think of as uniquely human. They are largely what distinguish us from our proto-chimpanzee ancestors in terms of our abilities to accumulate culture. What is it about the human brain that facilitated these abilities? How did we evolve the capacities to become cultural animals?

You and Your Big Brain

The high-fidelity cultural learning and sophisticated language skills that are uniquely possessed by humans would seem to depend on considerable cognitive resources. Indeed, humans do have quite enormous brains. Our brain size, as determined by the **encephalization quotient**—the ratio of the brain weight of an animal to that predicted for a comparable animal of the same body size—is approximately 4.6. That is, our brain is about four to five times larger than that of other mammals our size. This is the largest encephalization quotient of any mammal (Martin, 1981), except for the very tiny, yet remarkably big-brained, shrew. The size of our brains is surely relevant for understanding our skills of cultural learning.

Having such a large brain, however, does have its costs. Brains require an enormous amount of energy to operate. You can think of the big brain in your skull as being akin to a massive, gas-guzzling jet engine that consumes about 16% of all of your basal metabolism. That is, if you were to eat a dozen eggs, the energy from two of those eggs would be devoted solely to keeping your brain operating (and to thinking about this question), leaving just 10 of the eggs to take care of the rest of your body, including such tasks as breathing, digestion, homeostasis, and locomotion. This is a lot of energy intake, especially as our brains constitute only about 2% of our body weight. In contrast, the average mammal gets by with much less energy—only 3% of their basal metabolism is used by their brains. Some other mammals, such as marsupials, get by with the equivalent of a rubber-band-powered gizmo that uses up only about 1% of their basal metabolism (Aiello & Wheeler, 1995; Richerson & Boyd, 2005), leaving them with a lot of other resources to take care of the rest of their physical needs. Given the huge operating costs for large brains, there must have been some significant selective advantage for humans to get them.

Humans Versus Chimpanzees

In trying to understand why humans developed such big brains, let's consider how human brains compare to those of our closest evolutionary ancestors, primates. Primates also have unusually large brains for mammals, and chimpanzees, in particular, stand out. However, although chimpanzees have large brains, the encephalization quotient of humans is almost double theirs. Over the 5 to 7 million years of evolution that separate humans and chimpanzees, our brains grew at a quite rapid pace. It was necessary for our bodies to change in other ways to accommodate the very large energy intake of our massive brains.

One physical change in our bodies is evident in the opening story of this chapter, in which Snookie the chimpanzee mercilessly thrashed all human competitors. Compared with chimpanzees, and especially gorillas and orangutans, humans have considerably less muscle mass. The mass of the various muscles in chimpanzees' arms and legs, when scaled to the segment length of those limbs, is about 27% larger than it is for humans (Thorpe, Crompton, Gunther, Ker, & Alexander, 1999). Although having less muscle mass came with the cost of less strength for humans, it allowed a larger portion of our energy to be consumed by our brains. If we hadn't lost muscle mass over evolution, we would have needed to consume more calories to be able to have both large muscles and a large brain, which would have put us at a disadvantage when food supplies were short. So as we became a weaker ape, we were able to redirect some of the energy used up by those muscles to make us a smarter ape.

However, our relatively weaker muscles played only a small part in allowing for the expansion of our brains. More important, over the past few million years of evolution, our bodies changed in another, more dramatic way that freed up a lot of our energy consumption: Our guts became much shorter. The digestive tract, consisting of the stomach, the small intestine, and especially the large intestine, is about 60% smaller in humans than what would be expected in a primate of our body weight (Martin, Chivers, MacLarnon, & Hladik, 1985). Because the digestive tract is another huge consumer of energy, this smaller digestive tract saves humans approximately 10% of their daily energy expenditures (Aiello & Wheeler, 1995). By spending much less energy digesting their food, humans could afford to spend much more energy evolving a larger brain that allowed them to spend more time thinking about other things. If humans would have had both a larger gut and a larger brain, they would have had to spend a much larger portion of their day eating to get the sufficient energy to operate both of these.

You might notice an apparent contradiction here: If the purpose of the digestive tract is to extract energy from food, then how could humans direct more energy to their brains if their digestive tracts became smaller? Wouldn't a smaller digestive tract mean that they could extract less energy from their food? For smaller guts to have allowed humans to have more energy available for their brains, humans would have had to have more efficient digestion per unit of their digestion tract compared with chimpanzees. But how could this be possible? The biological anthropologist Richard Wrangham (2009) offers an intriguing answer to this question: Humans learned how to do much of their digestion *outside* of their bodies. That is, they learned how to cook their food.

When we cook food, we alter it in a number of ways. Some of those changes create a net loss: For example, the cooking process causes food to lose some of its energy through dripping, it can lead to a loss in some vitamins, and it produces some kinds of proteins that we aren't able to digest. It is largely on the basis of these costs that some people have sought to pursue a raw diet. However, there is a big upside to cooking: It substantially increases the amount of energy that we can extract from food. Cooking denatures proteins, gelatinizes starch, and makes all food considerably softer, thus requiring less energy for our bodies to digest them (Eastwood, 2003). It enables us to eat a wider variety of different kinds of food than what we could consume raw. It also reduces the amount of chewing that is necessary, which has led to humans' jaw muscles and teeth also being much smaller than those of chimpanzees. The average human spends approximately one hour per day chewing food, in contrast with the six hours a day spent chewing by chimpanzees (Wrangham, 2009). Researchers have found a direct negative relationship between the number of hours available for feeding and the low caloric yield of raw foods and the number of brain neurons that a mammal can develop (Fonseca-Azvedo & Herculano-Houzel, 2012). By cooking our food, we were able to evolve a much smaller digestive tract, which freed up much energy to be used by our brains.

This account suggests that it wasn't so much that humans' larger and smarter brains allowed them to figure out how to cook; rather, cooking, which appears to have emerged quite early in the hominid ancestral record (likely somewhere between 800,000 and 1.5 million years ago, although the dates are disputed; Goren-Inbar et al., 2004; James, 1989), allowed humans to have larger and smarter brains. Cooking, a cultural invention, is thus partly responsible for our biological nature. In sum, it is because of the trade-offs in these various competing forces that humans ultimately became the scrawny, short-gutted, and big-brained apes that we are.

What Is the Evolutionary Advantage of a Large Brain?

These changes in our physical evolution allowed humans to develop much larger brains compared with other primates. But this does not address why humans would benefit from having larger brains in the first place. What was the evolutionary advantage for humans to have such large and costly brains? To best answer this question, it is useful to first consider what kinds of evolutionary advantages existed for other primates to have large brains, because, as noted earlier, primates themselves have unusually large brains compared with other kinds of mammals.

How primates' brains got to be as large as they are has been a matter of some debate. Let's explore a number of the theories that have been proposed to explain how particular aspects of primates' lives would have exerted selection pressures that would have favored large brains. One such theory rests on the observation that many primates eat a lot of fruit. There are good reasons to eat fruit. Fruit is rich in vitamins, carbohydrates, and calories, and fruits tend to be available in concentrated patches. The challenge with having a diet based on fruit, however, is that it is ripe for only brief periods. To live off a diet of fruit, you need to keep in mind where the various fruit trees are located and when they would likely be bearing ripe fruit. Perhaps the selection for big brains in primates was driven by the need for cognitive abilities that would help them keep a mental map of the short-lived and patchily distributed fruit that was around them (Clutton-Brock & Harvey, 1980). Those primates that had better skills at remembering where the fruit was would have been more likely to eat well and to have surviving offspring than those who were stumbling about aimlessly trying to find some ripe bananas.

A second theory regarding the relevance of the diet of primates has also been offered to account for the evolution of primate brains. A number of primate species rely on food sources that require a fair bit of ingenuity to access them. For example, some primate food sources include nuts and seeds encased in hard shells that need to be cracked open, tubers that need to be dug up, and termites that need to be fished out of their mounds. These "extractive" food sources are often worth pursuing because they tend to be rich in protein and energy. Perhaps the cognitive skills needed to allow primates to extract these valuable foods served as the selective force for larger brains (Parker & Gibson, 1977). Those primates that were smart enough to figure out how to open the nuts and get themselves a nutritious meal would have had more surviving offspring than those that were left to eat less nutritious food.

A third theory to account for primates' big brains is the complexity of their social worlds. Most species of primates live in complex social groups. Clear power hierarchies exist within these groups, and individuals form various relationships and alliances with each other that are often communicated through their regular grooming activities. Within these groups there are conflicts, power struggles, and opportunities for cooperation, nepotism, and reciprocity. To function well in a highly social community, one must be able to outmaneuver others within it, which requires attending to a highly complex series of relations. Perhaps it was the great cognitive demands inherent in social living that led to the evolution of large primate brains (Humphrey, 1976). This theory has become known as the **social brain hypothesis** (Dunbar, 1998). Those primates that were most successful at navigating the intricate and elaborate webs of social relationships would have been more likely to attract mates, secure resources, and protect themselves and their offspring from dangers than those that were left to fend for themselves.

Psychologists do more than just armchair theorizing, and the value of theories is ultimately judged by assessing which theories are most consistent with the available evidence. The three competing theories were evaluated to see which one was best able to account for the evolution of primates' large brains (Dunbar, 1992). To do so, researchers calculated the ratio of the volume of the neocortex (the outermost layer of the brain that is concerned with higher functions, such as sensory perception, motor control, and conscious thought) to the volume of the rest of the brain. This is known as the **neocortex ratio,** and it has been used as a proxy measure of intelligence, because the most notable way that primate brains differ from those of other mammals is that the primate neocortexes are larger. Furthermore, much research conducted with functional magnetic resonance imaging (fMRI) has revealed that problem solving tends to be focused in the neocortex. Researchers compared the neocortex ratios across a number of primate species, while attending to variables relevant to the three competing hypotheses. Namely, the percentage of fruit in the diets of each of the primate species was calculated; the foraging styles of the different primate species were categorized as being focused on either extractive or nonextractive foods; and the average group size that the different primate species lived in was calculated. The three graphs plotting these three variables against neocortex ratios are shown in **Figure 2.7**. Each of the dots in the figures indicates a different species of primates.

First, looking at Figure 2.7a, we can see the relation between neocortex size and the percentage of fruit in the diets of various primate species. The individual primate species are pretty much scattered randomly across the graph, indicating that these two variables are uncorrelated. There is not much support here for the notion that the cognitive skills required to find ripe fruit drove the evolution of primate brains.

Second, Figure 2.7b tests whether the average neocortex ratio is larger for those primates that engaged in extractive foraging strategies than for those primates that used nonextractive techniques. Overall, there was little difference in neocortex ratio between these two groups. This analysis thus failed to provide support for the notion that the challenges of obtaining hard-to-extract foods is what selected for primate intelligence.

Third, as can be seen in Figure 2.7c, there is a rather clear relation between neocortex ratio and average group size for the different species of primates. Those primates that lived in larger social groups tended to have larger neocortex ratios. This is consistent with the notion that the complexities of social living selected for cognitive skills that allowed individual primates to successfully navigate their social worlds. Parallel findings have emerged for other kinds of animals: More social species of whales, carnivores, ungulates, and birds have larger brains than closely related species that are less social (Burish, Kueh, & Wang, 2004; Perez-Barberia, Shultz, & Dunbar, 2007). Living in large social groups is associated with having larger brains across species within numerous taxonomic orders.

The social brain hypothesis is thus the best supported of these accounts for why primates got their large brains. Indeed, there is much other evidence that some species of primates are able to attend to rather complex social relationships. For example, in one study researchers placed speakers around the jungle where vervet monkeys

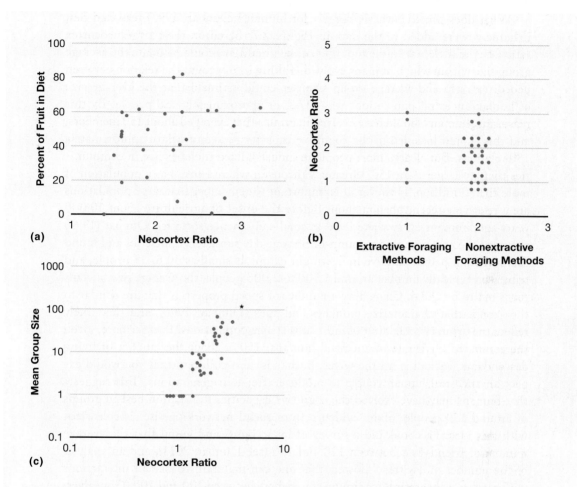

FIGURE 2.7 (a) The relation between neocortex ratio and the percentage of fruit in the diet of various primate species. (b) The relation between neocortex ratio and whether a primate species uses extractive or nonextractive foraging methods. (c) The relation between average group size and neocortex ratio of various species of primates (Dunbar, 1993).

lived, and they played back the recorded distress calls of juvenile monkeys (Cheney & Seyfarth, 1990). Not only did the mothers of those distressed juveniles react, showing that the mothers recognized the sound of their offspring's voices, but the other females also reacted, by looking at the juvenile's mother, indicating that they too recognized the sound of the voice as belonging to that mother's offspring. Primates tend to be highly social animals, and social behavior requires considerable cognitive skills.

What does this hypothesis suggest for humans? Dunbar (1993) reasoned that if humans were added to the data in Figure 2.7c based on their large neocortex ratio (see the little star in the top right of the graph), we could estimate the average group size within which humans evolved. Taking into account the relation between neocortex ratio and average group size, we could estimate that the average size of human ancestral populations was 147.8, or approximately 150 people. By this reasoning, humans should have evolved in groups that averaged about 150 members, and this should have led to the cognitive capacity to keep track of approximately 150 relations. But clearly, most people in industrialized societies live in communities that are larger than 150. Greater Vancouver, where I live, has a population of more than 2 million. However, it is important to remember that large populations are a relatively recent phenomenon. Before the onset of agriculture about 10,000 years ago, humans everywhere lived in small subsistence societies. Dunbar (1993) surveyed the ethnographic accounts of present-day subsistence societies and found that although people can live in overnight camps as small as 30 to 35 people, and tribes can typically number around 1,500 to 2,000 people, the average size of clans turns out to be 148.4. Clans have a number of social properties that are similar to the groups that characterize monkeys and apes (Dunbar, 1996), and they likely reflect the primary social unit of most subsistence populations. Furthermore, given the estimated birth rate of ancestral humans, 150 is about the number of living descendants (including all the wives, husbands, and children) that you would expect an ancestral human couple to produce after four generations. This suggests that humans may have evolved the cognitive capacities to function best in groups of around 150 people. Some evidence from social networking sites is consistent with this idea: Facebook did a survey of its accounts and found that the average number of friends was between 120 and 130 (see Dunbar, 2011), and an analysis of the number of Twitter followers that one can maintain consistent interactions with reaches a theoretical maximum somewhere between 100 and 200 (Goncalves, Perra, & Vespignani, 2011). Now, of course social media sites make it possible for individuals to greatly surpass this number; some people maintain thousands of Facebook "friends," and Justin Bieber somehow has attracted more than 50 million Twitter followers. On the surface this would seem to violate Dunbar's number; however, the vast majority of these relationships are typically quite tenuous, and wouldn't meet the criteria of a meaningful mutual relationship. In sum, humans appear to have evolved the cognitive capacities to maintain relationships of around 150 people, as this is the group size that they appeared to live in in ancestral environments. Any groups that were larger than 150 became too unwieldy to manage without some kind of formal institutional structure, yet smaller groups would lose the advantages of large numbers. One particular advantage of large groups, as we discussed before, is that it facilitates cultural evolution.

Human Brains Are for Learning from Each Other

Because human brains are so much larger than the brains of other primates, you might expect humans to be smarter than other primates on virtually all intellectually demanding tasks. But, actually, it appears that there are only some kinds of tasks where we have a clear edge on our most intelligent primate cousins, such as chimpanzees. For many kinds of cognitive tasks, chimpanzees can give us humans a real run for our money. One study compared university students to chimpanzees on a working memory task, where numbers were very briefly flashed on a screen and the participant then had to tap the screen in the places where the numbers had appeared in order of the numbers. While most humans could beat most of the chimps, the champion of this game came from Team Chimpanzee: At the most difficult level of the game, when the numbers were flashed for only 0.2 second, a 5-year old chimp named Ayumu performed the best of all participants, human or chimp (Inoue & Matsuzawa, 2007; see **Figure 2.8**). Likewise, when chimps were pitted against adult humans in a strategic conflict game, where participants earned points by either trying to match or mismatch what their partner was going to do, on average the chimps outperformed the humans (Martin, Bhui, Bossaerts, Matsuzawa, & Camerer, 2014). Hence, humans don't seem

FIGURE 2.8 Ayumu demonstrating his human-besting working memory skills.

to have an overwhelming intellectual advantage over chimpanzees for all kinds of tasks, despite our much larger brains.

As discussed earlier, the social brain hypothesis suggests that primates got their large brains because of the challenges involved in social living and that this was especially so for humans, given their unusually large social groups. However, although primates are highly social mammals, in many ways humans can be said to be an "ultra-social" species (Boyd & Richerson, 1998): Humans tend to be far more engaged with others around them than do any other primates. We are constantly attending to what others are doing, we gossip about others all the time, our behaviors are guided a great deal by what others around us are doing, and we learn by imitating others. The very large differences in the sociality of humans versus other primates parallels the very large differences in brain size between the species. This raises the possibility that humans derive particular benefits from social living that justifies the huge energetic expense of their massive brains. Is there any evidence for this claim?

One study contrasted the cognitive skills of 2.5-year-old human children with those of chimpanzees and orangutans to identify the kinds of skills that differentiate the species (Herrmann et al., 2007). The participants were provided with two kinds of problem-solving tasks: physical and social. The physical problem-solving tasks involved presenting the participants with a desired object that was unavailable to them unless they could figure out a way of acquiring it with the tools at hand. For example, the participants had to figure out how to put a stick through a hole in order to pull a desired object toward them. The social problem-solving tasks also involved the retrieval of a desired object from an apparatus; however, with the social tasks the participants first observed a model solve the problem. They could only solve the task if they did the same behaviors that were performed by the model. How did the participants do?

Figure 2.9a shows the performance of the three species on the physical problem-solving tasks: There was no significant difference across the species. When it comes to these kinds of tasks, 2.5-year-old children are only about as smart as other apes. This suggests that the evolution of the extra-large brains of humans did not likely occur in order to solve physical problems, because there is not a particular human advantage for these tasks, at least when looking at young children.

In contrast, **Figure 2.9b** shows the performance on the social problem-solving tasks. Here is where the humans really shone: The 2.5-year-olds were far more likely to do precisely what the model did compared with either species of ape. Rather, a common response of the chimps and orangutans was to try to figure out how to solve the problem on their own, using their own emulative learning styles. The human kids, on the other hand, did precisely the same set of steps that they saw the model do. A variety of specific kinds of subtasks made up the social problem-solving tasks, and the single subtask that humans most outperformed the other

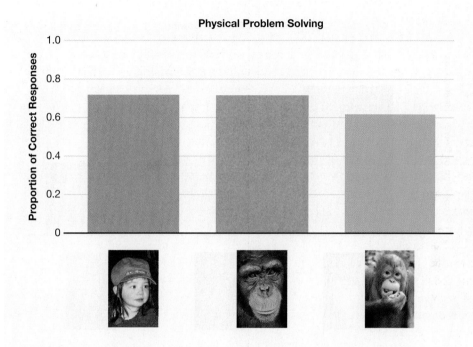

FIGURE 2.9A The performance of 2.5-year-old children, chimpanzees, and orangutans on physical problem-solving tasks.

apes on was the imitation subtask. On this task, most of the 2.5-year-olds got 100% correct, whereas most of the apes scored 0% correct. The humans were engaged in cultural learning.

This difference in an ability to learn from others can help make sense of why humans are the only species that has real cultural accumulation. By being able to learn so well from others, we're in a position to build upon the innovations of others. This unique human ability is clearly visible in the following study (see Dean, Kendal, Schapiro, Thierry, & Laland, 2012): Small groups of human children (3-4 years old) competed with similarly sized groups of chimpanzees and of capuchin monkeys—a highly social species thought to be the most intelligent of New World monkeys. They were given a puzzle box to solve, and solving the puzzle required learning a series of three steps that needed to be performed in a precise order. The puzzle was designed to capture the sequential processes involved in cultural accumulation—the third step could not be completed without completing the first two steps in order. For each

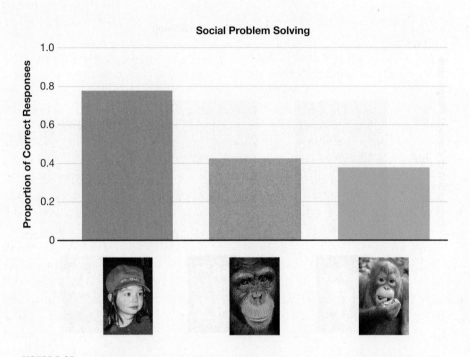

FIGURE 2.9B The performance of 2.5-year-old children, chimpanzees, and orangutans on social problem-solving tasks (Herrmann et al., 2007).

successfully performed step, the participants were given increasingly valuable rewards (carrots, apples, grapes, or increasingly desirable stickers for the children). How did the different species do on the task? After dozens of hours of presentation with the puzzle task, only 2 of the 30 capuchins were able to solve Stage 2, and none of them solved Stage 3. The chimpanzees did a little better: After dozens of hours, 4 of 33 chimps reaching Stage 2, and 1 reached Stage 3. In contrast, 15 of the 35 children made it to Stage 3, despite having the boxes for less than 10% of the time of the other primates. The children were able to go through the different steps, and thus their cultural learning accumulated, because they were more likely than the other primates to imitate each other, were more likely to teach each other, and were more likely to reward each other by sharing their stickers—all of these behaviors predicted successful performance among the children. In contrast, there were no instances of teaching or sharing among the chimpanzees and capuchins, and there was very little imitation going on for them as well. The intellectual advantages that the children had over their primate cousins were precisely those kinds of skills that fostered the accumulation of culture.

These results suggest that the primary way that humans differ from other primates is in terms of their ability to learn from others. Chimps, orangutans, and capuchins are all highly intelligent species with excellent problem-solving abilities, good working memory, fast reaction times, and good strategic skills. Moreover, the imitation skills of these species are the best that have been documented among nonhuman primates. But their abilities to learn from others pales in comparison to those of humans. These enhanced abilities to learn from others is what leads to the accumulation of culture, which appears to be the key advantage that humans derived from their larger brains. If this reasoning is correct, then the primary forces that drove the evolution of the costly human brain were associated with our being able to attend to, and accurately understand, the intentions and activities of a reasonably large group of individuals with whom we regularly interacted. Being able to interact with and learn from a reasonably large group of people meant that we were more likely to find talented models that we could imitate and learn from, and ultimately develop new skills that would be adaptive for us. By developing the cognitive capacities associated with cultural learning, even if those adaptations required a lot of energy to sustain them, humans were able to adapt to the various challenges they encountered in the diverse ecologies within which they settled.

Thinking about it this way suggests that humans did not just evolve biologically to the point that they could cross over a magic threshold and become cultural beings. Rather, the ability to engage in cultural learning itself was a selective force that has shaped human evolution since humans last shared common ancestors with other primates (see Henrich, 2015; Richerson & Boyd, 2005). The earlier example of our hominid ancestors learning how to cook demonstrates how cultural learning played an important role in our biological evolution. Culture, was, in the words of anthropologist Clifford Geertz (1973), a central "ingredient" to human evolution. We evolved to depend on cultural learning, and over the millennia we have continually become more dependent on this learning. Those of our ancestors who were best able to engage in cultural learning were the ones most likely to have surviving offspring. Culture and the biology of the human brain are thus inextricably bound. Humans evolved to be a cultural species.

SUMMARY

Humans are unique in the animal kingdom for being so dependent on cultural learning. Although other animals are capable of creative kinds of learning such as emulative learning, there is scant evidence for imitative learning in other species, as they lack the rich theory of mind that would enable them to understand the perspective of others well. Likewise, humans are unique in having complex language capabilities. Language greatly facilitates cultural learning by allowing communication among individuals. A theory of mind and sophisticated language skills are necessary for cultural accumulation, whereby cultural innovations build on ones that are already learned. Other species do not appear to have any appreciable degrees of cultural accumulation.

Humans differ physically from other apes in terms of having larger brains, less muscle mass, and shorter digestive tracts. The latter was made possible by humans learning how to cook their food.

Much of the human brain, particularly the regions that differ appreciably in size from those of other mammals, appears to have been selected primarily to engage in cultural learning. Humans evolved to be able to function in large social groups, which offered more cultural learning opportunities.

THINK ABOUT IT

1. In what ways do some animals have culture?
2. What are some consequences of humans being attracted to prestigious others?
3. What are the respective advantages of emulative and imitative learning?
4. Where should we expect to see the most rapid cultural accumulation in the near future? Explain why.
5. What does it mean to say that humans live in cultural worlds?
6. What is the relation between cooking food and having a big brain?
7. Given what we know about chimpanzee intelligence, if humans went extinct what kind of chimpanzee society would you expect to develop? Would they take over the world, as in the movie *Planet of the Apes*?

KEY TERMS

These Dinka girls are applying facial decorations for a wedding celebration. Despite sharing the same ecology, crops, and lifestock with the nearby Nuer, the Dinka's cultural practices differ from those of the Nuer in many ways, showing the power of transmitted culture.

3

CULTURAL EVOLUTION

There are many behaviors that you distinctly avoid engaging in because they are considered to be "bad manners." However, many of the manners that you are aware of have not emerged to address universal human problems but instead are the result of cultural learning. This fact becomes clear when we consider how manners vary across cultures. For example, when you enter a Japanese house, it is good manners to remove your shoes, point them toward the door, and put on a pair of slippers, which are to be removed when you enter a room with a tatami mat or are to be exchanged for a pair of special "toilet slippers" upon entering the restroom. And, as I can testify from personal experience, it's a guaranteed show-stopper if you ever forget to remove the toilet slippers when you sit down to eat at the dining table. In contrast, for many Americans shoes come off only when they are taking a shower or going to bed. Manners differ across cultures because people are socialized to different sets of norms and customs.

The evidence for the cultural foundation of manners is even stronger when we consider how manners have changed over time. The German sociologist Norbert Elias, in his classic work *The Civilizing Process* (1939/1994), argues that Western Europe, and likewise other modernizing cultures, was transformed as the manners of the aristocracy slowly trickled down to govern the behavior of the lower classes as well. People became "civilized" as a growing set of rules and norms came to regulate the behaviors of people across all classes of society. Elias provided a sampling of many of these manners.

For example, consider the maxim offered in a 15th-century German book of table manners: "It is unseemly to blow your nose in the tablecloth." Today this advice remains equally sound, but now it somehow goes without saying. You can't help wondering who were the runny-nosed readers that the author had in mind when he wrote this useful piece of guidance. Blowing your nose was a common topic in older manners books, and one's technique was seen to indicate one's status. As a 16th-century Dutch manners book stated: "To blow your nose

"Not so loud, sweetie. We're in Europe."

on your hat or clothing is rustic, and to do so with the arm or elbow befits a tradesman; nor is it much more polite to use the hand, if you immediately smear the snot on your garment. It is proper to wipe the nostrils with a handkerchief, and to do this while turning away if more honourable people are present." Here we can see how what was formerly the etiquette for only the upper classes came to govern the manners for all classes of people.

A section in Elias's book titled "On Spitting" reveals another way in which current manners have diverged from the past (**Figure 3.1**). Advice from the Middle Ages recommended: "Do not spit into the basin when you wash your hands, but beside it," or "Do not spit across the table in the manner of hunters." By the 18th century, spitting etiquette had progressed from the norms of the Middle

FIGURE 3.1 In past centuries, spittoons were regular fixtures in many public locations in the United States, so that people could spit indoors without making a mess. This is a photo of the luxurious lobby of the Brown Palace Hotel in Denver, Colorado, taken around 1900. The vessel in the foreground is a spittoon, signifying a very different attitude toward spitting than is present in the United States today.

Ages. Advice included the following: "Frequent spitting is disagreeable. When it is necessary you should conceal it as much as possible, and avoid soiling either persons or their clothes, no matter who they are." By the late 19th century, however, spitting was far less tolerated, although still very common: "Spitting is at all times a disgusting habit. I need say nothing more than—never indulge in it." As the centuries passed, greater and greater emphasis was placed on acting in so-called civilized ways.

One reason manners have changed over time is that people's views of what is healthy have also changed. For example, in the 16th century it was seen as unhealthy to refrain from either spitting or from passing wind. These behaviors have become less tolerated as it is no longer considered healthy to engage in them. And some differences in manners of the past simply reflect changing norms that are quite arbitrary as to what is considered polite. For example, medieval eating etiquette prescribed, "You should always eat with the outside hand; if a companion sits on your right, eat with your left hand." A 16th-century recommendation said, "If a serviette is given, lay it on your left shoulder or arm." A 19th-century manners book offered the following: "I may hint that no epicure ever yet put knife to apple, and that an orange should be peeled with a spoon." These table manners appear as arbitrary as the current Western norms for salad forks to be on the far left of the plate, for soup to precede a main course, or for wine to be served in glasses that are held by the stem.

These transformations in manners over time are instances of an obvious fact: Cultures change. Behavior considered polite a few centuries ago would not necessarily be appropriate today. Standards of politeness, as well as many other cultural norms, have changed over generations. Cultures continue to evolve; when your parents were your age, they likely participated in a quite distinct culture from what you do today, even if they grew up in the same neighborhood as you. Cultures are not monolithic and frozen entities but rather are fluid and constantly evolving as new ideas emerge and conditions change. Hence, it is important to keep in mind that the studies discussed in this book in which different cultures are contrasted represent a snapshot in time, and the findings very well might not hold for later generations.

In this chapter we will explore where cultural variation comes from and how cultures are able to both change and persist over time. The fact that cultures do often change and evolve, and that psychological processes likewise change and evolve, underscores a theme in this book—that experiences shape our psychology. But before we can understand how cultural experiences come to shape the ways we think, we first must understand how cultures come to be.

Where Does Cultural Variation Come From?

There are few questions more challenging in the social sciences than the question of what causes cultural variation. This issue has been considered from a variety of disciplines outside of psychology, and we will consider some of those perspectives in this chapter. It is immediately apparent that cultures around the world vary, often tremendously, in their practices, social structures, diets, economic systems, technologies, religious beliefs, and, as this book argues, psychology. Why cultures vary in these ways defies any single answer—rather, we can come to understand cultural variation by considering a variety of different forces that come into play.

Ecological and Geographical Variation

One way that we can consider how cultural variation comes to be is to consider the ecologies within which people live. By the late Pleistocene era (about 20,000 years ago), humans had already settled in a more diverse range of physical environments than any other species. And it is quite obvious that these different environments affected the ways that people went about living their daily lives. Some of the ways that physical environments affect culture are quite direct. For example, there are no large indigenous mammals in Hawaii, and native Hawaiians do not have any hunting traditions. This contrasts sharply with the !Kung of the Kalahari who live in an environment surrounded by large animals and who derive much of their caloric intake by hunting them. The kinds of foods that are available within a given ecology affect the kinds of foraging behaviors that people engage in.

These ecological differences can have some indirect effects on cultures as well. Different physical ecologies do not just affect the diets of people; the different foraging behaviors can also come to affect how the societies are structured and the values that people come to adopt.

"I don't know how it started, either. All I know is that it's part of our corporate culture."

For example, cultural variation in gender roles can arise from the different ecologies within which people live (Gilmore, 1990). In those cultures where the environment is harsh and requires courage and physical prowess to secure a living (e.g., places where large game is hunted, or risky deep-sea fishing is performed), cultures of masculinity that value the strength and toughness of males are more likely to emerge. For example, on the South Pacific island of Truk, men traditionally had to go on dangerous deep-sea fishing expeditions to secure food for their families. At the same time, the Trukese greatly value masculinity, which is manifested by young men engaging in frequent violent drunken melees with knives and clubs. In contrast, in cultures in which the environment is more benign and food is plentiful and more easily acquired, more androgynous gender roles are more likely to emerge (see Cohen, 2001). For example, men in Tahiti do not hunt; the shallow lagoons provide ample fishing without needing to venture into more treacherous waters, and the rich volcanic soils allow for the easy harvesting of taro, cassava, coconuts, and fruit. There is virtually no warfare or feuding in Tahiti, and there is little evidence that masculinity is a matter of much concern for Tahitians. In general, a survey of the norms for masculinity across diverse ecological contexts led one anthropologist to conclude that "the harsher the environment and the scarcer the resources, the more manhood is stressed as the inspiration and the goal. The correlation could not be more clear, concrete, or compelling" (Gilmore, 1990, p. 224). The physical environments that we live in shape the array of lifestyles that are possible. How much do you think your own culture is the way that it is because of the physical environment around you?

SMALL DIFFERENCES CAN HAVE LARGE EFFECTS. Sometimes what might seem to be small variations in ecologies can lead to dramatically different cultures, especially as they unfold over time. Consider the following historical event: In 1532, Francisco Pizarro, leading a group of 168 Spanish soldiers, met with the Incan emperor Atahuallpa in the Peruvian highland town of Cajamarca. At the time, the Incans were the largest and most advanced state in the Americas, and Atahuallpa was surrounded by 80,000 soldiers when Pizarro met with him. Within the day, Pizarro's men had captured the emperor and killed about 7,000 of his soldiers. In a series of other similarly lopsided battles, Pizarro and his small band of soldiers continued on their rampage, and ultimately the Spaniards conquered the Incan empire. Jared Diamond, in his Pulitzer Prize–winning book on cultural and geographic variability, *Guns, Germs, and Steel* (1997), raises some simple yet profound questions about this event. How was it that Pizarro and his vastly outnumbered band of soldiers succeeded in overthrowing the Incan empire? Why didn't the Incans defeat Pizarro, or why didn't the Incans go over to Europe to conquer the Spanish instead?

These questions can be addressed by looking at both proximal and distal causes. **Proximal causes** are those that have direct and immediate relations with their effects.

At a proximal level, the Spaniards had the political organization that drew on the experiences of thousands of years of written history, along with oceangoing ships that allowed them to reach the Americas. They had steel swords and steel armor, and guns that easily bested the stone clubs, slingshots, and quilt armor of the Incans. The Spaniards also had horses, which allowed them to outmaneuver and overtake the Incans, who were all on foot. Furthermore, the Incan empire at the time was divided because of a smallpox epidemic that had been spread across the Americas by the first Spanish explorers and had decimated the population. These proximal advantages are largely what led to Pizarro's conquest of Atahuallpa.

However, these Spanish advantages over the Incans just push the questions back further. Why did the Spaniards have the technologies, the horses, and the long written history that the Incans didn't have? Why did the Spanish germs kill the Incans—and not the reverse? To address these questions we need to consider the distal causes. **Distal causes** are those initial differences that lead to effects over long periods, often through indirect relations. Diamond proposes that rather subtle differences in the geography of Eurasia and the Americas are important in helping to address why the Spanish defeated the Incans. First, in a region known as the Fertile Crescent, which straddled the Middle East from what is now Iran up to Turkey and over to Egypt, there existed a unique collection of plant species (wheat, barley, peas, lentils) and animal species (sheep, goats, pigs, donkeys, cows) that were especially suitable for domestication. These species ultimately provided the basis for the development of Western agriculture, and no other region in the world has had as many plant or animal species that are suitable for domestication. Furthermore, these domesticated species quickly spread both East and West because many populated areas shared a similar latitude and, hence, a climate similar to that of the Fertile Crescent (in contrast, agricultural developments by the Mayans in Mexico were unlikely to reach the Incans in Peru because the regions are far apart in terms of latitude and climate). This difference exists because the major continental axis of Eurasia runs east to west, whereas the major continental axes of the Americas and Africa run north to south (**Figure 3.2**). The birth of agriculture enabled these formerly nomadic people to adopt sedentary lifestyles that allowed them to benefit from creating tools and artifacts because they wouldn't have to carry them all the time. Also, agriculture allowed for enough food production that some people could devote their activities to non-food-producing tasks, such as working to create various tools and innovations. These benefits, together with the greater exchange of ideas permitted by the denser populations in Eurasia, allowed for inventions such as steel, ships, and writing systems to emerge much earlier there than in the Americas.

Second, the domestication of various animal species in the Fertile Crescent caused humans in Eurasia to live in close proximity with animals for thousands of years. Living close to animals led many diseases that originated in animal species (measles, tuberculosis, smallpox, influenza) to cross over and infect humans as well.

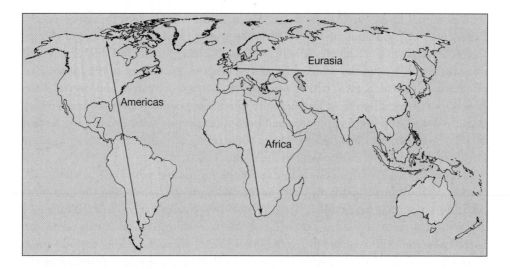

FIGURE 3.2 The major continental axes (Diamond, 1997).

Furthermore, the settlements in Eurasia became more densely populated because of the food surplus provided by agriculture, so any contagious diseases that were caught by one person were likely to spread to many others as well. Diamond proposes that thousands of years of dense populations living among livestock in Eurasia led to the development of many diseases over the centuries that the survivors and their descendants ultimately developed resistance to. These diseases would later prove to be enormously virulent when they were introduced to people in the Americas, where the population had not developed resistances to them. In sum, Diamond proposes that minor geographical differences in the availability of easy-to-domesticate species of plants and animals, and the position of Eurasia, stretching for thousands of miles from east to west along the same latitude and climate, allowed people in Eurasia to develop complex societies, writing systems, tools, weapons, and resistance to deadly germs much earlier than people in other parts of the globe could. Diamond's thesis is a powerful argument that cultural differences can originate in geographical differences.

Even cultural differences in ways of thinking can be influenced by geographic differences. Consider this example from China: The two key cereal crops in China are wheat and rice, which require quite different cultivation practices (**Figure 3.3**). Rice, when cultivated in paddies, is grown in plots of standing water. Rice farming can only be done in areas with sufficient rainfall, and the water needs to be collected and channeled through irrigation canals to the paddies. The channeling of this shared water source to individual farmers' respective paddies requires a lot of coordination and cooperation with other families. Moreover, rice farming is labor intensive. In contrast, wheat is grown in fields with typically very little irrigation. A farmer's family does not need to cooperate as much with their neighbors when growing wheat, and relatively less labor is required.

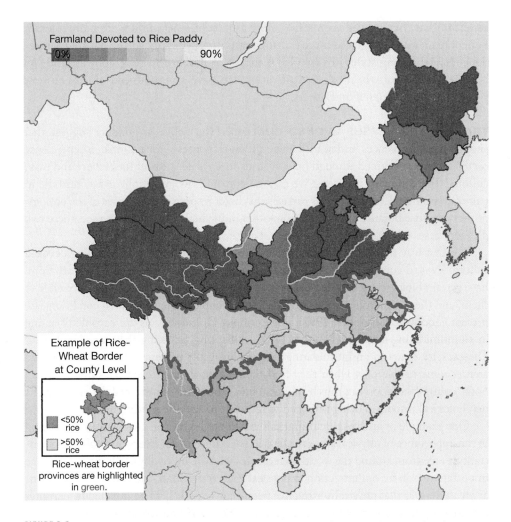

FIGURE 3.3 The areas in red produced more wheat than rice, whereas the areas in beige produced more rice than wheat. People who lived in the predominantly rice-growing regions showed more evidence of interdependent thinking and holistic reasoning than those who lived in the predominantly wheat-growing regions.

Source: Figure 1 from T. Talhelm, et. al. "Large-scale psychological differences within China explained by rice versus wheat agriculture." *Science* 344(6184):603-608. May 2014. Copyright © 2014, American Association for the Advancement of *Science*. Reprinted with permission from AAAS.

A recent study compared Chinese university students depending on whether they were from largely wheat-growing or rice-growing counties (Talhelm et al., 2014). Despite the fact that these different counties were in close physical proximity (on either side of the Yangtze River, which forms somewhat of a boundary between the wheat-growing and rice-growing communities), and that the vast majority of the students were not directly involved in farming themselves, there were pronounced cultural differences in the ways of thinking between these different regions. In the rice-growing regions, people showed more evidence of interdependent thinking styles, in that they viewed themselves more as part of a network, were more tolerant of nepotism, and engaged in more holistic reasoning (we'll revisit the nature of inter-dependent thinking styles in Chapters 6 and 9). Whether the geography around you is more suitable for wheat or rice cultivation can have a pronounced impact on how you think about yourself and others.

TRANSMITTED VERSUS EVOKED CULTURE. The above arguments suggest that geographical differences lead to different cultural responses—for example, a dependence on food sources obtained through bravery leads to a greater respect for bravery and mas-culinity. There are two ways that we can understand how geography can contribute to cultural variation. Cultural norms can arise as direct responses to features of the ecology, or they can arise because of learning from other individuals. As you'll soon see, these two different bases of cultural variability are not always clearly separable.

The first way that different geographies can affect cultural norms is through **evoked culture**. Evoked culture is the notion that all people, regardless of where they are from, have certain biologically encoded behavioral repertoires that are potentially accessible to them, and these repertoires are engaged when the appropriate situational conditions are present (Tooby & Cosmides, 1992). For example, all individuals are capable of acting in an intimidating manner when they or their offspring are being threatened by others. The capacity to act in an intimidating way is universally present; however, it is evoked among some people only when they find themselves or their loved ones under threat. Some cultural variation can thus be understood as the result of universal domain-specific psychological responses being activated in response to specific conditions.

One example of an evoked cultural difference can be seen in cross-cultural variation in the importance of physical attractiveness in selecting a mate. Everything else held con-stant, people from around the world prefer mates who are more physically attractive. One important reason for our attraction to physically attractive mates, according to evolution-ary reasoning, is that physically attractive people are less likely to be infected by parasites (parasitic infections can cause asymmetry and blemishes, which tend to be viewed as unattractive) and are thus, on average, healthier. Because our ancestors who were at-tracted to healthy mates had more surviving offspring than those who were attracted to unhealthy mates, humans have inherited preferences for attractive mates.

However, there are many other characteristics that we find attractive in mates aside from their physical beauty, such as their intelligence, kindness, sense of humor, and so on. In many contexts these other characteristics can come to be valued more than physical at-tractiveness. This would especially be true in contexts with little variability in the health of potential mates, because physical attractiveness would be a less useful basis for select-ing a mate. However, if people are living in an environment with pronounced threats from various parasites (such as those causing leprosy, malaria, boils, or syphilis), it should be more important to select physically attractive mates to better ensure that one will have surviving offspring. To support this reasoning, the prevalence of various parasites in 29 different cultures, as well as the importance that people in those cultures placed on physical attractiveness in choosing mates, were assessed in one study (Gangestad, Haselton, & Buss, 2006). The study revealed that the more parasites prevalent in a culture, the more people emphasized the physical attractiveness of potential mates. This finding suggests that people all have the potential to value physical attractiveness; however, this motivation for selecting attractive mates is most strongly activated in an environment where the health of mates is less certain. Variation in geography—in this case, in terms of parasite prevalence—differentially evokes universal aspects of our psychology. Evoked culture is thus tied to particular geographical environments: When one moves to a new environment, new behavioral responses should be evoked.

A second way that geography leads to cultural variation is that people come to learn about particular cultural practices through social learning or by modeling others who live near them. This is known as **transmitted culture**. For example, if you observe your neighbor planting wheat seeds and notice the benefits that she earned for doing so, you might adopt this cultural practice for yourself. The vast majority of the cultural differences discussed in this book can be best understood in terms of the results of transmitted culture. Although transmitted culture typically begins in a particular geographic area (because we are more likely to learn from those people with whom we interact regularly), it does not necessarily stay bound to a particular geography. Unlike evoked culture, transmitted culture can travel with people when they to new environments. People can bring their transmitted ideas with them, and cultures can spread past their initial set of geographic conditions.

Often, however, the distinction between evoked and transmitted culture is not clear-cut. A particular behavioral script (e.g., a heightened preference for attractive mates) might be activated by a specific situational variable (e.g., prevalence of parasites); however, if that behavioral script becomes a norm, then that norm might be learned by others, and thus transmitted to future generations. These cultural norms can continue to be transmitted even in contexts where the initial situational variable (e.g., prevalence of parasites) is no longer present. Indeed, it would seem that transmitted culture is always involved in maintaining cultural norms, even when evoked cultural responses are also present (e.g., Norenzayan, 2006).

Ecological variation and evoked culture represent important reasons underlying cultural variability. However, there is much more to cultural variation than just variation in ecologies. For example, consider two cultures, the Dinka and the Nuer, that coexist in the marshlands of southern Sudan (**Figure 3.4**). These cultures have coexisted in the same region for more than a century, and they live a migratory existence in which they grow millet and corn in the wet season and move about to let their cattle graze in the dry season. However, despite the fact that people from these two cultures live in the same ecology, share a similar technology, raise similar crops and livestock, and are descended from the same ancestors from about a thousand years ago, their cultures are different in a number of pronounced ways. The Nuer maintain larger

FIGURE 3.4 Striking cultural differences between (a) the Dinka and (b) the Nuer of southern Sudan highlight the limits of geography's influence on culture.

herds of cattle and rely largely on milk from their herds, whereas the Dinka regularly slaughter their herds and rely on the meat. The Dinka tribal memberships are based on who lives next to whom in the wet season, whereas the Nuer base kinship on the male line. Furthermore, the Nuer tribes are far larger and more militarily powerful than the Dinka. The Nuer also have very costly and inflexible dowry payments that are incurred when daughters are married, whereas the Dinka have small and flexible payments. The same geography thus results in quite different cultural practices (see Richerson & Boyd, 2005, for a review).

Likewise, the limits of ecological variation on culture are evident in a landmark study by the anthropologist Robert Edgerton (1971), who contrasted culture against ecology. Edgerton studied four East African tribes (the Sebei, Pokot, Kamba, and Hehe) that each had multiple communities living in different ecological settings. For example, some communities from all four of the tribes lived in moist highlands where they subsisted largely through farming, whereas other communities from each of the four tribes lived in dry lowlands where they subsisted largely through herding. Edgerton contrasted the attitudes of these various communities. If people's attitudes are largely a product of ecology, then the communities that farmed should show attitudes that are largely similar and should appear different from the communities that herded. In contrast, if people's attitudes are largely the product of transmitted culture, then the different communities within each tribe should show attitudes that are quite similar to each other, and different from the attitudes of the other tribes, regardless of whether they lived in farming regions or in herding regions. Edgerton found that for the majority of attitudes, tribal affiliation was a better predictor of people's attitudes than was their primary means of subsistence (see Richerson & Boyd, 2005, for a review). Again, these findings demonstrate that although ecology is a key component of cultural variation, much cultural variation is transmitted in ways that are largely independent of ecology.

Here's a thought experiment to illustrate how transmitted culture tends to be of more importance than evoked culture (see Boyd, Richerson, & Henrich, 2011). Imagine that you're left to survive by yourself on King William Island, located far to the north in the Canadian Arctic. To make the task easier, you're provided with various kinds of equipment and supplies that will last you for one year, so that you'll have time to familiarize yourself with your new surroundings before having to eke it out on your own. Do you think you'd be able to figure out how to survive?

I'm sorry to inform you, but I think most likely you'd fail. You see, this experiment has already been conducted. In 1845 Captain Sir John Franklin departed England on an expedition to discover the Northwest Passage, a northern route connecting the Atlantic and Pacific Oceans. It was the best-equipped expedition in the history of British polar exploration. Franklin's ships ran aground near King William Island and the 128 men were left to fend for themselves as they awaited help (**Figure 3.5**). Two years later, after their supplies had all run out, hypothermia, scurvy, and starvation (which ultimately led to cannibalism among the survivors) killed the last of the remaining crew members. It is perhaps not surprising that the men were unable to

FIGURE 3.5 Franklin's men perished in the Canadian Arctic because the cultural knowledge necessary to survive there was never transmitted to them.

survive in such a hostile environment. Not surprising, except that King William Island was home to numerous settlements of Netsilik, an Inuit group, who have been living in the area for thousands of years. The Netsilik have coped with the hostile environment just fine, and they have done so with only the supplies and tools that they have been able to fashion from local materials.

If evoked culture were the primary determinant of people's repertoire of behaviors, we would have expected that the same hostile environment would have evoked the same survival responses among Franklin's crew as among the Netsilik. But we see that the behavioral responses that have been transmitted from generations of Netsilik have provided them with the means to survive in this environment, whereas the accumulated cultural knowledge of 19th-century Britons was not suited for long-term survival in the Canadian Arctic. Interestingly, the Norwegian explorer Roald Amundsen spent two years on King William Island in 1903–1904, and he and his men survived just fine; they had sought out the nearby Netsilik and learned from them how to hunt seals, make fur clothing, and acquire other survival skills. The key for survival on King William Island rested on cumulative cultural ideas regarding how to subsist and survive in the hostile environment. These essential ideas were only available through cultural transmission, and unfortunately for the members of the Franklin expedition, they were not transmitted to them.

Understanding cultural variability thus requires us to look at both the evoked culture that originates in the surrounding geography and the transmitted culture that spreads the norms that develop. An important question to consider, then, is why some ideas are transmitted whereas others are not.

How Do Ideas Catch On?

It was the worst natural disaster in U.S. history. After Hurricane Katrina slammed into New Orleans in the summer of 2005 and damaged the levees holding back the waters of Lake Pontchartrain, the city began to fill up like a bathtub. More than 1,500 people were killed in the flooding, and property damage was estimated to be about $75 billion. Over the next several days, as assistance was ineffective and slow in coming, the news reported many extremely disturbing events coming out of New Orleans. Rescue helicopters were being shot at, a 7-year-old rape victim was found with a slit throat, sharks were swimming in the floodwaters, gang rapes and gang violence were rampant, and the Convention Center and Superdome were live-in morgues, stacked with dozens of dead bodies, with people murdering each other inside. The world recoiled in shock at the violence and chaos of the aftermath of Katrina. However, as reporters researched the origins of the stories that were being reported, it turned out that virtually none of them were true. Some were based on exaggerations (one person was murdered in the Superdome, and a total of 10 people died while at the Convention Center and Superdome); however, most of the stories that were circulated turned out to be completely fabricated—false rumors that arose in the chaos of the aftermath (Welch, 2005).

Rumors are of course not limited to Katrina. Rumors arise in all kinds of situations, particularly in times of war or disaster. For example, in World War II, people were fed a daily ration of rumors, the majority of which were simply untrue. There were rumors that thousands of soldiers' bodies had washed ashore at various towns (the town names varied), that crab meat packed by the Japanese contained ground glass, and that the entire American Pacific Fleet had been destroyed at Pearl Harbor (Knapp, 1944). Rumors are fueled by a lack of information, creating an environment in which facts become extremely valuable, and their spread is fanned by strong emotional feelings.

The study of rumors is informative because it can indicate what kinds of ideas come to be spread and become common within a culture. Cultural evolution requires that certain ideas be passed on to others (i.e., people must be motivated to share some information) and that those ideas be selectively retained (i.e., people recall that information out of the barrage of information that they are exposed to each day). Cultures change when new ideas become widely shared among their populations. The study of cultural evolution is an important and rapidly growing enterprise, although it has proven to be a challenging topic to study.

Parallels Between Biological and Cultural Evolution

Many aspects of cultural evolution can be informed by looking at the processes of biological evolution (Collard, Shennan, & Tehrani, 2005; Dawkins, 1976; Mesoudi, Whiten, & Laland, 2006). Biological evolution occurs when certain genes become more common in populations than they were in the past. It operates through **natural selection**. Natural selection is the evolutionary process that occurs when the following three conditions are present: (1) Individual variability exists among members of a species on certain traits (e.g., some antelopes can run faster than other antelopes); (2) those traits are associated with different reproductive rates (e.g., faster antelopes are better able to outrun predators than slower antelopes and are thus more likely to produce surviving offspring); and (3) those traits have a hereditary basis (e.g., the offspring of faster antelopes tend to be faster than the offspring of slower antelopes). If all three conditions are present, with enough time you will have natural selection. With each new generation the proportion of faster antelopes in the population will increase, and ultimately the species will change over time. However, the ecological world is extremely complex, and numerous trade-offs are involved with respect to any given trait. For example, faster antelopes might require more calories to support their additional muscle mass, and when food is scarce, slower antelopes, who are in need of fewer calories, would have a survival advantage over the faster antelopes. It is the balance of all the selective pressures that a species faces in a given environment that affects which individual members will survive to pass on their genes to the next generation.

Natural selection has parallels in cultural evolution, as some ideas are more likely to attract adherents than others and thus become more common in subsequent generations. As ideas become more common in a population, we have the beginning of the cultural evolution of norms. For example, as described at the beginning of the chapter, specific cultural norms for appropriate table manners have become more common from generation to generation in Western culture. Like fast-running antelopes, cultural norms for not spitting at the table or for not blowing your nose in the tablecloth have had a selective advantage over the norms for engaging in these behaviors. Note, importantly, that "selection" for cultural evolution is not tied to genes. Certain ideas or norms are more likely to be retained or shared compared with other ideas or norms.

Biological evolution and cultural evolution are not identical processes, however. One difference is that genes are copied very faithfully from one generation to the next, with copying errors (mutations) being very rare and emerging randomly, by chance. In contrast, copying errors are much more common for cultural ideas, and these errors are often intentional innovations that are planned, rather than random accidents. People don't have to wait for cultural ideas to mutate by chance but can actively work toward changing cultural ideas to better fit their needs.

A second key difference is that genes can only be passed vertically from parents to offspring, and the evolution of genes is an enormously slow and gradual process that occurs across many, many generations, as the percentage of individuals carrying certain genetic variants slowly changes over time. In contrast, a cultural idea can pass horizontally from one person to anyone else, it can be transmitted to many people in an instant (e.g., think of how quickly attitudes toward flying changed on September 11, 2001), and people can elaborate on, change, and extend the cultural ideas quickly as they learn them. Cultural evolution can thus occur at extremely rapid speeds, such as when a new fad takes off, a political revolution is sparked by perceptions of an unjust event, or broad societal changes occur as a result of the introduction of a new technology, such as the Internet.

A third difference is that cultural ideas do not have to be adaptive (i.e., result in more surviving offspring) to become common, unlike evolutionary processes with genes. Many cultural ideas spread even though they are quite maladaptive. Consider the cultural practice among the Fore of New Guinea of engaging in ritualized cannibalism, in which the Fore honor their dead by consuming parts of their bodies. This practice became popular despite the fact that it often leads to its practitioners developing the degenerative disease called *kuru*, which has killed more than 2,000 Fore (Durham, 1991). The fact that an idea can come to catch on, even though the individuals who follow this idea may be more likely to die themselves, demonstrates how the forces of cultural evolution occur in terms that are independent from the processes of biological evolution. Cultural evolution is powerful enough that ideas can spread even if as many as 50% of those who follow the ideas lose their lives from doing so (Cavalli-Sforza & Feldman, 1981). One does not have to look hard through history to find many examples of extremely harmful ideas that nonetheless quickly spread through populations (such as National Socialism in the 1920s and 1930s in Germany or the Cultural Revolution in the 1960s and 1970s in China).

Factors That Cause Ideas to Spread

Cultural evolution involves the spreading of new ideas. But what makes an idea likely to spread? Why do some ideas spread like wildfire, whereas other ideas never leave the inventor? Understanding what motivates individuals to communicate and remember ideas is key to understanding how ideas spread across populations.

Communicable Ideas Spread

For ideas to spread, they need to have some way of moving from one person's head to another. The most direct way for this to occur is through language; however, some ideas might be more likely to be communicated than others. For example, some ideas are difficult to summarize succinctly, some ideas might seem to be less useful or pertinent, and some ideas might be deemed too socially undesirable for people to express them to others. These kinds of ideas would seem to be less likely to spread than ones people are eager to communicate to others.

One way to investigate culturally shared ideas has been to look at the stereotypes that people have of certain cultural groups (Schaller, Conway, & Tanchuk, 2002). These stereotypes vary tremendously from place to place and across historical time. For example, in the 19th century, a relatively common stereotype in the United States was that the Irish were obese, wasteful, and violent hard-drinking monkeys, as depicted in **Figure 3.6**. Today, the circumstances of the Irish in the United States have improved so much that it is hard to believe that these crude kinds of stereotypes about them ever existed. This reflects how negative stereotypes about cultures tend to be motivated by beliefs that stem from particular circumstances, such as a conflict over resources (e.g., new Irish immigrants competing for low-paying jobs with poorer Americans), the remnants of historical conflicts (e.g., the centuries-old struggles between Great Britain and Ireland), disenfranchisement, and ignorance about a group's cultural practices.

Stereotypes can thus be seen to reflect shared ideas that people have in particular cultural contexts about some specific cultural groups. It would seem, then, that the content of stereotypes would be influenced by the kinds of ideas that people were most likely to communicate. If some ideas were rarely communicated about various ethnic groups, then these ideas would be less likely to become part of any shared stereotypes that might exist (for example, see

THE USUAL IRISH WAY OF DOING THINGS.

FIGURE 3.6 Anti-Irish prejudice was common throughout the United States in the late 19th century, as shown in this cartoon published in 1871.

Martin et al., 2014). In one study, participants were asked to consider how character-istic a number of trait words were for what they believed others thought about certain ethnic groups (Schaller et al., 2002). Participants were asked what they believed *others* thought because, in general, people are more willing to discuss the contents of stereotypes that they think other people have than they are to discuss the contents of stereotypes that they have—people usually don't like to admit that they think about others in stereotypical ways. Also, participants were asked how likely they were to use those traits in describing other people that they knew. The researchers found that for relatively common ethnic groups in Vancouver (e.g., people of European, Chinese, and East Indian descent), people said that the trait words that were the most characteristic of the shared stereotypes were also the words that were most commonly used to communicate information about others. In contrast, for less common ethnic groups in Vancouver (e.g., those with smaller local populations, such as First Nations tribes), there was no correlation between the communicability of traits and the likelihood that they were characteristic of stereotypes, because people apparently rarely discussed these less common groups. That is, culturally shared stereotypes tend to be formed based on the kinds of traits that people are most likely to communicate, and for the kinds of groups that people are most likely to be talking about.

Of course, when we communicate our ideas, not everyone is equally likely to be our communication partner. Quite simply, we are far more likely to communicate ideas with people we see regularly than with those we rarely or never meet. Because of this obvious fact, people tend to be more influenced by the ideas of those with whom they regularly interact. **Dynamic social impact theory** posits that individuals come to influence each other, and they do so primarily in terms of how often the individuals interact, which ultimately leads to clusters of like-minded people who are separated by geography—cultures, in other words (Latané, 1996). Dynamic social impact theory is thus one account for the origin of culture: Norms develop among those who communicate with each other regularly. For example, there is clear evidence of people sharing many similarities with those who cluster around them in terms of dialect, crime rate, self-concepts, political attitudes, product consumptions, and lifestyles (Harton & Bourgeois, 2004; Mark, 1998; Plaut, Markus, & Lachman, 2002; Weiss, 1994).

Our behaviors have an influence on others because each of us is connected to those around us through a web of relationships. Some people have relatively few relationships, so fewer people have direct influence on them, and they themselves have direct influence on only a few others. Other people have a large number of relationships and are thus influenced by a large number of people, and vice versa. The burgeoning study of social networks has revealed how our behaviors come to influence others through the individual relationships that connect us with others. For example, in an upcoming election, I may plan on voting. When I let a friend know that I plan on voting, my friend will be more likely to vote himself. And if my friend now is more likely to plan to vote, then he will subsequently come to increase the likelihood that his other friends will vote, and so on. The burgeoning study of social networks has revealed how the actions that we engage in can come to influence others whom we don't even know ourselves, by spreading them through our friends and then their friends. Research finds that we can come to have an influence on others across a broad array of life outcomes, such as how happy we are, how overweight we are, and the kinds of products we purchase (for a review see Christakis and Fowler, 2009).

Here is one example of how we influence others through our relationships. In one study, students' attitudes were surveyed at the beginning of the year and then at later points throughout the school year (Cullum & Harton, 2007). The researchers kept track of the individuals who were the students' roommates, housemates, and residence hallmates over that time. In the vast majority of cases, the assignments to rooms, houses, and residence halls was conducted randomly. Over the course of the year, students came to have attitudes that were similar to the attitudes of the people with whom they shared a common living space. This change in attitudes was especially true of those attitudes that participants viewed to be personally important at the beginning of the semester and, consequently, were discussed most with their peers over time. Attitudes came to be quite similar within houses and dining halls but remained different between houses and dining halls. In effect, the researchers documented the formation of some microcultures within people's living quarters. Cultures thus emerge when people communicate with those around them, and people are most likely to communicate information that is personally relevant to them. Can you identify any microcultures that might have developed around you and your friends?

Useful Ideas Spread

Humans are an ultra-social species, and one way that our social orientation is highly visible is that we like to help others. If there is a way that we can easily help someone else, especially if there is little cost to ourselves, we feel a strong urge to do so. Helping others gives us a reputation for being a co-operator and increases the likelihood that others will in turn help us when they have the chance. Indeed, our strong desire to help each other is a critical adaptation that further distinguishes humans from our primate relatives and has allowed us to thrive in such diverse environments. And perhaps the easiest way that we can be of service to our friends and neighbors is by sharing information with them.

Think about occasions when you had some useful knowledge that others did not. Imagine that you had learned that a bridge was closed because of an accident, that the room for an upcoming examination had been changed, that the newest iPhone was in stock at your university's bookstore, or that there was a 2-for-1 sale at your neighborhood coffee shop. When you meet a friend who you know would find this information useful, what do you do? That's easy—you'll have a strong desire to tell her about your useful news. It may even be the first thing that you say to her. And social media have capitalized on this desire, as they allow people to easily share whatever useful information they encounter with their on-line friends.

In his book, *Contagious: Why Things Catch On*, Jonah Berger (2013) describes how this desire to share useful information can sometimes result in the most seemingly banal of events going viral. He describes a YouTube video posted by an 86-year-old grandfather, showing his surprisingly easy way of shucking corn with a microwave. (You can watch the video here: http://www.youtube.com/watch?v=YnBF6bv4Oe4.) Despite the video being only about as interesting as watching someone's grandfather shuck corn, in the first three years after its release, the video was watched more than 8 million times! Simply, people wanted to be the ones that shared this highly practical piece of information with their friends and family. By sharing useful information, we make ourselves more useful, and thus valuable as a relationship partner.

Emotional Ideas Spread

When I was a child going trick-or-treating on Halloween, my mother had a rule that she had to inspect all of the candy before we were allowed to eat it. Anything that was not wrapped or was in an opened package was confiscated, for fears that a nasty neighbor had inserted razor blades in it or had spiked it with poison. This seemed like a reasonable precaution at the time, as we had all heard many tales of children who had been killed from such booby-trapped candy. *Newsweek* published an article in 1975, right before Halloween, that warned, "In recent years, several children have died and hundreds have narrowly escaped injury from razor blades, sewing needles, and shards of glass purposefully put into their goodies by adults." However, in a study of every single reported Halloween incident since 1958, only two deaths were substantiated—both of which were caused by the unfortunate children's parents rather than by sadistic strangers (Best & Horiuchi, 1985). In only a few incidents had children received minor cuts from sharp objects in candy bags (the most serious injury required 11 stitches), but the large majority of the reports were hoaxes enacted either by the children or by their parents seeking to extort money through lawsuits and insurance scams. There was little evidence that children were endangered by taking candy from strangers; the problems seemed to stem largely from a few kids taking candy from their dysfunctional parents.

So if booby-trapped Halloween candies are such rare events, how did fears of them ever lead to the belief that several children had been killed by them? Such stories are just one of many kinds of urban or **contemporary legends** that have spread through various cultures. Contemporary legends are simply fictional stories that are told in modern societies as though they are true. Of concern to psychologists are the reasons these legends spread (Heath, Bell, & Sternberg, 2001).

Heath et al. (2001) proposed that rumors and legends are more likely to spread when they can evoke a shared emotional reaction among people. People appear motivated to share emotions with others because doing so allows them to connect with others. Social interactions should be facilitated to the extent that people feel their partners are experiencing similar feelings as themselves. Rumors or legends that spark strong feelings should thus facilitate a sense of shared connection with others. Heath and colleagues investigated this hypothesis by creating a number of variants on some contemporary legends to see whether participants felt motivated to pass the stories on to others. For example, one story that participants read referred to a man who found a dead rat inside a soda bottle. One group of participants read a variant of the story that was designed to elicit in readers only a *small* amount of emotion (disgust, in this case). It went like this:

> Before he drank anything he saw that there was a dead rat inside.

A second version of the story was designed to lead to a *moderate* degree of emotional response in the readers.

> About halfway through he saw that there was a dead rat inside.

And a third version of the story was written so that it should create a *strong* emotional response. Brace yourself.

> He swallowed something lumpy and saw that there were pieces of a dead rat inside.

Participants each read 12 stories, varying in emotional impact, and were then asked a number of questions about their reactions to the stories and whether they would be willing to pass the story along to others. A variety of features of the stories increased people's willingness to pass along the stories. In terms of informational features, people were more motivated to spread the stories if the stories were plausible and if they felt the stories would cause them to change their behaviors—that is, people were motivated to communicate stories that contained potentially useful information. Furthermore, the more emotion the stories elicited (i.e., the more interesting, joyful, contemptible, or disgusting they were), the more likely people were to say they would pass them on. In addition to the informational value of the stories, then, people are motivated to pass on stories that convey a lot of emotion. Emotional ideas are more likely to spread through a culture than are unemotional ones (also see Harber & Cohen, 2005).

Minimally Counterintuitive Ideas Persist

One source of evolution of cultural ideas is evident in religions and myths around the world. For example, almost every culture has a creation myth—a story for how the world came to be. The Fulani believe that the world was created from a drop of milk; according to Japanese mythology, the world was created from brine dripping from the tip of the Jewel-spear of Heaven; Judeo-Christian beliefs state that God created the heavens and the earth in six days. It is not possible for all of these conflicting creation myths to be literally true, and it may be that none of these beliefs are literally true, so religions and myths can be considered as cultural ideas that successfully catch on and spread through cultures. What influences the extent to which particular myths or beliefs come to be shared across a population?

Atran and Norenzayan (2004) propose that not all stories are equally memorable. Rather, the kinds of stories that are especially likely to persist in our memories are ones that contain a few **minimally counterintuitive ideas**. "Minimally counterintuitive" means statements that are surprising and unusual in the sense that they violate our expectations but are not too outlandish. In the case of a religious text, such as the Bible, the vast majority of the text describes rather ordinary events, and those ordinary events are interspersed with occasional "counterintuitive" events, such as a talking bush, a virgin birth, or miracles such as water turned into wine. Atran and Norenzayan propose that such kinds of narratives—mostly ordinary, intuitive events sprinkled with the occasional counterintuitive idea—are the most likely to persist in our memories and survive many retellings. One demonstration of this found that participants who were asked to remember and retell Native American folk tales remembered approximately 92% of minimally counterintuitive items, but only 71% of intuitive ones (Barrett & Nyhof, 2001; also see Boyer & Ramble, 2001). The minimally counterintuitive ideas were recalled better than intuitive ideas.

Atran and Norenzayan tested their hypothesis by providing participants with sets of statements that included many two- and three-word statements that varied in their intuitiveness. Participants were later asked to recall the statements they had read. Some statements were designed to be intuitive (e.g., a chanting man), some were designed to be minimally counterintuitive (e.g., a melting grandfather), and some were designed to be maximally counterintuitive (e.g., a squinting wilting brick). Participants were later asked to recall the events. Immediately after learning the statements, participants tended to have the best recall for the intuitive statements and the worst recall for the maximally counterintuitive ones. However, this initial preferential memory for intuitive statements did not seem to last. Participants were contacted again, one week later, and asked to recall what they had learned. They had the best recall for those sets of statements that were mostly intuitive but also contained a few minimally counterintuitive ones. That is, sets of ideas that were largely intuitive, with the occasional counterintuitive idea interspersed, were the most memorable after a long period.

Similarly, another study explored the kinds of statements that were included in folk tales by the Brothers Grimm. Some of these folk tales have been quite successful and have become part of the cultural landscape. For example, it is quite likely that you are familiar with the stories of "Little Red Riding Hood," "Hansel and Gretel," and "Cinderella." However, some of the other folk tales by the Brothers Grimm have been much less successful. For example, you likely have never heard of the stories "Farmer Little," "Hans My Hedgehog," or "The Donkey Cabbage" (**Figure 3.7**). One study (Norenzayan, Atran, Faulkner, & Schaller, 2006) investigated 42 folk tales by the Brothers Grimm and had trained raters count the number of counterintuitive elements in each of the tales (e.g., talking mirrors, a house made of gingerbread). The researchers then did a search on Google for the number of times each of the folk tales was listed. The results indicated that the most successful folk tales (the ones with the most Google hits) tended to have two to three counterintuitive elements in the story. In contrast, the least successful folk tales had a broad range of counterintuitive

FIGURE 3.7 The Grimms' tale of "The Donkey Cabbage" failed to catch on as well as some of their other tales.

elements, ranging from zero to six, and no clear pattern was discernible among the unpopular stories. Again, there was evidence that narratives that are largely intuitive but contain a couple of violations of expectations end up being the most memorable. The secret to a good story that will get passed on thus appears to be one that, for the most part, is a tale of everyday expected events, with the occasional unexpected element.

How Have Cultures Been Changing?

The notion that cultures evolve does not refer to just the distant past. Cultures are always evolving, and they continue to change today. How have cultures been evolving over recent decades?

Cultures Are Becoming Increasingly Interconnected

Different cultures have always been in contact with each other, and trade, intermarriage, political alliances, immigration, and sharing of ideas and technologies have always occurred across cultures. However, as a series of technological innovations have reduced the costs of transportation and eased the process of long-distance communication, cultures have become far more interconnected than ever before. These increasing interconnections allow ideas that emerge in one culture to have an influence on people in other cultures, thereby hastening the process of cultural evolution. What happens tomorrow in Paris, then, is not just a matter for Parisians and the French but is something that can potentially affect people all over the world.

Furthermore, in many ways these interconnections among cultures are resulting in the formation of a global culture. Many large companies are now global entities that have outgrown their cultural boundaries. For example, Sony, IKEA, and Exxon each do more than three-quarters of their business outside their respective home countries of Japan, Sweden, and the United States (Barber, 1995). Across much of the world today, people are drinking the same Starbucks coffee, using the same Microsoft software, and driving the same Toyotas. Much of popular culture also transcends national borders (see **Figure 3.8**). MTV

FIGURE 3.8 The world has become increasingly interconnected, such that people from around the world are exposed to many of the same cultural products and ideas.

has been available in 71 countries around the world, and thus people everywhere are exposed to the same kinds of themes that are conveyed in many music videos, such as embracing freedom, defying authority, celebrating youth, and promoting sexuality (Barber, 1995). Hollywood movies, too, are watched the world over. In a typical year, 9 or 10 of the top 10 grossing movies in countries such as Argentina, Kazakhstan, the Philippines, Russia, and South Africa are Hollywood productions (Rosenthal, 2004), communicating largely American cultural values. Of course, nothing can compete with the Internet in spreading cultural information across national boundaries.

Does globalization mean that we are destined to all become citizens of a homogenous world culture? Probably not, because this trend toward globalization is simultaneously paralleled by an opposing trend toward increasing tribalism, such as the dissolution of many former Eastern bloc countries into smaller and more culturally distinct nations, independence movements for Quebec and Scotland to separate from Canada and the United Kingdom, respectively, and Muslim fundamentalists battling Muslim secularists throughout the Mideast and South Asia. As Michael Ignatieff stated, "The key narrative of the new world order is disintegration of states" (1994, p. 5). The title of a popular book by political scientist Benjamin Barber (1995), *Jihad vs. McWorld,* nicely encapsulates these coexisting forces of motivations for cultural distinctiveness appearing alongside motivations for global homogeneity. Barber argues that as cultures around the world are penetrated by global companies and largely American popular culture, one common reaction has been for people to reject the globalizing force in an effort to return to the traditional cultures of their past. Sometimes these nationalistic sentiments are wrapped in religious overtones, and sometimes they are expressed violently, as a jihad, or holy war.

Likewise, although different cultures around the world are exposed to the same global products and popular culture, there is increasing cultural heterogeneity within the borders of many countries, as many nations receive immigrants from around the world. Ethnically diverse cities such as New York, Singapore, Sydney, and Toronto in many ways are microcosms of the world at large, each having many distinct ethnic enclaves coexisting within their boundaries. Somewhat paradoxically, then, there are trends toward cultural homogeneity at a global level and toward cultural heterogeneity at a more local level. Interconnections between culture thus do not just breed homogeneity but also serve to underscore cultural differences. How do you think people's ways of thinking are affected as the world becomes more interconnected? This is a topic that we'll explore in Chapter 7.

Many Cultures Are Becoming More Individualistic

One important dimension of culture that will be discussed and contrasted throughout this book is individualism versus collectivism. Cultures that are **individualistic** include a variety of practices and customs that encourage individuals to place their own personal goals ahead of those of the collective and to consider how they are distinct from others (Triandis, 1989a). For example, some practices common in individualistic cultures include the tracking of children at school, college-age children being encouraged to move out of their parents' homes, workers being given meritocratic pay at the office, employees being given individual offices or cubicles, and people choosing to put their elderly relatives in retirement homes. In contrast, cultures that are **collectivistic** include many cultural practices, institutions, and customs that encourage individuals to place relatively more emphasis on collective goals—specifically, the goals of one's ingroups. For example, collectivistic cultures often include cultural practices such as children sleeping with their parents, classes of schoolchildren being promoted together to the next grade regardless of the performance of some individual children, marriages being arranged by parents, companies compensating their employees on the basis of how long they have been employed, and extended families living under one roof. As you'll see later in several chapters of this book, the dimension of individualism and collectivism is important for understanding many cultural differences in a wide variety of different psychological processes.

Although an analysis of contemporary cultures around the world reveals how much cultures vary in the degree to which they can be considered individualistic or collectivistic (see Chapter 6 for more on this), it is important to remember that cross-cultural comparisons make contrasts at a single point in time. We can also consider how cultures have changed across time, and such analyses reveal much about how some cultures have become more individualistic over recent decades.

In his bestselling book *Bowling Alone* (2000), political scientist Robert Putnam made the case that social life in the United States has changed considerably since the 1960s. As he argued, up until the 1960s people were more socially engaged and civically active than they have been in recent years. This societal transformation is evident in a wide variety of social measures. Compared with the early 21st century, people in the 1960s were far more likely to entertain at home, vote, obey traffic laws, be members of the Parent-Teacher Association, belong to a union, have dinner together as a family, hang out at bars or nightclubs, play cards, socialize with neighbors, hold a position in a club or organization, and trust each other. And, as captured in the title of his book, whereas bowling remains a popular activity in the United States, in the past most bowlers were part of a league that met weekly to bowl and socialize, whereas today they are more likely to bowl on an ad hoc basis, either with friends or by themselves. In general, Americans are less likely to participate in formal groups than they were in the past. They are spending more time by themselves, and they are participating in fewer organizational activities. These changes have been occurring gradually over the past few decades. Yet, it is important to note that Putnam's data were largely collected before the rise of the Internet and social-networking technologies. How do you think the rise of Facebook, Twitter, and texting has influenced people's social relations?

Importantly, however, the changes Putnam documented appear to be generational changes. For the most part, people who are over the age of 60 are as socially engaged as those who were over the age of 60 in past decades. Older Americans do not appear to be any less socially engaged. In contrast, it is the younger generations of Americans who have come to differ the most from previous generations of young Americans. That is, younger Americans appear to be more individualistic, on average, than their parents, and as the American population slowly becomes replaced with people who were born in more recent decades, the culture is changing accordingly.

There are many other ways that we can see how America has become more individualistic across time. For one, they are giving their children more unique names. In 1880, approximately 65% of baby boys and 55% of baby girls received one of the 50 most popular names of those years. In 2007, in contrast, the percentages of babies receiving one of the top 50 names was less than half of the 1880 percentages. Instead, unique names came to represent a much larger share of names (Twenge, Abebe, & Campbell, 2010). As another example, from 1980 to 2007, song lyrics from popular music contained progressively fewer collective pronouns such as "we" or "us" and came to use more individual pronouns such as "I," "me," and "mine" (DeWall, Pond, Campbell, & Twenge, 2011); this trend is also evident in the use of pronouns in books published in the same time frame (Twenge, Campbell, & Gentile, 2013). Analyses of the frequency of words used in books published in the United States over the past two centuries show increasing use of words that emphasize aspects of individualism, such as "choose," "unique," "self," and "individual," which are contrasted with a decreasing use of words reflecting individual's obligations to others, such as "obedience," "authority," "obliged," and "belong" (**Figure 3.9;** Greenfield, 2013).

Moreover, there has been an increasing orientation toward money and materialism (which tends to go together with individualism; Vohs, Mead, & Goode, 2006), over recent decades (Twenge & Kasser, 2007). In contrast to those from the Baby Boom and Gen-X generations (born between 1943 and 1981), Millennials (born between 1982 and 1999) are more likely to report valuing being well-off financially and are less likely to report caring about developing a meaningful philosophy of life or being politically engaged (Twenge, Campbell, & Freeman, 2012). Likewise, words related to moral character and virtue have declined in frequency in published American books over recent decades (Kesebir & Kesebir, 2012). The one exception to this general trend of increasing materialism and individualism was that American high school students surveyed during the Great Recession (2008–2010) showed less materialism and less individualism than students surveyed in the years prior to the recession, in 2004–2006 (Park, Twenge, & Greenfield, 2014). In general, economic hardship is often associated with more communitarian values and less materialism (Inglehart & Baker, 2000).

A key question to consider here is: Why are we seeing these changes? What is causing Americans to become more individualistic? In Putnam's data, he was able to look at a number of sources of evidence to reach some interesting conclusions. First, increasing pressures of time and money have competed with people's time for

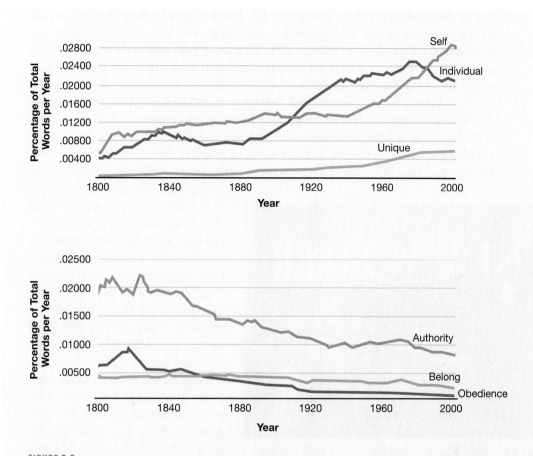

FIGURE 3.9 Changes in word frequencies in books published in the United States (from Greenfield, 2013; data from Google NGram Viewer).

being socially engaged. Many surveys reveal that Americans feel more financially pressed than before, even though real incomes have been rising, and time pressures have increased as two-career families have become more common. However, this is only a small piece of the puzzle—Putnam estimates its contribution to explaining American's increasing individualism to be only 10%. A second small contributor (also estimated at around 10%) is the increasing suburbanization of America, which results in people spending more time in their cars and in their homes and being less likely to run into friends and neighbors during the day. A larger culprit (approximately 25%) behind the transformation that Putnam identifies is electronic entertainment, especially television, which leads people to isolate themselves and engage in more passive forms of entertainment (**Figure 3.10**). Interestingly, Putnam documents how the younger generations even watch TV differently from the way their parents and grandparents do, as they are more likely to turn the TV on even if there is nothing in particular that they have in mind to watch; the older generations are more likely to watch TV only when there is a particular show that they want to see.

The largest cause of this cultural change remains the most difficult to identify directly. Approximately half of the variance behind the increasing individualism rests with the different lifestyles between the younger and older generations. It is not altogether clear what causes the older generations to watch television differently from the younger ones, or for the older generations to be more socially connected than the younger ones, but Putnam proposes that having lived through World War II is a key factor in this generational shift. The war united the country for a common cause more than any event since, and Putnam suggests that this critical episode changed all of those who experienced it, making them embedded in their social groups, with a sense of shared fate, that subsequent generations have not felt. Whether this single transformational experience is largely behind the dramatic generational changes in social engagement is not clear; however, at this point it is the single variable that has the most empirical support.

This trend of increasing individualism is not solely an American event. Indeed, if Putnam is correct in identifying the key culprits behind this cultural transformation as television, lack of a recent national unifying event such as World War II, and to a lesser extent, increasingly suburban lifestyles and women entering the workforce, then we would expect that there would be trends of increasing individualism wherever these usual suspects are found—that is, in

FIGURE 3.10 This Chris Ware cover illustration from *The New Yorker* contrasting Thanksgiving dinners in 1942 and 2006 captures Putnam's arguments about cultural change in the United States.

most industrialized and developing cultures. For example, the same pattern of books containing more individual-centred words over time was also found in the United Kingdom (Greenfield, 2013). Likewise, Hamamura (2012) identified some variables to indicate changes in individualism, and he found that Japan has also shown increasing individualism over the past few decades for some of these measures. For example, since 1950, the divorce rate in Japan has increased while the average household size has decreased, similar to trends in the United States during this period. Likewise, Japanese today value independence in their children more than they did a few decades ago. On the other hand, some measures indicate *decreasing* individualism in Japan, such as an increased importance placed on social obligation, with a corresponding decrease in the importance placed on individual rights. For the most part, however, Hamamura's data reveal increasing degrees of individualism in both the United States and Japan. That both Japan and the United States are showing some evidence for increases in individualism, and given the worldwide trend toward increasing globalization discussed earlier, it is likely that similar cultural changes are also evident in other industrialized cultures.

These changes raise the question of whether these trends will continue in the future. Is the world destined to become an increasingly individualistic environment? If technology continues to provide leisure that is socially isolating, if people continue to have too many work commitments to have time to be socially engaged, and if there are no more events such as World War II to lead citizens to feel a common fate with their compatriots, then this trend very well might continue for some time. Alternatively, perhaps there is a maximum degree of individualism that people can comfortably tolerate, and on reaching that point people might react and begin to reject cultural practices that decrease their social engagement. However, it is useful to remember that we are not very adept at being able to identify the future cultural changes that will occur over the next several decades. A decade ago, for example, few people would have predicted the dramatic rise in social-networking technologies.

Furthermore, as you'll see in many studies discussed throughout this book, although Japan and the United States have both become more individualistic over the past few decades, there are still pronounced cultural differences in their psychologies. Likewise, striking cultural differences remain in many psychological phenomena among people from cultures around the world. Despite recent growth in individualistic tendencies worldwide, cultures today remain different in many important ways that affect the ways we think. We have much to learn as cultures from around the world continue to evolve in front of us.

People in Many Cultures Are Becoming More Intelligent

One of the most remarkable findings regarding cultural change is that people seem to be getting smarter. On average, across all cultures for which there is adequate longitudinal data, people in the current generation have higher IQ scores than those from earlier generations. This trend has been dubbed the "Flynn effect" after the researcher who first identified it. A review of changes in IQ scores in 14 nations revealed that the average increase in IQ was between 5 and 25 points per generation (Flynn, 1987). Subsequent research has revealed that the pattern extends to other countries as well (Flynn, 1994). These are not trivial changes. IQ is reported in standardized scores, with a mean of 100 and a standard deviation of 15. This suggests that if the performance of a given sample is standardized, only about 2% have IQ scores below 70 (which is often viewed as a cutoff for a classification of mental retardation), and only about 2% have IQ scores over 130 (which is often viewed as a cutoff for being classified as "gifted"). IQ has been increasing at a rate of approximately 6 points per decade in many countries around the world. If this trend could be extended back into the past (a big if), this means that a person who is tested with an IQ of only 70 today (and is thus in the bottom 2% of the population of her contemporary peers) would be about as smart as a person who was tested with an IQ of 130 a century ago (and thus would have been in the top 2% of her peers back then). These massive gains in IQ remain controversial as people debate what IQ tests really measure.

The measurement of intelligence is one of the most contentious issues in psychology. When asked for a definition of "intelligence," the standard answer given by many psychologists is to demur and say that intelligence is what intelligence tests measure. This tautological answer reflects the difficulty in identifying a universal definition of intelligence. Is one's ability to construct a kayak out of driftwood and sealskin, and use it to hunt a walrus in the darkness of an Arctic winter, a good measure of intelligence? Arguably yes, and if so, we would expect that Inuit hunters would score far higher on this intelligence test than would people from other cultural contexts. Is one's ability to solve algebraic puzzles a good measure of intelligence? The answer here is also arguably yes, and again we would expect better performance among those who have participated in contexts with much algebraic learning. It is exceedingly difficult to conceive of intelligence outside of a particular cultural context, which makes it challenging to understand what the pattern of increasing IQ scores across generations is telling us.

As a further challenge to understanding what the Flynn effect means, not all measures of "intelligence" have been showing the same increases over time. The one striking exception to the general pattern of increasing IQ scores has been the findings that scores on the Scholastic Aptitude Test (SAT) have been *decreasing* in the United States over past decades. One argument for why SAT scores have been falling is that the SAT measures acquired knowledge: In particular, the verbal component of the SAT measures a good deal of difficult vocabulary. There is much evidence that people are reading less and are gaining more information from TV, the Internet, and computer games than in previous generations. Although TV viewing might prompt certain kinds of learning (more about this later), it does not allow for much development of vocabulary, because most TV programming communicates at about a fourth-grade vocabulary level (Healy, 1990). If people are not reading as much today as they did in past generations, and are not developing as large a vocabulary, then their verbal SAT scores would go down (Greenfield, 1998).

Some other commonly used IQ tests, such as the Wechsler, the Otis, and the CTMM, have shown moderate gains over time. However, the IQ test that shows the largest increase across time is the Raven's Matrices, which was originally developed as a "culture-free" measure of IQ, as it doesn't require any specific cultural knowledge or language skills. An example of the type of questions included on the test is shown in **Figure 3.11** (the answer is given at the end of the chapter). To answer the question, the test taker must choose which of the six numbered alternatives best fits into the bottom right corner of the matrix. Raven's Matrices is thus often viewed as the purest measure of intelligence, although the fact that cultures of recent decades score higher on it than those cultures of past decades reveals that it is by no means "culture-free" (see Greenfield, 1998, for more discussion on this). Performance on the Raven's Matrices involves basic problem-solving skills, an area where people seem to be making the most improvement. Why would that be?

A number of explanations have been proposed for this increase in IQ. One argument is that IQ is a proxy for health, as one can develop a fully functioning mind only with adequate nutrition. Hence, it follows that as dietary nutrition has improved around the world, accordingly so has IQ (Lynn, 1989). However, evidence for improvements of nutrition around the world do not closely parallel those of IQ gains, rendering this account incapable of explaining much of the global increase in IQ (Flynn, 1999).

Another argument is that the world is becoming a far more complex place than it used to be, and navigating it successfully requires much learning and practice with demanding problem-solving tasks, which ultimately influences one's intelligence. One indicator of the increasing complexity of the world is represented in the amount

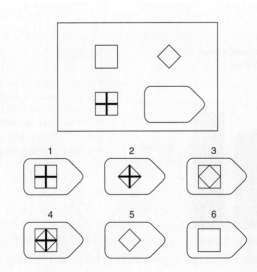

FIGURE 3.11

A simulated item from the Raven's Matrices IQ test.

of education that is needed in order to get a good job. Of men born in 1890 in the United States, only 27% had more than an eighth-grade education, and only 9% had any schooling after high school (Goldin, 1998; only male data are provided, as at this time relatively few women entered the workforce). In 2012, the percentage of Americans over the age of 25 (both men and women) who had more than an eighth-grade education was approximately 94%; 58% had some schooling after high school, and approximately 11% had postgraduate degrees (U.S. Census Bureau, 2014). The percentage of 25-year-olds and older with a bachelor's degree has increased consistently across decades (**Figure 3.12**). Similar trends hold for post-graduate degrees: For example, the number of PhDs granted per year at Canadian universities increased by 64% from 1988 to 1998 (Statistics Canada, 2001).

Whereas most adults got by with less than an eighth-grade education in the early part of the 20th century, today most adults get by with some college education, and an ever-growing proportion are obtaining postgraduate degrees. As the world becomes more complex, succeeding in it requires understanding in a broader array of domains, and this is facilitated by education. Most likely, the trend toward increasing average levels of education will continue for some time. Importantly, however, the increasing number of years of higher education by itself cannot account for the overall increase in IQ, because IQ has also been rising among those who do not go on to higher education.

Another argument for the effect that increasing complexity has on people's growing intelligence comes from an unlikely source: pop culture. The key proponent of this view, Steven Johnson (2005), argues that popular culture has become progressively more complex and challenging over the past half-century. For example, he notes that television dramas of the 1950s, such as the police drama *Dragnet*, consisted of a single story line that Sergeant Joe Friday pursued from the beginning scene to the very end.

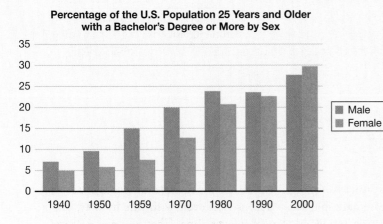

Percentage of the U.S. Population 25 Years and Older with a Bachelor's Degree or More by Sex

FIGURE 3.12

The percentage of the U.S. population with at least a bachelor's degree has steadily increased over the past century, with particularly notable increases among women.

Each scene built on the subsequent one, and the viewer had to follow only one story. Watching *Dragnet* was not a very challenging exercise and, arguably, did little to develop one's intelligence. In contrast, Johnson argues that since that time, many of the programs on television have become steadily more complex. For example, the hit HBO drama *The Sopranos* involved more than 20 recurring characters who were typically involved in about a dozen different story lines per episode, some of which were connected to events that happened in previous seasons. Likewise, many other recent shows, such as *Game of Thrones, The Wire,* and *Lost,* are equally complex. To be sure, there is still no shortage of mindless offerings on television today (case in point: *Keeping Up with the Kardashians*). However, Johnson makes a good argument that the average program broadcast today has grown progressively more complicated, and that even the mindless programs today are more challenging than the mindless ones of the 1950s.

Furthermore, electronic entertainment is not limited to television, as an evolution has occurred in the complexity of video games as well. I grew up playing *Space Invaders,* a game in which one could choose between moving left or moving right while shooting at a grid of descending blobs (aliens, I guess) before they shot you. There is no comparison between the complexity of *Space Invaders* and the complexity of many video games today, such as *Dark Souls II, Civilization V,* or multiplayer online battle arena (MOBA) games such as *League of Legends*. For example, Johnson notes that the game *Grand Theft Auto III* has a walk-through, which explains how to play the game, that is 53,000 words long—about one-third the length of this textbook. In addition to the visceral thrills of shooting at opponents or trying to run over them, playing video games involves a lot of problem-solving skills and very complex plots. The increasing complexity of popular games and television programs shows that people are demanding greater challenges from their entertainment. If Johnson's thesis is correct, the complexity of our entertainment is making us smarter, and that is leading us to demand more challenging entertainment, which further develops our problem-solving skills.

In sum, in every culture for which there are good longitudinal data on intelligence tests, IQ scores have been rising over past decades, in particular for tests from the Raven's Matrices. As of yet, there is no widely accepted explanation for this increase, but it most certainly reflects some kind of change in the cultural environments in which people are participating.

In the Face of Change, How Do Cultures Persist?

As discussed earlier, cultures are highly fluid and continue to change across time. Perhaps the more remarkable fact, then, is that even with this fluidity, cultures also have an enduring tendency to persist over time. That is, once cultural habits get established, many of them remain entrenched across generations, despite the great amount of change that those generations encounter. The notion that cultures can persist over time is central to many of the key theories discussed later in this book (e.g., see Nisbett & Cohen, 1996; Nisbett, Peng, Choi, & Norenzayan, 2001; Weber, 1904/1992). These theories propose that cultures have surprising abilities to retain much of their shape and many of their characteristics across centuries.

There is much evidence that cultures persist a great deal across time (see Cohen, 2001; Richerson & Boyd, 2005). An example of cultural persistence for a psychological characteristic can be seen by comparing people from various countries around the world with the descendants of immigrants to the United States from those same countries. For example, how similar are the experiences of Swedes living in Sweden to the experiences of Swedish Americans? Does the culture of people's ancestors shape how they think today? One domain in which this question has been explored is with respect to **subjective well-being**. Subjective well-being is the feeling of how satisfied one is with one's life. There is much evidence for striking cultural variability in the average levels of subjective well-being reported by people from different countries. For example, among European nations, Scandinavian nations score particularly high in their citizens' average level of subjective well-being, whereas eastern European nations score rather low, and many central European nations fall in between. (We'll return to discuss and make sense of cultural differences in subjective well-being in Chapter 10.)

How well are these cultural differences in subjective well-being preserved in the descendants of immigrants to the United States from those countries? This question was explored by contrasting the well-being scores of people who were born in America and who reported a single ethnic identity with the average well-being scores of various countries around the world (Rice & Steele, 2004). The research revealed two notable things. First, there was much less variability among the American samples than among the samples from other countries around the world. Not surprisingly, people who were born and raised in the United States share many similar cultural experiences, which leads them to have somewhat similar well-being scores. Second, despite the fact that the range of well-being scores among the American samples was much narrower than that of the international samples, there was still a clear pattern among the American samples. A strikingly large positive correlation ($r = .62$) was found between the average well-being scores for people in American ethnic groups and the well-being scores for the countries from which those ethnic groups were originally descended. That is, Americans of Scandinavian descent tended to have the highest well-being scores, followed by Americans of central European descent, and followed by Americans of eastern European descent. Furthermore, this pattern remained even after statistically controlling for any variation in socioeconomic status, age, education, and a number of other variables. Apparently, people learn cultural traditions from their families that affect their well-being and these traditions are passed down through the generations, even after their ancestors have moved to the United States. Similar parallels between American ethnic groups and their countries of origin have been found in people's attitudes toward income redistribution (Luttmer & Singhal, 2011). The ways that people think thus are not just due to the influence of the mainstream culture with which they interact but are also influenced by cultural traditions of their ancestors, some of which might date back many generations.

For another example of cultural persistence, consider the game of Japanese baseball. Baseball was imported into Japan from the United States in the late 19th century. Both countries use the same baseball rulebook; however, as former Los Angeles Dodger Reggie Smith said after playing his first season as a Tokyo Giant, "This isn't baseball; it only looks like it." Robert Whiting (1990) describes the many differences between Japanese and American baseball in his book *You Gotta Have Wa*. Indigenous Japanese sports were traditionally the martial arts (e.g., sumo, kendo, judo, karate)—activities dedicated to self-discipline and the refinement of the human spirit. Baseball was a foreign import that was grafted onto this existing culture, and the echoes of the indigenous sports remain. For example, training camp for professional baseball in the United States starts in the spring and consists of 3 to 4 hours of practice a day, typically in a southern locale such as Florida, with much time for swimming and golf in between. In contrast, Japanese training camp is held in the frigid winter; players typically are on the field for 7 hours, run approximately 10 miles a day, and then return to the dormitory for strategy sessions and indoor workouts. As Warren Cromartie, a former player for the Montreal Expos and Tokyo Giants, stated when describing Japanese training camp, "It makes boot camp look like a church social." Also, in comparison with its American counterpart, Japanese baseball involves far more plays in which the individual makes a sacrifice for the benefit of the team, such as the sacrifice bunt, and teams work to prevent members of the other team from losing face, such as avoiding three-pitch strikeouts or extremely lopsided victories. Even though the games are played by the same set of rules, Japanese and American baseball reflect the respective cultural backgrounds from which they have evolved.

Cultural Innovations Build on Previous Structures

Why should aspects of culture persist across time, especially as people from those cultures face new challenges, technological innovations, and historical changes? An exploration of the biological evolution of species can illuminate one reason that cultural elements have a tendency to persist. The evolution of new species is constrained by traits of the ancestors from which those species evolved. For example, bats are small mammals that evolved a number of particular adaptations, including wings. The wings did not grow out of nothing; rather, bats' wings emerged from a series of gradual adaptations over the evolutionary record as their forelimbs became more and more adapted to flight until they became fully functioning wings and rather useless arms. It was a far more straightforward process to have a series of incremental adaptations leading arms to evolve into wings than it would have been for wings to have somehow grown, say, out of the backs of bats. This example underscores a critical point about biological evolution: Adaptations are constrained by previously existing structures. If you were to design a flying mammal from scratch, you might very well want to create a bat that had both wings *and* arms. A bat with arms would appear to be more effective because it could carry its prey or hold its offspring. But with evolution you don't start from scratch; you are always making very small adjustments to a preexisting set of circumstances, and those circumstances influence the evolutionary path that is followed.

Likewise, cultures do not emerge out of a vacuum. The thread of every cultural innovation must be woven into an existing web of beliefs and practices. The culture of 21st-century America grew out of the culture of 20th-century America, which grew out of the culture of the 19th century, and so on. Along the way, American culture evolved from the cultures of the first settlements and adapted to a set of emerging ideas, technological innovations, continuing migrations of people, and responses to a series of particular historical events. We can be certain that 22nd-century American culture will in many ways be different from 21st-century American culture. However, these future changes will be modifications to the preexisting cultural foundation rather than a new culture cut from whole cloth, and in many ways we can confidently predict that 22nd-century America will remain distinctively American. Existing cultural habits influence and constrain the evolution of new cultural habits.

A number of examples of striking cultural persistence reveal the strong role that early cultural structures came to influence cultural norms many centuries later. For example, in medieval Italy the northern regions had a number of egalitarian institutions (e.g., guilds, neighborhood associations) whereas the southern regions did not. During that time the south of Italy was ruled by Norman kings in an autocratic manner that engendered much corruption and distrust among families. A highly centralized Italian state was created in the 1870s, and the same laws and reforms were applied across all of Italy. However, since then, northern Italian regions have built powerful and competent regional government organizations, whereas the southern regions have made comparatively little progress and remain the least civic regions of the country (Putnam, Leonardi, & Nanetti, 1993). Regional differences in Italy today thus mirror the differences that were present 800 years ago.

Likewise, particular prejudices can persist in certain regions across centuries. In the 14th century, when the bubonic plague was killing large swaths of the European population, many people suspected the deaths had been caused by Jews poisoning the wells. This belief led to pogroms in many cities across Germany, where there were mass killings of Jews in retaliation for their incorrectly suspected role in the plague. Six centuries later, during the rise of the Nazi party in Germany, anti-Semitism again led to pogroms against the Jews. A recent analysis finds that the German cities that had Jewish pogroms in the 14th century were the same cities that had higher rates of violence against Jews in the 1920s and had higher support for the Nazi party (Voigtländer & Voth, 2012). As horrific as they are, these feelings of anti-Semitism were passed down from generation to generation in the regions in which the prejudice was strongest several centuries ago.

Another depressing example of the powerful influence past cultural structures have on future cultural developments can be seen in the economic development of sub-Saharan Africa. On average, African economic performance over the past half century has been poor. However, there is considerable variability across regions of sub-Saharan Africa, with countries like Botswana, Swaziland and Namibia faring reasonably well, and countries like Malawi, Zimbabwe, and Liberia faring quite poorly. Can these differences in economic development be understood in terms of cultural persistence?

The economist Nathan Nunn (2008) submits that a key factor underlying Africa's uneven economic development has been the unexpected lingering aftereffects of the slave trade. There were numerous slave trades in Africa from approximately 1400 to 1900 that resulted in millions of Africans being violently captured and thrown into slavery. Manning (1990) estimates that by 1850 Africa's population was only half of what it would have been had the slave trades not occurred. In regions where slaves were most frequently captured (**Figure 3.13**), a fear of capture spread, and people were motivated to acquire weapons, such as swords and firearms, to defend themselves. However, these weapons could most easily be acquired from Europeans in exchange for slaves, which led to a "gun–slave cycle" (Lovejoy, 2000) in which villages raided each other to capture slaves in order to purchase weapons to protect themselves from being caught and enslaved by their own neighbors. Hence, in many parts of Africa, people developed a deep mistrust of those around them. Nunn argues that this mistrust continues to this day and is responsible for the lower economic development of many parts of Africa (**Figure 3.14**). Indeed, Nunn found that (controlling for a host of variables such as coastline, population density in 1400, percent of the population that was Islamic, temperature, and presence of natural resources, such gold, oil, and diamonds) those countries that exported many slaves have a lower GDP today. Further, this relation between slavery and economic development appears to be the result of increased mistrust in the countries with many slaves (Nunn & Wantchekon, 2011). The events that happened centuries ago still reverberate in African cultures today.

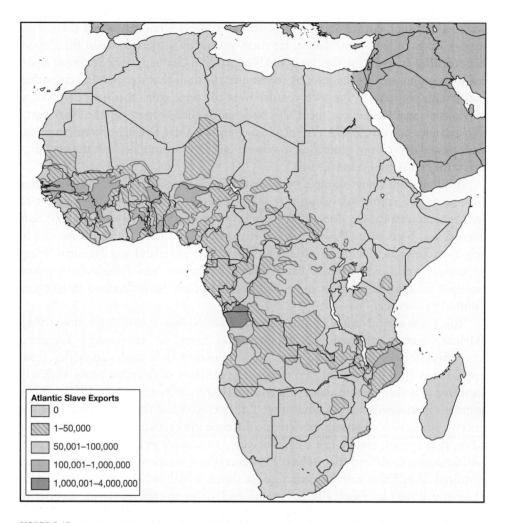

FIGURE 3.13   Number of slaves from individual African countries that were shipped across the Atlantic.

Early Conditions Have Disproportionate Influence on Cultural Evolution

Because cultures evolve from their past circumstances, the early conditions of a culture matter a great deal with respect to how cultures subsequently evolve. In the same way that the direction you take in your first few steps of a long journey by foot determines your path more than the direction you take in your last few steps, the early conditions of a culture likewise have greater influence in shaping a culture's long-term evolution than later conditions do. The critical role of early

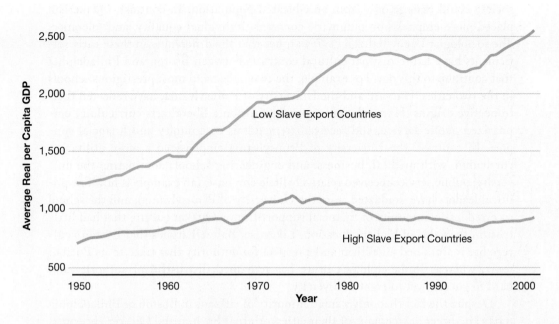

FIGURE 3.14 Those African countries that exported more slaves from the 15th to the 19th centuries have lower GDPs than those that exported fewer slaves. The slave trade created a sense of mistrust that has persisted for centuries and undermines these nations' economies.

Source: Figure 8 from Nathan Nunn, "The Long-Term Effects of Africa's Slave Trades," *The Quarterly Journal of Economics*, February 2008, 123(1), pp. 139-176. Copyright © 2008, Oxford University Press. Reprinted by permission of Oxford University Press.

conditions is one important reason that cultural differences can persist across time. Although people from cultures from around the world are encountering many similar experiences in this age of globalization, each culture is following a path with a distinctive origin. These distinctive origins preserve many cultural differences across time.

We can see much evidence for the significance of early settlements by contrasting different regions within the United States that were settled by different populations (for some excellent discussions of this see Fischer, 1989; Woodard, 2011). For example, in the 17th century, Boston was settled largely by Puritans whereas Philadelphia was settled largely by Quakers. Although these were both Protestant sects that shared many similarities, there were also some key differences in the views of Puritans and Quakers. Puritanism emphasized respect for authority and the importance of applying one's wealth and social position to community goals. Furthermore, many of the original Puritans who first settled in Massachusetts were highly educated intellectuals (including more than 100 graduates from Oxford and Cambridge), and they felt that their dream of forming a utopian society could emerge only from an educated population. In contrast, Quakerism placed more emphasis on pragmatic concerns, individual equality, and tolerance. The sociologist Digby Baltzell (1979) argues that the differences in these early settlements have led to distinct cultural contrasts between Boston and Philadelphia that continue to this day. For example, the two oldest and most prestigious schools in the two cities, Harvard and the University of Pennsylvania, have reflected their respective origins. Harvard was originally built on a liberal arts curriculum, emphasized public service, and received tremendous community and financial support. In contrast, the University of Pennsylvania emphasized a more utilitarian curriculum with medical, business, and engineering schools dominating the university; public service received relatively little emphasis (an example is how few political leaders have graduated from the University of Pennsylvania); and the school received less community or financial support from a Quaker culture that had little trust in the value of higher education. Likewise, Baltzell argues that Boston's culture has maintained an elitism and a respect for authority that trace to its Puritan roots, whereas Philadelphia's culture has remained distrustful of authority and hard to govern, yet tolerant of diversity.

Despite the fact that only a small minority of citizens in Boston or Philadelphia today are direct descendants of their cities' original Puritan and Quaker ancestors, and relatively few continue to practice Puritan or Quaker faiths, the cultures of both cities have continued to persist since they were first founded by European settlers. All people who were subsequently born in, or emigrated to, Boston and Philadelphia have needed to adjust themselves to the prevailing cultural traditions, and this has perpetuated the distinctive cultures. Similar arguments have been made for why the U.S. South continues to have more of a culture of honor than the North (Nisbett & Cohen, 1996; see Chapter 4) and why New York City remains a world center for finance since it was founded by a Dutch trading company that governed the city's affairs for the first decades of its existence (Woodard, 2011). The first settlers to a region can have a profound impact on that region's culture centuries later.

Researchers have tried to isolate the effects of initial conditions on the development of cultural norms by studying changing norms in the laboratory. In one study, participants entered a completely dark room in groups of four people (Jacobs & Campbell, 1961). These four people were tested to see whether they would form any kind of microculture that persisted across time. Their task was to look at a small light on the opposite wall and to report how far they thought the light moved. The light was actually attached to the wall, so any perceived movement was entirely illusory and a product of the **autokinetic effect**. The autokinetic effect is caused by the involuntary saccadic movements of the eyes, which, in the dark, create the illusion of movement. The task was set up so that people reported out loud how much they saw the light move. The first person to report was a confederate of the experimenter, and he reported that the light had moved 16 inches, which is considerably more than the amount of movement that the average person tested alone reports (mean of 3.8 inches). There is much ambiguity in this task, so people tend to conform to other people's reported judgments—in this way, norms develop among groups with regard to how much they believe the light is moving. After the confederate reported 16 inches, most of the other members of the group also begin to "see" the light move at about 16 inches. In sum, a microculture was produced where four people had adapted to a norm of seeing the light move about 16 inches. At the end of the trial, in which everyone had reported how much he or she saw the light move, one person would leave the room (the first person to leave the room was the confederate) and be replaced by a new participant. After four trials, then, the group has a completely different membership from what it had started with, as all four members would have been replaced with new people. This continued for 11 generations, resulting in a total of 11 microcultures of four people each, with each microculture having a slightly different membership from the previous one.

The experimenters wanted to see how long the confederate's initial report would continue to influence the subsequent participants. Although the estimates began to gradually drift toward the mean of the control group (i.e., 3.8 inches), the influence of the confederate's judgment persisted for five generations after he or she left. Even though there were no longer any members from the original group who had been exposed to the confederate's rather large estimate, people continued to see the light as moving more than had those who were tested by themselves. Initial conditions thus do indeed influence later generations, although their effects can diminish over time. A weakness of this particular study is that these experimental "cultures" are very different from ones in real life, as in them a few strangers have only the most limited of interactions with regard to an unusual task and for a short period. One would expect that the effects of initial conditions would persist more if people participated in the cultures for a longer period, as they do in real life.

Pluralistic Ignorance Is a Force for Cultural Persistence

Here is an interesting finding: Students at Princeton stated that they believed that most others at their school approved of the large quantities of alcohol that were regularly consumed at campus events. However, that same survey revealed that most students themselves said that they were not so comfortable with the amount of alcohol being consumed (Prentice & Miller, 1996). If people were accurate in assessing others' feelings toward alcoholic consumption, we would expect that people's self-assessments averaged across the sample would be similar to the average of their assessments of other people's feelings toward alcohol. That there was a difference indicates a bias: Why would people assume that others have more accepting attitudes toward heavy drinking than they themselves do?

This is an example of pluralistic ignorance, a mechanism that further leads to cultural persistence. **Pluralistic ignorance** is the tendency for people to collectively misinterpret the thoughts that underlie other people's behaviors. Often we try to figure out what others are thinking, but really, all we have to go on is what people tell us or our observations of how they behave. We can be pretty accurate in inferring others' thoughts when people's statements or behaviors accurately reflect their private thoughts. For example, if I tell you I don't like olives, it would be quite reasonable for you to assume that my private feelings toward olives are similarly negative. I have no reason to mislead you about my feelings for olives. However, in other kinds of situations, people's behaviors and statements are not accurate reflections of their thoughts. Some kinds of behaviors or statements are socially desirable—that is, they make others think more positively of us. People are likely to make socially desirable statements because they wish to maintain a positive impression. In the case of the Princeton students, people assumed that their own private thoughts of being uncomfortable with the amount of alcoholic consumption were more conservative than their fellow students' opinions. This bias exists because people apparently feel it is socially undesirable to publicly express that their classmates are drinking too much, so such thoughts are rarely stated publicly. On the other hand, thoughts that it is fun to drink to excess appear to be more socially desirable and are more regularly stated, which yields a false impression of a consensus that students like to drink to abandon. Because some thoughts are more likely to be publicly expressed than others, people come to collectively misrepresent what other people's true feelings are.

Interestingly, the precise opposite case of pluralistic ignorance existed in the United States in the early 20th century. During that time Prohibition was in effect, a legal ban on the public sale and consumption of alcohol (**Figure 3.15**). Prohibition never had majority support, but it *seemed* to have public support because few people were willing to publicly argue in favor of keeping alcohol legal, apparently because open support of alcohol was socially undesirable at that

FIGURE 3.15 Prohibition lasted as long as it did in the United States, in part, because of pluralistic ignorance. People's public behaviors communicated more negative attitudes toward alcohol than what the majority of people believed privately at the time.

time. Once polls were conducted and clear evidence was collected on the strength of anti-Prohibition feelings, the pluralistic ignorance was eliminated and Prohibition came to an abrupt end (Katz & Schnack, 1938). Other examples of pluralistic ignorance that currently exist in college student samples are that people believe their peers are more interested in "hooking up" than they are (Lambert, Kahn, & Apple, 2003) and that people believe others hold more politically correct beliefs than they do (Van Boven, 2000). These biases exist because it tends to be socially desirable on some college campuses to talk about hooking up and to espouse politically correct views.

Pluralistic ignorance is relevant to cultural persistence because people are influenced by what they *believe* other people feel rather than by what other people *actually* feel. If I think that I'm the only one who is uncomfortable about the amount of drinking on campus, then I am likely to be shy about expressing my concern and may go along with others and drink excessively myself, thereby further contributing to the misconception and perpetuating the drinking culture. Through the mechanisms of pluralistic ignorance, a culture that includes the practice of heavy drinking on campus can thus come to persist even when a majority of people do not privately endorse the practice themselves.

Furthermore, people's willingness to openly discuss certain topics is not just a matter of social desirability. In some cultural contexts, particularly those with totalitarian governments, there can be significant risks for openly discussing some topics. It is likely that in such contexts there will be even less congruence between what people say and what they privately think, and thus there should be greater degrees of cultural persistence (Cohen, 2001). A disturbing example of pluralistic ignorance was identified by Hannah Arendt in her controversial analysis of the rise of National Socialism in Germany (Arendt, 1964). Arendt viewed the extensive German cooperation with National Socialism to be caused not by evil motives but by thoughtlessness and mass conformity (Cohen, 2001). In Nazi Germany it seemed safer to go along with the fascist crowd than to risk speaking publicly against the growing horrors. As long as everyone else seemed to be in support of the actions of the Third Reich, people collectively convinced each other that they were pursuing the right tack, and the culture persisted until it met an abrupt and violent end in World War II.

The correct answer to the Raven's Matrices item in Figure 3.11 is 2.

SUMMARY

Cultures are not fixed entities but continually evolve over time. Norms that were common a generation ago are not necessarily common any more.

Cultures vary, and it is challenging to understand where the variation comes from. One source of variation is the geographical environment. Different environments afford different subsistence patterns, and these can lead to different cultural practices. Sometimes what might appear to be minor geographical variants can lead to large cultural differences.

Cultural variability emerges through one of two mechanisms. Transmitted culture is the process by which one learns a cultural idea from another. Evoked culture is the notion that some behavioral responses are universally available to people, but they only become engaged when appropriate triggering conditions are present.

Cultural evolution occurs when ideas spread. Ideas are most likely to spread if they are communicated, if they are useful, if they involve strong emotions, and if the ideas are largely intuitive, with a few unexpected elements.

In the past few decades, many cultures have been changing around the world in similar ways. There is evidence that cultures are becoming more interconnected, that individualism is growing in industrialized countries, and that average IQ levels have been increasing.

Although cultures are always changing, many elements and patterns persist over time. Cultural evolution involves changes to preexisting conditions, so early conditions of a culture can have a large influence on how cultures evolve over time. Pluralistic ignorance is one mechanism that also leads cultures to persist across time.

THINK ABOUT IT

1. What aspects of your own cultures do you think have been shaped by the local geography?
2. In what ways is biological evolution similar to and different from cultural evolution?
3. What makes an idea more likely to spread?
4. Why have so many cultures around the world become more individualistic over recent decades?
5. This chapter discussed how around the world cultures have been becoming more interconnected, individualistic, and intelligent. How do you think the world's cultures will change over the course of your lifetime?
6. What are the forces that keep cultures stable across time?

KEY TERMS

These are Zinacantecan women at the market. When researchers gave these women standardized questionnaires that are commonly used in psychological research, the participants became annoyed. The questionnaires included a series of similar questions that violated Zinacantecan conversational norms and offended the participants.

4

METHODS FOR STUDYING CULTURE AND PSYCHOLOGY

CHAPTER OUTLINE

W hat do you do if you want to study how culture influences the ways that people think? Consider what happened when the cultural psychologist Patricia Greenfield tried to study the psychology of the Zinacantecans, an indigenous people living in Mexico. She wanted to interview the Zinacantecans to find out about their experiences in textile production (see Greenfield, 1997). She went about interviewing the Zinacantecans using the same kinds of surveys that have been validated many times with Western, largely college-educated populations. But these same surveys didn't work so well with the Zinacantecans. One implicit understanding involved with survey methodology is that each of the questions is independent; the different questions do not necessarily take on the form of a conversation. Researchers rely on this convention, and the result is that one standard methodological technique used in survey research is to ask participants about the same issue in a number of items that vary slightly. A measure of extraversion, for example, typically does not have just one item but more often a dozen or more items that all assess the extent to which one acts in extraverted ways. There are psychometric benefits to asking people similar questions over and over again: reducing concerns with random error, ensuring that people's responses pertain to the underlying construct and not to various tangential aspects of each item. Zinacantecans, however, approached Greenfield's survey with an expectation that the interaction would follow their conversational norms—that is, when you give an answer to someone's question, the questioner then doesn't just ignore your answer and go ahead and ask another question that sounds almost the same as before. Greenfield found that her standard, ordinarily methodologically sound interview technique just seemed to make her Zinacantecan participants angry, as if they couldn't understand how she could be so stupid as to keep asking the same question over and over again!

As this one example demonstrates, psychologists are often in a difficult position. Our object of study is the mind, which, fascinating as it is to study, is a black box that doesn't reveal itself to us readily. It is extremely challenging to collect sound and compelling evidence for psychological phenomena, as they are by nature elusive, abstract, and invisible. With current technology we still know strikingly little about how specific psychological phenomena are produced and represented in the brain (although we are making great progress).

Consider the challenge of trying to understand our own thought processes. It would seem that if anyone should know about what's going on inside someone's head, it would be the owner of that head. However, much of our own psychological experience occurs completely beyond our awareness. For example, research has revealed that we often don't really know how we feel (Schacter & Singer, 1962), what we have remembered (Loftus, 1993), whether we've enjoyed a task (Festinger, 1957), or the reasons we like something (Nisbett & Wilson, 1977). It is for these reasons that experimental psychologists rarely investigate psychological processes by asking subjects directly about their experiences. People are usually able to come up with answers to such questions, answers that they often are quite convinced are true, but research reveals, in many situations, that people's answers can be outright wrong.

If we don't have good access to our own psychological experiences, consider how much more difficult it is to try to discern someone else's psychological experiences. What is your roommate thinking about right now? What did she mean when she said that your fashion sense was "unique"? Has she really forgiven you for the time she thought you were flirting with her boyfriend? We're often skating on thin ice in trying to confidently assess what is going on in the minds of others. The problem for cultural psychologists is that these difficulties are multiplied many times over when trying to understand the minds of people from another culture.

The goal of this chapter is to learn how to design studies to study culture and psychology. How can we go about investigating how people think in cultures that are different from our own? Later I list some methodological concerns that are inherent in the study of people from other cultures (see Cohen, 2007, for a more detailed review). Although some of these concerns seem particularly daunting, you'll see that—with appropriate consideration, creativity, and effort—we are able to surmount them, gathering compelling data that give us a very nice perspective on what exactly is going on in the heads of people from other cultures.

The study of culture and psychology touches clearly on the two central themes that guide this book. First, the goal of many cultural studies is either to demonstrate similarities across cultures in the ways that people think (thereby reflecting universal psychological tendencies) or to demonstrate cultural differences (thereby reflecting culturally shaped psychological tendencies). Second, for those ways of thinking in which cultural differences emerge, many studies are designed with the express purpose of understanding how people's different experiences in their cultures resulted in their different ways of thinking. How do people's experiences shape the ways that they think?

Considerations for Conducting Research Across Cultures

Studying people from other cultures involves some issues that are unique compared with those involved in studying people from one's own culture. Because the study of culture's influence on psychological processes cuts across virtually all subfields of human psychology, researchers often utilize methods that are commonly used in the study of those subfields. For example, people studying culture and personality tend to rely on the methods of the personality psychologist, the study of culture and cognition utilizes methods from the field of cognitive psychology, those studying culture and neuroscience use the various tools of neuroscience, the study of culture and mental health borrows from the methods of clinical psychology, and so on. Each of these methods has its own strengths and weaknesses. As David Funder (2007) emphasizes, psychological data are only clues, and clues are always ambiguous. The problem for cultural psychologists is that not only do they inherit the standard ambiguities of whatever methods they adopt from other subfields, but many of these methods create further ambiguities when applied to the study of people from other cultures (Cohen, 2007). In this chapter I describe various strategies by which researchers can improve their ability to assess the psychological states of people from other cultures.

What Cultures Should We Study?

There are thousands of cultures around the world. How can we go about deciding which ones to study? In general, it's not recommended to use a "shotgun" method for studying cultures and to randomly select cultures to study. Although such an approach might reveal some unexpected cultural differences, interpreting the results can be very difficult if there is no theory guiding the selection of the cultures. Rather, you will more likely find meaningful and easy-to-interpret results if you let your research question guide your choice of research samples.

One common approach for selecting cultures is to choose samples based on a theoretical variable that you are investigating. For example, if you are interested in exploring how collectivism shapes the ways people view their relationships, your research would fare well by selecting cultures that clearly differ in terms of their collectivism. If you contrast how people view their relationships between two cultures that vary in their degree of collectivism and you find a significant cultural difference, you would have some preliminary evidence to suggest that collectivism shapes how people view their relationships. You could then follow up with some other strategies that are discussed later in this chapter. Alternatively, if you found no difference between two cultures in how people view their relationships, this would suggest that collectivism and people's views of relationships are unrelated. One good way to choose your samples, then, is to look for cultures that vary on a specific theoretical dimension of interest, such as collectivism.

Sometimes you might want to explore the degree of universality of a particular psychological finding. Is a particular way of thinking peculiar to North American culture, or does it characterize the way of thinking of humans everywhere? A good first step would be to select two cultures that vary greatly on as many theoretically relevant dimensions as possible, such as language, geography, philosophical traditions, level of education, or social practices. If a similarity is found in a particular psychological process between two cultures that are maximally different, this would be compelling evidence for a high degree of universality for that process. For example, as we discussed in Chapter 2, humans are unique in developing a rich theory of mind, and they

FIGURE 4.1 The Baka live in quite different circumstances from those in industrialized cultures. Here's a Baka family in Cameroon preparing a meal.

do so at a young age. Is the development of a rich theory of mind a product of having participated in a complex industrialized culture, or is this something that emerges in all human contexts? One study explored this question by examining how two sets of children did on a measure of a "theory of mind," contrasting Western children with Baka children, members of a pygmy people who live in the rainforests of southeast Cameroon (Avis & Harris, 1991). The Baka are nonliterate hunter-gatherers with little or no exposure to Western philosophical ideas, so the Baka and Western children represent sharply divergent cultural contexts (see **Figure 4.1**). Despite this great difference between the cultures, children performed extremely similarly on the experimental tasks, suggesting that the development of a theory of mind is highly similar across the world—a good example of an accessibility universal. The researchers were able to make a convincing case for the universality of a theory of mind by selecting cultures that differed maximally from each other.

Making Meaningful Comparisons Across Cultures

After one has selected the cultures to study, it is critical that the researcher design a study so that the results can be meaningfully interpreted. What kinds of steps should a researcher take to ensure that the research findings provide a fair contrast of the cultures?

THE IMPORTANCE OF DEVELOPING KNOWLEDGE ABOUT THE CULTURES UNDER STUDY. For the most part, psychologists in many other fields have one key advantage over cultural psychologists in that they are studying people who are usually from their own culture and thus are likely to think in ways similar to themselves. They can thus rely on a healthy dose of introspection, everyday observations, and intuitions to guide their development of theories and hypotheses. Cultural psychologists, in contrast, are often studying people from a different culture, and it is not always clear how much the researcher's own experiences would generalize to the people she is studying. Consider the following example described by Richard Shweder (1997), regarding what can happen if researchers study a culture with which they are unfamiliar:

> A team of psychologists from Scandinavia was doing comparative research [on] variations in the "universal" family meal. They wired ahead to a prominent local psychologist in this rural area of India and asked him to arrange for a family meal. . . . Being civil and polite, he did so, without ever telling them that in rural India there is no such thing as a family meal. The Scandinavian research team spent a few days in the area. The local psychologist convinced some family to sit down at a table together and food was served and they were filmed. But everyone was uncomfortable. Avoidance relationships were being violated. People kept getting up from the table and leaving. No one ever explained to the visitors that family meals should not be presumed to be part of some universal grid. They returned home, coded the materials, and made some sort of inference about what was going on, without really ever understanding what was really going on. (p. 155)

The moral of this story is to make sure you know something about what you are studying! In this example, it is difficult to draw any meaningful conclusions about rural Indian family meals because they don't really exist in the context where they were studied. If the researchers had more knowledge about the culture prior to investigating it, they would have been able to conduct their research in a far more effective way. Thus, what should always be the initial step in studying people from other cultures is to learn something about the culture under study. A little bit of knowledge can go a long way in avoiding costly and embarrassing mistakes.

One can learn about another culture in a variety of ways. Perhaps the simplest way is to read existing texts and ethnographies about the culture. Ethnographies usually contain rich descriptions of a culture, or a particular situation or group of people within a culture, derived from extensive observation and interaction by an anthropologist. We can learn an extraordinary amount from the rich cultural detail provided in ethnographies. Moreover, in most cases the kinds of data derived from ethnographies is complementary to the kinds of data collected by the more empirical and hypothesis-driven methods of psychologists—such as the methods that I describe in the other chapters of this book.

Given the challenges inherent in studying psychology within another culture, it would seem that researchers would be at a distinct disadvantage if they did not have access to the vivid cultural detail that is provided in ethnographies. However, learning about a culture through books and ethnographies limits you to learning about the ideas that the author felt were relevant, and this might not shed much light on the phenomena that you are interested in studying. Moreover, much of what is described through ethnographic observation is information filtered through the ethnographer's own peculiar set of beliefs, biases, and values. There are many instances in which two ethnographers describe the same culture in strikingly different ways (e.g., Freeman, 1983; Mead, 1928).

Another approach is to find a collaborator who is from the culture you are studying and who is interested in pursuing the same research with you. The more involved your collaborator is in the project, the more likely you are to avoid the situation that happened to the researchers studying the Indian family dinner. Much research in cultural psychology is conducted in collaboration with people who are from the cultures the researchers are studying. For example, the study of cultural psychology received a tremendous boost when the American social psychologist Hazel Markus compared notes with the Japanese social psychologist Shinobu Kitayama and realized that there were significant and meaningful gaps in the ways that the self-concept appeared in their respective cultures (Markus & Kitayama, 1991). The International Association of Cross-Cultural Psychology is an organization of researchers studying culture and psychology from all around the world, and its members routinely find members from other countries to collaborate with on cross-cultural projects. Much important cross-cultural research would likely never be conducted if researchers did not collaborate across cultures.

Alternatively, another effective strategy is to immerse oneself in another culture to learn it firsthand. This is an excellent way to gain a rich understanding of another culture, but it can be time-consuming and costly. In my own case, much of my cross-cultural research has explored ways of thinking in Japan, and this research has been enormously aided by the experiences that I had living in Japan for two years prior to starting graduate school, and again living there as a researcher while I was conducting many of the studies. To this day, my research plans are still shaped by things that I observed while living in Japan. There is no substitute for firsthand experience.

Some combination of the above strategies is probably the optimal way to learn about other cultures. It can take a lot of time to develop a rich understanding of a culture; however, such efforts to ensure that one's research is culturally informed are important for conducting successful studies.

CONTRASTING HIGHLY DIFFERENT CULTURES VERSUS SIMILAR CULTURES. Are there any special considerations that need to be taken into account

FIGURE 4.2 The anthropologist David Tracer conducting a third-party punishment game experiment with an Au woman in Papua New Guinea.

when contrasting cultures that are especially different (see **Figure 4.2**)? It might not seem obvious to you, but if you are reading this book in a course at a college or university, you are engaging in a set of culturally learned skills about acquiring knowledge. You are considering the information in this textbook from a variety of culturally learned perspectives: You might critique some of the ideas presented here, you might try to memorize some in order to do well on an exam, you might expect to discuss the ramifications of these ideas with your instructor in class. You have learned how to go about considering and studying academic topics in textbooks. There are many cultures around the world that do not have formal systems of education, and we would expect that people from such cultures wouldn't respond to this textbook in the same way that you do. As much as I would like to think that what I have written here is universally relevant and important, I imagine that in much of the world people wouldn't have much use for this book other than for starting a fire.

There are also culturally learned skills regarding completing surveys or participating in psychological studies. By now you have participated in countless surveys in your life—for example, when a marketing research firm calls your house, when you evaluate your instructor at the end of a course, or when you fill out the registration

card after purchasing some computer software. These kinds of experiences are common in industrialized cultures everywhere. Through such experiences you have gained much implicit knowledge about the survey process. For example, your experiences have led you to understand that when people ask your opinion on a survey they are not doing so to start a dispute with you; they are interested in your own unique opinion and they expect you to give an answer that is not necessarily the same as what your father thinks; your responses will be kept anonymous, and your response will not be met with some kind of reward or punishment based on how much the researcher agrees with you. This kind of implicit understanding of survey research by those surveyed is a prerequisite for researchers to be able to collect survey or questionnaire data. It would be meaningless to compare responses from people who have this understanding with those of respondents who did not. Hence, although the standard survey methodologies are useful for conducting cross-cultural research among people of industrialized societies who have comparable experiences, they are of less utility when exploring subsistence societies that don't share these kinds of research experiences.

Recall the difficulties Greenfield (1997) was having when trying to apply survey methodology while studying Zinacantecan girls. If we are to make meaningful comparisons across cultures, our participants must understand our questions or situations in equivalent ways. Having one's methods perceived in identical ways across different cultures is termed **methodological equivalence**. A variety of statistical techniques are applied to cross-cultural studies of survey data to increase such equivalence. However, when the cultures are not comparably familiar with the research setting, ensuring methodological equivalence is a more challenging endeavour; we have to adapt our procedures so that they are understandable in each culture we study, which sometimes results in using a slightly different procedure in each culture (Triandis, 1994). Some experimental control is lost when we use different procedures in the different cultures that we are comparing. There is an unavoidable trade-off in experimental control versus comparable meaning when studying extremely diverse cultures.

Because of the challenges inherent in creating methodologically equivalent studies across cultures, the vast majority of cross-cultural research has been conducted between industrialized societies: By far, the most common comparisons are between North Americans and East Asians. When cultures are similar in their familiarity with research settings, we can often use the same methods between cultures. Likewise, studying college students from different cultures also lends itself to making meaningful comparisons, as students the world over tend to be familiar with many of the kinds of procedures used in psychological studies (and college students tend to be an easily accessible sample for most university researchers). Most of the studies covered in this book were conducted with such samples.

However, there can be some pronounced costs to cross-cultural studies that focus solely on targeting university students in industrialized societies. What kinds of problems do you think emerge when psychologists overemphasize students in their samples? First, as we saw in Chapter 1 in the discussion of WEIRD people, there is a significant problem with **generalizability**—do the findings generalize to populations other than the samples that were studied? It is not always clear how well findings that emerge from college students generalize to nonstudent populations. It is possible that the cultural differences exist only between student populations but might not exist between other populations, such as between elementary school children, or between elderly populations. We are less able to confidently generalize our results if we do not have much evidence from a diverse range of samples.

Second, there is a problem with the **power** of the studies. *Power* refers to the capability of your study to detect an effect (which in studies of culture is usually a cross-cultural difference) to the extent that such an effect really exists. Power reflects the quality of the design of your study—is your study designed so that it is sensitive enough to identify the anticipated effect? It is possible that one's hypothesis is correct but that the study has insufficient power to be able to provide support for it. In cross-cultural studies, you can think of culture as the **independent variable** (i.e., the variable that is varied or manipulated), and if researchers contrast two similar cultures, they would not have as much variance in their independent variable as if they had compared two very dissimilar cultures. The more variance in the independent variable, the more likely that an effect will be detected in the **dependent variable** (i.e., the variable that you measure). Students from industrialized societies share many similar experiences, so a failure to find cultural differences in a phenomenon between such populations (e.g., Japanese versus American students) does not necessarily mean that the phenomenon is not influenced by culture; it could instead mean that you don't have a powerful enough contrast to be able to detect the influences of culture. Comparisons of more divergent cultures (such as Americans versus a traditional hunter-gatherer society) might reveal pronounced differences in the phenomenon. In this way, a comparison between students of industrialized societies is a rather conservative, and less powerful, investigation of the effects of culture. If cultural differences emerge with such similar samples, we can often assume that the effects of culture would be at least as pronounced with more divergent samples. This is one reason why so much cross-cultural research has focused on university students.

Conducting Cross-Cultural Research with Surveys

One of the most common ways of conducting cross-cultural research is to use surveys. That is, participants are asked for their responses to a series of questions, usually presented in the format of an anonymous questionnaire. There are several unique challenges to conducting survey research across cultures, including problems with translation, various types of response biases, reference-group effects, and deprivation effects.

TRANSLATION OF QUESTIONNAIRE ITEMS. One rather obvious challenge unique to studying cultural differences in psychology is that the research participants and the researchers often speak different languages. If you've ever traveled in a place where you don't speak the local language and the locals don't speak your language, you've probably discovered how hard it can be sometimes to get even a concrete question answered, such as "Where is the nearest bank machine?" When dealing with topics that are far less concrete, such as emotions, values, narratives, or personality traits, these communication difficulties become even more problematic.

One potential solution to this problem is to keep all of your materials in the original language, such as English, and study only people who are bilingual with English and their native language. This avoids the costs and challenges associated with translating the materials; however, can you think of any problems that such a strategy might entail for learning about how culture affects how people think? First, your participants will likely have poorer English skills than your translators. Your data would be meaningless if your participants did not have the requisite language skills to understand what was being asked of them. Second, one has to be concerned about whether those in a culture who have good English capabilities are representative of their cultures. It is likely that respondents from a non-English-speaking, non-Western culture who are fluent in English have had more exposure to Western products, culture, and ideas and might be more Westernized than their non-English-speaking compatriots. This would decrease the likelihood of finding cultural differences that might exist more generally in the population.

Another problem in giving bilingual respondents materials in English and comparing their answers with those of native English speakers is (as we'll see in Chapter 7) that the language we're thinking in can greatly affect the way we're thinking. Much research has found that bilingual participants respond differently when tested in their native language and in their second language (Bond, 1983; Ross, Xun, & Wilson, 2002). For example, Sussman and Rosenfeld (1982) observed that when speaking their native languages, Venezuelans sat closer to each other than Japanese did, while Americans fell in between (see **Figure 4.3**). However, when the participants conversed in English, they all sat about the same distance from each other, regardless of culture. Apparently, when people are responding in English, they start thinking in ways that are more characteristic of native English speakers. In general, a minimal step to take for providing a strong test of whether cultural differences exist is to translate the materials (e.g., Berry & Annis, 1974; Cole & Scribner, 1974).

However, translating psychological materials is not as easy a task as you might expect. One demonstration of how intertwined culture and psychology are is that many psychological terms do not have equivalents in other languages. For example, there are emotion words from many languages that do not have an equivalent counterpart in English (e.g., *amae* in Japanese, *schadenfreude* in German, *fago* in Ifaluk). Likewise, many English psychological terms have no equivalent in other languages—for example, there is no direct translation of the term "self-esteem" into Chinese (Miller, Wang, Sandel, & Cho, 2002). Questions such as "Do you have high self-esteem?" or "Do you regularly experience *amae*?" would yield dubious results in some cultures. To allow for meaningful cross-cultural comparisons, it is crucial that we ask questions that have comparable meaning across cultures.

FIGURE 4.3 Japanese typically maintain a larger interpersonal distance between acquaintances than do Latin Americans.

Having an accurate translation of your psychological materials is a necessary precondition for doing good cross-cultural research. Given this necessity, it's crucial that researchers be extra cautious in ensuring that their materials are translated well. How can we go about ensuring a good translation? My favored approach is to be sure that at least one of the primary investigators on a project is fully bilingual in the languages that are being compared. This person is then in a good position to assess whether the materials are capturing the subtle nuances of the intentions of the research questions. Psychological meanings are complex, and many of the nuances can easily be lost in translation unless a translator has a rich understanding of what the questions are asking. A bilingual investigator will be able to compare the translated materials with the originals (and with any back-translations; see below) and will be in a good position to assess whether the translations are accurate. In the field of professional translations, this is the most commonly used method (Wilss, 1982). This process is further improved if a number of the primary investigators are bilingual so that they can discuss any of the most problematic translations and resolve them through consensus. There will always be a number of problematic phrases or words that require discussion between the translators and the investigators to ensure that the literal meaning is captured and that the translations do not sound awkward or unnatural.

In many instances, however, it's impossible for researchers to secure collaborators who are both fluent in the languages of interest and intimately involved with the project. In this situation the researcher is somewhat at the mercy of the translators. It's a bit too much of a blind leap of faith to hope that whatever

TABLE 4.1

The perils of translation: examples of translations gone wrong

Location	Sign
Chinese hotel	Notice: Please don't accept strangler's invitation, so as not to be cheated.
Chinese store	Please don't touch yourself. Let us help you to try out.
Cambodian hotel	Wishing you "Bong Voyage."
Hong Kong bathroom	For keeping the toilet clean and tidy, please dump at the dust bin.
Japanese street	When carrying a parasol, please be careful to get in the way of other people around you.
Japanese drugstore	We make up prescriptions.
Bucharest hotel lobby	The lift is being fixed for the next day. During that time we regret that you will be unbearable.
Paris hotel elevator	Please leave your values at the front desk.
Athens hotel	Visitors are expected to complain at the office between the hours of 9 and 11 a.m. daily.
Japanese hotel	You are invited to take advantage of the chambermaid.
Paris dress shop	Dresses for street walking.
German campground	It is strictly forbidden on our black forest camping site that people of different sex, for instance, men and women, live together in one tent unless they are married with each other for that purpose.
Soviet weekly newspaper	There will be a Moscow Exhibition of Arts by 15,000 Soviet Republic painters and sculptors. These were executed over the past two years.
Majorcan shop	Here speeching American.

Sources: Samples from Lederer (1987) and www.engrish.com.

translator has been hired has captured the nuances of the meanings included in the materials (**Table 4.1**). A strategy that can reduce the size of this leap of faith is to use the **back-translation** method (e.g., Brislin, 1970). Here's how it works. Imagine that you want to compare Americans and Indonesians, you've developed all of your materials in English, and you need to have them translated into Indonesian. You would hire one translator to translate the original English materials into Indonesian. You would then hire another translator to translate the translated Indonesian materials back into English. The result would be two different English versions of your

"You'll have to phrase it another way. They have no word for 'fetch.'"

materials (the original one and the back-translated one), and you would carefully compare these two. There are likely to be some differences between the two English versions. The researcher would then discuss the problematic places with the two translators and, through a series of back-and-forth discussions, reach a consensus on how to alter the materials (either the English version, the Indonesian version, or both) so that they would be equivalent. One weakness of the back-translation method is that it might result in a very unnatural or hard-to-understand translation, even though the literal meaning is preserved. For example, idioms such as "it's a piece of cake," "beat around the bush," or "let the cat out of the bag" might be preserved word for word in a back-translation, but these expressions would likely be completely unintelligible in the other language.

In sum, reliable and valid cultural differences are more likely to be found with well-translated materials. Because cross-cultural comparisons are meaningful only if participants understand the materials in the same way, it's always important to get the best translation possible, even though securing a good translation might be time-consuming and costly.

RESPONSE BIASES. Once you have a translation of your materials that you are confident with, you are ready to start recruiting participants to complete your survey. However, interpreting and comparing survey responses from people of different cultures is far more challenging than interpreting those from within a single culture. Researchers want to be able to assume that people's responses on a survey are an accurate reflection of how they truly feel, so that if you compare people's responses between cultures and find a difference, you could conclude that people from the different cultures really do differ in their thoughts. However, it often isn't this simple—in many ways, what people are thinking and how they answer a survey question might not be exactly the same because of the existence of response biases. Response biases are factors that distort the accuracy of a person's responses to surveys and they become especially problematic when we compare groups that differ in their response biases. For example, one kind of response bias is known as **socially desirable responding**. People who strongly show this bias are motivated to be evaluated positively by others, and as a result they might disguise their true feelings to appear more socially desirable.

So, for example, imagine that people in Culture A view it to be socially desirable to appear modest, whereas those in Culture B view it to be socially desirable to appear confident. If you compared people's responses to a measure that assessed self-reported leadership ability, you might very well find that people in Culture B had higher self-reported leadership scores than people in Culture A. But this cultural difference could potentially be due solely to the different kinds of socially desirable responding and not at all to actual cultural differences in leadership ability—we can't confidently draw conclusions by accepting people's responses at face value. One way of addressing this particular response bias is to design studies that assess the construct of interest (e.g., leadership ability) without having people directly report on it (we'll discuss this particular example more in Chapter 8 when we discuss self-enhancing motivations). In the following sections I describe the challenges involved in a few other kinds of response biases and strategies for surmounting them.

MODERACY AND EXTREMITY BIASES. Often, psychological materials present participants with statements, and the participants indicate their agreement by choosing a number from a scale—for example, a scale that runs from 1 (strongly disagree) to 7 (strongly agree). However, there is a tendency for people from different cultures to vary in terms of how likely they are to express their agreement in a moderate fashion—that is, by choosing an item close to the midpoint of the scale (e.g., choosing a 5 on a 7-point scale)—or to express their agreement in an extreme fashion—that is, by choosing an item close to the end of the scale (e.g., choosing a 7 on a 7-point scale). The former is known as a moderacy bias and the latter as an extremity bias.

There is considerable cultural variation on this dimension. African-Americans and Hispanic-Americans tend to give more extreme responses than Americans of European descent do (Bachman & O'Malley, 1984; Hui & Triandis, 1989). For example, a Hispanic respondent might be more likely to indicate his agreement with a statement such as "I am impulsive" by circling a 6 on a 7-point scale, whereas a non-Hispanic with the same degree of impulsivity might indicate his agreement by circling a 5. The Hispanic participant's response thus appears more extreme than the non-Hispanic's because of a habitual way of responding to questions, even though they do not differ in their actual degree of impulsivity. Likewise, East Asians tend to be more moderate in their responses than European-Americans are (Chen, Lee, & Stevenson, 1995; Zax & Takahashi, 1967). Furthermore, East Asians show a greater moderacy bias when they complete the materials in their native language than when they complete them in English (Kuroda, Hayashi, & Suzuki, 1986).

Moderacy and extremity biases are response biases, because they affect how an individual responds to an item *independent of the content* of the item. Such response biases are problematic for cultural comparisons because if cultures vary in how people respond to questions, this will affect any conclusions that we can draw when comparing average scores across cultures.

Moderacy and extremity biases can be controlled for in certain situations. One simple strategy is to avoid providing participants with a set of responses that has a middle answer. For example, rather than having people indicate their answers on a 7-point scale, you could have them respond with a simple "Yes/No" format. Because there is no middle response option, you do not need to be concerned that some cultural groups might be more likely to select it. However, this approach might not provide you with a sensitive enough measure to detect nuanced differences in opinion across individuals.

If you are interested in assessing how people feel across a broad range of items or content domains, you might consider *standardizing* your data before conducting cross-cultural comparisons (e.g., Bond, 1988). In standardization, each participant's scores are first averaged, and then the individual items are assessed with respect to how much they deviate from the participant's own personal average. The standardized scores (also known as z scores) indicate how participants respond to each item compared with their typical way of responding. The participants' responses are no longer kept in the original metric, such as the 7-point scale that was written in the questionnaire, but rather are expressed in terms of the number of standard deviations by which they depart from the participant's own personal average. Standardizing dramatically alters the data, but it preserves the individual's own pattern of responses. It shows us which items the individual agreed with most and which items the individual disagreed with most. It allows us to compare the patterns of responses across individuals or across cultures by statistically forcing everyone to have a uniform response style, thereby eliminating the problems with moderacy and extremity biases. However, there is an important catch: Standardizing assumes that the average level of response is identical across cultures (that is, everyone's scores are forced to have an average z score of 0). This assumption might not be especially problematic when we are looking for patterns of responses across a broad array of measures—for example, if we provide people with an inventory of many different personality traits. It might not be unreasonable to assume in this case that everyone has about the same amount of personality, although some traits are more pronounced than others in each person. However, if we are comparing individuals or cultures on just a few different constructs, we cannot confidently assume that people share the same average response. For example, consider what would happen if we wanted to compare cultures on a 10-item measure of talkativeness. We might be concerned about moderacy and extremity biases, so we would first standardize our data. However, this standardization statistically forces every individual to have the identical level of talkativeness: Everyone's average response is set to a z score of 0. Standardization could thus not tell us which culture is more talkative, as the two cultures would be equated at the same level of talkativeness. Standardizing is a powerful statistical tool, but it does alter a data set, and sometimes in problematic ways, depending on the comparisons we are trying to make. It is appropriate only when we are interested in cultural differences in the *pattern* of responses and not when we want to compare the *average level* of responses across cultures in a single measure.

ACQUIESCENCE BIAS. People also differ in the extent to which they tend to agree with statements they encounter. Some people might be more prone to agree with any item they read, whereas others might be prone to disagree with them. A tendency to agree with most statements is known as an **acquiescence bias** and is an issue for cross-cultural comparisons. Imagine that you're interested in assessing people's feelings toward the government's foreign policy. Individuals are presented with several items that ask them to evaluate various aspects of the government's foreign policy, and then a total approval score is calculated by summing up their answers to the individual questions. You can imagine that people who tend to agree somewhat with almost any statement would score quite high on this foreign policy approval measure, even if they were not big fans of the government's policies. They could earn a high score simply because they find most statements agreeable, regardless of the content. This bias would make it very hard to compare the individual's true degree of approval with that of another person who tends to find most statements to be disagreeable, regardless of content.

The acquiescence bias is a problem for cross-cultural research because cultures differ in their tendencies to agree with items (e.g., Grimm & Church, 1999; Marin, Gamba, & Marin, 1992; Ross & Mirowsky, 1984). Much work has revealed that East Asians tend to have a relatively holistic way of looking at the world (something that we'll return to in Chapter 9), and one consequence is that there are more possible truths in a holistic world. That is, to the extent that the world is an interconnected place that is always changing, which is how it appears with a holistic point of view, then most statements have some truth in them. For example, the statements "I am introverted" and "I am extraverted" both contain some truth if one takes on a holistic perspective. In some situations a person may feel introverted, and in some she might feel extraverted, so these are both truths, and a holistic person would endorse both of them (e.g., Choi & Choi, 2002). If people in some cultures have a predisposition to see the truth in more statements than those in another culture, this will lead to cultural differences in responses, independent from the content of the items.

There is a straightforward solution to the acquiescence bias that is commonly applied when researchers construct trait measures. Typically, half of the items in a measure are designed to be reverse-scored—that is, they are written so that agreeing with them indicates an opinion opposite to that measured in the construct. For example, if we were to measure self-esteem, we would want to ensure that half of our items indicated low self-esteem (e.g., "I feel like a failure") and half indicated high self-esteem (e.g., "I have many great talents"). A person's total self-esteem score would be calculated by first reverse-scoring the responses for the items written in the direction of low self-esteem (i.e., on a 7-point scale, we would need to change the 7's to 1's, the 6's to 2's, the 5's to 3's, and leave the 4's as 4's) and then adding all of these together with the items written in the direction of high self-esteem. By ensuring that half the items are reverse-scored, any acquiescing tendency would be canceled out because individuals would be agreeing with items that both increase their total score (the positively worded items) and items that decrease their total score (the negatively worded items), thereby neutralizing the effects of this bias. Alternatively, standardizing the data would also neutralize acquiescence biases; however, standardization can be problematic, as noted earlier.

REFERENCE-GROUP EFFECTS. **Figure 4.4** illustrates another problem with comparing survey results across cultures. This is a picture of me (second from the right in the back row) together with the other teaching staff from Obama Junior High School in Nagasaki prefecture, where I taught for a couple of years

FIGURE 4.4   The author (back row, second from right) with the other faculty from Obama Junior High School.

after receiving my undergraduate degree. This picture is very special to me, and one reason is that it is probably the only picture that I have in which I am the tallest person.

You see, in Canada, I'm never the tallest person around. I'm 5' 8" which makes me about 2 inches shorter than the average male in Canada. But when I'm in Japan, I am often one of the taller people in any group (although I regretfully note that I've been losing my edge, as the average height of the Japanese has been increasing over the past few decades; see Chapter 13). At least in terms of height, I really am big in Japan. I was the tallest person at Obama Junior High School, I sometimes bumped my head on doorframes in older houses, I could see over most people's heads in a crowded subway train, and I wasn't able to buy shoes in the small town of Obama because they didn't carry a size as large as mine. On the other hand, when I am in the Netherlands, which has the tallest average height in the world, I feel very short indeed.

Now, of course, my actual height, as measured with a tape measure, does not change when I travel between Canada, Japan, and the Netherlands. But if you ask people the same height as me to rate themselves on a scale of 1 to 7 for a statement such as "I am tall," you will get different answers in these three different countries. In Japan, people of my height would probably rate themselves around a 5 or 6, in Canada they'd probably rate themselves around a 2 or 3, and in the Netherlands they'd likely rate themselves around a 1. The same height would yield a different response to the statement, "I am tall" in these different contexts, and that's because the statement "I am tall" does not have the precise same meaning in all cultures.

The reason that such a simple statement as "I am tall" can take on different meanings across cultures is that people in different cultures use different standards to answer the questions. As much research in social psychology has revealed, people tend to evaluate themselves by comparing themselves with others—similar others (Festinger, 1954). When we are assessing ourselves in terms of how tall, intelligent, or punctual we are, what matters is how tall, intelligent, or punctual we view ourselves *compared to most other people around us*. This point is critical for cross-cultural research because people from different cultures tend to evaluate themselves by comparing themselves to *different reference groups* and thus to different standards. This is a problem for cross-cultural research because usually we are interested in assessing cultures by a single standard. This problem is known as the **reference-group effect** (Heine, Lehman, Peng, & Greenholtz, 2002; Peng, Nisbett, & Wong, 1997). Research has shown that reference-group effects are potentially problematic whenever we are comparing cultures on how much they agree with statements with subjective response formats.

One classic example of the reference-group effect was a study from before the civil rights movement that found that African-American soldiers in the North were less satisfied than those in the South because they compared themselves primarily to civilian African-Americans who were better off in the North than in the South (Stouffer, Suchman, DeVinney, Star, & Williams, 1949). In this situation, the reference-group effect leads one to make the exact opposite conclusion (i.e., Southern African-American soldiers were better off than Northern ones) than a more objective comparison would indicate.

Another example of the reference-group effect comes from a curious pattern that regularly emerges when comparing schools and countries on academic achievement. If you ask individual students how talented they are at academic pursuits, you will find that those who say they have higher academic abilities also tend to actually perform better at school—there's a positive correlation between what students think about their academic abilities and their actual achievement in their schoolwork. This makes sense. However, when you look across schools and countries, this relation gets reversed. Students who are from the schools and countries that perform the best on international measures of academic achievement tend to rate their academic abilities as *worse* than those from the worst-performing schools and from the worst-performing countries (e.g., Shen & Tam, 2008). This pattern doesn't make sense until it's considered from the perspective of reference groups—students from top-performing schools and top-performing countries are comparing themselves to a higher standard of performance than those in the schools and countries that aren't doing as well (Van de Gaer, Grisay, Schulz, & Gebhardt, 2012).

One technique for correcting the problems associated with the reference-group effect is to avoid subjective measures that might have different standards in the groups being compared. Instead, one is often better off using more concrete measures that will be perceived more similarly across cultures. Measures can be made more concrete either by changing the content of the item or by changing the response format. For example, a statement such as "I am helpful" can be interpreted quite differently depending on a culture's standards for what kinds of behaviors are perceived to be helpful. In contrast, a statement such as "If a friend of mine needed help with his studies, I would be willing to cancel my own plans to spend the evening helping him" is more concrete in describing the situation in terms of what kind of help is needed and what kinds of sacrifices are made.

The more concrete the scenario, the less likely it is that people from different cultures would interpret the meaning differently. However, more concrete scenarios also tend to be more specific (e.g., one could be helpful in situations other than helping a friend study). To ensure that you are adequately covering the range of helpful behaviors, you would want to create a number of items that indicated helping behaviors. Past research reveals that more-concrete items better capture cultural differences than more-subjective ones (e.g., Heine et al., 2001a; Peng et al., 1997; Takemura, Yuki, Kashima, & Halloran, 2004). Also, you could make your questions more concrete by altering the response format. Some response formats are quite subjective, such as indicating one's endorsement by choosing a number from a scale that ranges from "strongly disagree" to "strongly agree"—this is the most common response format used in psychological surveys. It is subjective in that respondents are able to determine for themselves what kind of agreement corresponds to "strongly agree" (e.g., Biernat & Manis, 1994). A more concrete response option would be to provide some quantitative descriptions, such as "At least once a day" or "10–20% of the time," which do not provide much room for different interpretations. Likewise, one can reduce the range of interpretations for an item by asking participants to make a forced choice between two or more response alternatives—for example, "Which of these two responses would you be more likely to choose if you were in such a situation?" This removes concerns over reference-group effects because people are no longer answering the question by comparing themselves to some imagined standard but rather are comparing two or more response options and are making their choice from them. Efforts to change response formats in this way have been shown to improve the validity of cross-cultural comparisons as well (Peng et al., 1997).

Some other kinds of measures are well protected from reference-group effects. For example, many cross-cultural studies have employed behavioral measures that do not rely on people's understanding of how they compare against others (e.g., Sussman & Rosenfeld, 1982; Vandello & Cohen, 2003). For example, Levine and Norenzayan (1999) investigated the pace of life in 31 cultures by examining behavioral measures. They calculated the pace of life by timing how long it took people to walk a certain distance on a busy street, by checking how accurate the clocks were in banks, and by timing how long it took a postal worker to sell them a stamp. These measures appear reliable in that they are better correlated with other measures relevant to the pace of life than self-report measures are (see Heine, Buchtel, & Norenzayan, 2008).

Likewise, physiological measures are especially protected from reference-group concerns (Cohen, Nisbett, Bowdle, & Schwarz, 1996). For example, one study investigated the autonomic nervous system responses of the Minangkabau of West Sumatra (Levenson, Ekman, Heider, & Friesen, 1992). Although physiological measures are often difficult and costly to obtain, especially in remote cultures, they are especially powerful for cross-cultural study because they occur independently of the various response biases that challenge questionnaire work.

DEPRIVATION EFFECTS. Consider the results of the following study that investigated values in 38 countries around the world (Schwartz, 1994). One question asked how much people valued "enjoying life" and "pleasure." The findings showed that East Germans scored the third highest of all the countries on this dimension, while Italians scored the second lowest (Schwartz, 1994). Another study found that Americans value "humility" more than Chinese do, whereas Chinese value "choosing one's own goals" more than Americans (Peng et al., 1997). Do these findings fit with the stereotypes that you have for these cultures? Evidence from a variety of other sources stands in conflict with these findings from the value measures. Why do Italians rate "pleasure" as so unimportant compared to other nationalities when they

"Could you walk a little faster, buddy? This is New York."

simultaneously have developed a lifestyle that emphasizes good food, leisurely breaks in cafes, opera, art, and long summer vacations?

The disconnect that is sometimes observed between self-report measures of values and other indicators is a challenge for cross-cultural investigations. One way to make sense of this disconnect is to consider what people *actually* have in contrast to what they would *like* to have. Consider the question, "How much do you value personal safety?" Clearly, personal safety is of importance to everyone, everywhere. But it would seem that people start thinking about their personal safety more, and would be more willing to make sacrifices in order to secure it, in situations where their personal safety is most at risk. It is when your safety is vulnerable that you are likely most concerned with it, and at other times you might be quite willing to forget about it. The issue with this for measuring values across cultures is that we might expect that in cultures where there is chronically less personal safety that people express valuing it *more*. This is known as the **deprivation effect**, and it poses a serious challenge to the investigation of values (Peng et al., 1997). It can thus be problematic to make inferences about a culture from the values that people endorse the most. There is no straightforward technique to correct for the deprivation effect other than to investigate whether the results from self-report measures of values converge with the results from other sources of evidence regarding values. The existence of the deprivation effect forces us to be cautious in interpreting what is valued in different cultures.

As you can see, several methodological that make it difficult to compare subjective questionnaire responses across cultures. Although there are some strategies to reduce the impact of these challenges, which I described above, cross-cultural comparisons of means of questionnaires remain potentially misleading. My own personal view of these kinds of comparisons (which is admittedly more critical than that of most other researchers) is that we should be suspicious of any cultural differences that are identified by comparing means across subjective questionnaire measures unless the patterns converge with findings from other methods.

Although the use of subjective self-report measures makes it problematic to compare average scores *across* cultures, these measures can be extremely useful for identifying individual differences *within* a culture. For example, British students who score high on a measure of extraversion can be assumed to be more extraverted than British students who score low on the same measure. Because the within-culture validity of subjective self-report measures is preserved, these measures are extremely useful for identifying correlations between different constructs within cultures—for example, investigating whether extraversion and self-esteem are related. These measures work fine *within* cultures because cultural members tend to *share the same response biases and reference groups*. On the other hand, subjective self-report measures do not work as well *between* cultures because the members from the different cultural groups potentially have *different response styles and reference groups,* thereby obscuring the comparisons.

Conducting Cross-Cultural Research with Experiments

In addition to standard survey methods, much psychological research in cultural psychology employs the experimental method. The experiment is a powerful methodological tool that can reveal much that straightforward questionnaires are not always able to do. Many psychologists get quite excited about a nice experimental design because of their confidence that it allows us to draw inferences about the findings. In general, the experiment is the method of choice for psychological research. Most of the research examples in this textbook are derived from the experimental method.

The experimental method involves the manipulation of an independent variable and measurement of the influence that this manipulation has on a dependent variable. It allows researchers to be confident in their exploration of the relation between the independent variable and the dependent variable because all other extraneous influences can be held constant. If the only aspect of the study that varies is the independent variable, we can be confident that any differences in the dependent variable must be due to that independent variable. The independent variable can be said to *cause* the change in the dependent variable. Such experimental control greatly increases the power of our investigations.

In cross-cultural studies, one important independent variable—cultural background—is *not* manipulated, because it can't be. This means that comparisons of cultures are not true experiments but are quasi-experiments. However, even though this one independent variable is beyond the experimenter's ability to control, many other independent variables can be manipulated to give cross-cultural researchers a great deal of experimental control in their studies.

Two kinds of manipulations of independent variables can be performed in psychological research. One kind is a **between-groups manipulation,** in which different groups of participants receive different levels of the independent variable. The groups that receive each level of the independent variable are referred to as "conditions." Between-groups manipulations require *random assignment* such that each participant has an equal chance of being assigned to any given condition. Random assignment ensures that the participants in the different conditions are statistically equivalent at the beginning of the study. Any differences in their responses, or behaviors, that are observed must be due to the independent variable, as this is the only thing that differs systematically between the experimental conditions. For example, let's imagine that we're interested in exploring whether people are more persuaded by fast-talking salespeople or by slow-talking salespeople. In this case, each participant would be randomly assigned to listen to either a fast-talking salesperson or a slow-talking one, and we would measure their persuasion and compare these across conditions.

A second kind of manipulation is a **within-groups manipulation**. In this case, each participant receives more than one level of the independent variable. Within-groups manipulations do not involve random assignment because *every* participant receives all the levels of the independent variable. In other words, each participant is assigned to all of the conditions. Let's return to our example of exploring persuasion by fast- and slow-talking salespeople. To manipulate the independent variable, talking speed, with a within-subjects design, we would first assess participants' persuasion by a fast-talking salesperson and then by a slow-talking salesperson. One factor that is important in within-groups designs is to provide participants with different orders of the conditions. If we want to be certain that people respond to the fast-talkers differently from the slow-talkers, we want to rule out the possibility that people are differently persuaded by whatever salesperson they encounter first compared with the salesperson that they encounter second. Hence, we would have one group of participants hear the fast-talking salesperson before the slow-talking one, and another group hear the slow-talking salesperson before the fast-talking one. Then we would be able to explore whether the order of the conditions affected people's responses (the astute reader might notice that in this hypothetical study the order of the conditions is a between-groups manipulation). Because all participants are included in both the fast-talking and slow-talking conditions, we can again be confident that any differences in the responses of participants to the conditions are due solely to the independent variable and not to other factors.

The experimental method is not limited to laboratory situations but can also be utilized in questionnaire research (questionnaires can include different conditions too). A clear virtue of manipulating independent variables in cultural research is that doing so can provide us with a comparison that is not limited by the response biases associated with questionnaire research. As you now know, these response biases influence how participants respond to self-report items, making it problematic to compare mean scores directly across cultures, as we end up comparing apples to oranges. However, if we can make comparisons *within* cultures, or within individuals, which the experimental method allows, these response biases are no longer a concern, because the comparison is across groups that *share a response bias*. The experimental method, then, allows us to get back to comparing apples with apples, despite people's response biases.

For example, imagine that you are interested in investigating how Jamaicans and Indians view people with high status. A nonexperimental method would simply ask individuals to rate a particular high-status person on a number of traits. Let's imagine that this study showed that, on average, the Jamaicans evaluated the high-status person more positively than the Indians did. However, because of response biases, we would not be able to confidently assess whether this finding reflected different attitudes toward the high-status person or different response biases.

In contrast, an experimental approach would include more than one condition. In one condition, participants would rate the high-status person. In a second condition, participants would evaluate a person of moderate social status. And perhaps in a third condition, participants would evaluate a person of low social status. Now we would be able to compare how the different individuals were evaluated *within* the cultures. That is, we could see, for example, whether Indians evaluated the high-status person significantly more positively than either the low- or moderate-status person. This would allow us to see how big an impact status has on Indians' evaluations. Note that this kind of analysis is protected from the response biases described above, because even if Indians and Jamaicans have different reference groups, moderacy biases, or acquiescence norms, we are explicitly comparing Indians with Indians, so these response biases are not affecting our comparisons.

Once we have determined the impact of status within each culture, we can then compare the magnitude of this impact *between* cultures. The experimental method changes our between-culture comparison from one of comparing the *magnitude of means* across cultures (which is problematic) to one of comparing the *pattern of means* across cultures (which is fine). The experimental method is an excellent solution for correcting the methodological challenges in cultural research. Many of the studies in cultural psychology with greatest impact have used this method.

Neuroscience Methods

In recent years, much of psychology has become increasingly interested in methodological advances that allow for the study of the specific brain mechanisms that are associated with psychological processes. Cultural psychology has been no exception. There has been a tremendous amount of recent research in the incipient field of cultural neuroscience that has used various kinds of neuroscience methods to understand how neural events vary alongside cultural traits. For example, much recent research has used functional magnetic resonance imaging (fMRI), which produces a high-resolution image of the brain by tracking changes in the blood's oxygen levels throughout the brain. By comparing fMRI images across different cognitive tasks and across cultural groups, researchers are able to identify cultural differences in the particular regions of the brain that are most activated when people are engaging in a variety of cognitive tasks

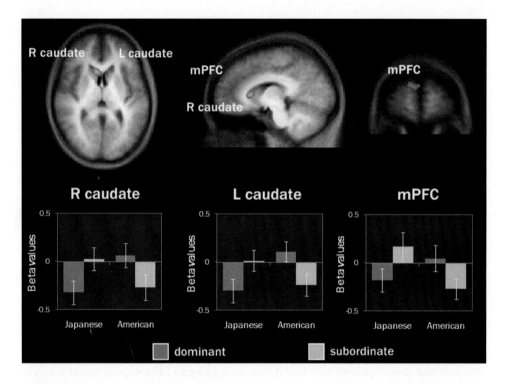

FIGURE 4.5 An example of an fMRI scan comparing Japanese and Americans in how they respond to pictures that indicated either dominant or subordinate poses. The highlighted brain regions are associated with reward-related processing, suggesting that Americans had relatively more positive reactions to the dominant poses whereas the Japanese had relatively more positive reactions to the subordinate poses (Freeman et al., 2009).

(e.g., Adams et al., 2010; Chiao et al., 2009; Freeman, Rule, Adams, & Ambady, 2009; see **Figure 4.5**).

Another method commonly used in cross-cultural studies is to measure brain activity at certain electrodes placed along the scalp using an electroencephalograph (EEG). This method is used to measure electrical patterns that follow the presentation of specific events, and it can identify temporal patterns of activation to those events that are divergent across cultures (e.g., Goto, Ando, Huang, Yee, & Lewis, 2000; Murata, Moser, & Kitayama, 2013; Varnum, Na, Murata, & Kitayama, 2012). An advantage of studies using EEG is that it provides a more precise assessment of the time course of brain activity, although it is not as accurate at localizing brain regions as fMRI.

Cross-cultural studies that have used these methods have demonstrated how participating in different cultural situations can lead to different ways of thinking, and the methods allow us to see the precise neural mechanisms that underlie these differences. In addition, there is a growing body of research that employs molecular genetic technologies to assess how gene frequencies vary across populations (e.g., Chen, Burton, Greenberger, & Dmitrieva, 1999; Chiao & Blizinsky, 2010) and to identify how particular genes are differentially associated with particular ways of thinking across cultures (e.g., Kim et al., 2010a; Kitayama et al., 2014). These are all emerging technologies that cross-cultural researchers are just beginning to employ. We'll discuss several examples of research that use these newer methods in later chapters.

Some Methods Particular to the Study of Culture

Surveys, experiments, and neuroscience methods are not specific to cultural psychology but are characteristic of the ways we test hypotheses in all of psychology, and the sciences more generally. There are some methods, however, that lend themselves especially well to the study of cultural psychology.

Situation Sampling

One inherent shortcoming in cross-cultural research is that we're unable to manipulate our participants' cultural background. From a scientific point of view, the ideal way to conduct a cross-cultural experiment would be to assign cultures to our participants. That is, we would need to take newly born infants who did not have any cultural experiences and randomly assign some of them to be raised in, say, an American cultural condition and some others to be raised in a Bolivian cultural condition; a third group would be assigned to a "control" condition raised without any culture at all. Everything else would be kept completely constant throughout their lives. Then we could measure whatever dependent variable interested us. If we found any differences, we could be certain that they were due to the different cultural experiences that our participants had. I must confess that I sometimes fantasize about running studies like this because of all that we could learn. For obvious ethical and practical reasons, however, we cannot go around enculturating people into different cultural worlds. Because of these limitations, we usually resort to contrasting individuals who have grown up in different cultures.

One methodological technique provides a practical, and ethical, way of getting one step closer to my fantasized experimental methodology (Kitayama, Markus, Matsumoto, & Norasakkunkit, 1997; Morling, Kitayama, & Miyamoto, 2002). Called **situation sampling**, this methodology utilizes the fact that cultures do not affect people in the abstract; they affect people in particular, concrete ways. You can think of your day as consisting of a series of situations that you've experienced. You woke up, you stumbled into the shower to get clean, you had a shouting match with your roommate over an apparent missing bottle of conditioner, you received a phone call from a furniture store telling you that the sofa you ordered was going to be delayed, and so on. The ways in which our cultures affect us is that they provide us with particular kinds of situations that we encounter on a regular basis. In different cultures, people regularly encounter a different collection of situations. It is our experiences in these culturally shaped situations that lead us to adopt habitual ways of thinking about ourselves and our worlds.

The underlying idea of the situation sampling methodology is that if researchers can see how people respond to situations that are regularly experienced by people in another culture, they can get a viewpoint into how cultures shape people's ways of thinking. The situation sampling method involves a two-step process. First, participants from at least two cultures are asked to describe a number of situations they have experienced in which something specific has happened. For example, in one study, Japanese and American participants were asked to list situations in which their self-esteem had either increased or decreased (Kitayama et al., 1997). In the second step, different groups of participants are asked to participate in the study. This second set of participants is provided with a list of the situations that have been generated by the first set of participants, and they are asked to imagine how they would have felt if they had been in those situations themselves. In the Kitayama and colleagues study, this second set of participants were asked to indicate how much they thought their self-esteem would have increased or decreased had they been in those specific situations. Importantly, in this second stage, participants are provided with situations generated by *both* of the comparison cultures. That is, American participants think about how they would feel both in the situations generated by other Americans and in situations generated by Japanese, and vice versa for the Japanese participants. In this way, we can get an idea of how Americans and Japanese would respond if they were participating in the other group's cultural worlds. It is similar to being an exchange student. We can get a viewpoint into how Japanized Americans and Americanized Japanese behave, thereby learning a great deal about the ways culture shapes psychology.

This methodology allows the researcher to do a couple of kinds of analyses. First, the researcher can explore whether there are differences in the ways people from different cultures respond to the situations in Step 2. If, regardless of the situation that participants imagine, people in one culture indicate that they would consistently respond differently from people in the other culture, this suggests that there are learned cultural experiences that have become habitualized by people such that they govern people's reactions across all kinds of situations. For example, in the above study, Japanese participants indicated that their self-esteem would increase less than that of Americans in the self-esteem-increasing situations, and that their self-esteem would decrease more than that of Americans in the self-esteem-decreasing situations. This suggests that Japanese are habitually more attentive to situations that afford opportunities for self-criticism, whereas Americans are habitually more attentive to situations that allow them to boost the positivity of their self-views. We will explore the reasons behind this cultural difference when we discuss self-esteem in Chapter 8.

Second, the situation sampling methodology allows the researcher to explore whether the cultural origin of the situations that participants listed in Step 1 are responded to differently by participants in Step 2. To the extent that situations from one culture are consistently responded to differently from situations from another culture, this would suggest that the two cultures provide participants with different kinds of experiences. For example, in the above study, both American and Japanese participants in Step 2 reported that their self-esteem would decrease more when they responded to Japanese-made self-esteem-decreasing situations than when they responded to American-made ones. Likewise, both Americans and Japanese reported that their self-esteem would increase more when they responded to American-made self-esteem-increasing situations than to Japanese-made ones. This suggests that the kinds of experiences people encounter in the United States are especially conducive to boosting self-esteem, whereas the kinds of experiences people regularly encounter in Japan lead people to be especially self-critical. These two kinds of analyses afforded by the situation sampling methodology allow us to identify both the kinds of cultural experiences people regularly encounter in different cultures and the habitual responses they tend to develop. It is a powerful methodological tool, although the two-step procedure makes it a time-consuming technique to use.

Cultural Priming

Situation sampling is not the only method available to help us come closer to the idealized goal of being able to manipulate culture. Another technique involves the "priming" or activation of cultural ideas within participants. **Cultural priming** works by making certain ideas more accessible to participants, and to the extent that those ideas are associated with cultural meaning systems, we can investigate what happens when people start to think about certain cultural ideas.

Although cultures differ quite profoundly in their most common ways of thinking, for the most part it appears that these differences are ones of degree rather than of kind. That is, there are some ways of thinking that might be more uncommon in Culture A than in Culture B; however, those ways of thinking are likely still present to a limited degree in Culture A as well. There are a few exceptions to this pattern (i.e., there are ways of thinking that appear to emerge only with certain cultural experiences—nonuniversals; Norenzayan & Heine, 2005), but in general, most of the psychological processes that have been studied thus far are at least existential universals that exist in varying degrees across cultures.

For example, one way of thinking that varies across cultures is the extent to which one views oneself as distinct from others (independent) or as connected with others (interdependent). We'll explore this way of thinking in more detail in Chapter 6, but for now suffice it to say that cultures vary in the extent to which they habitually think of themselves in either of these two ways. One study demonstrated that thoughts about independent aspects of the self are more characteristic of Americans than of Chinese, and thoughts of interdependent aspects of the self are more characteristic of Chinese than of Americans (Trafimow, Triandis, & Goto, 1991). The researchers hypothesized that people could be led to consider more independent aspects of themselves if thoughts about people's distinctness could be activated in their minds; likewise, people could be led to consider more interdependent aspects of themselves if thoughts about people's relations were activated. American and Chinese participants were asked to think either of how they were different from others (an independence prime) or how they were similar to their family and friends (an interdependence prime). Then participants were asked to describe themselves in an open-ended survey. Interestingly, when Chinese participants encountered the independence prime, their self-descriptions became more similar to the ways that Americans typically describe themselves, and when Americans encountered the interdependence prime, their self-descriptions became more similar to the ways that Chinese typically describe themselves. In other words, when cultural ideas are activated that are more common in another culture, people start thinking in ways that are more similar to the thinking of people from that culture. Much recent research has explored how a wide variety of ways to prime cultural ideas in people's minds can effectively lead people to think and act in culturally distinct ways (e.g., Hong, Morris, Chiu, & Benet-Martinez, 2000; Kühnen, Hannover, & Schubert, 2001; Oyserman & Lee, 2008). We'll return to priming methods when we consider the minds of bicultural people in Chapter 7.

Culture-Level Measures

The goal of much research in cultural psychology is to assess how cultures affect people's thinking, and the most common way of pursuing this goal is to measure people's thoughts in an effort to see the effects of culture. However, before we can be confident that the psychological processes that we're investigating have been influenced by culture, it's important that we have a confident understanding of what the cultures are like in the first place. That is, we need a way to measure cultures.

For the most part, psychologists tend to be interested in data that allow us to test hypotheses. The kinds of methods we've been discussing thus far have pertained to collecting data to test hypotheses about people, but how can we collect data that allow us to test hypotheses about culture? In principle, the cultural data should be similar in nature to those of psychological hypothesis testing in that they should be (1) objective and capable of being replicated by others and (2) quantifiable so that we can conduct statistical analyses to determine whether our hypotheses are supported. The challenge is to appropriate the kinds of methods that psychologists have mastered for the study of people and apply these to the study of cultures.

Cultural psychologists have used such empirical methods to investigate the kinds of cultural messages to which individuals are habitually exposed. The cultural messages that we encounter are highly relevant to cultural psychologists because they reflect the ideas that are communicated to individuals by participating in their cultures. A careful analysis of the messages that people are exposed to on a regular basis can provide us with a nice perspective on the ways that cultures influence their members.

We encounter a barrage of cultural messages from all kinds of sources as we go about our daily lives. A first step in studying these messages is to focus our investigation on an identifiable and quantifiable subset of them. A variety of domains of cultural messages lend themselves well to this kind of investigation. Past research has explored cultural messages in domains as diverse as magazine advertisements (Han & Shavit, 1994), laws (Cohen, 1996), newspaper articles (Morris & Peng, 1994), fairy tales (Doyle & Doyle, 2001), children's stories (McClelland, 1961), sports coverage (Markus, Uchida, Omoregie, Townsend, & Kitayama, 2006), web pages (Wang, Masuda, Ito, & Rashid, 2012), and personal ads (Parekh & Beresin, 2001).

As an illustration, consider some research that contrasted working-class and upper-middle-class Americans (Snibbe & Markus, 2005). The researchers reasoned that they could identify the different cultural messages these two groups were exposed to by attending to the lyrics of the music they most commonly listened to. Their surveys revealed that country music was more popular among working-class Americans, whereas rock music was more commonly listened to by upper-middle-class Americans. Exploring the lyrics from songs of these two genres, then, provides a window on the kinds of cultural messages that working-class and upper-middle-class Americans commonly encounter when listening to music.

A second step to take when studying cultural messages is to derive a specific hypothesis to test. For example, the researchers in the above study were interested in testing the hypothesis that working-class individuals were more commonly exposed to messages emphasizing resilience whereas upper-middle-class individuals were more in contact with messages that called for carving one's own unique path. This hypothesis can be tested by exploring whether such messages really are more common in the different genres of music.

Last, we need to come up with a way to transform our raw data (in this case, the actual song lyrics) into quantifiable data that lend themselves to a test of our hypothesis. This transformation involves coding the data—that is, deriving a set of categories that are consistent with particular cultural messages. For example, messages could be coded as to whether they emphasize something relevant to resilience (e.g., rebelling against authority) or to uniqueness (e.g., being unique or talented). Coders who are trained to identify the categories then go through the raw data in search of instances of specific cultural messages that fit into the different categories. Unfortunately, many coding decisions are quite subjective and, on occasion, the decisions are not obvious.

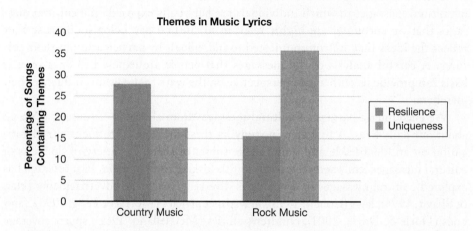

FIGURE 4.6 Country music listeners hear different cultural messages than rock music listeners.

To ensure that the coders' individual biases are not overly influencing the results, a couple of safeguards can be introduced. First, the coders can be kept blind to the hypotheses being tested—for example, in the above study the coders would not know that the researchers are expecting resilience categories to be more common in country than in rock music lyrics. Keeping the coders blind prevents their motivation to get good results from leaking into the subjective decisions they have to make. Second, multiple coders are employed, and some, or all, of the raw data are coded by more than one individual. Then, the experimenters can check to see whether the different coders are making the same decisions. If the different coders are making different decisions, this means that the data are not reliable and the coders need more training about the boundaries of the different categories. Once the coders have reached a consensus for all the decisions they have made, the data are considered reliable and can be statistically analyzed. For example, in the above study, analyses did indeed reveal that country music lyrics convey more messages about resilience and rock music lyrics more messages about uniqueness (see **Figure 4.6**).

The Challenge of Unpackaging

Many cross-cultural psychological studies find pronounced differences between cultures, and these differences reveal to us that there are ways in which people from different cultures have divergent experiences that affect their psychologies. Finding a cultural difference represents an important first step in understanding how culture influences psychological processes because it suggests that the psychological process under study is likely grounded in cultural experiences. However, a cultural difference by itself does not tell us *which* cultural experiences sustain it. There are myriad ways in which cultures differ from each other. Which of these ways are relevant to understanding the psychological process at hand? This question belies a particular challenge to cultural research. Cultures appear to us as "packaged" (Whiting, 1976)—that is, participating in a culture means that one is exposed to a broad network of practices and meanings that are presented to the individual as a whole. We are not able to separate the individual cultural practices and meanings from each other because they are always wrapped up together, as if in a package. If we are to deepen our understanding of how cultures and minds are intertwined, we need to "unpackage" the cultural differences to reveal the specific cultural experiences or variables that relate to the cultural difference. **Unpackaging** cultural findings means identifying the underlying variables that give rise to the cultural difference.

For example, consider the finding that Japanese scored higher than Americans on a measure of embarrassability (Singelis, Bond, Lai, & Sharkey, 1999). Why might we expect this cultural difference? Which of the multitude of cultural differences between Japanese and Americans can account for this difference? Is it because many Japanese take baths together with their parents until they reach puberty that they become more habitually embarrassed? Is it because American schools encourage children to express their own opinions more that they become less embarrassed? We could go on and on coming up with potential cultural explanations. The key to advancing our understanding would be to discover which cultural experiences are relevant.

How would one go about unpackaging the observed cultural differences in embarrassability? The first step would be to let a theory guide the researchers' search for potential underlying cultural variables. Much other research has revealed that Japanese tend to have more interdependent views of self than Americans do (Markus & Kitayama, 1991), something we'll return to in Chapter 6, and the researchers reasoned that a concern with interdependence and how one relates with close others might lead one to become more easily embarrassed. The next step in the unpackaging process of this study is to demonstrate that Japanese really do have more interdependent views of self than Americans. Indeed, this is what the researchers found. So now there is evidence that Japanese score higher than Americans on both embarrassability and on interdependence. The third necessary step in the unpackaging process is to demonstrate that the observed cultural differences in interdependence relate to the observed differences in embarrassability. In the case of this study, the researchers' approach was to correlate people's embarrassability scores and their interdependence scores within each culture. They found that these two variables were significantly related within both Japanese and American cultures. That is, those Japanese who were more interdependent reported feeling the most easily embarrassed, and likewise for Americans. The cultural difference in embarrassability has thus been successfully unpackaged. Unpackaging does not mean that you have necessarily identified all the variables behind a cultural difference, or even the most powerful variable. It does show you, however, that the variable you identified is at least partly responsible for the observed cultural difference.

Unpackaging cultural differences is a powerful analytical tool. It's a tool by which we can use cultural differences themselves to shed light on the nature of underlying processes. Discovering cultural differences increases not only our understanding of how culture and psychology are interrelated, but also our understanding of the psychological processes themselves. If the above study hadn't first identified the cultural difference in embarrassability, we might never have learned about the important relationship between embarrassability and interdependence. Knowing about this relation enables us to better understand the nature of embarrassability by focusing our exploration on the aspects of interdependence that lead to heightened embarrassment. Similar to how neuroscientists often study the cognitive deficits of people with brain injuries as a tool for discovering what parts of the brain are associated with what kinds of cognitive abilities, cultural psychologists can also learn more about particular psychological phenomena by identifying cultures that engage in these phenomena relatively more or less than other cultures. Learning about the minds of people from other cultures helps us to understand our own minds better as well.

Conducting Cross-Cultural Research with Multiple Methods

A key point to realize about research is that no single study is perfect. Every study has potential methodological shortcomings or alternative theoretical explanations. In fact, one important skill that students learn in graduate school in psychology is precisely how to come up with alternative explanations for virtually any study they encounter. This is viewed as a good exercise in critical thinking. To the extent that compelling alternative accounts can be offered, we become less confident in the conclusions of the study. Just because there are alternative explanations for every study does not mean that every study is worthless. Each study still provides us with a valuable perspective; however, no single study can provide us with a complete picture.

Because of this fact, a more compelling case is always made when researchers utilize multiple methods in their research. If a finding is observed with one method, it is good practice for the researcher to try to replicate it with a different kind of method. The more divergent the methods across the different studies, the more compelling a convergent set of findings would be. If each study provides one perspective, then multiple studies will give us a more complete picture from multiple perspectives. Researchers tend to get especially excited about multiple studies with divergent methods, as this kind of approach is largely resistant to alternative accounts because any alternative explanation must apply to all the methods that were explored.

We rely on the principle of **Occam's razor**, which states that any theory should make as few assumptions as possible, eliminating, or "shaving off," any extraneous assumptions. All else held equal, then, Occam's razor maintains that the simpler theory is more likely to be correct. Hence, if a researcher conducts four studies on a topic, each using a different method, and these results all converge with his predictions, the researcher's own account would be more compelling than an account that offered four separate alternative explanations for each of his individual studies. A single explanation is more parsimonious and more likely to be correct than four separate explanations. Multiple methods are important for all kinds of scientific research, but they are especially so in cultural psychology because of the methodological challenges involved (e.g., Triandis, McCusker, & Hui, 1990).

Case Study: The Culture of Honor in the Southern United States

In many things we learn, the best educational device is a good example. I can think of no better way to learn about how to conduct cross-cultural psychological research than to read about a research program conducted by some of the most skilled methodological craftsmen.

Richard Nisbett and Dov Cohen (Cohen et al., 1996; Cohen, Vandello, Puente, & Rantilla, 1999; Nisbett, 1993; Nisbett & Cohen, 1996) launched a large-scale investigation of an intriguing cultural difference that they had noticed: Why does the U.S. South seem so much more violent than the North? Their observation that the South is an especially violent place is not new. Early in the country's settlement, a number of observers noted that the South seemed to have a penchant for violent activities and outbursts (de Tocqueville, 1835/1969; Gastil, 1989). From the 18th century on, the South has had a greater number of lynchings, sniper attacks, feuds, homicides, and duels than the North (Fischer, 1989; Gastil, 1989; Nisbett & Cohen, 1996). The South has also had more tolerance for other aggressive pursuits. In the colonial days in the South, there were many gruesome reports of "no-holds-barred" fights, in which participants resorted to eye-gouging and biting off noses and ears (Fischer, 1989), and there was participation in violent games such as "gander-pulling" (in which the object of the game was to ride by on horseback and try to yank the head off a live, greased goose hanging upside-down from a tree; Fischer, 1989) or "purring" (in which the goal was to kick your opponent in the shins until he lost his grip on your shoulder; McWhiney, 1988). While this was going on, the Puritans in New England were inventing baseball. Furthermore, from colonial times to the present, the South has historically been more tolerant of corporal punishment of children, of capital punishment, and of gun ownership and has been more supportive of the United States engaging in wars when compared with the North (see Cohen, 1996, for a review).

Such regional differences in violence continue to this day. For example, high school students in the South are more likely than those in the North to report having brought a weapon to school in the previous month, and there have been more school shootings in Southern states than in Northern ones (Brown, Ostermann, & Barnes, 2009). How can we make sense of this greater tolerance for violence in the South than in the North?

A number of explanations have been offered. For example, the South's higher rates of violence have been attributed to the more uncomfortably hot temperatures (people tend to become more frustrated and violent when the weather is uncomfortable; Anderson, 1989), the greater poverty (people might resort to more drastic, and potentially violent, attempts to improve their quality of life if they can't afford the bare necessities), and the longer history of slavery (treating some people inhumanely might have led to a greater tolerance for violent behavior more generally; e.g., de Tocqueville, 1835/1969).

Nisbett and Cohen's own explanation is unique, and it might strike you as rather bizarre. They argue that there have historically been more herders in the South (i.e., people raising cows, pigs, and sheep) than in the North and this has given rise to a violent **culture of honor** that has continued to persist until this day. A culture of honor is one in which people (especially men) strive to protect their reputation through aggression. This is admittedly an unusual explanation for the regional differences in violence, and when we encounter these kinds of extraordinary claims, we require extraordinary evidence to be convinced. Nisbett and Cohen tried to marshal the kind of compelling evidence necessary to support such an unusual hypothesis, and I highlight their research program as an exemplary way to study cultural psychology.

Before considering Nisbett and Cohen's methodological approach, let's first explore why herders should be expected to be more violent. Imagine you're a herder and your family's wealth is tied up in the 10 pigs you own. One night, while you're sleeping, someone comes by and opens up the pen and steals all your pigs (**Figure 4.7**). Now you're in trouble, as your family's wealth has literally vanished overnight. In contrast, imagine you're a farmer with a field full of wheat. There isn't much thieves can do—they're probably not going to stick around to harvest your crops for you. In sum, herders face a particular kind of threat that farmers do not: Their wealth is portable. This threat is exacerbated because herding tends to be practiced on rather marginal land, which can't support large populations, making it very difficult to police. Herders would seem to live a rather precarious existence indeed.

What is one to do if one's livelihood can be easily stolen and there isn't much of a police force around to guard it? Nisbett and Cohen propose that you'll fare better if you can develop a reputation as someone who maintains his sense of honor. In this case, others come to think of you as someone who is likely to respond with violence when people try to take advantage of you. Of course, if you wait until someone steals your herd before you demonstrate that you're not someone to be messed with, this would be too late. You'd want to develop this reputation beforehand, and a good way to do so would be to show that you are prepared to respond with violence to any threat to your honor—for example, if someone insults you or makes a pass at your girlfriend. Note that Nisbett and Cohen's rationale here is not limited to herders in the United

FIGURE 4.7 In the late 19th century there was a famous multigenerational feud between the Hatfields (pictured above) and the McCoys in the borderlands between West Virginia and Kentucky. The feud apparently started with the reputed theft of a single pig, and fits well with a culture of honor account.

States but applies to herders everywhere. And they discuss some evidence that this kind of culture of honor develops in other places where there has historically been a lot of herding—for example, the Scotch-Irish borderlands of Britain (from which the first settlers of the South came, and brought their culture with them; Fischer, 1989), many countries in the Middle East (recall the violent rhetoric of Saddam Hussein and his threats that the United States would drown in its own blood), and some traditional societies in Africa (Galaty & Bonte, 1991).

That, in a nutshell, is Nisbett and Cohen's theory. Now what kind of evidence could they collect to make a convincing case of it? The particular strength of their research program, as you'll see, is in using a wide array of methods to test their hypothesis.

One kind of evidence they gathered was *archival data* (see Nisbett & Cohen, 1996). Archival data exist in accumulated documents or records of a culture. Although there is not much of an archival database out there on attitudes toward violence in general, there is an extremely detailed database on police records of homicides. If the South's violence is due to a culture of honor, we shouldn't expect that all kinds of homicide would be higher in the South than in the North. Rather, specifically *argument-related murders,* in which people are compelled to defend their honor, should be higher. Nisbett and Cohen show that, overall, this pattern is true; however, the pattern is especially pronounced when you contrast the rural South with the rural North. It is in the rural South where culture of honor norms should persist more strongly, as they are that much closer to the traditional herding cultures from which these norms originated. Furthermore, within the rural South the homicide rate is more than twice as large in the hills and dry plains where livestock are raised as in the moist plains where farming is practiced. This finding by itself lends support to the culture of honor explanation for Southern violence over the other competing hypotheses. Because the herding regions do not differ much from the farming regions in terms of either income or temperature, the hypotheses that the South is more violent because of its poverty or high temperatures loses plausibility. And because, prior to the Civil War, slaves were far more numerous in the farming regions (which are heavily labor dependent) than they were in the herding regions, the South's history with slavery can also not explain why the homicide rate is higher in the herding regions than in the farming regions. This is one piece of evidence for Nisbett and Cohen's culture of honor explanation.

Another kind of evidence that they recruited was survey data (see Cohen & Nisbett, 1994). They contacted people by phone who lived in either the South or North and asked them to respond to some attitude items and some scenarios regarding the appropriateness of violence. They found that Southerners were more likely than Northerners to agree that a man has the right to kill a person to defend his family or home. However, Southerners were not more likely than Northerners to agree with statements about violence in general. Southerners were only more likely than Northerners to have more positive attitudes toward violence when it related to defending their families or honor. Respondents were also asked to imagine a guy named Fred in a variety of scenarios in which some bad things happened to him. In one version, they were told to imagine that Fred's 16-year-old daughter was sexually assaulted. Respondents were asked whether they felt that Fred would be "extremely justified" to go out and shoot the assailant; 23% of Northern respondents agreed, compared with 47% of Southerners. Again, the regional differences were evident only for scenarios that involved defending one's family or honor. Score another point for Nisbett and Cohen.

Nisbett and Cohen aspired to get some *physiological measures* to support the idea that Southerners respond with violence to insults. One thing we've learned from physiological research is that when people are ready to aggress, their testosterone levels rise (e.g., Mazur, 1985). Nisbett and Cohen reasoned that if the culture of honor theory was correct, you should see evidence of testosterone rising in Southerners but not in Northerners following an insult. The challenge for Nisbett and Cohen, then, was to find a good way to insult people in an experimentally controlled situation. Here's what they did (see Cohen et al., 1996, for a more detailed description): Participants (who were all non-Hispanic White male students at the University of Michigan who had grown up either in the North or the South) came into the lab. Half were randomly assigned to an "insult condition" in which they were instructed to walk down a room between a wall and a long row of tables to pick up a questionnaire to fill out. Along the way they encountered a confederate of the experimenter, posing as a rather uptight research assistant, busily digging in the open drawer of a file cabinet, which blocked the participant's path. The confederate looked rather frustrated that he had to close the file drawer to let the participant by, and the participant passed him and picked up his questionnaire. But on his way back, the participant discovered that the confederate had the file drawer open again and again was blocking his path. This time the confederate looked thoroughly ticked off at being interrupted once more. He slammed the door shut, bumped his shoulder into the participant as he walked by, and said, "Asshole!" Before the startled participant had the chance to react, the confederate exited through a door marked "Photo Lab" that locked behind him (which was a good thing, as some participants tried to go after him). The insult had been delivered and the hapless participant was left alone to stew in his juices. The other half of the participants were in a control condition in which they were never insulted by the confederate.

The dependent variable was the change in participants' testosterone level throughout the experiment. The participants were asked to give saliva samples at various times through the experiment under a false explanation that the study was about task performance and blood sugar levels. The experimenters analyzed participants' testosterone level as it was measured both before and several minutes after the insult, and it was compared between Northerners and Southerners.

As **Figure 4.8** shows, Southerners who had been insulted showed a sharp spike in testosterone level. The insult made them angry and poised to aggress. In contrast, Northerners did not show a significant difference in testosterone level between the two conditions. They had little reaction to the insult. Indeed, other measures showed that the Northerners found the insult to be quite humorous, apparently as it reflected

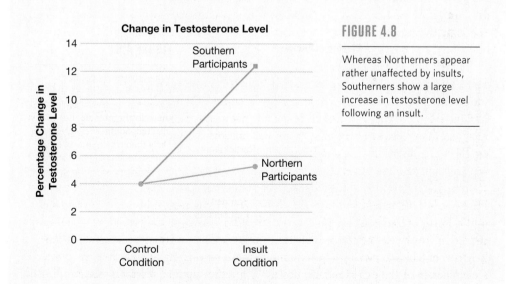

Change in Testosterone Level

FIGURE 4.8

Whereas Northerners appear rather unaffected by insults, Southerners show a large increase in testosterone level following an insult.

a problem with the confederate. The Southerners showed clear signs of anger, because in a culture of honor a challenge to one's honor is a problem for oneself. This is further evidence for Nisbett and Cohen's theory.

The kinds of data that are perhaps most exciting for many psychologists are *behavioral measures*. Ultimately, we're interested in the kinds of things people do; however, behavioral measures are usually extremely difficult to get. They're especially challenging in studies of aggression, as one thing that is not acceptable is for your participants to leave your experiment with their experimental credit and a black eye. How can you measure aggression in a way in which no one actually gets hurt? Being creative methodologists, Cohen and colleagues (1996) figured that they could tap into aggressive behaviors by staging a game of "chicken" with the participant.

They ran another study using the same "asshole" manipulation described above. After the participants had been insulted (or not, for those in the control condition), they were told that they had to proceed to another laboratory for the next part of the study. The way to the other lab was through a narrow hallway that had a row of tables along either side. Once the participant had started his trek down the hallway, the experimenter signaled for a second confederate to begin his role. This confederate was chosen for his physical characteristics. Namely, he was 6' 3", weighed 250 pounds, and played on the offensive line of his college football team. His instructions were clear: Walk toward the participant at a quick pace and be sure *not* to give way. The participant thus had the choice of either stepping aside or being flattened by this oncoming freight train. The dependent measure was how close the participant got to this second confederate before yielding way. As **Figure 4.9** shows, there was a clear

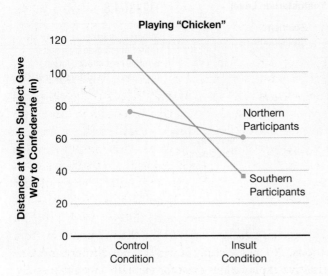

Playing "Chicken"

Distance at Which Subject Gave Way to Confederate (in)

Northern Participants

Southern Participants

Control Condition   Insult Condition

FIGURE 4.9

When they have not been insulted, Southerners yield to an oncoming person earlier than Northerners do. But when insulted, Southerners are more likely than Northerners to confront an oncoming person.

cultural difference. Northerners showed no significant difference in their behaviors between the insult and control conditions. Southerners, in contrast, showed a pronounced difference. When they were not insulted, they yielded much earlier than the Northern subjects did—perhaps showing some of that famous Southern hospitality. When they had been insulted, in stark contrast, they went right up to the face of the second confederate. This is a clear example of the culture of honor. It is interesting that they showed this aggressive stance even though the second confederate had never insulted them. The desire to show that one was a tough guy and not to be messed with was active in their minds and carried over to their interactions with a new person. This is yet another piece of evidence in support of Nisbett and Cohen's theory.

Another way to test the theory of the culture of honor is to see if there are regional differences in people's tolerance for insult-related aggression out in the real world. Cohen and Nisbett (1997) conducted a *field experiment* to test this hypothesis. Field experiments are those conducted outside the laboratory in the real world, with participants who are typically not aware they are in a study. The real advantage of the field experiment is that we can be confident we are observing patterns that generalize to the real world and are not just limited to the artificial confines of the laboratory.

Cohen and Nisbett conducted their study by mailing out letters to employers around the United States. Some of these offices were in the North, and some were in the South. The letters specified that the applicant, a 27-year-old male who was fresh out of prison, was looking for a job. However, there were two different versions of these letters. In an "honor letter" condition, the applicant explained that he had served time for manslaughter because he had killed a man who had slept with his girlfriend and who had teased him about it publicly. The applicant described how he had told the victim to "take it back, or else"—meaning the public insult—and when it wasn't taken back, he had grabbed a pipe and killed the victim in anger. In a "control letter" condition, the applicant explained that he had served time for stealing a car. The dependent variable of interest was the warmth of the letter that the employer sent in return. As might be expected from what we've seen thus far, the Southern employers were more sympathetic to the applicant in the "honor letter" condition than the Northern employers were, but there were no regional differences in warmth in the "control letter" condition. The culture of honor still appears to be operating in the South. This is yet another demonstration in favor of Nisbett and Cohen's account for the greater violence in the South.

Nisbett and Cohen have conducted a number of other studies using diverse methodologies that further converge to support their hypothesis, but I think you've gotten the point by now, so I won't go into those. Why their research program is so compelling is that they were able to find support for their hypotheses from such a diverse range of methods. No single study is perfect, not Nisbett and Cohen's, or anyone else's. Alternative explanations exist for virtually any given study. However, when you utilize a diverse range of methods and continually find convergent evidence for your hypotheses, these alternative explanations fall by the wayside. You might wonder, for example, how representative of Southern culture were the Southern students attending classes at the University of Michigan. That would be a good point, and it's a valid challenge to the testosterone study. However, that point cannot account for the findings in the field experiment or in the archival evidence.

Unless there is an alternative explanation that can account for the results in all of the experiments, we're left to accept the one explanation that can account for all the findings. That is, the South has a culture of honor that leads people (particularly white men) to respond aggressively to insults or threats to their honor, and this seems to be associated with the herding background of the South's initial European settlers. This doesn't mean that other competing theories that might arise in the future don't warrant our attention; however, unless they are consistent with the wide array of findings presented here, they'll pale in comparison to Nisbett and Cohen's theory. As noted before, research across cultures is particularly prone to methodological challenges, raising many alternative explanations for each study, and because of this, a multiple-method approach is especially valuable in cultural psychology. Our confidence in a theory increases with the number of different ways a researcher can provide support for it.

SUMMARY

Cross-cultural psychological research presents a set of unique methodological challenges. As a first step, it is crucial to learn something about the culture you are studying. Also, it is important to ensure that there is methodological equivalence between the cultures that you are comparing.

In survey research, a variety of issues pose validity problems for comparisons of cultures, particularly for questionnaires with subjective questions. These issues include problems inherent in translating materials, response biases such as moderacy and extremity biases, acquiescence biases, reference-group effects, and deprivation effects. There are some methodological and analytic strategies to deal with most of these problems; however, the best solution would seem to be to avoid comparisons of means of questionnaire responses whenever possible.

The experiment provides a method that transcends the methodological shortcomings of comparing means across cultures. Furthermore, any scientific investigation is improved when multiple methods are adopted in the search for convergent findings.

Many methodological developments are particular to the study of culture. An inherent limitation of cross-cultural research is that the primary independent variable, culture, cannot be manipulated by the experimenter because participants arrive at experiments already enculturated. Two methods that approximate experimental manipulations of cultural background are the situation sampling and cultural priming techniques. Cultures can also be studied directly, either through quantitative analyses or the presence of particular cultural variables.

Cultural differences beg for explanations, and the "unpackaging" method allows for the identification of other psychological processes that relate to the cultural differences that have been observed. Unpackaging allows cultural psychological studies not only to significantly advance our investigation of the cultures under study but also to provide an added level of explanation for why psychological processes operate as they do in a given culture.

THINK ABOUT IT

1. What are some tradeoffs between deciding to compare two highly different cultures (such as Dutch undergraduate students versus Hadza hunter and gatherers from Tanzania) versus two more similar cultures (such as Dutch undergraduate students versus American undergraduate students)?
2. What are some of the challenges to consider if you want to compare two cultures on a survey that measured talkativeness?
3. What are some advantages of using the experimental method in cross-cultural research?
4. Why would researchers want to "unpackage" a cultural difference?
5. What are the advantages of using multiple methods in research?
6. Why is a culture of honor associated with herding?
7. Can you think of other contexts where you might find a culture of honor?

KEY TERMS

Methodological
  Equivalence, 123
Generalizability, 124
Power, 124
Independent Variable, 124
Dependent Variable, 124
Back-Translation, 127
Response Biases, 128

Socially Desirable
  Responding, 128
Acquiescence Bias, 131
Reference-Group Effect, 133
Deprivation Effect, 136
Between-Groups
  Manipulation, 137

Within-Groups
  Manipulation, 138
Situation Sampling, 141
Cultural Priming, 143
Unpackaging, 147
Occam's Razor, 148
Culture of Honor, 150

This Cameroonian mother provides her infant with far more direct personal contact than what is typically found among European mothers and infants.

5

DEVELOPMENT AND SOCIALIZATION

ulture shapes many of the norms that govern our behavior. Take the question of interpersonal space. When you have a conversation with someone, you stand a certain distance from that person. Quite a range of distances allow for a functional conversation. You could communicate fine if you were just 1 foot away, and you could also communicate fine if you were 15 feet away. However, people don't usually use the full range of possible distances when they have conversations. Rather, within a culture there is usually an implicitly understood "appropriate" conversation distance that people unconsciously adopt. If someone starts off a conversation from either too great or too small a distance, people will usually adjust where they are standing until they have reestablished the appropriate distance, and these adjustments occur for the most minor deviations from the norm. Furthermore, these appropriate distances vary across cultures. For example, in Venezuela the typical conversation distance is 32 inches, in the United States it is 35 inches, and in Japan it is 40 inches (Sussman & Rosenfeld, 1982). Compared with Americans, Venezuelans prefer closer conversational distances, and Japanese prefer wider conversational distances.

Upon learning about this cultural difference, or any of the others covered in this book, you might ask this: How did Venezuelans come to prefer closer interpersonal spaces and Japanese to prefer more-distant interpersonal spaces than Americans? How did cultures get inside people's heads in the first place? There seem to be at least two distinct possibilities for the origins of these cultural differences. One is that Venezuelans, Japanese, and Americans were born that way. That is, Venezuelans tend to have more of an inherited genetic predisposition to prefer closer interpersonal distances, and Japanese have inherited tendencies to prefer greater interpersonal distances, whereas Americans were born preferring intermediate interpersonal distances. Although it is possible that the genes underlying inherited psychological traits are not distributed equally across the globe (see Chiao & Blizinsky, 2010), there is as yet no good evidence for such kinds of population differences in genes underlying differences in ways of thinking (we'll discuss genetic variation more in Chapter 13). Rather, there is much acculturation research that finds weaker cultural differences among those who have moved to other cultures (e.g., Heine & Lehman, 2004).

The second possibility to account for such cultural differences is that people of different cultural backgrounds come into the world with rather similar genetic temperaments, yet interact with different environments as they grow up. According to this perspective, it is their early experiences with their environments that lead Venezuelans to prefer closer interpersonal distances, Japanese to prefer greater interpersonal distances, and Americans to prefer intermediate distances. That is, people acquire their cultures through socialization. The field of cultural psychology has largely explored this second explanation.

This chapter explores how people come to be socialized into particular cultural worlds. How do people acquire culture? How do child-rearing experiences differ around the world? This chapter addresses the two guiding themes of this book: first, how universal predispositions become shaped in culturally specific ways, and second, how people's experiences, particularly when they are infants and children, come to influence the ways they think.

Universal Brains Develop into Culturally Variable Minds

The starting assumption of cultural psychology is that we are all cultural beings. One key adaptation that enabled humans to distinguish themselves from their proto-chimpanzee ancestors was the ability to learn and accumulate cultural information so well. This adaptation allowed humans to learn the requisite technologies and skills to stake out a successful existence in such diverse environments as the ice-encased Arctic hinterland, the thick Amazonian jungle, the parched Kalahari desert, and the dog-eat-dog corporate world of Wall Street. Without this ability to learn cultural information, we would likely still be competing with our distant chimpanzee relatives over territorial rights to some termite mounds. The ability to acquire cultural knowledge has allowed us to succeed in an amazingly diverse array of environments.

The key point about cultural knowledge and skills is that they are not in our heads from the beginning. This contrasts with other important kinds of knowledge and skills that we see in other species. Salmon do not have to be taught how to find their way back from the ocean to the stream where they were born. That knowledge is instinctual. Cats do not need to be taught to go into their hunting position when they hear something rustle in the grass. These kinds of skills are hard-wired, although certain environmental experiences might be necessary to trigger them. In contrast, humans are not born with the knowledge of how to hunt a seal with a handmade kayak and harpoon, catch a howler monkey with a poisoned blow dart, collect the morning dew in emptied ostrich eggshells, or close a seven-figure advertising deal with a multinational firm on Madison Avenue. We must learn these skills, and we have certain biological potentials that enable us to learn them well. We come into this world cultureless, but we are prepared to adjust to and seize meaning from any environment with which we are presented (see **Figure 5.1**).

That people from different cultures come into this world so similarly yet end up having such different life experiences attests to the powerful role that socialization occupies in influencing who we become. As the cultural anthropologist Clifford Geertz (1973) famously asserted, "We all begin with the natural equipment to live a thousand kinds of life but end in the end having lived only one" (p. 45). This suggests that fundamentally our nature is that of a cultural being. Our universal biological foundation is shaped by

FIGURE 5.1 One example of the many ways that children grow up to learn cultural ideas. Here is a San toddler in the Kalahari desert in Botswana observing how his father makes fire.

our experiences, such that we are able to thrive in an extremely broad array of cultural environments. Who we are is greatly influenced by the cultural worlds into which we are socialized. And all humans have been socialized into some kind of cultural environment that influences how they perceive and understand themselves and their worlds.

Sensitive Periods for Cultural Socialization

It would seem that if humans evolved as cultural beings, we should see evidence that the human brain is preprogrammed to learn cultural meaning systems. One such source of evidence would be an indication that there is a sensitive period for being enculturated. A

sensitive period is a period of time in an organism's development that allows for the relatively easy acquisition of a set of skills. If an organism misses that chance to acquire those skills, it would have a difficult time doing so later, after the sensitive period has expired.

There is a trade-off between an organism's ability to learn new behaviors that suit its new environment and its abilities to specialize in behaviors that are effective in particular environments (see Auld, Agrawal, & Relyea, 2010; Pigliucci, 2005). Some organisms specialize shortly after birth, such as goslings imprinting on the first caretakers they encounter and following them as though they were their mothers. Other organisms, such as humans, can continue to specialize throughout their lives in some domains, as your ability to learn cultural psychology demonstrates. Indeed, human cultural learning continues throughout the lifespan, although the developmental trajectory of learning can vary across cultures (e.g., Grossmann et al., 2012). Most species go through a critical developmental transition from emphasizing the acquisition of new skills to emphasizing the specialization and the exploitation of the skills that have already been acquired. These developmental transitions indicate the existence of a sensitive period.

Sensitive Periods for Language Acquisition

Have you ever learned a second language? How easy was it for you to speak the new language flawlessly? Likely, the success of your experiences has depended on how old you were when you started to learn the new language.

How people go about acquiring languages is the question that has attracted the vast majority of research on sensitive periods in humans. Language ability is a hallmark human characteristic, and although there are rudimentary language skills in some other species (Seyfarth, Cheney, & Marler, 1980), no other species is as dependent on language skills or has as complex a language system as humans. It is easy to imagine how language skills provided a survival advantage to humans. Being able to describe to others where the dangers are, to coordinate each other's behaviors to increase the success of a hunt, to discover and share the precise social dynamics that are occurring among your allies and competitors, and to say the right things so that you can attract a mate—all of these advantages suggest that those humans who were able to communicate most effectively were more likely to produce surviving offspring than those who were not. Because language skills confer such an obvious evolutionary advantage, there should be evidence of a sensitive period for language acquisition.

One source of evidence for such a sensitive period is with respect to people's abilities to discriminate among different sounds. Humans are capable of producing, recognizing, and using approximately 150 phonemes (units of sound) in communication; however, no language uses more than 70 of them (Brown, 1991). This means that many phonemes that are used in various languages around the world are not used in other languages. Interestingly, people are not able to discriminate easily between some phonemes that are not in their own language. For example, the Japanese language does not have separate phonemes for the sounds "la" and "ra." Likewise, the Japanese language does not have a phoneme for "va," although it does have a phoneme for the closely related sound of "ba." Consequently, an adult who was exposed only to the Japanese language cannot perceive the differences between "la"s and "ra"s, or between "ba"s and "va"s—phonemes that sound obviously different to English speakers. To native Japanese-speaking adults who never learned English as a child, the words "rubber" and "lover" sound the same, a fact that has surely led to some embarrassing cross-cultural misunderstandings!

So, how do English speakers learn to distinguish between sounds that sound the same to Japanese speakers? Research suggests that young infants can discriminate among all the phonemes that humans are able to produce. We come into this world able to recognize all kinds of different sounds. However, when we learn a language, it is functional to perceive sounds categorically. That is, it's easier to understand an utterance if we can recognize that any sound that falls within a particular range is a "la," and that any sound that falls within a slightly different range is a "ra." If we did not perceive sounds categorically, we would have a most difficult time understanding the sounds that we hear.

As we are exposed to a language, we begin to categorize sounds in ways that are used by that language. And this begins early in life—very early. Within the first year, infants already begin to lose the ability to distinguish between closely related sounds that are not in their own language. For example, as **Figure 5.2** shows, native

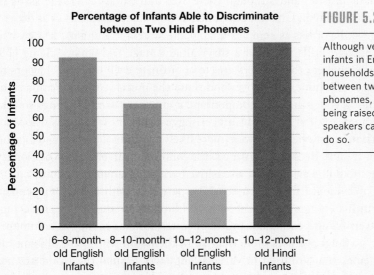

FIGURE 5.2

Although very young infants in English-speaking households can distinguish between two Hindi phonemes, older infants being raised by English speakers can no longer do so.

English-speaking babies of 6–8 months can reliably distinguish between two sounds from the Hindi language, but 10–12-month-old native English speakers cannot (Werker & Tees, 1984). Even 4-day-old infants already begin to show a preference for the rhythm of sounds from their own language over other languages (Mehler, Jusczyk, & Lambertz, 1988). Humans appear to come into this world ready to attend to the sounds that they hear communicated in language and to separate those from all the other noises they encounter. The universal human ability of being able to distinguish all possible phonemes gets whittled down to the ability to perceive and categorize only the phonemes heard during the critical window of language development.

This research suggests that we are biologically prepared to attend to human speech as soon as we come into this world. And this preference for speech (we are not especially attentive to many other kinds of sound as babies; Vouloumanos & Werker, 2004) predisposes us to start picking up languages at an early age. However, in the process of learning a language, our brains need to organize language sounds and other features in order to recognize them. Early in life (before puberty) our brains are especially pliable for organizing themselves in response to language input. Later on, however, our brains are not as flexible. As a result, humans are better at acquiring and mastering languages early in life (both first and second languages, although adults may initially outstrip children when they begin to learn a second language; Johnson & Newport, 1989), but this capacity declines with age, especially with respect to aspects such as accent and grammar (Lenneberg, 1967; Newport, 1991). For example, deaf children who first learn sign language late in childhood do not learn it as well as either deaf children who learn it earlier in childhood or children who become deaf later in childhood and learn sign language as their second language (Mayberry, 1993).

The differences in language competence can be quite striking among members of a family who were of different ages at the time they immigrated to a new country. For example, Henry Kissinger, former secretary of state of the United States, was 15 when his family moved to this country from Germany. His younger brother, Walter, was 14 at the time. After decades of living in the United States, Henry's English always preserved a thick German accent. Walter, on the other hand, speaks with no German accent whatsoever. When asked why his brother still spoke with an accent, Walter replied, "Because Henry doesn't listen!" However little Henry may have listened, a more likely explanation for his German accent is that he started learning English after his sensitive period for acquiring languages was for the most part closed. It is much more difficult to master a language if you start learning it after the sensitive period has expired.

Another source of evidence for this sensitive period in language acquisition comes from studies of bilingual individuals' brains. In these studies, people are placed in fMRI scanners to see which parts of their brain are active while they are listening to different languages. For bilinguals who learned their second language later in life, one part of the brain is active when they hear their second language and another when they hear their native language (both parts are in Broca's area). In contrast, bilinguals who learned their second language early in life showed activation in the same part of the brain, regardless of whether they were hearing their second language or their native one (Kim, Relkin, & Lee, 1997; also see Chee et al., 1999). This is evidence that early in life the language center of the brain is quite flexible at attuning itself to various kinds of linguistic input. After the sensitive period starts to close, however, those regions of the brain are no longer as capable of being restructured to accommodate the new language (also see related work by Perani, Paulesu, & Galles, 1998).

The most compelling kind of evidence that one could gather to test whether humans have a sensitive period for language acquisition would be to experimentally raise some children with no language input until they were 15 or so and then try to teach the unfortunate subjects a language and measure their performance. This is sometimes called the "forbidden experiment," and you'll be happy to know that psychologists don't run these kinds of studies. However, there are a few tragic instances of children whose real-life situations have mirrored this forbidden experiment (see **Figure 5.3**). In

FIGURE 5.3 A Cambodian woman, Rochom P'ngieng, apparently lived in the jungle on her own from the ages of 8 to 26. Her attempts to reintegrate into society have been fraught with difficulties (MacKinnon, 2009).

1800 in France, someone found a feral 12-year-old boy who had apparently lived in the wild for most of his life. This Wild Boy of Aveyron, as he was called, was coached to speak for several years by a teacher. The coaching had little success, however, and the boy was able to learn to speak only two words: "milk" and "ohmyGod." Indeed, he never developed into a fully functioning adult and was able to live only "a kind of vegetative life, sunk in inaccessible torpor, capable only of detached and half-articulate sounds, or silent from an absence of ideas" (Newton, 2002, p. 101).

Another instance was an appalling case of child abuse. A young Californian girl named Genie was raised alone in silence, either tethered to a potty chair or confined to a cagelike crib until the age of 13. Poor Genie's vocabulary at the time of discovery in 1970 consisted of two words: "stopit" and "nomore." Many people were involved in Genie's rehabilitation, including various scientists and foster parents. However, despite her considerable intelligence, Genie never developed any mastery over grammar or syntax (although she did develop a good-sized vocabulary). A poignant example of one of her sentences as an adult was "Think about Mama love Genie" (Newton, 2002, p. 27). Despite decades of exposure to her only language, Genie has not been able to attain the grammatical competence of a 4-year-old. More recently, another victim of horrendous child abuse in the United States, known as "the girl in the window" and made famous by coverage on the *Oprah* show, was raised in silence until the age of 6, from which time she was moved to a caring adoptive family. Despite the parents' efforts, the now teenaged girl remains severely cognitively disabled and has very little language capacity ("How 'The Girl in the Window' Is Doing," 2014).

These tragic instances lack the rigorous experimental control that would allow us to draw firm conclusions (but see a controlled experimental study conducted in impoverished Romanian orphanages suggesting that early experiences with caregivers are critical for language and cognitive development; Nelson, Fox, & Zeanah, 2013), and it is clearly possible that the children's language difficulties might have stemmed from the abuse they experienced rather than their lack of language exposure. Nonetheless, these case studies are very much in line with what you would expect from efforts to learn a first language after the sensitive period has ended.

The tragic stories of the Aveyron boy, Rochom P'ngieng, Genie, and the girl in the window, as well as the volumes of research on language acquisition, demonstrate that we all come into the world with similar language-learning capabilities, yet some of us have those capabilities directed toward learning English, and others toward learning Hindi or any other of the more than 3,000 languages spoken on the planet. We are born biologically prepared to learn a language, and our early experiences determine how our minds process the different kinds of human speech we later encounter. We are socialized to understand different languages. English speakers do not have English-speaking genes, and Hindi speakers do not have Hindi-speaking genes. We differ in our experiences—especially our early experiences—and this leads our minds to process the linguistic input that we hear in greatly different ways.

Sensitive Periods for Acquiring Culture

Learning a language is a necessary aspect of being socialized into a particular culture. As the linguist Edward Sapir put it, "Language is a great force of socialization, probably the greatest that exists" (Mandelbaum, 1951, p. 15). Language and culture are both meaning systems that we acquire through our social interactions, and they depend greatly on each other. Some would say that language is a part of culture—the communicating function of culture. Because learning a language and being socialized in a culture are so closely intertwined, we should expect some similarities between language acquisition and cultural acquisition more generally. Is there a sensitive period for acquiring cultural knowledge?

Measuring the acquisition of culture, unfortunately, is much less straightforward than measuring the acquisition of language. I've always been rather envious of linguists because languages around the world are different in such concrete ways that they are easy to measure. Each language has its own grammar, accent, syntax, morphology, and vocabulary. Cultures are far less tangible to study than languages. Whereas it's easy to determine whether someone has mastered a particular language, it's not as straightforward to determine whether someone has mastered a particular culture. An inability to distinguish between the words "rubber" and "lover," for example, is a pretty reliable indicator that one is not a native English speaker. It is much more challenging to identify ways of understanding the world that can indicate whether one has acquired a particular cultural meaning system. How could we investigate whether people have a sensitive period for acquiring culture?

My students, Benjamin Cheung and Maciej Chudek, and I thought that studying the ways immigrants adapt to a new culture might provide evidence of a sensitive period for culture acquisition. Immigrants have been born into one particular cultural context and then at some point in their lives have moved into another (we'll discuss the acculturation experiences of such multicultural people in more detail in Chapter 7). We reasoned that immigrants who move to a new culture after a sensitive window had closed would have a difficult time adjusting to their new culture. To investigate this idea, we targeted a large group of immigrants who had moved from the same origin to the same host culture at different ages. We selected Hong Kong immigrants to Vancouver, Canada, because tens of thousands have made this move over the past couple of decades, and have done so at different ages (Cheung, Chudek, & Heine, 2011). We asked the participants questions about their identification with Hong Kong, such as whether it was important for them to maintain or develop Chinese cultural practices, and questions about how much they identified with Canada, such as whether they enjoyed Canadian jokes and humor. Their answers across the various questions were summarized to indicate their identification with Chinese and Canadian culture, and these summaries were analyzed to see whether age of immigration and number of years spent in Canada correlated to their levels of cultural identification.

What did we find? First, we found that identification with Chinese culture was not predicted by any of the variables in our study—whether people moved to Canada at a young or old age and whether they had been there for a short or long time did not influence their Chinese identification. Perhaps this is due to their being recognized as being of Chinese descent by other Canadians, or by them being able to continue to participate in Chinese cultural activities because of the large local Chinese community in Vancouver. Identification with Canadian culture, however, yielded a different effect, which is summarized in **Figure 5.4.** The graph is broken into three panels to distinguish the different age groups at time of immigration. As the panel on the left shows, those immigrants who arrived in Canada before the age of 15 more strongly identified with Canadian culture the longer they lived there. Those who had been in Canada for 20 years identified with Canada more than those who had been in Canada only 5 years, indicating that they continued to acquire Canadian culture with time. The middle panel shows that those who moved to Canada between the ages of 16 and 30 did not come to identify more with Canada the longer they were in Canada. They did not seem to acquire any more Canadian culture over time. And, curiously, the right panel shows that those who arrived in Canada after the age of 31 came to

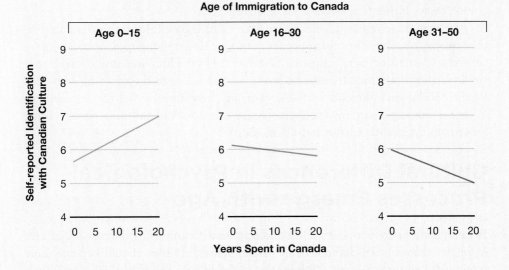

FIGURE 5.4 Hong Kong immigrants' identification with Canadian culture.

identify with Canada slightly less (the effect was not statistically reliable) the longer they were in Canada. It's possible that because a sensitive window for culture acquisition was largely closed for this latter group, repeated exposure to a culture that they had difficulty relating to became increasingly frustrating over time.

These findings are consistent with the existence of a sensitive window for culture acquisition that begins to close at around age 15, and some other studies have similarly found that when people attempt to learn a second culture later on in life they preserve an echo of the emotional repertoire of their host culture (also see McCauley & Henrich, 2006; Minoura, 1992; Tsai, Ying, & Lee, 2000). However, these results might be peculiar to Chinese immigrants' experience in Vancouver, given that they have such a large community (the second largest outside of Asia) and many are able to maintain a Chinese lifestyle there communicating largely in Chinese.

Other research has identified that the process of cultural acquisition does seem to unfold differently within ethnic enclaves such as that found in various cities' Chinatowns compared with more integrated neighborhoods (Schwartz, Unger, Zamboanga, & Szapocznik, 2010). Indeed, when we also attempted to document the same pattern with other immigrant groups throughout the United States where such ethnic enclaves were not as prevalent, we did not find such a specific cutoff of declining cultural acquisition at age 15, although we still found that the younger a person was at the time of immigration, the more likely he or she was to identify with American culture (Chudek, Cheung, & Heine, in press). We suspect that the more opportunities there are for immigrants to continue to live and communicate as they had in their heritage cultures, the more difficult it becomes to fully acquire their host culture's ways if they first arrive at an older age.

Although more research is necessary to draw firm conclusions, this developmental sequence of culture learning appears quite similar in timing to people's ability to acquire a second language (Johnson & Newport, 1989). Humans seem to have a sensitive window when they are especially adept at attending to the meanings provided by their social environments and at organizing their lives around these meanings. Whether this same pattern would emerge for other ways of thinking or with other groups of immigrants remains to be explored.

Cultural Differences in Psychological Processes Emerge with Age

Because humans are born cultureless and acquire their culture as they are socialized, it follows that cultural differences in psychological processes should become more pronounced with age. Young children from different cultures should appear relatively more similar to each other (although, as you'll soon see, there are still some cultural differences even among toddlers) than should older children, because younger children have been socialized less deeply into their cultures. Likewise, the most pronounced cultural differences should emerge for adults, because their minds have had much more time to be shaped by cultural experiences.

Conducting studies across different age groups is inherently challenging, and few studies have done this in different cultures. However, the few that have been done nicely highlight how people become socialized to think in culturally divergent ways. For example, consider people's beliefs about how the future will unfold. One way is to extrapolate linearly from the recent past to the present and on to the future. For example, the average house in the United States sold for approximately $268,000 in 2011, $278,000 in 2012, and $307,000 in 2013. What will the average house sell for in 2020? If we assume that the pattern of change continues linearly, then the average home should sell for well over $400,000 by 2020, which suggests that buying a house would be a terrific investment—it would seem like a sure bet. However, it's important to note that change can also occur nonlinearly. Indeed, the average house price was approximately $322,000 in 2007, $290,000 in 2008, and $257,000 in 2009. So, the pattern of house prices changed from decreasing in value (2007–2009) to increasing in value (2011–2013). And the pattern may well change again soon.

Some research reveals that East Asians and North Americans differ in how they expect the future to unfold (Ji, 2008). For example, North Americans are more likely to expect that trends will continue in the same direction as they have in the past. East Asians, in contrast, are more likely to expect that change will be nonlinear and that a decreasing trend will soon be followed with an increasing trend. This cultural difference has been explained in terms of cultural differences in dialectical ways of thinking, which we will explore in more detail in Chapter 9.

When are these cultural differences in perceptions of trends evident between Chinese and Canadians? In one study, children ages 7, 9, and 11 were brought into the laboratory (Ji, 2008). The children read a number of scenarios about a past state of affairs (e.g., they read about a child who was always sad) and were asked to predict a future state of affairs (e.g., how the child would feel tomorrow). The Chinese and Canadian 7-year-olds tended to respond quite similarly. In contrast, the Chinese 9-year-old children were more likely to expect a reversal of the trends compared with the Canadian 9-year-olds (they expected the child would start to feel better), and this cultural difference became slightly more pronounced among 11-year-olds (see **Figure 5.5**). Chinese and Canadian 7-year-olds are more similar in terms of their thoughts about the future than 9- and 11-year-olds are.

With age, people from different cultures diverge in their psychological experiences. These kinds of developmental patterns showing cultural differences increasing with age have been identified for a number of phenomena: explanations of others' behaviors (Miller, 1984; see Chapter 9), optimism (You, Fung, & Isaacowitz, 2009), and tendencies to focus on positive aspects of the self (Falbo, Poston, Triscari, & Zhang, 1997; see Chapter 8).

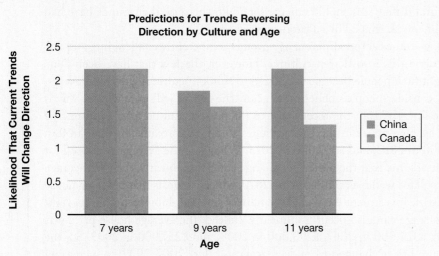

FIGURE 5.5

Seven-year-old Chinese and Canadian children make similar predictions about the future. As the children age, however, Canadian children come to expect that trends will change direction less often than Chinese children.

How Do Early Childhood Experiences Differ Across Cultures?

Acquiring a culture is thus a developmental process, and people are socialized into their respective cultural worlds by participating in specific cultural practices and institutions. The more one has engaged in a given cultural practice, the more one's ways of thinking become habitualized to respond to that practice. One key source of cultural practices that guide children's development is their interactions with their parents—the ways in which parents structure their children's early lives. How do parents and children around the world differ in their interactions?

Infants' Personal Space

Perhaps one of the most influential sources of cultural influence is the actual personal space within which we exist. Given this, it is quite striking to see the many different ways in which infants are raised around the world. The 2010 movie *Babies* nicely highlighted some of these differences by contrasting the lives of babies born in San Francisco, rural Mongolia, Tokyo, and rural Namibia. The Mongolian baby, Bayar, was swaddled up so tight that he could not move at all (**Figure 5.6**), whereas the Namibian baby, Ponijao, was always being held by her mother throughout the first several months of her life.

FIGURE 5.6 Bayar, from the movie *Babies,* was tightly swaddled for the first several months of his life.

In an extensive effort to document the different kinds of early life experiences around the world, Heidi Keller (2007) studied parenting interactions with 3-month-old infants in five diverse cultural contexts: urban middle-class Germans, urban middle-class Greeks, urban lower-class Costa Ricans, rural Indian Gujarati, and rural Cameroonians. The researchers made several unannounced visits to videotape mothers and their infants, resulting in about 100 minutes of observation per family. The researchers assessed several different behaviors of the mothers. For example, they calculated the amount of time the mother was in bodily contact with the infant. **Figure 5.7a** shows that there was considerable variation in this behavior, with the urban European infants spending most of their time not in contact with their mothers, whereas the infants from the other cultural groups spent the majority of the time being held by their mothers. Indeed, there was not a single observation of a Cameroonian infant when it was not being held by its mother.

Another variable that was assessed was the amount of time mothers made face-to-face contact with their infants. **Figure 5.7b** shows that the urban European infants spent most of their time in face-to-face contact with their mothers, but this was much less the case for the other groups, especially the Gujarati. Moreover, the responses of the German mothers were more contingent to the babies' cries and behaviors than was found with the Cameroonian mothers, and this cultural difference predicted how quickly the babies learned to recognize themselves in a mirror: The more responsive their mothers were to their cries, the younger the child

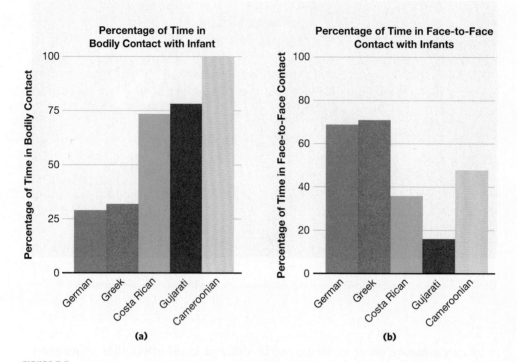

FIGURE 5.7 Percentage of mothers' time in face-to-face contact with infants.

was able to show self-recognition skills (Keller, Kartner, Borke, Yovsi, & Kleis, 2005). Learning that others will respond to their cries facilitates infants' recognition that they have a distinct identity.

In sum, the first experiences of infants vary quite dramatically around the world: Urban European babies tend to occupy their own physical space, and they are often in face-to-face contact with their mothers, putting them in a position to interact with their mothers as separate beings, as in turn-taking conversations, and their mothers are more responsive to their individual needs. In contrast, in the other cultural contexts the infants share the same physical space with their mothers, and are not as likely to be in a position to interact with their mothers through face-to-face contact.

Children's early physical experiences differ in other ways. In some regions of Africa, the Caribbean, and India, infants receive a daily massage and an exercise regime, such as stretching their limbs or putting them into sitting positions (Karasik, Adolph, Tamis-LeMonda, & Bornstein, 2010). These experiences shape their development, and those who receive this kind of massage and exercise begin to sit on their own and walk at earlier ages than those who do not (Hopkins & Westra, 1988; Super, 1976). Likewise, cultural practices such as putting infants to sleep on their backs, rather than on their stomachs, can delay when children begin to crawl, roll over, or learn to stand (Davis, Moon, Sachs, & Ottolini, 1998). In cultures that do not encourage crawling, large proportions of children never crawl but instead scoot along on their bums or proceed directly to walking (Hopkins & Westra, 1988). These different cultural experiences thus can affect the rate of children's physical development.

An important determinant of the personal space of infants is the product of one of the parents' first decisions: "Where do we put the baby?" This seemingly simple decision can tell us a lot about one's cultural values, and it largely influences the kind of environment in which the baby starts its life. And people from different cultures make this decision in strikingly different ways.

If you are of European descent and grew up in a North American household, odds are that your parents made this decision in one particular way. It is quite likely that your parents set aside a room in their house, perhaps decorating it with pastel colors and scenes of romping bunny rabbits, and put a crib in it for you to sleep in. That is, there is a cultural norm widely shared among many European-descent North American families that the "right way" to bring up children is to provide them with their own private rooms to grow up in, often starting the day that they return from the hospital.

As "right" as this way seems to many European-descent North Americans, people from many other cultural backgrounds have a very different view. For example, in a study of 136 societies, infants in two-thirds of these groups slept in the same bed as their mothers; in the majority of the other cases, infants slept in the same room as their mothers but in a different bed (Whiting, 1964). American parents were the only ones in a survey of 100 societies who created a separate room for the baby to sleep in (Burton & Whiting, 1961). In many societies, children continue to sleep in the same bed as their parents, or sometimes grandparents, until they are well into their primary school years. Furthermore, this practice of **co-sleeping** is also quite common in other subcultures in the United States—for example, among African-Americans, Asian-Americans, and Hispanics. The practice of people sleeping separately in their own beds has not yet been identified in a single subsistence society around the world. For example, among the Efe, a hunting-and-gathering culture from Zaire, it is not unusual for their small leaf huts to include the sleeping bodies of parents, their children, a grandparent, and a visitor, with their limbs all tangled together in one snoring mass (Worthman & Melby, 2002). Providing separate sleeping quarters for the baby, so common in much of North America, is a rather unusual cultural practice throughout the world.

One thing that I learned upon becoming a parent is the extent to which parenting decisions are moralized by others. That is, people tend to evaluate the decisions of parents as either "good" or "bad," and parents go through a lot of grief trying to ensure that they are raising their child in the best possible way. This tendency to moralize parenting decisions clearly extends to the decision of whether parents should allow their child to co-sleep with them. For example, America's most famous infant sleep expert, Dr. Richard Ferber, had the following to say about co-sleeping in his 1985 book: "If you find that you actually prefer to sleep with your infant, you should consider your own feelings very carefully." Dr. Ferber also states that "even if you and your child seem happy about his sharing your bed at night, and even if he seems to sleep well there, in the long run this habit will probably not be good for either of you." The moralization of co-sleeping is even more evident when we consider some guidance provided on this topic by two advice columnists, Ann Landers and Prudence:

Dear Ann Landers: I have three children, ages 2, 3, and 5. Here's my problem: All three end up in my bedroom during the night. Usually I know they are there, but I sleep right through it. . . . I'm newly divorced and there is no man in my bed, so the kids aren't disturbing anyone. . . . My mother tells me I must make the kids sleep in their own rooms. She says sometimes children who want to sleep with their parents need to be taken to a psychologist because their behavior indicates deeper problems. What do you say? Is it that big a deal when they are so young?
—**Wondering**

Dear Wondering: Usually, I tell parents to keep the kids out of their bed at night, but in your case I suspect the divorce has made them insecure. Talk to your pediatrician about the way to wean these kids away from this habit. You really do need professional guidance. . . . Good luck, dear. You have your hands full. (January 14, 1992; reported in Shweder, Jensen, & Goldstein, 1995)

Dear Prudence: I am writing you about a rather bizarre situation. My wife and I have been together for nearly 13 years. Things were great until the birth of our second child, a daughter.... Since the day our daughter came home, she has slept in our bed. The year before last we even bought a new, larger home so that our daughter would have her own bedroom. This improved nothing; our daughter still sleeps in our bed, and I have been retired to the family room couch. I love my wife and my daughter, but I am alone. I complain, only to be told that our daughter—nearly 7!—will be in her own room soon. At times these debates become loud, at which point I am told I am selfish and must not care about our daughter. I know that I am not selfish or uncaring. I am, however, considering a divorce. It is not something I want, but I no longer wish to live like a guest in my own home.
—**Lost and Lonely**

Dear Lost: Something obviously happened in year six of your marriage that made your wife decide she had reached her sexpiration date. Not only

does she have a 7-year-old chastity belt, but no kid in the second grade belongs in her mother's bed. The emotional turmoil for this child should be immeasurable. You certainly have the patience of a saint—a celibate one, at that—but you must now insist she see a counselor or mediator with you. If her problems cannot be dealt with, you will, indeed, have to divorce . . .
—**Prudie, promptly** (June 2, 2005, *Slate*)

As you can see, issues of children co-sleeping with parents are not seen as a matter of personal choice; rather, they are seen as behaviors that reflect the moral value of the parents. Making the "wrong" choice in where you let your child sleep is something that suggests that you need "professional guidance," is something that will cause the child "immeasurable emotional turmoil," indicates the reaching of a "sexpiration date," and necessitates divorce. Parenting decisions, and the ways that others in the culture respond to them, reflect the underlying values of a culture.

Why do you think European-descent North Americans are so much more likely than most of the rest of the world to view co-sleeping as a morally bad parenting decision? One possibility is that co-sleeping is something that you do only if you don't have enough space in your home to give the children their own rooms. Perhaps the big wide open spaces of the North American continent allowed the room to let children have their own privacy, whereas much of the rest of the world can't afford the luxury of having that much real estate, given higher population densities. Perhaps people in other cultures would also think it is better parenting to give their children their own private rooms, and the only thing preventing them from doing so is that their houses are not big enough.

Although the availability of space is an issue that must be relevant to the question of why people co-sleep, it is not the only issue. Consider the following study: Researchers approached people living in Chicago and in Orissa, India, and asked them how they would plan the sleeping arrangements for a hypothetical family that consisted of seven members: a father (f), mother (m), three sons ages 15, 11, and 8 (s15, s11, s8), and two daughters ages 14 and 3 (d14, d3) (Shweder et al., 1995). The participants were asked to imagine a variety of different space situations. In one case they have to figure out where everyone would sleep in a house that has only one room (that decision was easy); in other cases the house had two rooms, three rooms, and so on up to seven rooms.

There are many ways that you can arrange the families in the different room combinations. For example, in a house with three rooms there are 301 possible ways to divide up the sleeping arrangements of this hypothetical seven-member family. However, people do not see all of these 301 ways as equally appropriate. Rather, people in the different cultures tended to favor just a handful of possible solutions. When asked to divide up the family into these three rooms, people in the two cultures tended to reach quite different solutions. For example, here are two possible solutions: The 3-year-old daughter can be put in the same room as the mother and father, the 14-year-old daughter can share a room with the 8-year-old son, and the 15-year-old and 11-year-old sons can be together. A second arrangement is to put the father in a room with the 8-year-old son, put the 15-year-old and 11-year-old sons together, and put the mother in a room with both the 3-year-old and 14-year-old daughters. These two arrangements were viewed as the best three-room solution by 47% of the Indian respondents (see **Figure 5.8**). In stark contrast, not a single American participant viewed either of these as the best three-room solution. Rather, 88% of the Americans considered this the best solution: The father and mother are put in one room, the two daughters share a room, and the three sons share a room. The Indians saw this arrangement as best 47% of the time (there were a number of other different arrangements that were viewed as best by a few participants). Given the same resources, the Indians and Americans tended to come up with different solutions.

The different sleeping arrangements that were preferred between the two cultures tell us much about the underlying values of the cultures. The Indians seemed to be guided by four moral principles in deciding which sleeping arrangements were appropriate. The most important principle they adhered to was **incest avoidance.** That is, postpubescent members of the family of the opposite sex should not sleep in rooms together. The second most important principle for the Indians was **protection of the vulnerable.** According to this principle, young children who are needy and vulnerable should not be left alone at night. The principle that was third most important for the Indians was **female chastity anxiety.** This principle holds that unmarried postpubescent women should always be chaperoned to protect them from engaging in any sexual activity that would be viewed as shameful. The last principle to guide the Indians' decisions was **respect for hierarchy,** in which postpubescent boys are conferred social status by allowing them to not have to sleep with parents or young children.

The decisions made by Americans, in contrast, were governed by a rather different set of principles. The Americans were similar to the Indians in that they also viewed incest avoidance as the most important principle in deciding about sleeping arrangements. Indeed, incest avoidance is often discussed as a cultural universal whose breach has serious consequences, both in terms of destroying family relations and in potentially producing offspring that suffer from recessive genetic disorders (Westermarck, 1922). Two other moral principles were adhered to by Americans. The second most important principle for them was the **sacred couple,** in which participants believed that married couples should be given their own space for emotional intimacy and sexual privacy. This principle, prized by many Westerners, is violated in many cultures. For example, a review by Whiting and Whiting (1979) found that in

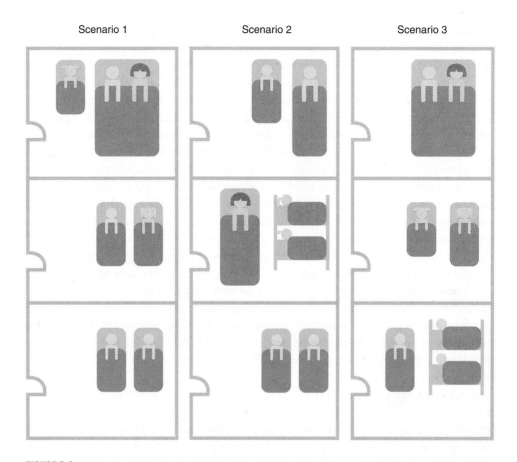

FIGURE 5.8 Indian participants viewed at least one of the first two sleeping arrangements to be about as desirable as the third one. In stark contrast, not a single American viewed either of the first two sleeping arrangements to be desirable. In contrast, the vast majority of Americans selected option 3 as the most desirable of the many different possible combinations of sleeping arrangements.

42% of herding and agricultural societies, the husbands and wives slept in separate rooms. The third most important principle for Americans was the **autonomy ideal**, a belief that young children who are needy and vulnerable should learn to be self-reliant and take care of themselves.

In sum, with the exception of a shared concern about avoiding potentially incestuous situations, different cultural values guided the Indians and the Americans in deciding about sleeping arrangements. Americans strive to protect the privacy of the married couple and encourage the development of independence among their children. In stark contrast, Indians prefer to keep their young children and postpubescent daughters from being alone and try to offer older boys the deference of not having to sleep with their parents or younger siblings. A simple decision about sleeping arrangements can tell us a lot about a culture's values.

North American children and children from many other cultures would thus appear to have very different early experiences. How do you think these different sleeping arrangements affect children's socialization? It would seem that North American children live in an environment where they are by themselves from a very early age and must cry out to their parents when they have needs to be taken care of. Children from many other cultures, in contrast, may live in an environment where their mother is always around—often, as in many cultures, the children are literally carried by their mother throughout the day. Mothers do not need to be called to, as they are always present to respond to the child's needs. Furthermore, the cultural variability in children's social worlds is not just limited to the nearness of their mothers. In many cultures around the world, children are raised in far closer proximity to various other people than Western children are. For example, whereas Scottish children spend more time with physical objects than they do with people, the precise opposite pattern is evident among Nigerian children (Agiobu-Kemmer, 1984). The social worlds of young children differ dramatically around the globe, and children are thus learning very different ideas about how to perceive themselves and their relations with others (see Rothbaum, Weisz, Pott, Miyake, & Morelli, 2000).

Parenting Styles

A popular dinnertime conversation among North American parents in early 2011 was the widespread news coverage of Amy Chua's book, *Battle Hymn of the Tiger Mom*. For a while, it seemed that almost every parent (and Chinese student) I met wanted to talk about it. Chua, who lives in New Haven, Connecticut, described her parenting experiences with her two daughters, and, frankly, many Western parents were shocked (**Figure 5.9**). Her list of rules for her daughters included: No playdates, no sleepovers, no TV or computer games, no choosing one's own extracurricular activities, and no being in school plays (or complaining about not being in a school play). The girls were required to practice violin or piano for 3 hours a day (no other instruments were acceptable) and to be the top student in class in every subject except gym and drama. Chua referred to her parenting style as "Chinese parenting," although even she acknowledged that her variant of it was extreme by Chinese (or any culture's) standards.

Following the publication of Chua's book, many newspaper articles and op-ed pieces appeared as parents debated the virtues and costs of strict parenting. A big part of the debate centered on an uncomfortable fact: Chua's children were remarkably successful at school and at music; they were straight-A students who ended up matriculating at Harvard and Yale, and one played piano at Carnegie Hall. As we'll

FIGURE 5.9   Amy Chua and her daughters.

discuss again later in this chapter, Chinese children really shine in their academic performance, particularly in math and science. Could it be that this over-the-top strict parenting style actually leads to successful children?

The most well-researched approach to understanding the effects of parenting styles has been Diana Baumrind's (1971) tripartite typology. **Authoritarian parenting** involves high demands on children, with strict rules and little open dialogue between parent and child. It typically involves low levels of warmth or responsiveness by the parents to the child's protests. **Authoritative parenting** is a child-centered approach in which parents hold high expectations of the maturity of their children, try to understand their children's feelings and teach them how to regulate those feelings, and encourage their children to be independent while maintaining limits and controls on their behaviors. This approach is associated with parental warmth, responsiveness, and democratic reasoning. **Permissive parenting** is characterized by parents being very involved with their children, with much expressed parental warmth and responsiveness, but placing few limits and controls on the children's behaviors. The results of research on these styles with Western populations have been fairly consistent: Authoritative parenting leads to the most desirable outcomes in terms of perceived parental warmth, acceptance, better school achievement, autonomy, and self-reliance (e.g., Leung, Lao, & Lam, 1998; Steinberg, Lamborn, Dornbusch, & Darling, 1992; Trommsdorff, 1985).

However, some have argued that Baumrind's typology is bound up in Western cultural understandings of development and does not adequately capture parenting styles elsewhere. At first glance, Chinese parenting styles, with Amy Chua's as an extreme example, would seem to be best described as authoritarian. Indeed, such kinds of strict parent-centered parenting are also common in other non-Western cultures, such as countries in East, Southeast, and South Asia, as well as in Egypt, Iran, Turkey, and Latin America (e.g., Dornbusch, Ritter, Leiderman, Roberts, & Fraleigh, 1987; Harwood, Miller, & Irizarry, 1995; Huang & Lamb, 2014; Kagicibasi, 1996; Rudy & Grusec, 2006). However, some elements of various non-Western cultures' dominant parenting styles are inconsistent with the authoritarian category. First, it is important to recognize that in many Asian cultures, infants and toddlers are often shown a great deal of indulgence with few demands or expectations placed on them until they reach school age, when parents become much stricter (e.g., Conroy, Hess, Azuma, & Kashiwagi, 1980; Kim, Kim, & Rue, 1997; Morrow, 1989); that is, there are different parental styles depending on the stage of development of the child. Second, the ways that warmth and responsiveness are communicated by parents vary considerably across cultures, and thus what might look like cold behavior in one culture is not perceived as cold in another. For example, Westerners are more likely to be explicit about communicating their feelings—by kissing and by telling their children that they love them—than are Asian parents (e.g., Chao & Tseng, 2002). Third, the authoritarian category has been argued to exclude one important element of parenting common in Chinese and various other non-Western parenting styles: the role of training. Chao (1994) argues that training (*jiao xun;* 教训) is a core part of Chinese parenting. It is an effort to have children adhere to socially desired behaviors, often by providing the child with explicit examples of proper behavior, and it entails much devotion and sacrifice on the part of the parents (for example, Amy Chua spent hours each day supervising her children's homework and piano practice). A Chinese taxonomy of parenting styles would likely have training as a core component.

The underlying cultural foundation of different parenting styles can be seen in that some parenting styles appear to produce different outcomes across cultures. For example, in contrast to the findings from various Western countries, strong parental control has been found to be associated with increased family cohesion, perceived parental warmth and acceptance, and better academic achievement in China, Japan, and Korea (Leung et al., 1998; Nomura, Noguchi, Saito, & Tezuka, 1995; Rohner & Pettengill, 1985; Steinberg, Dornbusch, & Brown, 1992; Trommsdorff & Iwawaki, 1989). One study found that whereas European-American high school students viewed any pressure by their mother to be largely negative, and indicative that they didn't feel supported by their mother,

Asian-American high school students didn't view maternal pressure in negative terms. Indeed, when Asian-American students reflected on their mother pressuring them to work hard on a task they were more motivated to complete a task on their own (Fu & Markus, 2014). As one researcher studying Japanese parenting noted, "Japanese adolescents even feel rejected by their parents when they experience only little parental control and a broader range of autonomy" (Trommsdorff, 1985). Strict and controlling parenting thus appears to have better outcomes in some cultures than others. On the other hand, authoritarian parenting styles have been found to be associated with more-stressed mothers (Su & Hynie, 2011) and to lead to increased psychological maladjustment among children across a variety of both Western and non-Western cultures, including Chinese (Qin, Pomerantz, & Wang, 2009; Sorkhabi, 2005). In general, children are less happy with strongly controlling parents, and this effect is found across many cultures (but see Rudy & Grusec, 2006, for an exception).

To summarize, although overly strict and controlling parenting can lead to many kinds of negative outcomes among people from Western cultures, in non-Western cultures it appears to be associated with increased family cohesion, and improved grades, but less-happy children. There are thus trade-offs involved in parenting styles, and whether strict and controlling parenting will yield desirable outcomes overall is dependent on what values a culture prioritizes (e.g., happiness or achievement).

Aside from their overall strictness, parenting styles differ across cultures in other ways. If you look in a North American bookstore for advice on parenting, you'll typically find whole sections devoted to the topic. For example, one strategy that is frequently emphasized in North American parenting books (e.g., the "Positive Discipline" series) is to acknowledge the child's feelings or perspective in order to gain his or her compliance. A North American mother might say, "I know you want to put paint on the cat. That looks like a lot of fun. But I don't want you to do that." The mother is thus empathizing with the child's perspective and is taking his lead. Does this sound like familiar or good parenting to you? Indeed, parenting strategies such as this, and of letting the child take the lead while the mother takes a supporting role and elaborates on the child's ideas and preferences, are very common among North Americans of higher socioeconomic status.

In contrast, interactions between children and their mothers in many other cultures are quite different. For example, recently there has been much interest in the parenting styles of French mothers (e.g., Druckerman, 2012; Le Billon, 2012), because to North Americans, French children come across as very well-behaved and seem to have far fewer dietary issues and weight problems (e.g., Musher-Eizenman, de Lauzon-Guillain, Holub, Leporc, & Charles, 2009). French parents seem much less likely to follow the child's lead, and instead offer more clear-cut rules that need to be followed. Similarly, Chinese mothers are more likely to lead the interactions and introduce the topics, while the children learn to take after their mother's lead (Haight, 1999; Wang, 2001; Wang, Leichtman, & Davies, 2000).

How might these different parenting styles affect how children develop? It would seem that the North American children come to learn that they are independent agents to which their mothers respond, whereas the Chinese children learn that they are relational beings who need to respond to their mothers. There is some evidence for this. In one study, for example, young European-American and Chinese children ages 3 to 8 were interviewed to ask about themselves and their early memories (Wang, 2004). Compared with the Chinese children, the American children were more likely to describe themselves with individualistic statements about their own qualities and preferences (e.g., "I like hockey" or "I'm a very smart person") and were less likely to describe themselves with collectivistic statements (e.g., "I am from Albany" or "I am in the second grade"; we'll explore this point in more detail in Chapter 6). American children were also less likely to refer to others when describing themselves, compared with the Chinese children. By an early age, then, children in different cultures are socialized to differentially attend to either individualistic or collectivistic aspects of themselves.

Other research finds that North American mothers are more likely to discuss their child's successes and positive emotional experiences with them, thereby emphasizing what the child is able to accomplish. In contrast, Chinese mothers are more likely to call attention to their child's mistakes and transgressions, thereby elaborating on how the child needs to change to fit in better (Miller, Wiley, Fung, & Liang, 1997; Wang, 2001). Indeed, Amy Chua regularly directed her children's attention to where they weren't doing well enough.

How do you think these early experiences might shape the way children tend to view themselves? Mothers play an important role in socializing their children to develop culturally appropriate ways of viewing themselves. And, as we have seen, mothers go about socializing their children in different ways across cultures.

Noun Biases

Another window into the early experiences of childhood is through language learning. Young children, typically around the age of 18 months, enter a period of accelerated word learning when their vocabularies begin to increase dramatically. A great deal of research has indicated, however, that this increase in vocabulary is not distributed equally across all different forms of words: The first words that young children tend to learn are nouns (e.g., Gentner, 1982; Huttenlocher & Smiley, 1987). This preponderance of nouns relative to verbs and other relational words in young children's vocabularies is known as a **noun bias**. The existence of this noun bias is informative with respect to the experiences that young children have.

Researchers have argued that the noun bias indicates that nouns are more salient, refer to more concrete concepts, and are easier to isolate from the environment than other words, such as verbs, and this is why children learn them first (Gentner, 1982; Gleitman, 1990). To the extent that this is true, we should see evidence of a noun bias everywhere and in every language. The majority of research on the noun bias has been conducted with North Americans, and there is a great deal of evidence that North American children tend to learn nouns much quicker than verbs. However, the noun bias is much more difficult to identify in some other cultural groups, particularly among East Asians. In one study, for example, Chinese toddlers were found to use more verbs than nouns (Tardif, 1996), and in another, there was no evidence of a noun bias among Korean toddlers (Choi & Gopnik, 1995). The noun bias does not appear to be as universal as it was originally supposed. Another study found that when North American college students are asked to guess a word that they couldn't hear in a conversation between a mother and child, they tended to guess that it was a noun (Lavin, Hall, & Waxman, 2006; also see Gillette, Gleitman, Gleitman, & Lederer, 1999), revealing a noun bias; Chinese-speaking college students, however, did not show this bias.

One possible explanation for this cultural difference is not a cultural explanation but a linguistic one. Perhaps there is something about the nature of languages that makes nouns or verbs more salient. Indeed, the structure of English is such that nouns tend to come in rather salient locations, such as at the end of the sentence, as in "He dented his new car." On the other hand, some East Asian languages (such as Japanese and Korean) place verbs in salient positions at the end of sentences. For example, to say that someone ate a cookie in Japanese, you would say the words in the order of "She cookie ate." Moreover, unlike in English, the Chinese, Japanese, and Korean languages all allow for nouns (and pronouns) to be dropped when the context is clear, so that the verbs remain in salient positions in the sentences. For example, to say "I love you" in Japanese, you can get away with just saying "Love," and it will be understood from the context who is loving whom. Indeed, if it's *not* clear from the context who is doing the loving and who is being loved, then you probably shouldn't be saying it! Perhaps, then, the cultural differences in noun biases simply reflect how various languages highlight nouns and verbs differently. This explanation may prove to be correct, although it still begs the question of why East Asian languages allow for noun or pronoun drops, whereas the English language (and many other Western languages) does not (Kashima & Kashima, 1998).

An alternative explanation is that young children learn to communicate about objects differently across cultures. How might a North American mother play with a 1-year-old with a toy, such as a truck? We might expect her to say something like "Look at this truck. It's a big, strong truck! Look, here's another truck. It's a yellow truck. It has black wheels. They can drive fast. Trucks, let's go to the garage." Such communications highlights how the truck is separate from its environment, and it describes the truck in terms of its characteristics. In contrast, an East Asian mother playing with her child and the same truck might say, "Here comes Daddy truck. He's saying hello to older brother truck. Daddy truck loves older brother truck. They're going to the beach together for a picnic." Such communication highlights relationships between the trucks. How might these kinds of conversations shape the way children attend to their worlds? One important line of research, which we'll return to in Chapter 9, is that Westerners tend to perceive the world in a more analytic fashion, seeing objects as discrete and separate, whereas East Asians are more likely to perceive the world in holistic terms, stressing the relations between objects (e.g., Nisbett, Peng, Choi, & Norenzayan, 2001). It is plausible that the cultural differences in the noun bias reflect this difference in thinking about the world.

Much research suggests that mothers' interactions with children do vary across cultures as in the example conversations above. North American mothers are more likely to call attention to objects than are East Asian mothers (Bornstein et al., 1992; Senzaki, Masuda, Takada, & Okada, 2014), and these differences are identifiable even among very young infants. Parents from all cultures will talk about children's toys with them; however, Western mothers tend to talk more about the toys, whereas East Asian mothers more often use those toys as part of a social routine (Tamis-LeMonda, Bornstein, & Cyphers, 1992). East Asian mothers more effectively communicate actions than North American mothers, whereas North American mothers more effectively communicate objects than East Asian mothers (Lavin, Hall, & Waxman, 2006; Lavin, Hall, & Leung, 2006). It appears that the early worlds of infants and toddlers vary in systematic ways. Western children are directed to attend to objects, whereas East Asian children are directed toward the relations among objects.

Difficult Developmental Transitions

Development does not always proceed linearly across the lifespan, with each month passed being associated with an equivalent amount of increased knowledge and maturity. Rather, there can be a number of key periods where children go through growing pains as they begin to transition to a new level of maturity. Two of these periods, which have received much attention, are "the terrible twos" and "adolescence."

The Terrible Twos

When my son reached 2 years of age, I learned to add some strict routines to my life. I used to not pay much attention, for example, to whether I pushed the elevator button as we left our apartment or I let someone else do it. But I learned that the success of the day hinged on being sure that I did not carelessly push the elevator button before my 2-year-old son had the chance to do so. Otherwise our day started off with a half-hour-long tantrum of inconsolable ear-splitting screams as my son vented his anger and frustration at having been deprived of his favorite task. It really was quite a spectacle. Other parents told me that this stage would end soon, and it was this belief that helped me get through the day. They said my son was in his "terrible twos."

The idea that children pass through a difficult transition during their early toddler years is viewed as a hallmark of development, at least by Americans (Wenar, 1982). Around the age of 2 there is an unmistakable increase in noncompliant and oppositional behavior (see **Figure 5.10**). Many 2-year-olds, my son included, will say "No" to virtually anything asked of them by their exasperated parents. Although this obstinacy tends to be very draining on parents, many Western researchers describe it as an important developmental milestone when the young toddler begins to establish his or her individuality, and this is seen as the foundation for mature relationships (e.g., Sroufe, 1979). Indeed, some forms of non-

FIGURE 5.10 Toddlers in individualistic cultures go through a period where they are more likely to show noncompliant and oppositional behavior than those in many other non-Western cultures.

compliance among American children have been shown to predict fewer behavioral problems later in life (Kuczynski & Kochanska, 1990). The tantrums of the terrible twos are seen to serve an important function in the young child's socialization to be a mature, verbally assertive individual.

What makes it all the harder to deal with the terrible twos as a parent is to discover that it doesn't have to be this bad. Two-year-olds in many other cultures are not as obstinate and difficult as in the United States. Particularly among various nomadic hunting societies, such as the Aka Pygmies of Africa, where children are held by a caretaker for much of the day, this developmental stage is not as evident (Hewlett, 1992). Among the Zinacantecans in Mexico, infants do not go through this transition of obstinacy. Rather than asserting control and striving for independence, Zincantecan 2-year-olds change their status from mother's baby to a member of the courtyard children's group (Edwards, 1994; Rogoff, 2003). Without the interactions with their parents that try to inculcate a sense of individualism and independence, these early and rather clumsy efforts to exert autonomy and control by young toddlers are rarely seen.

Similarly, Japanese toddlers have been shown to make fewer demands on their parents than their American counterparts and are less likely to assert their disobedience (Caudill & Schooler, 1973). Those occasions when Japanese toddlers do act unruly tend not to be viewed as signs of blossoming individuality but rather as indicators of their immaturity (Lebra, 1994). The developmental goal embraced by Japanese parents is much less a desire to see their children learn how to individuate and assert themselves than it is for them to learn how to accommodate to others and to become part of a harmonious social group (Rothbaum, Pott, Azuma, Miyake, & Weisz, 2000). Even by the very young age of 2, toddlers raised in American environments seem to be embracing aspects of autonomy and individualism through their clumsy efforts to exert control over their worlds. When, in contrast, children are raised with cultural goals of interdependence, such signs of noncompliance often appear to be replaced by efforts to fit in and belong.

Adolescent Rebellion

On Tuesday, April 20, 1999, two teenage students, Eric Harris and Dylan Klebold, walked into Columbine High School in Jefferson County, Colorado, carrying heavy artillery with the express purpose of killing their classmates. At the end of their horrific rampage, Harris and Klebold committed suicide, but not before killing 12 fellow students and a teacher and wounding 24 others. It was one of the deadliest school shootings the world has ever witnessed. Although it is difficult to offer a complete explanation for such an unusually rare and appalling event, one account is clearly relevant. Harris and Klebold were adolescents. And one thing that characterizes adolescence is that, more than any other developmental stage, it is often a period of great turmoil (although, thankfully, rarely as tumultuous as the lives of Harris and Klebold).

In the West, adolescence is typically described as a chaotic period of "storm and stress" when teens act out against authority figures, commit acts of delinquency and criminal behavior, suffer from a great deal of emotional stress, and are at risk for substance abuse and suicide. Hollywood has often portrayed the adolescent as angry, distraught, confused, and intentionally disobedient, as in the classic *Rebel Without a Cause*. Evidence for adolescence as a troubled period can also be seen by looking at historical trends when there were large concentrations of adolescents. During the 1960s, when all the Baby Boomers born in the years after World War II were in their teens, protests, demonstrations, and outright rebellion were almost daily occurrences.

Adolescence has also been viewed as an especially violent phase of life. The association between adolescence and violence has been perceived as so reliable that sociologists make predictions about crime rates by tracking the percentage of the population who are between the ages of 14 and 21 (e.g., Fox, 1978). Male adolescents seem to be especially violent when there are relatively few females around (Vandello, 2004), arguably because they are competing with each other for access to mates.

The traditional view of the turmoil of adolescence was that it arose from the hormonal changes associated with puberty (Hall, 1916). That is, it was considered a biological development as inevitable as changes in voice or the growth of breasts. However, there has since been a great deal of controversy surrounding the universality of adolescent rebellion. In 1928, Margaret Mead famously made the case that adolescents growing up in Western Samoa enjoyed a carefree and smooth transition to adulthood, somehow avoiding all the difficulties so common in the West. More than 50 years later, however, Mead's observations were challenged by Derek Freeman (1983), who argued that Samoan adolescence was at least as tumultuous as adolescence in the West, and he attributed Mead's allegedly mistaken observations to her informants, who teased her and made up stories. Despite the unresolved controversy in this one instance, there have been investigations from many other areas of the globe regarding the prevalence of adolescent rebellion.

One study reviewed the ethnographic database (specifically, the Human Relations Area Files, a record of all published ethnographies) to explore what the adolescent experience was like in 175 different pre-industrial societies (Schlegel & Barry, 1991). The researchers discovered evidence for both similarities and differences. On the one hand, all the cultures viewed adolescence as a distinct period of life, separate from childhood and adulthood, in which some restructuring and role-learning occurred. This suggests that adolescence itself is not a cultural invention and seems to be an existential universal. On the other hand, however, there were some pronounced cultural differences in the experiences of adolescents. Many cultures demonstrated tendencies for adolescents to act in the rebellious ways familiar to the West; however, this was by no

"I'm sorry, but so far medical science hasn't come up with a cure for adolescence."

means universal. Rather, expectations for such antisocial behaviors were present in only 44% of societies with respect to boys, and in only 18% of societies for girls. The majority of the cultures studied did not expect adolescents to behave especially disobediently. Furthermore, the notion that adolescence is universally associated with violence received little support. Rather, only 13% of societies expected adolescent boys to occasionally be violent, and only 3% of societies had such expectations for girls. Adolescence as a developmental stage that is associated with rebellion and violence thus does not meet the criteria to be categorized as a functional universal. There is important cultural variation.

Whether adolescence is a tumultuous life stage does not seem to be determined randomly. A number of investigations have identified some variables that predict whether a given society will likely be associated with difficult adolescent times. For example, the experiences of adolescents in Germany, Scotland, Japan, Bali, and Batak were compared, and the results indicated that both individualism and modernity seem to increase the difficulties in adolescence (Trommsdorff, 1995). In particular, there appears to be more conflict between children and their parents in individualistic societies, where children seem to view parental control as a constraint they must resist.

Some features of modern Western societies seem to be associated with increased adolescent distress. These include the sheer range of opportunities that confront children as societies industrialize and become more urbanized (Dasen, 2000). One task in adolescence is to learn how to accept adult roles. This is much more straightforward when there are fewer role distinctions and when youths are more in contact with adults, as they are in more traditional, agricultural societies. For example, if your parents are farmers and there really aren't any options available to you other than farming, you're probably not going to need to spend years racking your brain over what you're going to do with your life. The answer is straightforward: You're going to farm. In more complex modern societies, however, the range of available roles is quite staggering, and adolescents spend a longer period in school preparing for those roles while being kept largely separate from adults.

As the range of roles has grown over time, so has the problem of adolescence. It was in the late 19th century that novels about the struggles of adolescence first appeared in abundance, likely as a result of the greater array of choices available to adolescents (Baumeister, 1987). The number of choices has continued to grow, which has lengthened the period of adolescence, sometimes referred to as a "failure to launch," or "emerging adulthood" (Arnett, 2000). The transition to adulthood has been indicated by five milestones: completing school, leaving home, becoming financially independent, getting married, and having at least one child. In the United States in 1960, 77% of women and 65% of men had passed all five milestones by the age of 30. In 2000, fewer than half of women and less than one-third of men had done so by this age (Henig, 2010). With more choices available, more people are delaying making commitments to their choices, thereby extending their period of adolescence. This set of circumstances increases the stress and confusion of adolescents and appears to be largely responsible for the tumultuousness of adolescence in the West.

Socialization Through Education

Testimony to the argument that humans are dependent on their ability to acquire cultural information to succeed in life is the fact that you are reading this chapter right now. You're probably in your early twenties or older and are reading this chapter for a university or college course. Think about that for a moment. You've been around this planet for some time now. You passed the physical age some time ago that allows you to start reproducing and raising your own children, you're fully grown physically, your government recognizes you as an adult with full responsibilities, and yet you're still in school! Our cultural worlds are complex enough now that succeeding in them requires more than a decade of effort to acquire the necessary cultural information. We depend on this cultural information to excel, and it is no coincidence that as our cultural worlds become more complex, the average amount of education that people receive increases accordingly.

Given all the time we spend in school, we might question the kind of impact this long exposure to education has on our psychological experiences. How do you think formal schooling affects the ways people think? Obviously, schooling provides us with some explicit kinds of knowledge, both in terms of techniques that we learn (e.g., how to multiply fractions, how to identify the predicate in a sentence) and content that we absorb (e.g., the elements in the periodic table, the date of the signing of the Magna Carta). This is the kind of information that is covered in textbooks, is discussed in class, and shows up on exams. However, we learn other kinds of knowledge through formal schooling that is not explicitly taught. Schooling leads people to think in ways that are different from the thought processes of people who do not experience formal schooling. For example, schooling leads people to cluster information as they try to learn it, it improves perceptual skills for analyzing two-dimensional patterns (Rogoff, 1981) and it leads people to reflect more on how information is organized (Goody, 1977). Much research has documented the ways schooling affects how people think (e.g., Cole et al., 1971; Rogoff, 2003; Scribner & Cole, 1973). Education doesn't just teach you facts—it shapes how you think about the world generally.

A good example of the effects of education on thinking was demonstrated by the Soviet psychologist Alexander Luria in his experiments with uneducated peasants

FIGURE 5.11 Alexander Luria.

in Uzbekistan in the early 1930s (see **Figure 5.11**). He was interested in their ability to engage in taxonomic categorization—the way that they lumped items together using an abstract concept. For example, he presented some of his participants with the following four objects and asked which of them did not belong: a hammer, a saw, a log, and a hatchet. Solving this problem required people to abstract the common attributes or uses of the objects and to form a category—tools in this case. If you've already received an education, this task is straightforward. You may even have learned how to engage in such taxonomic categorization by watching *Sesame Street* and learning the song "One of These Things Is Not Like the Others." But in the absence of such education, people do not necessarily learn how to form such abstract categories. Luria was struck by how few of his uneducated participants could engage in taxonomic categorizations. Here are the exchanges between Luria and a couple of his participants while looking at the group of four objects (Luria, 1976):

Luria:	Which of these things could you call by one word?
Participant:	How's that? If you call all three of them a "hammer," that won't be right either.
Luria:	But one fellow picked three things—the hammer, saw, and hatchet—and said they were alike.
Participant:	A saw, a hammer, and a hatchet all have to work together. But the log has to be here too!
Luria:	Why do you think he picked these three things and not the log?
Participant:	Probably he's got a lot of firewood, but if we'll be left without firewood, we won't be able to do anything.

Here's another exchange with the same group of items.

Luria:	Which one doesn't belong?
Participant:	It's the hammer that doesn't fit! You can always work with a saw, but a hammer doesn't always suit the job; there's only a little you can do with it.
Luria:	Yet one fellow threw out the log. He said the hammer, saw, and hatchet were all alike in some way, but the log is different.
Participant:	If we're getting firewood for the stove, we could get rid of the hammer, but if it's planks we're fixing, we can do without the hatchet.

Luria:	If you had to put these in some kind of order, could you take the log out of the group?
Participant:	No, if you get rid of the log, what good would the others be?
Luria:	Suppose I put a dog here instead of the log?
Participant:	If it was a mad dog, you could beat it with the hatchet and the hammer and it would die.

Luria's participants were stuck on how the objects could be used together and could not follow his lead into thinking about the attributes that the objects all shared in common. Education thus seems to afford the skills underlying taxonomic categorization. As we'll see in Chapter 9, this kind of categorization is reflective of analytic reasoning, whereas attending to the relations among objects indicates a more holistic reasoning style.

Education also seems to facilitate abstract logical reasoning—that is, the ability to apply a rule on the basis of logical principles rather than on the basis of personal experience or familiarity. Consider this syllogism:

In the far north all bears are white.

Novaya Zemyla is in the far north.

What color are the bears in Novaya Zemyla?

To answer this question logically, one should set aside all knowledge one has about bears or Novaya Zemyla and just focus on the premises provided. The bears in Novaya Zemyla must be white, because the premises determine that this is so, and the content of the premises is arbitrary. However, when Luria (1976) presented this syllogism to uneducated people in Uzbekistan, the most common response he received was "You should ask the people who have been there and seen them." That is, his participants often seemed reluctant to generalize beyond what they could tell from practical experience, and they were sometimes unwilling to accept the premises of the syllogisms. One only could know about the color of bears in a region if they had some kind of direct experience there. Similarly, a reluctance to show abstract logical reasoning has been found among uneducated Kpelle, Vai, and Yucatecans (see Scribner, 1977, for a review). It is not that people with little education are unable to reason logically; rather, their reasoning is anchored to information with which they have direct experience, and they reason logically about that information. Together with education, then, comes a heightened willingness to consider information beyond what one has experienced or heard about firsthand, and to apply logical principles to it. This entails a shift from the concrete to the abstract.

Another way that we can see the influence of education on thinking is by considering how much of our intellectual capability is sustained by knowledge that is built into the ways that problems are framed. For example, could you calculate the answer to the following arithmetic problem?

$$
\begin{array}{r}
642 \\
\times\ 439 \\
\hline
\end{array}
$$

With a little thought and effort, you could probably solve this question if you applied the strategies that you learned in math class. That is, you could likely solve it by doing something like this.

$$
\begin{array}{r}
642 \\
\times\ 439 \\
\hline
=\ 5778 \\
1926 \\
2568 \\
\hline
=\ 281838 \\
\end{array}
$$

However, imagine that I had presented the same problem to you like this: $642 \times 439 = ?$ Or imagine I had asked you the same problem orally. The question is no longer so straightforward, is it? Being able to solve multiplication problems is greatly facilitated by placing the numbers in vertical arrays with columns. If the numbers are not properly aligned, the task is much more difficult. In an important way, then, the organization of the numbers into a vertical array accomplishes much of the thinking necessary to solve the problem. Without this cultural tool of vertically presented columns of numbers, we are hard-pressed to do multiplication. And we tend to be unaware of how dependent our thinking is on such cultural tools until we are in a situation in which that tool is not available to us. This suggests that, in some ways, we do not solve multiplication problems by ourselves. We do so in conjunction with the capabilities of our cultural tools (Wertsch, 1998). And the process of formal education provides us with many such tools.

It can thus be quite problematic to attempt to assess the intelligence of people with no formal schooling when testing skills that are shaped by education. In 1912, in a time of increasing racism in the United States as the country was admitting vast numbers of immigrants, the U.S. Public Health Service hired the psychologist H. H. Goddard to help screen out immigrants with "inferior minds," who were perceived as a threat. As new immigrants stepped off the boats at Ellis Island, they were asked various questions to assess their intelligence. Many of the immigrants had not had any schooling whatsoever, nor any exposure to the cultural context from which these questions were derived. The results of Goddard's testing were that 83% of Jews, 80% of Hungarians, 79% of Italians, and 87% of Russians were classified as "morons"—the technical term that Goddard invented to indicate poor intellectual functioning (see Gould, 1981, for an in-depth description of this period of intelligence testing). Obviously, Goddard's test did not provide an accurate assessment of the immigrants' true potential, and it underscores the challenges of comparing people's capabilities across cultures. Do you think it's possible to develop a way to accurately measure people's cognitive abilities that is equally valid for individuals everywhere in the world, regardless of their experiences?

Schooling thus plays an important role in shaping people's thinking. How could we go about identifying how schooling affects people's thinking? Would it work if we just found people with differing levels of education within a particular culture and then compared how they thought? Unfortunately, it is not straightforward to study the influences of formal education on thinking; a number of other variables might separate people who have received a great deal of formal schooling from those who have not. If we think about the difference in the use of clustering strategies between schooled and unschooled people, for example, it is possible that the difference between these two groups has nothing to do with schooling but with something that is related to schooling, such as intelligence. That is, remembering a list by clustering might be a strategy that requires a certain amount of intelligence, and the fact that people who have been to school use more clustering than those who have not might be because intelligent people are more likely to attend school in the first place. This is not an unreasonable challenge to comparisons of schooled and unschooled people, as there are likely many reasons that some people choose to, or are able to, receive an education that are relevant to how their minds work. The variable of whether a person has received formal schooling is confounded with the many other variables that might distinguish the kinds of people who receive education from those who do not.

One of the most ambitious attempts to explore the effects of schooling was conducted by Harold Stevenson (1982). He investigated neighborhoods in rural Peru where only 53% of children attend school and compared the family circumstances of children who attended school with those who did not (**Figure 5.12**). He found a number of differences between these two groups. For example, the parents of children who attended school generally had received more education, they were more likely to be literate, and they were more likely to have items in their home that might stimulate cognitive development—such as books, toys, or radios.

Because of these differences between the children who received education and those who did not, it is not appropriate to simply compare the cognitive differences between the two groups. You also need to statistically control for any relations between cognitive abilities and the various family circumstances that differed across the groups. Stevenson collected an enormous amount of data and was able to discern how schooled and unschooled children differed in ways that were independent from their family circumstances. Put simply, he found that a few years of schooling led to some rather dramatic effects on the cognitive abilities of children. Controlling for all the other variables, Stevenson still demonstrated that schooling led to improved contextual memory, spatial memory, serial memory, and visual and sequential analysis. That

FIGURE 5.12   An example of a rural Peruvian school.

is, the schooling led the children to process information in a more efficient manner. Formal schooling affects how people think.

Case Study: East Asians and Math Education

If education affects how we think, we might expect that any differences in the ways cultures go about educating their children might lead to cultural differences in psychological processes. Educational experiences are not constant across cultures. Rather, how societies opt to educate their children reflects their implicit beliefs about what kinds of knowledge are most important, what kinds of learning styles should be encouraged, and what kinds of teaching styles are most effective. The educational strategies that a culture adopts influence the ways its citizens think (Tweed & Lehman, 2002).

One way to investigate how schools affect the ways children think is to compare schools and students from different cultures in their performance in various subjects. Some subjects, such as reading and language arts, make for problematic comparisons across cultures because the languages, choice of reading materials, and writing styles often vary greatly across cultures. On the other hand, math is an especially appropriate subject for cross-cultural investigation because everywhere you go the answers are the same. Not surprisingly, much research has explored math performance in various cultures around the world. This research is very telling about how our schooling shapes the way we think.

One large-scale research program examined students' performance on math tests, focusing on students who grew up in East Asia and those who grew up in the United States (Stevenson & Stigler, 1992). The researchers administered the same math exam to groups of students in schools in cities in China, Japan, Taiwan, and the United States; the tests were matched along a number of demographic characteristics. Both first-grade and fifth-grade students were compared across the four cultures. **Figure 5.13** shows the performance of the schools on the math tests. Each dot in the figure represents the average performance for each of the schools.

The figure shows a number of quite remarkable trends. One is a far greater spread in the average math performance of each school among the American schools than among the schools of the other countries. That is, there are more similarities among schools in the East Asian countries, particularly in Japan and Taiwan, than among the U.S. schools. Second, on average, the students in the East Asian schools performed much better on the math test than the American students. Third, the cultural differences become even more pronounced as the children continue to participate in their respective educational systems. By the fifth grade, the best-performing U.S.

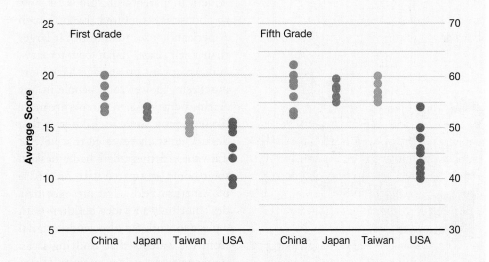

FIGURE 5.13 The dots represent the average math test scores for individual schools in different countries.

school in the study performs about the same as the worst school in each of the other countries. These are quite enormous differences in performance. And they are differences on a real-life concrete task: math tests. So how can we make sense of these cross-national differences?

First, it is important to note that there are some key differences in the way math is taught in the various schools. For example, at the time of the investigation, East Asian children spent more days in school (240 days per year in Japan versus 180 days per year in the United States); a greater percentage of class time was devoted to math education in the Asian schoolday than in the American; Asian teachers spent a greater percentage of time lecturing in the classroom compared with their American counterparts (90% in Taiwan compared with 46% in the United States); and Asian math lessons were far more likely to contain real-world examples than American lessons (approximately 80% of examples were real-world in Japan compared with about 10% of examples in American classes). Asian teachers also assigned more homework to students. Fifth-graders in the United States had less than half as much homework assigned to them as Taiwanese students (Stevenson & Stigler, 1992). Such teaching differences surely play an important role in how children learn math.

Second, psychological differences in the ways children and parents conceptualize learning are important to understanding these performance differences. Asian parents seem to view education as more central to their children's lives than American parents do. Look at how the house is structured. Even though American houses tend to be far larger than their East Asian counterparts, and Americans on average have more purchasing power than people in any Asian country, Asian parents are more likely to provide their children with a desk. One study revealed that 98% of Taiwanese fifth-graders had a desk in their home, compared with only 63% of American kids. The presence of a desk not only provides children with a place to work but also sends a signal from the parents that studying is an important and valued activity. There are also other cultural differences in education. For example, fifth-graders

"Big deal, an A in math.
That would be a D in any other country."

were asked to imagine that there was a wizard who would grant them anything they wished for (Stevenson, 1992). About 70% of the wishes listed by Chinese had to do with education—they wished for success in school or to be able to go to college. In contrast, only about 10% of American children wished for things relevant to education. And, tellingly, the most common wish among those 10% was to have *less* school! There are pronounced differences in how education is valued across cultures.

Third, the cultural differences in performance also seem to be related to the expectations of children and their mothers. On average, the East Asian children are doing so much better as a group on math tests than the American children that one might expect East Asian mothers to be especially satisfied with their children's performance. This does not seem to be the case; rather, the American mothers report being far more satisfied with their children's performance than the East Asian mothers—and this difference in standards seems to change with age. Compared with mothers of first-grade children, Chinese and Japanese mothers of fifth-grade children reported that a higher standard of achievement was necessary for them to be satisfied with their children's math performance. In stark contrast, the standards of American mothers were lower for their fifth-grade children than for their first-grade children. Over time, Chinese and Japanese mothers set higher and higher standards (Chua's "Tiger Moms") whereas American mothers set lower and lower standards. When mothers were asked to state the minimal standard that would lead them to be satisfied with their child's performance, American mothers gave a number that was considerably *below* the level at which they expected their child to perform. In contrast, East Asian mothers gave a number that was considerably *higher* than the level at which they expected their child to perform. Regardless of how well their children might have done on a test, East Asian mothers often direct their children's attention to the answers that they got wrong. Even when the children got 100% correct, some Chinese mothers responded by saying, "That's nothing to be proud of; you should get 100% every time" (Hess, Chang, & McDevitt, 1987). More generally, East Asian mothers direct their children's attention to their academic failures, in an effort to correct the shortcomings, whereas European-American mothers direct their children's attention to their successes (Ng, Pomerantz, & Lam, 2007). In sum, it appears to be far easier to meet standards of American mothers than East Asian mothers. This would suggest that American children have less reason to work hard at their studies than East Asian children.

A fourth factor underlying cultural differences in math performance can be traced to the languages themselves. Numbers are harder to learn in English than in Japanese, Korean, or Chinese, because there are more irregular number words in English. When East Asian speakers count past 10, their number words, both in how they are written and how they are pronounced, read "ten-one," "ten-two," "ten-three," and so on, up to 20, which is represented as "two-ten." Thirty is "three-ten," and so on. In contrast, English speakers have to learn a number of irregular number words and prefixes to count past 10, such as "eleven," "twelve," and "thirteen." Chinese preschoolers make fewer errors when they are learning to count than American children do (Miller & Stigler, 1987) because they have fewer unique number words to keep track of. Further, East Asian counting systems also incorporate the base-ten concept, which is necessary for learning how to do multidigit arithmetic, in a more straightforward way than English does. As a result, English speakers need more conceptual support for the base-ten concept than do speakers of East Asian languages (Fuson, Stigler, & Bartsch, 1988; Miura, 1987). This linguistic difference appears to contribute to the differences in the ease of learning basic mathematical concepts (Fuson, 1988; Gladwell, 2008; Miller, Smith, Zhu, & Zhang, 1995).

In sum, the convergence of a variety of cultural factors can be seen in the performance differences of math education between East Asian and American children. Education shapes the way that people think, but education practices themselves are also shaped by cultural attitudes, values, and even features of the language.

SUMMARY

People are not born with their cultures; they are born culture-free (or are at least conceived culture-free; in utero cultural experiences may possibly affect development); however, people begin attending to cultural information and being socialized by that information from very early in their lives. Becoming a cultural being is a developmental process, and as we age we are shaped more and more by the cultural practices and institutions in which we participate. This process is evident in that cultural differences in psychological processes tend to become more pronounced with age.

There is much evidence that a sensitive period exists for learning language, and other evidence suggests that this is true for learning cultural meaning systems as well. The existence of these sensitive periods suggests that people are biologically prepared to learn a language or culture in the initial years of life.

Various cultural practices differ across cultures, and these differences emerge at young ages. Infants have different kinds of personal space, including when they sleep. Across cultures, parents rely on different parenting styles to socialize their children. Children learn to attend differently to nouns and verbs across cultures, which is likely due to the ways that parents call their attention to features of objects or the relations among objects.

Cultures also differ in some key developmental transitions. The "terrible twos" is an infamous transition period that Western toddlers are likely to go through; however, the twos seem to be considerably less terrible in cultures where children are not encouraged to be as independent. Likewise, although adolescence is often viewed as a time of rebellion and aggression in the West, most subsistence societies around the world do not experience it this way.

Much of human socialization occurs through the schools, and the process of being educated shapes our thinking in quite profound ways. Moreover, cultures differ in the ways that they educate their children, and these differences affect the ways that children perform in their classes.

THINK ABOUT IT

1. Given that humans would seem to be better off if they could always acquire a language easily, why might there be sensitive periods for language acquisition?
2. If humans are biologically prepared to learn the surrounding culture, what kind of culture might you expect of children who are reared in the wild?
3. What are some implications that we might expect for immigrants if it becomes harder to acquire new cultural information after a certain age?
4. How do you think infants' perceptions of themselves and their relations with their mothers vary depending on whether or not they co-sleep?
5. What are some tradeoffs with strict parenting across cultures?
6. Why is adolescent rebellion more of a problem in modern industrialized societies than in nonindustrialized societies?
7. What are some reasons why children who attend schools in East Asia generally do better on math tests than students who attend schools in other countries?

KEY TERMS

Sensitive Period, 163
Co-Sleeping, 175
Incest Avoidance, 178
Protection of the Vulnerable, 178

Female Chastity Anxiety, 178
Respect For Hierarchy, 178
Sacred Couple, 178
Autonomy Ideal, 179

Authoritarian Parenting, 181
Authoritative Parenting, 181
Permissive Parenting, 181
Noun Bias, 184

A Japanese family sharing a meal. Japanese people tend to have more interdependent views of self compared with Westerners.

6

SELF AND PERSONALITY

n the summer of 2000, at the Olympic Games in Sydney, Australia, two gold-medal winners spoke to the media. Misty Hyman had just won the gold medal for the United States in women's swimming, specifically in the 200-meter butterfly stroke. She explained her victory to the press as follows: "I think I just stayed focused. It was time to show the world what I could do. I am just glad I was able to do it. I knew I could beat Suzy O'Neil, deep down in my heart I believed it, and I know this whole week the doubts kept creeping in, they were with me on the blocks, but I just said 'No, this is my night'" (see **Figure 6.1**). Around the same time, Naoko Takahashi had just won the gold medal for Japan in the women's marathon, and she explained her victory this way: "Here is the best coach in the world, the best manager in the world, and all of the people who support me—all of these things were getting together and became a gold medal. So I think I didn't get it alone, not only by myself" (from Markus, Uchida, Omoregie, Townsend, & Kitayama, 2006, p. 103). Although both athletes had received the same instructions from the International Olympic Organization about how to talk to the media, they offered quite different accounts of their victories. An analysis of the national media coverage of Japanese and American Olympic athletes of the 2000 Summer and 2002 Winter Olympics revealed that these two responses were not atypical; overall, Japanese and American athletes tended to explain their performance in ways that contrasted with each other (Markus et al., 2006). Americans focused more on how their performance reflected their own personal characteristics, whereas the Japanese focused more on how their performance was guided by the expectations of others.

FIGURE 6.1 Misty Hyman and Naoko Takahashi, Olympic champions.

These contrasting media accounts are not only indicative of people's different theories for athletic success, they reflect something more fundamental. They highlight some profound cultural differences in the ways people come to understand themselves. The heart of who we think we are, our self-concept, varies in important ways across cultures.

This chapter explores the role of culture in how we understand ourselves. We will investigate how culture shapes a number of key aspects of the self-concept. Furthermore, we will consider the role that gender plays in how we view ourselves, and the structure of people's personalities around the world. This chapter looks at the tensions between culturally universal and variable aspects of psychology. How similar to or different from people in other cultures around the world are we in our feelings of identity and our understanding of what makes us tick? This question has a number of profound implications as we explore the ways that cultural experiences shape our thinking.

Who Am I?

Sometimes, in the middle of the night, when we're all alone, we might ponder that most profound of questions: "Who am I?" This question is not only relevant to our existential musings but is also important in psychological research, because it addresses the nature of our self-concepts and the foundation of our identities. The self-concept holds a privileged position in psychology, as we'll see later, because the nature of our selves strongly influences the ways we perceive and interact with our social worlds.

Please take the opportunity now to think about the ways you would answer the question of "Who am I?" In **Figure 6.2**, write down 20 statements that begin with "I am _____." Complete the statements in the way that you feel best describes who you are. You'll get a lot more out of this chapter if you try to describe yourself in this way. This exercise is a well-used measure of the self-concept known, appropriately enough, as the Twenty-Statements Test (Kuhn & McPartland, 1954).

What do you think your self-description tells people about your cultural background? This exercise reveals the extent of culture's influence on people's identities in at least two ways: one rather superficial, and one much deeper. At the superficial level, your self-description might include some culturally shaped statements such as "I'm a Vancouver Canucks fan," or "I am a devotée of jazz." These statements are cultural products in that you can't be a fan of the Vancouver Canucks without having participated in a cultural meaning system that includes hockey as a spectator sport (or more specifically, one that includes the Canucks as a hockey team), nor can you view yourself as an aficionado of jazz if you haven't been exposed to the music and its surrounding culture. However, these kinds of self-statements might reveal only

---

TWENTY-STATEMENTS TEST

I am _____.   I am _____.

I am _____.   I am _____.

I am _____.   I am _____.

I am _____.   I am _____.

I am _____.   I am _____.

I am _____.   I am _____.

I am _____.   I am _____.

I am _____.   I am _____.

I am _____.   I am _____.

I am _____.   I am _____.

FIGURE 6.2   Who am I? Complete this questionnaire by listing 20 statements that best describe who you are.

a superficial influence of culture, because the culture is merely providing the *content* about the ways people think of themselves. That is, a consideration of culture's influences at this level does not say much about why we describe ourselves with these kinds of preferences. Indeed, if we imagine that we had instead been born and raised somewhere else, such as in Afghanistan, and described our identities in terms of our favorite sport of *buzkashi* (the national sport, which involves passing a goat carcass among players on horseback; **Figure 6.3**) and our preferences for folk music played on the *rohab* (something like an Afghani violin), our identities might not be all that different. We would still be defining ourselves in terms of sports and music, and the difference would be that we were exposed to different kinds of sports and music. It's possible, then, that we might appear highly similar across experiences in these two diverse cultural worlds and vary only in terms of the content of things that we would be thinking about.

There is a deeper and more penetrating influence of culture on self-descriptions that is harder to detect. This influence isn't seen so much in the content of the statements as in their structure. What categories of statements do we consider when we think about ourselves? For example, one type of statement that you might have included in your self-description is "I am creative." What does this type of statement have to say about how culture shapes the self-concept? At first glance, it would hardly seem to be culturally influenced, because there are creative people in all cultures of

FIGURE 6.3 *Buzkashi*, the national sport of Afghanistan.

the world. However, what is noteworthy about this kind of statement is that it reveals a specific kind of understanding about ourselves. That is, defining ourselves as creative individuals suggests that we think in terms of having enduring traits, such as creativity, that exist across situations. This kind of statement refers to an inner attribute about the self—creativity—that has a number of telling features: It is relatively abstract (it encapsulates different kinds of thoughts and behaviors across different situations); it is likely experienced as stable (we don't expect our creative aspect to dissipate during the summer vacation or after we get our degree); and it can exist by itself (we do not need others around to be creative). Hence, a simple statement about ourselves such as "I am creative" can suggest a variety of ways that we think about ourselves.

Contrast the above kind of statement about oneself with another kind that one could make—for example, "I am a younger brother." How does this statement reflect on a person's cultural background? At first glance this statement is not obviously culturally influenced, as there are younger brothers in all cultures of the world.

However, in a self-description it is telling. First, it implicates a significant other in one's self-concept. One can't be a younger brother unless one has an older brother or sister. It defines a role in terms of whatever ideas one has regarding appropriate behaviors or responsibilities that are relegated to younger brothers. It also emphasizes a hierarchical relationship because it underscores that one is younger than one's other siblings. In sum, this kind of statement highlights an experience of self that is connected with others, and in ways that are specific to the role of being a younger brother.

People all over the world are able to think of themselves in terms of both abstract psychological attributes and concrete roles and relationships. However, the degree to which they view themselves in these two separate ways varies significantly across cultures. Some cultures encourage people to focus on their enduring inner attributes, such as personality traits, attitudes, or abilities, as a means to understand themselves. Other cultures, in contrast, encourage people to focus on their connections with others by considering themselves in terms of concrete roles, relationships, and group memberships. Much research shows that people from different cultures view themselves in these different ways.

One study explored this question among Kenyans and Americans by asking people to describe themselves in the same way that you did with the Twenty-Statements Test (Ma & Schoeneman, 1997). Because Kenya is a developing society, the authors divided their Kenyan sample into groups that should theoretically vary in terms of how much they were exposed to Western cultural ways. They reasoned that Kenyan university students in Nairobi should be the most Westernized group in their sample (because they participate in an education system that was shaped by the country's British colonial past); employed adults in Nairobi might be slightly less Westernized; and traditional indigenous Kenyan groups, in this case the Samburu and the Masai, would be the least Westernized. These Kenyan groups were contrasted with a sample of American undergraduates. How did people from these different groups describe themselves?

The results were striking (see **Figure 6.4**). The most popular kinds of self-descriptions for the Americans were personal characteristics, such as their traits, attitudes, and abilities, which accounted for 48% of their self-descriptions. In contrast, these kinds of statements made up less than 2% of the Masai and Samburu self-descriptions. The statements made by the Masai and Samburu generally reflected their social identity—specifically, their roles and memberships, which accounted for more than 60% of their self-descriptions. In stark contrast, such statements accounted for only 7% of American self-descriptions (people also used some categories other than personal characteristics or social identity, such as their possessions or interests). It appears that the Masai and Samburu think of themselves in vastly different ways from those reported by American undergrads. It is important to note that Americans do sometimes think of themselves in terms of roles, and Masai and Samburu sometimes consider their own personality traits. However, the degree to which people from these

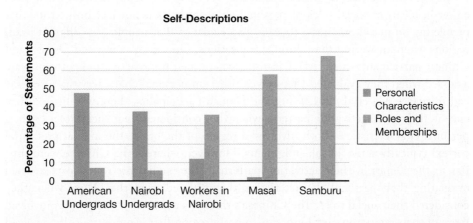

FIGURE 6.4 The proportion of self-descriptions that considered personal characteristics versus roles and memberships across cultural groups.

cultures consider these different aspects of themselves varies considerably. The other two Kenyan groups fell in between, with the university students being closer to the American pattern and the workers more closely resembling the Masai and Samburu patterns. These results suggest that the ways Kenyans and Americans think about themselves diverge profoundly.

This pattern of cultural differences is not unique to Kenyans and Americans. The Twenty-Statements Test is one of the most widely used cross-cultural psychological measures. The American pattern of emphasis on personal characteristics has emerged in many other Western cultures, such as those of Australia and Britain (Bochner, 1994), Sweden (Watkins, Yau, Dahlin, & Wondimu, 1997), and Canada (Leuers & Sonoda, 1999), whereas the Masai and Samburu pattern of a greater emphasis on roles and memberships appears in cultures from much of the rest of the world—for example, among Cook Islanders (Altrocchi & Altrocchi, 1995), Malaysians (Bochner, 1994), Chinese (Triandis, McCusker, & Hui, 1990), Native Americans (Fryberg & Markus, 2003), other African populations (Valchev, van de Vijver, Nel, Rothmann, & Meiring, 2013), Puerto Ricans (Hart, Lucca-Irizarry, & Damon, 1986), Indians (Dhawan, Roseman, Naidu, & Rettek, 1995), Japanese (Bond & Cheung, 1983), and Koreans (Rhee, Uleman, Lee, & Roman, 1995). Furthermore, these cultural differences are already evident among kindergarten-age children (Wang, 2004). Take a look at your own responses to the Twenty-Statements Test to see how much your self-concept is based on personal characteristics or on roles and memberships.

Moreover, this cultural difference in the ways that people understand themselves either in terms of social roles or personal characteristics is not just limited to what people say on questionnaires—there is also evidence that people use different brain regions when answering these kinds of questions. One study compared Danish and Chinese participants in an fMRI scanner, where their brain activation patterns were assessed when they evaluated themselves either on personal characteristics or on social roles (see Ma et al., 2012). For the Danish participants, there was little difference in their brain activation patterns when they considered their social roles or their personal characteristics—both involved a region of the brain (the medial prefrontal cortex) typically active in self-judgments. However, whereas the Chinese were similar to the Danes in their activation pattern in the medial prefrontal cortex when evaluating their personal characteristics, they differed from the Danes when they considered their social roles. The Chinese's thoughts about their social roles involved more of their temporoparietal junction, a brain region that is more typically involved in understanding other people's beliefs. This suggests that the Chinese participants were more likely thinking about other people's beliefs when they thought about their social roles when compared with Danes. The self-perceptions of people in these two cultures were associated with different patterns of brain activity.

This one difference in the way that people think about themselves has considerable importance in cultural psychology. Every human is ultimately a distinct individual, unique from everyone else; at the same time, we are also a highly social species. Our survival and fitness depend both on the things that we accomplish as individuals and on our abilities to interact successfully with others. As Jon Stewart (2010) put it, human history can be summarized as a series of attempts to reconcile the two fundamental truths offered by English poet John Donne ("No man is an island") and French philosopher Jean-Paul Sartre ("Hell is other people"). Given this, it is perhaps not surprising that the dimension underlying our proclivities to focus on how we are ultimately distinct from others or on how we are closely connected with others is the most researched psychological dimension across cultures.

Independent Versus Interdependent Views of Self

The findings from the study with Kenyans and Americans suggest that there are at least two ways people might see themselves. One way is reflected in many of the statements made by the American undergrads in that study. That is, the self can be thought to derive its identity from its inner attributes. These attributes are assumed to reflect an inner essence of the individual in that they are the basis of the individual's identity, they are viewed as stable across situations and across the lifespan, they are perceived to be unique (in the sense that no other individual possesses the same configuration of attributes), they are self-contained in that they are perceived to arise from the individual and not from interactions with others, they are viewed as significant for regulating behavior, and individuals feel an obligation to publicly advertise themselves in ways consistent with these attributes. Markus and Kitayama (1991) referred to this self-contained model of the self as the **independent view of self**.

Figure 6.5 represents a graphic view of this kind of self. A number of features from this illustration are key to understanding this kind of self-concept. First, note that the circle around the individual does not overlap with any of the borders surrounding its significant relationships. This shows that independent individuals experience their identities as largely distinct from their relationships. Second, the X's inside the circles reflect aspects of identity—the kinds of features that people consider when they think of themselves. The larger X's reflect the especially important self-defining aspects of identity. For those with independent selves, these important aspects tend to lie within the individual. Some examples of these aspects are a person's attitudes, personality traits, preferences, opinions, abilities, and individual qualities. Third, the border around the individual is drawn with a solid line, to indicate that the self is bounded, and as such, its experience is rather stable and does not change much from

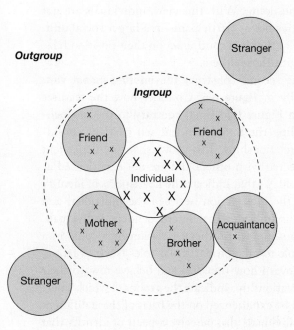

FIGURE 6.5

The independent view of self. The circles are drawn with either solid lines to indicate firm boundaries or dotted lines to indicate permeable boundaries. X's represent aspects of identity, and the larger X's indicate more-important and self-defining aspects.

situation to situation. The independent view of self is experienced as self-contained and exists as a relatively coherent and inviolate entity. Fourth, the border around the ingroup that separates one's close relations from one's more distant relations is drawn with a dotted line to indicate that it is fluid. This shows that others can move between the boundary of ingroup and outgroup relatively easily. Individuals with independent identities still feel much closer to ingroup than outgroup members; however, they do not view them in fundamentally distinct ways. The key boundary is between self and nonself, and, for the most part, others are viewed, and interacted with, as though they were nonself. In sum, independent selves tend to be viewed as distinct, autonomous entities whose identities are grounded in a variety of internal component features and who interact with other similarly independent entities.

Another way of considering the self is reflected in the kinds of statements commonly made by the Masai and Samburu. That is, the self can be viewed as a relational entity that is fundamentally connected to, and sustained by, a number of significant relationships. This is a profoundly different orientation of the individual. Rather than elaborating on how behavior and thoughts emanate from the individual's inner features, viewing oneself as part of an encompassing social relationship means that behavior is recognized as contingent upon perceptions of others' thoughts, feelings, and actions. When people are focused on how they are connected with others, it is important for them to consider how their behaviors will affect others; likewise, they must organize their own psychological experiences in response to what others are apparently thinking and doing. With this view, individuals are not perceived as separate and distinct entities but as participants in a larger social unit. Their experience of identity is reflexive in that it is contingent on their position relative to others, and their relationships with those others.

Markus and Kitayama labeled this second construct the **interdependent view of self**, which is represented graphically in **Figure 6.6**. Consider how the features in this figure contrast with those from Figure 6.5. First, contrary to the independent view of self, the border surrounding the interdependent self overlaps considerably with an individual's significant relationships. This shows that interdependent individuals' identities are closely connected with others and are not experienced as distinct, unique entities. Second, the bold X's that indicate the key aspects of identity for interdependent individuals rest at the intersection between the individual and his or her significant relationships. This indicates that interdependent individuals' identities are grounded in their relationships with others. Relationships come in a variety of forms, and they require people to take on particular roles (such as father, student, friend, lover, daughter) that govern how they feel and behave toward their relationship partners. Likewise, these relationships indicate the groups to which a person belongs, and his or her identity can be experienced on the basis of these different group memberships. Interdependent individuals also perceive aspects of identity that are based on internal characteristics, as shown in Figure 6.6; however, the small X's

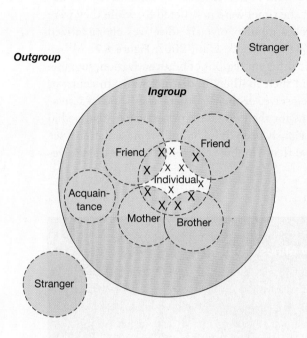

FIGURE 6.6

The interdependent view of self. The circles are drawn with either solid lines to indicate firm boundaries or dotted lines to indicate permeable boundaries. X's represent aspects of identity, and the larger X's indicate more important and self-defining aspects.

show that these are relatively less central to their identity. A third feature of the interdependent self is indicated by the dotted line that encapsulates the individual. This shows that the identity of the interdependent person is experienced as somewhat fluid in different situations. Depending on the situation, and the role that the person occupies in that situation, the person's experience of their self will vary accordingly. Last, the border that separates the ingroup from the outgroup is drawn with a solid line to indicate a relatively significant and stable distinction. Relationships with one's ingroup members are self-defining for those with interdependent selves; therefore, the people with whom these relationships are established assume considerable importance. People do not easily become ingroup members, nor do close relationships easily dissipate into outgroup relations. People with interdependent selves tend to view ingroup and outgroup members quite distinctly and may behave quite differently toward these individuals. In sum, interdependent selves consist largely of nodes within networks of individuals tied together by specific relationships whose identities are grounded in those relationships, and who are contrasted against other networks of individuals.

These cultural differences in the self-concept are not just theoretical—they can also be observed in brain activation patterns. In one experiment, Chinese and

Western participants (the Westerners were native English speakers from various countries who were living in China at the time) were instructed to, while they were in a fMRI scanner, consider how well a number of trait adjectives characterized themselves or their mothers (Zhu, Zhang, Fan, & Han, 2007; **Figure 6.7**). When doing this task, the Westerners showed different regions of brain activation, suggesting that they represent themselves and their mothers in distinct ways. In contrast, when the Chinese were evaluating themselves or their mothers, they showed activation patterns in the same brain regions for the two tasks (in particular, the medial prefrontal cortex, an area that has previously been linked to self-representations; see Heatherton et al., 2006). This suggests that Chinese representations for themselves

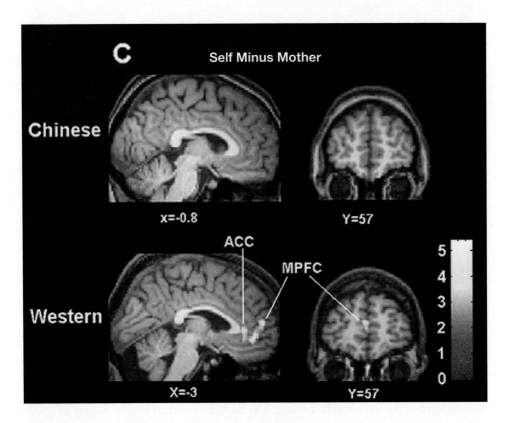

FIGURE 6.7 These are fMRI scans of the differences in brain activation patterns when participants were thinking about their mothers and when they were thinking about themselves. The Western participants showed more activation in the medial prefrontal cortex (and to a lesser extent the anterior cingulate cortex) when thinking about themselves than when thinking about their mothers. The Chinese participants showed the same pattern of activation regardless of whether they were thinking about themselves or their mothers.

and for their mothers are not that distinct and both reflect on the self-concept. Significant ingroup relationships form a core part of the self-concept for those with interdependent selves.

Identifying cultural differences in the self-concept has had important implications for psychology, because the self-concept shapes much about how people think—not just about themselves but about the world more generally. One metaphor that is often used to help make sense of how our minds work is the computer. Computers, like our minds, take in information, execute various programs or heuristics to process that information, and reach conclusions regarding the information considered. One important way that our minds differ from computers, however, is that we have self-concepts. Our self-concepts serve a number of key functions, and these functions represent some of the central themes of research in social psychology. Our self-concepts organize the information that we have about ourselves, they direct our attention to information that is viewed to be relevant, they shape the concerns that we have, they guide us in our choice of relationship partners and the kinds of relationships that we maintain, and they influence how we interpret situations, which, in turn, influences the emotional experiences that we have about them. In sum, the ways that people view themselves are central to topics of human cognition, motivation, emotions, and relationships. Understanding that there are different patterns in the way self-concepts are constructed across cultures enables us to make predictions about how specific psychological phenomena will also differ across cultures.

Relations with Ingroups and Outgroups

As Figures 6.5 and 6.6 indicate, people with independent selves have a number of close relationships with members of their ingroup; however, those relationships are less self-defining than are the corresponding relationships of those with more interdependent selves. Furthermore, people with independent selves have a rather permeable boundary between their ingroups and outgroups, whereas people with interdependent selves have a more clear-cut boundary between these groups. Why would we expect to see people with independent and interdependent selves having different views toward ingroups and outgroups?

Although ingroup relationships are surely essential in all cultures, they take on special significance among those with more interdependent views of self. Because ingroup relations are so critical for self-definition for people in more interdependent cultures and because they serve to direct appropriate behaviors in those contexts, it would be especially necessary to identify those with whom one has such significant relationships. Obligations to others are an important part of ingroup relations among interdependent people, so it is of vital importance for them to distinguish those toward whom they have obligations from those they do not. Becoming a member of an interdependent individual's ingroup is thus a rather substantial accomplishment, and such relationships should be entered cautiously. It is not easy for outgroup members to become part of the valued ingroup, and it is rare for a member of the ingroup to lose his or her privileged status and fall into the outgroup category. This would suggest that the boundary distinguishing ingroups from outgroups would be particularly salient for members of interdependent cultures.

In contrast, a more independent person is likely to perceive himself or herself as existing and functioning separately from the social environment; therefore, the people in that environment are relatively more tangential to the independent individual's identity. New relationships can be formed and old relationships can be dissolved without having a large impact on an independent person's perception of his or her identity. Hence, people with independent selves should be more willing to form new relationships, maintain larger networks of relationships, and be less distressed should any of those relationships fade away over time. The boundary distinguishing ingroups from outgroups is less consequential to self-construction for those with independent selves, and it should hence be experienced as rather fluid and permeable.

There is convergent evidence from a variety of sources of the heightened distinction between ingroups and outgroups among those who are more interdependent. Ethnographic research on the relationships among some collectivistic cultures, such as the Japanese, richly describes this pronounced difference in behavior between contexts involving ingroups (*uchi*) and those involving outgroups (*soto;* e.g., Bachnik, 1992). Language, customs, and obligations vary considerably depending on whether the other is an ingroup or outgroup member. Empirical evidence from several different paradigms highlights the cultural difference in the nature of the boundary between ingroups and outgroups. For example, one set of studies found that whereas Asian-Americans were more accurate than European-Americans in identifying the emotions experienced by their close friends, European-Americans were more accurate than Asian-Americans in identifying the emotions that were experienced by strangers (Ma-Kellams & Blascovich, 2012).

Yamagishi and colleagues (e.g., Yamagishi, Cook, & Watabe, 1998; Yamagishi & Yamagishi, 1994) developed a model to explain trust and commitment among people with independent and interdependent selves. They maintain that in a society characterized by strong group ties, feelings of trust are confined to that group. The stronger the bonds among members within a group, the weaker the ties between groups. One cannot have strong loyalties that conflict with each other. Hence, in places like Japan, where commitment to ingroup members is strong, there should be less of a willingness to cooperate with outgroup members. People with interdependent selves should focus their trust on people with whom they share some kind of relationship. Yamagishi and colleagues' research finds that Americans tend to have higher levels of general trust toward strangers than Japanese do (Yamagishi & Yamagishi, 1994).

Evidence for larger distinctions between ingroups and outgroups is also available from studies that have explored conformity pressures. As we'll discuss in Chapter 8, there has been much research on how conformity motivations differ across cultures. In general, people with more interdependent views of self are more likely to conform than those with more independent views of self (Bond & Smith, 1996). However, the conformity of people with interdependent selves appears to be more contingent on the nature of the majority group than it is for people with independent views of self. When in a situation with strangers, people with interdependent selves conform as much as those with independent selves, or even show some evidence of anti-conformity (e.g., Frager, 1970). However, in a situation with their peers, those with interdependent selves show evidence of heightened conformity; indeed, out of the 133 studies in which the Asch conformity paradigm has been tested (Bond & Smith, 1996), the two studies that revealed the largest amount of conformity involved Fijian Indian and Japanese participants (who both have largely interdependent selves) conforming to groups that included their peers (Chandra, 1973; Williams & Sogon, 1984). In contrast, the degree of conformity for Westerners did not appear to be contingent on the relationships between the subjects and those of the majority group.

In general, there is converging evidence that people with interdependent selves view ingroup members as an extension of themselves while maintaining distance from outgroup members. People with independent selves, in contrast, show a tendency to view themselves as distinct from all others, regardless of their relationships to the others. This finding highlights a problem in conducting research with groups across cultures. Many social psychological studies involve assessing how people behave in groups of strangers (e.g., Larson, Foster-Fishman, & Keys, 1994; Tajfel, 1970). More-interdependent people may feel especially distant from those strangers, and their behavior would likely be different from the behavior typically found in studies that have focused on more independent Western samples.

Individualism and Collectivism

Self-concepts are shaped by the cultural practices that direct what individuals attend to, value, believe, and are able to attain. So what shapes cultural practices? In addition to the constraints and affordances of the physical environment, cultural practices are also shaped by the kinds of self-concepts a culture's members have. In this way, culture and self can be said to make each other up (Shweder, 1990).

The two different views of self described by Markus and Kitayama are not randomly distributed across our planet but emerge in places where there are cultural practices that sustain them. For example, what kind of self do you think would be more likely to develop in a culture where children are typically provided with their own bedrooms, where college students earn their own money from summer jobs to help pay for their entertainment and college tuition, where employees are paid on the basis of how much profit they help the company earn, or where the elderly use their own savings to pay the costs of moving into retirement homes? As you may know from the previous chapters, such cultures are typically referred to as *individualistic* cultures. People participating in individualistic cultures are more likely to elaborate on independent aspects of themselves, and they come to feel distinct from others and emphasize the importance of being self-sufficient. Likewise, interdependent selves are more common in cultures where children typically co-sleep with their parents, where education is primarily a matter decided on by families, and where marriages may be arranged by parents, and so on—*collectivistic* cultures. People participating in a collectivistic culture are more likely to attend to interdependent aspects of their self-concepts, such as their close relationships and group memberships.

Where do we find individualistic and collectivistic cultures? This question was first explored a few decades ago by Geert Hofstede, a Dutch psychologist. Hofstede was hired by IBM to explore the values and concerns of their workers around the world. He gave questionnaires to 117,000 employees in IBM offices in 40 different countries. In addition to the items that IBM was interested in for assessing workers' interests and opinions, Hofstede also included some items that explored values purportedly related to individualism. He was able to map out the world in terms of its individualism by calculating an individualism score for each of the 40 countries; this map is presented in **Figure 6.8**. Hofstede's country scores show a clear and striking pattern. According to his data, the most individualistic country in the world is the United States, closely followed by other English-speaking countries and by Western European nations. On the other end of the distribution, countries that scored high in collectivism (or low in individualism) were various nations in Latin America and Asia. Other research has also found evidence of collectivism in countries in Asia, Africa, southern Europe, eastern Europe, and the South Pacific (e.g., Hofstede, 1983; Schwartz, 1994; Verkuyten & Masson, 1996).

In sum, if we took a head count around the world, we would surely find that most people participate in collectivistic cultures where interdependent selves are more common; these cultures likely encompass more than 80% of the world's population. Although interdependent selves thus appear to be more common throughout the world, most research in psychology has emerged in cultures where independent selves predominate. This raises a serious question: How well do the psychological theories that have been generated in Western cultural contexts apply to other cultures of the world?

Furthermore, one does not have to look in especially exotic places to find evidence of collectivism. Indeed, there are pronounced pockets of collectivism even in the United States. In one study, people from all 50 states were surveyed to calculate a collectivism score for each state (Vandello & Cohen, 1999). The state with the highest collectivism score by far was Hawaii, probably because of that state's large

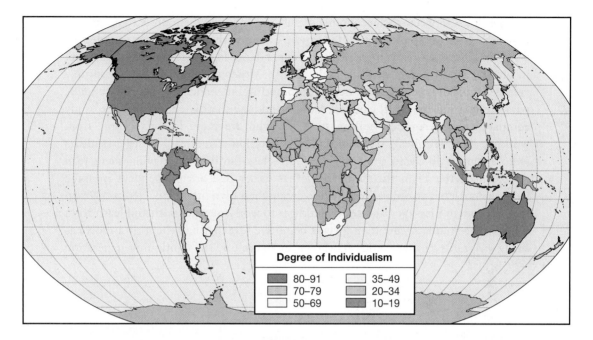

FIGURE 6.8 This map shows the degree of individualism and collectivism among IBM employees around the world. It shows a greater degree of individualism in Great Britain and in the United States, Canada, Australia, and New Zealand, which are former British colonies. Areas in gray were not surveyed in this study (based on data from Hofstede, 1980).

population of people with Asian ancestry. The next most collectivistic states were Utah and the states of the Confederate South. In contrast, the least collectivistic states were in the Mountain West, the Great Plains, the Northeast, and the Midwest. The other regions fell in between. Similar kinds of within-country differences in individualism have been found in Japan as well (Kitayama, Ishii, Imada, Takemura, & Ramaswamy, 2006).

Moreover, there is much research showing that individualism varies as a function of social class—specifically, people from higher socioeconomic backgrounds tend to be have more independent selves than those from poorer backgrounds, within the same country (for a review see Kraus, Piff, Mendoza-Denton, Rheinschmidt, & Keltner, 2012). For example, wealthier Icelandic children tend to describe themselves more in terms of inner psychological traits than poorer Icelandic children do (Hart & Edelstein, 1992), paralleling the cross-national differences in self-concepts discussed earlier. Likewise, middle-class American parents emphasize the importance of self-direction to their children, whereas working-class American parents place greater value on conforming to authority figures (Weininger & Lareau, 2009).

The links between socioeconomic status and individualism are strong enough that periods of economic growth tend to be linked with growing rates of independence and recessions with increasing interdependence (e.g., Grossmann & Varnum, in press; Park, Twenge, & Greenfield, 2014). Moreover, because American universities typically focus a great deal on promoting independence, poorer students, who are less independent, can feel more at odds with this emphasis. One study compared first-generation college students (who are more likely to come from working-class families) and continuing-generation American college students (who are more likely to come from middle-class families) by having them read a welcome letter from their university that either had an independent message (e.g., the university would allow them to create their own intellectual journey) or an interdependent message (e.g., they would get to work together with and learn from others). The students were then given a cognitive test that had them try to solve as many anagrams as they could. As shown in **Figure 6.9**, the continuing-generation

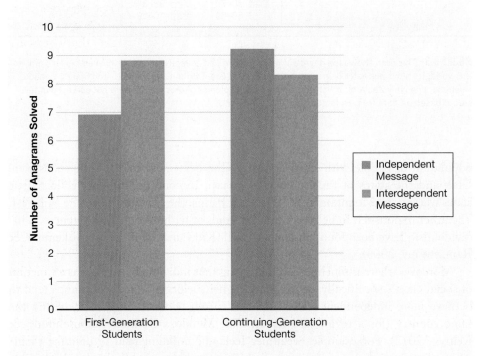

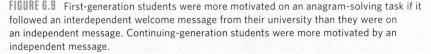

FIGURE 6.9 First-generation students were more motivated on an anagram-solving task if it followed an interdependent welcome message from their university than they were on an independent message. Continuing-generation students were more motivated by an independent message.

students tended to complete slightly more anagrams following an independent message, which indicates that they found this message to be motivating. In contrast, the first-generation students were more motivated to solve anagrams when they received an interdependent message. Interdependent messages are a better fit with American students from a working-class background (see Stephens, Fryberg, Markus, Johnson, & Covarrubias, 2012).

It is also worth noting that given that university students tend to be of higher socioeconomic status than nonstudents more generally, and that some of the highest concentrations of universities in the United States are in the Northeast and the Midwest where individualism is more pronounced, psychological research within the United States has been largely conducted with participants who are even more individualistic than most other Americans. Our understanding of what people are like has been biased by studying participants who are rather WEIRD in terms of their individualism.

We have a long way to go before having a clear understanding of the different kinds of psychologies that exist around the world. Cultural psychologists have started to make some progress by studying people from collectivistic cultures. However, the majority of this research, as you'll see, has been conducted with people from East Asian cultures, such as China, Korea, and Japan, with results usually compared to findings from Western samples. Some recent research—and I suspect that a growing proportion of future research as well—is beginning to consider the nature of psychological processes from many other cultures around the world.

Beyond Individualism and Collectivism

Research on the dimension of individualism and collectivism, and on the associated dimension of independent and interdependent self-concepts, has served as the foundation for many key cultural psychological theories. Perhaps this dimension may ultimately prove to be the most important one for capturing cultural variation; however, it is not the only dimension that we can consider. A number of other cultural dimensions have also been investigated by researchers across cultures. For example, the dimension of societal tightness versus looseness, which characterizes how strong cultural norms are and how tolerant cultures are of deviant behavior, has been found to predict many psychological phenomena, such as a prevention focus, impulse control, and self-regulation (Gelfand et al., 2011). Shalom Schwartz (1994; Schwartz & Boehnke, 2004) has looked at cultural values as a means of understanding cultural differences around the world and has created a broad framework of 10 cultural values that distinguish cultures: specifically, values for universalism, benevolence, conformity, tradition, security, power, achievement, hedonism, stimulation, and self-direction. Other cultural dimensions, such as power distance, uncertainty avoidance (Hofstede, 1980), vertical-horizontal social structure (Triandis, 1996), relationship structure (Fiske, 1992), context dependence (Hall, 1976), social cynicism, and social complexity (Leung & Bond, 2004), have also been developed. Thus far, none of these other dimensions have revealed the breadth of explanatory power or empirical support that individualism-collectivism has marshalled. However, these new dimensions have not yet received as much attention, and as we continue to explore these and other possible dimensions of cultures we will have a better system for understanding cultural variation. Hofstede (1980) launched an ambitious project in trying to map out the cultures of the world when he first conducted his massive study of cultural values of IBM workers. As our methods improve and our theories develop, we may one day be able to confidently realize his goals with a more extensive and sophisticated set of cultural dimensions.

A Note on Heterogeneity of Individuals and Cultures

It is much simpler to refer to people as though they had *either* an independent *or* an interdependent construal of self, as I've done in the preceding paragraphs. However, I use this dichotomy only as an explanatory device. In reality, people cannot be categorized so cleanly into these discrete categories; rather, the experience of self appears to follow a continuum. I'm sure you can think of times in your own life when, for example, you felt very connected with others, and times when you've felt very distinct. Every individual surely has both interdependent and independent aspects of self; however, people do vary considerably in the degree to which they are closer to the independent or the interdependent exemplars described earlier. As such, everyone occasionally experiences the self as a separate self-contained unit or as an interconnected, relational unit, and how people differ can be seen as the proportion of the time that they think of themselves in each of these ways, or as their default way of viewing themselves.

One important determinant of how often people experience themselves as independent or interdependent is the situations they encounter on a daily basis. Situations that highlight independent aspects of the self will be more frequently encountered when participating in an individualistic culture, in which cultural practices emphasize personal goals over collective ones. Likewise, situations that facilitate interdependent aspects of the self are more frequently encountered when individuals participate in collectivistic cultural contexts.

Not only are individuals more varied and complex than the schematics in Figures 6.5 and 6.6, but cultures, too, are highly variable and are resistant to simple categorization. As you've surely noted yourself, there are many ways that you differ from the people around you, and you know some individuals who seem to be more independent and others who are more interdependent. We all know people from our cultures who do not come close to approximating the prototypical individuals represented in Figure 6.5. All cultures are highly heterogeneous and contain a great variety of people (see **Figure 6.10**). When we speak of a culture as individualistic we mean that, on average, people in that culture are exposed to more cultural messages that encourage them to think in independent ways. Individuals will respond to those cultural messages in a variety of ways, with some embracing them more than others, and the fit between a given person's self-concept and the dominant surrounding culture is predictive of their behavior and well-being (e.g., Leung & Cohen, 2011; Zhang & Noels, 2012). The culture has some coherence in that people in the culture are exposed to a similar set of messages through the media, the institutions they belong to, and the norms and practices that are common. It is important to remind yourself every now and then as you are reading that the cultural differences this book describes reflect general patterns of differences, and not all-or-none statements.

FIGURE 6.10 People vary in terms of how they respond to dominant cultural norms. Some wholeheartedly accept them, some actively resist them, and some instead embrace subcultural norms that are at odds with the dominant culture.

Gender and Culture

The constructs of independence and interdependence have been useful for under-standing cultural variation in psychological processes. Could they also be useful for understanding differences between men and women? Indeed, a number of researchers have concluded that the features of interdependent identities seem more characteristic of women than of men, and likewise, the features of independent identities seem more characteristic of men than of women (e.g., Bakan, 1966; Gilligan, 1977). Do you believe men think in ways that are more prototypical of Western cultures and women think more in ways prototypical of non-Western cultures? Rather than saying that women are from Venus and men are from Mars, should we instead be saying that women are from Asia and men are from America?

One study directly explored this question (Kashima et al., 1995). The researchers asked men and women in Western (the United States and Australia) and Eastern (Japan and Korea) cultures to complete a number of different measures of independence and interdependence. The researchers combined all the measures and statistically extracted the underlying factors of these measures. That is, they simplified the large number of different items from the various scales into four underlying measures. These underlying factors were labelled *collectivism* (Sample item: "I am prepared to do things for my group at any time, even though I have to sacrifice my own interest"), *agency* (Sample item: "I stick to my opinions even when others don't support me"), *assertiveness* (Sample item: "I assert my opposition when I disagree strongly with the members of my group"), and *relatedness* (Sample item: "I feel like doing something for people in trouble because I can almost feel their pain"). For all these factors there were significant cultural differences—namely, the Western cultures scored higher on agency and assertiveness whereas the Eastern cultures scored higher on collectivism and relatedness.

"You know, in some cultures the male does things."

The researchers also compared the genders on these measures. Significant gender differences emerged on only one factor: relatedness, in which women scored higher than men. There were no gender differences for collectivism, agency, or assertiveness. This suggests that it is not accurate to say that women are like Asians and men are like Americans. Women are apparently more interdependent than men only with respect to their attention to others' feelings and concerns. They do not appear to differ on the other factors associated with individualism/collectivism.

And what can we make of these gender differences? Are they, too, the result of particular cultural practices? Do women score higher on relatedness than men because cultural norms dictate that women should be socialized to be more attentive to their relations than men? Or, alternatively, do these gender differences transcend cultural explanations?

CULTURE AND GENDER EQUALITY. There are clear cultural differences in the ways people view issues of gender equality. People in some cultures believe that women should be treated the same as men; in others, people believe that men should be granted more rights, privileges, and power than women. For example, women represent only about 3% of elected officials in Arab nations, whereas they represent 45% of the Swedish parliament. In Brazil, approximately the same percentage of men and women are literate; in Pakistan, twice as many men as women are literate. In sum, although there are some similarities in how men and women are perceived across the world, there are marked differences in the equality of the opportunities that men and women have.

One study used the Sex Role Ideology (Kalin & Tilby, 1978) scale in 14 countries to investigate people's attitudes toward how men and women should act (Williams & Best, 1990). This inventory includes items that reflect "traditional" views on gender (Sample item: "For the good of the family, a wife should have sexual relations with her husband whether she wants to or not") and more "modern" or "egalitarian" views (Sample item: "Marriage should not interfere with a woman's career any more than it does with a man's"). Men and women from each culture answered the items on a scale that ranged from 1 (very traditional gender views) to 7 (very egalitarian gender views). The means for the different countries are presented in **Table 6.1**.

Several findings from this study are noteworthy. First, there are some strikingly different views toward gender equality around the world. In the Netherlands, Finland, and Germany, on average, people expressed views that men and women should be treated quite similarly. In contrast, in India, Pakistan, and Nigeria, people tended to believe that the roles, obligations, and rights of men and women are clearly different (with men being perceived to have more rights than women). Second, regardless of where the data were collected, within a culture, men and

TABLE 6.1

Mean scores on the sex role ideology scale

	Males	Females
Netherlands	5.47	5.72
Finland	5.30	5.69
Germany	5.35	5.62
England	4.73	5.15
Italy	4.54	4.90
Venezuela	4.51	4.90
United States	4.05	4.66
Canada	4.09	4.54
Malaysia	4.05	4.01
Singapore	3.61	4.39
Japan	3.70	4.01
India	3.81	3.88
Pakistan	3.34	3.30
Nigeria	3.11	3.39

Higher numbers represent more egalitarian gender attitudes, whereas lower numbers represent more traditional gender attitudes.

women tended to share fairly similar views about gender equality. For example, women in India, Pakistan, and Nigeria are more likely to embrace traditional gender attitudes than are women from European nations. This suggests that attitudes toward gender equality are part of the cultural discourse and shape people's views in those cultures. Third, in every case except for two nonsignificant reversals (i.e., Malaysia and Pakistan), males had significantly more traditional gender views than females—probably because traditional gender views benefit men more than women.

A number of other variables were included in the study to explore what features of a culture predicted egalitarian gender views. One variable that seemed to have a large impact on gender views was the percentage of people in the country who embraced a particular religion. Countries in which a large percentage of the population practiced Christianity, in particular Protestantism, were more likely to have egalitarian gender views, whereas countries with a large percentage of Muslims were associated with more traditional gender views. It is intriguing to note that the geographical location of the cultures was also associated with gender views, with more northern countries expressing more-egalitarian views, and more southern countries expressing more-traditional gender views (although the authors did not speculate on whether this was anything more than a coincidence). Also, the more urbanized the country, on average, the more likely people were to have egalitarian views. Last, the country's individualism score (obtained from Hofstede's data summarized in Figure 6.8) also correlated positively with egalitarian views. As these are correlational data, it is not clear whether these are causes of greater gender equality or consequences of it.

Another perspective offers a historical take on the origin of gender norms. As discussed in Chapter 3, cultural norms can often persist for long periods because new cultural developments must be fit in with the older norms. And gender norms have persisted across some cultures for centuries. So what can we trace their beginnings to? Economist Ester Boserup (1970) proposed that a seemingly simple cultural innovation in agriculture had far-reaching implications for gender norms. There are two key ways that traditional agricultural cultivation is generally conducted. One is termed "shifting cultivation," which, among other things, is characterized by the earth being dug up with a tool similar to a contemporary garden hoe. Where shifting cultivation is practiced, women do most of the agricultural work, which entails planting and weeding, with their children nearby. The other major cultivation method is called "plow cultivation," in which a large animal is used to pull the plow to turn over the soil (**Figure 6.11**). There are certain efficiencies associated with plow cultivation; however, controlling the plow requires much muscular strength and quick bursts of energy, which is why it tends to be done by men, with their greater average muscle mass. Moreover, it is difficult to take care of children when controlling the plow, because the work requires much concentration, it cannot be stopped and resumed easily, and it can put nearby children at risk. In contrast, with shifting cultivation it is possible to tend to the children while working. Because child care is undertaken more by women than

FIGURE 6.11 A man cultivating a field with a plow.

men around the world, shifting cultivation is more likely to be adopted by women and plow cultivation is more likely to be adopted by men. In many societies where plow cultivation is practiced, women do not participate much at all in the labor sphere but instead tend almost exclusively to domestic affairs. Boserup argued that even when a country moved out of agriculture into industrial endeavors it tended to preserve some of the gender norms associated with its traditional cultivation methods.

Recently, the economists Alberto Alesina, Paola Giuliano, and Nathan Nunn (2011) tested Boserup's thesis by exploring whether historical use of the plow in the 19th century (and earlier) predicted current attitudes about gender roles and female labor force participation around the world. Controlling for numerous relevant variables, they found that places that adopted the plow as a primary agricultural tool centuries earlier have less egalitarian gender norms and less female participation in the labor force today. Furthermore, the researchers also looked within the United States to examine the labor participation of women immigrants to the United States. The same pattern emerged: Those woman immigrants who came from regions where the plow was being used centuries earlier were less likely to be participating in the U.S. workforce. Thus, whether your distant ancestors tended to use a plow to raise their crops appears to have a curious influence on whether your own mother worked outside the home.

GENDER AND ESSENTIALISM. Another way to consider how culture influences people's perceptions of gender is to determine which gender identity is viewed to be more **essentialized** (i.e., it is thought to reflect an underlying unchangeable essence). Which gender do you think is more essentialized? That is, which gender do you think has less flexible ways of being expressed in socially approved ways? Take the case of American culture. Research suggests that Americans tend to view male gender identity to be more essentialized than female gender identity (e.g., Feinman, 1981). For example, most Americans do not seem to find it disturbing or unusual for women to present themselves like men (such as wearing pants, getting their hair cut short, or not wearing facial makeup) or to participate in stereotypically male behaviors (e.g., girls playing with trucks, or girls playing ice hockey). This suggests that Americans do not essentialize female gender identity to a great degree. In contrast, many Americans do find it disturbing or unusual for men to present themselves as women (such as wearing dresses, high-heeled shoes, or lipstick) or to participate in stereotypically female behaviors (e.g., boys playing with dolls, or boys taking ballet lessons). This suggests that Americans view male identity to be less changeable and thus more essentialized. In general, the gender that is associated with more power in a culture is the one that is more likely to be essentialized.

Mahalingam investigated the way Hindu Indians viewed gender identity. He noted that in Hindu myths, many more male gods change into female ones than female goddesses change into male gods (Mahalingam, 2003). Hindu religion involves goddess worship, and many of the most powerful gods are female (e.g., Shakti, Kali, Durga, Maya; see **Figure 6.12**). According to Hindu religion, female identity is viewed as pure,

FIGURE 6.12 A statue of the Hindu goddess Durga.

strong, and powerful. This suggests that Indians should be more likely to essentialize female identity than male identity. Mahalingam conducted a number of studies to investigate this. In one study he asked Indian participants to imagine that Kumar (a male) had his brain switched with Mina (a female; Mahalingam & Rodriguez, 2003). How would we then expect Kumar's and Mina's bodies to act? On average, Indians felt that Kumar's body would act more like a woman if it had Mina's brain in it. In contrast, on average, they felt that Mina's body would continue to act like a woman, even with Kumar's brain in it. That is, they felt that the male gender identity was more mutable, and less essentialized, than the female gender identity (also see Mahalingam, 2003).

In sum, perceptions of gender identity vary significantly across cultures. Although more cultures need to be investigated to reach firm conclusions, it appears that when females are viewed as more powerful, they also have more essentialized identities, whereas the reverse holds true where males are viewed as more powerful.

Some Other Ways that Cultures Differ in the Self-Concept

Although the field of cultural psychology dates back to the 19th century, it had little theoretical foundation to build on until Markus and Kitayama provided this distinction between independent and interdependent selves. In this section we consider how cultural differences in independent and interdependent self-concepts lead to other differences in ways of thinking about the self.

Self-Consistency

One important way that the self-concept shapes our psychology is in how we think and behave across different situations. Some people seem to act pretty much the same across all different situations. Whether they're with their friends at a bar, with their colleagues at work, or with their family at home, they seem to be acting basically the same. These people would score very high on a measure of self-consistency. Regardless of the situation they are in, they behave largely in the same way. Other people seem to act quite differently depending on whom they are with. They might appear quiet and respectful with their professors, outspoken and opinionated with their friends, and caring and doting toward their grandparents. These people would score rather low on self-consistency. Different aspects of their identities are much more salient in some situations than in others.

Cultures vary considerably in the degree to which individuals are motivated to be consistent across situations. For example, consider the results of the following study

(Kanagawa, Cross, & Markus, 2001). The researchers wanted to investigate the effect of context on the ways people view themselves. They designed a simple but elegant study. College students from Japan and the United States were asked to complete the Twenty-Statements Test like the one at the beginning of this chapter. Straightforward enough. However, the researchers manipulated a variable that is rarely considered by people who conduct questionnaire research—namely, the context the participants were in at the time of the study. The researchers specifically varied who was sitting near the students when they filled out the questionnaire. In one condition, students completed the questionnaire in a professor's office with the professor present. In another condition, students sat next to a fellow student when they answered the items. In a third condition, the students completed the questionnaire in a large group that consisted of about 20–50 people. Finally, in a fourth condition, the students completed the questionnaire alone in a room.

A person's self-descriptions can be summarized in a variety of ways. Let's focus here on how positively participants described themselves. The researchers coded each statement to see if it referred to a positive feature or a negative feature about the self. They then calculated the ratio of positive to negative statements that students made about themselves. The findings are shown in **Table 6.2**.

First, looking at Table 6.2, we can see that the American responses, on average, were far more positive than the Japanese ones. We'll explore this puzzling finding more in Chapter 8. Second, the American responses looked quite similar across the four conditions. Although their responses varied a little depending on what condition they had been assigned to, for the most part their responses appeared to be rather unaffected by the situation. In contrast, the Japanese responses varied considerably across situations. They were much less self-critical when they were by themselves than when they were with others, especially when they were with a professor. The general positivity of Japanese individuals' attitudes toward themselves appears to vary depending on who is in the room with them.

TABLE 6.2

Positivity of self-descriptions across contexts

	In Professor's Office	With Fellow Student	In a Large Group	Alone
American	3.77	3.26	3.30	3.22
Japanese	.35	.69	.50	1.19

The values in the table represent the ratio of the number of positive statements that participants used to describe themselves compared with the number of negative statements.

This pattern of results challenges an implicit methodological assumption made when studying people's personalities. In the past, there was little concern about the context in which personality measures were used. They were assumed to work well across time and situation, as they should if people's self-concept exists separately from their contexts. Although this might be true for the measurement of independent selves, the results of the Japanese sample here call this assumption into question. Depending on the context, the same question can yield quite different results (for further evidence of the context specificity of the East Asian self also see Cousins, 1989, and Oishi, Diener, Scollon, & Biswas-Diener, 2004). Furthermore, it's not at all clear *which* context provides the most accurate or self-defining results. Which could be called the true self—the one measured in the solitary context or the one measured with peers? How should we describe a Japanese individual's self-concept if it appears quite different depending on whom the person is sitting near at the time? Do we describe it as the average across the different situations? At present we don't have good answers to these questions, but they reveal just how much of a challenge it is to study the interdependent view of self. Given that the theories and methods used in psychology have largely emerged from the study of people with predominantly independent views of self, we need to be careful when we try to use them to study people with different views of self-concept.

How consistently people view themselves is thus important for both our methods and our theories. The motivation to be consistent has held a privileged place in social psychology. Leon Festinger, one of the most influential social psychologists of all time, saw this motivation as underlying what is, perhaps, social psychology's favorite theory: **cognitive dissonance**. Festinger (1957) proposed that we have a powerful motivation to be consistent and that cognitive dissonance is the distressing feeling we have when we observe ourselves acting inconsistently. This distressing sense is disturbing enough that we feel a great need to rid ourselves of it. One way to do so would be to start acting more consistently. But often that can be very difficult to do. Another strategy would be to change our attitudes so that we no longer appear to be so inconsistent. This latter strategy is known as *dissonance reduction*. The premium that is placed on acting consistently is evident in the great lengths people will sometimes go to in convincing themselves that their actions are consistent.

One way we can see our desire to avoid dissonance is when we make choices. Often when we are making choices we must choose between two or more alternatives that are quite similar in their desirability, such as between an iPhone and an Android phone—it's not always obvious what is the best choice to make. But after people make a choice they often experience dissonance, and they do so because there are features of the alternatives that are inconsistent with them having made the best choice. To reduce these unpleasant feelings, people will often rationalize their decisions, and they do so by starting to view the elements that are consistent with them making a good decision (i.e., the positive features of their chosen alternative, and the negative features of their rejected alternatives) as *more* important and the elements that are inconsistent with their decision (i.e., the negative features of their chosen alternative, and the positive features of their rejected alternatives) as *less* important. These rationalizations typically happen *after* someone has made their decision, because this is when the potential inconsistencies emerge.

Do people from different cultures show similar kinds of dissonance reduction tendencies when they make decisions? It would seem that if individuals are motivated to be consistent with their roles rather than with their internal attributes (such as their attitudes), dissonance would be a different issue for those with interdependent self-concepts. An inconsistency between one's decisions and one's attitudes would not be as urgently in need of resolution.

We conducted a study to compare dissonance reduction tendencies between Japanese and Canadians when they make choices (Heine & Lehman, 1997b). We had Japanese and Canadian participants rate a list of 10 music CDs in terms of their desirability. They were then asked a number of questions about those CDs, including the first half of our dependent measure: "How much would you like to own this CD?" Then participants were presented with two of those CDs (namely, their fifth- and sixth-ranked choices) and were told that they could take one of those home as compensation for their participation. So the participants had to make a choice between two CDs that they had, on average, rated to be similarly desirable. After they had made their choice, we investigated whether they had rationalized their decision. The participants were again asked to evaluate all 10 CDs by answering the same question about how much they would like to own each one. Participants' ratings of the CDs that they made *after* they had chosen their CD were compared with their ratings made *before* they had chosen their CD. If people are rationalizing their decisions, they should prefer their chosen CD even more and like their rejected CD even less after they have made their decisions. The bigger the change in their preferences, the more people are rationalizing their decisions.

Did people try to rationalize their decisions? The Canadians showed clear evidence that they were rationalizing their decisions. This Canadian pattern replicates much past work on dissonance (Brehm, 1956; Steele, Spencer, & Lynch, 1993), demonstrating how people (or North Americans, at least) engage in postdecision dissonance reduction. The Japanese results, however, were strikingly different. The Japanese participants showed no tendency to rationalize their decisions. They did not appear to have much motivation to ensure that their decisions were consistent (also see Kashima, Siegal, Tanaka, & Kashima, 1992).

But is it reasonable to claim that Japanese don't have motivations to be consistent? More recent work has identified some different kinds of motivations for consistency among East Asians. One study found that East Asians will rationalize decisions that they make for *others*, which suggests a motivation to have their behaviors be consistent with others' expectations (Hoshino-Browne et al., 2005). In that study, Japanese who ordered food from a restaurant for others to eat showed more rationalization than when they were just ordering food for themselves. The opposite pattern emerged for European-Canadians. Likewise, Japanese were found to rationalize their decisions when they consider the decisions they think others would make, which also suggests a motivation to be consistent with others' decisions (Kitayama, Snibbe, & Markus, 2004). These studies suggest that East Asians are not less consistent than North Americans but are consistent in different ways. North Americans appear to aspire for consistency within themselves, whereas East Asians are concerned with being consistent with others. Hence, there is a similarity across cultures in motivations to keep something consistent; however, what people try to keep consistent varies across cultures. These differences in the kinds of consistency that people pursue can have marked effects on their behaviors.

One way to see the effects of motivations for consistency on people's behaviors is to look at how these motivations affect people's responses to advertisers. Our desire to be consistent is something that advertisers or fund-raisers play on to encourage us to give them more of our money. For example, if you've ever agreed to contribute money to someone raising funds for a particular cause, you'll likely be reminded of your past contributions the next time the fund-raiser contacts you. By reminding you that "you've helped us out before," the fund-raiser is trying to push your "need for consistency" buttons. After all, if you're the kind of person who has given money to a charity in the past and if your attitudes haven't changed much since then, you should be prepared to contribute money to the organization the next time they contact you as well. If you give on one occasion but not the other, you're not being very consistent. Fund-raisers exploit our desire for consistency all the time, and the value of consistency to us is obvious if we're often willing to pay money to preserve it (see Freedman & Fraser, 1966, for a striking demonstration of this motivation).

However, if people with interdependent self-concepts are less motivated for consistency within themselves, they should be less affected by fund-raisers who remind them of their past behaviors. On the other hand, as we have noted, such people tend to be especially attentive to others. This orientation toward others suggests that they might be motivated to act in ways consistent with how others similar to themselves have acted.

One study investigated this hypothesis among samples from Poland and the United States (Cialdini, Wosinka, Barrett, Butner, & Gornik-Durose, 1999). Although perhaps not as collectivistic as cultures in East Asia and Latin America, Poland is considerably more collectivistic than the United States (Reykowski, 1994). The authors hypothesized that this cultural difference should lead Poles to be more affected by trying to be consistent with how others have behaved, and Americans to be more affected by trying to be consistent with how they themselves have behaved in the past. Participants were asked to imagine how they would respond to a request by a marketing representative from Coca-Cola to take part in a survey about their beverage preferences. The kind and amount of consistency was varied across conditions. In a *self-consistency* condition, participants were asked to imagine that in the past they had always complied with similar requests. In a *peer-consistency* condition, participants were asked to imagine that their classmates always complied with similar requests. The dependent measure of this study was how likely participants thought they themselves would be to comply with the marketing representative's request.

The pattern of results nicely captured the authors' hypotheses. Looking at **Figure 6.13** we can see that the Americans were more influenced than the Poles by the information about their past performance. If Americans felt they had complied with these kinds of requests in the past, they assumed that they would be consistent and comply with them again. In contrast, the Poles were more influenced by the information about what their classmates had done. If their classmates had complied with these kinds of requests, Poles assumed that they would be consistent with their classmates' behaviors and comply as well. This suggests that marketers and fund-raisers in different cultures need to adopt different strategies to have maximal influence.

As much research has demonstrated, then, people with independent views of self are motivated to be consistent across situations. Why should people differ in their need to be consistent? Not all human behaviors are rational or necessarily functional within their cultures; however, when researchers are trying to understand why people behave in the ways they do, a good place to start is often to assume that people's behaviors are functional. This reasoning would suggest that people with independent views of themselves must realize some benefits when they act consistently. What are the favorable outcomes associated with acting consistently, and are these outcomes distributed equally across cultures?

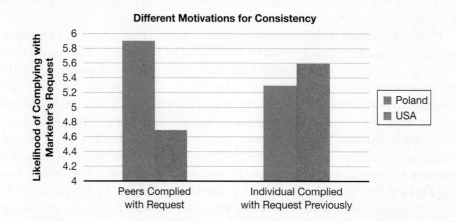

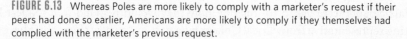

FIGURE 6.13 Whereas Poles are more likely to comply with a marketer's request if their peers had done so earlier, Americans are more likely to comply if they themselves had complied with the marketer's previous request.

These questions were investigated in a cross-cultural study (Suh, 2002). Koreans and Americans were compared with regard to their self-consistency. This was accomplished by asking people to indicate how well a list of traits characterized them in a number of different situations—for example, when they were with their friends, with their families, with a professor, or by themselves. A consistency coefficient was calculated for each individual, which revealed how similarly people viewed themselves across the different situations. Not surprisingly, given what we learned in the study that compared self-descriptions across the contexts in which they were written (Kanagawa et al., 2001), Koreans viewed themselves as far less similar across situations than Americans did.

The participants were also asked to complete a measure of their subjective well-being, which indicates how satisfied people are with their lives. Moreover, two informants (one friend and one family member) of each participant were asked to evaluate the participant in two ways: First, they were asked how socially skilled they thought the participant was. Second, they were asked how likable they thought the participant was. The individual's consistency coefficients were then correlated with both their well-being scores and the evaluations of the informants. The results are shown in **Table 6.3**. For Americans, there were strong positive correlations between consistency and each of the other variables. Likewise, other research has found that being consistent across situations was associated with higher feelings of authenticity for European-Americans but not for East Asians (English & Chen, 2011). Apparently, there are clear benefits in the United States for being consistent. People feel better about themselves if they see themselves as consistent, they feel authentic, and other people view them to be especially socially skilled and likable. Consistency has its rewards in the United States. Some of those rewards are evident in presidential elections, where the respective campaigns invariably criticize each other for appearing inconsistent (see **Figure 6.14**).

In contrast, in this study Koreans realized few benefits for being consistent. The correlations between consistency and the other desirable qualities were much smaller for the Korean sample. Being consistent in Korea is not associated as strongly with feeling good about oneself (see Campbell et al., 1996, for similar findings with Japanese) or with being perceived as especially socially skilled or likable. Koreans are likely less consistent across situations than Americans because there are fewer benefits in Korea for viewing oneself consistently in this way. We would expect just such a pattern when we consider the importance of adhering to the requirements of one's roles in an interdependent cultural context.

TABLE 6.3

Cross-cultural comparison of correlations with self-consistency.

	USA	Korea
Correlation with well-being	.44	.19
Correlation with social skills	.37	.12
Correlations with likability	.33	-.02

FIGURE 6.14 A common accusation in American presidential debates is that one's opponent is not acting consistently.

However, it is important to note that this documented tendency for East Asians to be less consistent across situations compared with Westerners does *not* mean that East Asians are unpredictable. East Asians do show much self-consistency; however, it is a different kind of consistency than that typically observed among Westerners. Although East Asians may feel differently about themselves *across* contexts, such as when they are with family compared with when they are with friends, they do show much consistency across time *within* each of these relationships (see English & Chen, 2007, 2011). Their "son self" remains fairly constant across their lifespan, as does their "drinking buddy self." Hence, the East Asian self-concept might best be characterized by an "if-then" profile, in which "if" refers to the relational context and "then" refers to the habitual way of thinking about oneself. For example, if Ben is with his parents, then he is highly diligent and eager to fulfill his obligations. It is a self-concept that remains stable across time (similar to Westerners); however, unlike that of Westerners, it varies across relationship contexts.

Self-Awareness

The self is a unique entity because it can be considered from two very different vantage points. On the one hand, we can consider ourselves from the perspective of the subject—that is, the "I" that observes and interacts with the world. When we take this perspective we are in a state of **subjective self-awareness**. In this state, our concerns are with the world outside of ourselves, and we are largely unaware of ourselves. Our attention is directed away from ourselves, from the inside out. This is the state that we are in when we are an audience member and our awareness is directed to the stage. On the other hand, we can consider ourselves from the perspective of an object, the same way that we perceive the rest of the world. That is, the self can be experienced as the "me" that is observed and interacted with by others. When we adopt this perspective, we are in a state of **objective self-awareness**. In this state, our concerns are directed specifically at ourselves, from the outside in. We are conscious of how we are being seen and evaluated by others.

How might we expect culture to affect people's self-awareness? Well, it would seem that individuals who have more of an interdependent view of self would tend to focus more on monitoring their sense of belongingness and connection with others than do those with more independent views of self. Indeed, if one is considering whether one is fitting in with others, one must take the perspective of an object and think about how others are viewing oneself: "Did I just offend Ravinder?" "Andres seems to like my sense of humor," and so on. In other words, interdependent individuals should be more likely to be considering themselves from the point of view of an audience. Is this really the case?

There are a few ways that we might expect cultural differences in self-awareness to emerge. First, consider how people would think about themselves if they were adopting an objective, outside-in perspective as opposed to a subjective, inside-out perspective of the self. If one is trying to fit in with others, or trying to meet the expectations of others, it would follow that their thoughts about themselves (e.g., "What kind of person am I?") would be guided by how they think *other* people are viewing them. For example, imagine that I believe that other people think that I am rude, and if I am in a state of objective self-awareness, then I should come to think of myself as rude as well. My self-views should be guided by impressions of how others view me. On the other hand, if I am in a state of subjective self-awareness, my thoughts about myself should be less affected by what I believe others might think about me.

Research has demonstrated that East Asians and Westerners do differ in their thoughts about themselves precisely along these lines. Consider the following experiment (Kim, Cohen, & Au, 2010). Hong Kong and American university students completed a bogus projective creativity test that was to be graded by a computer. The participants were told that two kinds of software would evaluate their performance: One was a program that had been well validated and the other was a newer program that had yet to be validated. The participants thus received two separate creativity scores, although, unbeknownst to the participants, everyone actually received the same two scores: one indicating that they had aced the task, and the other one indicating that their performance was only average. It wasn't clear which program yielded which score, so the participants were left with a rather ambiguous set of evaluations of their work. Then, through an elaborately staged ruse, one of their scores was accidentally revealed to a confederate who was pretending to be another participant. So the participants knew that one other person had seen one of their scores, and they knew which score the other person had seen. Later, the participants evaluated their own creativity levels. As shown in **Figure 6.15**, a striking pattern emerged: For the American participants, their self-evaluations were relatively unaffected by whether they thought another person had seen either their good score or their average score. This is consistent with them taking an inside-out perspective; they evaluated themselves based on their own subjective standards. In contrast, the Hong Kong participants' self-evaluations were affected by their knowledge of what another person knew about their performance. If their good score was seen by the other person, then participants evaluated their performance more positively; if their average score was seen by the other person, then participants evaluated their performance more negatively. The Hong Kong participants' self-evaluations appear to be the product of what they think others (in this case, a single other who is a stranger) think of them. Likewise, Asian-Americans have been shown to be more influenced by information about themselves if they believe that this is information is possessed by others (Kim & Cohen, 2010). This is evidence of them taking an outside-in perspective regarding themselves.

Here's another way that one's state of self-awareness can affect how one thinks: Remember back to a time when you were the center of attention. For example, think back to your high school graduation when you received your diploma in front of the

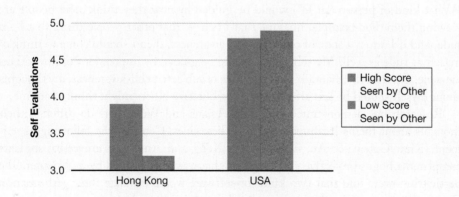

FIGURE 6.15 Whereas American self-evaluations were largely unaffected by whether someone else thought they had done well or had done poorly, Chinese self-evaluations were more positive when someone else thought they had done well rather than poorly.

whole auditorium. Think carefully about the image that comes to your mind about this event. Now, I'd like you to evaluate the imagery in your memory. One way that you might have conjured up this memory is from the perspective that you had as a subject at that time. That is, you could remember the images that you saw with your eyes as you walked up the stage, walked over to your principal, took the diploma that she handed to you, turned to the audience, and then walked off the other side of the stage. This kind of memory is called a "first-person" memory, because it contains the imagery that you experienced firsthand. Another way that you might recall your high school graduation is from the perspective of the audience. That is, you might recall seeing yourself walk up to the stage and over to the principal, receive your diploma from her, and then walk off the other side. Of course, this imagery was never available to you firsthand. To the extent that you have this kind of memory, it suggests that you were attending a lot to how you thought people in the audience were viewing you. Your thoughts of their perceptions leak into your own memory, providing you with some "third-person" imagery. Is the imagery from your memories of your high school graduation more consistent with a first-person perspective or a third-person perspective?

In one study, Asian-Canadians and European-descent-Canadians were contrasted on this kind of question (Cohen & Gunz, 2002). When controlling for the amount of imagery that people had for memories when they were *not* the center of attention (in which no one, interdependent or independent, should be taking on the perspective of the audience because the audience was not watching them), the Asian-Canadians revealed significantly more third-person imagery in their memories of being at the center of attention than did the Euro-Canadians across a variety of different situations (also see Grossmann & Kross, 2010, for related effects comparing Russians and Americans). These findings suggest that Asian-Canadians are so habitually considering the perspective of significant others that they start to see themselves in their mind's eye in terms of how they think they appear to others! And someone who is used to taking the perspective of others can actually become more skilled at imagining scenes as observed by someone who is in a different position. Asian-Americans have been shown to be better than Euro-Americans at imagining what is being seen in the mind's eye of others (see Wu & Keysar, 2007).

Another curious consequence associated with the perspective that one is taking about oneself is the accuracy of one's self-views. Who has the most accurate perspective of an individual? On the one hand, you might think that the most accurate assessment of an individual would be one made by the person who knows the individual the best—that is, the self. Indeed, the self is privy to a lifetime of experiences and private thoughts that others don't have. On the other hand, other people might have a more objective view about a target person. As we'll see in more in Chapter 8, people are motivated to view themselves in certain ways, which can often distort the accuracy of their self-assessments. Hence, assessments made by others might be more accurate because they would be less distorted by the ways that people *want* to view themselves.

Indeed, research with Americans has found, curiously, that although people are quite accurate in their judgments about the ways that others will behave, their judgments about how they themselves will behave is often not so accurate (Epley & Dunning, 2000). People seem to see themselves in ways that they would like to see themselves, whereas they see others in a more detached and objective way.

Are people with interdependent selves more accurate in their self-views? One study explored this question by examining the predictions made by children attending a summer school in Mallorca, Spain (Balcetis, Dunning, & Miller, 2008). The children came from several different countries, and these countries were divided into those that were primarily individualistic or primarily collectivistic. They were asked to complete a number of tasks, including one in which they were asked to imagine that they had been rewarded for their efforts by receiving 10 pieces of candy. They were asked to imagine that other students didn't perform as well as them and didn't receive as many pieces of candy, and that they could contribute some of their own candy to a common pool that would be shared with those other students. They were asked to predict how many candies they would give if they were in this hypothetical situation. Five days later, the children actually found themselves in this same situation, when they received 10 candies for their effort on a new task and were given the opportunity to contribute some to a common pool to be distributed to others. The researchers compared the children's earlier predictions with their actual donations. The children from individualistic cultures donated fewer candies than they had earlier predicted that they would, whereas the children from collectivistic cultures donated about the same number of candies as they had earlier predicted. The collectivistic children thus had made predictions for their future behavior that turned out to be more accurate than the individualistic ones, which is what one would expect if the collectivistic children were taking more of an objective perspective of themselves. Other studies revealed similar effects (Balcetis et al., 2008).

Much research on self-awareness, conducted with Westerners, has focused on how people's self-awareness can be changed by putting them in front of certain stimuli. For example, when people hear their own voices on an audiotape, see a video camera directed at them, or see themselves in a mirror, they are more likely to be in a state of objective self-awareness (Duval & Wicklund, 1972; see **Figure 6.16**). This research has shown that there are a number of predictable responses that Westerners show when they are put in a state of objective self-awareness. For example, they come to view themselves more self-critically as they become aware of how they might be falling short of their standards (e.g., Ickes, Wicklund, & Ferris, 1973). This is because people tend to be very critical when they are adopting the perspective of an audience, because they take on the role of the judge. And, as the judge, they tend to be fairly critical because they're always able to conjure up standards to compare themselves with that are higher than their current levels of performance.

If people with interdependent selves are chronically considering themselves from the perspective of an audience, what would happen if they encountered stimuli that

FIGURE 6.16 When people see themselves in a mirror, or hear their voices on a recording, they are more likely to be in a state of objective self-awareness and consider themselves in terms of how they are perceived by others.

put them in a state of objective self-awareness, such as being placed in front of a mirror? It would seem that seeing themselves in a mirror should have little impact on their self-perceptions because they are likely already in a state of objective self-awareness. We set out to test this hypothesis (Heine, Takemoto, Moskalenko, Lasaleta, & Henrich, 2008). Japanese and American students were either placed in front of a mirror or not, and were then asked to evaluate themselves on a measure of actual-ideal self-discrepancies. That is, they were asked to evaluate their actual selves and to evaluate the kind of person that they would ideally like to be. The magnitude of the discrepancy between these two self-evaluations indicates how self-critical individuals are feeling. The results (see **Figure 6.17**) showed that Americans became significantly more self-critical in front of a mirror than they were when no mirror was present. This finding replicates previous findings with Americans (Ickes et al., 1973). In contrast, Japanese were unaffected by the mirror. Regardless of whether they were viewing themselves in a mirror and seeing how they appear to the world or they were just thinking about themselves the way they typically do, they evaluated themselves in the same way. Apparently, the habitual self-view of Japanese is very similar to the perspective that they have in front of a mirror. It is perhaps also telling that Japanese and American self-discrepancies look quite similar when they are in front of a mirror.

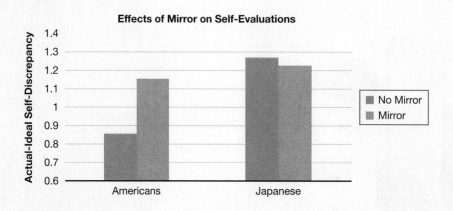

FIGURE 6.17   Whereas Americans are more self-critical when they are in front of a mirror than when they are not, Japanese self-evaluations are unaffected by the presence of a mirror.

When Americans are considering themselves as an object, as when they are in front of a mirror, they appear to be thinking thoughts about themselves that are similar to those the Japanese are, with or without a mirror.

Implicit Theories Regarding the Nature of the Self

The nature of our self-concept is shaped by our implicit theories about it. Implicit theories guide our interpretation of much of what happens in the world. For example, you might believe that it's dangerous to walk through a particular neighborhood by yourself late at night because of your belief that much violence occurs there, especially to solo pedestrians in the dark. Or you might believe that if you're on a date, you'll make a more favorable impression if you don't wear your rattiest pair of sneakers, because you believe that people on dates evaluate each other based on the clothes they are wearing. These theories are implicit in the sense that they represent a set of beliefs we take for granted, usually without engaging in much active hypothesis testing. Implicit theories are a great place to explore cultural influences on psychology because they reflect the beliefs that people have. In a number of significant domains in life the theories people have about the way things work can vary substantially across cultures (e.g., Chiu, Dweck, Tong, & Fu, 1997).

One kind of implicit theory is about the nature of our selves. For example, we might believe that our self-concepts are largely in flux and respond to the efforts we make. The belief that we can easily change, and are expected to change, is referred to as an **incremental theory of self** (e.g., Dweck & Leggett, 1988). This theory of self represents the belief that a person's abilities and traits are malleable and can be improved. The attributes that one possesses (for example, one's soccer-playing skill, one's extraversion, or one's intelligence) are not seen to remain constant across one's life but are perceived as reflecting how hard one has worked on them.

In contrast to this view, one could instead embrace a theory that aspects of the self are largely resistant to change, which is known as an **entity theory of self**. People who endorse this set of beliefs tend to view their abilities and traits as largely fixed, innate features of the self. Individuals with this view see their attributes to be largely inborn. As they get older, their attributes are viewed to stay largely the same. Which of these two implicit theories of the self best captures your own views?

Whether individuals possess more incremental theories or more entity theories for a given domain in life can have a large impact on the efforts they make. If people hold an incremental theory about intelligence, they will tend to think that how intelligent they are is due to how much they study. Studying hard is believed to make one more intelligent. The implication of embracing such a theory of intelligence is that if they aren't satisfied with their intelligence, they must not have made enough effort. People with incremental theories about intelligence should thus be strongly motivated to study hard, especially when their grades aren't as good as they want. There is always room for improvement if people hold incremental theories.

Entity theories, in contrast, suggest that aspects of the self reflect an essence of the individual—an essence that remains largely removed from the efforts a person makes. If people's attributes are stable over their lifetime and reflect self-defining characteristics, they should be less inclined to view their attributes as the products of their efforts. Indeed, to the extent that a person strongly embraces an entity theory of self, making continued efforts can suggest a problem. It might suggest that an individual's innate abilities are not adequate and that efforts are needed to compensate for them. People with entity theories of self should thus not make many efforts in the face of failure.

Much research has demonstrated that people holding an incremental theory of self respond to difficulties differently from those holding an entity theory of self. For example, when people embracing an entity theory of intelligence encounter a failure, they are more likely to blame their static intellectual ability. People with more incremental theories, in contrast, respond to failures by focusing on their efforts and the strategies they utilized (Henderson & Dweck, 1990). Also, people who are having trouble in their classes are more likely to take remedial courses if they embrace incremental theories of self than if they tend to favor entity theories (Hong, Chiu, Dweck, Lin, & Wan, 1999). If your abilities are a function of your efforts, it makes sense to increase your efforts when you're not doing well enough.

People from different cultures do indeed appear to differ in the extent to which they embrace incremental views of self. In *The Analects* (Slingerland, 2003), Confucius stated that "by nature people are similar; they diverge as the result of practice," reflecting the incremental view that individual differences are more the product of what people do (e.g., how much they study) rather than of their innate differences (see **Figure 6.18**). And there is much evidence that North Americans are less likely to hold an incremental view than people from some Asian cultures (e.g., Heine et al., 2001b; Norenzayan, Choi, & Nisbett, 2002; Rattan, Savani, Naidu, & Dweck, 2012). This makes sense when you consider the cultural differences in the consistency of the self that we discussed earlier. If your self varies from situation to situation, it seems unlikely that you would embrace an entity theory. These cultural differences are evident when you ask people to think about what leads to certain abilities. For example, more than 60% of Chinese high school students said that the key to success in math was to study hard. In contrast, less than 25% of American high school students felt this way (Stevenson & Stigler, 1992). Likewise, Japanese believe more than Americans that intelligence is based on how hard you try, rather than on what you are born with (Heine et al., 2001b). Compared with Americans, Indians are more likely to believe that almost everyone could become highly intelligent (Rattan et al., 2012). Moreover, when Americans are led to believe that high intelligence is attainable for a larger portion of the population,

FIGURE 6.18 People with more incremental views of self are more likely to see intelligence as the product of their efforts rather than as something that is innate.

they become more supportive of government policies to distribute rewards more equally between advantaged and disadvantaged groups (Rattan et al., 2012).

Given this pattern of cultural differences between various countries in Asia and North America, it might not be surprising to learn that different kinds of exams are given in the two cultures. To get into a good American university you typically need to get an acceptable score on the SAT. The SAT was originally designed to measure innate aptitudes and not efforts in one's classes. (It turns out that studying hard can increase one's SAT scores significantly. This has been a source of frustration for the test-makers, because the tests are no longer serving the function they were originally designed for, which has sparked much policy debate about their utility.) Also, IQ tests are regularly given in public schools in the states, and the results influence decisions on whether students should attend gifted or remedial classes. In contrast, in Japan, to get into a good university you need to do well on a university entrance exam that tests your mastery of a large amount of material (a sample question might be "Who built the Suez Canal and when?"). Successful performance on these tests is viewed to be largely due to how hard one studies for them. It is not unusual for students to spend much of their time in high school, and one or more years after graduation, attending cram schools to help them master the material. Furthermore, IQ test results are not given out in public schools, and teachers are averse to discussing differences in abilities among students (Tobin, Wu, & Davidson, 1989).

In addition to the different kinds of content that make up exams, the difficulty of exams may also vary based on whether a culture is operating more under an incremental model or more under an entity model. The Japanese bar exam for becoming a lawyer is notoriously difficult. Only 2.5% of people pass it each year, and those who do, on average, have failed the exam four times before ultimately succeeding (Hashimoto, 2007). In contrast, approximately two-thirds of those taking the American bar exam each year pass it, with about three-quarters of them passing it on their first attempt (National Conference of Bar Examiners, 2010). The people who make the exams can largely determine the passing rate by varying the exam's difficulty, and it's clear that the Japanese bar examiners are expecting most students to fail the exam the first time and to spend additional years studying after their first failure in order to improve their scores. In contrast, the American bar examiners have designed the exam so that most people pass it the first time and do not need to work at improving their scores. Japanese exam-makers thus appear to be operating more under an incremental theory than the American ones.

The various kinds of exams given in Japan and the United States reflect and sustain the different kinds of implicit theories of intelligence that people in these countries have. The different ways that we educate people shape the theories that people hold about the nature of intelligence; likewise, the theories that we have shape the decisions that our schools make for educating people. This is one way that we can see the mutual influence of cultural practices (such as entrance exams) and psychological processes (such as implicit theories of intelligence).

Personality

It goes without saying that people are different. Here, I'm not referring to the systematic differences that exist across cultures—the focus of much of this chapter. Rather, I'm referring to the obvious fact that people in any given culture differ from their compatriots in many important ways. For example, even though Barack Obama and Mitt Romney are similar in that they both were highly accomplished men trying to be elected president of the United States, in many ways, as repeatedly emphasized in their respective presidential campaigns, they have strikingly different personalities. The ways that people are different from each other have been a primary concern of the field of personality psychology.

One key approach in personality psychology has been to describe people in terms of underlying personality traits. There is no shortage of terms that can be used to describe people like Barack Obama or Mitt Romney (and they might not always be nice ones!), or anyone else you know. Indeed, by one count, there are approximately 18,000 personality trait words in the English language (Allport & Odbert, 1936). Some of these terms are probably familiar to you (e.g., *outgoing, conservative*), whereas others are probably not (e.g., *accrescent, vulnific*). We thus have a very rich vocabulary for categorizing people according to personality.

Many personality typologies have been proposed around the world that serve to classify people into different types. For example, the Roman physician Galen proposed that there were four basic types of human temperaments that depended on the balance of the four fluids, or humors, present in the body: blood, yellow bile, phlegm, and black bile. Ayurvedic medicine from India proposes that there are three metabolic body types, thus maintaining that one's metabolism rate provides the foundation of individual temperaments. A question asked by Japanese that often surprises Westerners is about their blood type, as the four blood types are perceived to underlie reliable differences in personality in Japan. In short, across cultures and history, people have come up with a remarkably diverse array of ways for explaining people's personalities.

The Five Factor Model of Personality

The approach most widely accepted by personality psychologists to view the different kinds of personality traits is the **Five Factor Model of personality,** or the "Big Five" (McCrae & Costa, 1987) although this model does have its critics; e.g., Block, 1995; McAdams, 1992). According to this model, there are five underlying personality traits, or "core traits." If you would attempt to measure people's personalities by use of any substantial list of personality traits (an extreme example would be the nearly 18,000 traits identified by Allport and Odbert), you would find a great deal of overlap among many of the traits, allowing the list to be reduced to a much smaller number. One reason for the overlap is that many trait terms are synonyms (e.g., shy, introverted, quiet) and likely do not reflect independent traits. Also, we could simplify our list of personality traits much further by noting how many seemingly distinct-sounding personality traits tend to have substantial correlations with other traits. For example, people who are more authoritarian in their personalities also tend to be more religious, conventional, and dogmatic; they tend to have negative attitudes toward obesity and homosexuality; and they tend to be less gregarious and less open to aesthetics and ideas (Butler, 2000). Because these traits correlate with each other, they cannot be said to represent independent traits.

Factor analysis is a technique used to identify groups of things that are alike or different. As an example, consider what kinds of athletic talents are needed in order to do well at a decathlon competition. The decathlon consists of 10 events, so to do well, it would seem that one would need to have 10 skills that are unique to those 10 events. But are all those skills so unique? Could we instead reduce those 10 skills to a smaller number? For example, the decathlon includes the 100-meter sprint and the 110-meter hurdles. Both of these events require speed. Likewise, the decathlon includes both the discus throw and the shot put, both of which require upper-body strength. If we did a similar analysis for all the sports in the decathlon, we might be able to identify some underlying "factors," such as speed and upper-body strength, that could predict how well one would do on all 10 events. Rather than needing to identify skills for all 10 events, then, we might be able to predict someone's performance in the decathlon by identifying only a few underlying skills. Factor analysis is the technique that allows us to do this. It can simplify a long list of items into a much shorter list of underlying factors by investigating the patterns of correlations among the various items.

In the case of personality testing, factor analysis has been used to reduce the great number of personality traits to a much more manageable number. Specifically, in the Five Factor Model, there are only five underlying personality traits: **Openness to experience** reflects a person's intelligence and curiosity about the world. **Conscientiousness** indicates how responsible and dependable an individual is. **Extraversion** indicates how much an individual is active or dominant. **Agreeableness** is the extent to which a person tends to be warm and pleasant. Last, **neuroticism** is the degree to which an individual can be seen as emotionally unstable and unpredictable. These five traits (which can be remembered by the acronym OCEAN) are argued to be fundamental traits because they can't be reduced to a smaller number (i.e., the five factors are largely uncorrelated with each other).

The Five Factor Model proposes that all personality traits largely reflect some combination of these five core traits. That is, all personality traits should show significant correlations with at least one, if not more, of these core traits. To the extent that a personality trait consistently fails to correlate with any of the core traits, it would suggest that this trait itself is an additional core trait (if so, we would then have the Six Factor Model). However, this is not to say that there is nothing more to any specific personality trait than some combination of the Big Five core traits. For example, although a sense of humor correlates positively with extraversion and not with any of the other Big Five traits, there likely is something about a sense of humor that goes well beyond just extraversion (Saucier & Goldberg, 1998). Hence, the five factors can be seen to reflect the basic structure of personality, although there are some subtle, yet important, ways that individual traits can lie beyond this basic structure.

The idea that much of what entails personality can largely be understood by five factors is an important one, and it has led to much speculation about how well this model would generalize elsewhere. Do you think the five-factor structure is something basic about human nature, something that we should find in the personalities of people in all cultures that we examine? Can human personality be largely captured by these five specific traits? Alternatively, do you think the Five Factor Model reflects ideas about personhood that are limited to the West, where the bulk of this research has been conducted? A number of large and costly research projects have been launched to explore this fundamental question.

A questionnaire that measures the Big Five, the Revised Neuroticism, Extraversion, and Openness Personality Inventory (which goes by the catchy acronym of the NEO-PI-R; Costa & McCrae, 1992) has been distributed to thousands of people in dozens of cultures around the world. In one study, people from 50 different cultures used this scale to evaluate people that they know (McCrae et al., 2005b). The scale was translated into the local languages of the respective cultures. In all 50 cultures, people's responses organized themselves along the five factors, just as they do among Americans, for whom the scale was originally developed. Likewise, a number of other investigations have used the NEO-PI-R to have people evaluate themselves in many different cultures (Allik & McCrae, 2004; Yik, Russell, Ahn, Fernandez-Dols, & Suzuki, 2002). These studies have largely revealed a similar pattern of results: Around the world people seem to think of themselves and others in terms of the same five basic personality traits. Moreover, in dozens of countries around the world people's personality seems to mature in rather similar ways, with people tending to become more agreeable, more conscientious, and less neurotic as they age (Bleidorn et al., 2013). Human nature appears to be such that personality traits organize themselves into five distinct clusters.

However, there are some limitations to this conclusion. First, one could raise the question of whether the Five Factor Model provides sufficient coverage to capture all the personality variation in the world. The cross-cultural research discussed above has shown that personality as measured by the same scale, the NEO-PI-R, has the same basic five dimensions everywhere. However, the NEO-PI-R was developed through the exploration of English personality terms, largely with Americans. Would we expect the same pattern to emerge if, in contrast, questionnaires were developed from trait terms that were derived from different languages and from different cultures? Do the Big Five personality dimensions emerge regardless of what traits one considers, or do they arise from the kinds of personality traits that are discussed in English?

A number of investigations have explored this question. An analysis of indigenous Chinese personality trait terms (Cheung et al., 1996) found a set of factors that were not the same as the Big Five; rather, four factors emerged that were captured by the following labels: dependability (reflecting responsibility, optimism, and trustworthiness), interpersonal relatedness (reflecting harmony, thrift, relational orientation, and tradition), social potency (reflecting leadership, adventurousness, and extraversion), and individualism (reflecting logical orientation, defensiveness, and self-orientation). Moreover, these researchers explored whether the four Chinese personality traits were similar to those from the Five Factor Model (Cheung, Cheung, Leung, Ward, & Leong, 2003). That analysis revealed substantial overlap between three of the factors; namely, neuroticism correlated with dependability, extraversion correlated with social potency, and individualism correlated with agreeableness. Openness to experience did not correlate with any of the Chinese factors (this factor is the least reliably found of the five factors), and interpersonal relatedness was uncorrelated with any of the Big Five factors. This suggests that interpersonal relatedness might be a sixth personality factor that is especially salient in Chinese culture. Whether interpersonal relatedness is a reliable sixth factor in Western samples has yet to be demonstrated.

Similar approaches have been taken in other cultures. An indigenous list of Filipino personality traits was developed and the underlying factors were explored through factor analysis (Church, Reyes, Katigbak, & Grimm, 1997; Church, Katigbak, & Reyes, 1998). This analysis revealed five traits that were highly similar to the Big Five; however, it revealed two additional factors—temperamentalness and a negative valence dimension—that did not correlate strongly with any of the Big Five. Similarly, an investigation of 11 different language groups in South Africa revealed nine underlying factors, some of which overlapped with the Big Five, but other factors, such as integrity, and relationship harmony, did not (Nel et al., 2012). Studies of other languages tend to also capture some additional factors to the Big Five (Benet-Martinez & Waller, 1995, 1997; Saucier, Georgiades, Tsaousis, & Goldberg, 2005). Moreover, whereas some studies conducted in other languages reveal evidence for factors in addition to the Big Five, other studies sometimes do not find evidence for all five of the Big Five traits (DeRaad et al., 2010)—in particular, openness to experience is the trait that emerges the least consistently in studies conducted in other languages (e.g., Di Blas & Forzi, 1998; Szirmák & De Raad, 1994). In general, such investigations reveal that although the Five Factor Model does appear to be fairly cross-culturally robust, it does not seem to provide an exhaustive list of personality traits in other cultures. When personality structures are explored with indigenous personality terms, some additional dimensions emerge.

One other limitation to the conclusion that the Five Factor Model is a universal description of human personality is to note that the vast majority of the studies have explored it in WEIRD samples. What would personality look like if rather than studying large industrialized populations of students, you instead looked at subsistence societies around the world? For example, one study measured the personality of a large number of the Tsimane, a forager-horticultural group living in the Bolivian Amazon, using a modified interview measure of the Five Factor Model (Gurven, von Rueden, Massenkoff, Kaplan, & Vie, 2013;

FIGURE 6.19   A group of Tsimane women and their children.

see **Figure 6.19**). In general, it produced very little evidence in support of the Big Five—the individual items did not correlate well with each other to form distinct traits, and the Tsimane appeared to have personality that was explained better by just two personality factors—neither of which approximated any of the Big Five. Other studies with nonindustrialized populations have similarly found that the individual items do not cohere as well to form clear traits compared with WEIRD samples (e.g., Alvergne, Jokela, & Lummaa, 2010; Piedmont, Bain, McCrae, & Costa, 2002; McCrae et al., 2005b). It's possible that the weaker support for the Five Factor Model in nonindustrialized cultures is the result of the participants being less familiar with answering questions in this format, distorting our ability to see the underlying factors. More research with other subsistence populations and with different kinds of methods is needed to draw firmer conclusions about the generalizability of the Five Factor Model outside of WEIRD societies.

Given that the evidence that the structure of personality is reasonably similar across a broad array of cultures, researchers have begun to compare mean levels of personality traits across cultures. For example, one investigation has uncovered different personality regions within the United States: The north central Great Plains, especially around Minnesota and Wisconsin, is the epicenter for a Friendly

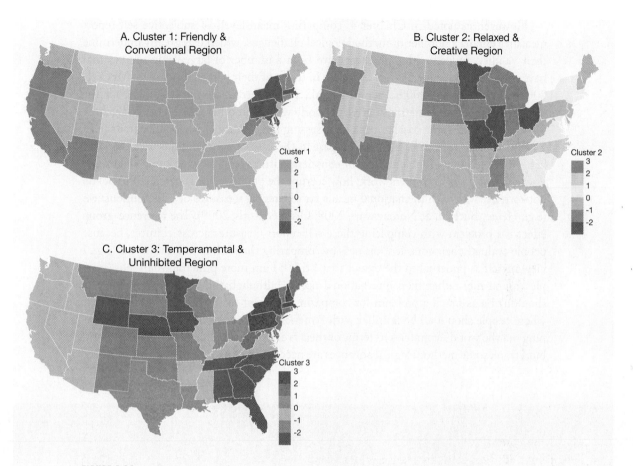

A. Cluster 1: Friendly &
Conventional Region

B. Cluster 2: Relaxed &
Creative Region

C. Cluster 3: Temperamental &
Uninhibited Region

FIGURE 6.20 Different clusters of personality traits exist across the continental United States.

and Conventional cluster, as residents are the highest in the country for the traits of extraversion, agreeableness, and conscientiousness (see **Figure 6.20**); the Western states, from Oregon down through to Arizona, house the Relaxed and Creative Cluster, where there is the lowest Neuroticism and the highest openness to experience; and the Northeastern states, especially New York and Massachusetts, are home to the Temperamental and Uninhibited Cluster, where people score the highest on neuroticism and the lowest on conscientiousness (Rentfrow et al., 2013).

Many other investigations have assessed the personality profiles of countries from around the world. The goal of this enterprise is laudable; it is an effort to map out the world in terms of personality traits—for example, to identify the countries where the most extraverted or the least agreeable people reside. Such information would obviously be of great utility in understanding psychological similarities and differences across cultures.

However, as noted in Chapter 4, comparing mean levels of subjective self-report measures entails a number of methodological challenges, which can greatly undermine their validity. Indeed, although there have been a number of large-scale surveys that have produced rank orderings of countries in terms of their personalities (e.g., McCrae, 2002; McCrae et al., 2005a; Schmitt et al., 2007; Terracciano et al., 2005), for the most part these rank orderings correlate poorly with each other (see Heine & Buchtel, 2009) and violate some basic criteria for assessing the validity of personality traits (e.g., Campbell & Fiske, 1959). Further, at least in the case of conscientiousness, objective behaviors and demographic indices of conscientiousness (e.g., how accurate clocks are, how efficiently postal workers work, how corrupt the public sector is perceived to be) do not correlate well with the national means for self-report measures of conscientiousness (e.g., Heine, Buchtel, & Norenzayan, 2008; Oishi & Roth, 2009). The reference-group effect is a problem with comparing these self-report measures across cultures, because people evaluate their conscientiousness by comparing themselves to local norms (e.g., I view myself as punctual to the extent that I think I am more punctual than most people around me) rather than international norms (although the reference-group effect shouldn't be as much a problem for comparing different regions of the United States, where people should all be familiar with American national norms). The goal of mapping out the world's countries in terms of their average personalities remains important, but I think some methodological advances are necessary before we can do this accurately.

SUMMARY

The self-concept is central to much of psychological research, and it varies in important and systematic ways across cultures. Individuals who participate in cultural practices and scripts common in individualistic cultures are likely to develop an independent view of self, in which they tend to highlight how they are separate from others and how their identity is based on inner attributes that are relatively stable across time and situation. In contrast, individuals who participate in cultural practices and scripts more commonly found in collectivistic cultures are more likely to develop interdependent views of self, in which their connections with significant others are emphasized and they tend to see their identity as largely arising from social roles, memberships, and relationships.

Because people do not respond to information from the world directly, but only encounter it in terms of how it is organized by their self-concepts, cultural differences in self-concepts importantly implicate a wide variety of psychological processes. A few ways that we can see psychological consequences for these cultural differences in views of self are that people from individualistic cultures tend to strive for more consistency in their actions, are more frequently in a state of subjective self-awareness, and are more likely to conceive of many attributes as stable entities, in contrast to the views of people from more collectivistic cultures. In later chapters we will see how these differences in the self-concept are associated with a variety of other psychological experiences, such as emotions, motivations, cognitions, and relationships.

People everywhere can consider themselves and others in terms of personality traits. Research indicates that personality structure appears quite similar across diverse cultural contexts; the Five Factor Model of personality is largely supported in many cultures around the world. However, there is some evidence that the Five Factor Model is not sufficient to account for all the personality variability in some cultures, because inventories generated from indigenous terms in some cultures reveal additional factors, and the evidence from subsistence societies is not as consistent as that found with industrialized samples. Also, the extent to which the five personality traits are common in particular cultures likely varies considerably around the world; however, there are significant methodological challenges to the validity of these comparisons.

THINK ABOUT IT

1. Do you think your own self-concept is more similar to the independent exemplar or the interdependent exemplar?
2. Why do you think independence versus interdependence is such a critical dimension for understanding how cultures differ?
3. In what ways are the self-concepts of women similar to Asians and in what ways are the self-concepts of men similar to Americans?
4. Why are people with interdependent selves more likely to act differently across different situations?
5. What do you think are some ways that people's thoughts about their selves would differ if they were taking an inside-out perspective versus an outside-in one?
6. Do you think about intelligence more from an incremental or from an entity-based perspective?
7. Which of the Big Five personality traits best characterize you? Which of the traits do you think best characterize others from your culture? Are they the same traits?

KEY TERMS

Independent View of Self, 211

Interdependent View of
  Self, 212

Essentialized Gender, 228

Cognitive Dissonance, 231

Subjective Self-Awareness, 237

Objective Self-Awareness, 237

Incremental Theory of
  Self, 243

Entity Theory of Self, 243

Five Factor Model of
  Personality, 246

Openness to Experience, 247

Conscientiousness, 247

Extraversion, 247

Agreeableness, 247

Neuroticism, 247

Ken Decker is a Tsimshian artist. The Tsimshian have had an easier time acculturating to the European colonists in North America than members of some other tribes (such as the Eastern Cree), because their original society shared more features in common with that of Europe.

7

LIVING IN MULTICULTURAL WORLDS

ichaelle Jean was born in Port-au-Prince, Haiti, a country that was discovered in 1492 by the explorer Christopher Columbus. When Columbus
arrived in Haiti and planted the flag of Spain, the country was populated
almost exclusively by the Arawak people. Early in the 17th century,
British, Dutch, and French pirates established bases on the island, and
ultimately the French claimed control of the country in 1664. For almost three
centuries, the Spanish and French colonists imported slaves to Haiti from Ghana,
Nigeria, Togo, Benin, and the Ivory Coast to develop Haiti's sugarcane and coffee industries. Many of Jean's ancestors were slaves who had intermarried with
the Arawak as well as with Spanish and French colonists. When Jean was 11,
her family left Haiti and moved to a town in rural Quebec. She attended college in Montreal and in Italy and married a filmmaker from France. Jean is fluent
in French, English, Spanish, Italian, and Haitian Kreyol. Her critics maintain that
she was actively involved in the Quebec separatist movement. In 2005 Jean was
appointed by Queen Elizabeth II to be the governor general of Canada—that is,
she was the Canadian representative of the monarch of England.

So here's a question. Considering the historical and cultural context of
Jean's ancestry and the experiences that she has had in her own life, what is
Michaelle Jean's culture?

FIGURE 7.1 People with multicultural
backgrounds, such as Michaelle Jean, highlight
how heterogeneous cultures often are.

Obviously, no simple statement can meaningfully encapsulate her cultural background. Haiti has
been populated by people from many different parts
of the globe, and Jean herself has lived in a number of different countries and has been exposed to
a diverse array of cultural messages. Her biography
highlights a real challenge for studying cultures. In
many ways, "cultures" don't really exist. That is, cultures are not homogenous entities with clear-cut
boundaries (**Figure 7.1**). Today there are no large societies anywhere that include only people from one
cultural background. Even the most homogeneous
societies contain individuals with different cultural
heritages, traditions, religions, and languages. Moreover, those parts of the world where most psychological research is conducted (North America, Western
Europe, and Australia) have witnessed some of the
greatest and most diverse influxes of immigration.
These exchanges of people are not only occurring
between neighboring countries with fairly similar
cultural backgrounds, such as between Canada and
the United States, but also include the migrations of

people across the farthest extents of the globe. For example, the city of Toronto contains more immigrants than it does nonimmigrants, and in the past decade the vast majority of these immigrants have come from non-Western nations. This cultural diversity makes it rather futile to make any specific statements about the culture of Toronto that would apply to all its citizens.

Currently, worldwide, an estimated 130 million people are living in countries they were not born in—approximately the same number as the population of Japan (**Figure 7.2**). In the United States, about 10% of the population has immigrated from another country (Suarez-Orozco & Suzrez-Orozco, 2001). For some immigrant groups within the United States the numbers are more striking: 59% of Latino-American children and 90% of Asian-American children were either born outside the United States or are second-generation residents (Zhou, 1997). With such large numbers of people crossing borders, encountering people from different cultures has become a common experience for most people. In contrast, in much of the world just a few centuries ago, the only people who regularly encountered individuals from distant cultures were explorers, diplomats, marauding warriors, and merchants. I often fantasize about how much easier it would have been to be a cultural psychologist back then, when cultures were relatively distinct and homogenous and comparisons between cultures would have

FIGURE 7.2 What culture is represented here?

been more clear-cut. Alas, with such little contact between people of divergent cultural backgrounds, the world would have had little use for us at that time.

Although the ever-increasing contact between cultures has complicated comparisons of their psychological processes, it has paved the way for investigating a different series of fascinating psychological questions. What happens to people's psychology when they move to a culture that is different from the one where they were raised? What are some of the psychological costs of being a member of a culture that is actively discriminated against by others? How are people's minds different if they have lived in two distinct cultures throughout their lives? Do some people fare better in this experience than others? As the world continues to globalize and as experiences with other cultures become the norm rather than the exception, these questions take on fundamental importance. I think they represent the most pressing issues that cultural psychologists will face over the years to come.

This chapter explores how people's psychology is affected when they move to a new culture. Research that tracks migrating people across time demonstrates, perhaps more clearly than other topics in this book, how an individual's experiences shape his or her psychological processes.

Difficulties in Studying Acculturation

Acculturation is the process by which people migrate to and learn a culture that is different from their original (or heritage) culture. The study of acculturation is beset by unique difficulties and challenges. Thousands of studies relevant to acculturation have been conducted, but extracting a set of generalizable findings or any cumulative theories from them is difficult (Furnham & Bochner, 1986; Rudmin, 2003; Ward, 1996). Despite its great importance, the literature on acculturation remains more contradictory, less coherent, and less empirically grounded than that for any other topic in this book, although as you'll see there are many key points that emerge quite reliably.

Reaching consistent conclusions on acculturation is difficult for researchers because acculturating individuals have such widely varying experiences. How do you think these experiences might differ? People move to a new country for many reasons: Some are moving to be closer to family members; some move to seek fame and fortune; some move because they are refugees and have no choice but to leave their countries; some are moving through a series of different countries, as their parents have jobs that require them to keep changing residences; some leave to study abroad with the intention of returning to their home country after graduating; and some move as young children because their parents decide that it is in the family's best interest.

Acculturating individuals can also move to dramatically different kinds of environments. Some move to cultural ghettos in which they can speak their original language and keep their old cultural traditions without having to interact much with members of their new host culture; some move to a rather homogenous neighborhood where they are the only ones who appear different; some move to an environment that actively discriminates against people from their cultural background; and some move to diverse expatriate neighborhoods that consist largely of people who have recently migrated from places all over the globe (see **Figure 7.3**).

Furthermore, people move to cultures that vary in their similarity to their heritage culture. Some move from a rural community in their home country to an urban center in their new culture; some move to a place where the dominant language, religion, and cultural practices are similar to those of their heritage culture; and some move to a cultural environment that is different from their own in almost every respect.

Complicating matters even more, different individuals have very different personalities, goals, and expectations that affect their acculturation experiences. In sum, few commonalities occur for all acculturating individuals, which makes it challenging to

FIGURE 7.3 The environments that immigrants move to can vary tremendously. Some live in cultural ghettos where they can speak their heritage language and maintain their heritage cultural traditions, such as San Francisco's Chinatown.

identify common patterns (Chirkov, 2009; Schwartz et al., 2010). Nevertheless, several key points can be extracted from this very diverse field of study.

What Happens When People Move to a New Culture?

One clear issue of agreement emerges from the very diverse literature on acculturation: Moving to a new culture involves psychological adjustment. This adjustment occurs over a wide variety of domains—acquiring a new language, learning new interpersonal and social behaviors, becoming accustomed to new values, often becoming a member of a minority group, and adjusting one's self-concept (e.g., Berry & Kim, 1988; Church, 1982; Furnham & Bochner, 1986; LaFromboise, Coleman, & Gerton, 1993). For example, the longer immigrants spend in a new culture, the more similar their emotional experiences become to those of other people living in that culture (De Leersnyder, Mesquita, & Kim, 2011); and the more people adapt to a new culture, the more they acquire the host culture's norms for relating to others (Zhang & Li, 2014). Given the influence that culture has on psychology, the adjustment that individuals go through when they move to a new culture can be enormous. How do people experience this adjustment?

Changes in Attitudes Toward the Host Culture

A number of studies have explored how migrants' psychological adjustment to new cultures unfolds across time. **Migrants** are defined as those who move from a **heritage culture** (their original culture) to a **host culture** (their new culture) and include those who intend to stay only temporarily (known as **sojourners**) and those who intend to move permanently (known as **immigrants**). A classic investigation was conducted on the adjustment experiences of Norwegian Fulbright scholars in the United States (Lysgaard, 1955). In that study an adjustment pattern was identified that was shared by many of the grantees. The experiences of these participants tracked what is described as a U-shaped curve, shown in **Figure 7.4**. The y axis indicates how positive the migrants feel about their host country. In the first few months of their experiences, the migrants were having an especially positive time in their visit. They were enjoying the new experiences, meeting new people, trying new foods, communicating with people in a foreign language, and feeling the excitement of participating in a novel and exotic environment. This stage has been labeled, appropriately, the "honeymoon stage" (Oberg, 1960). It is the existence of the honeymoon stage that keeps the tourism industry in business. Most travelers do not stick around in a new culture long enough to move past this stage, and they thus tend to view their experiences in new cultures to be, for the most part, pleasant and exciting.

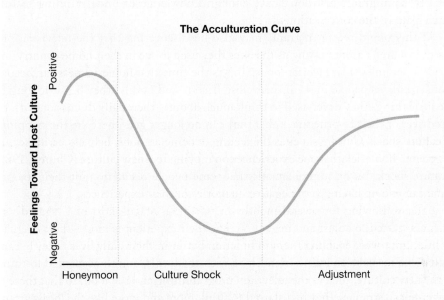

FIGURE 7.4 A common pattern of adjustment to acculturation is a U-shaped curve. In the first few months people often have very positive feelings about the host culture, but over time this gives way to the negative feelings associated with culture shock. With time, people adjust to their new host culture and often develop positive feelings toward it.

Unfortunately, like other honeymoons, at some point the fun and excitement usually comes to an end. Following this honeymoon stage most visitors turn a corner and begin to have increasingly negative views about their host culture. In fact, in the next few months—specifically, in Lysgaard's data, between 6 and 18 months—participants typically experienced the most negative feelings of their sojourn in a stage that has been labeled the "crisis" or "culture shock" stage (Oberg, 1960). In this stage, the thrill of having novel and exotic experiences wears off and these experiences become tiring and difficult. At this stage recent migrants often realize that their language skills are not yet good enough for them to fully function in the new environment. They realize that they do not have a rich enough understanding of how the system works to thrive. The people they initially met who were interested in them because they were exotic and different are no longer so interested in those differences. Others have already heard their stories about what the weather is like in their hometown, what kinds of sports are popular, or which seemingly bizarre foods they eat during their holiday festivals. Now others are interested in talking about things and events that are of concern to locals in the host culture, and recent migrants just don't have enough knowledge or understanding to fully participate in the conversations.

At this point, recent migrants may also be discovering that the television programs just aren't as interesting as the ones they used to see in their home country, and they start to miss their favorite foods. This is the time that homesickness can become quite strong, as people miss all their close friends and family; they begin to long for the little things they never used to think much about—their daily discussion with the bus driver or their favorite snack that they can no longer get. These are the symptoms of **culture shock**. Culture shock is the feeling of being anxious, helpless, irritable, and in general, homesick that one experiences on moving to a new culture (Church, 1982). Culture shock can be so problematic that some people decide to quit their sojourn; some can end up having very negative memories of their experiences.

After wallowing for several months in this crisis stage, most of Lysgaard's sojourners started to adjust and began to enjoy their experiences more. Their language abilities improved, enabling them to function better in their daily lives. They became better able to make enduring friendships with the locals, and they adapted to things in the new culture, such as the television programming and the food, so that these no longer felt so strange. They had started to think more and more like the locals around them. This stage, labeled the "adjustment" phase, tends to extend over a number of years, and with time, people become more and more proficient at functioning in their new culture.

Some research have found that this U-shaped adjustment curve is not limited to experiences in a foreign country (Gullahorn & Gullahorn, 1963). Sojourners can go through the same adjustment stages *after* they return to their home country. Initially on returning, people are elated to see their families and friends again and to be able to eat their favorite foods. However, it is not uncommon for people soon to experience "reverse culture shock" and find themselves puzzling over why they do not quite feel at home anymore and why they feel somewhat alienated from those around them. Their home culture often does not seem quite the same as they remembered it, and they are no longer an especially good fit. This unsettling sense also gives way to an adjustment period as they gradually acclimate themselves to the familiar life they once knew.

The U-shaped pattern of adjustment to new cultures seems to characterize the experiences of many migrants, and a number of other researchers have found evidence that tends to be consistent with this model, although the timing of the stages varies considerably (e.g., Oberg, 1960; Richardson, 1974; Zheng & Berry, 1991). However, as you might imagine, the range of experiences that people have when moving to a new culture varies tremendously, and this U-shaped curve does not characterize the adjustment pattern of everyone's experiences (Church, 1982). In particular, some research has found that the initial honeymoon stage is not evident for many sojourners and migrants (Guthrie & Zektick, 1967; Ward & Kennedy,

1995). For many people, the first few weeks at the beginning of an extended stay are characterized by a lot of anxiety that prevents them from feeling much excitement about their new experience.

One societal feature of a host culture that seems to influence the acculturating individuals' adjustment is the ease with which migrants can be accommodated by the host culture. Lysgaard's original study of sojourners' adjustment investigated Norwegians moving to the United States. The United States is a country of immigrants and is one of the most ethnically diverse nations in the world. People from a wide variety of backgrounds have come to view the United States as their home and have adjusted accordingly. In contrast, Japan is a country that is relatively ethnically homogenous: indeed, more than 98% of people living in Japan are Japanese. Trying to adjust as a migrant to a homogenous society would seem to be inherently more challenging. Regardless of how well people learn the customs or master the language, they will always stand out as different from the other 98% who are ethnically Japanese.

One study tracked the acculturation experiences of a few hundred migrants to Japan and did not replicate the U-shaped curve that Lysgaard had found (Hsiao-Ying, 1995). Instead, a rather pessimistic L-shaped curve was identified, which shared the honeymoon and crisis stages found in Lysgaard's work but did not find any evidence for the adjustment stage. Sadly, those who had lived in Japan for more than 5 years were just as negative toward Japan as those who had been there for just over 1 year and who appeared to be in the depths of the crisis stage. It is possible that in homogenous societies the adjustment phase just takes longer; had the researcher studied more individuals who had been there much longer (i.e., more than 10 years), she might have found evidence for the adjustment stage. Nonetheless, the success of people's acculturation experiences seems to be influenced by the homogeneity of the society to which they are trying to acculturate.

Who Adjusts Better?

Of all the experiences that people adjust to, few affect more aspects of their lives than moving to a new culture. It would not be surprising to learn that people tend to respond differently to the myriad challenges posed by acculturation, depending both on the situation that they are in and their temperament. Acculturation experiences are diverse enough that we cannot predict how well a given person has adjusted to his or her new culture just on the basis of how many years the individual has spent there (Rhee, Uleman, Lee, & Roman, 1995). What are some factors that influence how people will adjust to their acculturation experiences?

CULTURAL DISTANCE. In acculturation, people have to learn the lifestyles of a new culture. How successful they will be in acquiring the necessary information to thrive in a new culture is influenced by how much learning they need to do. Imagine someone is moving to a new cultural context in which absolutely everything is different. Such a situation would require a tremendous amount of learning, and most people would find it very difficult. In contrast, if someone moves to a new culture that is highly similar to his or her heritage culture, there would be less learning to do and fewer difficulties. So one factor that should predict a person's success in adjusting to a new culture is the amount of cultural distance between the heritage culture and the host culture. **Cultural distance** is the difference between two cultures in their overall ways of life. We can hypothesize that the more cultural distance someone needs to travel, the more difficulty that person will have acculturating.

One way to test this hypothesis is to compare performance on various measures of acculturation across countries. An indirect measure of acculturation is language performance. Many studies show that one of the best predictors of acculturative success is language ability (e.g., Gullahorn & Gullahorn, 1963; Ying & Liese, 1991), and people's confidence in their mastery over the host culture's language greatly affects how they identify with that culture (Noels, Pon, & Clement, 1996). There are many similarities between language and culture, and a very good proxy for how familiar a person is with a culture is his or her skill with its language. Hence, the easier it is for migrants to learn the language of their host culture, the better they should fare in the acculturation process.

One source of data for assessing how easily people learn the language of the host culture is average country scores on the Test of English as a Foreign Language (TOEFL). International students who wish to study at a school in an English-speaking country typically need to take the TOEFL to gain admittance. Although average country scores on the TOEFL are influenced by many factors—such as the country's GNP and the percentage of students in the country who take the exam—these scores also vary considerably based on the participants' own mother language (**Table 7.1**). Those who grew up speaking languages that are highly similar to English (e.g., Germanic languages such as Dutch or German) perform better than those who grew up speaking other European languages that are a little more distant (e.g., Romance languages, such as French and Spanish). Moreover, speakers of Indo-European languages tend to perform better on the TOEFL than those who grew up speaking languages from highly distant language families, such as Kazakh or Japanese (Educational Testing Service, 2014). The ease with which people learn English is influenced by how distant their mother tongue is from English, and thus how much new learning is involved.

Cultural distance encapsulates more than just language. Many other skills must be mastered when people move to a new culture. For example, they also have to learn how to accomplish everyday tasks such as making friends and figuring out how to find a doctor, where to go to get a driver's license, or how to cook the strange-looking foods sold at the market.

A number of studies have investigated how well people acculturate depending on how much overall cultural distance migrants must cover. Ward and Kennedy (1995) compared the adjustment of Malaysian university students in New Zealand (a culture that is quite different from their own) and another group of Malaysian students in Singapore (a culture that is fairly similar to their own). The students completed a measure of sociocultural adjustment that assessed their daily problems in navigating through the new culture. After spending almost 3 years, on average, in the two countries, the Malaysian students who were studying in Singapore reported having fewer difficulties than those who were studying in New Zealand. Apparently, Malaysians, on average, seem to fit in better in culturally close Singapore than in more culturally distant New Zealand, and they consequently had an easier time getting by in Singapore.

Other studies have found that sojourners from more distant cultures suffer from more distress, require more medical consultations (Babiker, Cox, & Miller, 1980), and have more social difficulties in general (Furnham & Bochner, 1982) than those who traverse less cultural distance. In particular, cultural distance seems to make it difficult to establish and maintain interpersonal relationships with members of the host culture.

People do not actually have to leave their country to be confronted with the need to acculturate to a new set of values. Various indigenous groups have found themselves, through no choice of their own, having to adjust to a culture imposed on them by a colonial force. For example, many distinct indigenous native populations throughout Canada have had to deal with the onslaught of cultural traditions forced on them by European settlers. These various indigenous cultures provide an excellent test case for investigating the impact of cultural distance on acculturation. Although none of them had to do any traveling to encounter mainstream Canadian culture, each of these cultures vary considerably from each other in terms of their own traditions. Some indigenous Canadian tribes, such as the Tsimshian of the Northwest Pacific Coast region, engaged in subsistence practices (primarily fishing for salmon and shellfish) that allowed them to accumulate large quantities of food and establish permanent, highly stratified settlements long before they had any contact with Europeans. In contrast, other tribes, such as the Eastern Cree, who live just below the tree line in Northern Quebec, engage in subsistence practices (primarily winter hunting and summer fishing) that do not allow them to accumulate much food, so some of the bands are migratory and have low sociocultural stratification. Other tribes, such as

TABLE 7.1

Average scores on the Test of English as a Foreign Language (TOEFL)

Mother Tongue	Average TOEFL Score
Dutch	100
German	97
French	86
Spanish	85
Farsi (Persian)	82
Vietnamese	78
Afrikaans	77
Turkish	76
Kazakh	76
Japanese	70

the Carrier, who live on the Rocky Mountain Plateau of northern British Columbia, also engage in hunting and fishing like the Eastern Cree. However, because they have the possibility of accumulating large numbers of salmon at the headwaters of some rivers, and because their culture was influenced by the geographically close Tsimshian, the Carrier represent a culture with a moderate degree of food accumulation and social stratification. Berry and Annis (1974) reasoned that the complex social stratification of the permanent settlements of the Tsimshian was more similar to mainstream Canadian culture than were the less socially stratified, somewhat migratory patterns among the Eastern Cree, and the moderate stratification of the Carrier should be in between. Hence, they predicted that there should be a greater degree of acculturative stress among the Eastern Cree than among the Carrier, who, in turn, would experience more acculturative stress than the Tsimshian. Indeed, this is exactly what they found for a variety of measures of acculturative stress: The Tsimshian acculturated to mainstream Canadian culture with the fewest difficulties, the Eastern Cree had the most signs of stress, and the Carrier were intermediate. Again, we can see that cultural distance reliably predicts how difficult one's acculturation experiences will be.

Cultural distance is thus a useful variable for helping us predict who will fare the best in acculturating. However, people vary a great deal within cultures. They come in all sorts of psychological shapes and sizes, and it would seem that some people would fare better in the acculturation experience than others, regardless of what culture they are from. What kinds of individuals would have the easiest time acculturating?

CULTURAL FIT. One way this question has been explored is to see whether acculturation occurs more smoothly for those who are a better **cultural fit** with their host culture. Cultural fit is the degree to which an individual's personality is more similar to the dominant cultural values in the host culture. It would seem that the greater the cultural fit of a person with the host culture, the more easily he or she should acculturate to it. This hypothesis has been explored in a number of ways.

First, consider the personality trait of extraversion, which reflects a general orientation toward seeking active stimulation from the environment and of being rather outgoing. People who score high on extraversion are more likely to move to other countries (Silventoinen et al., 2008), particularly to urban areas (Jokela, Elovainio, Kivimäki, & Keltikangas-Järvinen, 2008), when compared with those who are less extraverted. Countries or regions of the world that were largely populated by immigrants should thus be expected to have disproportionate numbers of people with temperaments, such as extraversion, that motivated them to immigrate in the first place (Kitayama, Ishii, Imada, Takemura, & Ramaswamy, 2006; Turner, 1920).

Some researchers have proposed that because extraversion should facilitate communication everywhere, extraverts should always fare better in the acculturation experience compared with introverts (Gardner, 1962). However, some studies have found that the relation between extraversion and acculturative success is considerably more complicated than it first appears. For example, one study found that Malaysians and Singaporeans who scored high on extraversion demonstrated more signs of psychological well-being while living in New Zealand than those who scored low (Searle & Ward, 1990). In contrast, however, another study found that English-speaking expatriates living in Singapore who scored high on extraversion reported feeling more boredom, frustration, depression, and health problems than those who scored low. Extraversion thus does not always facilitate acculturation (Armes & Ward, 1989). Rather, it appears that an extraverted personality makes a better cultural fit in New Zealand than it does in Singapore, and extraverts will fare better in the acculturation experience only where they fit in well with the culture. More generally, highly extraverted immigrants fare better in terms of their well-being when they immigrate to countries with overall more pronounced levels of extraversion (Fulmer et al., 2010). Likewise, people with more independent self-concepts have been found to suffer less distress in acculturating to the United States than people with more interdependent self-concepts (Cross, 1995), and people who have patterns of emotions that are more similar to those from the host culture report experiencing greater relational well-being (De Leersnyder, Mesquita, Kim, Eom, & Choi, 2014).

The key role that cultural fit plays in successful adjustment can also be seen when first-generation students begin college in the United States. On average, first-generation students in the United States are more likely to be from a working class background than those whose parents also went to college, and they tend to have more interdependent views of self. Because American universities tend to have relatively independent norms that emphasize making choices and becoming unique, the first-generation students' more interdependent orientation is often a poor fit with these norms, and they can experience more stress because of this (Stephens & Fryberg et al., 2012; Stephens, Townsend, Markus, & Phillips, 2012). In general, acculturation is more straightforward if one's sense of self fits well with one's host cultural environment.

ACCULTURATION STRATEGIES. Much psychological research has focused on people's acculturation strategies. John Berry and colleagues (e.g., Berry & Sam, 1997) have proposed that two issues are critical to the outcome of one's acculturation. The first is whether people attempt to participate in the larger society of their host culture. Do people have positive attitudes toward their host culture, and are they actively seeking to fit in it? This issue reflects how motivated people are to acquire an identity consistent with that of the host culture. The second issue is whether people are striving to maintain their own heritage culture and identity as members of that culture. Do people have positive attitudes toward their heritage culture, and are they actively seeking ways to preserve the traditions of their heritage culture? Those who have positive attitudes towards their heritage culture are said to be maintaining an ethnic identity (Phinney & Ong, 2007).

These two issues lead to distinct strategies that are proposed to influence the likelihood that one will experience psychological stress in the acculturation process (Berry, Phinney, Sam, & Vedder, 2006). Furthermore, these two issues are proposed to be independent, such that it is possible for someone to possess positive attitudes toward both their heritage and host cultures, negative attitudes toward both cultures, or positive attitudes toward one and negative attitudes toward the other. A person's acculturation strategies are measured by a questionnaire, an example of which is shown in **Table 7.2**. The four different acculturation strategies that people might have are shown graphically in **Figure 7.5**.

The strategy that involves attempts to fit in and fully participate in the host culture while at the same time striving to maintain the traditions of one's heritage culture is known as the **integration strategy**. People using this strategy have positive views toward both their heritage and their host culture—they are seeking the best of both worlds. Conversely, the strategy that involves little or no effort to participate in the host culture or to maintain the traditions of the heritage culture is known as the **marginalization strategy**. People using this strategy have negative views toward both their heritage and their host cultures. This strategy is relatively rare and is theoretically puzzling (who do people identify with if not either their heritage or host cultures?). It may be something pursued more by people who have grown up in multiple cultures across their childhood (who are sometimes termed "Third Culture Kids"; Pollock

TABLE 7.2

Sample items from the Vancouver Index of Acculturation

1. I often participate in my heritage cultural traditions.

2. I often participate in mainstream North American cultural traditions.

3. I am interested in having friends from my heritage culture.

4. I am interesting in having North American friends.

5. I believe in the values of my heritage culture.

6. I believe in mainstream North American values.

7. I enjoy the humor and jokes of my heritage culture.

8. I enjoy typical North American jokes and humor.

9. I would be willing to marry a North American person.

10. I would be willing to marry a person from my heritage culture.

Source: Ryder, Alden, & Paulhus (2000).

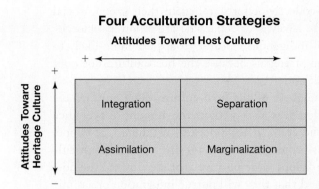

Four Acculturation Strategies

Attitudes Toward Host Culture

FIGURE 7.5

Positive or negative attitudes toward one's host or heritage cultures yield four different acculturation strategies.

& Van Reken, 2009), and thus they often identify more as global citizens. Some others have proposed that marginalization should not be considered a genuine "strategy" (e.g., Del Pilar & Udasco, 2004); it may, indeed, reflect little more than neuroticism.

On the opposite diagonal of the figure are two mixed strategies. The **assimilation strategy** involves an attempt to fit in and fully participate in the host culture while making little or no effort to maintain the traditions of one's heritage culture. It involves having positive attitudes toward the host culture and negative attitudes toward the heritage culture. It reflects a desire to leave behind the ancestral past so as to fit in with the host culture. Last, the **separation strategy** involves efforts to maintain the traditions of the heritage culture while making little or no effort to participate in the host culture. This strategy is composed of positive attitudes toward the heritage culture and negative attitudes toward the host culture. People pursuing separation strategies do not wish to acculturate to the host culture. They would prefer to continue to exist in the cultural world of their heritage culture.

In general, the most common strategy people are likely to pursue is the integration strategy. The least common strategy, in contrast, is the marginalization strategy, whereas assimilation and separation strategies fall in between, with neither being clearly more common than the other. A variety of factors influence which strategy a migrant is likely to pursue. In general, a person will not strive to fit into the host culture if that culture shows a good deal of prejudice toward the individual's own cultural group. Furthermore, people who have physical features that distinguish them from the majority of those in their host culture will likely experience more prejudice than people who have physical features that allow them to blend in with their host culture; thus, more physically distinct ethnic groups are more likely to maintain negative attitudes toward the host culture and pursue separation or marginalization strategies

(Berry, Kim, Power, Young, & Bujaki, 1989). Physically distinct ethnic groups are also more likely to actively support collective efforts to benefit their group's social position (Lalonde & Cameron, 1993). Likewise, people who are of lower socioeconomic status or who are members of indigenous cultural groups are more likely to pursue separation or marginalization strategies because the host culture does not typically offer them much that they desire.

The extent to which majority members of the host culture value cultural diversity and tolerance of cultural differences also predicts the amount of prejudice that immigrants experience (Guimond et al., 2013; Smeekes, Verkuyten, & Poppe, 2012). Moreover, when host cultures promote tolerance for diversity and multiculturalism, migrants are more likely to adopt more positive attitudes toward the host culture, which increases the likelihood that they will pursue integration or assimilation strategies. In addition, the acculturation strategy that one adopts might vary across situations: for example, Turkish immigrants in the Netherlands often show an integration strategy in public situations, where they publicly act in mainstream Dutch ways, yet some will simultaneously show a separation strategy in private, rejecting mainstream Dutch ways when they are in an entirely Turkish immigrant setting (Arends-Toth & van de Vijver, 2003).

The four acculturation strategies are hypothesized to yield different outcomes in the acculturation process. Specifically, the strategy that is hypothesized to result in the lowest degree of acculturative stress is the integration strategy, and much research shows that this strategy yields the most favourable outcomes (e.g., Berry et al., 1989; Nguyen & Benet-Martinez, 2013; but see Rudmin, 2003 for a contrary view). One possibility for the success of integration is that this strategy incorporates some protective features, such as a lack of prejudice and discrimination, involvement in two cultural communities and having access to two support groups, having a clear ethnic identity, and having a flexible personality that allows for this (Berry, 1997; Schwartz et al., 2010). The least successful strategy is marginalization, which involves rejection of the dominant society, a loss of one's original culture, and weakened social support. Assimilation and separation strategies are proposed to be intermediate in terms of their mental health outcomes. A potential cost of assimilation is the loss of one's heritage culture and accompanying social support networks, along with a sense of disconnection with the past. Separation strategies bear the cost of rejecting the host culture and all the protective features that it encapsulates, which often is accompanied by the individuals themselves being rejected by the host culture.

Some Pitfalls of Acculturation

The discussion thus far assumes that the adjustment migrants undergo when moving to a new culture is largely a good thing. That is, people acquire a set of skills, habits, and ways of thinking that work effectively in the new culture. However, it is quite possible that not all cultural habits picked up along the way are inherently desirable. For example, American culture is an outlier among the world's industrialized cultures on a great many dimensions (see Lipset, 1996, for a review), and as we will discuss in more detail in Chapter 13, one of these is physical weight. On average, Americans are among some of the heaviest people on the planet, and there are considerable health costs to the weight gains that American cultural habits have produced. Immigrants who move to the United States are not immune to the consequences of American eating habits. One study found that among immigrants who had lived in the United States for less than a year, only 8% were obese. In contrast, among those who had lived in the country for 15 years, 19% were obese. This number approached the obesity rate of 22% for American-born residents (Goel, McCarthy, Phillips, & Wee, 2004).

Parallel findings also emerge for Latinos who move to the United States. They not only got heavier the longer they were in the United States; they also became more likely to engage in less-healthy behaviors, such as smoking and drinking (although, in contrast, they also became more likely to exercise). These changes in lifestyle that came with acculturation are associated with a variety of adverse health outcomes for acculturated Latino-Americans compared with their less acculturated peers (Abraido-Lanza, Chao, & Florez, 2005; Allen et al., 2008; Corral & Landrine, 2008).

A similar pattern can be seen among Japanese immigrants to the United States. The Japanese have the longest average expected lifespan of any major nation in the world, and they have remarkably low rates of coronary heart disease. However, Japanese who emigrate to the United States are more likely to get coronary heart disease than those who stay in Japan, although this increased risk for heart disease is evident only among those Japanese immigrants who have acculturated to an American lifestyle (Marmot & Syme, 1976). In contrast, Japanese immigrants who continue to embrace Japanese cultural traditions do not show any increased risk for heart disease. The difference in risk for heart disease was quite enormous—the more-acculturated immigrants were three to five times more likely to have heart problems. It is still not clear from this study precisely what aspects of Japanese culture protect one from risk factors for heart disease (one of my Japanese friends is quite sure it's the miso soup).

There are other ways in which acculturating individuals can fare worse over time. One study found that among Vietnamese immigrants in New Orleans, the better they did in school, the more upwardly mobile they were, and the fewer delinquent acts they committed, the *less* they were integrated into the broader community (Zhou & Bankston, 1998). Because many immigrant groups are disadvantaged and discriminated against, they often live in poorer neighborhoods where the surrounding community is more likely to be struggling and is often caught up with problems of crime and dropping out of school. Somewhat ironically, those immigrants that assimilate into the surrounding community can end up having more difficulties than the ones who resist the cultural values of the community

FIGURE 7.6 A still from the 2008 movie *Gran Torino* showing a poorly acculturated Hmong (who is continuing his studies and has a job) being bullied by other more acculturated Hmong (who are gang members).

(**Figure 7.6**). Another study found that because European-American adolescents are more likely to disrespect authority figures than Latino adolescents are, the more that Latino immigrants were acculturated to the mainstream culture surrounding them, the less seriously they took their studies and the worse they performed in school (Suarez-Orozco & Suarez-Orozco, 1995). Suffice it to say that not all cultural habits lead to positive outcomes, and immigrants who pick up these less-desirable habits will also suffer their consequences.

Different but Often Unequal

One might conclude from my rather Panglossian description of the acculturation experience that immigration is like getting used to a new pair of shoes. Although in the beginning there are some times of discomfort, over time, people happily grow into a comfortable and accepting new environment. For some people, the acculturation experience may indeed be a relatively painless, gradual process of adjustment that continues to improve over time as they become fully integrated into a multicultural community. However, one of the saddest facts of human existence remains that people from different cultures are not all treated with equal respect. Prejudice and discrimination have always been rampant, particularly within countries where people of different ethnic backgrounds interact. For many people in the world, the experience of moving to a new culture is fraught with active discrimination, systematic disenfranchisement, unjust treatment, mocking and humiliation, violence, and perhaps even threats to their lives. Moreover, the experience of prejudice against minorities is not limited to those who move to a new culture but also extends to those who have ancestors who are from a different cultural background. What are the consequences of living in a multicultural world in which some of the cultures are actively discriminated against?

One way that discrimination can affect acculturation experiences is evident in how majority members of a culture often view minority members. For many minority members of a culture, when asked the ubiquitous getting-to-know-you question "Where are you from?" the follow-up question is often "No, where are you *really* from?" This question highlights how the immigrant or minority member is perceived to not really be from the host culture—his or her appearance betrays that the person's ancestors come from some other part of the world, and the questioner is suggesting that the person doesn't really belong. This experience, which is quite common to many minority members, is known as **identity denial**, in which an individual's cultural identity is called into question because he or she doesn't seem to match the prototype of the culture (see **Figure 7.7**).

Identity denial is typically a frustrating and demoralizing experience. One set of studies investigated how Asian-Americans would respond to identity-denying suggestions that they weren't prototypical Americans, such as being asked, "Do you speak English?" or being told, "Actually, you have to be an American to be in this study." Following these identity-denying prompts, Asian-Americans were more likely to demonstrate their authentic American identity compared with those who were not confronted with identity-denying statements. For example, when asked to list the names of popular American TV shows or to list the number of American practices they engaged in (such as what music they listened to, or what sports they played), Asian-Americans who had their identity denied came up with longer lists of TV shows and American practices than either those Asian-Americans who did not have their identity denied or White Americans (Cheryan & Monin, 2005). Another study found that Asian-Americans would actually

FIGURE 7.7 As an Indian-American celebrity, Mindy Kaling has sometimes expressed frustration that she is asked questions that White celebrities don't get, such as what ethnicity she is interested in dating, or what she thinks about diversity in TV.

order less healthy, but more typically American food (such as hamburgers or Philly cheesesteaks) when they had first been asked if they spoke English than those who did not have their American identity questioned (Guendelman, Cheryan, & Monin, 2011). The identity-denied Asian-Americans wished to publicly affirm their American identity. Moreover, even being the recipient of a positive stereotype (e.g., Asians are good at math) can sometimes lead to bad feelings, because the individual feels depersonalized and their sense of individual identity is threated (Siy & Cheryan, 2013).

The consequences of discrimination can be far-reaching, and some of the most powerful and unsettling research on this topic has been conducted by Claude Steele and colleagues. Focusing on African-Americans, Steele highlighted a disturbing finding: African-Americans tend to drop out of school at far greater rates than do European-Americans, and this trend is apparent even among those students who are the most qualified (Steele, 1992). What is causing highly qualified African-American students to do worse in their studies?

Steele proposes that **stereotype threat** can account for a lot of the differences in the ways that African-American and European-Americans identify with their studies. Stereotype threat is the fear that one might do something that will inadvertently confirm a negative stereotype about one's group. Stereotypes represent cultural beliefs— that is, they are shared beliefs among members of a culture. It is not necessary that you believe the stereotypes to be aware of them; belief and knowledge about stereotypes are separate. Part of growing up in American culture is being exposed to the stereotypes that are sometimes discussed, whether one believes them or not. A relevant example is the stereotype that African-Americans fare worse on intellectual tasks. People experience stereotype threat when they realize that they are at risk for confirming a negative stereotype, and in so doing, they end up proving the stereotype. For example, if you are an African-American engaged in a difficult intellectual task, it is likely that this negative stereotype about African-Americans will come to mind. The stereotype states that African-Americans have difficulty with challenging intellectual tasks and there you are, an African-American having difficulty with a challenging intellectual task. You are at risk for proving the stereotype.

Steele and colleagues have shown through a number of elegant experiments that a variety of things happen to people when they are in a state of stereotype threat. First, they get quite stressed as they realize the parallels between their own performance and the stereotype. Some studies have found that their blood pressure increases (Blascovich, Spencer, Quinn, & Steele, 2001), their working memory capacity decreases (Schmader & Johns, 2003), and they start showing evidence that they are thinking about the stereotype because they are more likely to be thinking of words like "dumb," "loser," and "black" (Steele & Aronson, 1995).

Most problematic, however, is that people who are under stereotype threat while taking a test start to do worse on the test. In one study, African-American and European-American Stanford students took a test that consisted of some verbal items from the Graduate Record Examination (Steele & Aronson, 1995). As any of you who have taken this exam know, these items are quite difficult. In one condition, students simply took the test that was framed to them as a psychological task. In a second condition, prior to taking the test the students were asked to check a box that identified their race. The dependent measure was how many items people were able to answer correctly. As shown in **Figure 7.8,** there was clear evidence of stereotype threat. In the "no race prime" condition, the African-American and European-American students did equally well when controlling for SAT scores. In this condition, no stereotype was activated and thus no one's performance was affected. In the "race prime" condition, the performance of the European-Americans was unaffected—there is no widely shared stereotype regarding the performance of European-Americans on verbal tests, so there was no impact on performance. However, in the "race prime" condition, African-Americans performed significantly worse than they had in the "no race prime" condition. The stereotype that African-Americans do worse on intellectual tasks was activated, and this dramatically interfered with their performance. Merely indicating their race caused them to do worse. This study demonstrated that when people experience stereotype threat they often end up acting in ways that are precisely consistent with the stereotype, and their behavior ends up proving it. And because ethnic minorities so often receive the brunt of negative stereotypes around the world, they are at risk for stereotype threat and proving the stereotypes.

Although much of this research has targeted the experiences of African-Americans, this effect generalizes broadly to virtually all stereotyped groups. Comparable findings

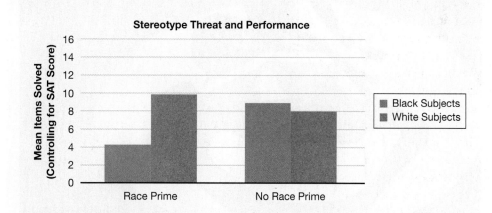

FIGURE 7.8 When asked to indicate their race prior to taking a difficult verbal test, African-Americans perform worse on the test than African-Americans who are not asked to indicate their race. In contrast, indicating one's race has no impact on European-Americans' test performance.

have shown that women perform worse on math tests when reminded of their gender (Shih, Pittinsky, & Ambady, 1999), European-American students perform worse on an athletic task when reminded of their race (Stone, Lynch, & Sjomeling, 1999), low-caste Indians do worse on an intellectual task when their caste is made salient (Hoff & Pandey, 2004), and the elderly perform worse on memory tasks when reminded of their age (Hess, Auman, & Colcombe, 2003).

Sometimes the effects of stereotype threat can even be elicited by what may seem to be positive reminders of a stereotype. For example, consider what stereotypes might be associated with Native Americans as embodied in various Native American mascots across the United States. Chief Wahoo is the cartoon caricature of the mascot for the Cleveland Indians baseball team (**Figure 7.9**). Although the mascot looks more affable than threatening, is hugely popular among Cleveland fans and—according to a much-critiqued poll conducted by *Sports Illustrated*—most Native Americans (King, Staurowsky, Baca, Davis, & Pewewardy, 2002), a question arises regarding how Native Americans might respond to reminders of this stereotypical image: Does this seemingly harmless caricature of Native Americans produce harmless consequences? Researchers explored this question by presenting Native Americans with one of a

FIGURE 7.9 Chief Wahoo of the Cleveland Indians. Despite its appearance as an affable caricature, Native Americans feel worse about their community when they encounter this mascot.

variety of stereotypical portrayals of Native Americans, such as Chief Wahoo, Chief Illiniwek (the mascot for the University of Illinois until 2007), or Disney's Pocahontas. Following these presentations, participants completed measures of self-esteem, their community esteem (i.e., how much they value and respect their own community), and their own achievement goals. The results showed that those Native Americans who were shown one of the stereotypical portrayals of Native Americans displayed lower self-esteem, less pride in their community, and fewer achievement goals compared with Native Americans who did not see the stereotypical portrayals (Fryberg, Markus, Oyserman, & Stone, 2008). That is, despite looking fun and harmless, these stereotypical portrayals of Native Americans appeared to elicit stereotype threat among them.

The authors argue that Native Americans felt worse about themselves and their communities because these stereotyped representations communicated the limited ways in which others view them. Given that Native Americans are a relatively invisible minority group to most Americans because they represent a small percentage of the population, often live on isolated reservations, and rarely appear in mainstream media (e.g., Mastro & Greenberg, 2000), these few stereotypical portrayals stand to greatly influence the way that Native Americans are perceived by others. When these portrayals seem out of touch with reality, even if they're the product of good intentions, it can have negative consequences for Native Americans.

The existence of stereotype threat can make the acculturation process of disadvantaged minorities difficult indeed. Knowing that others expect you to fare poorly and then encountering occasions in which you succumb to stereotype threat can have long-term negative consequences. People may begin to cope with the stress of stereotype threat by disidentifying with the stereotyped domain (e.g., performing well in school) and adopting strategies to avoid reminders of the stereotype (e.g., dropping out of school), thus perpetuating the stereotype. However, now that researchers have identified this striking obstacle that thwarts the integration efforts of disadvantaged minorities, they are developing solutions to combat stereotype threat (e.g., Cohen, Garcia, Apfel, & Master, 2006; Good, Aronson, & Inzlicht, 2003). One particularly effective way of combating stereotype threat is simply to learn about its existence (Johns, Schmader, & Martens, 2005). There are many reasons to remain optimistic that the deleterious consequences of stereotype threat will someday be reduced.

Furthermore, although having a distinct cultural background is sometimes associated with discrimination and the kinds of problems that stem from stereotype threat, being from a distinctive group can also have psychological benefits. People with a distinctive cultural background are more likely to come to strongly identify with their group and to increase their loyalty toward it—their distinctive group membership becomes an important source of meaning and self-esteem in their lives (Brewer, 1991). In contrast, majority-group memberships play a far smaller role in people's identities. For example, there are few White, heterosexual males in North

America who identify strongly with their groups, because memberships in majority groups or groups associated with power are typically quite invisible to the members themselves. The stronger sense of group identification that people from distinctive cultural backgrounds possess can create many positive feelings about both the individual and the group, and these appear to serve an important function for coping with the discrimination that they sometimes experience (Schmitt & Branscombe, 2002).

Multicultural People

Thus far, we have discussed how people fare in the acculturation process. A separate question to consider is how people who have been exposed to multiple cultural worldviews organize their different experiences. Do their experiences get all mixed up and averaged together? For example, does a Peruvian who has moved to the United States end up feeling emotions that are roughly halfway between those common in Peru and those common in the States? The tendency for bicultural people to evince psychological tendencies between those of their two cultures is termed **blending**. Alternatively, do multicultural people end up with multiple selves—feeling and thinking like a Peruvian in Peruvian contexts, and feeling and thinking like an American in American contexts? The tendency for bicultural people to switch between different cultural selves is termed **frame-switching** (or alternation). Which of these two possibilities, the blending model or the frame-switching model, best captures the ways multicultural people deal with their experiences in multiple worlds? There is evidence for both.

Evidence for Blending

If multicultural people respond to their experiences in different cultures by blending and averaging those experiences, we would expect them to show responses on psychological measures that are intermediate to responses of monocultural people from the different cultures. Asian-Americans, for example, would be expected to think not quite like either mainstream Americans or Asians but in some way that lies between the two. Many cross-cultural studies do include a bicultural sample in addition to two monocultural samples. The most common pattern of findings is evidence for blending—that is, the bicultural sample shows a pattern somewhere between the two monocultural samples (e.g., De Leersnyder et al., 2011; Heine & Hamamura, 2007; Kitayama, Markus, Matsumoto, & Norasakkunkit, 1997; Norenzayan, Choi, & Nisbett, 2002; Tsai, Simeonova, & Watanabe, 2004).

My colleagues and I explored the acculturation of self-esteem among people of East Asian descent who moved to Canada. As we'll discuss in detail in Chapter 8, North Americans are much more likely to elaborate on positive aspects about themselves and to have higher self-esteem than East Asians. To investigate what happens to self-esteem when one moves from a culture that tends to have lower rates of self-esteem to a culture that tends to have higher rates, we measured the self-esteem of Japanese exchange students living in Canada at two points in time: a few days after they arrived in Canada, and then 7 months later (Heine & Lehman, 2004). As you can see in **Figure 7.10**, the Japanese students' self-esteem scores were significantly higher after they had been in Canada for a while than when they had just arrived. We also measured the self-esteem of Canadian English teachers who were moving to Japan at two points in time: a couple of weeks before they left Canada and then after they had been in Japan for 7 months. The teachers' self-esteem scores were significantly lower after having spent some time in Japan. This suggests that people are exposed to novel cultural information when they move to a new culture. The information that people are exposed to in Canada appears to encourage them to focus on their strengths, whereas the information that people are exposed to in Japan appears to encourage them to focus on their weaknesses. Moreover, this exposure to new cultural information seems to affect the self-concept rather quickly—we found evidence of significant changes after only 7 months.

This study suggests that acculturative change in the self-concept can occur relatively quickly. A related question is how long does it take for people to completely acculturate to the norms of a host culture? Is 7 months of living in Canada enough to make a Japanese exchange student psychologically Canadian? In another study we investigated this question by comparing the self-esteem of several thousand students in Japan and Canada (Heine & Lehman, 2004). This large group of students was divided into subsamples that tracked a continuum with respect to their exposure to

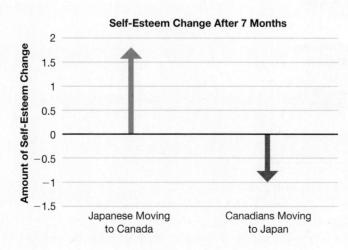

Self-Esteem Change After 7 Months

Amount of Self-Esteem Change

Japanese Moving to Canada

Canadians Moving to Japan

FIGURE 7.10

After living in Canada for 7 months, Japanese show a significant increase in self-esteem, whereas after living in Japan for 7 months, Canadians show a significant decrease in self-esteem. People's self-esteem scores moved in the direction of the dominant norms for self-esteem in their host cultures.

North American culture. In order of increasing exposure to North American culture, these categories were (1) Japanese who had never been outside Japan, (2) Japanese who had spent time in a Western country, (3) recent East Asian immigrants to Canada (who had been in Canada less than 7 years), (4) East Asians who immigrated to Canada more than 7 years ago, (5) second-generation Asian-descent Canadians, (6) third-generation Asian-descent Canadians, and finally, (7) European-descent Canadians. The self-esteem scores of these subsamples were contrasted. As you can see in **Figure 7.11**, this classification resulted in a clear relation between exposure to North American culture and self-esteem. The longer those of Asian descent had spent participating in North American culture, the higher their self-esteem scores. More-over, it wasn't until those of Asian descent had been in Canada for three generations

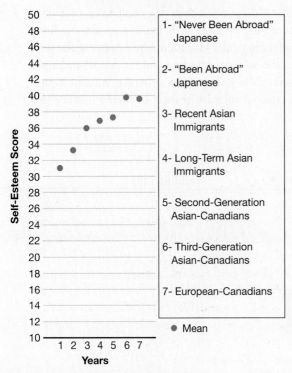

Self-Esteem and Exposure to North American Culture

1- "Never Been Abroad" Japanese

2- "Been Abroad" Japanese

3- Recent Asian Immigrants

4- Long-Term Asian Immigrants

5- Second-Generation Asian-Canadians

6- Third-Generation Asian-Canadians

7- European-Canadians

● Mean

Years

Exposure to North American Culture

FIGURE 7.11

On average, the more exposure one has to North American culture, the higher one's self-esteem. It appears to take three generations of living in Canada for the self-esteem of East Asians to fully approximate that of European-Canadians.

(that is, their grandparents had immigrated to Canada) that their self-esteem scores reached the level of European-Canadians' scores.

Apparently, at least with respect to self-esteem, acculturative changes in the self-concept extend across a long period of time. For self-esteem, it appears to take three generations to become fully acculturated. It remains to be seen, however, whether acculturative changes are as slow for people from all cultural backgrounds. It is possible that East Asians take longer to acculturate to North America than immigrants from Europe because East Asians have a greater cultural distance to traverse. Moreover, it is not at all clear whether different psychological processes acculturate at the same rate. There has been scant research mapping out how psychological processes change with acculturation, and we do not know how well the findings shown in Figure 7.11 would generalize to other psychological phenomena or to people acculturating from different cultural backgrounds (also see McCrae, Yik, Trapnell, Bond, & Paulhus, 1998).

Evidence for Frame-Switching

The previous two studies provide evidence that is consistent with a blending view of acculturation. Over time spent in North America, the average person of East Asian descent comes to more closely resemble European-Americans and to less closely resemble East Asians living in East Asia. However, another interpretation is still possible to explain these findings. Perhaps in these two studies people were either thinking like North Americans *or* they were thinking like East Asians. It is possible that after a few months of life in Canada, only a small percentage of East Asians were thinking like North Americans. After 7 years in Canada, in contrast, a larger percentage of East Asians might have been thinking like North Americans, and after three generations, virtually 100% of Asian-Canadians were thinking like European-Canadians. That is, rather than each person's self-concept being blended a little over time as new Western cultural experiences were slowly poured in, it is possible instead that the percentage of people thinking in Western ways increased with exposure to North American culture.

This alternative account of multicultural experience presupposes that multicultural people can develop multiple selves, each equipped to deal with a specific cultural environment. According to this frame-switching or alternation view, multicultural people do not develop a blended self-concept that is an admixture of the different cultures they are exposed to, nor do they lose their heritage-culture self once they have mastered their host culture self. Rather, this hypothesis maintains that multicultural people develop mastery over both cultural worlds and develop divergent selves that can be selectively activated by different cultural contexts (e.g., LaFromboise et al., 1993).

If we again use language as a proxy for culture, it becomes clear that the frame-switching hypothesis makes more sense than a blending hypothesis. For example, native Indonesian speakers who move to a predominantly English-speaking country do not end up speaking a blended language of "Englonesian." Rather, they usually speak Indonesian in Indonesian contexts and English in English contexts. Bilinguals learn to switch between languages depending on the context they are in. Although some people who emigrate may never learn the new language of their host culture completely fluently, and some migrants might largely forget the language of their heritage culture, there does not seem to be much blending of languages, aside from intermixing the occasional word or expression when talking with other bilinguals. To the extent that navigating multiple cultures is similar to navigating multiple languages, we would expect that people can also frame-switch or alternate between different cultures.

Indeed, from the subjective perspective of the multicultural person, there is much discussion about frame-switching between cultural contexts. For example, more than a century ago the sociologist W. E. B. Du Bois (1903/1989) claimed that African-Americans experienced continual switching between "two souls, two thoughts, two unreconciled strivings, two warring ideals" (p. 5). The cultures of mainstream America and that of African-Americans (in particular, that of inner-city African-Americans) continue to be different enough that people need to learn how to behave differently depending on which context they are in. The sociologist Elijah Anderson (1999) describes in great detail how inner-city African-American children quickly learn to discriminate between the norms and unwritten rules that govern their schools and mainstream society and those that govern the streets. "Code-switching," as this particular kind of cultural frame-switching is referred to, is an essential skill for inner-city children to learn if they are to survive and succeed in these two divergent cultural contexts. Anderson argues that such children must learn to switch between the "code of the decent" and the "code of the street" as they deal with people in their school culture and their street culture. The code of the street permeates many aspects of life—in particular, the development of a reputation that one is tough and is not to be messed with. The only way an inner-city child can succeed, Anderson argues, is to be able to switch effectively between these two codes.

This code-switching has been discussed largely among sociologists in terms of the ways people need to *act and present themselves to others* in their respective cultures. When on the street, people must follow the code of the street, but when among "the decents," they need to act in ways that are congruent with mainstream American society (see **Figure 7.12**). However, it is possible that this tendency to oscillate between two different cultural worlds is not isolated to the ways people act and present themselves to others—it might possibly affect the ways people are thinking at a basic psychological level as well.

Hong, Morris, Chiu, and Benet-Martinez (2000) proposed that multiculturals do engage in frame-switching and that it should be evident in how their minds operate at the most fundamental level. Borrowing from information science, Hong and colleagues propose that culture is represented in the brain as a network of specific

FIGURE 7.12 President Obama's Republican critics have sometimes complained that he talks in a different way to black audiences than he does to white ones.

information. For example, people exposed to American culture would have a set of ideas in their heads that cluster together, such as independence, confidence, freedom, individual rights, and the Statue of Liberty. These ideas are networked together in the sense that they usually come in clusters. That is, people who are thinking about independence should be more likely to think of confidence and individual rights than those who are thinking about interdependence, because confidence and individual rights are more commonly associated with independence than interdependence. The mind forms links between those constructs that tend to get activated together, and thus activating one construct that is part of a network should activate the other constructs of the network. Because information is dispersed in people's minds through networks, people who are "primed" or exposed to one part of an information network should be more likely to think in other ways that are part of that same network.

Consider this dramatic demonstration of priming. College students participated in a task requiring them to unscramble some sentences (Bargh, Chen, & Burrows, 1996). Half of the students unscrambled sentences that contained some words related to the elderly—*wrinkle, old, knits,* and *bingo.* The other half unscrambled sentences that contained neutral words. At the end of the study, participants left by walking down a hallway. Unknown to them, an observer timed how long it took them to walk that hallway. Remarkably, participants who had been exposed to words related to the elderly walked significantly slower than those who had been exposed to the neutral words. The reason is that people have a number of ideas associated with the elderly that form an information network, one of which is that elderly people tend to move quite slowly. Activating part of the information network (having people think of words like bingo and wrinkle) leads to related ideas and behaviors (such as walking slowly) to become activated as well.

Hong and colleagues applied this same kind of reasoning in their investigations of how the minds of multicultural people operate. They reasoned that people who were exposed to multiple cultural worlds would have multiple information networks in their heads. For example, a Chinese-American would have an information network regarding Chinese ideas and one regarding American ideas. Hong and colleagues reasoned that if people exposed to both Chinese and American cultures were primed with things that reminded them of the different cultures, they could be led to think in ways that are more consistent with the primed culture.

In one study they conducted, attributions were investigated among Westernized Chinese students in Hong Kong (Hong et al., 2000). They reasoned that having been educated in a former British colony, and in English, these students had had exposure to both Western and Chinese ways. One point that we'll be discussing in Chapter 9 is that Chinese are more likely to explain people's behaviors in terms of external attributions (e.g., situational factors cause people to act the ways that they do), whereas Americans are more likely to explain people's behaviors in terms of internal attributions (e.g., personality factors cause people to act the ways they do; Morris & Peng, 1994).

Quite remarkably, this pattern of results holds not only for how people explain the behaviors of humans but also for how they explain the behaviors of fish (**Figure 7.13**). That is, Chinese are more likely to make external attributions to explain why a single fish is swimming ahead of a group (e.g., the fish is being chased by others), whereas Americans are more likely to explain the fish's behavior in terms of internal attributions (e.g., the fish is leading the others).

Hong and colleagues were interested in how Hong Kong Chinese would explain the fish's behavior.

FIGURE 7.13 Is the front fish being chased by the others, or is it leading the others?

They reasoned that the answer to this question is "it depends"—it depends on which cultural knowledge network has been activated. If Hong Kong Chinese are thinking Chinese thoughts, they should explain the fish's behavior in terms of the pressures from the group it is in. In contrast, if they are thinking American thoughts, they should explain the fish's behavior in terms of its individual desires. They manipulated the kinds of thoughts the Hong Kong Chinese were having by showing them a number of cultural icons. Those in the "Chinese prime" condition were shown such pictures as a Chinese dragon, the Chinese Emperor's Summer Palace, a rice farmer, the Great Wall, and a mythical Chinese dancer. They were then asked to write several sentences about Chinese culture. In contrast, those in the "American prime" condition were shown pictures of Mickey Mouse, the U.S. Capitol building, a cowboy, Mt. Rushmore, and the Statue of Liberty and were asked to write some sentences about American culture. They also had a "neutral prime" condition, in which participants viewed pictures of environmental scenes. Then, the participants saw computer images of fish swimming across the screen and were asked to explain their behavior.

Their results are quite striking, a shown in **Figure 7.14**. Students who saw the American primes explained the fish's behavior less in terms of the group's influence than those in a neutral prime condition. Likewise, those who saw the Chinese primes explained the fish's behavior more in terms of the group influencing it than those in the neutral prime condition. The Hong Kong Chinese were capable of explaining the fish's behavior in either the typically American or the typically Chinese way. They switched cultural frames depending on which cultural information network was activated.

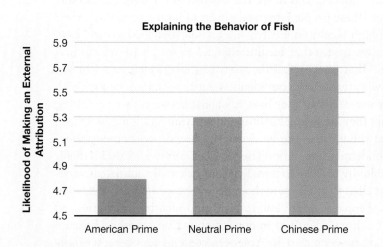

Explaining the Behavior of Fish

Likelihood of Making an External Attribution (y-axis: 4.5, 4.7, 4.9, 5.1, 5.3, 5.5, 5.7, 5.9)

American Prime   Neutral Prime   Chinese Prime

FIGURE 7.14

Hong Kong Chinese who are primed with American icons are less likely to make external attributions to explain the behavior of a single fish, whereas those primed with Chinese icons are more likely to make external attributions.

This is a profound finding and extends our understanding of frame-switching in dramatic ways. It is likely that the kind of code-switching people have discussed regarding African-Americans shifting between the "code of the street" and the "code of the decents" is a largely conscious process. That is, people are likely aware that they are adjusting their behaviors to fit in better with whichever group they are among. The findings of the study by Hong and colleagues, in contrast, surely do not represent conscious responses. People do not have an explicit idea in their head that Americans explain a fish's behaviors by making internal attributions whereas Chinese explain a fish's behavior by making external attributions. You probably did not know this fact about how people explain the behavior of fish before reading this book. Yet despite being unaware of these specific kinds of cultural information, the participants still ended up thinking in ways that were consistent with the primes they saw.

Apparently, when thinking "American" thoughts, people are more likely to think of a broad array of thoughts, many of which they are not aware of but that include the implicit notion that focusing on individuals is the way to explain behavior. These thoughts are associated with other thoughts, such as pictures of Mickey Mouse, not because of any causal relation between Mickey Mouse and internal attributions but because these thoughts tend to occur together. When thinking about Mickey Mouse, people are thinking about "American ideas" more generally, which increases the likelihood that they will explain the behaviors of fish by focusing on the individuals. Bicultural people can shift between cultural frames with as small a prompt as thinking about a handful of pictures (also see Wong & Hong, 2005).

Not all biculturals should necessarily frame-switch to the same degree, and they should vary based on their degree of **bicultural identity integration**, which is the extent to which people see their two cultural identities as compatible or in opposition to each other. Some biculturals, for example, tend to see their two cultural identities as quite compatible with each other. These people integrate aspects of both cultures into their everyday lives—they have high bicultural identity integration (Benet-Martinez, Leu, Lee, & Morris, 2002). In contrast, other biculturals tend to see their two cultural identities as in opposition. That is, they feel that they can identify either with, say, their Chinese identity or with their American identity, but they cannot identify with both simultaneously. They may feel that they have to choose between their identities, depending on the situation; they are low in bicultural identity integration.

One hypothesis is that the greatest frame-switching should occur among those who are high in bicultural identity integration (Benet-Martinez et al., 2002). This is because these people can fluidly react to external cues in culturally consistent ways. For example, Chinese cues elicit their Chinese thoughts whereas American cues elicit their American thoughts. People who are low in bicultural identity integration, in contrast, tend to see their cultural identities in opposition with each other. Because of this, for example, when these people are in American contexts they feel especially Chinese, and when they are in Chinese contexts they feel especially American. The two identities feel largely opposed. Consequently, being primed with their culture should not lead them to react in culturally consistent ways. There is good evidence to support this hypothesis. In one study, the only biculturals who showed the kind of frame-switching identified by Hong and colleagues were those who scored high on a bicultural identity integration measure (Benet-Martinez et al., 2002).

Other kinds of primes that can lead people to frame-switching have also been explored. Because language and culture are so intimately connected, it is probably not surprising to hear that language can activate a cultural frame. Indeed, it seems that bilingual people tend to frame-switch when they shift between their languages. For example, bilingual Chinese-Canadians and Hong Kong students were far more likely to describe themselves in positive terms when answering questionnaires in English than when answering them in Chinese, which is consistent with a broad pattern of cultural differences in self-enhancing motivations that will be discussed in Chapter 8 (Lee, Oyserman, & Bond, 2010; Ross, Xun, & Wilson, 2002). Similarly, a study conducted with Arab-Israelis who are bilingual in Arabic and Hebrew found that this group had more negative associations with Jewish names when they were presented in Arabic than when they were presented in Hebrew, and the reverse was true for their associations with Arabic names (Danziger & Ward, 2010). The language that people speak seems to activate an associated cultural network, and this influences how they think (Chen & Bond, 2010; Marian & Kaushanskaya, 2004). When bilinguals switch between languages, they are not just bringing different vocabularies and grammars to mind—they seem to be bringing different selves to mind as well.

Although findings such as these provide clear evidence that bicultural individuals can be primed to think in culturally distinct ways, a question to consider is whether this effect is limited to biculturals. Indeed, it is debatable about just how bicultural Hong Kong Chinese are in the first place. One could argue that rather than the individual Hong Kong Chinese participants being exposed to two different cultural worlds, it might be more accurate to say that the participants are all exposed to a single, multifaceted culture. Hong Kong surely is not unique in being a country that is influenced by multiple cultural influences. That would seem to characterize virtually any large city today. Would we expect to find, then, that people who are traditionally thought of as monocultural might also have access to multiple cultural frames?

For example, one study contrasted Chinese and American students in terms of how they viewed the importance of a tennis game that was framed either as trying to secure a win (which is consistent with something called a *promotion orientation*— trying to achieve a positive outcome—which is discussed more in Chapter 8) or as trying to avoid a loss (which indicates a *prevention orientation*, where people try to avoid a negative outcome; Lee, Aaker, & Gardner, 2000). The Americans viewed the situation in which the player was trying to secure a win as more important than one in which he was trying to avoid a loss. Apparently, then, Americans tend to maintain promotion orientations. In contrast, the Chinese viewed the situation of trying to avoid a loss as more important than the one in which the player was trying to secure a win. Chinese appear to maintain prevention orientations.

The researchers were interested in whether this cultural difference had anything to do with the fact that Chinese tend to be more interdependent than Americans. Perhaps interdependence is associated with a prevention orientation. One way they tested this was to see whether Americans would also become more prevention oriented if they were led to think about their interdependence. They had Americans again consider which kind of tennis game was more important; however, the researchers manipulated whether the Americans were considering an individual's performance or a team's performance. The authors reasoned that an individual competition highlights one's independence, whereas a team performance highlights one's interdependence. Interestingly, they found a pattern of results that paralleled the cultural differences. That is, Americans who considered an *individual's* tennis game adopted a promotion orientation in that they viewed efforts to secure a win more important than efforts to avoid a loss. In contrast, Americans who considered a *team's* tennis game adopted a prevention orientation in that they viewed efforts to avoid a loss more important than efforts to secure a win. In sum, Americans could be led to think like Chinese with the priming of information that was related to interdependence—a key aspect of Chinese self-concepts. This priming was possible even though it's probably fair to assume that the American participants had very little knowledge of or exposure to Chinese culture. Yet they could think like Chinese when they considered the situation from an interdependent perspective.

The results of this study, as well as those from many other similar ones (e.g., Kühnen, Hannover, & Schubert, 2001; Mandel, 2003; Oyserman & Lee, 2008; Trafimow, Triandis, & Goto, 1991), highlight that bicultural people are not the only ones who have access to multiple knowledge structures. But how could this be? How could Americans be primed to think in a way that is more characteristic of people in another culture that they don't know much about? The results of these studies suggest that although some ideas (such as independence or promotion orientations) might be more common among Americans than other ideas (such as interdependence or prevention orientations), these less-common ideas are still present within American culture—that is, they are at least existential universals. Americans too sometimes think of themselves as interdependent and are concerned with a prevention orientation. Because of this, they too develop a knowledge network of ideas that are associated with interdependence and prevention orientations. Once a knowledge network exists, when any part of that network is activated through priming, the other parts of the network should also be activated. Hence, even monocultural people can probably be primed to think in ways that are more similar to other cultures to the extent that those ways of thinking are sometimes present in their own minds. Biculturals are not the only ones who can frame-switch.

However, we might wonder whether biculturals would be more adept than monoculturals at frame-switching because they might have more clearly demarcated information networks. Because biculturals often live in two distinct cultural worlds, it is likely that there would be a clearer division between their two views of self. For example, we might expect that a Chinese-American can feel and act very Chinese when with her extended family, yet feel very American when with her friends at school. If her experiences as Chinese or American are so clearly distinct from each other, it follows that the information networks regarding "Chinese" ways of thinking and "American" ways of thinking would be relatively nonoverlapping networks, with very strong linkages within each cultural mindset. In contrast, monoculturals might have relatively looser knowledge networks around concepts such as independence and interdependence, and thereby would react relatively less consistently to primes they might encounter.

This question was investigated in a study that compared biculturals (Asian-Americans) and monoculturals (European-Americans—they are considered monocultural because mainstream American culture has been more influenced by people of European descent) with respect to how easily they could be primed (Gardner, Gabriel, & Dean, 2004). The participants were primed with either independent or interdependent aspects of themselves. The priming was accomplished by having participants read one of two versions of a paragraph that described a trip to the city. The independent prime version of the paragraph included only singular pronouns, such as *I, me,* and *mine,* whereas the interdependent prime version of the paragraph was identical except that it included plural pronouns such as *we, us,* and *our.* Then participants were asked to rate the importance of certain values. Some of the values represented individualistic concerns, such as freedom, independence, and choosing one's own goals. Other values reflected collectivistic goals, such as belongingness, friendship, and respect for the elderly. The values that Asian-Americans and European-Americans rated were compared across priming conditions. The results are shown in **Figure 7.15**.

A number of trends are indicated by this figure. First, people who were primed with independence rated the individualistic values as more important and the collectivist values as less important, compared to those primed with interdependence. This shows that everyone is capable of frame-shifting. Second, regardless of the prime they received, European-Americans rated the individualistic values as more important than Asian-Americans did, whereas Asian-Americans rated the collectivistic values as more important than European-Americans did. This shows that the overall cultural difference in values emerged as expected. Third, this figure also shows that the primes had a weaker effect for European-Americans (i.e., the gap between the independent and interdependent primes is significantly smaller) than they did for Asian-Americans. That is, Asian-Americans showed more pronounced frame-switching than the European-Americans (also see Oyserman & Lee, 2008). This provides nice evidence that although everyone can frame-shift, biculturals do so more strongly, which is likely because they have more distinct and clear-cut knowledge networks consistent with their two cultural selves. Further research suggests that this frame-switching is

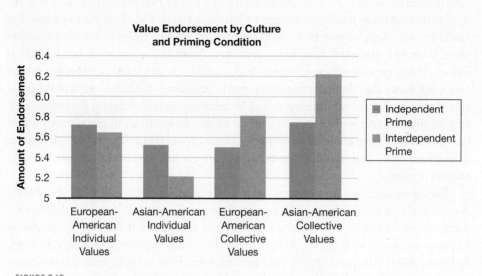

FIGURE 7.15 The values of Asian-Americans are more affected by independence and interdependence primes than the values of European-Americans are.

especially prevalent among biculturals who were born in North America compared with those who immigrated (Cameron & Lalonde, 1994; Tsai, Ying, & Lee, 2000). This may be because North American–born biculturals have a lifetime of bicultural experiences and have thus developed especially efficient frame-switching strategies, compared with immigrants who lived monocultural existences for much of their lives.

Multicultural People May Be More Creative

In 2013, the director Ang Lee won the Oscar for best director for *Life of Pi*, a story depicting the soul-searching journey of an Indian boy stuck on a raft with a Bengal tiger. He had paved the way for this honor with a series of successful movies that were produced both in his native Taiwan (where he lived until the age of 21), such as *The Wedding Banquet, Eat Drink Man Woman*, and *Crouching Tiger, Hidden Dragon*, and in Hollywood. What is perhaps noteworthy about Lee's films, particularly his Hollywood productions, is that he has had great success in directing movies that would seem to be worlds apart from his Taiwanese background. For example, Lee also won the Oscar for best director for his 2006 movie *Brokeback Mountain*, an epic love story about two gay cowboys (see **Figure 7.16**). His 1995 film *Sense and Sensibility* was a period piece about 19th-century British socialites, and his 1997 film *The Ice Storm* delved into the emotional vacuum surrounding two affluent suburban New England families during the 1970s. How could a Taiwanese emigrant come to have such penetrating insight into the minds of 19th-century British gentry, suburban New Englanders, Indian castaways, and gay cowboys?

Lee credits some of his success to the fact that he has multicultural experiences. Often referred to as an "outsider's outsider," Lee has been able to approach his subjects in a more naive way, free of the expectations that govern the perceptions of cultural insiders. *Time* magazine called him "a cosmopolitan chameleon [who] seems at home in any culture while viewing it with an outsider's ironic acuity" (Corliss, 2001). Looking in from the outside, Lee feels that he is able to see things differently, and perhaps even more accurately or objectively, than those who are shackled by conventional wisdom. He is able to take on a different perspective of a cultural situation than those who are immersed in it themselves.

However, Lee's creative success, impressive as it is, is perhaps not all that surprising given his multicultural experiences. People have noted for decades that

FIGURE 7.16   Ang Lee is a good example of a highly creative person who has had experiences living in different cultural environments. Here he is on the set of *Brokeback Mountain*.

many creative individuals have produced some of their most famous works during or following a stint abroad. For example, the American author Ernest Hemingway wrote *The Sun Also Rises* while living in France; the French painter Paul Gauguin created his most famous paintings while living in Tahiti; and the German composer George Handel composed his most famous works while living in England. One possible explanation for this recurring pattern is that there is something about adjusting to life in another culture that makes people more creative (see Leung, Maddux, Galinsky, & Chiu, 2008). Indeed, one key feature of creative insight is that people come to see something from a new and different perspective. Adjusting to life in another culture might provide the perspective that allows people to see things differently. For example, the American author Richard Wright, who wrote many of his novels in France, reflected on his time in France by noting that "once I went (abroad) it was extremely exciting for me to become a new personality, to be detached from everything that bound me, noticing everything that was different. That noticing of difference was very important" (Csikszentmihalyi, 1996, p. 129). Having more than one perspective available might well lead people to see the world in novel ways, which could foster creative thinking.

A number of studies have investigated the links between multicultural experiences and creative thinking. For example, in one study, researchers found that people who had lived in more than one culture were more likely to come up with outside-the-box creative solutions to a problem than those who had lived in only one culture (Maddux & Galinsky, 2009). Furthermore, they found that those who had merely visited other cultures as tourists did not show any comparative creativity advantage. Visiting other cultures is quite different from living in another culture, because the former does not involve any adjustment on the part of the individual. Visitors are free to observe and note differences, but like sojourners in the honeymoon stage, they haven't yet gone through the long adjustment period that is necessary for acculturation. Adjusting to life in a new culture is more likely to provide one with an additional perspective, and this appears to be associated with enhanced creativity.

Several studies have found that living in other cultures leads to more creative thinking across a wide variety of measures (e.g., Maddux, Adam, & Galinsky, 2010). This effect is stronger when the different cultures that one has had exposure to span greater cultural distance (Cheung & Leung, 2013) and when multicultural individuals feel that their cultural identities are blended (Saad, Damian, Benet-Martinez, Moons, & Robins, 2013). Moreover, organizational teams that have members from more than one culture show evidence for enhanced creativity above and beyond that of their individual members (Tadmor, Satterstrom, Jang, & Polzer, 2012). One reason that multicultural experiences foster creative thinking is that living in different cultures fosters a way of thinking called **integrative complexity**—a willingness and ability to acknowledge and consider different viewpoints on the same issue (Suedfeld, Tetlock, & Streufert, 1992). For example, one study found that after living in a new culture for 10 months people scored higher on a measure of integrative complexity (Maddux, Bivolaru, Hafenbrack, Tadmor, & Galinsky, 2014) and that the enhanced performance by multiculturals on creativity tasks was in part due to their higher integrative complexity scores (Tadmor, Galinsky, & Maddux, 2012).

Although these findings have been explained as the result of multicultural experiences causing enhanced creativity, it is possible that the effects are due to a very different kind of explanation—that is, perhaps creative people are more interested in moving and adjusting to new cultures in the first place. Both of these causal accounts appear to be true. For example, researchers have identified personality traits that predict who will be most likely to seek cross-cultural experiences. In general, people who score higher on measures of openness to experience, extraversion, and conscientiousness show the greatest interest in cross-cultural experiences (Stürmer et al., 2013; Zimmermann & Neyer, 2013). Given that openness to experiences is generally predictive of creativity, this is consistent with the notion that creative people might be more likely to choose to move to other countries. On the other hand, there is also evidence for the other causal account. People's openness to experience has been shown to increase when they move to another culture (Zimmermann & Neyer, 2013).

One study sought to disentangle the competing causal accounts of creativity and multicultural experiences by ensuring that *all* of the participants were people who had lived in more than one culture. Then these participants were primed to either think about *adapting* to life in another culture or think about *observing* another culture. A third group did not receive any prime and served as the control group. If the researchers were correct in the idea that multicultural experiences lead to creativity, rather than the reverse causal order, we should see enhanced creativity only among those primed to think about adapting to another culture. In this study, following the prime, participants were instructed to draw an alien unlike anything that had ever been observed on earth. Objective judges, who were blind to the participants' priming condition, then evaluated the drawings based on their number of novel features. As shown in **Figure 7.17**, those who were primed to think about adjusting to a new culture drew aliens that were judged to be more creative than those of the other two groups (Maddux & Galinsky, 2009). This is evidence that it is the act of adapting to a new culture that leads to more creativity.

The effects of multicultural experiences on creativity are not just limited to performance in lab studies. One study investigated the creativity of professional fashion designers (Godart, Maddux, Shipilov, & Galinsky, in press). The fashion industry maintains a trade magazine, the *Journal du Textile,* which surveys industrial

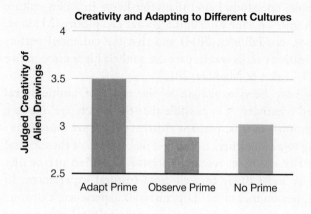

Creativity and Adapting to Different Cultures

FIGURE 7.17

The evaluation of the alien drawings by objective judges revealed that the participants who were primed for adapting to a new culture showed more creativity in their drawings than participants under other conditions.

buyers' ratings of the creative innovations of the various fashion collections in fashion shows. The multicultural experiences of the creative directors of leading fashion houses were used to see how well they predicted the creative innovation ratings of the journal. The researchers calculated the breadth of the creative directors' cultural experiences (i.e., the number of countries they had lived in), the depth of their experiences (i.e., the number of years they had spent living abroad), and the cultural distance between the countries that they had lived in. The results are shown in **Figure 7.18**. There was a curvilinear relation between the number of countries a creative director had lived in and the ratings of his or her creative innovations: The most creative directors had lived in two to three different cultures. There was a nearly linear relation between the years that people had lived abroad and the ratings of their creative innovations—generally, the more years one had lived abroad, the higher one's rated creativity. And there was a curvilinear relation between the cultural distance between the different cultures they had lived and their rated creativity—those who had lived in cultures that were moderately different from each other were rated as the most creative. Fashion appears to be one industry in which there are real benefits to having had multicultural experiences. Other studies have also found evidence for greater professional success with multicultural experiences (Maddux et al., 2014; Tadmor, Galinsky, & Maddux, 2012).

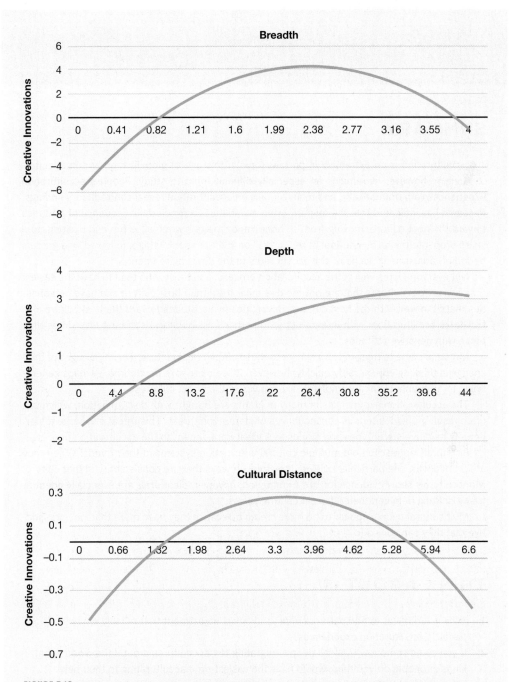

FIGURE 7.18 The number of creative innovations of the creative directors of fashion houses is predicted as a function of the number of countries they've lived in (breadth), the amount of time they've lived there (depth), and how culturally distant those countries are from each other (cultural distance).

SUMMARY

Acculturation is an extremely important topic in this age of globalization and multiculturalism; however, it remains an especially difficult topic to study. People's acculturation experiences vary dramatically, and many studies on acculturation reveal contradictory findings. Research has indicated that the migrant often experiences a predictable sequence of attitudes toward the host culture, moving from a "honeymoon stage," when all is fun and exciting, to a sharp drop into the turbulent pool of the "crisis" or "culture shock" stage, followed by a gradual period of "adjustment" as he or she acculturates to the new environment.

Not everyone fares well in the acculturation process, and those who tend to have the easiest time come from cultures that are not too dissimilar from their host culture and have personalities that fit in well with the host culture. Having positive attitudes toward the host culture also facilitates acculturation, with integrators (and perhaps assimilators) suffering less stress than those with negative attitudes.

Migrants come to think in ways similar to those of their host culture. The initial signs of their change in thinking appear fairly quickly; however, it seems to take much time, perhaps generations, for migrants to think completely like natives of their host cultures.

The acculturation experiences of many migrants are fraught with discrimination, which can often result in the deleterious consequences of stereotype threat. This threat can serve to perpetuate negative stereotypes and stands as a great impediment to the acculturation process.

Biculturals appear to hold multiple cultural information systems in their minds. When they are primed with one particular culture, they think in ways that are consistent with that culture. Monoculturals show evidence for this priming too; however, biculturals are especially adept at frame-shifting between their different cultural selves.

Multicultural people appear to be more creative because they have more than one perspective that they can consider.

THINK ABOUT IT

1. Why is it difficult to find patterns of psychological adjustment that reliably apply to all people's acculturation experiences?
2. If you could somehow track all people migrating to new cultures around the world, what kinds of people do you think would have the easiest time acculturating to their new homes? What kinds would have the toughest time?
3. If you could design a society that would allow immigrants to have the most positive outcomes in their acculturation experiences, what kind of society would you create?

4. Why is integration typically viewed as the most successful acculturation strategy? How does stereotype threat come to undermine the performance of negatively stereotyped groups?
5. Why do multicultural people tend to be more creative?

KEY TERMS

Acculturation, 258
Migrants, 260
Heritage Culture, 260
Host Culture, 260
Sojourners, 260
Immigrants, 260
Culture Shock, 262

Cultural Distance, 264
Cultural Fit, 266
Integration Strategy, 268
Marginalization Strategy, 268
Assimilation Strategy, 269
Separation Strategy, 269
Identity Denial, 273

Stereotype Threat, 274
Blending, 278
Frame-Switching, 278
Bicultural Identity
   Integration, 286
Integrative Complexity, 292

Indians do not seem to be as motivated to make individual choices compared with Americans.

8

MOTIVATION

Assuming that you're a student somewhere taking a course on culture and psychology, I'd like you to consider this question: "Why are you a student?" You might have many different answers for this question. You may be a student because you want to enhance your status in society, or because you are captivated by learning new things. You might want the bigger paychecks down the road, or to please your parents. You may be trying to delay finding a job. Or you may be doing it because it's what everyone else seems to be doing. Perhaps all of these reasons, and others, apply to your case.

This might seem like a simple, or even banal, question to ask. However, your underlying reasons speak to your motivations, and these reflect a great deal about how you understand yourself and the world around you. As this chapter will show, the kinds of things that motivate people vary in important ways across cultures. To have a better understanding of ourselves and of people from other cultures, we need to learn about what drives us and others. We need to consider what makes people tick.

Simply put, we are motivated to pursue the things we want and to avoid the things we don't want. To a certain extent, these things are very similar to what others around the world also want or don't want. We all desire things that improve the quality of our lives, such as getting access to material rewards, having stimulating relationships, and earning the respect of our peers (Kenrick, Li, & Butner, 2003). However, the ways we get access to those nice rewards, the kinds of relationships we might find stimulating, and the ways by which we secure the respect of our peers are influenced considerably by our cultural environments. Moreover, the decisions that we make in our lives involve trade-offs, such as the one you might have made in deciding to live a student's life for a few years rather than take the money you would have earned if you had started a career fresh out of high school. The trade-offs we are willing to accept reflect how we value different outcomes, and our values, in turn, are shaped a great deal by culture (e.g., Schwartz & Bilsky, 1990). As you read this chapter, you may realize that the reasons that you have for being a student, or for explaining any of the other behaviors you engage in, speak a great deal to the cultural experiences you have had growing up.

This chapter explores how some fundamental motivations vary across different cultural contexts. We will discuss how the concerns people have, and how people work toward addressing those concerns, are shaped by their cultural experiences. We will consider questions such as these: "How universal are needs for self-esteem?" "How are people from different cultures motivated to seek control?" "Are people from different cultures equally likely to strive to fit in with others?" The notion that people's experiences shape their psychology is the primary theme that guides the discussion of this chapter.

Motivations for Self-Enhancement and Self-Esteem

Many research ideas are sparked by events witnessed in everyday life. Some of my own research has contrasted Japanese and North Americans in their motivations, and many of the ideas I studied stemmed from experiences I had living in Japan. Upon receiving my B.A., I spent two years in a small town in southwestern Japan teaching English at a junior high school. In many ways it was an ideal place for a budding cultural psychologist, because the town had been somewhat isolated from Western influences. Indeed, I was the first Westerner to have lived in the town, and this set the stage for a 2-year comedy/drama of mutual cross-cultural misunderstandings. Such misunderstandings can often lead to the discovery of interesting cross-cultural differences.

One occasion in particular sticks in my mind. It was the very last day of the school year, and a Japanese teacher and I were preparing a lesson we would co-teach to a class of graduating ninth-grade students. We thought it would be fun if I would give the class a graduation speech in English and the Japanese teacher would translate any of the words the class didn't understand. So I went in front of the class and started saying the kinds of things I'd heard at graduation speeches while I was growing up in Canada. For example, I told them how proud I was of how well they had learned their English. And I went on about how talented they were, how they each had such special individual strengths, and I wrapped things up by urging them to remember that they could accomplish anything they wanted as long as they believed in themselves.

Well, the bit about their learning English well was something of an exaggeration because no one in the class seemed to understand a word of my speech. So the Japanese teacher, who had been taking notes throughout my speech, started to give an accurate word-by-word translation. And as I was looking out at the class during his translation I saw the class look progressively more and more confused and uncomfortable, until finally the students erupted into a bout of enormous laughter. But the Japanese teacher, who was always really good, seemed to sense the awkwardness of the moment, and he quickly changed gears. As I listened to his apparent "translation" of my speech, I noticed that he was now saying things that had never been in my original speech. He told them, for example, that if they thought English class in junior high school had been hard, that they would be rudely surprised because high school English was going to be far more difficult. And he reminded them that they were sorely lacking some basic English skills as none of them had been able to understand my very simple speech. He emphasized that they had an enormously difficult task ahead of them, and that they were going to have to put in very long hours and to keep persisting at their studies.

I remember at the time wondering what on earth the Japanese teacher was trying to do. That's not how you motivate people—telling them how difficult things are going to be and emphasizing how poor their skills are. But to my surprise, looking out at the class, the students started to stand up straight, had a look of determination in their eyes, and responded in unison with a powerful *"Hai!"*—a "Yes, sir!"—and they looked ready to take on the world. Of course, this is the effect I had been trying to achieve with my feel-good "You're all terrific" speech, but my words had failed miserably. This was not an isolated incident, and throughout my 2 years as a teacher I was chastised many times by the other teachers for praising the students too much. As they told me, "How can you expect them to keep trying if you're telling them that they're already good enough?" This seemed to suggest a key cultural difference in how people are motivated, and that was an idea that I followed up on over the years with a number of studies.

My own tendency to put a positive spin on the students' strengths reflected a powerful motivation that has received much research attention: **Self-enhancement** is the motivation to view oneself positively. Research (which has primarily been conducted with North Americans) reveals that people apparently have a strong need to view themselves positively. This need is evident across a diverse array of methodologies. First, you can see evidence of this motivation when you look at measures of **self-esteem**. Self-esteem is the positivity of your overall evaluation of yourself. When people are asked to complete a self-esteem measure, the vast majority are found to have high self-esteem. For example, we found that 93% of one very large sample of European-Canadians had self-esteem scores that were above the midpoint of the scale (Heine, Lehman, Markus, & Kitayama, 1999). That's a lot of high-self-esteem folks walking around. You can measure your own self-esteem by completing the self-esteem scale in **Table 8.1**.

You can also see evidence for self-enhancement motivations in measures of self-serving biases. **Self-serving biases** are tendencies for people to exaggerate how good they think they are. One study that demonstrated self-serving biases asked American college professors to evaluate how good they were at being at a professor (Cross, 1977). Can you guess what percentage thought that they were better than the average American college professor? Ninety-four percent! Now, we say that this is a bias because 94% of people clearly cannot be better than average. That's not how average works. Approximately 50% of people are better than average in any given domain, and approximately 50% are worse than average. I imagine that you wouldn't have a hard time deciding which of your professors you think are above or below average, and your evaluations would likely be closer to the distributions governed by the laws of statistics. Obviously, these professors did not have a very accurate or objective perspective when they evaluated themselves. Much research has revealed that one important reason people have such biased views of themselves is that they are motivated to view themselves positively.

TABLE 8.1

The Rosenberg Self-esteem Scale

	Strongly Disagree			Strongly Agree
I feel that I'm a person of worth, at least on an equal basis with others.	1	2	3	4
I feel that I have a number of good qualities.	1	2	3	4
*All in all, I am inclined to feel that I am a failure.	1	2	3	4
I am able to do things as well as most other people.	1	2	3	4
*I feel I do not have much to be proud of.	1	2	3	4
I take a positive attitude toward myself.	1	2	3	4
On the whole, I am satisfied with myself.	1	2	3	4
*I wish I could have more respect for myself.	1	2	3	4
*I certainly feel useless at times.	1	2	3	4
*At times I think I'm no good at all.	1	2	3	4

Items with an * are reverse scored. For those items, substract your answer from 5 to get your score. Then add all your individual scores. The lowest possible score is 10 and the highest is 40, with the midpoint being 25.

Source: Rosenberg (1965).

In case you're chuckling about how out of touch these professors are, it's informative to note that self-serving biases are not confined to academics. They've been reliably observed among elementary school children, high school students, college students, and working adults (see Taylor & Brown, 1988, for a review). Take a minute to think about whether you would evaluate yourself as above or below average for each of the following characteristics: ability to get along well with others, creativity, considerateness, driving ability, loyalty, dependability. My bet is that you think you're above average for all of these. Now it's possible that you might very well be better than average on all of them. Some people surely are. However, one thing that helps sustain these unrealistically positive self-assessments is that people rarely encounter concrete information in these domains. Without this information, there is nothing to prove that one is not above average. In other domains of life in which a person's relative standing compared to others is more clearly observable, such as height, calculus ability, or free-throw shooting skills, people are much less likely to hold such unrealistic views of themselves (Dunning,

FIGURE 8.1 Is this a pose of self-enhancement?

Meyerowitz, & Holzberg, 1989). People are quite accurate about their standing when they encounter incontrovertible evidence; however, in its absence they're likely to interpret the evidence in the most favorable way or just round upward when given half the chance (also see Kunda, 1990). This is evidence for people's motivations for self-enhancement (see **Figure 8.1**).

Perhaps the most striking evidence of people's motivation to view themselves positively comes from studies that investigate what people sometimes do to secure a positive evaluation of themselves when they encounter unfavorable information about themselves. A prospective romantic partner may rejects one's advances, or maybe one gets poor grades in classes. How do people go about keeping a positive self-view when their experiences aren't providing them with much to feel positive about?

Well, it turns out that people who are motivated to secure a positive self-view are often resourceful enough to figure out a way to get one. For example, if you get a bad grade in class, you could try several strategies to make yourself feel good again. You might engage in **downward social comparison** by comparing your performance with the performance of someone who is doing even worse than you (Festinger, 1954). When we compare ourselves to someone who is worse off than us, we create a favorable comparison that casts our own performance in a positive light. So an easy way to feel better about the C you received on your paper is to hang out with the people who got D's. This is usually a good occasion to avoid the people who got the A's— when we compare our performance with someone who is doing better than we are, this is known as an **upward social comparison**. In many kinds of situations, upward social comparisons tend to be rather painful because the contrast can make your own performance look that much worse (although there are important exceptions to this pattern; Lockwood & Kunda, 1997).

Another strategy you might try is **compensatory self-enhancement** (e.g., Baumeister & Jones, 1978), in which you acknowledge the poor grade you got in class but instead start to think about your excellent clarinet-playing skills. When engaging in this strategy you can focus on, and perhaps exaggerate, how good you are at something unrelated to your setback so that you can compensate for the pain of your failure and can again self-enhance by recruiting other kinds of positive thoughts about yourself. You might also try **discounting** your setback. Discounting is reducing the perceived importance of the domain in which you performed poorly (e.g., Simon, Greenberg, & Brehm, 1995). For example, to ease the sting from your bad grade, you might say something to yourself like, "Who really cares about chemistry anyway? I'm not going to become a chemist." Alternatively, you might try to make an **external attribution** for your poor performance. With an external attribution, people attribute the cause of their actions to something outside themselves, in contrast to an **internal attribution**, in which people locate the cause within ourselves, such as our abilities (e.g., Zuckerman, 1979). Hence, we can shift the blame for our poor grade elsewhere and think to ourselves, "The professor was impossible to understand," or "I didn't have enough time to prepare for the exam because of my cousin's wedding."

Or, you might try **basking in the reflected glory** of a successful group to which you belong. We do such basking when we emphasize our connection to successfully performing others and feel better about ourselves by sharing in the warm glow of the others' success. For example, research reveals that people are more likely to refer to their university's football team with the pronoun "we" than "they" if the team has recently won a game and if the individual has just done poorly himself or herself on a test (Cialdini et al., 1976). People wish to rid themselves of the bad feelings of their poor performance by aligning themselves with their more successful football team.

In sum, we have an impressive arsenal of tactics to protect and enhance our self-views. Given the range of strategies we have to choose from, it becomes less surprising that so many people do have such high self-esteem and such unrealistically positive views of themselves.

CULTURAL VARIATION IN SELF-ENHANCING MOTIVATIONS. The evidence from this psychological research, then, quite clearly shows that motivations for positive self-views are powerful and pervasive. However, given that the vast majority of research conducted on this topic has involved WEIRD participants, we might question whether this tendency is also found in countries where interdependent self-controls are more common. This is a reasonable concern, because much research has identified a pronounced positive relationship between independent self-construals and self-esteem within a variety of cultures (e.g., Oyserman, Coon, & Kemmelmeier, 2002; Singelis, Bond, Lai, & Sharkey, 1999). Would people from more collectivistic backgrounds show similarly strong motivations to enhance themselves?

One study investigated this question by comparing the positivity of self-views of Mexican-American and European-American preschool and elementary-school children (Tropp & Wright, 2003). The children were shown the photographs of eight other children and a photograph of themselves. They were asked to choose the photographs of the children who possessed a number of positive characteristics, such as "Who is smart?" or "Who is nice?" Overall, the children from both cultural groups tended to view themselves quite positively and usually included their own pictures. However, the European-Americans did so even more, choosing their picture for 92% of the positive characteristics, whereas Mexican-Americans did so for 82% of theirs. Even at this young age there is evidence of cultural variation in positive self-views.

A similar question was explored by contrasting Native American and European-American university students (Fryberg & Markus, 2003). The students were asked to describe themselves in an open-ended questionnaire. Similar to the findings with Mexican-Americans, the self-views of the Native Americans were less positive than those of the European-Americans. Indeed, the Native Americans listed fewer than half as many positive statements about themselves as the European-Americans did. Because Native Americans tend to have less independent self-concepts than European-Americans, these findings are again consistent with the argument that independence and self-enhancement are related. However, there do seem to be some exceptions to this rule, as some collectivistic cultures (e.g., the Maori in New Zealand [Harrington & Liu, 2002], African-Americans in the United States [Major, Spencer, Schmader, Wolfe, & Crocker, 1998], Israeli Druze [Kurman, 2001], or Indians who are making predictions about their futures; Joshi & Carter, 2013) have shown levels of self-enhancement comparable to those found in more individualistic settings.

The cultural variation in self-enhancement is even more striking when we compare North Americans of European descent to people living in East Asia, particularly those from China, Japan, and Korea. Whereas 93% of European-Canadians have high self-esteem, only about 55% of Japanese do (Heine et al., 1999). Likewise, tendencies to show self-serving biases are far less common among East Asian samples than Western ones (e.g., Norasakkunkit & Kalick, 2002). These differences in positive self-views are sustained by the ways people attend to and interpret events in the world. Consider the following study: Japanese and American college students were asked to list as many success or failure experiences they could remember having had in their lives (Endo & Meijer, 2004). The American pattern suggested a self-enhancing tendency in that Americans listed more success memories than failure memories (62% vs. 38%), whereas Japanese listed slightly fewer success memories than failure ones (48% vs. 52%). Unless American life really does provide people with more winning experiences and Japanese life provides people with more losing ones, we can conclude that Americans find successes more memorable, probably because they think about them more, whereas Japanese tend to find failures more memorable, because they think about these more. Much other research is consistent with this conclusion (e.g., Hamamura & Heine, 2007; Kitayama, Markus, Matsumoto, & Norasakkunkit, 1997; Kurman, Yoshihara-Tanaka, & Elkoshi, 2003).

Indeed, research on self-enhancing tendencies among people of East Asian descent shows a striking lack of enhancement motivations. For example, if we consider the tactics that people (or at least North Americans) have been shown to use to recruit positive self-views, which we discussed earlier, we find pronounced cultural variations. For example, after experiencing a failure, Asian-Canadians were three times more likely to seek upward social comparison targets than downward ones, whereas European-Canadians sought about as many upward as downward comparison targets (White & Lehman, 2005). North Americans often compensate for their failures by inflating their self-assessments in other unrelated domains; however, Japanese show the reverse tendency (Heine, Kitayama, & Lehman, 2001a). Whereas after failing on a task North Americans tend to discount the importance of the task, Japanese view the task as even more important (Heine et al., 2001b). Much research reveals that North Americans tend to make more external attributions for their failures, but Japanese often make more external attributions for their successes (e.g., Endo & Meijer, 2004). And whereas Americans tend to bask in the reflected glory of their sports teams, Japanese sports fans are likely to be more critical of their own teams than of the opposition (Snibbe, Kitayama, Markus, & Suzuki, 2003). These cultural differences are pronounced, they are evident across a broad range of different methodologies (29 different methodologies, at last count; Heine & Hamamura, 2007), and the East Asian samples often show a tendency to exaggerate a negative self-view. Do East Asians really view themselves in more self-critical terms than North Americans do? Can you think of any other alternative explanations for why East Asians appear to self-enhance less?

"Why are you special?
Because I'm your mommy, and I'm special."

One alternative possibility is that East Asians really are just as motivated as Westerners to evaluate themselves positively; however, various Western biases in our research methodologies prevent us from seeing these motivations. For example, East Asians may be more motivated to enhance their group selves rather than their individual selves, and comparisons of people's individual self-enhancing tendencies don't capture group self-enhancing motivations. This hypothesis is intriguing; however, many studies find that Westerners show stronger motivations than East Asians to enhance their group selves as well (e.g., Heine & Lehman, 1997a; Snibbe et al., 2003), which challenges this alternative explanation.

East Asians' relatively self-critical views appear to generalize from their individual selves to their groups. Actually, the extent of the spreading self-criticism appears to be even broader than this. A robust finding from the economic literature is the *endowment effect,* which is the tendency for people to value objects more once they own them, and have endowed them with their own positive qualities. It is because of the endowment effect that you come across classified ads on Craigslist from people who seem to be asking far too much for their used junk. An important component of the endowment effect is that people see a connection between their objects and their selves, and once an object is owned, people's self-views tend to color the objects (Gawronski, Bodenhausen, & Becker, 2007). But because Westerners tend to be self-enhancing, while East Asians do not, evaluations of owned objects also differ across cultures. The endowment effect is significantly stronger in Western samples than in East Asian ones, and in some situations East Asians even appear to show a reverse effect (Maddux et al., 2010). Actually, the cultural diversity of the endowment effect is quite extensive—recent research has found an absence of the endowment effect among the Hadza, a tribe of hunter-gathers from Northern Tanzania, unless they have had much exposure to modern society and markets (Apicella, Azevedo, Christakis, & Fowler, 2014; see **Figure 8.2**).

Another possibility is that East Asians value a different set of traits from those that have been explored in research thus far, and if they were asked to evaluate themselves

FIGURE 8.2 Coren Apicella working with Hadza of Tanzania where she found a striking absence of motivations for an endowment effect among those who had little exposure to markets.

on especially important traits, the cultural differences would be reduced. Although some evidence supports this alternative account using one method (e.g., Brown & Kobayashi, 2002; Sedikides, Gaertner, & Toguchi, 2003), several other methods have been used reveal the opposite pattern. A look at all the published studies on this topic stands in contradiction of this account (see Heine, Kitayama, & Hamamura, 2007, for a review).

Another possibility is that these studies are not measuring people's "true" feelings but are instead tapping into differences in cultural norms for describing oneself. That is, East Asians may just be feigning modesty in these studies (and perhaps Westerners are feigning their bravado; see Kurman, 2003). One source of evidence that is consistent with this idea is that East Asians appear to feel as good about themselves as Westerners do based on answers to a test that measures unconscious associations between the self and other positive and negative words (Falk, Heine, Takemura, Zhang, & Hsu, 2015; Kitayama & Uchida, 2003). This evidence suggests that East Asians *like* themselves as much as Westerners do. However, when it comes to assessments of their *competence*, East Asians appear to be more self-critical (also see Tafarodi & Swann, 1996). Even studies that investigate people in anonymous situations and use hidden behavioral measures (e.g., Heine et al., 2001b; Takata, 2003) or indirect measures (Falk & Heine, in press) find clear evidence for this cultural difference in how they evaluate themselves. Overall, the research provides converging evidence that East Asians do not have as strong a desire as Westerners to view themselves positively.

ORIGINS OF CULTURAL DIFFERENCES IN SELF-ENHANCEMENT. Now how might this cultural difference in self-views emerge? A short answer would be that people learn self-enhancement motivations as they grow up in their culture. In one set of studies, parents in Taiwan and the United States were interviewed regarding their attitudes toward child rearing (Miller, Wang, Sandel, & Cho, 2002; Miller, Wiley, Fung, & Liang, 1997). It was found that parents often used stories about the child's past behaviors to socialize them. Can you recall the kinds of stories your parents told you as a child? Interestingly, the stories that were more often told by European-American parents focused on a past success of the child. In stark contrast, Taiwanese parents were more likely to tell stories about past transgressions of the child (Miller et al., 1997; also see similar findings by Ng et al., 2007; Wang, 2004). American stories thus focused children's attention on their strengths, whereas Taiwanese stories were more likely to focus the children's attention on areas that needed correcting. Furthermore, when researchers explicitly asked parents what they thought about self-esteem, they got highly divergent answers from the two groups (Miller et al., 2002). The European-American parents viewed self-esteem as central to child rearing and saw it as a positive quality that enhanced children's development and that should be cultivated by parents. The Taiwanese parents, in contrast, had little to say about the words that most closely approximated "self-esteem" (it's telling that there is no direct translation of self-esteem in many East Asian languages), and what they did have to say was often somewhat negative—for example, expressing the belief that too much self-esteem can lead to frustration when things aren't working out well for the children. Similarly, North American schools are more likely than their East Asian counterparts to make efforts to inculcate self-esteem in students (e.g., Lewis, 1995; Stevenson & Stigler, 1992). In sum, cultural environments in North America and East Asia provide different opportunities for learning whether positive self-views are desirable or not.

However, this answer is not complete. If we learn our attitudes about self-esteem from our parents and schools, then where did our parents and schools get these views in the first place? One way to address this question is to look at the emergence of motivations for positive self-views over time. Unfortunately, for those of us who are interested in investigating this kind of question, the history of motivations hasn't provided us with a fossil record. We need to look for some rather indirect evidence to see changes in motivations over time. Baumeister (1987) explored this question through an analysis of some historical literature. First, this analysis revealed that the notion of individual selves didn't really emerge in Western literature until the 12th century, when the Christian concept of the Last Judgment changed from being an issue of the salvation of collectives to the salvation of individual souls. It was also around this time that literature began to use devices based on the idea that different characters had different perspectives of events (Hanning, 1977). Furthermore, not until the 16th century and the birth of the Protestant Reformation did something akin to self-enhancing motivations first become clearly evident. Many of the early Protestant sects maintained a belief in **predestination,** the idea that before people were born, it had already been determined whether they would be one of the fortunate "elect" who would spend eternity in blessed heaven after passing or would be one of the wretched many doomed to burn in hell forever. Which group a person was assigned to was a distinction that obviously mattered a great deal to members of these Protestant sects. Because no one had access to God's ledger to determine whether he or she was on the right list, people had to rely on cues to discern their fates. The primary cue that a person was part of the elect was that he or she possessed absolute certainty about this fact. Any doubt regarding whether an individual was of the elect was to be seen as proof that the person was not, so individuals became highly motivated to interpret events in their lives as signs that God was viewing them favorably. The distinction between spending eternity in heaven or in hell was a sufficient motivator to lead people to make great efforts to interpret their situation in a favorable light. With this, it was argued, motivations for self-enhancement grew (also see Weintraub, 1978). We'll return to consider the key role of the belief in predestination in other motivations later in this chapter.

The Protestant Reformation may have been a helpful impetus in the growth of self-enhancing motivations; however, given that there is evidence of such motivations in many non-Protestant nations, this cannot be the whole story. There is a clear positive relation between independence/individualism and self-esteem, and this relation is found within both individualistic and collectivistic cultures (the correlation ranges from .33 to .51; Heine, 2003). Why might these two constructs tend to go hand in hand? One way to understand this is to consider what happens when the self-concept becomes more and more focused on the lone individual, as it does in individualism. When one's beliefs start to migrate to the idea "I'm all that I've got," there would seem to be a greater need to view oneself positively. If "all that I've got" is not very good, this would seem to be a real problem for the individual. Cultural messages common in individualistic cultures encourage people to be self-sufficient and not to rely on others (e.g., Markus & Kitayama, 1991). It would be extremely difficult to achieve these goals if one did not view oneself positively. This reasoning suggests that as cultures become more individualistic, rendering people more concerned with being able to take care of themselves and to carve their own paths, there should be a corresponding motivation to view oneself positively. However, an alternative perspective is that motivations for self-enhancement are stronger in some cultures not due to individualism but rather to economic inequality, as people are motivated to think of themselves as better than others when there are pronounced differences in economic opportunities (Loughnan et al., 2011).

We can see evidence for this relation between individualism and self-esteem by looking at the United States. As noted in Chapter 3, much evidence suggests that the United States has become more individualistic since the 1960s. For example, people are spending less time with their families, the divorce rate has increased, and people are less likely to get involved in community organizations (e.g., Putnam, 2000; Rosen, 1998; Twenge, Campbell, & Gentile, 2013). Evidence also suggests that self-esteem has been rising in the United States over the same period (Gentile, Twenge, & Campbell, 2010; Twenge & Campbell, 2001). **Figure 8.3** shows this relation clearly. Americans who have recently graduated from college had considerably higher self-esteem when they were in college than their parents' generation did when they were in college. A similar pattern has emerged for American students' assessments of various abilities—the percentage of people who view themselves as better than average has significantly grown over the past 50 years (Twenge, Campbell, & Gentile, 2012). It follows that wherever individualism has been increasing we should see an increase in self-esteem and positive self-assessments. Another example is that narcissism is higher in younger generations of Chinese than in older generations, and

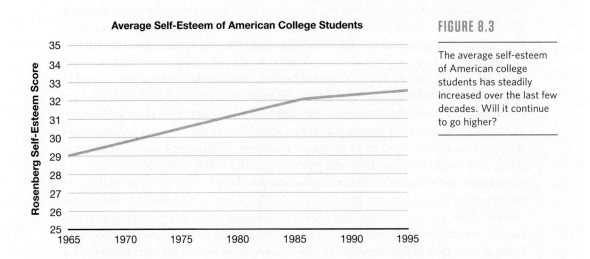

Average Self-Esteem of American College Students

FIGURE 8.3

The average self-esteem of American college students has steadily increased over the last few decades. Will it continue to go higher?

in those who are in a one-child family compared with those in a multi-child family (Cai, Kwan, & Sedikides, 2012; also see Cameron et al., 2013). Cultural messages and institutions change and adapt over time, and it follows that psychological processes, such as motivations for self-esteem, will change as well.

Motivations for Face and Self-Improvement

Another way to address the question of why motivations for positive self-views vary across cultures is to consider the different kinds of positive views that a person might desire. One way of having a positive self-view is to have high self-esteem. That is, the individual views himself or herself positively. Another way is to have a good deal of "face." Face is an interesting concept that is of considerable importance in much of the world, although many Westerners don't have a great understanding of it (see Ting-Toomey, 1994). Indeed, the expression "to lose face" entered the English language only in the late 19th century as a direct translation from Chinese (Oxford English Dictionary, 1989). **Face** has been defined as the amount of social value others give you if you live up to the standards associated with your position (e.g., Ho, 1976). The higher your social position, the greater the amount of face available to you. Hence, the president of a company has a lot of face, whereas the person in the mailroom has very little. Face can also be shared by groups. For example, in the 2008 Olympics in Beijing, the overall success of the event was seen by many Chinese to boost the face of all of China.

In hierarchical, collectivist societies, such as the kinds found in East Asia, face takes on special importance. What matters is not how positively you think of yourself but whether significant others think you're doing well. If others grant you face, you'll enjoy all the perquisites that come with the enhanced status and power. In such a cultural context, people can become highly motivated to maintain and enhance their face. Can you think how people's motivations would differ whether they are trying to maintain face or they are trying to build self-esteem?

A first important characteristic of face is that it's more easily lost than gained. Because the amount of face you have access to is determined by your position, you can't readily increase your face unless you get a promotion. This renders face as something that is difficult to enhance. However, face is lost whenever individuals fail to live up to the standards of their roles (Ho, 1976). For example, if a company gets caught up in an embarrassing scandal, the president of the company will lose face, or if a child is expelled from school, the child and his family will lose face. Face is always vulnerable, and because others determine a person's face, people must count on the goodwill of others to be able to maintain their face. Given that face is so easily lost, a good strategy is for people to adopt a cautious approach and try to ensure that they are not acting in a way that might lead others to reject them (Hamamura & Heine, 2008). If they can attend to any potential weaknesses and work toward correcting them by improving themselves, they should decrease the chance that others will view them as having lost face.

This kind of defensive, cautious approach to not losing something is known as a **prevention orientation**. This is in contrast with a concern over advancing oneself and aspiring for gains, which is known as a **promotion orientation** (Higgins, 1996). These two orientations are fundamentally different, are evident across a wide range of species (e.g., Jones, Larkins, & Hughes, 1996), and are even associated with activation in different hemispheres of the brain (Tucker & Williamson, 1984). When we are engaged in a promotion focus we are trying to secure good things, and when we are engaged in a prevention focus we are trying to avoid bad things. A loss of face is one of those bad things that people are motivated to avoid.

If a concern with face leads to a prevention orientation, and East Asians are more concerned with face, we should expect to see greater evidence of prevention orientations among them. Much research has confirmed this pattern (e.g., Elliot, Chirkov, Kim, & Sheldon, 2001; Lee et al., 2000; Lockwood, Marshall, & Sadler, 2005). In one study, for example, book reviews for the best-selling books on Amazon.com and Amazon.co.jp (Japanese Amazon) were compared (Hamamura et al., 2009). The researchers identified the reviews that were rated as most helpful by other visitors to the site, and these reviews were coded for how much promotion information (e.g., "the book has great character development,") and prevention information (e.g., "it bored me silly") that they contained. The American book reviews contained more promotion information than the Japanese ones, and likewise, the Japanese reviews contained more prevention information than the American ones.

How do you think a promotion focus or prevention focus might affect how people respond to the successes and failures they encounter in their lives? It would seem that if people have a promotion focus, they will strive for opportunities for advancement and, as such, should focus their efforts on things they can do well, because these will provide more opportunities for success. Things they do poorly, in contrast, should be avoided, because they are not likely to lead to success. In contrast, people with a prevention focus should focus their efforts on things they don't do well, because correcting shortcomings will help them avoid a failure. This suggests that East Asians and Westerners should respond quite differently to successes and failures. Is this the case?

My colleagues and I asked Japanese and Canadian participants to come into the laboratory where they privately received false feedback that they had done either very well or very poorly on a creativity test (Heine et al., 2001b). The participants were then left alone in a room with another set of creativity items and were timed on how long they persisted on this task. The results are shown in **Figure 8.4**. The Canadians persisted significantly longer after success than failure, a finding that replicates much work that has been done on persistence research in the West (e.g., Feather, 1966; Pyszczynski & Greenberg, 1983). In stark contrast, the Japanese persisted

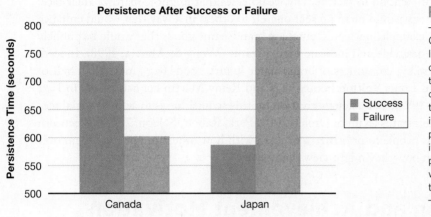

FIGURE 8.4

Canadians are more likely to persist longer on a task if they think they are talented at it compared to when they think they are poor at it. In contrast, Japanese persist longer on a task if they think they are poor at it compared to when they think they are talented at it.

significantly longer after failure than success. Apparently, the Canadians, maintaining a promotion focus, were more interested in working on things they did well, because these were more likely to provide them opportunities to view themselves positively. The Japanese, in contrast, maintaining a prevention focus, were more interested in working on the things they did poorly, apparently so they could improve themselves and be less likely to fail in the future. This **self-improvement** motivation, a desire to seek out potential weaknesses and work on correcting them, is a strong motivation in East Asian contexts (e.g., Kitayama et al., 1997).

Interestingly, this cultural difference has even been shown to influence people's choice of leisure activities. Oishi and Diener (2003) found that when given a choice to play either basketball or darts, European-Americans tend to choose the activity they do well whereas Asian-Americans do not (also see Peters & Williams, 2006). Parents also encounter this, as East Asian parents are more likely to call their children's attention to their weaknesses, whereas Western parents direct their children's attention to their strengths (Miller, et al. 1997; Ng et al., 2007). More generally, East Asians are more likely than Westerners to focus on the process underlying actions (such as improving) than on the goal of the action (such as becoming talented; Miyamoto, Knoepfler, Ishii, K., & Ji, 2013).

A second characteristic of face is that it involves a concern with how others are viewing oneself. Unlike self-esteem, which involves the individual evaluating himself or herself, face is maintained only when others evaluate oneself positively. As we discussed in Chapter 6, East Asians do attend more to the perspective of others than Westerners do (e.g., Kim, Cohen, & Au, 2010; Wu & Keysar, 2007), and this is a key component of face maintenance. What kind of steps might people take to ensure that others think of them positively? One strategy, as discussed earlier, would be to take a prevention orientation to identify any weaknesses that might jeopardize their face. A second strategy would be to present oneself to others in a way that would enhance one's face. For example, one could purchase brand-name goods that would be publicly recognized as desirable and indicate higher status (Wong & Ahuvia, 1998). Indeed, East Asians are big consumers of brand-name luxury goods (e.g., more than half of the business in Louis Vuitton luxury bags and Remy Martin cognac occurs in East Asia; Wilson, 1994), and a key motivation for this acquisition is to achieve social recognition of their status (Kim & Drolet, 2009; Park, Rabolt, & Jeon, 2008). A concern with face leads people to prioritize a concern with how others might view them over a concern with how they might view themselves.

Religion and Achievement Motivation

The studies I've discussed demonstrate how motivations for achievement in the face of success and failure vary across cultures. What motivates people to achieve has been a question that has attracted much interest. And what is perhaps the most profound cultural psychological theory that was ever proposed targeted this question. In 1904–1905 Max Weber (**Figure 8.5**) published a highly influential and controversial series of essays titled *The Protestant Ethic and the Spirit of Capitalism*. Weber's work has been enormously impactful, so we will look closely at it—and at some of its implications for modern cultural psychology.

Weber was interested in how the radical doctrine of capitalism was able to emerge out of the traditional economies of the medieval era. Capitalism encapsulated a way of thinking that was dramatically different from anything that had existed before in the Western world. At the time Weber published his ideas, the dominant theory came from Karl Marx, who proposed that capitalism emerged as the result of a surplus of capital that accumulated during the shift from an agricultural economy to an industrial one. In contrast to the economic determinism of Marxism, Weber viewed capitalism as the product of people's deriving meaning from a particular cultural context. He proposed that capitalism grew out of a belief system that was rooted in a number of cultural ideas that began emerging in the 16th and 17th centuries in Western Europe and in

FIGURE 8.5 Max Weber maintained that a particular set of cultural meanings associated with the Protestant Reformation allowed for the birth of capitalism.

North America. The ideas that became the foundation for capitalism were ones that grew out of the Protestant Reformation.

Protestantism initially emerged as a reaction to some perceived corruption in the medieval Catholic Church, but it contained ideas that shaped much more than the spiritual lives of its followers and, ultimately, of the societies that were built around it. One idea to emerge from Protestantism was the notion that individuals were able to communicate with God directly and thus were not dependent on the Church as an intermediary. As a result, Protestants emphasized literacy training more than Catholics, so that people would be able to read the Bible for themselves. The individualized relation that formed between each person and God has been argued to be central to the blossoming of individualism that emerged during the Reformation and continues to influence much of Western society today.

A related idea emerged out of this individualized relation between God and each person. Martin Luther, the founder of Protestantism, proposed that each individual had a **calling**—that is, a unique God-given purpose to fulfill during his or her mortal existence. The idea was that we are all God's servants in the world and that we are each given a specific duty or job to take care of while we tend the planet. In addition, God gives each individual the unique skills and capabilities needed to fulfill his or her calling, and it is incumbent upon individuals to discover their calling. The highest moral duty that individuals were believed to have was to serve God well by working hard at their calling. By developing this notion of a calling, Luther was able to imbue daily labor with a spiritual significance that had traditionally been reserved for religious activities such as prayer and ritual. With the Protestant Reformation, work had become a moral obligation rather than something necessary for subsistence. Weber maintained that this shift in attitude had an enormous impact on society. Furthermore, because Protestants came to view work as a spiritual task, they wished to avoid debasing it by holding a casual or unprofessional attitude. Protestants felt that people should take their work very seriously.

As discussed earlier in this chapter, some early sects of Protestantism (in particular, some early Puritan sects, which included Calvinism, Pietism, and Baptism) proposed the radical idea of predestination—the idea that God had already determined, before they were even born, who was going to heaven and who was going to hell. Weber proposed that this belief in predestination played a key role in the development of capitalism. How might a belief in predestination affect one's attitude toward work? You might expect that, if their fates were predetermined, people might respond by deciding to have a good time while on earth, because there isn't anything they could do to change their fates anyway. They might as well just live it up while they can. However, apparently this interpretation was rarely seized upon. Rather, the notion of predestination brought with it "a feeling of unprecedented inner loneliness" (Weber, 1904/1992, p. 104) that individuals were highly motivated to escape by convincing themselves that they were one of the privileged elect.

No one knew for sure whether they were among the elect, although a feeling of certainty of one's elect status was the best sign that one could come by. The evidence for this certainty was seen to lie in the products of one's efforts to fulfill one's calling. It was believed that God would not reward those who were doomed to burn in hell, so any sign of material success was perceived as evidence that one was of the elect. Furthermore, because one's time on earth was to be spent serving God through one's calling, rather than enjoying the fruits of one's labor (the fun times for Puritans were not perceived to begin until after they had died and gone to heaven), any accumulated wealth was to be reinvested to further one's efforts and to accumulate even more wealth and evidence of one's status among the elect. Modern capitalism, as Weber viewed it, was thus concerned with the accumulation of wealth for its own sake, and not for the sake of the material pleasures it brought. Weber proposed that it was in this fertile soil of ideas that capitalism took root and blossomed.

The notion that predestination was key to the Protestant sects that initially populated the United States might be surprising to many good Protestants out there today, because predestination is no longer a belief of contemporary Protestant sects. Firm beliefs in predestination lasted only a couple of generations, probably because it is not the kind of idea that has much lasting appeal (Landes, 1999). However, Weber proposed that it lasted long enough to be converted into a more enduring secular code of behavior that included honesty, hard work, seriousness, and the thrifty use of money and time. These attitudes toward work can be seen in some influential Puritan writings from the early days of the United States: Benjamin Franklin (who was raised in a Calvinist family) reminded people that "Early to bed, early to rise makes a man healthy, wealthy and wise" and that "God helps them that help themselves." John Wesley, the founder of the Methodists, the largest religious denomination in the United States, explicitly exhorted "all Christians to gain all they can, and to save all they can; that is, in effect to grow rich" (Weber, 1904/1992, p. 175). It is these secular attitudes that Weber argued spread throughout Protestant communities, particularly in the United States, and laid the foundation for the development of capitalism.

What do you think of Weber's thesis? As you might imagine, Weber's ideas were, and continue to be, controversial. Nonetheless, there is much evidence that is consistent with Weber's thesis (see Uhlmann & Sanchez-Burks, 2014). For example, in Germany, Protestant counties in the 19th century were wealthier than Catholic counties, and this was associated with greater literacy in the Protestant regions (Becker & Woessmann, 2009). A consideration of per capita income among countries of the world found that nations that were largely Protestant earned more than those that were mixed Protestant and Catholic, and that these earned more than those nations that were predominantly Catholic (Furnham, 1990). A recent analysis found that Protestants, and people living in Protestant societies more generally, consider the prospect of being unemployed as more of a blow to their well-being than non-Protestants and people living in non-Protestant societies do

(Van Hoom & Maseland, 2013). People living in Protestant countries also have more pro-market economic attitudes than ones living in non-Protestant ones (Hayward & Kemmelmeier, 2011). A few decades ago, it was observed that Protestants in the United States were more likely to enter high-status, nonmanual occupations than Catholics of the same occupational origin, controlling for a variety of other societal variables (Jackson, Fox, & Crockett, 1970). In the mid-20th century a study revealed that Protestant nations were far more industrialized than their Catholic counterparts (McClelland, 1961), and religious differences accounted for much of that (Cavalcanti, Parente, & Zhao, 2007).

These examples mostly reflect culture-level variables that differ between societies with predominantly Catholic or Protestant influences. There are also examples of differences in psychological variables between individual Catholics and Protestants. One variable to consider is the degree of individualism that exists in Protestant countries compared with other countries. The six most individualistic countries in the world according to Hofstede's (1980) measures are largely Protestant (see Figure 6.8), whereas the least individualistic Western societies are largely Catholic. (Countries dominated by various Asian religions also tend to score low in individualism.) Pronounced differences in the embracing of an intrinsic work ethic were observed between Western European Catholics and mainstream Protestants (interestingly, the relation was clear by contrasting individuals of different religions *within* countries and by comparing countries), as evident in a measure of work values (Giorgi & Marsh, 1990).

The Protestant ethic has been associated with negative attitudes toward laziness and being overweight (Quinn & Crocker, 1999). McClelland's (1961) classic cross-cultural comparison of Weber's thesis found that Protestant parents expected their children to become self-reliant at an earlier age compared with Catholic parents. McClelland also investigated the stories written by young boys and found that those written by German Protestants had more evidence of strong achievement motivations than those written by German Catholics.

However, some cross-cultural research comparing the average scores from self-report measures of the Protestant work ethic has provided evidence that is not obviously consistent with Weber's thesis (e.g., Furnham, Bond, & Heaven, 1993). Given the methodological challenges of comparing means across cultures in self-report surveys described in Chapter 4, and the great diversity in measures that have been used to measure the Protestant work ethic (Furnham, 1990), it is hard to know what to make of this mixed pattern of results. Laboratory studies that manipulate independent variables in controlled settings would be especially useful to explore Weber's thesis.

A variety of laboratory experiments have explored some hypotheses derived from Weber's theory, and we'll go over some of them here. One key idea was that Protestantism resulted in work becoming seen as a spiritual task. Hence, we would expect that Protestants who were led to think about spiritual quests should become motivated to work harder. A recent study tested this hypothesis by priming American and Canadian participants outside of their awareness with words related to salvation (or neutral words in a control condition), and they were then given a work task to complete (Uhlmann, Poehlman, Tannenbaum, & Bargh, 2011). The results found that Americans who were primed about salvation worked harder on the subsequent task than did those who were primed with neutral words. This indicates that notions of hard work and salvation are implicitly linked for Americans. Curiously, this pattern occurred regardless of whether or not the American participants were religious, providing some evidence for Weber's claim that ideas about predestination became secularized, and thus part of the American cultural fabric, even for those without Protestant beliefs. In contrast, the Canadian participants did not work any harder when primed with ideas about salvation, suggesting that an implicit link between salvation and working was not evident for them.

A second notion of Weber's thesis is that, when working, Protestants should be entirely focused on their work and thus maintain a rather detached attitude toward potential distractions, such as other people, because of the sacred nature of their work (Hampden-Turner & Trompenaars, 1993; Sanchez-Burks, 2005). This idea stems from the teaching of John Calvin, the founder of Calvinism, who argued that when people work on their calling, they should maintain an air of unsentimental professionalism in their conduct with each other. Calvin's justification for this impersonal and focused attitude toward work was that a casual attitude and idle socializing were evil because they detracted from one's work for God in their calling (Bendix, 1977). To perform good work, then, one should "focus on the task" and "be professional" (Sanchez-Burks, 2005). On the other hand, when not working, Protestants should feel free to switch back to a more relaxed style. Hence, working hard is okay, and playing hard is okay, but the idea is not to mix the two.

Much research does suggest that American Protestants take on more of a professional and non-casual attitude toward their work than other groups. For example, when Anglo-American and Mexican students were shown a video of a workgroup meeting, the Mexicans later showed significantly better recall of interpersonal information from the meeting than the (largely Protestant) Americans did; the Americans were focused primarily on the work task at hand (Sanchez-Burks, Nisbett, & Ybarra, 2000). Likewise, another study found that American-born office workers were more likely to decorate their own cubicles in a professional manner (with fewer personal items) than immigrants to the United States were (Heaphy, Sanchez-Burks, & Ashford, 2011). Similarly, Americans who were considering a hypothetical job candidate reacted more negatively than Indians did when the candidate mentioned nonwork roles and activities; the Americans preferred candidates who only discussed information directly relevant to the job (Uhlmann, Heaphy, Ashford, Zhu, & Sanchez-Burks, 2013). In another study, Protestant Americans were found to focus only on work-related tasks and pay less attention to relational cues from others, in contrast to non-Protestant Americans who attended to relational cues as well as their work. When Protestants are actually working, they do not seem to have much interest in anything else.

A key point about Weber's argument was that Protestant anxiety about salvation was the driving force behind their work ethic and that this was coupled with a Protestant worldview that maintained that people are inherently wicked and depraved. Any encounters with thoughts that one was behaving in a way that was less than holy should thus motivate Protestants to work even harder at their calling, in an effort to convince themselves that they are still among the elect, despite their occasional failings. In contrast to Protestantism, Judaism and Catholicism are less likely to see humans as fundamentally bad, and they have emphasized the emotion of guilt, which should be dwelled upon and suffered, as a motivator for people to strive to become better (see Chapter 12 for more discussion about religious differences in morality). So a question arises about whether Protestants might be more likely than Jews and Catholics to channel their thoughts of depravity toward productive ends.

This hypothesis might sound rather absurd; however, some recent evidence finds support for it. Kim, Zeppenfeld, and Cohen (2013) looked through a large archival database of a set of high-IQ American children from the 1920s who were followed longitudinally throughout their lives. In the 1950s the participants, then adults, were asked whether they had any anxieties or problems with respect to sex in their lives. Reasoning that, for Protestants, such anxieties might be experienced as concerns with their own depravity, the authors explored how productive those individuals with sex anxieties were compared with those who didn't have such anxieties, and compared these groups across religions. Intriguingly, those Protestants with sexual anxieties were more than twice as productive in their careers, particularly in creative pursuits, than Protestants without such anxieties. In contrast, sexual anxiety was unrelated to the productivity of Jews and Catholics.

Following up on this finding, the authors created a lab study in which they induced some male American students to consider sexually depraved thoughts (through an elaborate scheme, they led participants to unconsciously entertain sexual thoughts about their sisters) and put others in a control condition in which such thoughts were not primed. The participants were then given the opportunity to make sculptures out of clay. A series of local art experts judged the sculptures (blind to condition) and, remarkably, concluded that the best sculptures were made by the Protestant men who were led to have the depraved thoughts. The depravity manipulation had no impact on the sculptures of the Jews and Catholics. Thus, a Protestant drive to be creative and productive may be based on an effort to rid oneself of any thoughts that might not be spiritually pure (also see Cohen, Kim, & Hudson, 2014). As someone who was raised Protestant myself, working hard now to write this book, I can't help but wonder where my own motivations are coming from.

In sum, to the extent that Max Weber was correct more than a century ago, we can understand that some motivations toward work come from religious ideas that people encounter in their cultures. Weber's thesis remains controversial, but a great deal of evidence supporting it has been marshaled from a variety of disciplines. It is difficult to account for this evidence without accepting the basic tenets of his theory. Laboratory investigations of Protestant ideology are relatively new to psychology, and there will surely be further challenges and validations of Weber's thesis in the future.

Agency and Control

Perhaps the most fundamental way that culture can shape motivations is through perceptions of control. All organisms have their needs and desires. A critical challenge for organisms is to work within the constraints of their environments toward achieving those needs and desires. Given that humans, unlike other organisms, live in cultural environments, getting what we want requires us to make efforts that are constrained by what our cultures lead us to believe about how the world works. Imagine, for example, what you would do if you wanted to get a raise from your boss. You might believe that you would have more luck getting that raise if you ask your boss directly for it, if you compliment your boss on his new business plan, if you start working extra hard, if you secure a competing offer from another potential employer, or if you keep your mouth shut and don't rock the boat. Which strategy you pursue reflects the theories you have about how you can exert control over your environment with respect to getting raises, and these theories come from your beliefs about yourself and your environment.

One theory people have that is relevant to the experiences of control is whether they perceive their identities to be easily malleable and changeable or stable and fixed. Recall from Chapter 6 that these two implicit theories are known as incremental and entity theories of self, respectively. In addition to the implicit theories people have about the malleability of the self, they have implicit theories about the malleability of the world. For example, we can see the world as something that is fixed and beyond our control to change (an **entity theory of the world**), or we can think of the world as flexible and responsive to our efforts to change it (an **incremental theory of the world**). To the extent that different cultures perceive selves and their social worlds to be more or less fluid and malleable, they will possess different theories about how individuals can, should, and do act.

Su and colleagues (1999) offer a nice metaphor to capture the potential ways that people's selves and social worlds can be malleable. Imagine that you want to build a stone wall. You might try a couple of different approaches. One is to emphasize the integrity of the wall at the expense of the individual stones. That is, you could have a clear plan of the shape of the wall that you want to erect. You could choose stones that are approximately the correct size and carve them down so that they fit perfectly into the wall. The stones would change to accommodate the wall. An alternative way to build the wall would be to allow the wall to take on the shape of the individual stones. You could choose stones that are roughly of the right size and shape and assemble them into the wall. If a stone that you chose had a bumpy protuberance, then the wall would likewise have that same bump. The wall would change in shape to reflect the nature of the individual stones. The enterprise of stone-wall building will vary a great deal depending on whether you view the individual stones or the resultant wall as flexible and capable of being changed.

In many ways, life is like building a stone wall, with people as the stones. On occasions there are clear social constraints that individuals must adjust themselves to; at other times social relationships and organizations will change to adjust themselves to the nature of their individual members. Although we sometimes see ourselves as more flexible than our social worlds and other times see the social worlds as potentially more malleable than we are, the extent to which we hold these beliefs can vary importantly across cultures.

Primary and Secondary Control

Rothbaum, Weisz, and Snyder (1982) proposed that there are at least two ways people can gain control in their lives. The first way was labeled **primary control**. People achieve a sense of primary control by striving to shape existing realities to fit their perceptions, goals, or wishes. Primary control is an extensively researched construct in psychology, and it also goes under the related names of an *internal locus of control, influence,* and *agency.* It's the kind of control you perceive when you decide you want a hamburger and you go down to a burger joint to get yourself one. The chain of events that is initiated to get that hamburger into your stomach is predicated on a belief that you have the efficacy to influence your social environment to get what you want.

Rothbaum and colleagues proposed another kind of control that has been less researched by psychologists, which they labeled **secondary control**. People achieve a sense of secondary control when they attempt to align themselves with existing realities, leaving the realities unchanged but exerting control over the psychological impact of these realities. It involves accepting one's circumstances (Morling & Evered, 2006). Secondary control, also known as *adjustment,* is related to the construct of an *external locus of control.* It's the kind of control that you perceive when you're with a group of people going for lunch and the group decides to get pizza, and you come to feel that pizza is just what you'd like for lunch. Your desires and goals adjust themselves to what your environment is most likely to provide. Which kind of control do you think you experience more often?

Although everyone experiences primary and secondary control on occasion, cultures do differ in the extent to which people engage in these two strategies. In hierarchical collectivistic cultures, such as in East Asia, the social world remains somewhat impervious to efforts by a lone individual to change things (e.g., Chiu, Dweck, Tong,

& Fu, 1997). Power and agency tend to be concentrated in groups or in leaders of groups, or it is mandated by the role that one occupies; therefore, there are many domains in which the individual is unable to exert much influence. Likewise, as we discussed in Chapter 6, East Asians are more likely to have a flexible and incremental view of themselves. When the individual is perceived to be more mutable than the social world, we'd expect people to be quite willing to adjust themselves to fit in better with the demands of their social worlds.

In contrast, people from Western cultures tend to stress the malleability of the world relative to the individual (Su et al., 1999). In the Bible, for example, God told Adam that he would have dominion over all the earth; the world was there for humans to change and use to their liking. This belief persists in the West and is manifest in the view that the individual has potential control of shaping the world to fit his or her own desires. When people view individuals to be the center of experience and action, they accordingly look to individuals as a source of control. Moreover, the independent self, as discussed in Chapter 6, is perceived as relatively immutable and consistent. This view of self as an immutable entity, working within the context of a mutable world, sustains a perception of primary control.

Weisz, Rothbaum, and Blackburn (1984) see many socializing experiences in Japan that lead Japanese to be more comfortable with engaging in secondary control strategies. For example, Japanese infants spend much more time in contact with their mothers and thus learn to adjust themselves to what their mothers are doing. Japanese workers change jobs far less frequently than their Western counterparts, and it is not uncommon for workers to be promised lifetime employment—a system ensuring that employees learn to adjust themselves to whatever demands the company places on them. This can be contrasted with clear primary control attitudes expressed in such American popular songs as "Take This Job and Shove It" and "My Way." Weisz and colleagues propose that these and other socialization experiences lead people to seek strategies of control that are most likely to lead to beneficial consequences within the constraints of their respective cultural environments.

One study that investigated whether control strategies differed between Japanese and Americans, in line with the hypotheses of Weisz and colleagues, was conducted by Morling (2000). Having attended several aerobics classes in both Japan and the United States, Morling noticed some differences in attitudes that seemed to speak to different control strategies. She created a questionnaire that addressed people's reasons for choosing their aerobics classes and what they tended to do when the instructor initiated a move that was too difficult for them; she passed it out to students in aerobics classes in Japan and the United States. Her results are very informative. For example, when asked why they chose the particular class they did, Americans were more likely than Japanese to say it was because the class was at a convenient time for them (i.e., they chose to exercise when they wanted), whereas Japanese were more likely to say it was because the class was of the appropriate level for them (i.e., they adjusted their schedules so that they would be a better fit with the class). Also, when asked what they did when the instructor initiated a move that was too difficult for them, Japanese were more likely than Americans to say that they would try hard to keep up (i.e., they adjusted their routine to the instructors' standards), whereas Americans were more likely than Japanese to say that they would do their own move instead (i.e., their preferences determined their routine). Both Japanese and Americans take aerobics classes for the same goal—to get into shape; however, we can still see the different control strategies that are pursued to realize this goal.

Further work has found parallel evidence for differences between Japanese and Americans in their control strategies (Morling, Kitayama, & Miyamoto, 2002). In one study, participants were asked to list occasions when they had either tried to influence the people or objects around them (i.e., primary control experiences) or tried to adjust themselves to the people or objects around them (i.e., secondary control experiences). As shown in **Figure 8.6**, Americans were better able to recall the situations in which they had influenced others than those in which they had adjusted to others; Japanese remembered more adjusting situations than influencing ones. The term "secondary control" might thus be a misnomer in Japan, because this type of control appears to be more common there than "primary control." However, both Japanese and Americans reported that influencing situations felt more powerful than adjusting ones, suggesting that primary control might be universally experienced as powerful

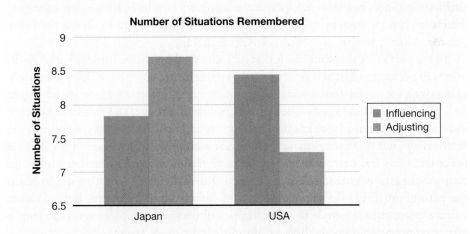

FIGURE 8.6 Japanese recall more adjusting situations than influencing ones, whereas Americans recall more influencing situations than adjusting ones. This suggests that primary and secondary control experiences are not equally common across the two cultures.

(primary control may thus be a good candidate for a functional universal). Despite the apparent universality of the perceived power in primary control situations, Japanese reported feeling more powerful about their adjusting situations than the Americans did. This cultural difference was evident in the way participants described their adjusting experiences. For example, Americans were more likely than Japanese to report feeling that they were compelled to adjust, as though it was against their will. They often described their experiences as something that they "had to do"—for example, "I had to adjust last school year when my roommate's boyfriend moved into our house." In contrast, the Japanese situations rarely indicated that the individual felt compelled to adjust or that the adjustment experience was negative.

In sum, experiences of primary control seem to be more frequent among people from Western than Eastern cultural backgrounds, and a variety of other studies have reported comparable findings (e.g., Bond & Tornatzky, 1973; Chang, Chua, & Toh, 1997; Mahler, 1974; Seginer, Trommsdorff, & Essau, 1993). Likewise, the East Asian pattern of relatively weaker feelings of primary control has also been found in African samples (e.g., Smith, Trompenaars, & Dugan, 1995). More generally, the experience of primary control is desired so much in individualistic cultures that when people feel less personal control over their life outcomes they tend to feel much anxiety. In contrast, this relation between feelings of personal control and anxiety is significantly weaker among people from collectivistic cultures (Cheng, Cheung, Chio, & Chan, 2013). Moreover, the kind of control one strives for can be seen in the ways that people use religion to help them deal with future life events. For example, Christians are more likely to use a primary control strategy to try to change future events by petitioning God's help through prayer; in contrast, Hindu Indians show more of a secondary control strategy of adjusting to situations by striving to divine the future (Young, Morris, Burrus, Krishnan, & Regmi, 2011).

Being part of a group can mean that an individual must sometimes go along with others to get along well. Secondary control strategies are an effective means for managing one's successful functioning in group contexts. However, if we spend a great deal of our time thinking of ourselves as members of groups, and thinking of others in terms of the groups to which they belong, we might also think of control in a different way. That is, we might start to perceive groups as agents, as entities that can make decisions and exert control. The idea of groups as agents is rather unfamiliar to psychologists, who tend to equate agency with individuals, and this might reflect the path of our field's development, growing largely out of Western, individualistic cultural contexts. Do people in collectivistic cultures see groups as agents in similar ways that people in individualistic cultures see individuals as agents?

One way this question has been investigated was to analyze how newspapers in different countries referred to the agents implicated in scandals involving rogue stock traders (Menon, Morris, Chiu, & Hong, 1999). For example, in 1995 the British stock trader Nick Leeson was convicted of fraud for his part in a scandal that resulted in the loss of more than a billion dollars and the ultimate collapse of his employer, Baring's Bank. Menon and colleagues were interested in how newspapers in the United States and Japan (specifically, the *New York Times* and *Asahi Shinbun*) reported this and various other rogue trader scandals that were in the news. Did they consider the problem as ultimately lying with the individual, such as Nick Leeson, or did they consider the problem to be due to the management of the organization, such as Baring's Bank? Who ultimately had responsibility, and thus control, over the event?

The researchers analyzed the articles about the scandals and checked the frequency with which the articles addressed the individuals involved or the organizations that employed them. As shown in **Figure 8.7**, the *New York Times* was more likely to explore the scandals in terms of the problems with the individual trader. In stark contrast, however, the *Asahi Shinbun* focused its reporting on the problems inherent in the organizations that could allow this scandal to occur. Note that these newspaper stories were about the identical scandals, and this pattern of results was obtained for scandals that occurred in both the West and Japan. Apparently, Japanese are more likely to see events in the world as occurring due to the behaviors and decisions of groups, whereas Americans tend to understand events in terms of the individuals involved (also see related work by Markus, Uchida, Omoregie, Townsend, & Kitayama,

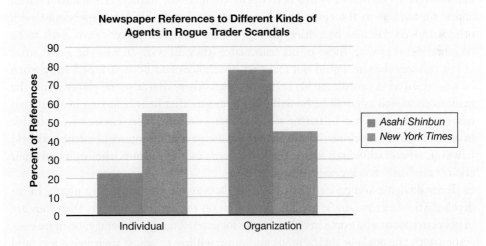

FIGURE 8.7 In explaining rogue trader scandals, Japanese newspapers tend to focus more on the organizations involved than on the individuals, whereas American newspapers tend to focus more on the individuals than on the organizations.

2006; Yamaguchi, Gelfand, Ohashi, & Zemba, 2003). The same event can be understood quite differently depending on one's view of agency.

Making Choices

One way that people can exercise control over their worlds is by making choices. By deciding where we live, what food we'll have for dinner, and what time we'll wake up in the morning, we're able to structure our lives so that they match our desires. We make countless choices every day, and they are perhaps the most direct way we engage in primary control strategies.

Choice is something that is surely valued everywhere; however, the extent to which people value choice, and exercise it, is influenced by the contexts they are in. If we imagine situations in which individuals are quite separate from others, for example, such as an author who lives alone and works at home, we can see that she has a great deal of freedom in the kinds of choices she makes every day. She might be free to sleep when she wants, eat what she wants, and work when she wants. Many of her goals would be personal, and there would be few interpersonal constraints on her daily choices. In contrast, imagine a situation in which many individuals are interdependent with others, such as players on a professional basketball team. Choices that individuals make regarding their basketball playing are clearly no longer free of interpersonal constraints. A player does not have the choice to go to practice when he feels like it, to get extremely drunk the night before a big game, or to shoot the ball himself if a teammate is in a better place to make the basket. His behaviors must adjust themselves to the constraints imposed on him by his interdependence with others. Indeed, because becoming part of a team renders a player's own goals to be largely consistent with those of his teammates (they all want to win the game, after all), it is likely that he would not feel that his choices had been stripped away when he was required to coordinate his behaviors with others. Because the player wants the team to do as well as possible, he will want to ensure that he is behaving in a way that maximizes the likelihood that the team will win. In sum, more choices are available to individuals acting alone than to those who are part of an interdependent network; however, when individuals share the same goals as their group, the limits on their choices are likely not experienced as aversive.

Individualistic and collectivistic cultures also vary on this same continuum. In individualistic societies people are less dependent on the actions of others than they are in collectivistic ones. People in collectivistic societies should, on average, be more concerned with the goals of their groups and more willing to adjust their behaviors (and reduce their choices) to coordinate with the actions of the group toward those goals.

Perhaps the strongest evidence for cultural variation in the valuation of choice can be seen in the domains in which people exercise free choice. Most Westerners, for example, spend a good portion of their time obsessing about a few key choices that will have a big impact on their lives: "What kind of job should I get?" "Who should I marry?" "Where should we live?" "Should we have kids, and if so, how many and when?" These tend to be seen as personal decisions, or decisions between a couple. Many people take years to decide these issues and often evaluate their lives with respect to the success of these decisions. Would you be willing to allow other people to make these decisions for you?

In many parts of the world, important decisions such as these are seen to reflect on the entire extended family, and often they are not made by the individual but by his or her parents. "What kind of job should I get?" *"You'll take over the family business."* "Who should I marry?" *"We've found someone for you from a good family on the other side of town."* "Where should we live?" *"You'll live with the husband's family."* "Should we have kids?" *"Yes, starting as soon as possible, and as many as possible."*

The influence of our cultural socialization is readily apparent here, as most Westerners have an extremely difficult time imagining not making these kinds of choices on their own. Given that many Westerners assume that the success of their lives and their happiness is contingent on these decisions, they assume that having these choices relegated to others—for example, to their parents—would result in a life of misery. I think this is a reasonable reaction to the extent that a person is solely focused on his or her personal goals. However, remember that in collectivistic societies (where parental decision making is more common) individuals tend to identify with their group's goals. If you also want what is best for your extended family, it very well might not feel like you are being stripped of your freedom to choose, but that you are engaging in actions that were thoughtfully and wisely decided as furthering your family's goals.

It is important to remember that we're not talking about individuals surrendering their choices to a random number generator or to their arch-rival; the ones who are making the decisions care a great deal about them and know a lot about their personal needs and the family's needs. We can likely suspect that choices made at random or by someone who doesn't care much for us would not serve our needs well, but choices made by a caring person who is considering our own personal and family interests may serve us just fine. This is a critical distinction for understanding why individuals in collectivistic cultures are willing to allow some choices to be made for them by others. For example, one set of studies used a situation-sampling methodology to compare Americans and Indians in terms of their reactions to how they responded when others tried to influence their choices (Savani, Morris, Naidu, Kumar, & Berlia, 2011). A number of telling findings emerged. First, when individuals listed situations in which someone had tried to influence their decisions in the past, the Indians assumed the influencer was doing this more for altruistic rather than selfish reasons, whereas the Americans assumed the opposite. The studies also found that Indians were more likely than Americans to say they would go along and make decisions in accordance with the influencers' preferences. In addition, the studies found that Americans (and

Indians) were more likely to say they would make decisions in accordance with the influencer's preferences in the Indian-made situations than in the American-made ones—the Indian situations were somehow able to convey more of a sense that the influencer could help them make a better decision.

There's much evidence to show how choices are viewed differently across cultures. In Indian contexts, in particular, there is relatively little emphasis on making choices in life, and this can be seen in a number of ways. First, making choices appears to be more difficult for Indians than for Americans; Indians take significantly more time to make choices than do Americans (Savani, Markus, & Conner, 2008). Second, Indians don't respond as negatively when they are deprived of the opportunity to choose when compared with Americans (Savani et al., 2008). Indians, and people from numerous other non-Western cultures, also indicate that they have less free choice in their lives compared with North Americans (Inglehart, Basanez, & Moreno, 1998). Choices do not appear to play as large a role in Indian life as they do for North Americans (see **Figure 8.8**).

Furthermore, choices appear to *mean* something different for Indians compared with Americans. Americans see more of their actions as reflections of their choices. In

FIGURE 8.8 Indians are more likely to make choices based on the preferences of significant others compared with Americans.

one study, Americans and Indians living in the United States were guided through an identical set of behaviors; they entered a room and selected which of two seats to sit in, they selected one of two consent forms to complete, they selected one of two pens to sign their names, and so on. At the end of the study they were asked how many choices they had made during the course of the experiment, and Americans indicated that they had made almost twice as many choices as Indians. Furthermore, the longer the Indian participants had lived in the United States, the more likely they were to identify their various actions as "choices" (Savani, Markus, Naidu, Kumar, & Berlia, 2010). Also, when reflecting on real-life actions that they had taken (such as picking a topic for a class project or purchasing a computer), Americans were more likely to view their decisions as reflecting personal choices. The more important the action, the more likely Americans were to identify it as a personal choice, whereas, for Indians, the more important the action, the *less* likely they were to view it as a personal choice (Savani et al., 2010).

This finding can perhaps be better understood by considering what guides the selections for people from the two cultures. Choices don't seem to reflect personal preferences as much for Indians as for Americans. When Americans are given an opportunity to choose something, they almost always select the option that they prefer: If a Ford Mustang is an American individual's favorite kind of car, that person is likely to choose a Mustang when given a choice among cars. But the link between preferences and choices isn't as tight among Indians—they are less likely to choose their favorite option (Savani et al., 2008). Their choices are guided by other considerations, such as what significant other people might prefer that they do. In particular, Indians are more likely than Americans to defer to the views of an authority's expectations when making their choices (Savani, Morris, & Naidu, 2012).

The important role of the preferences of others in people's choices is nicely demonstrated in the following study. Fifth-grade students were recruited from two elementary schools in the San Francisco Bay area (Iyengar & Lepper, 1999). The students whose results were analyzed were those of European-American background and those of East Asian background. The Asian-American students all spoke an Asian language at home with their families. These students were invited to play a computerized math game called Space Quest. Their task was to ensure that their ship had enough fuel to reach Planet Ektar to save the world from imminent disaster. They received points along the way for answering arithmetic problems correctly, and if they reached 50 points before their computerized opponent did, they won the game.

The students were randomly assigned to one of three conditions. In the *personal choice* condition, the students were allowed to make a number of choices that were all irrelevant to their success in the game. For example, they could choose which of four icons would represent their spaceship and which of four names they would give to their spaceship. Students in this condition had the freedom to choose for themselves. In the *outgroup choice* condition, students saw the same four options for the spaceship icons and possible names; however, one of these four was highlighted and they were told "These are the spaceships that are available for you. We're giving you the one shown below because that was what most of the third-graders at the last school wanted." Students in this condition did not have the freedom to make this choice; instead, the choice was made for them by someone whose opinion they did not value very highly (the researchers conducted a pretest and discovered that fifth-graders have very little respect for third-graders from other schools). Last, students in the *ingroup choice* condition were shown the same options and were told that they were assigned to a particular spaceship because "that was what most of the students in your class wanted." That is, the students did not have the freedom to choose, but they could expect that their fellow classmates likely made pretty good decisions. The students then all had the opportunity to play the Space Quest game for 20 minutes. The dependent variable was how many games they attempted during that time (a measure that should indicate how much intrinsic motivation the students had toward the game). The results were rather striking (**Figure 8.9**).

The students of European background attempted the most games when they got to choose their own spaceships. They played significantly fewer games when either the third-graders or their classmates made their choices for them. That is, the European-American students seemed to react rather negatively to the idea that others were making choices for them, regardless of who those others were.

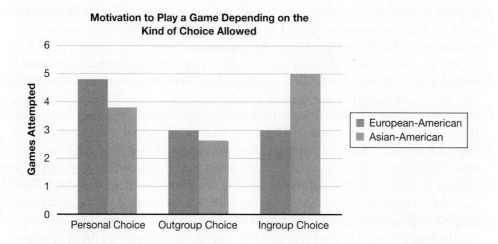

FIGURE 8.9 European-Americans made more attempts to play a game in which they made choices than a game in which others made the choices. In contrast, Asian-Americans made more attempts to play a game in which an ingroup member made choices for them than one in which either an outgroup member made the choices or they made the choices themselves.

In contrast, the Asian-American students attempted the most games when their classmates chose their spaceships for them. Indeed, they seemed to be more motivated to play the game in this condition than when they made their own choices. However, like the European-Americans, they were not very motivated when an undesirable other (the third-graders from another school) made their choices for them. The Asian-Americans thus shared some similarities but some important differences with the European-Americans in regard to their attitudes toward choices. Like the European-Americans, they seemed to be motivated when they made their own choices and were not motivated when an undesirable other made their choices for them. However, in stark contrast with the European-Americans, Asian-American students seemed especially motivated when a trusted other made choices for them (a similar pattern was found in another study when the children were told that their mothers had made the choices for them). Apparently, Asian-Americans viewed the situation of their ingroups making choices for them as opportunities to promote harmony and a sense of belongingness with their other group members. European-Americans seemed to view the same situation as something that stripped them of their freedom to choose.

In general, making individual choices seems to be especially valued in individualistic cultures, and this appears to be the most true in the United States—the world champion of individualism. One study contrasted people from the United States with those from France, Germany, Italy, Switzerland, and the United Kingdom. Participants were asked whether they would prefer a choice of 10 ice cream flavors or 50 ice cream flavors. The majority of people in each of the European cultures said they would prefer a choice among only 10 flavors, whereas in the United States, a majority of people said they would prefer a choice among 50 flavors (Rozin, Fischler, Shields, & Masson, 2006). Likewise, Americans (and Britons) prefer to have more choices on menus from upscale restaurants than citizens of the other European countries do (Rozin et al., 2006). The American results are especially interesting because research reveals that, even for Americans, too much choice is aversive. Although Americans will reliably tell you that they prefer having many choices, their behaviors indicate that they actually fare better when they have only a few choices to make (Iyengar & Lepper, 2000). Having too much choice can be quite debilitating at times, as making choices requires a great deal of cognitive resources (Schwartz, 2004).

Because people in collectivistic cultures tend to identify with group goals more than people in individualistic cultures do, they should be more content

"Can I overwhelm you with a menu?"

with exchanging some individual control for control by valued others. There are other ways, however, that we can see cultural differences in perceived control. In the 20th century many countries embarked on an enormous real-life experiment as various governments around the world became communist. There were many consequences of communism, both positive and negative; however, one consequence was that there was less relation between an individual's efforts and an individual's outcomes. For example, a communist farmer who wanted to increase his wealth could not simply devote more energies to tending his crops. Doing so might increase his crop yield, but this increased yield would go to the country as a whole rather than to his own private livelihood. To the extent that individuals' efforts are not clearly linked to their outcomes, they should experience relatively less feelings of primary control.

The Cold War was at its peak when the Soviets erected the Berlin Wall in 1961. Despite the great human suffering that this sad historical event caused, it also resulted in a unique opportunity to explore the psychological consequences of communism. Prior to World War II, Berlin was a unified city that shared a common culture and history. After the city was divided into two, the Western half continued from its democratic and capitalist prewar past, whereas the Eastern half became communist. Because people in the two halves shared a common heritage, we should expect that any psychological differences between people on the two sides are likely due to the different experiences they encountered with their respective political and economic systems. Unfortunately, the governments had other things on their agenda than cross-cultural psychological research, and few researchers were granted access to the divided city.

One exception is the work of Oettingen and colleagues (Oettingen, Little, Lindenberger, & Baltes, 1994; Oettingen & Seligman, 1990). These researchers visited the two Germanys prior to unification and were able to conduct a number of interesting cross-cultural experiments. In one series of studies they passed out questionnaires to elementary school children in both East and West Berlin to investigate the students' perceptions of control and efficacy. For example, children were asked to respond to the item "If I want to do well in school, I can." To the extent that one has feelings of primary control and efficacy, one should endorse this item. It reflects people's beliefs about whether they can change their behavior to effect a positive outcome in their studies. The researchers found that the West Berlin children endorsed this item significantly more than the children from East Berlin. Their findings across the items from the questionnaire and the different studies they conducted were consistent with this pattern: West German children felt that they had more control (at least in their schoolwork) than East German children. Would you think that this difference is due to the specific policies that were enacted within their respective school systems, or from attitudes that the students learned from life outside of school?

It would seem that decreased feelings of control might be associated with some psychological costs. Much research with people (and animals) has revealed that when individuals are unable to avoid harmful situations, they can experience something known as **learned helplessness**. In learned helplessness, an individual feels that he or she is unable to control or avoid unpleasant events, and the person will suffer from stress and potentially depression (e.g., Abramson, Seligman, & Teasdale, 1978). If East Germans had less control over their life outcomes than West Germans, we might expect that they should show signs of learned helplessness. Oettingen and Seligman (1990) investigated whether people in East and West Berlin differed in signs of learned helplessness, notably depression. Although the researchers were not allowed to collect questionnaire data from adults in East Berlin, they were resourceful in trying to measure depression in another way. They visited bars in East and West Berlin and observed the customers there. They looked for any behavioral signs of depression, such as frowns, slumped body postures, or a lack of expressive gestures. Their results showed a clear pattern: East Berliners were far more likely to be showing overt signs of depression than West Berliners (**Figure 8.10**). A reasonable interpretation of their data is that East Germans felt greater learned helplessness because they had less direct control over the outcomes in their lives.

Many kinds of contexts afford or constrain a sense of control, with a democracy and a totalitarian government being two such examples. We can also see cultural variation in perceptions of control if we look within 21st-century democratic countries, such as the United States. As noted in Chapter 1, the vast majority of psychological research is conducted with a limited sample that is not only largely restricted to participants from Western cultural backgrounds but is also usually further

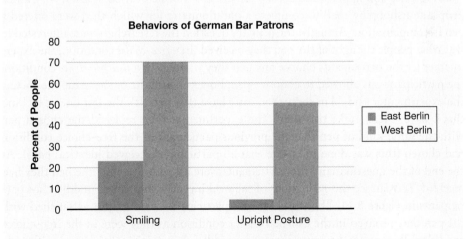

FIGURE 8.10   Bar patrons in East Berlin showed more outward signs of depression than bar patrons in West Berlin.

limited to college students from those same cultural backgrounds. College students are not necessarily representative of humankind; one way they differ from the rest of the population is that they are more likely to be from upper-middle-class backgrounds and are more likely later to raise their own families in an upper-middle-class environment. Non-college-educated people, in contrast, are more likely to be from lower-middle-class or working-class backgrounds.

How might we expect people of upper-middle-class backgrounds to differ in their perceptions of control from those with working-class backgrounds? One obvious way is that working-class people earn less money and have fewer choices available because of that. If your income is not large enough, you can't consider some of the choices that wealthier people routinely make (e.g., whether to send their children to private schools, whether to pay for the best medical care, whether to move to a safe neighborhood, or whether to go on a resort vacation). With fewer financial resources, people must accept many situations in life rather than being able to choose from a range of alternatives. Indeed, research has found that income correlates positively with feelings of control (e.g., Johnson & Krueger, 2005). Working-class people and upper-middle-class people also have different kinds of relationships; the working-class individuals tend to have fewer friends, they live closer to them, they have more frequent contact with family, and they rely more on relatives for material assistance (Allan, 1979). In sum, working-class adults participate in a different cultural world from that of upper-middle-class adults; they are more likely to face hardships in their lives, and they have less control over these hardships compared to upper-middle-class people.

Snibbe & Markus (2005) explored differences in control experiences by comparing working-class and upper-middle-class Americans. In one of their studies, they asked people at a shopping mall to complete a questionnaire for which they were offered a pen in compensation. Actually, the primary question the researchers were interested in was what people thought of the pen they received. In a *free-choice* condition, the experimenter let the participants choose any pen they wanted. In a *usurped choice* condition, the participant was allowed to choose a pen; however, after he or she made the choice, the experimenter said, "I'm sorry. You can't have that pen. It's the last one of its kind that I have. Here—take this one." The experimenter then replaced the chosen pen with the same kind of pen that the previous participant in the free-choice condition had chosen (this was done to ensure that all participants received identical pens). At the end of the questionnaire the participants were asked to evaluate the pen they had received. You can see the evaluations of the working-class and upper-middle-class participants in **Figure 8.11**. The working-class participants were almost as satisfied with the pen they received in the usurped choice condition as they were in the free-choice condition. In contrast, however, the upper-middle-class participants were significantly less satisfied when their choice had been taken away from them.

The researchers argue that upper-middle-class Americans are raised to favor choices and to express themselves through their choices. As such, they learn to respond quite

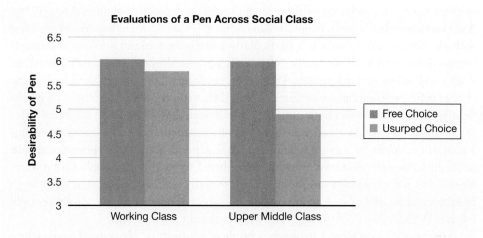

FIGURE 8.11 Whereas upper-middle-class people prefer pens that they chose themselves over those they did not choose, the preferences of working-class people were not affected by who chose the pens.

negatively when they believe that they do not have any choice in a situation. In contrast, working-class Americans grow up learning that much of what people encounter in life is beyond their control and that a good way to maintain one's independence is to emphasize one's integrity and resilience during tough times. This orientation leads them to accept and cope with occasions when they don't end up with what they wanted. Several other studies further support this result (see Snibbe & Markus, 2005). Even within a country, we can see clear differences in people's perceptions of choice and control. Do you think there are other phenomena discussed in this book that might appear quite different if the samples were working-class people instead of college students?

Motivations to Fit In or to Stick Out

On many occasions when we're deciding how to behave in a group, we can decide to go either of two ways. First, we can strive to act in a way that fits in well with others, thereby increasing group harmony at the expense of our own individual distinctiveness. Alternatively, we can decide to act in such a way that we stick out from others, highlighting our uniqueness at the potential risk of not getting along so well with others. People are often in the position to make such a decision, and the way they reach their decisions is influenced by their cultures.

Perhaps the most dramatic exploration of how people decide whether they should fit in or stick out was conducted by the eminent social psychologist Solomon Asch (1956). Asch was interested in when people would conform—that is, when they would go along with the crowd. Conformity is a particularly interesting topic in a Western context, because it tends to be viewed rather negatively in most Western societies; however, as Asch's and others' research reveals, Westerners conform all the time. Take a look at the clothes you're wearing right now. Surely you feel that you chose what clothes you would wear today; however, you might notice that the choice that you reached is quite similar to that made by your closest friends. For example, you're probably *not* currently wearing a zoot suit, a corset, or a grungy flannel shirt. The point here is that these clothes are not fashionable now, or at least not when and where I wrote this paragraph. Often when we feel that we're making a unique choice, we're really making choices that allow us to fit in to consensually agreed-upon norms for how good, interesting, responsible people behave. We are often conforming, even when we're not aware of it.

Asch wanted to explore a stronger example of conformity. He wanted to see when people would conform and clearly be aware that they were doing so. His experiment proceeded like this. A participant would arrive in the lab to take part in a study that was supposedly about visual perception. Sitting beside this person in the lab were a number of other students who appeared to be participants as well. The experimenter gave the group an extremely straightforward task. They were shown three lines of clearly different lengths and were asked which one of those three was the same length as the target line (**Figure 8.12**). The correct answer was obvious to everyone. Asch

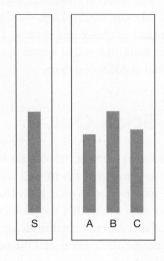

FIGURE 8.12

The kinds of stimuli used in Solomon Asch's study of conformity. Participants were presented with the sample line (S) and asked which of the other three lines' length matched the sample.

found that hardly anyone got the answer wrong when tested individually. However, before the individual had the chance to offer his or her own answer, a number of the other "participants" (who were actually confederates of the experimenter) answered and, with apparent certainty, indicated a line that was clearly different from the target line. When it was the participant's turn, he or she had a choice to make. Should he or she offer the answer that appears obviously correct, even though it contradicts what everyone else was saying? Or should the person go along with the group and offer what appears to be a patently wrong answer? Remarkably, 75% of Asch's American subjects conformed on at least 1 of the 12 trials of the experiment. Conformity is common indeed.

So what was motivating people in Asch's study to conform? An answer can be seen in a variant of the study that Asch conducted (1962). Rather than have a subject give his answer after hearing several confederates give what was an obviously incorrect answer, Asch reversed the situation. He had one confederate give what was clearly an incorrect answer after having several real subjects offer the correct answer before him. When the confederate did this, the rest of the participants turned around and laughed at him! Apparently, deciding to stand up against a crowd can be so ludicrous that people find it quite funny. It seemed so ridiculous that even the experimenter couldn't help laughing! One potential cost of not conforming is that people might laugh at you.

There are other social costs to not conforming. People tend to take an active dislike to those who won't conform. An early study instructed a confederate to offer a dissenting opinion to a group (Schacter, 1951). Later the group was required to reduce their size by choosing one person to leave. Not surprising to anyone who has watched episodes of the reality TV programs like *Survivor* or *Big Brother*, it was the dissenter who was quickly voted out of the group. People would rather not associate with those who won't agree with others. If you won't go along, you likely won't get along. It's rather ironic that those people whom we hold in high esteem for standing out from the crowd and forging their own paths, such as Galileo, Martin Luther King Jr., Darwin, and Gandhi, were often widely hated during their own lifetimes for expressing such counter-normative ideas. There are pronounced social costs to not conforming.

Given these social costs, we would expect that people from cultures that are more socially cohesive would be more willing to conform. The social costs of dissenting must be considerably greater in collectivistic societies in which people feel more obligation to their ingroup members and have a stronger motivation to achieve a sense of belongingness; for example, Koreans were more likely than Americans to report devaluing and avoiding others who stuck out from the group in some atypical way (Kinias, Kim, Hafenbrack, & Lee, 2014). The Asch study has been a popular one, and it's been replicated well over 100 times all around the globe. A meta-analysis of these studies revealed one clear trend: Although Americans show a great deal of conformity in the Asch paradigm, people from more collectivistic cultures conform even more, especially when they are conforming to their ingroups (Bond & Smith, 1996). Motivations to fit in are more powerful in cultural contexts that encourage people to maintain strong relationships with others.

In contrast to a motivation to conform, we can also consider people's motivations to stick out and to be unique. Why might people be motivated to think of themselves as different from others? How would you think this motivation might be related to independent and interdependent views of self? As you've already learned, people with independent views of self see their identity as ultimately grounded in their individual qualities. Their identity is not shared with others and thus is perceived to be fundamentally unique. Maintaining a view of oneself that is consistent with cultural values of independence, then, should be aided by striving to view oneself as a unique and special individual. In contrast, a motivation to be different should not be so pronounced among those who value interdependence, where concerns with fitting in are more important.

Is there evidence in support of this hypothesis? Consider the following clever experiment (Kim & Markus, 1999): People who were in the departure lounge at the San Francisco airport were approached while waiting for their flights. Participants of Asian descent who were waiting for a flight to East Asia and Americans of European descent who were waiting for a flight to a non-Asian destination were approached. Participants were asked to fill out a brief questionnaire and, in return for their time, they were offered a pen. The experimenter had a bag full of red and green pens; she would pull out a handful of five of them and ask each person to choose a pen. By doing this the experimenter ensured that all passengers had to make a choice between pens of two different colors and that they also had to choose between pens that were either of a majority color (three or four pens of the same color) or of a minority color (one or two pens of the same color). About half the time the majority color was red, and about half the time the majority color was green. The findings were quite striking, as seen in **Figure 8.13**. The European-Americans were much more likely to choose the pen of the minority color, regardless of what that color was. Somehow, it seemed that European-Americans viewed pens of a relatively unique color—in terms of its minority number—as more desirable. In stark contrast, the East Asians were more likely to choose the pen of the majority color, considering the less unusual pen more desirable. Apparently, European-Americans desire to express their uniqueness by making what they think are unique choices, whereas East Asians desire to express their belongingness by making what they think are common choices.

Other analyses and studies corroborated that the participants made these divergent choices because of distinct self-expressive motives and not, for example, because the East Asians were trying to avoid taking the experimenter's last red pen (Kim & Markus, 1999; also see Kim & Drolet, 2003). Likewise, when asked to do a simple drawing task, such as coloring geometric patterns, European-Americans' drawings were judged to be more unique than East Asian drawings, and these preferences for

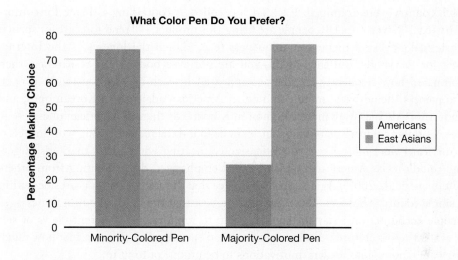

FIGURE 8.13 When given the choice, Americans tend to prefer minority-colored pens, whereas East Asians prefer majority-colored pens.

unique drawings were found to correlate with measures of acculturation to North America (Ishii, Miyamoto, Rule, & Toriyama, 2014). Similarly, research has also found that working-class Americans, like the East Asians in these studies, are also less likely to prefer unique objects compared with middle-class Americans (Stephens, Markus, & Townsend, 2007). Other research that has explored motivations for uniqueness in quite different ways finds that when people from collectivist cultures are motivated to be distinctive they are most likely to do so in terms of their social position (Becker et al., 2012).

Motivations for uniqueness are thus quite different between cultures. An important question to consider is how these particular motivations, and cultural ideas more generally, come to be so widespread within cultures yet so different between cultures. Obviously, these ideas must somehow be communicated to individuals within these cultures. How might we go about exploring the ways ideas are communicated differently across cultures?

One strategy would be to look at messages in advertisements. Advertisers are savvy folks, and their job is to persuade people. The kind of message that would be most persuasive is one that reflects ideas that are widely shared within a culture. One study investigated themes in magazine advertisements in Korea and the United States, evaluating them as expressing either uniqueness or conformity (Kim & Markus, 1999).

Several categories of magazines (e.g., business magazines, women's magazines) from each country were examined. Each ad was coded as containing a theme for conformity (e.g., "Seven out of 10 people are using this product," "Trend forecast for spring: Pastel colors!") or a theme for uniqueness (e.g., "Ditch the Joneses," "The Internet isn't for everybody. But then again, you are not everybody"). The researchers then compared how frequently the themes appeared in each ad. As you might expect, uniqueness themes were more common in American ads than in Korean ones, and conformity themes were more common in Korean ads than in American ones.

A similar comparison of magazine car ads found that ads targeting working-class Americans were more likely to emphasize connecting with others than ads targeting middle-class Americans, which instead emphasized differentiating from others (Stephens et al., 2007). Again, this is evidence that different cultures co-reside within a single country's borders. These findings suggest that the kinds of cultural messages people encounter on a day-to-day basis help to reinforce the different views of self prevalent across cultures. The next time you look at magazine ads, consider how much they are tapping into readers' motivations to be unique or to fit in.

SUMMARY

Why people act in the ways they do is a question that reveals their underlying motivations. These motivations are influenced in a variety of ways through cultural backgrounds. For example, the motivation to view oneself positively is shaped by culture. North Americans of European descent are especially concerned about their self-esteem, and they engage in a variety of tactics to boost the positivity of their own self-view. East Asians, in contrast, tend to be more concerned about face, and they use a preventive, self-improving tactic to ensure that they maintain it.

Motivations to work hard are moralized in cultures with predominant Protestant populations, apparently because of ideas stemming from early Protestant sects that such hard work on one's calling (and the material rewards that were thus accumulated) were evidence that God viewed one favorably.

Striking evidence of culture's influence on motivations can be seen in studies of control and choice. In collectivistic cultures, individuals are often in situations in which they must yield their own preferences to others. In such situations they can better exercise control by altering their personal expectations and preferences than by trying to change the outcome. This kind of control, known as "secondary control," is more evident among people from East Asian than Western backgrounds. Other situations prevent individuals from being able to exercise much control, such as being a citizen in a totalitarian society or being in the working class in the United States. People from these backgrounds are less likely to pursue their own choices and are more willing to accept what they have received.

Cultures also shape motivations to fit in or to stick out in a group. People from collectivistic backgrounds are more motivated to maintain harmonious relationships, and this can be facilitated by acting in ways consistent with the behavior of others. Individualists, in contrast, are more motivated to stick out and to perceive themselves as unique.

THINK ABOUT IT

1. Why do you think self-esteem appears to be increasing over the past several decades?
2. What do you think are some societal consequences from this increase in self-esteem?
3. How does comparing your performance on a task with others affect the positivity of your self-feelings?
4. What are some key ways that self-esteem differs from face?
5. How does Weber argue that the Protestant Reformation contributed to achievement motivations?
6. What are some ways that students use primary and secondary control when preparing for an exam?
7. How do Indians make choices compared with Americans?
8. Why do you think Americans seem to value choice so much compared with people in other countries?
9. Why did people conform so often in the Asch conformity study?

KEY TERMS

Unlike English, the languages of many Australian Aboriginal groups do not have words for relativistic direction terms, such as "right" or "left." They encode and describe all spatial experiences in terms of the cardinal directions.

9

COGNITION AND PERCEPTION

magine that you are walking through a museum and come across some art from different cultures. You may find terra cotta figurines from Nigeria, totem poles from the Pacific Northwest, Chulucanas pottery from Peru, marble statues from Greece, or bronze Buddhas from Thailand. Indeed, if there is one thing that varies tremendously across cultures, and across historical time, it is artistic traditions. But what can we make of the different traditions we see? Are they just a matter of convention, where, for some reason, a certain style became popular at a particular time and place and subsequent artists responded to that style, either by emulating it or challenging it? Or could these differences tell us something about the underlying psychology of people from those cultures?

This is a question that Taka Masuda and colleagues (Masuda, Gonzalez, Kwan, & Nisbett, 2008) have considered. As he visited art galleries in Europe and East Asia, Masuda noticed some striking differences in the paintings produced in the various countries. One thing he observed (and later documented empirically) is that the horizons in landscape scenes were painted considerably higher (about 15% higher on average) in East Asian pictures than in Western ones. Second, he noted that figures in portraits were much larger in Western pictures than in East Asian ones (on average, the Western faces were three times as large). These cultural differences emerged consistently across a variety of themes and styles (**Figure 9.1**).

So what might these differences in artistic convention be telling us? Perhaps they simply reflect the vagaries of fashion, and for some reason high horizons and small portrait figures came into vogue in East Asia in ways that they didn't in Europe. Many would view this as the only acceptable account of cultural differences in artistic traditions. However, Masuda, his supervisor Richard Nisbett, and their colleagues have offered a much bolder interpretation: East Asian art looks different from Western art because people from these cultures are literally *seeing* the world differently. They argue that these different artistic styles reflect some fundamental differences in basic cognitive and perceptual processes between these two cultures (Masuda, Gonzalez et al., 2008; Nisbett, 2003).

Now, an argument for cultural variation in basic cognitive and perceptual processes is a bold one indeed. If there is a hierarchy of the different fields within psychology, the study of cognition and perception is seen by many to be the field that occupies the throne. Research on cognition and perception is esteemed so much because it purports to be informing us about the most elementary and essential psychological processes. Researchers in this field question how the human mind works—how the brain is able to process the streams of information that people encounter as they go about our their lives. Such researchers are striving to isolate the building blocks of psychological experiences, the images the eyes perceive, the ways the brain encodes and retrieves memories,

FIGURE 9.1 The painting by the Flemish artist Berckheyde (top) and the one by the Japanese artist Hokusai (bottom) are both landscape river scenes. However, Berckheyde painted the horizon at a lower level than Hokusai did. On the next page, the portrait on the left is by French painter Blanche, and the portrait on the right is by a Chinese painter of the Qing dynasty. The subject of the French portrait occupies a larger portion of the painting than the subjects of the Chinese portrait. These differences in style are commonly found between Western and Eastern artists.

FIGURE 9.1 *continued*

how people categorize information, and the ways people understand the objects and events they encounter. Given the fundamental questions that occupy
researchers of cognition and perception, it is quite remarkable that it is in this
domain that some of the clearest evidence for cross-cultural variability appears.
This recently found and quickly growing body of evidence for cultural variability
in cognition and perception is calling into question some very basic assumptions
that psychologists have held about how the mind operates.

   This chapter explores the ways basic cognitive and perceptual processes
vary across cultures. Some questions that we'll investigate are: "Do people
from different cultures think and see the world differently?" "Do people attend
to different kinds of information when they communicate with others?" and
"Does our language affect the ways we think?" The exploration of cultural variation in cognition and perception is guided by the two themes of this book.
First, there are cognitive tools that are universally available to people; however,
as you'll see, in some of these studies it appears that these tools are not always
used with the same frequency or for the same purpose. Second, the cultural
differences that do appear in these basic cognitive and perceptual processes
arise because of the different experiences that people have growing up in their
respective cultures.

Analytic and Holistic Thinking

To understand the differences in the painting styles between East Asia and the West, we need to take a step back. First, consider the following question: "Which of these three is least like the other two? A dog, a carrot, and a rabbit." When answering this question, people typically give one of two kinds of answers (Chiu, 1972; Ji, Zhang, & Nisbett, 2004). One common answer is the carrot. Both the dog and the rabbit are animals, so they share common attributes that differ from the attributes of the carrot, which is a vegetable. Recall from Chapter 5 that this kind of answer reflects a *taxonomic* categorization strategy in that the stimuli are grouped according to the perceived similarity of their attributes. Taxonomic categorization answers are especially common among Westerners in these kinds of studies. The second common answer is the dog. Rabbits and carrots go together because rabbits eat carrots. Rabbits and carrots have a relationship, which dogs don't share. This kind of answer reflects a *thematic* categorization strategy in that the stimuli are grouped together on the basis of causal, temporal, or spatial relationships among them. Thematic categorization is especially common among East Asians. This difference in categorization strategies reflects an underlying difference in the ways that people attend to their worlds. Nisbett and colleagues (Nisbett, 2003; Nisbett, Peng, Choi, & Norenzayan, 2001) refer to these ways of attending to the world as analytic and holistic thinking.

Analytic thinking is characterized by a focus on objects and their attributes. Objects are perceived as existing independently from their contexts they are understood in terms of their component parts. The attributes that make up objects are used as a basis for categorizing them, and a set of fixed abstract rules is used to predict and explain the behavior of these objects. As we'll soon see, analytic thinking, in general, is more common in Western cultures than it is elsewhere, particularly in East Asia (i.e., China, Japan, and Korea).

In contrast, **holistic thinking** is characterized by an orientation to the context as a whole. It represents an associative way of thinking, which gives attention to the relations among objects and among the objects and the surrounding context. Objects are understood in terms of how they relate to the rest of the context, and their behavior is predicted and explained on the basis of those relationships. Holistic thinking also emphasizes knowledge gained through experience rather than the application of fixed abstract rules. Holistic thinking is more common in East Asian and other cultures than in Western cultures.

The origins of analytic and holistic thinking are argued to arise from the different social experiences people have within individualistic and collectivistic societies. As we discussed in Chapter 5, people in collectivistic societies tend to be socialized in relational contexts and to have their attention directed at relational concerns (e.g., Lavin, Hall, & Waxman, 2006; Tamis-LeMonda, Bornstein, & Cyphers, 1992; Wang &

Conway, 2004). People in individualistic societies, in contrast, are more likely to be socialized to be independent and to have their attention focused on objects (e.g., Bornstein et al., 1992; Wang & Conway, 2004). These kinds of cultural experiences lead people to have either primarily independent or interdependent self-concepts.

If you recall from Chapter 6, people with independent self-concepts come to understand others by focusing on their inner attributes and attending less to relationships. People with interdependent self-concepts, in contrast, tend to conceive of people in terms of their relationships with others. Nisbett and colleagues argue that these cultural differences in ways of understanding *people* also shape the kinds of information people attend to in their physical environments (also see Kühnen, Hannover, & Schubert, 2001; Kühnen & Oyserman, 2002).

Nisbett and colleagues further suggest that these cultural differences in analytic versus holistic thinking between Westerners and East Asians were also present between Greeks and Chinese 2,500 years ago. Analytic thinking is evident in the Platonic perspective that the world is a collection of discrete, unchanging objects that can be categorized by reference to a set of universal properties. Such thinking can be seen in Aristotle's view that a stone falls through the air because the stone possesses the property of "gravity" and that a log floats on water because the log possesses the property of "levity." Analytic thinking is further evident in the Greek development of an elaborate formal logic system that searched for the truth according to abstract rules and syllogisms that existed independently of observations.

In contrast, holistic thinking was evident among the ancient Chinese in that their intellectual traditions of Confucianism, Taoism, and Buddhism emphasized harmony, interconnectedness, and change. Although the Greek preference for discrete concepts and abstract principles led to the invention of science, the Chinese tendency to view the world as consisting of continuously interacting substances led them to discover the concept of action at a distance 2,000 years before Galileo did. For example, the Chinese had knowledge of magnetism, acoustic resonance, and the moon's role in the tides long before Westerners did, even though they lacked a scientific tradition at the time (Nisbett, 2003). Holistic thinking is further evident among the Chinese medical traditions and in the culture's emphasis on harmony among people and nature. According to Nisbett and colleagues, cultural differences in ways of thinking between Westerners and East Asians persist to this day because ancient Greece and Confucian China provided the intellectual groundwork from which modern Western and East Asian societies have evolved.

How analytic and holistic thinking styles took root in ancient Greece and Confucian China is not well understood (although, see Nisbett, 2003, for some informed conjectures). Some research suggests that holistic thinking is quite widespread throughout the world and that analytic thinking is the relatively unusual thinking style, in that it is largely restricted to people who have had much contact with Western society or education systems (see Varnum, Grossman, Kitayama, & Nisbett,

2010). For example, one study found that Arabs showed at least as much evidence of holistic thinking as Chinese did (Norenzayan, Choi, & Peng, 2007). Russians are more holistic in their thinking than Americans (Grossman & Varnum, 2011), as are Turkish farmers and fishermen (Uskul, Kitayama, & Nisbett, 2008). Even within cultures there are parallel differences—working-class Americans and Russians are more holistic than their middle-class compatriots (Grossman & Varnum, 2011).

My former colleague, Joe Henrich, relayed a story to me about visiting the Mapuche in Chile, a local indigenous population of subsistence farmers, to investigate holistic and analytic thinking. He asked people to make a decision about the task described above—namely, of a dog, a carrot, and a rabbit, which does not belong? Almost everyone he spoke with gave the holistic response and said that the dog didn't belong because the carrot had a relationship to the rabbit. After many holistic answers he finally found someone who gave him what seemed to be an analytic answer, as he said that the carrot didn't belong. Henrich, relieved at finding some evidence for analytic thinking at last, then asked the man why the carrot didn't belong. The man answered that it was because the dog took care of the rabbit (which apparently it did in his household)! In sum, there is evidence that holistic thinking characterizes people from much of the globe. Interestingly, the same places where holistic thinking are found are also the places where there has traditionally been little psychological research. We may well have overestimated the pervasiveness of analytic thinking.

This hypothesized cultural difference in analytic and holistic thinking styles manifests in a number of rather profound ways. In the following sections I provide a fairly long description of the many ways this cultural difference has been shown to emerge in some very basic psychological processes. Much of this work has been conducted by Richard Nisbett and his former students, who have primarily focused on comparisons of North Americans and East Asians, although many of the findings from East Asians are seen in other non-Western cultures as well.

Attention

One of the most fundamental psychological processes is *attention*—that is, at a given time, where one's cognitive activity is directed. It follows that analytic thinkers, who tend to perceive the world as consisting of discrete objects, would be more likely to focus their attention on separate parts of a scene—those parts that represent discrete objects of interest. In contrast, holistic thinkers, who tend to perceive the world as consisting of an interrelated whole, should direct their attention more broadly, across an entire scene.

An early finding from the psychoanalytic tradition lent support to the idea that East Asians and Westerners showed different attention to stimuli. In 1949 some European-Americans and Chinese-Americans were asked to describe what they saw

FIGURE 9.2 An example of a Rorschach ink blot.

in some Rorschach ink blots (Abel & Hsu, 1949). The Rorschach is a projective test in which people report what they see in an ambiguous stimulus (see **Figure 9.2**). The results revealed that these two groups of Americans apparently saw things quite differently. The European-Americans were more likely to describe what they saw based on a single aspect of the card—say, a little blotch on the bottom that looked like a Ferrari. In contrast, the Chinese-Americans were more likely to give "whole-card" responses, describing what they saw based on the entire image.

This finding was largely ignored by the field for about 50 years, because no one had any way of making sense of this cultural difference. Perhaps it was a fluke. However, many other studies have built on this intriguing finding and have extended it in important ways.

For example, to the extent that East Asians habitually perceive the world in holistic terms, they should be especially good at certain kinds of tasks; the attention that holistic thinkers direct to the entire scene should mean that they would be especially good at detecting relations among different events. This hypothesis was investigated by showing American and Chinese students pairs of pictures on a computer (Ji, Peng, & Nisbett, 2000). The pairings were set so that when one picture was shown (e.g., a lightbulb), the other picture (e.g., a coin) was shown 0% of the time, 40% of the time, 60% of the time, or 100% of the time. Later the participants were shown just one of the pictures (e.g., the lightbulb) and asked the likelihood that the other picture (e.g., the coin) would appear beside it. To succeed at this task, you have to be especially good at attending to the relations between these different pictures, something that holistic thinkers should do well. The results indicated that the Chinese estimates of the likelihood that the correct picture would appear were more accurate than the estimates of the Americans. Apparently, Americans focused more on the individual objects than they did on the relations between the objects.

There are other kinds of tasks for which holistic thinkers should perform especially *badly*. Their tendency to focus on entire scenes should mean they would do poorly on tasks that require separating a scene into its component parts. An example is the rod-and-frame task, as shown in **Figure 9.3**. The goal is to say whether the rod is pointing straight up. What makes this task challenging, however, is that the frame around the rod is rotated independently and thus it provides misleading information. To be able to do the rod-and-frame task properly, you have to be able to ignore the misleading information of the frame and focus solely on the rod. Analytic thinkers, with their tendency to perceive the world as separate objects, should fare well on this

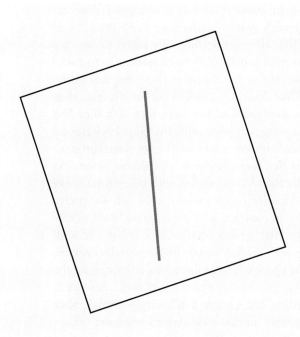

FIGURE 9.3

Rod-and-frame task. In this task, the rod and the surrounding frame are rotated independently. The frame provides misleading information about the angle of the rod, so it is necessary to ignore the frame to correctly identify the angle of the rod. People who are high on field independence can do this task well.

task. Analytic thinkers tend to show **field independence**—that is, they can separate objects from their background fields. Holistic thinkers, in contrast, tend to show **field dependence**, in that they tend to view objects as bound to their backgrounds.

Research shows that people's ability to judge the rod's angle while ignoring the frame relates to their general social orientation. People who attend a lot to others develop more of an orientation toward the field. Those who are more outgoing are more field dependent than people who are more introverted (Witkin, 1969). Similarly, farmers who live in societies where they must coordinate their actions with others are more field dependent than people who hunt and gather or who herd animals (Witkin & Berry, 1975). Likewise, religious training in Calvinism, which emphasizes the independence of individuals, leads people to be more field independent than atheists or people with training in Catholicism or Judaism (Colzato et al., 2010; Colzato, van den Wildenberg, & Hommel, 2008). People in industrialized societies also tend to be quite field independent, except for people living in highly industrialized East Asia, where clear evidence for field dependence is found. That is, in general, East Asians do relatively poorly on tasks such as the rod and frame (Ji et al., 2000; Kitayama, Duffy, Kawamura, & Larsen, 2003).

This field dependence identified among East Asians has been further investigated in a number of other studies. Consider what people see when they look at a scene. In one study, American and Japanese participants were shown some animated computer images of an underwater scene, complete with swimming fish, waving seaweed, and floating bubbles (Masuda & Nisbett, 2001). The participants were asked to describe what they saw. The Japanese participants made about 60% more references to background objects than the Americans, who tended to talk more about the fish at the center of the scene. After the participants had described a number of these scenes, they were then shown some additional scenes that included the same focal fish they had seen before. However, some of those fish were presented with the same background they had appeared in earlier, whereas other fish were shown with a novel background. The participants were asked whether they had seen the fish in the picture before. As shown in **Figure 9.4**, regardless of whether the fish was shown with its original background or with a novel background, the American's recognition of the fish was pretty much the same. The Japanese participants, in contrast, were much more likely to recognize the fish when it was with the original background than when it was paired with the novel background. They seem to have seen the fish and the background scenery as bound together. When the background is changed, the fish no longer look quite the same. And because the researchers were concerned that the results could have been influenced because the Japanese participants had greater familiarity with fish, they replicated the study with photos of American animals and American scenery. They found the same pattern of findings as with the fish. When looking at the identical scenes, Americans and Japanese appear to be perceiving them differently.

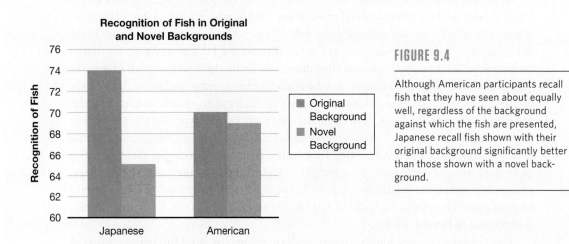

FIGURE 9.4

Although American participants recall fish that they have seen about equally well, regardless of the background against which the fish are presented, Japanese recall fish shown with their original background significantly better than those shown with a novel background.

This cultural difference in how people attend to parts of scenes is also evident at the neural level. Gutchess et al. (2006) placed East Asians and American participants in an fMRI scanner and showed them pictures of either individual objects (such as an elephant alone), empty background scenes (such as a savannah scene, with no animals), or an embedded scene (such as an elephant in a savannah). The American subjects showed more activation of object-processing regions in the brain (such as the bilateral middle termporal gyrus, left superior parietal gyrus, and right superior temporal gyrus) compared with the East Asians. In contrast, no cultural variation was found in areas associated with processing contexts and backgrounds. Moreover, other research found that the cultural differences in object processing are more pronounced in comparisons of elderly East Asians and elderly Westerners than in comparisons of younger East Asians and Westerners (Goh et al., 2007). Apparently, as people age, their neural functions continue to be shaped by normative cultural attention patterns. These studies show that people rely on different brain regions for processing visual information in scenes (for a review see Park & Huang, 2010).

Now, these findings raise a big question. Are people from different cultures really seeing things differently, or are they processing the same information differently? It's possible that Westerners think of objects as more important than East Asians do, and they thus end up reflecting on these more, which is evident in their brain activity. On the other hand, it's also possible that cultural differences in how people make sense of their worlds guides them to look at scenes differently, leading them to encounter different kinds of visual information.

The best way to provide an answer to this important question is to use an eye-tracker, a device with which researchers can determine precisely where someone is looking at any given instant. What would happen if the eye movements of East Asians and Westerners were contrasted? In one study, Japanese and American participants looked at some animated scenes on a computer (Masuda, Ellsworth et al., 2008). In one scene they saw a target person in the foreground surrounded by other people in the background. Each of the people was showing an emotional facial expression. Sometimes the background faces showed expressions inconsistent with the target person (e.g., the target person was smiling but the background people were frowning), and sometimes they showed expressions consistent with the target person. The task for the participants was to identify the emotion the target person was experiencing. The results showed, first, that Japanese judgments of the target person's emotional expression were influenced by the expressions of the people in the background. In contrast, the expressions of the background people had no impact on the judgments of the faces for the Americans. This again provides evidence that East Asians attend more to the background context than Westerners do.

In this study, the participants viewed the scenes while they were connected to an eye-tracker, so every movement of their eye was monitored. The test question was whether people from the two cultures were looking at the same things.

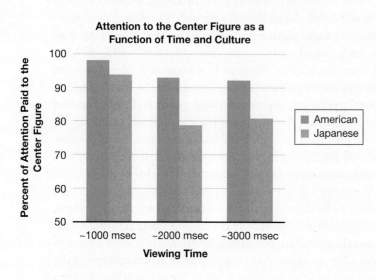

FIGURE 9.5

When looking at a picture, Americans focus more on the center figure than Japanese do, especially after the first second has passed. Japanese spend a relatively larger amount of time focusing on parts of the background.

Figure 9.5 shows the percentage of time participants were looking at the central figure compared to the background. In the first 1,000 milliseconds there is little cultural difference (although this difference is significant). That is, both Americans and Japanese are spending more than 90% of the time looking at the target figure, with the American percentage a little higher than the Japanese. In the next two 1,000-millisecond intervals, people in both cultures start to look a little more at the background. But this is especially so for Japanese. Whereas the Americans are still devoting more than 90% of their attention to the central figure, the Japanese are devoting somewhere between 70% and 80%. Furthermore, this pattern does not seem to be limited to scenes in which the background is composed of other people, which arguably might be more interesting for those with more interdependent selves. Similar cultural differences have been found when Chinese and American students looked at inanimate scenes (Chua, Boland, & Nisbett, 2005). Again, the Americans were more likely to attend to the foreground objects than the Chinese, who looked more at the background. Furthermore, the Chinese participants made more saccades than the Americans. **Saccades** are the extremely quick eye movements that shift people's gaze from one fixation point to another. Compared to the Americans, the Chinese were more systematically scanning the entire scene. By systematically scanning scenes, Asians are better able to detect changes in backgrounds than Westerners are (Miyamoto, Nisbett, & Masuda, 2006); however, Westerners' tendencies to attend to focal objects allows them to outperform Asians on tasks requiring keeping track of multiple objects (Savani & Markus, 2012).

These studies suggest, quite remarkably, that people from different cultures are not seeing the same things, even when they are looking at identical scenes. The stimuli perceived by our brains are different across cultures. Our eye movements occur largely outside of our voluntary control, suggesting just how deeply these cultural differences in attention lie. East Asians have been socialized from such a young age to attend to relationships that they do so unconsciously by continually scanning scenes. Westerners, in contrast, have been socialized to attend to focal objects, and they thus habitually tend to direct their attention at such objects.

This brings us back to the paintings that we saw at the beginning of this chapter. If you recall, Masuda and colleagues found that horizons tend to be painted significantly higher in East Asian paintings than in Western ones. A higher horizon calls attention to the depth of the setting and allows for all the different objects and places within a scene to be seen in relation to each other, whereas a lower horizon reduces the range of the scene that is visible. The East Asian paintings thus naturally direct an audience's eyes to the relations among the different objects and places within a scene, whereas Western paintings tend to direct an audience's attention to particular focal objects. The same kinds of physical landscape scenes are represented quite differently by artists depending on their cultural background.

Likewise, Western portraits tend to show larger figures than East Asian ones. The larger figures, in particular the larger faces, serve to focus one's attention on the portrayed individual. The figure comes to dominate the scene and stands apart from the background. In contrast, in the East Asian portrait the individual remains firmly ensconced within the surrounding context. Comparing the two portraits, it is not difficult to tell which culture has cultivated more of a sense that individuals are distinct and autonomous centers of agency.

It is possible, however, that the differences in the paintings reflect old artistic conventions rather than the aesthetic preferences that people currently have. To investigate whether cultural differences in perception affect the art people produce today, Masuda and colleagues asked participants to draw some pictures on their own (Masuda, Gonzalez et al., 2008). Specifically, American and East Asian college students were asked to draw a landscape scene within 5 minutes that contained at least a house, a tree, a river, a person, and a horizon. They were told they could draw any additional objects that they wanted. A couple of representative examples are shown in **Figure 9.6**. Two characteristics of the drawings were analyzed. First, as in the paintings, the height of the horizon in the picture was measured. Replicating the findings from the paintings in the art museums, East Asians drew a horizon that was significantly higher in the picture than it was for the Americans. Also, the East Asians tended to provide a more complex background in their drawings, in that they included 75% more contextual objects than did the Americans. Overall, East Asians were more likely than Americans to situate their objects in context. Likewise, when taking photographs of others, East Asians include more of the background

FIGURE 9.6 The house on the left is a representative landscape drawing by an American participant in Masuda and colleagues' study, and the one on the right is a representative drawing by a Japanese participant. The American drawings had lower horizons and fewer objects to contextualize the scene (Masuda, Gonzalez et al., 2008).

in the frame and have smaller figures in their portraits, compared with Americans (Masuda, Gonzalez et al., 2008). These predilections carry over to shape the pictures that people choose to include of themselves on their Facebook pages: East Asian Facebook photos have smaller figures and larger backgrounds compared with American ones (Huang & Park, 2013).

East Asian art thus seems to contain busier scenes than Western art—the Western art is more likely to direct your attention to the foreground, either by including low horizons or big central figures. Could these differences in aesthetic styles be reflected in other aspects of daily life across cultures? It seems that they can. First, consider how the actual landscapes around us may differ across cultures. Miyamoto et al. (2006) compared pictures of landscapes in Japan and the United States—specifically, according to a fixed set of rules they took photographs from post offices and schools in cities of comparable size in the two countries and then analyzed the number of boundaries in the scenes. The Japanese scenes actually contained more boundaries and edges then the American ones—the physical landscape in urban areas is literally busier in Japan than in the United States.

Living in a busier physical environment seems to foster the ability to attend to a lot of information at once. Research by Wang, Masuda, Ito, and Rashid (2012) explored how people from different cultures presented information to others. For example, in one study they looked at how scientists presented their findings in conference posters. They compared the posters of scientists from North America and scientists from East Asian universities who were presenting at the same international (and English-speaking) conferences. When the posters contained multiple studies (but not briefer posters that described just one study), the East Asian participants had busier posters, with more words than the North American participants.

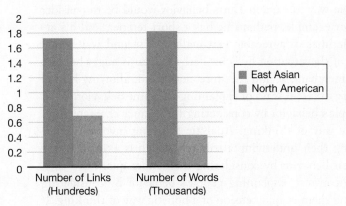

FIGURE 9.7

The main governmental and university web portals from East Asian websites contain a larger number of links and words than their North American counterparts. It seems that regular exposure to busier websites makes East Asians more efficient than North Americans at navigating them.

The researchers also looked at governmental and university websites in East Asia and North America. They compared a number of dimensions of the official portals for each of the websites. The East Asian websites were much longer (as indicated by the scrollbar being smaller) than the North American websites and had significantly more links and words (**Figure 9.7**). Simply put, the East Asian websites were busier, with more information for people to navigate.

And it seems that the regular exposure to busier environments among East Asian facilitates their ability to process busy scenes: Wang et al. (2012) conducted another study in which they timed how long it took European-Canadian and East Asian students to find a series of images buried in a busy website. When the websites were short, there was no cultural difference in how long it took participants to find the images. However, when the websites were long, the East Asian students were significantly quicker than the European-Canadians at finding the hidden images. East Asian experience with attending more to backgrounds, and in living in busier physical spaces, is associated with better skills for finding details in a busy scene.

Understanding Other People's Behaviors

Whether a person is attending in a holistic manner or in an analytic manner has a number of important consequences. For example, consider how an individual would go about understanding another person's behaviors. Imagine you see an acquaintance,

Dan, in a store arguing angrily with a shop clerk. You might very well wonder why Dan is behaving like this. One way to explain Dan's behavior would be to consider his internal characteristics. For example, perhaps he has a short temper, and his arguing is evidence of his sometimes disagreeable personality. A second way would be to consider characteristics of the situation he is in. Perhaps Dan is angry because he purchased some defective merchandise and the store clerk is not allowing him to exchange it. These are two very different ways of explaining the same behavior.

Trying to understand people's behavior by considering their inner characteristics is an extension of an analytic way of thinking. Analytic thinking involves understanding objects by identifying their underlying attributes, which is akin to trying to understand people and their behavior by considering their inner qualities—such as their personality traits. In contrast, explaining people's behavior by considering how the situation is influencing them is an extension of a holistic way of thinking. It requires considering the individual's relations with his or her context. Given what we know about cultural differences in analytic and holistic ways of thinking, we would expect Westerners to be more likely to explain people's behaviors in terms of their underlying dispositions (i.e., they will make **dispositional attributions**) and East Asians—and perhaps people from other cultural backgrounds as well—to be more likely to explain people's behaviors in terms of contextual variables (i.e., they will make **situational attributions**).

The Fundamental Attribution Error

Imagine you experienced the following: You read an essay written in the 1960s by a person who was asked to write about Fidel Castro, who at the time was widely perceived as the United States' number-one enemy. The essay makes a number of arguments that are clearly pro-Castro. What do you think the essay writer's true attitudes were toward Castro? Well, you would have no reason to doubt the writer's motives, so you would surely assume that he or she had favorable attitudes toward Castro. And you would likely assume that the writer had negative attitudes toward Castro if the essay included many anti-Castro arguments. It is perfectly reasonable to assume that the essay writer expressed his or her true attitudes. Now, however, imagine that before reading the essay you are told that the writer had been instructed to write with a perspective that was to be used in a debate—that is, those who wrote pro-Castro essays had been told to write an essay defending Castro, whereas those who wrote anti-Castro essays had been told to write an essay criticizing Castro. Your task remains the same: identifying the essay writer's true attitudes toward Castro. What do you think?

Well, it's not so straightforward now, because we shouldn't assume that the writer expressed his or her true attitude due to the instructions to take a particular position. Really, the essay tells us virtually nothing about the writer's true attitudes. However, as Jones and Harris (1967) found in a classic social psychological study, people still assumed that the person who was instructed to write a pro-Castro essay had positive attitudes toward Castro and that the person who was instructed to write an anti-Castro essay had negative attitudes toward Castro. That is, they attributed the behavior of writing the essay to reflecting the essay writer's underlying personality even though it was clear to them that the writers had no choice in what they wrote. This tendency to ignore situational information (such as the conditions under which the writers wrote their essays) while focusing on dispositional information (the essay writers' assumed attitudes) is known as the **fundamental attribution error**. It is termed "fundamental" because it is viewed to be deeply ingrained in us. When we see people acting, we assume they are doing so because of their underlying dispositions, and we tend to ignore the situational constraints that might be driving their behavior.

However, as with so many other psychological phenomena, this research was conducted almost exclusively with North American participants. A natural question emerged: How fundamental is the fundamental attribution error? Is it a universal tendency to explain other people's behaviors primarily in terms of their personality while ignoring situational influences?

The anthropologist Clifford Geertz suggests that it is not. He asserts that people in some other cultures—for example, the Balinese—do not tend to conceive of people's behaviors in terms of underlying dispositions but instead see them as emerging out of the roles people have (Geertz, 1975). This idea was developed further by Shweder and Bourne (1982), who contrasted Indians and Americans in terms of the ways they described others. Indians from the state of Orissa tended to describe others by saying things like, "She brings cakes to my family on festival days." In contrast, Americans were more likely to say things like, "She is friendly." That is, Americans were more likely to conceive of people in terms of abstract personality traits than the Indians, who attended to others in terms of the concrete behaviors they engaged in.

Comparable cultural differences in tendencies to focus on traits is also evident in a number of other experimental paradigms (e.g., Argyle, Shimoda, & Little, 1978; Maass, Karasawa, Politi, & Suga, 2006; Zarate, Uleman, & Voils, 2001). For example, when participants memorized a series of facial photographs that were matched with descriptions of behaviors (e.g., stopped to help a tourist with directions), the implied trait words (e.g., helpful) were more strongly linked to the photos for European-Americans than they were for Asian-Americans, showing that the behavior was more likely to be interpreted by the European-Americans as indicating an underlying trait (Na & Kitayama, 2011).

This question was further explored in an attempt to learn the age at which these different ways of understanding people's behaviors emerges across cultures. In one study, children (8, 11, and 15 years of age) and university students were recruited from India and the United States (Miller, 1984). The participants were asked to describe a situation when someone had behaved in either a prosocial manner or a deviant manner and then to explain why the person had behaved that way. Here is an example of a deviant behavior described by an Indian participant:

> This concerns a motorcycle accident. The back wheel burst on the motorcycle. The passenger sitting in the rear jumped. The moment the passenger fell, he struck his head on the pavement. The driver of the motorcycle—who is an attorney—as he was on his way to court for some work, just took the passenger to a local hospital and went on and attended to his court work. I personally feel the motorcycle driver did a wrong thing. The driver left the passenger there without consulting the doctor concerning the seriousness of the injury—the gravity of the situation—whether the passenger should be shifted immediately—and he went on to court. So ultimately the passenger died.

The reasons people gave for the actor's behaviors were examined, noting, in particular, whether they made explanations that referred to the actor's general disposition or to the context. (Other reasons for the actor's behavior are not included here.) **Figure 9.8**

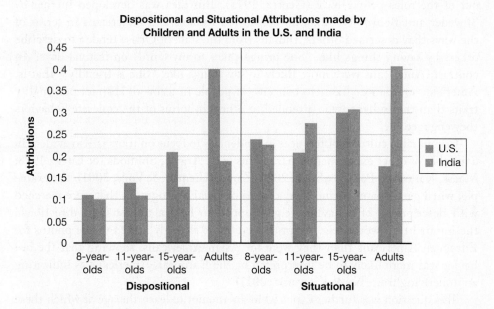

FIGURE 9.8 Although Indian and American children show similar attribution patterns, as Americans get older they tend to make more dispositional attributions, and as Indians get older they tend to make more situational attributions.

reveals that the 8-year-olds gave quite similar responses between the two cultures. However, as the American sample got older, they were more likely to make dispositional attributions, whereas their situational attributions remained largely unchanged. In contrast, as the Indian sample got older, they made more situational attributions whereas their dispositional attributions did not change significantly. By the time they were adults, the Americans showed clear evidence for the fundamental attribution error by explaining people's behaviors as largely due to their personalities. In contrast, the Indian adults did not show any evidence of the fundamental attribution error; rather, they showed evidence of a *reverse* fundamental attribution error because they tended to focus more on the situation than on the disposition. The fundamental attribution error does not look so fundamental anymore.

This cultural difference in the way people explain the behavior of others has some important consequences (e.g., Lee, Hallahan, & Herzog, 1996). For example, how do we make sense of a person's behavior when it is illegal or causes great harm to others? Do we blame the person or the situation they were in? This question was investigated by exploring the way newspaper articles described instances of behaviors that were undeniably antisocial—namely, mass murder (Morris & Peng, 1994). One instance was of a Chinese graduate student living in the United States who, on losing an award and failing to get a job, returned to school to kill his supervisor and several others. A second instance was of an American postal worker who, on losing his job, returned to work and, well, "went postal" and killed his supervisor and several others. Both of these stories were covered in the *New York Times* and the *World Journal,* the leading English and Chinese language newspapers. The researchers analyzed newspaper articles about the two events and noted each occasion when the reporters offered details about the disposition of the accused (e.g., having a "very bad temper," being "mentally unstable") or about the situation that was relevant to the killings (e.g., had a "rivalry with a slain student," "had been recently fired"). Regardless of the particular story, the American stories overall made more references to the disposition of the accused than to the situation. In stark contrast, the Chinese stories made more references to the situations that had provoked the accused than to the person's disposition. Even the causes of extreme behaviors are interpreted differently across cultures. Indeed, these results suggest that courts in different cultures likely view responsibility for crimes in quite different ways (for a striking contrast of how criminal responsibility is viewed in the Japanese and American legal systems, see Hamilton & Sanders, 1992).

These findings suggest that personality information is not seen as equally important for explaining the behavior of others in all cultural contexts, although the cultural differences are most pronounced when the situational information is made highly salient (e.g., Choi & Nisbett, 1998). Even though the structure of personality appears to be largely similar across cultures (see Chapter 6), Westerners tend to use personality information more for understanding others (and themselves) than East Asians do (also see Cousins, 1989; Suh, 2002).

Cultural differences in making dispositional attributions extend far more broadly than differences between East Asians and Westerners. People from many other non-Western cultural contexts show a pattern similar to East Asians (Church et al., 2006). Moreover, religious groups differ in their attributions as well. For example, recent findings show that American Protestants are more likely than American Catholics to make dispositional attributions. Moreover, this difference between the sects appears to be a function of Protestants having a greater commitment to the idea that people have individual souls (Li et al., 2012). If people believe that God is judging them on the basis of what their soul has done, it follows that they are more likely to view the soul as being the cause of the individual's behaviors. In addition, people's socioeconomic status predicts the kinds of attributions that people make: Working-class Americans make more situational attributions, and fewer dispositional attributions, than middle-class Americans (Kluegel & Smith, 1986; Kraus, Cote, & Keltner, 2010). The same kinds of social class differences in explaining other people's behaviors have also been found in France (Beauvois & Dubois, 1988), Russia (Grossmann & Varnum, 2011), and India (Mahalingam, 2003, 2007; for a review, see Kraus, Piff, Mendoza-Denton, Rheinschmidt, & Keltner, 2012).

Reasoning Styles

Another indication that an analytic or holistic orientation affects people's thinking is in the ways they reason. For example, if analytic thinkers tend to view the world as operating according to a set of universal abstract rules and laws, they will apply such rules and laws when they try to make sense of a situation. This is termed **rule-based reasoning**. In contrast, holistic thinkers should be more likely to make sense of a situation by considering the relationships among objects or events. They should look for evidence of events clustering together, such as a similarity among events or of temporal contiguity of events. This is termed **associative reasoning.** This suggests that analytic and holistic thinkers might go about solving problems in quite different ways.

Look at **Figure 9.9**. There are two groups of flowers and there are two target objects. The task for you is to decide which target flower, A or B, is more similar to those in Group 1 and which is more similar to those in Group 2. What do you think?

This example is tricky because it pits two reasoning styles against each other. If you are to make the decision based on the application of an abstract rule, you would conclude that Flower A goes with Group 2 and Flower B goes with Group 1. The reason is that the only characteristic that consistently distinguishes the flowers in Groups 1 and 2 is the shape of the stems. All the flowers in Group 1 have a curved stem whereas all of the flowers in Group 2 have a straight stem. Applying this rule would lead you to conclude that Flower A belongs to Group 2 and Flower B to Group 1. This way of thinking would be an example of rule-based reasoning.

FIGURE 9.9 To which group do the two target flowers belong? This stimulus pits associative reasoning against rule-based reasoning. Target object A belongs to Group 1 by associative reasoning but it belongs to Group 2 according to rule-based reasoning.

In contrast, if you were to base your decision on the overall similarity of the target flowers to the groups, you would have reached a different conclusion. Flower A resembles most of the flowers in Group 1 because most of the flowers in that group have round petals, have one leaf, and have only one circle. Likewise, Flower B resembles the family of flowers in Group 2. However, none of those features characterize all the flowers in the group, so these resemblances do not become rules; they would be an example of associative reasoning. Therefore, in this picture rule-based reasoning leads to a different solution than would be reached with associative reasoning.

American and East Asian participants were presented with a set of pictures like this, each of which involved a conflict between the application of a rule and family resemblance judgments (Norenzayan, Smith, Kim, & Nisbett, 2002). When presented with such stimuli, European-Americans were more likely to base their decisions on the application of the rule whereas East Asians were more likely to base their decision on the perceived resemblances of the stimuli. As would be expected, Asian-Americans fell in between the other two groups (**Figure 9.10**).

Note, however, that this study shows that East Asians are more likely to use holistic reasoning in a situation when there is a *conflict* between an analytic and a holistic solution. In situations when there is no conflict, Westerners should be able

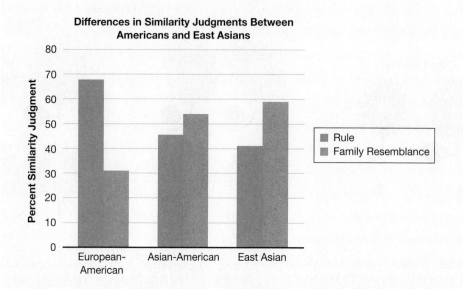

FIGURE 9.10 When deciding whether two stimuli are similar, European-Americans rely more on rule-based reasoning, whereas East Asians rely more on associative reasoning.

to engage in holistic reasoning and East Asians should be able to rely on analytic reasoning strategies. One domain in which we see problems that require purely analytic reasoning strategies is in most math and science problems. Because these problems typically do not have the kind of conflict between holistic and analytic strategies that we saw in the studies by Norenzayan and colleagues, East Asians should have no difficulty solving them, even though they involve analytic thinking. As we saw in Chapter 5, if anything, East Asians tend to excel on purely analytical problems.

Another way that holistic or analytic thinking influences reasoning styles is in the kinds of information people perceive to be relevant to a task. A truly holistic thinker is aware of the countless ways that things in the world are related to each other. For example, putting pressure on a point on one's heel could be seen to help relieve a headache. A drop in the stock market could be seen to influence the birth rate. Holistic thinkers tend to see actions as having distal, and sometimes unexpected, consequences. In contrast, analytic thinkers should focus their attention on the relations between a relatively small number of discrete objects or events. For example, one billiard ball is seen to move when another collides with it. Cutting taxes is seen to increase the amount of disposable income consumers have. Analytic thinkers should be more concerned with *direct* relations between objects or events (see Maddux & Yuki, 2006).

Imagine, as participants in a study were asked, how you would go about solving a murder mystery (Choi, Dalal, Kim-Prieto, & Park, 2003). All you know is that a graduate student is suspected of killing his advisor. You have 97 items of information that you can consider to help you crack the case. Some of these seem to be directly relevant to solving the murder—for example, what the graduate student was supposedly doing on the night in question, or whether the graduate student had a history of violence. In contrast, the direct relevance of some of the items is not so clear—for example, the graduate student's favorite color or the way the professor was dressed. What information would you use to solve the murder?

The answer to this question appears to differ between Koreans and Americans. When given the opportunity to exclude any information they found to be irrelevant to the case, Americans discarded more information than Koreans did. For more-analytical Americans, the murder mystery could best be solved by focusing only on those items that were most relevant to the case. In contrast, the more holistic Koreans felt that a greater number of the items had possible relations with the murder. For holistic thinkers the world consists of many overlapping and related events. Some details that might seem trivial at first glance could ultimately prove to be relevant.

Toleration of Contradiction

In addition to the holistic view that everything is fundamentally interconnected, East Asians seem to share a corresponding view that reality is continually in flux. This sense of the ultimate fluidity of reality is captured in the T'ai chi, the symbol that encompasses the Yin and the Yang (**Figure 9.11**). The Yin and the Yang represent opposites (literally, they mean the moon and the sun), and they indicate that the universe is constantly in flux, moving from one opposite pole to the other and back again. The darkness of the night will yield to the brightness of the day, which will lead to the darkness again, and the cycle will continue to repeat. This belief in a fluid and cyclical reality is perhaps most clearly evident in the writings of Lao Tzu, the legendary founder of Taoism. In the *Tao Te Ching* he said, "To shrink something, you need to expand it first. To weaken something, you need to strengthen it first. To abolish something, you need to flourish it first. To take

FIGURE 9.11 The T'ai chi.

something, you need to give it first" (Lao Tzu, 2000). This view not only highlights that reality is in flux but also indicates that opposing truths can be simultaneously accepted.

Around the time of Lao Tzu, a few thousand miles away Aristotle was offering a very different scheme for making sense of the world around us. He proposed the law of non-contradiction, in which he submitted that no statement could be both true and false, and thus "A" could not equal "not A." This law is at the heart of much of logical reasoning. In stark contrast to this Aristotelian law, ancient Chinese thought, as captured in the *I-Ching* (*The Book of Changes;* 1991), includes a principle of contradiction. Because everything is perceived to be fundamentally connected with everything else and constantly in flux, real contradiction ceases to exist. If "A" is connected with "not A," and if "A" is always changing into "not A," then "A" is no longer in contradiction with "not A." With this orientation toward the world, contradiction is not something to be rejected, but should be accepted. This acceptance of contradiction has been termed **naive dialecticism** (Peng & Nisbett, 1999). It reflects a profoundly different way of making sense of the world compared with Western logical reasoning.

Consider the following two arguments:

A: A sociologist who surveyed college students from 100 universities claimed that there is a high correlation among female college students between smoking and being skinny.

B: A biologist who studied nicotine addiction asserted that heavy doses of nicotine often lead to becoming overweight.

Can you see the apparent contradiction in these two arguments? One argument is that smoking leads to weight loss whereas the other is that smoking leads to weight gain. They are not strictly contradictory, as it is possible for both of them to be true, even from a logical perspective. However, the general thrusts of the arguments are in opposition to each other. Take a moment to think about how compelling you view these two arguments to be.

Chinese and American students were given these arguments as well as a number of other contradictory pairs (Peng & Nisbett, 1999). Half the participants received only one argument (either Argument A or Argument B) and were asked to indicate how compelling they found it to be. As shown in the left halves of the two figures in **Figure 9.12**, both Americans and Chinese who received only Argument A tended to view it as more compelling than those who received only Argument B. Because these participants saw only one argument, they did not witness any potential contradiction. The other half of the participants were asked to evaluate both of the contradictory arguments. These participants saw a potential contradiction. How did seeing the contradiction affect their evaluations of the arguments?

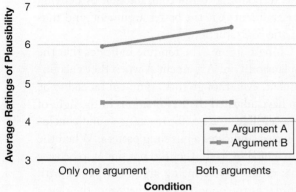

**Perceived Plausibility of an Argument
Based on Condition in American Students**

FIGURE 9.12

When Americans encounter two contradictory arguments, they come to view the better argument as even more compelling than when they encounter this same argument by itself. In contrast, when Chinese encounter two contradictory arguments, they come to view the weaker argument as more compelling than when it is presented by itself.

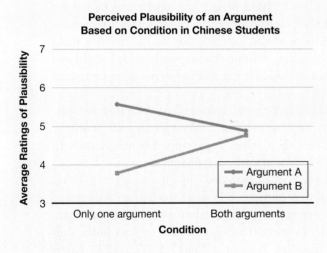

**Perceived Plausibility of an Argument
Based on Condition in Chinese Students**

First, let's look at the right half of the American figure. These participants read both of the contradictory arguments. The top line in the graph indicates that Americans who encountered the contradictory Argument B were even more convinced that Argument A was compelling than those who had read only Argument A. This is a puzzling response, although it is consistent with some past research with Westerners (Lord, Ross, & Lepper, 1979). It would seem that if participants did not find Argument

B to be compelling, a normative strategy would be to ignore it, or perhaps to hedge their bets by being a little less confident in Argument A. But the Americans who saw Argument B instead responded by being even *more* confident in the plausibility of Argument A. The Americans were thus responding to the contradiction by denying that it exists—they are confident that Argument A is the better argument, and thus they are denying that there is a problematic contradiction.

Next, look at the right half of the Chinese figure. The top line indicates that the Chinese became less convinced in the plausibility of Argument A when they encountered an apparently contradictory argument, even though that argument tended to be viewed as less plausible. They appear to have adjusted their evaluations in the light of the evidence, which would seem to be a sensible strategy for reaching sound conclusions. The bottom line of the figure, however, indicates a puzzling pattern. When the Chinese participants encountered Argument B by itself, they did not find it to be very plausible. However, when they saw this rather unconvincing argument paired with the more compelling Argument A that makes the opposite case, they were then *more* convinced by the rather implausible Argument B. The idea that smoking is associated with weight gain was compelling to them only if they had also read an argument that smoking was associated with weight loss! My helplessly undialectical mind cannot make heads or tails of this kind of reasoning. Apparently, the Chinese are reacting to the arguments in that they have noticed the contradiction and it reminds them that the world is often contradictory, making it difficult to say which side is right and which is wrong. The contradiction is accepted as it is, and they do not seem motivated to get rid of it.

This greater tolerance for contradiction found among East Asians is not just evident in how they reason about the external world. We can also see it in the ways that people think of themselves; their selves appear more contradictory. In one study, for example, Chinese and American participants were asked to describe themselves in an open-ended questionnaire (Spencer-Rodgers, Peng, Wang, & Hou, 2004). The Chinese were significantly more likely than Americans to provide statements that were in apparent contradiction with each other (e.g., Chinese individuals would provide answers that suggested they had both high self-esteem and low self-esteem; also see Bagozzi, Wong, & Yi, 1999). Likewise, other research has found that Koreans would endorse items that suggested they were introverted *and* that they were extraverted (Choi & Choi, 2002), and Japanese were more likely than Canadians to hold contradictory views of their personalities (Hamamura, Heine, & Paulhus, 2008). These more contradictory self-views among East Asians are also associated with less consistency in their self-concepts (Boucher, 2011). Moreover, while having contradictory self-views in the United States is associated with feelings of anxiety and depression, in Japan there was no relation between how contradictory one's self-views are and how anxious and depressed they are (Brown, 2013). Likewise, experiencing contradictory emotions is associated with better health outcomes in Japan than in the United States (Miyamoto & Ryff, 2011). In sum, East Asians appear to hold views about themselves that are more contradictory than those held by North Americans. Even within themselves, East Asians can tolerate apparent contradictions.

Because East Asians more than Westerners perceive life as fluid and changing, other interesting cultural differences emerge in the ways people think. Westerners also understand that the world changes; however, it appears that their views on change are slightly different from those of East Asians. Relative to East Asians, Westerners appear to view change as occurring in more linear ways. For example, if a stock has risen over the past year, it will likely rise again next year. The earth has grown warmer over the past few decades, indicating that it will continue to grow warmer over the next few as well. The birth rate has dropped over the past generation so it will probably continue to drop over the next generation. Change appears to occur in rather static and predictable ways.

In contrast, East Asians appear to believe that change itself happens in rather fluid and unpredictable ways. Consider the following story, which is known to almost every Chinese:

> One day an old farmer's horse ran away from him. His neighbors came by to comfort him, but he said, "How can you know it isn't a good thing?" And a few days later, his horse came back, bringing a wild horse with it. His neighbors came to congratulate the old man, who said, "How can you know it isn't a bad thing?" A few weeks later, the old man's son was trying to ride the horse and he fell off, breaking his leg. When the neighbors came over to express condolences, the old man said, "How can you know it isn't a good thing?" The next month a war broke out, and all the able-bodied young men were recruited to fight it. The old man's son did not have to go because of his broken leg, and he survived with his father. (cited in Ji, 2005)

This story shows that change can happen at any time and often in precisely the opposite way one is anticipating. To the extent that this story captures widely shared beliefs among East Asians, we would expect differences in the ways people predict how the future will unfold. One study investigated this question by providing Chinese and American students with a number of graphs indicating the past performance of a number of trends, such as the global economy growth rates or the worldwide death rate for cancer (Ji, Nisbett, & Su, 2001). Participants were asked to estimate what they thought would happen over the next few years. The Chinese were almost twice as likely as Americans to predict that the trend would reverse direction in the future, whereas Americans were more likely than Chinese to assume that the trend would continue in the same direction as in the past. This nonlinear perspective of change among Chinese is associated with them being more contrarian investors: Relative to Canadians, Chinese are more willing to buy stocks that are falling in value and are more willing to sell stocks that are rising in value (Ji, Zhang, & Guo, 2008). These cultural differences in predictions about the future are made more complex in that East Asians have been shown to place more value on things that have happened in the past compared with the future, whereas the opposite pattern has been found for North Americans (Guo, Ji, Spina, & Zhang, 2012). This suggests that attitudes toward the future vary considerably across cultures and that East Asians have quite different expectations and predictions about the future compared with Westerners.

Creative Thinking

Aside from analytic and holistic thinking, one additional way of thinking has received much attention across cultures: creative thinking. How does creativity compare across cultures? Are people in some cultures more creative than others?

Much of the cross-cultural study of creativity has contrasted Westerners and East Asians. Some have noted that by certain measures of creativity, Westerners seem to fare better: For example, Nobel Prizes have been disproportionately awarded to people in Western cultures (Switzerland is the per capita leader), and relatively few have gone to people in East Asian countries, particularly China (Kanazawa, 2006; but note that Chinese scientific innovations arguably led the world in the 15th century; Needham, 1956). Likewise, some have argued that Asian art, in comparison with Western art, tends to be more about mastering the techniques of a model rather than producing original works and that Asians have excelled more in genres such as classical music in which disciplined reproduction is prioritized ahead of novelty (Morris & Leung, 2010; Yoshihara, 2007). Socratic learning styles that originated in Greece put more emphasis on self-discovery compared with Confucian styles of learning that emphasized the mastery of material (Tweed & Lehman, 2002). These perspectives have focused on the aspects of creativity that appear more encouraged in the West.

However, to compare cultures on creativity, we have to consider what creativity is in the first place. Here's a useful definition that has guided much research on the topic: Creativity is the generation of ideas that are both (a) novel and (b) useful and appropriate (Amabile, 1983). Both of these components are necessary to be considered creative. For example, a hammer made out of Jell-O and ladybugs would certainly be novel, but it wouldn't be useful in any meaningful sense. And a useful hammer might be one made with a steel head attached to a wooden handle, but it wouldn't be novel if it was the same as the one in your toolbox. A creative hammer would have to be useful but in a novel way. When you separate creativity into these two separate components, cultural comparisons become more nuanced.

In general, the generation of novel ideas appears to be facilitated by individualism, and Westerners, accordingly, appear to generate more ideas than East Asians. It's possible that a greater motivation for uniqueness (see Chapter 8) underlies this tendency.

Westerners prefer novel objects more than East Asians do (e.g., Kim & Markus, 1999), they generate a larger number of ideas when they are primed with individualistic thoughts than collectivistic ones (Goncalo & Staw, 2006), and Asian-Americans show more divergent thinking when primed with American culture compared with Asian culture (Mok & Morris, 2010), at least when they have an integrated bicultural identity (see Chapter 7). The novelty part of the creativity equation appears to be facilitated by individualism and Western cultural experiences.

Perhaps the novelty-individualism link for Western creativity can also be seen in the tendencies for Western artists to be more likely than the average person to suffer from mental illness. There are many famous instances of the disturbed creative genius in the West (think of Vincent van Gogh cutting off his own ear, or Ernest Hemingway's suicidal end), and an analysis of creative works finds that this is indeed a reliable pattern. However, an analysis of Chinese creative geniuses does not find as strong a link between creativity and mental illness (Simonton & Ting, 2010). It's possible that a continual push toward novelty, rather than usefulness, is associated with more mental disturbances.

However, as I've noted, a focus solely on novelty can sometimes lead to some highly original but entirely useless ideas. Good creative ideas involve novel solutions that are appropriate for the problems at hand. Collectivism appears to be associated with the generation of useful rather than novel ideas (Erez & Nouri, 2010). In collective contexts people are socialized to be concerned about the opinions of others and to find solutions that will fit with the goals of the members of their groups. This orientation toward finding practical solutions that can fit within an existing set of social concerns appears to lead to skills for creating useful ideas more generally. For example, Nouri, Erez, Rockstuhl, & Ang (2008) documented that when Singaporeans were working with another person, they elaborated more on the appropriateness of their ideas than when they were by themselves, yet they became less original in their ideas. In contrast, Israelis were not affected by the presence of others in the same way. In another study, Dutch participants who were motivated to do their best on a brainstorming task came up with more original, but not more useful, ideas compared with those who were not motivated to do their best. In contrast, when Korean participants were especially motivated, they came up with more useful ideas, but not more original ones (Bechtoldt, De Dreu, Nijstad, & Choi, 2010). The useful component of creative ideas seems to be promoted in East Asian contexts.

One other way that we can see cultural differences between useful and novel ideas is in the kinds of innovations that cultures produce. When a new idea comes around, one can make a distinction between ideas that are breakthrough innovations—that are utterly different game-changers from anything before—and ideas that make smaller, incremental improvements. In general, more-collectivistic East Asian cultures, with their emphasis on useful ideas, are more likely to foster incremental innovations, whereas more-individualistic Western cultures, with their emphasis on novel ideas, encourage more breakthrough ones (Herbig & Palumbo, 1996). For example, Japan is the world leader in terms of the number of patents it receives each year (Brocklehurst, 2005), although most of these patents represent incremental improvements, particularly in the areas of telecommunications, information technology, and electronics. Apparently, different firms have cultures that favor either incremental or breakthrough innovations—even within the same country, companies that produce many incremental innovations rarely produce breakthrough innovations (Dunlap-Hinkler, Kotabe, & Mudambi, 2010)—and East Asian contexts are more likely to foster an environment for incremental innovations. Incremental innovations highlight the important role of useful ideas, because they typically involve modifying an idea to better fit with the practical constraints around it.

In sum, there are two key components of creative ideas, novelty and usefulness, and individualistic and collectivistic cultures encourage these two differently. Perhaps, then, the optimal creative team would include both people from individualistic and collectivistic cultures so that they could capitalize on their respective strengths. Supporting this, the most creative ideas in one study were found when team members were primed with both individualistic and collectivistic ideas (Bechtoldt, Choi, & Nijstad, 2012), and the most creative ideas in another study emerged when people were exposed to aspects of multiple cultures (Leung & Chiu, 2010). Multicultural environments may indeed have an advantage for producing more creative ideas (recall the discussion on multicultural selves and creativity from Chapter 7).

Talking and Thinking

Having a spoken language is one key way that humans differ from other species, and language has been argued to be, in part, responsible for humans' impressive cultural achievements. However, there is more to the story than just that humans talk. We also need to consider why humans talk and the consequences of talking. Interestingly, this very basic task of talking has some dramatically different implications for the ways people think across cultures.

Consider this excerpt from a newspaper article reported in the *San Jose Mercury News* (cited in Kim, 2002):

> A professor . . . encourages his Asian students to speak up in class by making it part of the class grade. He makes speaking in front of the class mandatory for some assignments. "Once they understand this is the norm you expect, they'll get used to it," he says. "But you have to make it clear." (Lubman, 1998, p. A12)

This reporter is focusing on an issue that is commonly discussed in colleges and universities with a large population of students of Asian descent. Often, students of Asian background speak up less in class than those of other cultural backgrounds (Tweed & Lehman, 2002). This relative silence is often viewed as a cause for concern and tends to be perceived by professors and other students as shyness or even a lack of interest in the class. Drawing these kinds of inferences reveals an assumption that talking reflects thinking and engagement in class. Heejung Kim (2002), however, argues that this assumption about talking is very much grounded in Western cultural practices, and that talking can affect people from different cultures in quite different ways.

Talking and language have held a privileged position in much of Western intellectual history. Kim notes that among the ancient Greeks, Homer concluded that there was no greater skill than to be a good debater, and Socrates thought that knowledge existed within people and could be revealed only through verbal reasoning. In Judeo-Christian beliefs the "Word" was viewed as sacred because of its divine power to create. Within the United States the freedom to speak one's mind is a birthright, protected by the First Amendment to the Constitution. Speaking is valued in the West because it is viewed as an act of self-expression and as inextricably bound to thought.

In contrast, however, in many East Asian cultural traditions there has been considerably less emphasis on talking, if not outright suspicion of the spoken word. Lao Tzu wrote, "He who knows does not speak. He who speaks does not know." Practitioners of many Eastern religions pursue truth through silent meditation rather than through spoken prayer. And as a Korean proverb states, "An empty cart makes more noise." In many ways, Eastern cultural traditions have not cultivated a belief that thought and speech are closely related.

There are rather pronounced cultural differences in speech among young children. Japanese mothers have been shown to speak less to their young children than their American counterparts (Caudill & Weinstein, 1969), and Chinese infants as young as 7 months have been shown to vocalize less in response to laboratory events than European-American infants (Kagan, Kearsley, & Zelazo, 1977). Comparable differences have also been found among older children (Minami, 1994). It is important to understand that less speech does not necessarily mean less communication. Indeed, the closer the relationship, the more people are likely to rely on nonverbal communication rather than the spoken word (Azuma, 1986; Clancy, 1986), a point to which we'll soon return. Nonetheless, the data on the development of speech among East Asian compared to Western children is suggestive that talking might have different implications across cultures.

Kim (2002) reasoned that if talking really does have a different relation with thinking for East Asians and Westerners, we should see variations in performance on cognitive tasks depending on whether participants are asked to speak. Namely, expressing one's thoughts out loud should interfere with the performance of East Asians on cognitive tasks, whereas it should have little impact on the performance of Westerners. To investigate this question, participants were asked to complete a version of Raven's Progressive Matrices, the nonverbal IQ test discussed in Chapter 3.

The participants were all born in the United States and had English as their native language. Half of them were of European descent, and half of them were of East Asian descent (their parents were all born in an East Asian country). The 20-item test was separated into two halves of 10 items each. For the first 10 items of the test, the participants were asked to sit alone in a room and to work through the test without speaking at all. For the second 10 items the participants remained by themselves in a room, but they received one of two sets of instructions. Participants assigned to a "thinking aloud" condition were asked to talk aloud into a computer microphone as they worked through the second half of the test. The participants were simply vocalizing their thoughts as they solved the items. In contrast, participants who were assigned to an "articulatory suppression" condition were instructed to repeat the alphabet out loud into a computer microphone as they worked on the items. (I'll explain the rationale for the articulatory suppression condition later.) The key variable was the number of items in the second half of the study that participants answered correctly in the allotted time period compared to the number they had answered correctly in the first half.

First, look at the left half of **Figure 9.13**. These scores reveal the impact that talking aloud had on the performance of participants compared to answering the items in silence. The European-Americans performed about the same on the test when they were speaking as when they were silent (the difference between the two conditions is not significant). This suggests that talking and thinking are very much

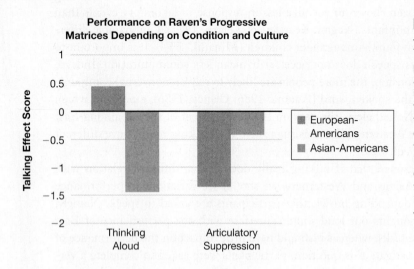

Performance on Raven's Progressive Matrices Depending on Condition and Culture

Talking Effect Score

Thinking Aloud   Articulatory Suppression

■ European-Americans
■ Asian-Americans

FIGURE 9.13

Thinking aloud impairs the performance of Asian-Americans on IQ test items, although saying the alphabet aloud while thinking has little impact on their scores. In contrast, thinking aloud has little impact on the performance of European-Americans, whereas reciting the alphabet impairs their performance.

related for European-Americans. In stark contrast, however, Asian-Americans performed significantly worse on the test when they were talking aloud. Expressing their thoughts out loud interfered with their thinking. This suggests that, at least for the kinds of items in Raven's Progressive Matrices, Asian-Americans perform better if they are able to think quietly to themselves. Rather than indicating a lack of engagement among Asian-Americans, silence in the classroom often might indicate some good thinking.

So why does this cultural difference exist? As we learned earlier, people of Asian descent are more likely to engage in holistic thinking whereas Westerners are more likely to engage in analytic thinking. Holistic thinking involves an attention to the whole and the perception of how various parts are interrelated. The nature of holistic thinking makes it difficult to express in words because speech is ultimately a sequential task. When you speak, one idea follows another. You can't easily describe multiple relations at once. In contrast, analytic thinking, with the emphasis on focusing on separate parts, lends itself very well to the spoken word. Each part can be described separately and sequentially. As such, speech is likely to interfere with performance on holistic tasks.

Some evidence of the interference between speech and holistic thinking can be seen when people are asked to describe faces. Faces consist of various parts; however, people, including Westerners, tend to see them more as interrelated wholes. For example, in one study people were shown a number of pictures of faces and were asked to describe each face they saw (Schooler & Engstler-Schooler, 1990; also see Alogna et al., 2014). In describing the picture of Tom Cruise, people might say something like, "He has thickish eyebrows, a big smile, dark hair, and is very attractive." However, those few observations hardly do justice to Tom Cruise's face. You've surely seen hundreds of faces that would fit this description, but they do not look like Tom Cruise. There is much more to his face, and to anyone's, than the few statements people can offer in describing them. After describing the faces they saw, participants looked at another set of faces and were asked to indicate which ones they had seen before. Interestingly, the results indicated that people were better able to recognize the faces they had previously seen if they had *not* tried to describe them before. Apparently, their verbal descriptions interfered with their ability to process the face as a whole, causing them to have poorer recall.

Kim reasoned that if Asian-Americans were indeed thinking holistically as they tried to solve the items in the Raven's test, they should be relatively unaffected by a verbal task that was unrelated to the test. This was the purpose of including the articulatory suppression condition in her study. Participants in that condition recited the alphabet while trying to solve the Raven's items. She reasoned that in this condition, the Asian-Americans should be free to think about the items in the test in the way that was most natural to them (i.e., considering the relations among the different parts of the items holistically), and they could then engage in the separate, and not very demanding, task of reciting the alphabet. Because these two tasks are so different, they should cause little interference with each other and performance should be largely unaffected. In contrast, however, if talking and thinking are fundamentally connected for European-Americans, being asked to recite the alphabet while thinking about something else should be challenging. European-Americans in the articulatory suppression condition must engage in two verbal tasks at once: their verbal thoughts about how to solve the Raven's items, and their verbal thoughts associated with the alphabet.

The results, as indicated in the right half of Figure 9.13, support this reasoning. European-Americans did very poorly on the IQ task when they were reciting the alphabet, indicating that their thoughts while solving that task apparently were verbal and were interfered with by their verbal recitation of the alphabet. In contrast, reciting the alphabet had no significant effect on the performance of the Asian-Americans. This suggests that the thoughts in the Asian-American participants' heads while solving the Raven's items were largely nonverbal thoughts. There thus seem to be some profound cultural differences in the ways people think, verbally or nonverbally, at least for the kinds of items in the Raven's test.

This cultural difference in the relation between talking and thinking has other implications as well. If what you say is viewed to be consistent with what is in your head, then speech can serve an important role for self-expression. To the extent that talking and thinking are viewed as intertwined, it is reasonable for others to infer things about you based on what you say. People can reveal themselves to the world by the things they say. In contrast, if talking is not so intimately connected with thinking, people will see less of a connection between what one says and who one is.

Are there cultural differences in the relation of speech and self-expression? To investigate this question, European-Americans and Asian-Americans were asked to complete a questionnaire and were then given four pens to choose from as compensation (Kim & Sherman, 2007). In one condition, participants were asked to write down which pen they would like; in the other, they never expressed their choice verbally. Then they were allowed to take a pen. However, after they had taken their pen, the experimenter asked for it back, saying that it was the last one she had, and she gave the participant an obviously inferior pen to replace it. Next, the participants completed another survey that included some questions about their satisfaction with the pen they received. Not surprisingly, people in general were not especially happy with the inferior pen they had received after the experimenter took away their chosen pen. However, what was noteworthy was that the European-American evaluations of the pen hinged on whether they had earlier been asked to express their pen choice verbally (**Figure 9.14**). Those who had expressed their choice verbally for the pen that was taken from them were less satisfied with the inferior pen than those who did not express their choice. In contrast, the evaluations of the Asian-Americans

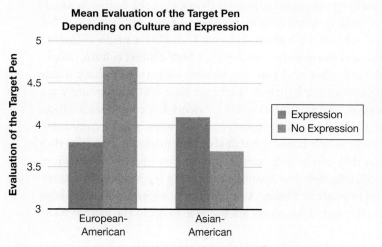

Mean Evaluation of the Target Pen Depending on Culture and Expression

FIGURE 9.14

European-Americans who verbally expressed their pen preferences evaluated a pen that was forced upon them more negatively than those who did not express a pen preference earlier. Asian-Americans' pen evaluations were unaffected by whether they had expressed their preferences.

were not significantly affected by expressing their choice. It seems that for the European-Americans, stating their choice was an act of self-expression and resulted in a greater feeling of commitment toward the soon-to-be usurped pen. In contrast, expressing their choices had little impact for the Asian-Americans and suggests that verbal self-expression is less of a concern for them.

Explicit Versus Implicit Communication

There is more to communicating with others than just expressing in words what you want to say. Much of what is communicated in the course of a conversation goes beyond the actual words that are used and is expressed in nonverbal gestures, facial expressions, and voice tone. You may have discovered, for example, how easy it can be to inadvertently upset someone in an email or a text message exchange. When the person cannot see your smile and wink, or hear the jovial tone of your voice, it is not always clear from what you have written whether you are making a joke or are saying something rude. All the nonverbal cues that are so important for effective communication are absent. Hence, people often resort to adding emoticons or abbreviations such as ;-) or LOL to their email or text messages to add the nonverbal contextual cues that are lacking in these exchanges.

Although nonverbal communication is a big part of communication in all cultures, there are some rather pronounced cultural differences in the degree to which communication relies on explicit verbal information versus more implicit nonverbal cues. In explaining these cultural differences, Edward Hall (1976) made a distinction between high-context and low-context cultures. In a **high-context culture**, people are deeply involved with each other, and this involvement leads them to have much shared information that guides their behavior. There are clear and appropriate ways of behaving in each situation, and this information is widely shared and understood so it does not need to be explicitly communicated. Much of what is to be communicated can be inferred because people have a great deal of information in common that they can rely on, and thus they can be less explicit in what they say. In contrast, in a **low-context culture** there is relatively less involvement among individuals, and there is less shared information to guide behavior. As a result, it is necessary for people to communicate in more explicit detail, as others are less able to fill in the gaps of what is not said.

East Asian cultures are good examples of high-context cultures, whereas North American, and English-speaking cultures more generally, are good examples of low-context ones. Typically, what is conveyed in some East Asian languages is considerably less explicit than what is communicated in English. As an English speaker who has struggled with learning Japanese, I can testify that the difference in the explicitness of the language can be extremely challenging. A question in Japan such as, "Is it okay if I park my car here?" might very well be answered with a pause, a strained look on the face, and only the words "Well, a little." It has taken years of effort for my helplessly explicit mind to learn that the words that are said in many situations are sometimes less important than the way they are said. A pause and a strained look on one's face sends a signal that is very clear to any native Japanese speaker, yet still remains rather opaque to me, that the person has information to communicate to me that he thinks I will find dissatisfying—namely, that it's not okay for me to park my car there. The key information is conveyed nonverbally, with the content of the words sometimes being rather empty.

One real-life situation in which nonverbal information is not communicated is when people leave messages on answering machines. Such messages do not allow speakers to receive any nonverbal cues about how their conversation partner is responding to their message. Rather, the speaker is left to deliver his or her entire message without any feedback. Given this situation, it is not surprising that people tend not to like speaking to answering machines. However, speaking to machines should be especially challenging for Japanese given their reliance on nonverbal communication. Indeed, research reveals that Japanese tend to actively avoid leaving messages on answering machines and are less than half as likely as Americans to do so. Furthermore, the reasons that Japanese offer for not liking answering machines are different from the ones offered by Americans. Americans say they don't like answering machines because they are worried that the target person might not check his or her messages, whereas Japanese don't like answering machines because they say that it's hard to speak without getting feedback (Miyamoto & Schwarz, 2006).

Furthermore, Japanese seem to struggle much more than Americans when actually trying to leave a message on a machine. In one study, Japanese and American participants left a message on an answering machine while engaging in a demanding cognitive task. Although the two cultures did not differ in their performance on the cognitive task prior to leaving a message, while speaking into the answering machine the Japanese's performance on the cognitive task fell significantly below that of the Americans (Miyamoto & Schwarz, 2006). Apparently, it is far more cognitively demanding for Japanese to leave a message because they are trying hard to imagine how their target person will react to it.

Some clever lab experiments have further demonstrated a cultural difference in people's reliance on nonverbal communications (Ishii, Reyes, & Kitayama, 2003; Kitayama & Ishii, 2002). Japanese and American participants were presented aurally with words that were either pleasant (e.g., grateful, refreshment) or unpleasant (e.g., bitter, complaint), and these words were accompanied by either a pleasant-sounding tone or an unpleasant-sounding tone. For some of the words the explicit meaning matched the tone, and for some the meaning of the words was opposite to the tone in which it was delivered. The participants were instructed either to ignore the tone of the word and answer whether the meaning of the word was pleasant or unpleasant or to ignore the meaning of the word and comment on whether the tone sounded pleasant or unpleasant. The key variable of interest was how long it took participants to respond when the tone and the meaning of the words were in conflict. The Americans showed more interference in their judgments about the vocal tone (while ignoring the meaning of the words) than they did when making judgments about the meaning of the words (while ignoring the vocal tone). This suggests that they chronically attend to the meaning of what is said more than they do to the tone in which it is spoken. In contrast, the Japanese participants showed the opposite pattern of results. Japanese showed more interference when they needed to attend to the meaning of the word and ignore the tone than they did when attending to the tone while ignoring the meaning. This suggests that Japanese are habitually attending to the tone in which things are said more than they are to the precise content of what is being said.

One alternative explanation to account for these results is that there is something about the Japanese language that requires people to attend to tone more than for English. If this were the case, then the cultural differences would simply reflect the linguistic skills required by the languages rather than a cultural difference. To test for this alternative account, the researchers replicated the study with another high-context culture that used two languages. Specifically, Filipinos are collectivist, and many are fluent in both Tagalog and English. If Filipinos have more difficulty ignoring vocal tones than the meaning regardless of the language they are speaking, this would suggest that the findings reflect cultural differences in attention to context rather than features of the language. Indeed, this is precisely what the researchers found (see Ishii et al., 2003).

Linguistic Relativity

The results of the study by Ishii and colleagues demonstrate that specific features of the Tagalog and English languages do not explain why Filipinos attend to vocal tones more than Americans do. However, the question raised here is an interesting one to explore more generally. How much does the language we speak affect how we think? This question was first formally proposed by Edward Sapir and his student Benjamin Whorf and has become known as the Sapir-Whorf hypothesis, or more commonly, the **Whorfian (or linguistic relativity) hypothesis** (Whorf, 1956). The strongest version of this hypothesis is that language determines how we think—that is, we are unable to do much thinking on a topic if we don't have the relevant words available to us. This strong version of the hypothesis has been almost universally rejected. Much thought clearly occurs outside of language; for example, prelinguistic infants and toddlers show evidence for quite complex thinking in the absence of language. A weaker version of this hypothesis is that the language we speak affects how we think. It is mostly with re-spect to the weaker version that there has been much debate, controversy, and research.

The Whorfian hypothesis has a certain amount of intuitive appeal, and it has independently been proposed by a number of eminent thinkers (see Hunt & Agnoli, 1991, for a review). For example, Herodotus claimed that the Greeks and Egyptians thought differently because the Greeks wrote from left to right whereas the Egyptians wrote from right to left (Fishman, 1980). Two thousand years later Einstein (1954) wrote, "Thus we may conclude that the mental development of the individual, and his way of forming concepts, depends to a high degree upon language. This makes us realize to what extent the same language means the same mentality. In this sense, thinking and language are linked together" (p. 336). George Orwell also realized the power of language on thought in his dark futuristic novel *1984,* in which the secret police developed a new language, "Newspeak," as a way of controlling the thoughts of the people. And today we can still see evidence that the Whorfian hypothesis is taken seriously in the movement for people to speak in terms that are "politically correct," or to use words that are deemed to be consistent with desired outcomes. The reasoning is that if we use words such as "physically challenged" rather than "handicapped" to describe people confined to wheelchairs, we will be more likely to think of these people as being capable and competent, which should serve to empower them.

In many ways, the words that we speak are assumed to affect the ways that we think. The reasoning for this is not that one language *allows* people to think about certain ideas but rather that one language *obliges* people to think about certain ideas (Deutscher, 2010). In German, for example, inanimate objects are assigned a gender—bridges are feminine, for instance. So when Germans think about bridges, they are obliged to think about gender in ways that English-speaking people are not (Phillips & Boroditsky, 2003).

Despite the intuitive appeal of the Whorfian hypothesis, it has been subject to some of the most intense debate and controversy in the field of psycholinguistics (e.g., Pinker, 1994; Roberson, Davies, & Davidoff, 2000). What kind of hard evidence is there for the Whorfian hypothesis? You can imagine how useful cross-cultural research could be for testing this hypothesis. One obvious way that many cultures differ from each other is in the languages that their people speak. And it is not just that different languages have different words for the same objects—the English horse is called a *cheval* in French and a *hevonen* in Finnish. Rather, numerous words and concepts simply do not exist in many languages of the world. The question is thus whether people who speak different languages think in some different ways as well.

LINGUISTIC RELATIVITY AND COLOR PERCEPTION. Much of the debate over the Whorfian hypothesis has occurred in the context of color perception and memory. Color is an especially appropriate domain for investigating this question because, perceptually, color is a continuous variable that extends gradually through all the hues of the rainbow, yet linguistically it is a discrete variable, as we have particular color terms for certain ranges of light wavelengths within the color spectrum. More important, different languages parse the spectrum of colors in dramatically divergent ways.

An analysis of the different color lexicons known for all the subsistence societies around the world that have been investigated has revealed some intriguing patterns (Berlin & Kay, 1969). There is tremendous diversity in the ways people label colors, and this diversity emerges in systematic ways. All known languages have a minimum of two color terms. The one identified language (Dani) with only two terms has words that roughly correspond to "black" (which included all dark-hued colors) and "white" (which included all lighter hues). Next in line are languages that have precisely three color terms. All of the languages with three color terms have words that roughly correspond to black, white, and red (which included some oranges, yellows, browns, pinks, and purples, with red being the focus of the category). Languages that have precisely four color terms have words that approximate the colors of black, white, red, and either green or yellow. Languages with five color terms have the same words, including words for *both* green and yellow. Languages with six color terms add blue to the list, and languages with seven terms include a word for brown. And languages with eight color terms add either purple, pink, gray, or orange to the list. Furthermore, the focal point of each of these color categories (e.g., the most prototypical green in an array of different shades of green) is largely similar across language groups. In sum, people who speak different languages carve up the color spectrum in some rather divergent ways; however, these differences do not emerge arbitrarily, and there are some strikingly consistent patterns across languages.

Does the fact that people from different cultures have carved up the color spectrum differently affect how they perceive colors? Take the example of the English color term "blue." English speakers use this word to refer to the color of the sky, blueberries, and the South Pacific Ocean. The Japanese word for blue is *ao,* and this word is also used to refer to the color of the sky, blueberries, and the South Pacific Ocean, but the same term is used to refer to the color of a lawn, a freshly shaven scalp, and what English speakers would call a green traffic signal. A Whorfian question automatically arises: When Japanese and English speakers look at the same patch of lawn, are they actually perceiving the same color?

The strongest test of this kind of question has been conducted by contrasting people who speak languages that differ the most in terms of their color lexicons (Japanese color terms, for the most part, map quite clearly onto their English counterparts, making for a weaker comparison). Rosch Heider (1972; Rosch Heider & Olivier, 1972) conducted a seminal series of studies investigating this question. She visited the Dugum Dani, a stone-age agricultural population living in Irian Jaya whose aforementioned language purportedly has only two color terms. Rosch Heider contrasted the performance of this group on a variety of color perception tasks with that of English-speaking Americans. The results of her studies indicated that the Dani remembered colors in similar ways to Americans, despite having such divergent color categories. Furthermore, the Dani could learn and recall new words that were associated with colors that corresponded with the foci of the eight basic chromatic categories of English more easily than they could learn words for colors that occupied intermediate points along the color spectrum. In sum, the evidence suggested that color perception and memory were largely independent from the color words that were in a language. The results of these studies were enormously influential and were interpreted as providing convincing evidence that language does not affect color perception; also, the results more generally were interpreted to suggest that the Whorfian hypothesis was untenable in other domains as well.

Rosch Heider's studies were largely perceived as having the final say on the Whorfian debate over the next 30 years, despite the fact that various researchers called attention to a number of potentially serious flaws in the experimental design and interpretation of these studies (e.g., Lucy & Shweder, 1979; Ratner, 1989; Saunders & Van Brakel, 1997) and that several calls for the need to replicate these findings went unheeded (e.g., Davies, 1997; Gellantly, 1995). More recently, research by Roberson and colleagues (Roberson, Davidoff, Davies, & Shapiro, 2005; Roberson et al., 2000) has attempted to address some of the criticisms of Rosch Heider's earlier studies.

Roberson and colleagues (2000) studied monolingual Berinmo speakers from isolated villages in Papua, New Guinea, whose language contains five basic color terms corresponding, roughly, to black (*kel*), white (*wap*), red (*mehi*), yellow (*wor*), and green (*nol*). In addition, Roberson and colleagues (2005) investigated monolingual Himba speakers, who are seminomadic cattle herders from Namibia. The Himba language also contains five basic color terms, which, likewise, correspond roughly to black (*zoozu*), white (*vapa*), red (*serandu*), yellow (*dumbu*), and green (*burou*), although the boundaries of these colors differ somewhat from those of the Berinmo (**Figure 9.15**).

English naming

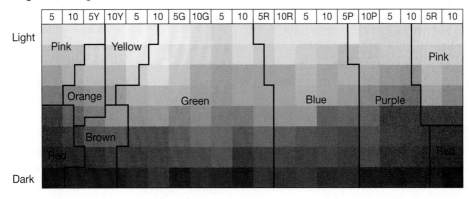

Berinmo naming

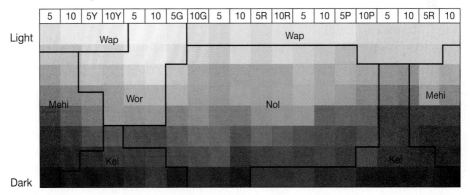

Himba naming

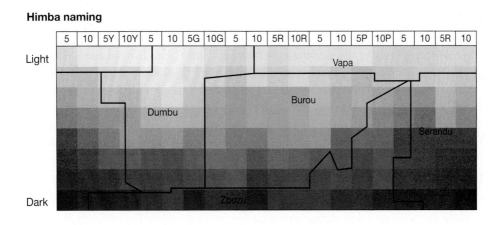

FIGURE 9.15 These are the different boundaries associated with the color labels in English, Himba, and Berinmo.

Although there is much overlap between the color boundaries and exemplars for the three languages, there are some clear differences.

Roberson and colleagues (2000, 2005) replicated the same basic methodology of Rosch Heider and contrasted the performance of the Berinmo and Himba with English-speaking Britons. First, their replications of Rosch Heider's work called into question the evidence for universal color perception on a number of rather technical grounds. Simply put, they found considerable evidence for cultural variation in the ways that people in the different cultures learned and remembered colors. Second, they included some studies that went beyond some perceived shortcomings in the original methodology of Rosch Heider. The Roberson studies were based on the idea that different color categories should affect people's **categorical perception** of colors. Much research has shown that we tend to perceive stimuli in categorical terms—that is, we tend to perceive stimuli as belonging to separate and discrete categories, even though the stimuli may gradually differ from each other along a continuum. For example, there is a continuum of sounds that exists between the phonemes of "ba" and "pa"; however, any sound that exists along that continuum is perceived by English speakers as either "ba" or "pa," and not as something in between (Macmillan, 1987).

Roberson and colleagues reasoned that a good test of whether color labels influence perception would be whether people given different color labels are similarly affected by the boundaries that exist between color categories. Participants were shown three different colored chips and were asked which of two chips, Chip 1 or Chip 2, was more similar to the target chip (**Figure 9.16**). The chips were chosen so that the target chip was equally distant from Chips 1 and 2 in terms of hue; however, Chips 1 and 2 fell into two different perceptual categories. For example, Chip 1 is typically labeled green by English speakers whereas Chip 2 was typically labeled blue. Furthermore, the target chip was usually labeled green. Most English speakers showed some evidence for categorical perception, as they were more likely to say that the target chip was more similar to Chip 1 than to Chip 2, because the target chip and Chip 1 shared the same category, whereas the target chip and Chip 2 did not.

Likewise, Roberson and colleagues also included triads of color chips based on the color categories of the Berinmo and of the Himba. English speakers, Berinmo speakers, and Himba speakers were shown a number of such triads and asked to indicate which chip was more similar in color to the target chip. As can be seen in **Figure 9.17**, there was some evidence that people from the different cultures made different choices. Namely, the English speakers were most likely to make judgments in line with categorical perception for stimuli that crossed the blue–green boundary. In contrast, the Berinmo speakers were most likely to show evidence for categorical perception when they discriminated between two stimuli that crossed the *nol–wor* boundary. Likewise, the Himba speakers were most likely to discriminate between

Try for Yourself: Perception of colors

Which chip, 1 or 2, is more similar to the color in target chip below?

English boundaries

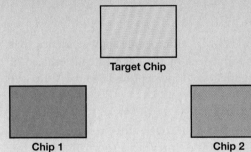

Target Chip

Chip 1   **Chip 2**

Again, which chip, 1 or 2, is more similar to the color in target chip below?

Berinmo boundaries

Target Chip

Chip 1   **Chip 2**

Result:
Most English speakers select Chip 1 for the first one, whereas Berinmo speakers are equally likely to select Chip 1 as they are Chip 2. In contrast, English speakers are equally likely to select Chip 1 as Chip 2 in the second example, whereas Berinmo speakers tend to choose Chip 1.

Explanation:
For the first example, both the Target Chip and Chip 1 fall within the English category of green whereas Chip 2 is usually perceived as slightly blue. Berinmo color categories don't distinguish Chips 1 and 2. For the second example, Berinmo color categories distinguish Chips 1 and 2 whereas English color categories do not. The color categories in one's language influence perception at the boundaries of those categories.

FIGURE 9.16

People are asked to judge whether Chip 1 or Chip 2 is more similar to the target chip. Even though Chips 1 and 2 are actually equally distant from the target chip in terms of hue, most English speakers would say that both Chips 1 and the target chip fall within the category of green, whereas Chip 2 falls within the category of blue. Because of this, most English speakers see Chip 1 as more similar to the target chip than Chip 2 is.

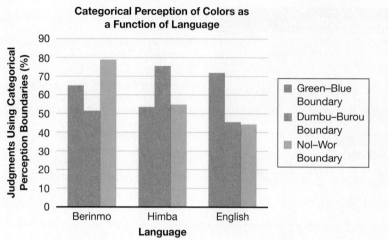

FIGURE 9.17

People make more judgments consistent with categorical perception for stimuli that cross the boundary between two color labels in their own language, compared with stimuli that cross a color-label boundary in other languages.

colors that crossed the *dumbu–burou* boundary. In sum, people show evidence that their perception of the different colors is influenced by the color categories used in their respective languages. Language can affect color perception (also see Winawer et al., 2007).

LINGUISTIC RELATIVITY AND ODOR PERCEPTION. This research on linguistic influences on color perception is important as it reveals a shortcoming in the imaginations of researchers. Psychological researchers, who are almost exclusively from industrialized societies, have access to many color words and are hard-pressed to imagine what color perception could be like in a society where such words didn't exist. The reverse situation may also be true. One domain where the English language is relatively impoverished is that there aren't many words used to describe odors. English speakers may try to compare the odor of one thing to another, such as describing the bouquet of a wine to be reminiscent of coffee, banana, and cloves, with olive tapenade notes, but they have few basic odor terms, beyond words such as "stinky" or "fragrant." Moreover, as a review of the literature on olfaction concluded, "Humans are astonishingly bad at odor identification and naming" (Yeshurun & Sobel, 2010). However, it's worth noting that almost all of the studies that this review was based on were of speakers of European languages, which all suffer from a paucity of odor terms.

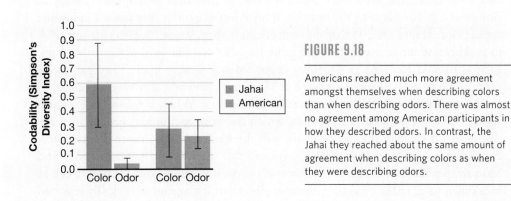

FIGURE 9.18

Americans reached much more agreement amongst themselves when describing colors than when describing odors. There was almost no agreement among American participants in how they described odors. In contrast, the Jahai they reached about the same amount of agreement when describing colors as when they were describing odors.

In contrast, the Jahai, a group of nomadic hunter-gatherers living in the Malay peninsula, have a much larger lexicon of olfaction words. One study compared native Jahai speakers with American English speakers in their ability to name both a set of odors (e.g., cinnamon, gasoline, onion) and a set of colors (e.g., red, blue, black; Majid & Burenhult, 2014). The participants were presented with the smells and color chips and were asked to freely describe them. The researchers looked to see how much agreement there was between the participants. The Americans did very well on the color naming, reaching much agreement in the color words that they used to describe the color chips. However, the Americans performed quite abysmally in the odor naming, with very little agreement among them (**Figure 9.18**). In contrast, the Jahai did about as well in naming the odors as they did in naming the colors—the Jahai had less agreement than the Americans in naming the colors (reflecting their smaller color lexicon) and had more agreement than the American in naming the odors. It is possible that if English speakers learned a larger set of olfaction words they might also become better at recognizing different odors.

LINGUISTIC RELATIVITY AND PERCEPTIONS OF AGENCY. Another example of how language can shape the ways that people think is in terms of perceptions of agency. When describing an accident in English, people commonly use an agentive description. For example, one might describe Justin Timberlake and Janet Jackson's famous wardrobe malfunction as "Justin tore the bodice." Less commonly used in English are more nonagentive sentences, such as "The bodice tore." Interestingly, people who heard the former description viewed Timberlake to be more at fault, and assigned a larger fine, than those who heard the latter description (Fausey & Boroditsky, 2010). Hearing the sentence framed in an agentive way made Timberlake appear more responsible. Perhaps not surprisingly then, when English speakers wish to avoid blame for an event, they are more likely to describe it in nonagentive ways, such as Ronald Reagan's famous *mea culpa:* "Mistakes were made." In Spanish, in contrast, nonagentive expressions such as "*Se rompio el florero*" ("The vase broke itself") are more common. A Whorfian question then arises: When English and Spanish speakers observe unintentional actions, which are more commonly encoded in agentive terms in English than in Spanish, will the speakers recall those events differently? Fausey and Boroditsky (2011) explored this question by having English and Spanish speakers watch videos that showed people involved in some actions (such as breaking a vase) either by acting intentionally (in which agency is typically reported *both* in English and in Spanish) or unintentionally (in which agency is more likely to be reported in English than in Spanish). Later, the participants were shown pictures of different people and were asked to recall which one had broken the vase. The English and Spanish speakers were equally accurate when identifying the targets who had acted intentionally (the languages do not differ in how they describe intentional agency); however, the English speakers were more accurate than the Spanish speakers in recalling who had broken the vase unintentionally. Apparently, by not being obliged to encode for agency in unintentional behaviors, Spanish speakers attended less to who had actually broken the vase and were less likely to recall that fact.

LINGUISTIC RELATIVITY AND SPATIAL PERCEPTION. Linguistic relativity can also be considered in terms of people's spatial descriptions. Every language has the capability of describing how objects are distributed in space, yet there are some rather fundamental ways that languages differ in how they do this. English speakers often identify locations based on their position relative to the speaker, using terms such as left, right, front, and back. For example, you may guide shoppers through a supermarket freezer by letting them know that the frozen peas are located in front of the Brussels sprouts and to the left of the pyrogies. These directions would no longer be applicable if the person approached the freezer from the other side; they would be reversed—reflecting their relativistic basis. The directions are accurate only from the perspective of the speaker. In contrast, the same kinds of directions as given by speakers of Guugu Yimithirr, an aboriginal group in Australia, would not include any of these relative terms. Rather, the person would be guided by saying that the peas are located east of the Brussels sprouts and south of the pyrogies, a set of directions that are not influenced by the location of the speaker. That is, speakers of Guugu Yimithirr identify space in absolute terms, as described by the cardinal points on a compass. The Whorfian question that arises from the linguistic differences between speakers of English and Guugu Yimithirr is whether people who speak these languages differ in their thinking as well.

Because Guugu Ymithirr lacks relativistic direction terms, it would seem that its speakers would need to be constantly attending to cardinal directions when interacting with their world. Otherwise, they would have no way of describing spatial locations if they were subsequently asked about what they had seen. In contrast, English speakers would not need to attend to cardinal directions because they can conceive of space, and communicate it to others, using terms relative to the location of their bodies.

How might people who speak different languages recall scenes they encounter? One study sought to test a Whorfian question of whether Guugu Ymithirr speakers and Dutch speakers (Dutch is like English in having relative direction terms) would remember scenes differently (Levinson, 1997). For example, in one study, participants were shown a row of figures of a cow, a pig, and a person on a table

"O.K., there's the sun, so that direction is 'up.'"

in one room (**Figure 9.19**). In that room, the table was against the north wall, so participants were facing north. Then they were asked to go to a different room that had a similar table containing the same figures, except now the table was against the south wall, so participants were facing south. The participants were asked to re-create the same scene they had witnessed in the other room. Most of the Dutch respondents tended to re-create the scenes based on their own position relative to the animals. Because the cow was left of the pig which was left of the person in the original room, they maintained these relative positions in the new room. In stark contrast, most of the Guugu Ymithirr speakers re-created the scenes in absolute terms. That is, because the cow had been west of the pig which had been west of the person in the first room facing north, when they were in the second room facing south they preserved the positioning of these animals relative to the cardinal directions. This meant that the cow was now placed to the right of the pig which was to the right of the person—the exact opposite of the arrangement the Dutch speakers had produced!

Apparently, even when entering different rooms in a building, the Guugu Ymithirr speakers are constantly attending to which direction is which. The Whorfian explanation is that because their spatial language is based solely on the cardinal directions, they conceive of the arrangement of their world only with respect to these directions. Dutch speakers, in contrast, elaborate more on directions relative to their physical selves, so it is less useful to attend to the cardinal directions in most

Dutch and Guugu Ymthirr Perceptions of the Spatial Arrangement of Objects

Original stimulus shown (participant facing north)

Most common Dutch solution (participants facing south)

Most common Guugu Ymithirr solution (participants facing south)

FIGURE 9.19

After viewing a group of stimuli, Dutch and Guugu Ymithirr participants were brought into another room facing a different direction. When asked to arrange the same stimuli to match their earlier order, Dutch participants arranged the items from right to left, and Guugu Ymithirr participants arranged them from east to west.

situations. The Guugu Ymithirr tendency to conceive of directions in ways that are not relative to their bodily location appears to be more common among subsistence populations throughout the world and is also more similar to the ways that chimpanzees understand directions (Haun, Rapold, Call, Janzen, & Levinson, 2006). It appears that the tendency to attend to directions relative to one's own egocentric position is a relatively recent development, and one that is peculiar to some industrialized cultures.

Following up on this work, some preliminary research by Lera Boroditsky and Alice Gaby has explored whether languages with different spatial referencing would also influence the ways that people represent the passage of time. Building on earlier research (Boroditsky, 2000) demonstrating that people's understanding of time is grounded in their understanding of space, Boroditsky and Gaby (2010) reasoned that English speakers tend to see time as passing from the left to the right. So, for example, if English speakers were to arrange the pictures in **Figure 9.20** (photos of Lera Boroditsky's grandfather at various ages) in the correct temporal sequence, they would arrange them from left to right, and they would do so regardless of what direction they were facing.

The idea that left is perceived as the origin of time in English is somewhat arbitrary and is likely determined by the fact that English is written from the left to the right. In contrast, Arabic is written from the right to the left, and Arabic speakers likewise see time passing from the right to the left. The important point is that for English speakers, time passes from one relative spatial marker (the left side of one's body) to another (the right side), and this does not change depending on the direction one is facing. Boroditsky and Gaby investigated Australian aborigines from the village of Pormpuraaw, who, like the Guugu Ymithirr, tend to use only absolute spatial markers when referring to directions. Among those in Pormpuraaw, time is seen to pass from the east to the west, tracking the sun's movement across the sky. The preliminary analyses suggest that when they were asked to arrange the pictures in Figure 9.20 in temporal sequence, they tended to arrange the pictures from east to west. This means that when they sat in a room facing south, they usually arranged the pictures in the same way as English speakers, because east is on their left side. However, when they sat in a room facing north, they often arranged the pictures in the exact opposite order from English speakers, with the pictures going from right (east) to left (west)! This further demonstrates how spatial perception, and time perception,

FIGURE 9.20 English speakers think of time as passing from left to right, whereas Australian aborigines think of time as passing from east to west. Hence, an aborigine would chronologically arrange the pictures differently depending on the direction he or she is facing.

are grounded in the linguistic markers available in one's language (for other examples of cultural and linguistic influences on time perception see Boroditsky, Fuhran, & McCormick, 2011; de la Fuente, Santiago, Roman, Dumitrache, & Casasanto, 2014).

NUMERICAL COGNITION. The studies regarding color and spatial perception are consistent with a weak version of the Whorfian hypothesis. That is, the results support the notion that the language differences between the cultural groups influenced the way the participants thought about the tasks. Language can influence thought.

Is there *any* support for a stronger version of the Whorfian hypothesis—namely, the notion that we are unable to think about something unless we have the corresponding language available to us? As I noted earlier, the strong version of the Whorfian hypothesis has been almost universally rejected. Indeed, many of the challenges to Whorfian arguments have been those that reject the strong version of the hypothesis. For example, Berlin and Kay's (1969) findings regarding the patterns of color categories across cultures, as well as the similarities in the focal colors of those categories, are evidence that color categories are not arbitrary nor solely dependent on the language that one speaks.

The kind of evidence that would be necessary to support the strong version of the Whorfian hypothesis would need to demonstrate that people cannot entertain some concepts in the absence of the appropriate words. Despite the many studies that provide evidence against the strong Whorfian argument, there is one line of research that may provide support for it.

In many ways it would seem that mathematics is one domain that is independent from culture. After all, mathematicians and physicians have proved the existence of various mathematical principles that occur outside of our cultural worlds, such as Einstein's famous equation, $E = mc^2$. This equation is as true in America as it is in the Amazon or in the constellation of Andromeda. Mathematical principles exist outside of culture, regardless of our ability to understand them.

However, mathematics is also a domain in which we can see pronounced cultural variation in people's understanding. You most likely learned a base-10 number system at school; however, this is a system that itself is a cultural invention and that has not always been around. The Mayans and Aztecs had a base-20 number system and the ancient Babylonians had a base-60 number system. The ancient Romans, despite all their technological achievements, did not have an understanding of the concept of zero, which was invented by Hindus in India in around the third century. Likewise, there was no real conception of probability in the West before Pascal invented one in the 17th century. People in many cultures today learn to do calculations on an abacus, and those who do tend to conceive of numbers in a different way from those who do not, as is evident in the kinds of errors they make. Our ability to reason with numbers very much reflects the experiences we have had in our cultures, and most modern industrial cultures have developed to the point that they require their citizens to spend years learning how to think in mathematical terms.

The most compelling evidence that much of our competence with mathematics and numbers is learned through cultural experiences, rather than being innate, comes from looking at the numerical systems of various subsistence societies. A number of cultures have relatively impoverished number systems. For example, the Piraha, a tribe from the Lowland Amazon region of Brazil, has a number system that contains only the numbers 1, 2, and "many." They have no terms for any specific numbers greater than 2. The strong test of the Whorfian hypothesis that begs to be asked here is whether people who do not have number terms in their language can understand the concepts of those numbers.

The Piraha have been studied to investigate the kinds of mathematical computations they are able to do. In one of the studies the researcher placed a number of nuts in a can (Gordon, 2004). The participants were then shown the nuts in the can and were allowed to inspect them for some time. The experimenter then removed the can from view of the participants and would remove one nut at a time. After each nut was removed, the participants were asked whether there were any nuts remaining in the can. The participants did well on this task when there were initially up to two nuts in the can; however, their performance steadily dropped in trials that contained increasing numbers of nuts. Those participants who were shown a can containing six nuts rarely were able to correctly determine when the last nut was removed. They did not seem to be able to perform this task well with numbers larger than 2.

In another task participants were shown an array of objects—for example, five batteries. They were then given some nuts and asked to place out the same number of nuts as there were batteries (see **Figure 9.21**). Similar to the nuts in the can task, participants could do this task well with small numbers; however, their performance deteriorated considerably as the numbers got larger (for similar findings with another culture, the Mundurucu of the Amazon, see Pica, Lerner, Izard, & Dehaene, 2004). However, in all the tasks conducted, the magnitude of the errors that the Piraha made increased with the magnitude of the numbers they were asked to estimate. This suggests that although the Piraha do not have concepts for specific numbers greater than 2, they do seem able to have rough quantity estimation skills. They know, for example, that 12 batteries is a larger quantity than 8 batteries, even if they can't distinguish between more similar quantities, such as between 8 and 9 batteries. This suggests that rough quantity estimation skills might be innate whereas numerical skills beyond 2 are acquired through cultural experiences. Parallel findings for the development of numerical competence in children is also consistent with this notion (Dehaene, 1997). Studies with some other cultures with limited number lexicons, such as speakers of Warlpiri in the Northern Territory of Australia, have found that people may use spatial strategies of trying to match the pattern of a set of objects to estimate quantities in the absence of numbers (Butterworth, Reeve, & Reynolds, 2011).

FIGURE 9.21 A Piraha man attempting to match the number of batteries shown to him.

In sum, in the absence of linguistic terms for specific numbers, people from some cultural groups do not seem able to understand the associated numerical concepts. This is some evidence for the strongest version of the Whorfian hypothesis (but for other interpretations of these findings see Everett, 2005; Gelman & Gallistel, 2004).

Cultures that have few number terms also seem to map numbers onto space differently. The way that people in industrialized societies learn about numbers is linear—the distance between 17 and 18 is understood to be the same as the distance between 1 and 2. Each unit is of the same magnitude in a linear scale, and when we are counting, we are counting in linear units. However, without the cultural input, people do not have an innate linear sense of numbers (Nunez, 2011). Research with kindergarten-age American children, who have not yet mastered numeric concepts, reveals that rather than having a linear sense of numbers, they have what seems to be a logarithmic sense. They see larger amounts of space between small numbers than they do between large numbers. For example, they identify the number 10 to exist approximately halfway between the numbers 1 and 100, which is what its logarithmic value is (Siegler & Opfer, 2003). As they get older, they come to have a more and more linear understanding of numbers. Likewise, research with Mundurucu adults, an Amazonian indigenous group with few number words, also finds that they map numbers onto space logarithmically (Dehaene, Izard, Spelke, & Pica, 2008). This suggests that humans' default understanding of numbers may be logarithmic and that we only come to have a linear understanding of numbers by training and exposure to linear numeric terms (for another interpretation, see Cantlon, Cordes, Libertus, & Brannon, 2009).

To summarize, the literature on linguistic relativity has been controversial since the Whorfian hypothesis was first proposed. For decades, Rosch Heider's early results had been viewed as evidence that color perception occurred independently of language, and conclusions from those findings had been generalized to challenge all Whorfian questions. However, more recent studies have called into question those initial findings, and compelling evidence for Whorfian effects has now emerged across a number of domains. The debate is by no means over, however, and with the Whorfian door propped open again we might see researchers attempt to explore linguistic relativity in a wider array of domains than those considered before. To the extent that Whorf was correct, it follows that there should be much variation in psychological processes across cultures because languages diverge so much from each other. The Whorfian hypothesis provides a useful tool with which to make predictions for the kinds of cultural differences that are likely to emerge.

SUMMARY

The field of cognition and perception is concerned with some of the most basic and fundamental operations of the mind. Yet it is within this field that some of the clearest evidence for cultural variation has emerged.

The most-researched cultural distinction regarding cognition has been the contrast of East Asians and Westerners in their thinking styles. Westerners tend to reason in analytic ways; they view objects as static and separate from each other and understand those objects on the basis of their internal properties and how they correspond to abstract rules and principles. In contrast, East Asians (and people from many other cultural traditions) tend to reason in holistic ways, understanding objects and events as being fundamentally connected with each other, bound to a background context, continually changing, and governed by harmonious relations.

Much evidence has been amassed to support this distinction between Westerners reasoning analytically and East Asians reasoning holistically. East Asians perform relatively better on tasks that involve detecting relations among events, whereas Westerners perform relatively better on tasks requiring separation of an object from its background. East Asians tend to see foreground objects as bound to their background context, whereas Westerners focus on foreground objects and relatively ignore the background. This cultural difference appears to be driven by where people are looking, as East Asians are more likely to scan an entire scene whereas Westerners devote more of their visual attention to focal objects. These cultural differences in perceptual habits are also identifiable in aesthetic preferences. East Asian art tends to emphasize the context by consisting of relatively small figures and scenes with relatively high horizons in contrast to Western pictures, where figures are relatively large and horizons are low.

These differences in analytic and holistic thinking affect how people from different cultures understand others. Westerners are more likely than East Asians to explain the behavior of others as arising from their dispositions, whereas East Asians are more likely to view behavior as being a function of situational constraints.

Westerners are more likely than East Asians to rely on abstract rules for reasoning. When abstract rules conflict with information about similarity, East Asians tend to prefer the similarity information whereas Westerners prefer the abstract rules.

The tendency for analytic thinkers to view objects as separate and internally consistent means that contradiction cannot be tolerated. In contrast, the tendency for holistic thinkers to view the world as consisting of fluid and interrelated parts leads to a belief that contradiction is natural. East Asians thus seem less troubled than Westerners by contradiction in the world and in themselves. Furthermore, East Asians tend to see even change as changing, and they are less likely to view the future as unfolding linearly compared with Westerners.

Creativity manifests differently across cultures. Creative solutions are both novel and useful, and Westerners tend to excel at coming up with novel ideas whereas East Asians are better at producing useful ideas.

Speaking is an inherently analytic act, as ideas are expressed sequentially, one after the other. Hence, it should not be especially difficult for Westerners to speak while they are thinking, because both speaking and thinking involve analytic thought. In contrast, holistic thoughts are difficult to express verbally. East Asians show some interference between thinking and speaking, at least for some kinds of problems. East Asians tend to perform worse at a simultaneous task when they are speaking out loud, whereas speaking has no impact on the performance of Westerners.

People in high-context cultures should attend more to nonverbal cues and rely less on explicit language, whereas those in low-context cultures need to attend carefully to explicit communication. East Asians have an easier time ignoring the explicit content of what is communicated, whereas Westerners find it easier to ignore the tone with which something is said.

The Whorfian hypothesis suggests that the language people use affects their thoughts. Although this hypothesis was rejected for a few decades, recent research has found much evidence in support of it. People perceive color differently depending on the color terms that are available in their language, and similar differences exist for the perceptions of odor; language affects how people attend to agency and how they perceive spatial arrangements of things; and people in cultures whose language lacks terms for some numbers do not seem to be able to understand the associated numerical concepts.

THINK ABOUT IT

1. What are the differences between analytic and holistic thinking?
2. Why would East Asians be more comfortable with busier webpages than Westerners?
3. How might cultural differences in attribution styles affect how people assign punishment to lawbreakers?
4. Why are Chinese more likely to be contrarian stock investors than Canadians?
5. What aspects of individualism and collectivism are associated with creative thinking?
6. If talking interferes with thinking more for East Asian students than Western students, should class participation be rewarded to the same degree in different cultures? What do you think should be done in multicultural classes?
7. Do people who speak languages with different color terms see colors differently? What evidence suggests that they do, and what suggests that they don't?
8. How do people who speak languages that do not have many number terms think about quantities?

KEY TERMS

Analytic Thinking, 349

Holistic Thinking, 349

Field Independence, 353

Field Dependence, 353

Saccades, 356

Dispositional Attributions, 360

Situational Attributions, 360

Fundamental Attribution
   Error, 361

Rule-Based Reasoning, 364

Associative Reasoning, 364

Naive Dialecticism, 368

High-Context Culture, 380

Low-Context Culture, 380

Whorfian Hypothesis, 382

Linguistic Relativity
   Hypothesis, 382

Categorical Perception, 386

Russians attending the memorial service for President Boris Yeltsin. Ruminating on life's difficulties does not have the same negative consequences for Russians as it does for Americans.

10

EMOTIONS

iget is a key emotion in the life of the Ilongot—an indigenous hunting-and-gathering tribe that lives in the Northern Philippines. One cannot really understand many of the customs of the Ilongot unless one understands *liget*. But understanding *liget* is somewhat of a challenge for English speakers because the concept does not map neatly onto any English emotion terms. The closest approximation is a combination of the English words "anger," "passion," and "energy." The anthropologist Michelle Rosaldo (1980) provides a detailed account of *liget* among the Ilongot, with whom she lived for a number of years. *Liget* is experienced when one is insulted, disappointed, or irritated, but especially when one is envious of another. It can be aroused by all-night songfests, pride of accomplishments, or the death of a loved one. *Liget* is seen as a wellspring of energy. When an individual's *liget* gets worked up, it can allow the person to work in the fields all day or to climb high in the trees. As one of Rosaldo's informants said, "If it were not for *liget,* we'd have no life, we'd never work." *Liget* is something that derives from interactions among people, particularly when they compete against each other and become envious of others' accomplishments. It is also sometimes cultivated through various magic rituals. *Liget* is believed to exist in concentrated form in semen, and thus it is assumed to be more common among men than among women (although women can, at times, feel much *liget* as well). But primarily, *liget* is possessed by striving youths, energetic hunters, and violent men (**Figure 10.1**).

FIGURE 10.1 Two Ilongot youth engaged in a ritual duel.

The most dramatic demonstration of *liget* occurs in the Ilongot head-hunting rituals. Until the 1970s, the Ilongot frequently engaged in head-hunting raids on neighboring tribes. When asked why they killed others in these raids, the men would answer that they kill because of *liget*. Head hunting was a demonstration of the strong feelings of *liget* that were believed to make men great. On these raids, men would play reed flutes and pound their heads to heighten their *liget* as they headed off on a trek to a distant village. Once their *liget* had reached a crescendo, further fueled by chewing on the narcotic leaves of the betel nut, they would rush in and attack their victim. The attack would end when the victor would toss the severed head of his victim high into the air. After the raid had ended, the victors would sing a celebratory song, put flowery reeds in their hair, and return to their villages empowered, glorified, and full of *liget*.

A question to consider here is, How universal is the emotion *liget*? Do you think you have ever felt *liget*? Not its display in a head-hunting ritual, of course, but the emotion itself—a frothy feeling of anger, passion, and energy that can lead either to extreme concentration and productivity or to chaos. Likewise, do you think the Ilongot might ever feel the same kinds of emotions that you do? For example, think of a situation that has made you embarrassed, and how you felt at that time. Now imagine how you think Ilongots would feel in that same situation. Do you think they would feel the same as you did, or would their emotions be different? If you think their feelings would be different, do you think they could ever have the same kinds of feelings that you experienced in your situation?

I imagine that it's difficult for you to answer these questions. It's hard enough to imagine how someone else from our own culture would feel, let alone someone from a culture as distant as the Ilongot. Yet these are precisely the kinds of questions that emotions researchers have been wrestling with. And I think "wrestling" is an apt metaphor in this case, because the question of whether emotional experiences are similar or different across cultures is one of the most contentious in cultural psychology.

The controversy regarding the role of culture and emotion focuses on a fundamental question that has guided our investigation in the other chapters in this book: To what extent are psychological experiences universal and to what extent are they shaped by cultural experiences? In the case of emotion, as you will see, strong arguments have been made for both cases—that emotions are experienced identically around the world and that cultural experiences determine the kinds of emotions one has. Scholarly debates are very important to a field, as they force researchers to sharpen their arguments and lead them to conduct clever studies that provide evidence to shed light on the disagreements. The study of culture and emotions is a classic example of such a debate, and this chapter considers the evidence regarding whether people's emotional experiences are similar or different across cultures. Let's take a stroll down the frontlines of this controversy.

What Is an Emotion?

Before we can begin a fruitful investigation into a topic, it's necessary to have a good understanding of what we are studying. But herein lies the rub. Emotions turn out to be remarkably difficult to define. For the most part, we feel that we can recognize our emotions easily enough. We feel quite sure that we know when we feel happy or afraid—these are highly salient and important experiences in our lives. In many ways, emotions are a central and focal part of our subjective worlds. Although emotions are perceived as central to the human experience, describing what they are is not at all straightforward. The controversy regarding the similarities and differences of people's emotional experience around the world is surely based on the disagreement about how we can define emotions in the first place. Let's consider two theoretical perspectives regarding the nature of emotions that have guided the debate regarding the universality or relativity of emotional experience: the James-Lange theory and the Two-Factor theory.

The James-Lange Theory of Emotions

As with so many other key ideas in American psychology, the study of emotions begins with William James (1950/1890; see **Figure 10.2**). James proposed a thought experiment in which we imagine that someone out for a hike has stumbled upon a bear. The hiker's heart starts pounding and he runs away, experiencing that highly salient emotion of fear. James's question was, "What is the fear that the hiker experienced in this situation?" Where precisely is the emotion here? His answer was that it was the hiker's pounding heart. That is, James proposed that emotions are the physiological responses or "bodily reverberations" to stimuli in the world. A contemporary of James, Carl Lange, proposed that these physiological responses were products of the autonomic nervous system, such as changes in heart rate, breathing, pupil dilation, tear secretion, blood flow to the skin, and stomach contractions, and their ideas became known as the **James-Lange theory of emotions.**

The James-Lange theory maintains that our bodies respond to stimuli in the world by preparing us to react in a survival-facilitating way (such as running away from the bear), and our emotions are our bodily changes that signal how we should behave. As James reasoned, what would be left of our feelings of joy, rage, love, or any emotion if we removed the heart palpitations, queasiness in the stomach, or muscle tension? We'd be left with a pure,

FIGURE 10.2 William James, the key founder of the James-Lange theory of emotions.

cold, intellectual state like that of Mr. Spock on *Star Trek*. According to James, emotions are precisely those physical sensations that make us feel human.

People of course have a wide variety of emotions, which suggests that people must also have an accordingly wide variety of bodily responses. James felt that each emotion word is the description of a different bodily state. Embarrassment is the sensation of blood rushing to the face, love is the feeling of one's stomach turning end over end, and fear is the sensation of a pounding heart. Emotions, according to this view, are all about physiological experiences. And some research has revealed support for the James-Lange theory by identifying distinctive physiological patterns that correspond to certain emotions (e.g., Ekman, Levenson, & Friesen, 1983; Levenson, 1992), although other surveys of the literature call into question the specificity of the physiological patterns associated with emotion (Barret, 2006; Cacioppo, Berntson, Larsen, Poehlmann, & Ito, 2000; Lindquist, Wager, Kober, Bliss-Moreau, & Barrett, 2012; Murphy, Nimmo-Smith, & Lawrence, 2003).

Since he first proposed it, James's theory of emotions has been expanded in many ways, so that emotions are no longer seen to be just the physiological experience but rather also include appraisals, nonverbal expressions, neural patterns, and subjective feelings (e.g., Barrett & Russell, 1999; Ellsworth, 1992; Mesquita & Frijda, 1992). However, the theory's focus on the physiological experience has been central to a number of other key theories on emotional experience (Ekman, 1972; LeDoux, 1996; Panksepp, 1998).

The Two-Factor Theory of Emotions

Not everyone saw things the same way as James. Another contemporary of James, Walter Cannon, quickly criticized the James-Lange theory because the autonomic nervous system seemed to be too clumsy and slow to be differentiated into all the emotional states people experience. In some ways, it seemed at the time that the key components of the autonomic nervous system—the sympathetic and parsympathetic nervous systems—were just either turned on or turned off. Cannon thought that such a simple and ponderous system could not provide the complexity to cover the wide array of emotions people feel. Those researchers who conceptualized the autonomic nervous system as too diffuse and ungainly offered a different take on what emotions are (for a review, see Barrett, 2006). Rather than seeing emotions as primarily consisting of physiological responses, this competing school of thought maintained that emotions are primarily the *interpretations* of those bodily responses. This view, the **Two-Factor theory of emotions** (named for the factors of the physiological signals and the interpretation of those signals), redirected the focus of emotions away from the physical body and into the mind.

Stanley Schacter (see **Figure 10.3**) and Jerome Singer (1962) were the most famous proponents of the two-factor theory. They contended that emotion researchers had neglected to study people's interpretations of their physiological sensations because the

FIGURE 10.3 Stanley Schacter, the key founder of the Two-Factor theory of emotions.

earlier studies and thought experiments had never separated people's interpretations from their actual physiological sensations. Their reasoning suggests that the hiker in James's thought experiment experienced fear at sensing his pounding heart because there was no other reasonable way to interpret his bodily sensations in that situation. One could imagine other situations in which the hiker's heart would be pounding—for example, being on a steamy date with an attractive partner—when the hiker would interpret his physiological sensations as indicating that he was in love. Schacter and Singer reasoned that we could identify the separate roles of the interpretation and the physiological sensation only if we disentangled them. Their way of doing so was to conduct an elaborate experiment that controlled for the source of participants' physiological arousal and their interpretation of that arousal.

To separate their participants' interpretations from the source of their arousal, Schacter and Singer (1962) needed to do two things. First, they needed to provide the participants with situational cues to guide their interpretation. They did so by having participants assigned to either a situation that was to lead them to interpret their feelings as euphoria or a situation that would lead them to interpret their feelings as anger. Those assigned to the "euphoria" condition were asked to complete a questionnaire in a lab stocked with props and a confederate whose job it was to get the participant in a giddy, playful mood. The confederate did this by playing with the props, such as shooting wads of paper at the participant with a slingshot, making paper airplanes, and playing with a hula hoop that was lying around. The researchers reasoned that participants in this condition should interpret any arousal they were feeling as due to their feeling giddy—or, in the experimenter's terminology, euphoric. In contrast, participants assigned to the "anger" condition completed a questionnaire alongside the same confederate, whose job here was to get the participant to join him in expressing his frustration and outrage at the rudeness of the items in the questionnaire. The questionnaire helped the confederate with this task because it included a list of rather insulting items, such as, "Which member of your immediate family does not bathe or wash regularly?" and "With how many men (other than your father) has your mother had extramarital relationships?" If that last question was not enough, the lowest answer that the participant could select as a response to it was "4 and under"! Participants in this condition should interpret any physiological arousal that they were feeling as due to their anger at being subjected to such an insulting situation.

The second factor that Schacter and Singer manipulated was the amount of physiological arousal the participants would be experiencing. Under the guise that the experiment was investigating how a new vitamin called Suproxin affected vision, participants were given an injection under one of three conditions. In the placebo condition, participants were given an injection of saline and were truthfully told that the injection would not have any side effects on their state of arousal. In the epinephrine-informed condition, participants were given an injection of epinephrine and were truthfully told that the injection would cause their arousal to increase. Epinephrine is the synthetic equivalent of adrenaline, a neurotransmitter that heightens arousal in the sympathetic nervous system. Last, in the epinephrine-uninformed condition, participants were given an injection of epinephrine but were falsely told that it *would not have any side effects* of increased arousal. This last condition was key; Participants should have felt a great deal of physiological arousal from the injection, but they wouldn't know where the arousal came from. Schacter and Singer reasoned that participants in this condition would look to the situation to interpret their feelings and would conclude that their arousal was due to their experiences in the situation— that is, either due to their giddy feelings from goofing around with the confederate in the euphoria condition or to their annoyance from being insulted in the anger condition. In contrast, the researchers predicted that participants in the placebo condition would experience little arousal and thus would experience little emotion. Likewise, those in the epinephrine-informed condition would experience little emotion because, although they experienced much physiological arousal, they would attribute it to the side effects of the injection they had received.

The results of the study largely supported Schacter and Singer's predictions. The strongest emotions were experienced by those in the epinephrine-uninformed condition. Participants in this condition were feeling a great deal of arousal but they had no good explanation for it. So they came to interpret their arousal by looking to the situation they were in. Those in the euphoria situation explained their arousal as a result of their feeling euphoric, whereas those in the anger situation attributed it to their feeling angry. The emotional experience came from participants interpreting their arousal in light of their beliefs of the situations that they were in. If the same physiological information can be interpreted as either euphoria or anger, two very distinct emotional experiences, this suggests that despite the different physiological patterns that different emotional states might have (e.g., Ekman et al., 1983; Levenson, 1992), people don't have an especially fine-tuned awareness of their bodily sensations. Much subsequent research, using a variety of manipulations of arousal and several measures of emotions (e.g., Dutton & Aron, 1974; Zillman, 1978), have converged to show that people look to cues from their environment to help them label their physical sensations.

The James-Lange theory and the Two-Factor theory suggest two very different origins for emotions, and these theories make different predictions regarding whether emotional experience is universal or culturally variable. If the various extensions of the James-Lange theory are correct—that emotions are largely based on the particular and specific physiological reactions that people have to various events—this suggests an evolutionary origin to human emotions. That is, if emotions are specific biological signals that alert people to events in their world, it would follow that this biological machinery must have been assembled through evolution. For example, the physiological signals of fear that we experience on encountering a bear in the woods serve us well in aiding to get our body out of harm's way. In the past, individuals who did not experience those physiological signals of fear were more likely to have been caught by the bear and thus wouldn't have had the chance to pass their genes down to the next generation. Over millions of generations these affective signals would have been adaptive for our ancestors, and the signals thus became part of our genetic code. And because we share the same genetic code, and we all shared the same ancestors up until very recently (it was not until about 60,000 years ago that some *Homo sapiens* first left Africa), we have all inherited these adaptive physiological signals. The James-Lange theory thus suggests that people in all cultures should have the same emotional experiences. In support of this, some research has identified distinctive physiological patterns of emotions that are similar among people from diverse cultural backgrounds (e.g., Levenson, Ekman, Heider, & Freisen, 1992; Tsai, Chentsova-Dutton, & Freire-Bebeau, 2002; but see Barrett, 2006, for a contrary view). The James-Lange theory, and other theories that focus on the centrality of physiology in emotions, make the case for universality in emotional experience.

On the other hand, if the Two-Factor theory of emotions is correct—that emotions are interpretations of physiological signals—this suggests that in addition to a physiological basis, emotions are grounded in the belief systems that shape people's interpretations (for a thorough discussion of this see Lindquist et al., 2012). Because belief systems are influenced a great deal by culture (e.g., Markus & Kitayama, 1991; Schwartz, 1994), the Two-Factor theory suggests that people might interpret their physiological signals in different ways across cultures. And research reveals important cultural differences in the experience of emotions (e.g., Kitayama, Mesquita, & Karasawa, 2006; Mesquita, 2001; Tsai, Knutson, & Fung, 2006). The Two-Factor theory, and other theories that focus on the centrality of interpretation in emotions, thus make the case for cultural variability in emotional experience.

Does Emotional Experience Vary Across Cultures?

As the preceding section suggests, the question of whether emotions vary across cultures hinges on how you conceive of emotions. Two aspects of emotions have received the most study: an objectively visible aspect, facial expressions; and a subjectively experienced aspect, people's descriptions of their emotional experiences. Let's consider each of these in turn.

Emotions and Facial Expressions

When you're happy, you tend to orchestrate the various muscles in your face to construct a beaming smile. Why is that? Did you learn by interacting with others that this was the appropriate way to express happiness in your culture? Or was the linkage between your happiness and your smiling hard-wired into your brain from birth? On the one hand, facial expressions are a means to communicate with others, and many other ways of communicating are heavily dependent on what people learn in their cultures. As an extreme example, consider what words you use to express happiness. In English, people say *happiness,* in Portuguese people say *felicidade,* and in Japanese people say *shiawase.* Around the world there seems to be a rather arbitrary pairing of phonemes with the experience of happiness. Might there not be a similarly arbitrary pairing of facial muscle movements with the experience of happiness as well? Perhaps in some cultures people frown when they're happy.

On the other hand, unlike languages, facial expressions often appear to be rather reflexive. The same facial expressions that adults make are made by very young infants (Izard, 1994), including those who were born blind and thus have never seen the expressions before (reviewed in Ekman, 1973). This suggests that facial expressions are part of our biological makeup, and because humans share the same biology everywhere, facial expressions should be the same worldwide.

EVIDENCE FOR CULTURAL UNIVERSALS IN FACIAL EXPRESSIONS. Charles Darwin (1872/1965) was one of the first scientists to seriously consider whether emotional facial expressions are common across all people of the world. If they are, this would suggest that the various facial expressions evolved as a product of natural selection—perhaps as means to communicate information before our species had the linguistic capabilities to describe feelings.

The researchers who have contributed the most in following up on Darwin's ideas have been Paul Ekman and his colleagues. Ekman and Friesen (1971) took thousands of photos of people making six different emotional expressions (anger, disgust, fear, happiness, sadness, and surprise). They reduced their set of photos to those that were most easily recognized by Americans and then showed this set to individuals in Argentina, Brazil, Chile, Japan, and the United States. The participants were asked to select which of a set of six emotion terms best matched the feeling that a person was showing in a photo. If people had no idea which emotions were expressed in the pictures, they would have identified about one out of six (16.7%) by guessing correctly (**Table 10.1**). However, the participants tended to identify the emotion correctly in 80% to 90% of the photos. That is, people in these five different cultures showed a great deal of agreement about what feelings the different facial poses were expressing. They paired smiles with happiness, scowls with anger, frowns with sadness, gapes with surprise, grimaces with disgust, and startles with fear. These findings are supportive of a claim for universals in emotional expression.

TABLE 10.1

Percentage correct in recognition of facial expressions across cultures

	Happiness	Disgust	Surprise	Sadness	Anger	Fear
USA	97	82	91	73	69	88
Brazil	97	86	82	82	82	77
Chile	90	85	88	90	76	78
Argentina	94	79	93	85	72	68
Japan	87	82	87	74	63	71

Source: Ekman & Friesen (1971).

However, demonstrating that a psychological process is universal is not such a straightforward task. It is possible, for example, that Ekman and Friesen obtained such similar responses among these different cultures because the cultures weren't all that different to begin with. The five cultures they had explored were all industrialized, literate cultures, and people from them had all been exposed to a lot of the same media images. For example, around the time that Ekman and Friesen were collecting their cross-cultural data, the Hollywood movie *Butch Cassidy and the Sundance Kid* had been playing in theaters in all five countries. Perhaps participants in those countries outside the United States learned that people smile to expressed happiness by watching Paul Newman's electric grin up on the silver screen. That is, even though Ekman and Friesen collected data from different cultures, it is possible that people from those cultures all *learned* to express emotions with their faces in ways that are similar across cultures. To be more confident that emotional expressions are universal, you would need to question people who hadn't had much experience with other cultures. Only then could you ensure that people had not learned how to interpret other cultures' typical emotional expressions but that the various cultures really did perceive emotional expressions in the same way.

Ekman's solution to addressing this shortcoming was to try to find a culture that had the least possible exposure to Western ways. He chose the Fore of the inner highlands of New Guinea. The Fore had not seen any movies or magazines, they didn't speak English or any other language influenced by a Western tongue, and they had never worked for Westerners. The Fore were from a culture that was one of the least exposed to Western ways on the planet. If the Fore made the same facial expressions that Westerners did, even though they had had virtually no contact with Westerners, the case for universality would be greatly strengthened. Ekman went to investigate whether the Fore would smile or frown when they were happy. What did he find?

It turns out the Fore smiled. And they frowned when they were sad, scowled when they were angry, and so on. Ekman demonstrated this by creating some stories appropriate for each of the six emotions. For example, he asked the Fore participants to imagine how they would feel, and to make a corresponding facial expression, in the following situations: (a) "Your friend has come, and you are happy," (b) "Your child has died," (c) "You are angry and about to fight," and (d) "You see a dead pig that has been lying there for a long time." In **Figure 10.4** you can see the kinds of

FIGURE 10.4 The expressions of Fore men when they were asked to show how their faces would appear if they experienced the following: (a) "Your friend has come and you are happy." (b) "Your child has died and you are sad." (c) "You are angry and about to fight." (d) "You see a dead pig that has been lying there for a long time."

facial expressions the Fore made in response to each of these situations (Ekman, Sorenson, & Friesen, 1969). The odds that by chance people would tend to make facial expressions so similar to the ones that you and I make, even though they have had no contact with our cultures, are extremely remote. This is strong evidence that some facial expressions are universally similar around the world (but see Barrett, Mesquita, & Gendron, 2011; Gendron, Roberson, van der Vyver, & Barrett, 2014; Jack, Garrod, Yu, Caldara, & Schyns, 2012; Russell, 1994 for challenges to this universality conclusion).

Ekman and colleagues proposed that there is a set of basic emotions that are universally recognized around the world. This basic set is argued to include at least six emotions: anger, fear, happiness, sadness, surprise, and disgust (**Figure 10.5**). Given Ekman's findings, you surely already know what each of the basic expressions looks like, but just to make sure, you can see examples of them here.

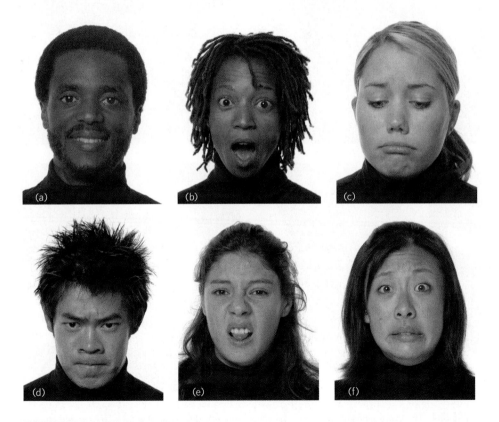

FIGURE 10.5 The six basic emotional expressions: (a) happiness, (b) surprise, (c) sadness, (d) anger, (e) disgust, and (f) fear.

FIGURE 10.6 The pride expression.

There is also debate over whether other emotions—in particular, contempt, shame, embarrassment, and interest—are universally recognized enough to justify being added to this set (e.g., Keltner, 1995). For example, there is good evidence that the expression of pride is universally recognized (e.g., Tracy & Robins, 2008). However, unlike the six basic emotions, the pride expression involves the whole body; it incorporates an erect posture, with the head tilted back, a slight smile on the face, and arms extending away from the body or held akimbo (**Figure 10.6**). People recognize this expression around the world as pride, and congenitally blind judo wrestlers from around the world spontaneously display elements of this pose after victories, despite never having seen it before themselves (Tracy & Matsumoto, 2008).

EVIDENCE FOR CULTURAL VARIABILITY IN FACIAL EXPRESSIONS. The above evidence, coupled with the findings from dozens of other studies on the topic gathered by Ekman and others, demonstrates that emotional expressions are not just something that people learn growing up. Although there may be a different word to express "happiness" in almost every language, everywhere around the world people communicate their happiness by orchestrating their facial muscles in a fairly similar way. This is clear evidence for a universal, biological substrate to emotional expressions. Given that movements of the facial muscles can be seen as part of the physiological component of emotions, it follows that in this domain of facial expression, we would see much evidence for universality. However, even here there is also some evidence for cultural variability.

Although Ekman and others' research clearly reveals that in every culture that has been studied people are able to recognize the facial expressions of the basic emotions, there are some intriguing cultural differences. For example, when shown pictures of posed facial expressions from one culture (for example, Americans of European descent), some cultures perform a little better than others. The success rates for identifying American-posed faces was better among English speakers than among speakers of other Indo-European languages (e.g., Swedish, Greek, Spanish), and these samples performed better than those who spoke non-Indo-European languages (e.g., Japanese, Turkish, Malaysian), and all of these groups performed better than those from pre-literate societies (e.g., the Fore and Dani from New Guinea; Russell, 1994). All groups performed significantly better than chance; however, Americans performed best of all at identifying the emotions posed by American actors.

Building on this observation, researchers conducted a meta-analysis of all the past research on cross-cultural recognition of facial expressions and noted that, on average, people were about 9% more accurate in judging the facial expressions of people from their own culture than those of another culture (with, on average, people showing about 58% accuracy overall; Elfenbein & Ambady, 2002). That is, there is a large universal component of recognizing facial expressions and a smaller culturally specific component. The link between certain facial expressions and inferred emotions thus appears to be a functional universal—the facial expressions are interpreted to indicate similar emotions across cultures, but the degree to which each expression is recognized varies across cultures.

The tendency to be better at recognizing the facial expressions of people from one's own culture can be seen in a variety of ways. For example, if you just show people pictures of people's eyes, without the rest of their face showing, and ask them to guess the emotion that the target is feeling, people do better when the target is from their own culture than from another culture (Adams et al., 2010; see **Figure 10.7**). This same task of judging the emotions by just looking at eyes is used in other research as part of a tool to diagnose people with autism. Curiously, then, people appear to be somewhat autistic when they interact with people from other cultures, struggling a bit to interpret what kinds of emotions they are feeling. People also show a stronger fear response as measured by brain imaging (i.e., they show greater activation of their amygdala) when they look at fear faces that are made by people in their own culture than those made by people of other cultures (Chiao et al., 2008). This demonstrates

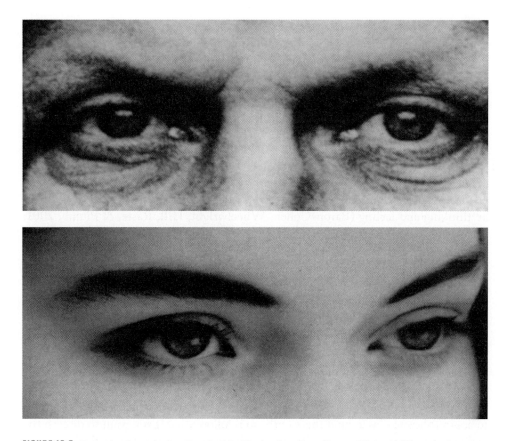

FIGURE 10.7   Examples from the Reading the Mind in the Eyes Test (Baron-Cohen, 2003).

that they are especially attentive to signs of fear as expressed in culturally familiar ways. Likewise, although research finds that people can predict the electability of political candidates within their own cultures just by looking at pictures of their faces, they aren't able to make the same kinds of accurate predictions when looking at pictures of candidates from other cultures (Rule et al., 2010).

In general, then, people are better at accurately perceiving the emotional expressions of people they have been exposed to more. Another example of this is that straight men were more accurate in judging the sexual orientations of men just by looking at their faces if they had had much past real-life experiences with gay men (Brambilla, Riva, & Rule, 2013). Hence, there are pronounced enough differences in facial expressions across cultures that people are more skilled at accurately identifying those expressions when they are made by people who are more familiar to them.

The differences in facial expressions of emotions across cultures are distinct enough that people can reliably guess the nationality of targets who are expressing emotions, even when the targets are of fairly similar cultural backgrounds. For example, Americans can guess better than chance whether a target is from the United States or Australia (Marsh, Elfenbein, & Ambady, 2007), or whether the target is Japanese or Japanese-American (Marsh, Elfenbein, & Ambady, 2003), just by looking at a target's face, but only when the target is expressing an emotion. Participants cannot make these same distinctions when the targets are showing neutral faces. Furthermore, people who are of a lower socioeconomic background are more accurate at identifying facial expressions of emotions, indicating that those who have relatively less status must attend more closely to what those of relatively higher status might be thinking and feeling (Baron-Cohen, Wheelwright, Hill, Raste, & Plumb, 2001; Kraus, Cote, & Keltner, 2010). In sum, although overall facial expressions of emotions are universally recognized at better than chance, people are especially adept at recognizing those expressions made by people from their own culture and those who are of higher perceived status than themselves.

Another way that cultures differ in how they interpret facial expression stems from the parts of the face to which they are attending. As we'll explore in the next section, people often don't express all of the feelings they are experiencing, and this tendency to modulate the feelings shown on one's face varies across cultures. In particular, Japanese people are more likely to conceal emotions they feel are potentially disruptive by presenting a more neutral or pleasant face than Americans (e.g., Ekman, 1972). However, it is more difficult to control the muscles around the eyes than it is to control the muscles around the mouth, so it follows that if you want to discern the feelings of someone who may be disguising their emotions, you should focus on their eyes. In contrast, the mouth is a much larger source of information than the eyes, so if you're expecting that people's feelings are being accurately broadcast by their faces, then you would fare best by attending to their relatively large mouths. One study investigated this hypothesis by showing Japanese and Americans photos of people's facial expressions in which the top half of the photos showed a different emotional expression than the bottom half (the researchers mixed and matched the halves from different photos). Participants were asked to decide what emotion the target person was expressing. The results revealed that the judgments of Japanese were more influenced by the top half of the photos (i.e., by looking at the eyes) than the judgments of Americans, and the judgments of Americans were more influenced by the bottom half of the photos (i.e., by looking at the mouths) than the judgments of Japanese (Yuki, Maddux, & Masuda, 2007).

Conceptually similar findings have emerged in studies showing that Europeans judged facial expressions by attending to both the eyes and the mouths, whereas East Asians did so by primarily attending to an area near the eyes (Blais, Jack, Scheepers, Fiset, & Caldara, 2008; Jack, Caldara, & Schyns, 2011). Moreover, there are different

FIGURE 10.8 Can the Japanese tendency to look relatively more at eyes than mouths when judging people's emotions help explain why anime characters have larger eyes than mouths?

patterns of neural activation when East Asians are looking at faces compared with Westerners, that are consistent with the differences in the facial regions that people from different cultures attend to (Goh et al., 2010). Perhaps it's because of this cultural difference in facial perception that Japanese anime characters typically have much bigger eyes than they do mouths (Takemoto, 2010; **Figure 10.8**).

Cultural Display Rules

Ekman and colleagues argue that the capacity to produce and recognize particular facial expressions is identical across cultures. What varies, they argue, are the **display rules** that cultures maintain for emotional expression (Ekman & Friesen, 1969). Display rules are the culturally specific rules that govern which facial expressions are appropriate in a given situation and how intensely they should be exhibited. Some cultures encourage people to display their emotions in clear, if not exaggerated, form. For example, among certain Arab populations it is dishonorable if a man does not respond to an insult with a great demonstration of anger (Abu-Lughod, 1986). Likewise, the Kaluli of New Guinea tend to show their emotions particularly intensely and dramatically (Schieffelin, 1979). Other cultures encourage people to express their emotions in muted form, or to conceal them altogether. For example, among the Utku Eskimos, public expressions of anger are strongly condemned (Briggs, 1970). Similarly, the Balinese have a preference for emotional "smoothness," where the emphasis is on avoiding strong displays of emotional feelings, for both positive and negative emotions (Geertz, 1983). This notion of display rules suggests that even though people in different cultures vary considerably in how strongly they express certain emotions, it is possible that they are all experiencing the same underlying feelings. Several studies have found evidence that cultures vary in the intensity and transparency with which people express their emotions in their faces (Ekman, 1972; Friesen, 1972; Matsumoto, Yoo, & Fontaine, 2008).

Evidence of cultural variability in display rules of emotion can also be found in hospitals. I am told that in a number of emergency rooms in North America it is not uncommon for some of the medical staff to privately joke among themselves by referring to some patients as having symptoms of AMS: acute Mediterranean syndrome. This syndrome refers to the observations by some ER personnel that people from many Mediterranean cultures communicate their discomfort and pain at several decibels louder than those from many other cultures. The medical staff identify some patients as having AMS to warn each other that they are likely to get an earful. The staff in these emergency rooms do not appear to have identified an illusory correlation. Much research corroborates their observations and finds that there are clear cultural differences in the ways pain is expressed. For example, one comparison of Italian and Irish clinical admissions to a hospital found that 57% of the Italians reported being in pain in contrast to only 33% of the Irish (Zola, 1966). Another study found that patients of Italian and Jewish backgrounds communicated their pain much more openly than those of Irish and Anglo backgrounds (Zborowski, 1969; also see Bates, Edwards, & Anderson, 1993), although some kinds of self-report measures of pain do not reveal consistent cultural differences (Zatzick & Dimsdale, 1990). Cultural differences in pain expression appear to be more pronounced among older patients than among younger ones (e.g., Koopman, Eisenthal, & Stoeckle, 1984), highlighting how emotional expression is shaped by cultural experiences over time. Whether the greater cries of pain of more emotionally expressive people lead to greater *experience* of pain is an interesting but difficult question to address.

In addition to governing the intensity with which emotions are expressed, display rules also shape the kinds of facial expressions that people might display. For example, when Americans are embarrassed they tend to make a facial expression along the lines of that shown on the left in **Figure 10.9**. They turn their head away, look down and to the side, smile with pressed lips, and touch their face. However, Indians often express their embarrassment by biting their tongues, as shown on the right in Figure 10.9. The expression shown on the left is recognized as embarrassment quite accurately by both Americans and Indians; however, the tongue bite is recognized as embarrassment by Indians but not Americans. This suggests that the tongue bite represents an expression that is voluntarily produced rather than reflexively generated (Haidt & Keltner, 1999). Voluntarily produced emotional expressions such as the tongue bite suggest the existence of cultural display rules that lead people to express idiosyncratic facial expressions, known as **ritualized displays,** that differ from the ostensibly universal facial expressions identified by Ekman and colleagues. Of course

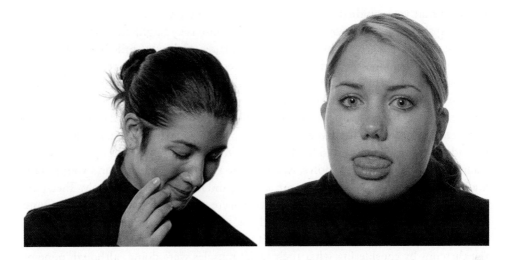

FIGURE 10.9 Americans and Indians both recognize the photo on the left as a prototypical embarrassment display. However, only people in India recognize the photo on the right as a ritualized display of embarrassment.

this adds a layer of complexity to the challenging task of interpreting emotional expressions across cultures. When we see someone's facial expression, it is not always clear whether we are looking at a universal facial expression or one governed by cultural display rules.

Facial Feedback Hypothesis

An important point about display rules is that they presuppose that emotional *experiences* are unaffected by facial expressions. The theory maintains that the experience of the basic emotions is more or less constant across cultures, although cultures vary in how they choose to display those facial emotions. However, are emotional experiences and expressions completely unrelated? One view, known as the **facial feedback hypothesis,** suggests that they are not. The facial feedback hypothesis proposes that one source of information we utilize when inferring our feelings is our facial expressions. So if we are trying to figure out if we feel happy, one clue that we might consider is whether we are smiling. After all, our faces are more likely to be smiling when we have happy feelings than when we have feelings of sadness or disgust. This correlation between our facial expressions and feelings might thus be relied on in interpreting our feelings.

One study investigated whether people's emotions were influenced by the expressions their faces were making (Strack, Martin, & Stepper, 1988). The researchers reasoned that you couldn't just ask people to make certain facial expressions before inquiring about their emotional experiences, because they might come to suspect the purpose of the study (e.g., why did the experimenter ask me to smile before he asked me to rate my happiness?), and this would affect the findings. As a result, the experimenters sought to manipulate people's facial muscles into a smile or frown without the participants being aware that they were actually smiling or frowning. Their unique solution was to ask participants to hold a pen in their mouth. One group was instructed to hold a pen between their teeth without having it touch their lips. A second group was instructed to hold a pen between their lips without having it touch their teeth. As **Figure 10.10** shows, when you do this the muscles around your mouth are in similar positions as when you are smiling and frowning, respectively. Then participants were asked to rate how amused they were with a number of cartoons. Quite remarkably, the pen-in-teeth group found the cartoons to be more amusing than the pen-in-lips group! Apparently, participants were inferring how amused they were by the cartoons by considering what their facial muscles were doing, although none of them appeared to be aware that they were doing so. There thus appears to be some wisdom to the advice to put on a happy face!

The facial feedback hypothesis suggests that culturally divergent display rules might affect more than just people's expressions of their emotions. If your culture encourages you to express your emotions clearly on your face, you may infer that you're feeling strong emotions, whereas if your culture encourages you to deamplify or mask

FIGURE 10.10 Facial muscle movements can affect the experience of emotion. People holding a pen between their teeth tend to find cartoons more amusing than people holding a pen between their lips.

your emotions, you might conclude that you're not feeling much emotion. American culture is one in which people are encouraged to express their emotions, whereas Japanese culture is one in which people are encouraged to exert considerable control over their emotional expressions. How do the cultures compare in their emotional experiences?

Cultural Variation in Intensity of Emotional Experience

A number of studies have compared the emotional experience of Japanese and Americans using a variety of techniques. For example, Japanese and American participants were asked to report on occasions when they had experienced certain emotions (Matsumoto, Kudoh, Scherer, & Wallbott, 1988). The Americans reported feeling those emotions longer and more intensely than the Japanese did. Similarly, in another study Japanese and American students completed a questionnaire a number of times per day over a week to indicate the emotions they had been experiencing (Mesquita & Karasawa, 2002). The Japanese were about three times as likely as Americans to report that they had *not* been feeling any emotions (see Kitayama, Markus, & Kurokawa, 2000 and Wang, 2004 for similar findings). Other research has found that East Asians are less attentive to their visceral states when compared with Westerners (Ma-Kellams, Blascovich, & McCall, 2012; Ryder et al., 2008); Ghanaians have also been found to attend less to their emotions than Americans (Dzokoto, 2010). These studies suggest that the cultural display rules governing the deamplifying and masking of emotions in East Asia might be leading East Asians to experience fewer and less intense emotions than Americans.

In some cultural contexts the expression of intense emotions may make it problematic to fit in well with others, particularly for the expression of such interpersonally disruptive emotions as anger. It can be difficult for an interdependent group to function well if members are angry with each other, particularly if someone lower in the hierarchy feels anger toward someone of higher status. The individual would appear to fare better by not expressing that anger. However, much research with Westerners has revealed that people with hostile tendencies are at increased risk for cardiovascular disease (e.g., Diamond, 1982; Mann, 1977). Furthermore, some have maintained that the reason hostility leads to cardiovascular disease is that hostile people have more occasions when they need to inhibit their anger. That is, some researchers maintain that it is the *suppression* of an anger response that causes difficulties in regulating one's heart rate, and thus a slower recovery of the heart rate following an initial angering event (e.g., Brosschot & Thayer, 1998). If the inhibition of anger leads to cardiovascular stress for people from all cultures, it would seem that people from cultures in which inhibition of anger is more common would suffer from more heart disease, because they would more often be trying to bottle up their angry feelings.

Alternatively, perhaps in cultures where the expression of anger is problematic, people tend to *experience* anger less intensely. This hypothesis was investigated in a couple of studies that compared Chinese-Canadians and European-Canadians in their anger responses (Anderson & Linden, 2006). In a first study, people were provided with some scenarios that typically provoke feelings of anger. For example, one scenario read, "You go with your family to a restaurant where the food is superb and prices are low, but the service is terrible. There are many people in the restaurant; you wait a quarter of an hour and the waiter has not yet come to your table to take your order." Participants were asked how angry they would be, and which of four strategies they would take. One strategy is to express the anger (e.g., to complain to the manager); a second strategy is to suppress outward signs of anger (e.g., to wait quietly, while getting angrier inside); a third strategy is to distract oneself from the anger source (e.g., change the topic of conversation); and a last strategy is to generate a less-angry appraisal of the event (e.g., convince yourself that the staff are very busy).

The results indicated two things: first, Chinese-Canadians, on average, found the scenarios to be less anger-provoking than the European-Canadians did. They imagined feeling less anger if they had been in those situations. Second, the most common response to the anger-provoking event for European-Canadians was to openly express their anger. In contrast, for the Chinese-Canadians, their most common response was to reappraise the situation in a less angry way or to make efforts to distract themselves from the anger-provoking event. That is, whereas the European-Canadians felt much anger and tended to express it openly, the Chinese-Canadians adopted strategies to minimize their anger response, and accordingly, felt less angry.

In a second study, participants were examined to see how they physiologically responded to an anger-provoking incident (Anderson & Linden, 2006). Chinese-Canadians and European-Canadians were brought into a lab where they were exposed to a rather rude and unprofessional experimenter. Throughout the course of the experiment, their blood pressure was measured. People from both cultural groups initially responded with similar degrees of anger to the obnoxious experimenter, as measured both by a self-report questionnaire and by their blood pressure. Both groups of participants showed an initial jump in their systolic blood pressure, which indicates an anger response. After that angry response, participants' blood pressure slowly dropped back down to baseline levels. Of interest here is that the blood pressure of the Chinese-Canadians recovered to baseline levels significantly more quickly than the blood pressure of European-Canadians (**Figure 10.11**). None of the participants openly expressed their anger to the experimenter (although some were given the opportunity to complete a written evaluation of the experimenter, which did not significantly influence the results), and thus participants were in a situation where they needed to inhibit the expression of their anger. Apparently,

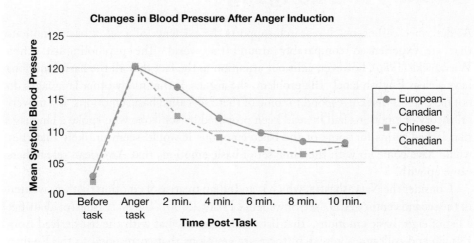

FIGURE 10.11 After being angered, Chinese-Canadians' blood pressure returns to its baseline level more quickly than European-Canadians' blood pressure does. This suggests that the Chinese-Canadians are not needing to devote as much effort toward suppressing their anger.

inhibiting anger led to a slower recovery of blood pressure for European-Canadians than it did for Chinese-Canadians. This suggests that the Chinese-Canadians experienced their anger less intensely than European-Canadians and were more comfortable with strategies that served to reduce their experience of anger, whereas the European-Canadians suffered from physiological consequences if they did not openly express their anger.

Similar findings have emerged in a number of other studies (Butler, Lee, & Gross, 2009; Mauss & Butler, 2010; Mauss, Butler, Roberts, & Chu, 2010). Moreover, other research has found that, compared with Americans, negative emotions in East Asians are associated with fewer negative health outcomes (Curhan et al., 2014; Miyamoto et al., 2013) and less of a neural response when suppressing their emotions, indicating that it is not as effortful for them to suppress negative emotions (Murata, Moser, & Kitayama, 2013).

Cultural display rules thus alter the ways that people express their emotions, which, in turn, can potentially alter their emotional experiences. To the extent that expressions of emotions are inextricably linked to the experience of emotions, this adds a further layer of complexity in evaluating the evidence for the universality or cultural variability of emotional experience.

Emotion and Language

As described earlier, much research supports the existence of a set of basic emotions that are experienced comparably around the world. The psycholinguist Anna Wierzbicka (1986), however, calls our attention to the fact that all the basic emotions have a clear English label. The problem, she argues, is that many other languages do not have labels that correspond to some of these so-called basic emotions. If a universal theory of emotions had instead been proposed by someone who spoke a language that lacked terms for some of the basic emotions it would seem unlikely that they would have come up with the same set of basic emotions that American researchers came up with.

Consider the Natyashastra, which is an Indian treatise of emotion that was written in the second century A.D. (see Shweder & Haidt, 2000). The Natyashastra identifies a list of eight basic emotions. That list overlaps somewhat with the list derived from Ekman and colleagues' research (there are emotions that correspond to the English terms of anger, fear, sadness, and disgust); however, it did not include words that corresponded to the basic emotions of happiness or surprise. Nor did it overlap with other contenders for the status of "basic emotions," such as pride, embarrassment, shame, interest, or contempt. Furthermore, the Natyashastra included four emotions that are not typically seen as "basic" emotions (love, amusement, enthusiasm, and wonder; Masson & Patwardhan, 1970). There thus appears to be some disagreement across cultures as to what the candidates for the "basic" emotions are.

Indeed, when it comes to exploring how different cultures describe their emotional experiences, we see tremendous cultural variation (Russell, 1991). On one extreme is the English language, which has more than 2,000 different emotion words. English speakers are particularly well equipped to describe the most subtle of variations in their emotional experience. On the other extreme is the Chewong of Malaysia, who have only eight emotion words (only three of which—anger, fear, and shame—map on to Ekman's basic emotions). Given this difference in the lexicons, it certainly is not surprising that so much interest in research on the emotions has emerged from English speakers and not from the Chewong.

The degree of cultural variation in emotional description is not just in terms of the number of emotion words that different groups have. People categorize their emotions in very different ways as well (Russell, 1991). For example, Luganda speakers in Uganda do not make a distinction between sorrow and anger. The Gidjingali aborigines of Australia use one word (*gurakadj*) to express both shame and fear. Samoans use one word, *alofa,* to express both love and pity. The Utku Eskimos do not distinguish between feelings of kindness and gratitude. The Ifaluk in Micronesia do not even have a word for "emotion" but instead lump all internal states together (Lutz, 1988). The emotional lexicon is carved up in remarkably different ways across cultures.

Furthermore, despite the enormous number of emotion words in the English language, there are many emotion words in other languages that have no equivalent in English. Some of these reflect feelings that English speakers are probably familiar with, even though the language doesn't contain a single term to express them. The best-known example is *schadenfreude*, the German term describing the feelings of pleasure that one gets when witnessing the hard times that befall another. Some other cases of novel emotion terms seem to express feelings that are not especially familiar to most English speakers, such as *liget*. Other less-familiar emotion words include the Javanese term *iklas,* which refers to somewhat pleasant feelings of frustration (Geertz, 1959) and the Japanese word *amae. Amae* captures the relatively pleasant feelings that one experiences when allowed to emphasize his or her dependence on another. It often involves tendencies to behave

"Schadenfreude Monthly"

inappropriately toward a close other, as a gesture to demonstrate how secure the relationship is (Niiya, Ellsworth, & Yamaguchi, 2006).

Personally, I have had a great deal of experience in Japan, and my occupation as a cultural psychologist demands a certain openness to culturally divergent ways of thinking. Nevertheless, my own experiences with *amae* situations are often frustrating and completely bewildering to me. I am quite certain that although I have a decent intellectual understanding of *amae,* I do not experience the emotion in the same way that most Japanese do. I think this is so because the kinds of inappropriate behaviors that demonstrate one's dependence on another carry different meanings for me, given my own Canadian cultural upbringing. I would argue that the cultural diversity in emotion terms arises from the different clusters of meanings that are frequently encountered in different cultures. For example, if inappropriate behaviors toward a loved one are consistently met with responses that indicate that your relationship is strong, this will lead to the pleasant cluster of feelings that constitutes *amae.* If the same behaviors are met with frustration or distancing from your loved one, you would appraise the situation differently and feel a different emotion.

Much cross-cultural research thus reveals that there are many exotic specimens in the emotion zoo. However, one important question to consider when looking at the dizzying array of emotion words around the world is: How much do the emotion words matter? Could it be that the labels are irrelevant to the experiences of emotion? Some researchers argue that the diversity in emotion terms is relatively meaningless because our language use does not affect our underlying psychological experience (e.g., Pinker, 1994). Other researchers view the diversity in emotion terms to be highly telling of cultural diversity in emotional experience (e.g., Russell, 1991). This disagreement gets to the heart of the controversial debate on linguistic relativity—that is, the extent to which the ways people think are influenced by the words they use, as discussed in Chapter 9. It is difficult to assess with any confidence the degree to which emotion labels affect emotional experience, because there aren't good physiological indicators of the nonbasic emotions. So we are hard pressed to evaluate whether English speakers experience *schadenfreude* as intensely, or with all the associated feelings and meanings, as German speakers do. At present, we can say that there is tremendous diversity in emotional experience across cultures in terms of how it is described in words, but whether this diversity is captured in people's own thoughts and internal states remains debatable.

Cultural Variation in Kinds of Emotional Experiences

In addition to research that has contrasted facial expressions and emotion terms across cultures, other research has attempted to investigate people's emotional experiences. How similar or different are people's daily emotional lives across cultures?

The differences between interdependent and independent selves provide a nice theoretical framework from which to draw hypotheses about how we might expect emotional experience to vary across cultures. People with interdependent selves are more concerned with maintaining a sense of interpersonal harmony and thus should be more aware of how events in the world affect others close to them as well as themselves. Those with independent selves, in contrast, should focus more intently on how events affect themselves, or how events might serve to distinguish themselves from others. This suggests that people with independent selves and interdependent selves will interpret situations differently—looking at situations as providing opportunities to distinguish themselves from others or to affect their relations with others.

This hypothesis was tested by comparing those from a more collectivistic culture (Surinamese and Turkish immigrants to Holland) with those from a more individualistic culture (mainstream Dutch citizens of Holland; Mesquita, 2001). In accordance with these very predictions, the Surinamese and Turks expressed more relational concerns and attended more closely to how situations affected others, compared with the Dutch. Moreover, the Surinamese and Turks were more likely than the Dutch to ensure that others attended to the same events, thereby sharing the experience with the participants. This suggests that the emotional experiences of those who are more interdependent are more interpersonally engaged than the emotional experiences among more independent individuals. Similar findings have emerged contrasting Mexicans and Americans—Mexicans are more likely to experience interpersonally engaging emotions and less likely to experience interpersonal disengaging emotions when compared with Americans (Savani, Alvarez, Mesquita, & Markus, 2013).

Moreover, we should expect that common cultural concerns should be associated with the kinds of emotions relevant to those concerns. For example, defending one's honor is a significant concern among Turks, whereas maintaining face is a particular concern among Japanese. The kinds of emotions that arise when people are concerned with defending their honor are feelings of anger and shame, and these are experienced more frequently in Turkey. In contrast, a concern with maintaining face is associated with feelings of shame but not anger, and in Japan people are far more likely to experience shame compared with anger (Boiger, Gungor, Karasawa, & Mesquita, 2014). In contrast, Americans are more likely to experience situations that lead to anger, but not those that lead to shame (Boiger, Mesquita, Uchida, & Barrett, 2013).

Similarly, research comparing the emotional experiences of American and Japanese Olympic athletes when describing their reactions to winning finds that Japanese athletes are more likely than their American counterparts to discuss their relationships when describing their emotions. Furthermore, when participants who read athletes' self-descriptions were asked to infer the emotions an athlete was feeling, Japanese participants inferred more emotions when the athlete mentioned relationships, whereas American participants inferred more emotions when the athlete focused only on herself (Uchida, Townsend, Markus, & Bergsieker, 2009). In other words, for Japanese, emotions are experienced more as interpersonal states that connect people to each other, whereas for Americans, emotions are experienced more as personal states that lie within individuals.

Along a similar line, descriptions of daily emotional experiences were compared among Japanese and Americans (Kitayama et al., 2000). People were provided with a number of emotions that varied on two dimensions and asked how often they experienced them. One dimension was whether the emotion was positive or negative (e.g., happy versus guilty). A second dimension was whether the emotion was interpersonally engaged or disengaged—that is, whether the experience involved connecting with others or distinguishing oneself from others. These two dimensions were combined to form four separate categories of emotions. Some examples of these categories are shown in **Table 10.2**.

The researchers were interested in assessing how good these various emotions felt. Toward this end, they correlated how often participants reported experiencing the positive interpersonally engaged and disengaged emotions with how often they reported feeling some general positive emotions, such as feeling happy, calm, or elated. The

TABLE 10.2

Emotion categories used in Kitayama et al.'s study of emotions associated with happiness

Positive Interpersonally Engaged Emotions	Negative Interpersonally Engaged Emotions
Respect	Ashamed
Shitashimi (friendly feelings)	*Oime* (indebted)
Positive Interpersonally Disengaged Emotions	**Negative Interpersonally Disengaged Emotions**
Proud	Anger
Yuetsukan (superior)	*Futekusare* (sulky feelings)

pattern of correlations was quite striking, as shown in **Table 10.3**. Those Japanese who reported feeling a great deal of positive interpersonally engaged emotions reported a lot more positive feelings in general. In contrast, Americans who reported feeling a great deal of positive interpersonally disengaged emotions reported much more positive feelings in general. In contrast, the positive interpersonally disengaged emotions for Japanese and the positive interpersonally engaged emotions for Americans were not closely tied to general positive feelings. This suggests that Japanese feel especially good when they're focusing on how their emotional experiences lead them to connect with others, whereas Americans feel especially good when they're dwelling on those emotional experiences that distinguish them from others. What makes people feel good appears to vary in important ways across cultures (also see Kitayama, Mesquita, & Karasawa, 2006; Uchida & Kitayama, 2009, for similar findings).

TABLE 10.3

Correlations between different types of positive emotions

	Positive Interpersonally Engaged Emotions and General Positive Emotions	Positive Interpersonally Disengaged Emotions and General Positive Emotions
Japanese	.58	.20
Americans	.30	.54

Cultural Variation in Subjective Well-Being and Happiness

Is happiness necessary for a good life? This is a rather heavy existential question, and it becomes much more challenging when you consider it from a cross-cultural perspective. Happiness is indeed a universal emotion, and people everywhere often pursue activities that make them happy. Happiness feels very good, and it signals to the individual that all is well. Furthermore, much research demonstrates that there are tangible benefits to being happy. For example, happiness is associated with increased longevity and career success, at least in North America where this research has been largely conducted (Lyubomirsky, King, & Diener, 2005). Given that happiness is so pleasurable and apparently has such beneficial consequences, shouldn't people in all cultures strive to maximize their degree of happiness?

Coming up with an answer to this question depends on how one views happiness. Happiness does seem to be a central value among many people from Western cultures. Indeed, the pursuit of happiness has been central enough to American culture that it was described as an "unalienable right" in the Declaration of Independence. This pursuit is alive and well in North America, and much of the West, as evidenced by the findings from many surveys that many Western countries report average levels of happiness that are far above neutral (Veenhoven, 2014).

However, happiness has not always had such a central role in Westerners' lives. In 1843, the British historian Thomas Carlyle noted that, "happiness our being's end and aim' [a famous quote on happiness from the English poet, Alexander Pope] is at bottom, if we will count well, not yet two centuries old in the world." Carlyle was referring to changes during the Enlightenment when the world began to be seen as a more rational and predictable place and happiness was believed to be achievable through efforts to pursue a good life. Prior to this shift, happiness was seen as largely the result of good luck. Indeed, the idea that happiness is a matter of good luck is still evident in most cultures in the world. When Oishi, Graham, Kesebir, and Galinha (2013) examined dictionary definitions of the word "happiness" in 30 countries, they found that definitions of happiness that included luck were in the dictionaries in all the countries except the United States, Spain, Argentina, Ecuador, India and Kenya. Perhaps not surprising, people who live in countries where happiness is defined as good luck report feeling less happy than those where luck is not seen as an important part of the definition.

Moreover, looking at definitions across time in American dictionaries reveals that the definition of happiness included the concept of good luck until 1961. Also, the same authors looked at how frequently the expressions "happy nation" and "happy person" were used in a Google NGram database of American books and found that uses of the term "happy nation" have steadily dropped over time, whereas the term

FIGURE 10.12 According to the Google NGram database of books published in the U.S., the use of the term "happy nation" has slowly dropped over time, whereas the use of the term "happy person" has steadily increased since the 1920s.

"happy person" has steadily risen (**Figure 10.12**). This suggests that happiness has been transformed over time in American English to reflect more of an individual's state, as opposed to that of a collective.

What does the cross-cultural literature have to say about happiness around the world? A great deal of research has explored how positive emotional experiences are distributed around the world. Much of this research has investigated cultural differences in **subjective well-being.** Subjective well-being is the feeling of how satisfied one is with one's life. Research consistently reveals that there are pronounced cultural differences in subjective well-being. In general, the nations that score highest on this measure are Scandinavian and Nordic countries, much of Latin America, various English-speaking countries, and Western Europe. On the low end are the former Soviet republics and some impoverished countries in Africa and South Asia (Diener, Diener, & Diener, 1995; Inglehart & Klingemann, 2000; Veenhoven, 2014). Around the world, people are not equally satisfied with their lives.

Well-being varies not only across cultures but across regions within cultures. In one investigation, various measures of subjective well-being were contrasted across five regions of the United States: New England, the Mountain region, West South

Central, West North Central, and East South Central (the researchers were unable to collect data from other regions; Plaut, Markus, & Lachman, 2002). Participants from each region evaluated their well-being in terms of their health, their sense of autonomy, their satisfaction with their identities, their emotions, their relations with others, and their sense of social responsibility. The researchers standardized their results so that people in each region could be compared with people from other regions on their well-being on these dimensions (i.e., positive z scores indicate that a region had scores that were on average higher than the national average). As can be seen in **Figure 10.13**, there was much variation in the well-being profiles across the country. People in New England and the Mountain states, on average, were faring better on most domains of well-being than other regions in the country were. Well-being thus varies both across countries and across regions within countries. Why would rates of well-being differ across cultures?

Many factors contribute to the overall satisfaction that people have with their lives. A not surprising one is wealth. On average, people who live in countries in which they have access to enough wealth to easily meet the basic needs of life tend to be considerably more satisfied than those who do not. Indeed, some of the

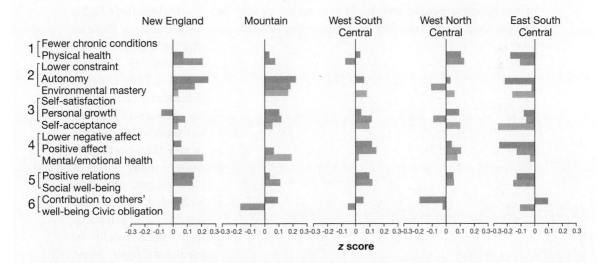

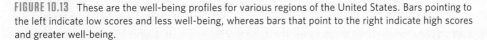

FIGURE 10.13 These are the well-being profiles for various regions of the United States. Bars pointing to the left indicate low scores and less well-being, whereas bars that point to the right indicate high scores and greater well-being.

least satisfied people in the international comparisons come from countries such as Bangladesh and Cameroon where many people don't have adequate food and clean water to survive easily. However, the relation between money and happiness is not universally strong. Money and happiness seem to be most closely connected at very low levels of wealth, where a few extra dollars can make the difference between surviving or not. For example, a strong correlation of .45 was found between income and life satisfaction among respondents in the slums of Calcutta (Biswas-Diener & Diener, 2002). The relation between income and subjective well-being is much smaller in developed nations, although it is still positive (Diener & Biswas-Diener, 2002). On average, once a country has an average GDP of at least 40% of that of the United States, there is no longer any pronounced relation between money and subjective well-being (Diener, Diener, & Diener, 1995). In sum, money can buy a lot of happiness if you're struggling to survive; however, it has much less impact if your basic needs have been met.

Another factor that predicts the subjective well-being of nations is human rights. On average, those countries that promote human rights the most tend to have the happiest citizens. Conversely, those countries in which people live under the constant threat of being thrown in jail for suspicions of plotting against the government are, on average, not as happy. The overall equality among people in a country is also associated with greater subjective well-being (Diener et al., 1995). The Scandinavian and Nordic nations, which have various social policies to minimize differences in opportunities among its citizens, tend to have some of the happiest people around. It seems that people feel good when their rights are not threatened and they have opportunities that are comparable to those of their neighbors.

These are the factors that have emerged consistently across studies. However, they do not seem to be the only factors that matter, because many nations have average subjective well-being scores that depart considerably from what would be predicted from these factors alone. In particular, many countries in Latin America show

"Right. Money isn't everything—what's the other thing again?"

average subjective well-being scores that are much higher than would be predicted by the variables of wealth, human rights, and equality (Diener, 2001), whereas countries in East Asia show much lower subjective well-being scores than would be predicted by these factors (Diener, Suh, Smith, & Shao, 1995). There must be other factors that influence well-being that have yet to be reliably identified.

The above research shows that a variety of factors predict subjective well-being in *similar* ways across nations. However, there also appear to be some factors that predict life satisfaction *differently* across cultures. Consider the question of whether the "good life" can be attained mostly by doing what a person would *like* to do or by doing what a person thinks he or she *should* do. In what kinds of cultural contexts might we expect people to base their life satisfaction on whether they are doing the kinds of things they would like to do? It would seem that if people have a more independent view of self, satisfaction with their lives should be based on whether they feel they are acting in ways consistent with their inner desires. If you recall, people with independent selves tend to view their identity as being grounded in inner attributes, such as their personality traits, attitudes, and opinions. If someone acts in ways consistent with those inner attributes, it should feel good, because this would represent a culturally appropriate way of being—that is, a good life, independent style. This question was investigated by exploring whether feelings of life satisfaction are more highly correlated with overall positive affect in individualistic cultures than in collectivist cultures (Suh, Diener, Oishi, & Triandis, 1998). Indeed, there was clear evidence to support this: People in individualistic societies were far more likely than those in collectivist societies to base their life satisfaction on how many positive emotions they were experiencing. Positive emotions appear to be seen as the basis of a good life in individualistic cultures.

So what is life satisfaction based on for people with more interdependent selves? Suh and colleagues reasoned that people with interdependent selves would feel good about their lives if they were living up to others' standards for being a good person. That is, if they felt they were highly respected by others, they might feel very good about their lives. Indeed, people in collectivistic cultures showed a higher correlation between their life-satisfaction scores and being respected by others for living up to cultural norms when compared with people from individualistic cultures. Living up to cultural norms seems to be viewed as the basis of a good life in collectivistic cultures.

Another key factor that influences people's judgments of life satisfaction is which theory they embrace regarding how happy they think they should feel. Some people think life should be full of happy experiences, whereas others believe life should consist of both the happy and sad times. The theory that you endorse will influence how you make sense of your satisfaction, regardless of your actual daily experiences. Consider the following study (Oishi, 2002). American participants were asked to complete a brief questionnaire at the end of every day to indicate how satisfied they had been that day. After doing this for 7 days, participants were also asked to think back over the past week in which they had been completing the questionnaire and to indicate how satisfied they had been with that week. The participants were divided into two samples: those of European descent and those of Asian descent. Participants from other cultural backgrounds were not included in the study.

The findings were quite revealing, as can be seen in **Figure 10.14**. When people looked back at their weeks, the European-Americans remembered having a much better week than the Asian-Americans did. At first glance, this difference would seem to suggest that the European-Americans encountered more satisfying events in their week than the Asian-Americans. However, if you look at the right side of the graph, you see how positively the participants rated their satisfaction each day of the week. There was no cultural difference here. That is, it seems that European-Americans and Asian-Americans were having comparable weeks in terms of the satisfying events that they experience, but the European-Americans were remembering their weeks as having been better than they really were, whereas the Asian-Americans seemed to be

FIGURE 10.14   European-Americans and Asian-Americans gave similar overall satisfaction ratings about their daily experiences. However, when both groups looked back on their experiences, European-Americans recalled them as being more satisfying than Asian-Americans did. This finding suggests that the recollections of European-Americans are being shaped by a theory that life should be more happy than the theory held by Asian-Americans.

remembering their weeks as having been about as good as they had experienced them. What can we make of this finding?

It seems that when people reflect on their day, they recall the events that happened and rate their satisfaction accordingly. However, when they consider a longer period, their estimates are more likely to reflect the theories they hold about what life should be like (e.g., Robinson & Clore, 2002). European-Americans appear to be operating under an implicit theory that they should be happy, whereas Asian-Americans seem to operate under the theory that emotional experience, like other aspects of life, should be balanced and consist of both positive and negative experiences (Rodgers, Peng, Wang, & Hou, 2004). This dialectical view on emotions means that East Asians can simultaneously experience both positive and negative emotions (Miyamoto, Uchida, & Ellsworth, 2010). These findings indicate that when people think back over their lives, they are likely to interpret their feelings with respect to these culturally divergent theories, but when they consider their feelings at a given time, those theories do not come much into play. It is quite possible that many of the observed cultural differences in subjective well-being are based on the different theories that people from different cultures have about how they should be feeling about their lives.

Interpreting cultural differences in happiness is made more difficult by the findings that positive emotions appear to have different meanings and consequences across cultures. A guiding assumption underlying research on happiness is the expectation that people necessarily want to be happy and that it would always be better if one were only a little bit happier. But this notion that happiness as "our being's end and aim" is found equally across cultures appears to be questionable. Consider for a moment why it is that you chose your college major. Was it because it seemed like the prudent thing to do, or did you think that having this particular major would ultimately make your life happier than if you didn't have it? Do we make decisions in our lives to make ourselves feel happier?

One study investigated the role of predicting happy feelings when making decisions. Canadian students were asked to make a number of forced-choice decisions. For example, they were provided a description of two different computer games and were asked to choose one of them to play. One of the games was described as being quite fun and enjoyable, whereas the other was described as one that could improve one's thinking skills and boost one's grades. The results indicated that European-Canadians were more likely to choose the fun game, whereas Asian-Canadians were more likely to choose the useful game (Falk, Dunn, & Norenzayan, 2010). Similar findings emerged when students were asked to select university courses from a fictitious set of course descriptions; European-Canadians were more likely to choose the courses that sounded fun and interesting compared with Asian-Canadians, who focused more on the perceived utility of the courses. Asian-Canadians seem less interested in the idea of doing things for the sake of anticipated positive feelings compared with European-Canadians. Life appears to be less about a pursuit of happiness for people with Asian cultural experiences than it does for Westerners.

One reason that Asians might be less interested in positive feelings compared with Westerners is that there may be fewer benefits for them of having especially positive feelings. There is some evidence for this: Whereas European-Americans who report experiencing many positive emotions also report experiencing less depression, East Asians who report having many positive emotions are no less at risk for depression than those East Asians who report having very few positive emotions (Leu, Wang, & Koo, 2011). That is, positive feelings do not seem to carry the same protection against depression in East Asia. Perhaps it's because positive feelings do not have the same beneficial consequences in East Asia that research finds that happiness-boosting activities do not seem to be as effective among East Asians as they are among Westerners (Layous, Lee, Choi, & Lyubomirsky, 2013).

Similarly, experiencing negative emotions does not appear to have the same consequences across cultures. Consider this quote from the Russian heroine of Woody Allen's 1975 satire of Russian novels, *Love and Death:* "To love is to suffer. To avoid suffering one must not love. But then one suffers from not loving. Therefore to love is to suffer; not to love is to suffer; to suffer is to suffer. To be happy is to love. To be happy, then, is to suffer, but suffering makes one unhappy. Therefore, to be unhappy, one must love or love to suffer or suffer from too much happiness. I hope you're getting this down." Woody Allen here is having fun with the stereotype that Russians live to suffer—that they dwell on all that is miserable in their lives and wallow in their despair. This is an observation that is commonly made about the Russian character. "That dark Russian spirit, brooding and complicated—Religion, society and morality are all tied up in the distrust of any amount of happiness. Even the children are worried all the time" (Wagman, 2008). It would follow that if the Russian stereotype is accurate, then all this dark brooding would be associated with increased levels of depression. But is this true?

To investigate this question, Russians and Americans were asked to read some vignettes in which a target has done something that has made her feel upset (Grossmann & Kross, 2010). For some of the vignettes, the target analyzes her feelings about why she's upset, whereas in the others she does not analyze her feelings. Participants were asked to indicate which of the vignettes more closely resembled their own coping tendencies. In addition, participants completed a measure of depression. The findings? Russians were more likely to identify with the target that reflected on her feelings than Americans did, reflecting the stereotype of the Russian brooder. Moreover, whereas those Americans who identified with the self-reflective target were more depressed than those who did not identify with that target, for Russians there was a trend in the opposite direction. Self-reflective Americans were considerably more depressed than self-reflective Russians. Similar findings emerged with other measures. This suggests that brooding over one's negative emotions, although common in Russia, does not lead Russians to feel more depressed, as it does for Americans. Wallowing in one's negative self-feelings does not have the same consequences across cultures.

The question of cultural variation in happiness is further complicated in that the *kinds* of positive emotions people desire also seem to vary considerably across cultures. Not all positive emotions are created equal. Some positive emotions, such as excitement and elation, involve a great deal of arousal. Other positive emotions, such as feeling calm or at peace, involve a low degree of arousal. Research by Jeanne Tsai and colleagues (Tsai, Knutson, & Fung, 2006) reveals that these two kinds of positive emotions are sought after differently by Americans and East Asians. Tsai and colleagues propose the notion of **ideal affect**—the kinds of feelings that people desire. They are the emotions that people are trying to achieve, so they structure their lives in order to increase the likelihood that they will experience these emotions. For most Americans, ideal affect contains positive emotions that are high in arousal, whereas for most East Asians ideal affect contains positive emotions that are low in arousal.

There is much evidence for this cultural difference across a wide array of life activities between the two cultural groups. For example, a comparison of facial expressions that were shown in characters in American and Taiwanese children's storybooks revealed that the American faces more often showed feelings of excitement and had significantly bigger smiles than the Taiwanese faces. The authors of these books seem to be aware of what their audiences want, as subsequent analyses revealed that European-American preschool children preferred the pictures of excited faces more than the Taiwanese preschoolers did, and they also felt more similar to the characters who were engaged in high-arousal activities; the Taiwanese children felt more similar to the characters engaged in low-arousal activities (Tsai, Louie, Chen, & Uchida, 2006).

Further evidence for this cultural difference can be seen in Christian and Buddhist teachings and practices. A content analysis of classic Christian and Buddhist texts (e.g., the Gospels of the Bible and the Lotus Sutra) as well as contemporary Christian and Buddhist self-help books revealed that high-arousal states were encouraged more in the Christian texts whereas low-arousal states were encouraged more in the Buddhist texts. Furthermore, some Christian sects include enthusiastic religious practices such as jumping, shouting, and applause; Buddhist religious practices emphasize meditation and the calming of one's mind (Tsai, Miao, & Seppala, 2007).

In addition, various activities encourage high- or low-arousal states, and cultures differ in the frequency with which they practice those activities. For example, European-Americans are more likely to engage in active individual activities such as jogging or rollerblading, whereas Asian-Americans are more likely to engage in passive activities such as sightseeing and picnicking (Gobster & Delgado, 1992;

FIGURE 10.15 East Asians are more likely than Americans to prefer low-arousal activities, and are less likely than Americans to prefer high-arousal activities.

see **Figure 10.15**). European-Americans are more likely to prefer fast-tempo and exciting music, whereas Chinese are more likely to prefer calm music (Tsai, Miao, & Seppala, 2007). In sum, European-Americans are more likely to engage in activities that lead to high-arousal positive states, whereas those from East Asian backgrounds aspire for more low-arousal positive states. Recent research reveals that Latin Americans prefer high-arousal positive emotions at least as much as (if not more than) Canadians or Americans (Ruby, Falk, Silberstein, Villa, & Heine, 2012). The pursuit of happiness across cultures, then, also appears to depend on the kinds of positive emotions people desire.

What can we conclude about cultural variation in the pursuit of happiness? First, it appears that cultures do differ in the average degree of well-being they experience and that these differences hinge, in part, on some universal relations between well-being and such variables as wealth (at low ends of the wealth spectrum), human rights, and equality. However, the question is also complicated because people in different cultures view happiness and positive emotions in quite different terms. Among Westerners, interpersonally disengaging acts feel especially good, subjective well-being is associated with positive feelings, people operate under the implicit theory that more positive feelings are better, positive emotions serve as a bulwark against depression, and high-arousal positive emotions are preferred. Among East Asians, in contrast, interpersonally engaging acts feel especially good, subjective well-being is associated with appropriate role behaviors, people operate under the implicit theory that it is good to experience both positive and negative feelings, positive emotions are not associated with less depression, and low-arousal positive emotions are more sought after. Cultures vary in their happiness, in part, because they have quite different ideas about what happiness is and what it is derived from.

Conclusions Regarding Cultural Variation in Emotions

The field of culture and emotions has experienced considerable debate regarding the role of culture in shaping the emotions. Much of this debate grows out of researchers' different conceptions of emotions and of the aspects of emotions they study. What can we conclude about cultural variation in emotional experience?

If we focus on facial expressions, there is good evidence for universality in emotions around the world. For the most part, people are universally adept at producing and recognizing facial expressions associated with the basic emotions. There is no evidence for accessibility universals here, however, because people perform worse when evaluating the facial expressions of those from other cultures than from their own.

Looking at emotional experience, there is more evidence for cultural diversity. People from different cultures vary in the intensity with which they experience emotions, the kinds of things that they feel best about, and the degree to which they experience positive versus negative feelings. Emotional experience varies more across cultures than people's facial expressions for the basic emotions.

Last, considering the emotional lexicon, there is tremendous variability in the kinds of words that people use to describe their experiences. Cultures vary not only in the number of emotion words that they have but also in the ways they carve up the emotional space, with many English emotion words not existing in other languages, and many non-English emotion words not existing in English.

SUMMARY

There is considerable debate about the best way to conceive of emotions. Some theories have focused more on the physiological markers of emotions; others focus more on the interpretive aspects of emotions. In general, theories that focus on the physiological aspects of emotions predict less cultural variability, while theories that focus on interpretive aspects of emotions expect much cultural variability.

Research on facial expressions reveals much consistency around the world in the ways that people recognize the basic emotions of fear, anger, happiness, sadness, surprise, and disgust. These expressions are not the product of cultural learning but reflect universal physiological reactions. However, some aspects of the ways people express their emotions are shaped by cultural learning, and people are less accurate at recognizing facial expressions of people from different cultures than of people from their own culture.

Cultures vary in the display rules that shape how emotions are expressed. Display rules guide both the intensity with which emotions are expressed and the ways they are expressed. Some cultures communicate their emotions more directly, whereas others express them in more moderated form.

Cultures vary tremendously in their vocabulary for emotions. Some cultures have many more emotion words than others, and there is often little overlap between these emotion words. For example, terms for the basic emotions are not represented in all languages, and many emotion words from other languages do not exist in English.

People with interdependent selves are more likely to interpret situations with regard to relational concerns than are people with independent selves. Also, people with interdependent selves are more likely to feel happy when they have interpersonally engaged positive emotions, whereas people with independent selves are more likely to feel happy when they experience interpersonally disengaged positive emotions.

Cultures around the world vary considerably in their degrees of subjective well-being. Subjective well-being is affected by such variables as wealth, protection of human rights, and income equality. People's reporting of their subjective well-being is also affected by whether they believe that life should be consistently good or that life is inherently composed of both good and bad events. Furthermore, some kinds of positive feelings, such as high-arousal states, are more desired in Western cultures, whereas low-arousal positive feelings are more desired among East Asian populations.

THINK ABOUT IT

1. Do you think you can experience the emotion *liget* in the same was as an Ilongot does? On what basis did you come up with an answer to this?
2. What is the primary difference between the James-Lange and the Two-Factor theories of emotion?
3. If you expressed your emotions with your face, would people from all over the world be equally accurate at identifying how you're feeling? Who do you think would be worst at accurately identifying your feelings?
4. Why do cultures vary in terms of what part of the face they attend to when judging other people's facial expressions?
5. How do cultural display rules influence the emotions that people actually experience?
6. Do you think you experience the emotion *schadenfreude* in the same way and to the same degree as the average German speaker?

7. Do you think the pursuit of happiness should be equally valued across cultures?
8. Why do you think that North Americans and Latin Americans tend to value high-arousal positive emotions more than East Asians do?

KEY TERMS

James-Lange Theory of
    Emotions, 404
Two-Factor Theory of
    Emotions, 405

Display Rules, 417
Ritualized Display, 418
Facial Feedback
    Hypothesis, 419

Subjective Well-Being, 430
Ideal Affect, 437

At this wedding ceremony in Guatemala, as in other parts of Latin America, *simpático* is a highly valued relational style.

11

INTERPERSONAL ATTRACTION AND CLOSE RELATIONSHIPS

ere's an observation of mine: Ryan Reynolds and Scarlett Johansson are two very attractive people (**Figure 11.1**). You might agree. In 2010, *People* and *GQ* anointed them "Sexiest Man Alive" and "Babe of the Year" respectively. So there seems to be some consensus among us that as physical attractiveness goes, Ryan Reynolds and Scarlett Johansson are about as good as it gets. But most of the readers of *People* and *GQ* and myself share a common cultural context. Most of us live in the West, watch movies that are by and large made in Hollywood, and see the same magazine covers in the checkout lines. So all of this raises an important question: Do people share the same standards of physical attractiveness around the world? Would Ryan Reynolds and Scarlett Johansson cause heads to turn in other parts of the world as well?

This chapter explores how culture shapes the ways people relate to others. It considers how people are attracted to others and how they form close relationships. We will consider such questions as these: How universal are standards

FIGURE 11.1 Scarlett Johansson and Ryan Reynolds are certainly considered attractive in the West. Would they be seen as attractive everywhere?

of interpersonal attraction? What kinds of relationships exist across cultures? Does the nature of friendships and romantic relationships vary across cultures? Our investigations of these and other questions are guided by a consideration of how people's experiences in their cultures shape their thinking, and we will also focus squarely on the contrast of universal versus culturally relative psychologies.

Interpersonal Attraction

Physical Attractiveness

Returning to the example of Ryan Reynolds and Scarlett Johansson, are there universal standards of attractiveness around the world? In answering that question we need to contrast the similarities and differences in the ways people go about trying to make themselves more attractive. A glance at some bodily decoration strategies around the world reveals a good deal of cultural variation in what is viewed as attractive (**Figure 11.2**). Consider the different ways people alter their faces to make themselves beautiful. Among the Paduang in Thailand, women elongate their necks by several inches by inserting an increasing number of brass rings around their necks as they grow up. Among the Mursi in Ethiopia, women stretch their lower lips by inserting progressively larger ceramic disks in a hole that has been cut through the lip. Mentawai women from Indonesia file their teeth into sharp points so they have smiles not that different from a shark. Ainu women of northern Japan often tattoo their faces in what looks like a moustache around their lips. Western women darken their eyelashes with mascara, trim their eyebrows, and paint their lips with lipstick. Indeed, it would seem that if anything is influenced by cultural norms and context, fashion would have to be near the top of the list. Moreover, it's not a coincidence that all of these examples of bodily decoration are of women, as around the world physical attractiveness is a more significant factor in interpersonal attraction for women than it is for men (although it's certainly also an important concern for men; Buss, 1989).

Charles Darwin (1871) too was struck by the cultural diversity in standards for what is considered an attractive face. Yet he also noticed some similarities across cultures, as he stated in one of his books: "Mr. Winwood Reade . . . who has had ample opportunities for observation, not only with the Negroes of the west coast of Africa, but those of the interior who have never associated with Europeans, is convinced that their ideas of beauty are, on the whole, the same as ours." Much research has supported Darwin's friend's observations that, despite the stunning array of fickle strategies humans adopt to make themselves more physically appealing, there are numerous commonalities across cultures in what is perceived as attractive (e.g., Cunningham, Roberts, Barbee, Druen, & Wu, 1995).

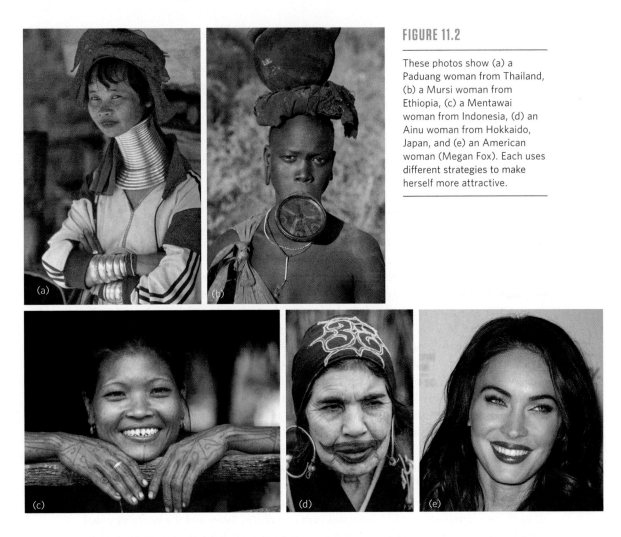

FIGURE 11.2

These photos show (a) a Paduang woman from Thailand, (b) a Mursi woman from Ethiopia, (c) a Mentawai woman from Indonesia, (d) an Ainu woman from Hokkaido, Japan, and (e) an American woman (Megan Fox). Each uses different strategies to make herself more attractive.

First, what kinds of faces are thought of as attractive? One variable that matters is complexion. Around the world there appears to be striking agreement here. Skin that looks free of blemishes, blotches, sores, and rashes is viewed as more attractive than skin that does not (Ford & Beach, 1951; Montagu, 1986). Indeed, a sizable portion of the multibillion-dollar cosmetics industry is directed at selling products that conceal anything that makes one's skin appear less than pristine. Why would people be so concerned with their complexions? According to evolutionary reasoning, people should be especially attracted to healthy mates who would likely produce healthy offspring that would survive. Note that this doesn't mean that people are consciously thinking about selecting healthy mates, but that their unconscious preferences for traits that are associated with health have been guided by natural selection. We do not know for sure how healthy people are by looking at them; however, blemishes and sores on their skin could be useful (although far from perfect) indicators regarding the presence of parasites or diseases. Responding to the apparent health of the skin could thus have been a useful heuristic for sizing up the health of one's potential mate in the ancestral environment. Our ancestors who preferred blemish-free skin would have been more likely to have healthy mates and to produce surviving offspring. As such, over time, preferences for perfect skin would have become more common in the human gene pool.

A second characteristic that appears to be universally viewed as attractive is bilateral symmetry. Simply put, we are most attracted to people whose left sides of their faces and bodies look identical to their right sides. The reason for this, according to evolutionary biologists (e.g., Gangestad, Thornhill, & Yeo, 1994), is that bilateral symmetry is an indicator of developmental stability. Given ideal growing conditions, an organism's right and left sides will develop identically. However, genetic mutations, pollution, pathogens, and stresses encountered in the womb can lead organisms to develop in slightly asymmetrical ways. The more asymmetrical someone is, the more likely he or she is to have various genetic mutations or to have developed in less than ideal circumstances, and the less likely the person is to be in prime health. Everyone has certain degrees of asymmetry and, in general, the less symmetrical someone appears, the less attractive he or she is perceived to be. An attraction to symmetry appears to be so fundamental that it is not limited to humans. Even more symmetrical scorpion flies are perceived as more attractive by other flies (i.e., they get more mates) than less symmetrical ones (Thornhill, 1992).

Thus far, evidence that people prefer symmetrical faces to asymmetrical ones has been found in all cultures studied, however, the preference for symmetry is even stronger in hunting-gathering populations, such as the Hadza in Tanzania (Little, Apicella, & Marlowe, 2007). Because the Hadza suffer from higher rates of infant mortality than cultures in industrialized societies, they should be especially attracted to any indicator of the health of their mates as a means of increasing their odds of having surviving offspring.

A third characteristic of attractive faces is that they tend to be average. Not average in the sense that we are especially attracted to people who are average in their attractiveness. Instead, this means that facial features that are close to the average in size and in configuration are perceived as most attractive. With a few notable exceptions (e.g., men tend to prefer some youthful features in women, whereas women prefer some masculine features in men; Cunningham, 1986; Cunningham, Barbee, & Pike, 1990), average-size noses, average-size eyes, average-size smiles, and average-size distances between the eyes, and so on are perceived as most attractive. At least two mechanisms seem to be at work here. First, people with average-size features are less likely to have genetic abnormalities than people with deviant features, thus reflecting genetic health (Rhodes et al., 2001). A second reason people prefer average features is that humans can quickly process something that resembles a prototype, and quick processing is associated with good feelings and feelings of attraction (Winkielman & Cacioppo, 2001). Average faces can be thought of as prototypes of faces.

Interestingly, the attractiveness of average faces appears to also hold in terms of how people view the attractiveness of those from other cultures, too, provided that they have had experiences with people from the other culture under study (Apicella, Little, & Marlowe, 2007). In one study, the faces of a number of European-Australians and a number of Japanese were averaged together, both within and across cultures, using computer software (Rhodes et al., 2005). In addition, faces from a number of Eurasians (i.e., people with both European and Asian ancestry) were averaged. Participants in both cultures viewed the average faces to be most attractive, regardless of the faces' culture of origin. The researchers also averaged the Australian and Japanese faces together. They found that the averaged Eurasian face and the averaged biracial face were the most attractive of all, particularly as judged by members of the opposite sex (**Figure 11.3**). Similar findings have emerged in looking at biracial

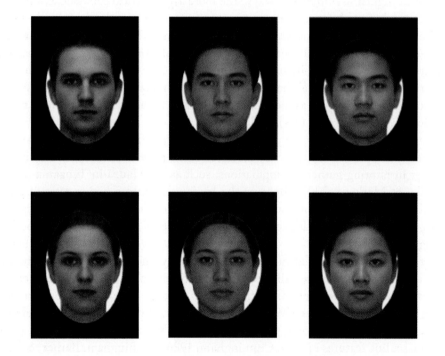

FIGURE 11.3 Average faces tend to be especially attractive. These photos were all created by averaging several other photos together. The photos on the left are averaged faces of Caucasian Australians, the photos on the right are averaged faces of Japanese, and the photos in the center are averaged faces of Eurasians. Most people find the averaged Eurasian faces to be the most attractive of the set of photos (Rhodes et al., 2005).

faces of Europeans and Africans (Little, Hockings, Apicella, & Sousa, 2012). It is not certain why multiracial faces are perceived as so attractive—one account is that people should be attracted to genetic diversity as a marker of healthy genes (Roberts et al., 2005). Another explanation is that multiracial represent the best average of all the faces the participants have encountered in their lives. Extending from this we would expect that a face that was the average of faces from all cultures in the world would be seen as the most attractive of all, especially in multicultural societies where people are exposed to faces from many different cultures.

The attractiveness of average features, however, does not seem to generalize well to perception of bodies. In general, it does not seem to be true that people are most attracted to those of average weight, average height, with average-size muscles, breasts, hips, and so on. Rather, the kinds of bodies that tend to be seen as most attractive are often those that depart considerably from the average.

One aspect of people's bodies that varies considerably in its perceived attractiveness across cultures (in particular for the perceived attractiveness of women) is weight. If you were to look at the covers of women's magazines in the West today, you likely would conclude that the kind of female body viewed as attractive is remarkably thin. If you opened those magazines and read some of the articles, you would also find a great deal of attention placed on weight loss, new diets, exercise regimes, and the occasional story about the high prevalence of eating disorders. Given how ubiquitous the images are for thin female models in Western culture, you might be tempted to conclude that preferences for thin female bodies are universal. Such a conclusion, however, would be grossly incorrect. Consider the conclusion about attractive bodies reached by Ford and Beach, an anthropologist and psychologist who wrote a highly influential book titled *Patterns of Sexual Behavior*. They looked at the standards of beauty in the United States in 1951 in conjunction with the standards of beauty they saw in the rest of the world's cultures; they concluded that it was a human universal that *heavier* women are viewed as the most attractive. The female models that currently grace the covers of fashion magazines prove that Ford and Beach's conclusion is obviously incorrect—at least in Western culture today, thin seems to be in.

The changes in the standards of what constitutes an especially beautiful female body as it was seen in the United States in 1951 and today are quite dramatic. The shift is even more dramatic when you look at the kinds of bodies that were glorified in the days of Peter Paul Rubens or Pierre-Auguste Renoir (**Figure 11.4**). What was prized as the ideal female form then is not the same as what appears to be prized now. The cultural differences in standards of beauty for female bodies differ not just across historical context but across current cultural ones as well. Much research has found that in some cultures people view the ideal female body to be far heavier than what is typically preferred among Westerners. The preference in many cultures within Africa is for heavier body weights for both men and women compared with the norms in the West (Cogan, Bhalla, Sefa-Dedeh, & Rothblum, 1996), and this has also been

FIGURE 11.4   The norms for an attractive female body have changed over time. (From left to right) Peter Paul Rubens's "The Three Graces" (1639), Auguste Renoir's "Nude Woman Seated" (1876), and British actress Keira Knightley (2013).

traditionally so in the South Pacific (Pollack, 1995). Indeed, in West Africa, the term "fat" is often viewed as complimentary, indicating strength and beauty (Cassidy, 1991). Within the United States as well, African-Americans have heavier ideal body weights than European-Americans and feel less social pressure toward thinness (Kumanyika, Wilson, & Guilford-Davenport, 1993; Neff, Sargent, McKeown, & Jackson, 1997). However, there are also signs that the beauty ideals that are embraced in the wealthy West are viewed as markers of high status and, to a certain degree, are spreading to some other parts of the world (e.g., Hall, 2013; Swami et al., 2010; Williams, Ricciardelli, McCabe, Waqa, & Bavadra, 2006). Nonetheless, there has been much variation in the kinds of bodies that are viewed as most attractive across time and place.

Hence, research suggests that although there is tremendous cultural variation in the ways that people make themselves fashionable, there is also much that humans agree on with respect to who is beautiful. Ryan Reynolds and Scarlett Johansson, in all likelihood, would be viewed as attractive anywhere they go, given their symmetry, clear complexion, and average-size features. However, they likely wouldn't be seen as the most beautiful people in some other contexts because there are specific cultural norms for attractiveness that they wouldn't meet. For example, Scarlett Johansson could perhaps boost her perceived attractiveness among Africans if she gained several pounds, and she could attract the attention of more Paduang if she stretched her neck a few inches. There are both universal and culturally specific features of physical attractiveness.

Other Bases of Interpersonal Attraction

Aside from physical characteristics, other processes influence whether we're attracted to someone either as a friend or a romantic partner. I'm going to go out on a limb and guess that none of the readers of this book are best friends with Rugi Ngoma from the village of Chitimba, Malawi. Am I correct? Well, then, please consider who your best friend is. Now think for a minute how you ended up becoming so close to your best friend but not with Rugi. Well, one difference between your best friend and Rugi is that you've surely met your best friend, and I'm guessing that you probably haven't met Rugi. This rather obvious point underscores an important aspect of how people form interpersonal relationships, known as the **propinquity effect** (Festinger, Schacter, & Back, 1950): People are more likely to become friends with people with whom they frequently interact. Pretty straightforward stuff. Recently, the Internet has allowed for many relationships to develop in cyberspace, but these still are based on interactions, virtual as they may be. Of relevance for cultural psychology, it is difficult to imagine a culture in which the propinquity effect would not hold true. It would seem to be a good candidate for an accessibility universal.

I imagine that the propinquity effect does not strike you as especially profound. It might even seem kind of silly to think that people have spent time and resources to research something as obvious as this. But a couple of features of the propinquity effect are not as obvious as they might seem. First, it is surprising to learn how powerful it is. People generally realize that they are more likely to develop relationships with people they see more frequently, although they probably don't realize just how much this affects their choice of friendships. Consider the friendships that were developed at the Maryland Police Academy in the early 1970s (Segal, 1974). At this academy, the new recruits were lined up in the alphabetical order of their last names, and this order influenced where they sat in class and where their dorm rooms were located. One study investigated the friendships that developed among the new police recruits. They were asked to nominate their closest friend at the academy. These nominations are presented in **Figure 11.5**. The numbers along the x and y axes represent the names of the recruits in alphabetical order. If people had based their choices of friends on something other than the alphabetical order of their names, the dots would be scattered randomly across the figure. In reality, as you can see, the choices of friends cluster closely toward the diagonal of the figure, meaning that the alphabetical ordering of the recruits' last names played a large role in determining whom they chose as friends. In fact, 45% of all the friendships were among those whose last name was adjacent to the chooser's name in alphabetical order, and the majority of

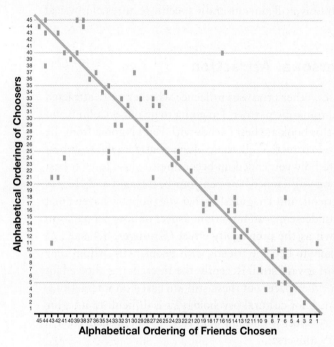

FIGURE 11.5

Trainees at the Maryland State Police Training Academy indicated whom among their fellow trainees they had befriended. The numbers along the bottom indicate the alphabetical order of friends chosen, whereas the numbers on the left indicate the alphabetical order of the choosers (Segal, 1974).

the other friendships were with people whose last names were within a few letters of the chooser's last name. The simple fact of who stood next to whom was more important in influencing these police recruits' selection of friends than their personalities, backgrounds, or religious beliefs. This study demonstrates how, in many ways, our friendships are not so much chosen by us but are chosen by the situational forces that bring us together.

A second nonobvious fact of the propinquity effect is in how it operates. One important basis of why propinquity is attractive is known as the **mere exposure effect**. That is, the more we are exposed to a stimulus the more we are attracted to it. This has been shown to be true for attraction to other people, foreign words, music, and a variety of inanimate stimuli. The attraction to frequently encountered stimuli appears to be due to the pleasant associations developed through classical conditioning, when one learns that a stimulus is not threatening (Zajonc, 2005) and to the pleasant affect associated with easy-to-process stimuli (Winkielman & Cacioppo, 2001). In addition, the mere exposure effect appears to be a cultural universal. For example, Japanese and Americans appear to be equally likely to come to like those people with whom they interact most frequently (Heine & Renshaw, 2002). This cross-cultural similarity in the mere exposure effect is not a surprise. Indeed, Zajonc and colleagues (1975) found that even chickens are more attracted to those chickens they had been exposed to the most. If chickens and American participants are showing evidence of the same psychological processes, then we shouldn't be surprised to learn that people from different cultures exhibit evidence of the same processes as well.

Similarity-Attraction Effect

Another powerful predictor of attraction is the **similarity-attraction effect.** People tend to be attracted to those who are most like themselves. Much research has shown that people are more likely to view someone as attractive either as a potential friend or a romantic partner if both are similar in their attitudes, economic background, personality, religion, social background, and activities (e.g., Byrne, 1961; Lydon, Jamieson, & Zanna, 1988; Newcomb, 1961). The similarity-attraction effect is one of the most powerful and reliably found predictors of whether people will become friends or romantic partners.

How universal is the similarity-attraction effect? In the study with the chickens described earlier, Zajonc and colleagues also investigated whether chickens were attracted to similar others. The chickens in that study were dyed either green or red while still in their eggs to make them look either similar to or different from each other. It turned out that the chickens showed no hint whatsoever of a similarity-attraction effect. They were not any more attracted to the similarly colored chickens than to the differently colored ones. This raises the possibility that the similarity-attraction effect is not as fundamental a psychological process as the mere exposure effect, since it is not found as broadly across species.

Does the similarity-attraction effect operate similarly in different cultures? Like many other psychological phenomena, the similarity-attraction effect has been studied almost exclusively in Western cultural contexts, where the evidence for its existence is quite unassailable. What might we find if we looked in a non-Western context? My colleagues and I explored this question by contrasting the similarity-attraction effect between Japanese and North Americans (Heine, Foster, & Spina, 2009). For example, in one study we had Japanese and Canadian participants come into a lab where they briefly met a stranger of the same sex and nationality. They then went into separate rooms and completed either a personality measure or a measure of their social background. Next they were shown what was apparently the personality or social background measure of the stranger. However, the profile of the stranger the participants saw had actually been filled out by the experimenter, who had made these "responses" highly similar to those of the participant (a high-similarity condition) or quite dissimilar (a low-similarity condition). Participants were then asked to indicate how much they felt they would like the stranger. As shown in

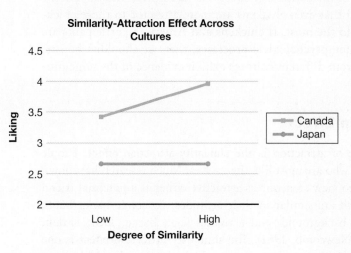

Similarity-Attraction Effect Across Cultures

FIGURE 11.6

Whereas Canadians better liked a stranger they considered very similar to themselves, Japanese attitudes toward strangers were largely unaffected by perceived similarity.

Figure 11.6, the Canadians showed evidence of the similarity-attraction effect, replicating much past research. They liked the highly similar person more than the dissimilar one. For the Japanese, in contrast, their liking for the stranger was unaffected by their apparent similarity. The pattern of results was identical regardless of whether participants found out about the stranger's personality or social background. Other studies also find that the similarity-attraction effect is stronger among North Americans than Japanese (Heine et al., 2009; Schug, Yuki, Horikawa, & Takemura, 2009). In some studies, Japanese show a similarity-attraction effect as well but it is consistently weaker than the North American effect.

Close Relationships

Humans are nothing if not social. In all cultures, most people live with others, eat with others, socialize with others, work with others, study with others, hang out with others, and sleep with others. We are born and raised in families, and most of us go on to create families of our own. Most of our work activities take place with others, and there are relatively few times in the day when most people are all alone. Most events in our lives unfold in the context of the relationships we have with others.

Furthermore, relationships not only occupy much of our time, they also represent some of our most significant concerns. Researchers who have systematically eavesdropped on people's conversations find that the most common topic of conversation is gossip about other people (Dunbar, Marriott, & Duncan, 1997). Studies that track people's happiness over time find that their happiest times are when they are with others (Csikszentmihalyi & Hunter, 2003). People's most emotionally wrenching experiences involve the break-up of relationships and the deaths of loved ones (Holmes & Rahe, 1967). In sum, relationships with others are concerns that dominate people's lives, and it would be impossible to have a good understanding of human nature unless we also considered how people relate to others. This social foundation of human nature is universal in that there are no cultures in which people live as lone individuals. Despite this universality, however, the ways that people go about relating to others vary in some predictable and important ways.

The Four Elementary Forms of Relationships

Given that this book has revealed some pronounced cultural differences in various psychological processes, it's perhaps not surprising to expect that cultures might differ in their kinds of relationships. How broad might this cultural variation be? Could people in some cultures have kinds of relationships that are completely unfamiliar to those in another culture?

Alan Fiske (1991, 1992) would argue that the answer to this question is a resounding "No." Although we do see tremendous variation across cultures with respect to relationships, Fiske claims that there is some underlying structure that is common to all forms of relationships in the world. Specifically, he argues that all relationships are based on one or more of four basic elements of sociality.

The first basic structure of relationship is known as **communal sharing**. With this view of relationships, the members of a group emphasize their common identity rather than consider their idiosyncrasies. In communal sharing every person is treated the same—each has the identical rights and privileges as every other member of that group. One domain where communal sharing is especially operative is within the family. People in a family typically do not keep explicit track of what is taken and what is contributed by each member. All typically take what they need and contribute what they can, without any recordkeeping. Usually, we would not expect that an older sister would deserve a larger piece of pie than a younger brother, or that the older sister would get more of a say on where the family should have their summer vacation than the younger brother does. Rather, the ideal in communal sharing is equality among all the members of the group. The resources tend to be pooled as belonging to the larger whole that transcends each of the individual members.

Of course, even within a family there is not complete equality. For example, the mother's opinion of what kinds of television programs a child should be able to watch might trump the child's own opinions. This reflects **authority ranking**, the second relational structure. Within authority-ranking relationships, people are linearly ordered along a hierarchical social dimension. People with higher ranking have prestige and privileges that those with lower ranking do not; however, subordinates are often entitled to receive protection and care from those above. A prototypical example of authority ranking in action is in the military, where rank determines benefits, power, duties, prestige, and obligations. The lower-ranked members earn less money, are allowed fewer privileges, and are obligated to follow the orders of those above them. Asymmetry underlies all authority-ranking relationships.

A third basic relational structure is **equality matching,** which is based on the idea of balance and reciprocity. People keep track of what is exchanged and are motivated to pay back what has been exchanged in equivalent terms. Although equality matching is perhaps the least familiar of the four relational structures to Westerners, it is quite common in many cultures around the world. Some examples of Western situations in which it operates are exchanging Christmas cards, taking turns, exchanging dinner invitations, and car pooling—people keep track of what they have received and the system is out of balance until they have paid back the original benefits in kind (see **Figure 11.7**). A non-Western example common in many societies throughout Africa, Asia, and the Caribbean is a rotating credit association (e.g., Fessler, 2002). On a fixed occasion, every family in a tribe makes an equivalent contribution of money to a pool and one family gets to take the entire amount. Each family gets a turn at this, so every handful of years each one enjoys a short period of wealth. People ensure that their contributions are equal and their chances of taking home the entire pot of money are also equal. Within equality-matching relationships, the relative position of individuals does not matter; each gets his or her own turn regardless of rank.

Market pricing is the last kind of relational structure. It is distinctive in that it is concerned with proportionality and ratios. All the features of benefits that are exchanged can be reduced to a single underlying dimension, usually money. Similar to equality matching, people expect to ultimately receive something equivalent to what they have given; however, in market pricing, both sides of the exchange usually occur at once, and different kinds of goods can be exchanged. So, for example, I can purchase your pound of coffee with a sack of flour and six seashells because we have calculated that both sides of the transaction are equal in value. Or I can get your assistance in repairing my leaky roof in exchange for $500 because we came to an agreement that this is what your time and skills are worth. With market pricing, members of a party calculate the ratios of the goods that are exchanged

FIGURE 11.7 Equality matching is a relational style where people exchange equivalent goods. This is the least common style among Westerners, although it's quite common in many other parts of the world. One example among Westerners is the exchanging of Christmas cards.

so that the transaction will be equivalent in value for both parties. The relative status of individuals in the transaction is irrelevant. The CEO of the company is charged the same amount for a quart of milk as the new recruit in the mailroom. Furthermore, the parties in the exchange do not have to have any kind of formalized relationship with each other. For example, two strangers can use eBay to complete a transaction by calculating an agreed-upon value of the exchange. Market pricing relationships are highly ubiquitous in Western society, and modern theories of economics view all transactions in these terms.

Fiske maintains that all kinds of human relationships are constructed out of one or more of these four basic elements. It is possible that people might have single relationships that are governed by all four elements. For example, within a family at dinner each person is allowed to eat until he or she is satisfied (communal sharing), the father might occupy the seat at the head of the table (authority ranking), for dessert each person can claim an equal-size cupcake (equality matching), and a child might be paid $1.00 for each time she loads the dishwasher (market pricing). These four relational elements are said to be operational in relationships in all cultures.

Despite the hypothesized universal presence of these elements, there is much cultural variation in the extent to which each operates. For example, market pricing is characteristic of a broader class of relationships within American culture today than it is among the Fore of New Guinea. Indeed, because market pricing can operate without any close relations between two individuals, it is especially common within more individualistic societies. Equality matching is emphasized more in many traditional subsistence societies around the world, where elaborate rituals are often involved in the reciprocal exchange of equally valued goods. For example, among the Trobriand Islanders, men take long and dangerous open-ocean journeys to exchange shell necklaces that have no "practical" value. Later on, the person who received the necklace is obligated to go on a similarly dangerous journey to exchange a similarly valued, and not especially practical, gift (Malinowski, 1922/1965). Likewise, East Asians also show stronger motivations for equality matching—they are more likely than North Americans to be reluctant to accept gifts because of the obligation they feel to reciprocate the gesture (Shen, Wan, & Wyer, 2011). Authority ranking characterizes a greater portion of behaviors in hierarchical class-based societies than in more egalitarian ones. And norms for communal sharing are stronger in India than they are in the United States (Miller et al., 2014). Moreover, the context in which communal sharing is most common in the West is in families; however, this often generalizes to the tribal level in many smaller societies, characterizing a significant proportion of relational exchanges there. In addition, within Western societies communal sharing appears to characterize a broader array of behaviors in relationships among people lower in socioeconomic status than among those of the highest status (see Kraus et al. 2012, for a review). Hence, although these relational structures serve the same function around the world, some cultures rely on particular structures more than others.

Friends and Enemies

Let's now consider some different kinds of relationships. First, it would seem that there are few things in life that are more special than friendships. Friends make good times more enjoyable and bad times less painful. They help us out when we're in need, they make us laugh, and they make us feel wanted and valuable. Friendships are important enough that they have been argued to be the key to success (Carnegie, 1936), and research has revealed that the quality of one's friendships is one of the best predictors of happiness (e.g., Csikszentmihalyi & Hunter, 2003). Most dramatic, perhaps, are the findings from research that having close friends increases the length of one's life (House, Landis, & Umberson, 1988).

Given the obvious pleasures and benefits associated with friendships, the following poem (Kyei & Schreckenbach, 1975, p. 59) is a puzzle:

Beware of friends.

Some are snakes under grass;

Some are lions in sheep's clothing;

Some are jealousies behind their façades of praises;

Some are just no good;

Beware of friends.

Why would we need to be wary of friends rather than trusting of them? Even more puzzling, this quote comes from a poem written by a Ghanaian and reflects a sentiment that is expressed quite commonly in West African worlds (Adams & Plaut, 2003)—a collectivistic cultural context (**Figure 11.8**). Why, in a cultural context that emphasizes people's fundamental connection with close others, can those others be viewed with such suspicion?

FIGURE 11.8 Some examples of bumper stickers frequently seen in Ghana.

Before we make sense of this puzzle, consider another question: Do you have any enemies? Let's define *enemies* as those who are wishing for your downfall or are trying to sabotage your progress. According to this definition, do you have enemies, and if so, who are they?

If you're like the majority of Americans who have participated in the research by Glenn Adams and colleagues, you probably can't think of any enemies you have. Only 26% of Americans in one study reported that they had any enemies (Adams, 2005). In contrast, 71% of Ghanaians claimed that they were the target of enemies. Although only a minority of Americans thought that others were plotting against them, a substantial majority of Ghanaians did. Furthermore, Americans who do feel they had enemies were more likely than the Ghanaians to view those enemies as coming from outside their group, such as those who held ethnic prejudices against their group. In contrast, Ghanaians were more likely to view their enemies as coming from within their ingroups—people such as neighbors, friends, or relatives (Adams, Anderson, & Adonu, 2004). The worlds of Ghanaian and American relationships appear to be very distant indeed.

At first glance, these cultural differences would seem to be at odds with what we would expect from the idea that people who are independent are more common in the United States and people who are interdependent are more common in Ghana. You might expect that the lone individual with few close ties or self-defining relationships would be the most vulnerable to enemies and most suspicious of friends. After all, if people who are independent choose to view themselves as autonomous and distinct from others, this might suggest that they don't trust others very much. On the other hand, people who are interdependent and who allow others to become so close as to be key self-defining aspects of their identity should be especially trusting of those others. But the data suggest the exact opposite. How can we resolve this paradox?

The root of this apparent contradiction can be traced to the nature of people's relationships, which loosely parallels the distinctions between independent and interdependent self-concepts. Those people with more independent views of self perceive the self as fundamentally disconnected from others, and the only reason that such people would form connections with others is because they choose to do so. Relationships form between two people with independent self-concepts when the people involved decide that it is to their advantage to form a relationship; otherwise, such people would remain in the default state of relations between independent individuals, which is a null relationship. No relationship develops unless independent individuals see a benefit to themselves (e.g., it would be fun; I'm attracted to them; the other person might have valuable information; a relationship might create future opportunities).

For example, consider how one of Adams's (2005) American participants responded to the question of whether he had an enemy: "For me, it's really nonproductive. . . . I won't entertain or I won't stay engaged with that type of person. I mean, they may try, but one of my strengths is that I am pretty good at that, weaving my way out of that maze." For this participant, enemies are not a problem because he chooses not to engage with them. He appears to simply avoid those people with whom relations might not be productive, and thus no relationship, and no enemyship, would ever develop.

RELATIONAL MOBILITY. A characteristic of many cultural contexts in which independent selves predominate is that people have the freedom to move between relationships. If one particular relationship is found to be insufficiently rewarding to devote appropriate relationship-maintenance efforts, it might be neglected and allowed to wither away, and the person might move on to form new relationships with others that could prove to be more rewarding. We can say that people in these contexts have **high relational mobility** (Yuki et al., 2007)—their relational ties are flexible enough, and opportunities for new relationships are available enough, that they feel they can find new relationships and not feel overly bound by their old relationships. What is perhaps one of the highest relationally mobile contexts is the life of the American college student (see **Figure 11.9**). Such students have typically moved away from home (and are thus not as bound by their past relationships), and they are living among many others (several thousands in the case of students at large universities) whom they meet in a variety of contexts, such as shared classes, shared dorms, shared student clubs, shared parties, and other shared interests. In such contexts, opportunities to form potential new relationships are abundant, and people often work to make themselves more attractive in case any new relationship opportunities arise.

FIGURE 11.9 Students at large universities are often in a situation of high relational mobility.

Now let's compare this situation with other contexts, particularly those populated with people with more interdependent self-concepts. As you'll recall, the interdependent self is primarily defined on the basis of one's close relationships. Ingroup relationships are not so much chosen by individuals as they are perceived to exist by default. One is born into a family within a network of relatives, and these relationships are not up for negotiation. They simply exist, whether one likes them or not. Furthermore, one is born into a neighborhood, goes to a school, and starts an occupation, and the people with whom one shares these contexts are also those with whom one has relationships. A person's relationships are tied to the interpersonal networks within which he or she exists. In interdependent contexts people do not so much choose whom they will have relationships with; instead, the relationships are perceived to exist naturally without negotiation—the default state between two such individuals is that they have a relationship. Interestingly, when people move to new cultures, they seem to acquire some of the new culture's attitudes toward relational mobility, although not all of them (Zhang & Li, 2014).

Furthermore, given the more unconditional and lasting attitudes toward relationships in these contexts, people can be said to have **low relational mobility**. They perceive that they have few opportunities to form new relationships, and their past relationships, and their commitments and obligations to them, continue to guide them. Relationships are viewed as stable, often lifelong connections that provide both benefits to the individuals involved and costs in order to maintain them.

However, relationships in low-relational-mobility contexts are not always positive. Some people really do not get along with each other, but if it is not an option to decide that they will not engage with each other, they will continue to have a relationship, albeit one that is frequently characterized by negative feelings. Perhaps the situation that comes closest to this for many Western people is with some in-laws. You might not like all of your in-laws, but you still have to maintain relationships with them. Despite, say, your negative feelings toward your father-in-law, you may still have to sit next to him at Thanksgiving dinner and listen to his objectionable political views, and continue to do this every year. In some instances in which people have unavoidable relationships with people with whom they do not get along, the relationships might develop into full-blown enemyships. Such a view seems to be expressed by one of Adams's (2005) Ghanaian participants: "The world is such that everybody is bound to have enemies."

This view proposes that people from different cultures form relationships for different reasons. Relationships in high-relational-mobility contexts are entered into, and are maintained, on a mutually voluntary basis. One can choose to make efforts to start a relationship, or one can choose to dissolve that relationship. The existence of a relationship is rather tenuous and requires that the people involved agree that the relationship is beneficial, and worth whatever efforts are put into maintaining it; otherwise it returns to the default status of a null relationship. This view would seem to be what is emphasized by Western social psychologists (who primarily study Western college students living highly relationally mobile lives), because the majority of research on relationships has targeted attraction and the formation of new relationships, especially romantic relationships, as well as the dissolution of those relationships. There is almost no mention of less-voluntary kinds of relationships, such as kin relations, within Western social psychological research (for an exception see Georgas et al., 2006). It seems that the theoretical model that guides this research is that relationships are conditional and voluntary, and will return to their null state if people move on to pursue other relational opportunities elsewhere.

In contrast, relationships in less relationally mobile contexts tend to be viewed in more unconditional terms. One is born into a relatively fixed interpersonal network—for example, one might be born the second daughter of the Ackah family, peanut farmers who live in a village just south of the town of Navrongo in Ghana. The relationships that one has with one's kin are not voluntary—the default state of relationships in this context is that these relationships simply exist, whether they are always rewarding or not, and that these enduring relationships come with a certain amount of obligations. This model of unconditional kinship relations appears to shape other relations that people in less relationally mobile contexts have; thus, relationships with friends, neighbors, and enemies tend to be perceived in unconditional, enduring terms.

One way that this difference in views of relationships can be detected is by exploring what people think about friends. Friendships are universal relationships—we see them in all cultures; however, the nature of these relationships can vary. One way that American friendships stand out is in terms of just how many of them there are. In his classic ethnography of 19th-century America, Alexis de Tocqueville (1835/2003) was struck by the ease with which Americans made new friends. Studies find that Americans report having more friends than people in other cultures (and these are real friends, not Facebook ones). For example, American college students reported having more friends than Ghanaian college students (Adams & Plaut, 2003), and American adults report an average social network size of 20.76 (Fung, Carstensen, & Lang, 2001), which compares with social network sizes of 13.23 among Hong Kong Chinese adults and 12.75 among German adults (Fung, Stoeber, Yeung, & Lang, 2008). A common reaction heard among many international people after their first encounters with Americans is how friendly they seem. The American sitting next to you on the plane may seem quite ready to share her life story with you and learn about yours, but she also might have no intention of ever seeing you again once the plane has landed. Compared with people from other cultures, Americans have rather casual attitudes toward forming friends.

Furthermore, the meaning of friendship appears to vary across cultures. In collectivistic contexts, an important aspect of friendship is to provide each other with advice, and, although this is common in individualistic contexts as well, among collectivists this advice is frequently offered regardless of whether one's friend wants to receive it. And although the offering of unsolicited advice is present in a variety of collectivistic cultures (such as in Turkey and Columbia; Bayraktaroglu, 2001; Fitch, 1998), it seems to be especially prevalent in Russia. As the BBC correspondent, James Rodgers, put it: "You can't really say 'Mind your own business!' in Russian. You can translate the phrase literally, but the concept is not well understood" (cited in Chentsova-Dutton & Vaughn, 2012). For example, in one study Russians were almost twice as likely as Americans to say that their last offering of advice was unsolicited, and in another study, the advice offered by Americans was found to be contingent on whether it was requested, whereas for Russians, the amount of advice offered was largely unaffected by whether or not it was requested (Chentsova-Dutton & Vaughn, 2012). In Russia, a big part of friendship seems to be to let your friends know how you think they should be leading their lives differently.

The meaning of friendship also differs between Ghanaians and Americans. When asked what they thought of someone who had a large number of friends, many Ghanaians (but few Americans) said that such a person would be rather foolish. One possible reason Ghanaians might not have as many friends as Americans, or might think of someone having a lot of friends as foolish, is reflected in how people describe friendships. Whereas the majority of Ghanaians emphasized that friends were people who would provide practical support, only a minority of Americans spontaneously listed this feature in their definition of friendship. For example, one Ghanaian participant described friends this way: "A friend is someone who is ready to help you, whether it is financially or socially, where there is a need. That's what I think is most important about a friend" (Adams & Plaut, 2003). This suggests that friendships among Ghanaians are perceived to involve more obligations than they do for Americans. Friendships are not just about sharing good times or deriving positive benefits; they also entail some substantial costs when obligations need to be fulfilled. A person with many friends, then, is a person who also has many obligations, and this fact would seem to underlie the relatively smaller friendship networks among Ghanaians.

A similar cautious attitude toward friends has been identified in East Asia, and relational mobility is the variable that best explains it. East Asians who are relatively high in relational mobility have attitudes toward friends that are similar to American attitudes; in contrast, those who score low on relational mobility are cautious toward friends, as in Ghana (Li, Adams, Kurtis, & Hamamura, in press).

The relationship landscape in a high-relational-mobility society should also affect the strategies that people use to maintain their relationships and to attract new relationships. If people are more free to choose their relationships, then any kinds of attributes that can attract potential new relationship partners should come to be of more value. In contrast, if people's relationship networks are largely stable, characteristics that attract people should be of relatively less utility. One way we can see this is in a relationship-attracting feature discussed earlier: similarity. People tend to be attracted to similar others, but this effect is less clear in some non-Western cultures, notably Japan. One study investigated why Americans show a stronger similarity-attraction effect than Japanese by asking participants to indicate how many new relationship opportunities they felt existed in their own lives. The findings revealed that Americans were more attracted to similarity and felt they had more opportunities for forming new relationships than the Japanese did. Moreover, the researchers demonstrated that this cultural difference in relational mobility could account for the cultural difference in the similarity-attraction effect (Schug et al., 2009). That is, because being attractive to others is more important in a high-relational-mobility context such as in the United States, people come to attend more to features that make someone more attractive, such as how similar they are. Likewise, in more relationally mobile contexts, people are more likely to strive to be unique, as their access to a broad network of potential relational partners will allow them to find like-minded others (Takemura, 2014). Moreover, more relationally mobile people work harder to maintain their existing relationships because they appear to recognize that their relationship partners might find more rewarding relationships elsewhere (Schug, Yuki, & Maddux, 2010).

The enhanced value of attractiveness in high-relational-mobility contexts is evident in another line of research. Much research conducted with Westerners has shown that physically attractive people have a number of more positive life outcomes than those who are less physically attractive, and these outcomes extend across a broad array of domains in ways that may seem patently unfair. For example, essays that are believed to have been written by an attractive author are evaluated more positively than ones believed to have been written by a less-attractive author (Landy & Sigall, 1974); attractive politicians get more votes than unattractive ones (Efrain & Patterson, 1974); attractive children are rated as smarter and better behaved by their teachers (Clifford & Walster, 1973); attractive MBA grads earn more money than less-attractive MBA grads (Frieze, Olson, & Russell, 1991); and attractive criminals get lighter sentences than less attractive ones (Stewart, 1980).

From a young age we learn implicitly that attractive people have more desirable characteristics than unattractive ones, such as when we learn of Cinderella's kindness and beauty in contrast to her evil and ugly stepsisters. One way that this tyranny of the beautiful has been explained is that because the first thing we often learn about someone is their level of attractiveness (we see it immediately when we first meet them), it is cognitively more straightforward to assume that they have other positive features as well, a phenomenon known as the "halo effect" (e.g., Kaplan, 1978).

However, most of this research has been conducted with highly relationally mobile North American samples, and a question arises as to whether the tyranny of the beautiful would be observed in the same way in less-mobile samples. If one had fewer opportunities to form new relationships, then physical attractiveness should be less valuable as an asset; there would be fewer people one could potentially attract. In one study, Ghanaian and American university students described their satisfaction with their general life outcomes and their friendships (Anderson, Adams, & Plaut, 2008). Moreover, photographs of the participants were evaluated for their physical attractiveness by judges from the participants' own cultures. The results indicated that, again, the tyranny of the beautiful was evident in the American sample, because the more-attractive Americans reported being more satisfied with their general life outcomes and friendships when compared with the less-attractive Americans. In contrast, the more attractive Ghanaians reported being *less* satisfied with their general life outcomes and their friendships than less attractive ones. That is, the tyranny of the beautiful did not seem to be evident in a Ghanaian context, arguably because Ghanaians have less relational mobility than Americans.

Parallel findings also emerge when more relationally mobile Americans who live in urban settings are compared with their less-mobile counterparts who live in rural settings. More-attractive urban American women tended to have greater well-being, but the same relation between attractiveness and well-being was not found among rural American women (Plaut, Adams, & Anderson, 2009).

RESIDENTIAL MOBILITY. Cultures differ in their relational mobility in yet another way: In some contexts people literally are more physically mobile—that is, they are more likely to change their place of residence. Americans have long been recognized as an especially mobile people (see Oishi, 2010). Alexis de Tocqueville made the following observation in the 19th century: "In the United States, a man will carefully construct a home in which to spend his old age and sell it before the roof is on. . . . He will settle in one place only to go off elsewhere shortly afterwards with a new set of desires" (1835/2003, p. 623). Given that people form relationships with those who live around them, what kinds of psychological effects does changing one's residence have?

In a fascinating series of studies, the cultural psychologist Shige Oishi has demonstrated the many diverse consequences that emerge when people change their residence. This evidence is available both by contrasting communities in which people frequently change residences with those where people stay more settled, and by comparing individuals who have moved multiple times in their lives with those who have not moved at all. For example, studies of American college students find that, compared with those who have not moved before, those who have moved multiple times in their lives (1) show more conditional loyalty to their colleges (that is, they identify with their colleges only when they are described positively, but not when they are described negatively; Oishi, Ishii, & Lun, 2009); (2) have more Facebook friends on campus (and continue to acquire more new Facebook friends over time; Seder & Oishi, 2008); (3) view their personality traits (which are immediately apparent upon meeting them) to be a more central part of their identity than their group

FIGURE 11.10 The state of Nevada has the highest residential mobility in the United States.

memberships (which take more time to learn from someone; Oishi, Lun, & Sherman, 2007); and (4) prefer large national chain stores, which are the same wherever you go (e.g., Starbucks, Walmart, Barnes & Noble), over local regional stores (Oishi, Miao, Koo, Kisling, & Ratliff, 2012).

In contrast to communities in which residency is more stable, American communities in which people are likely to move have, on average, (1) more fair-weather sports fans (i.e., attendance at professional sports events is more closely tied to the performance of the local teams, whereas people in residentially stable communities attend sporting events even when their teams are losing; Oishi et al., 2007); (2) higher crime rates and less pro-community action (Oishi et al., 2007; Sampson, Raudenbush, & Earls, 1997); and (3) more large national chain stores per capita (but not more regional stores) and more goods sold at those chain stores (Oishi et al., 2012; see **Figure 11.10**). In sum, living in a context in which one moves relatively frequently changes the kinds of relationships that people have and affects a variety of other attitudes and lifestyles. One reason that Americans appear to be as psychologically unusual as they are in the context of the world's cultures (e.g., Henrich et al., 2010) may be because of the relatively itinerant lifestyles that they lead.

SIMPÁTICO. Cultural differences in friendships can also be understood in terms of the ways that people tend to present themselves to others. In many Latin-American cultures, people place an emphasis on maintaining harmonious relationships, and on making expressive displays of graciousness, hospitality, and personal harmony (Sanchez-Burks, Nisbett, & Ybarra, 2000). This highly valued relational style is known as **simpático**, and Latin-Americans view achieving this state as an end in itself. Latin-Americans view their self-concepts to be more characterized by traits that reflect *simpático,* such as easygoing, respectful, courteous, and agreeable (Holloway, Waldrip, & Ickes, 2009; Ramirez-Esparza, Chung, Sierra-Otero, & Pennebaker, 2012). Latin-Americans also expect interactions with others to be dominated by positive social behaviors and to have fewer negative social behaviors, compared with the expectations of European-Americans (Triandis, Marin, Lisansky, & Betancourt, 1984).

These cultural differences are particularly evident in workplaces, where Latin-Americans show a clear preference for working in groups in which people strive to maintain a warm and hospitable atmosphere. In contrast, as discussed in Chapter 7, European-Americans (particularly Protestants) show a clear preference for staying focused on the task at hand (Sanchez-Burks et al., 2000). Latin-American dyads speak more, make more eye contact, and show more positive feelings than European- or African-American dyads. Interestingly, when European- or African-Americans were paired with a Latin-American partner, they rated the interaction as being more smooth, natural, and involving, and they showed more interest in interacting again in the future when compared with European- or African-American dyads (Holloway et al., 2009).

In general, Latin-Americans act in more sociable ways than European-Americans, and time-sampling studies find that they spend a greater proportion of their time socializing with others (Ramirez-Esparza, Mehl, Alvarez-Bermudez, & Pennebaker, 2009). The presence of Latin-Americans in groups often comes with their *simpático* relational concerns, which can sometimes make for a warmer exchange.

Love

Let's talk about love—that ineffable, indomitable, and invaluable commodity that likely occupies a substantial amount of your thoughts. Love has been written about, recited about, or sung about more than most any other topic, and psychologists too, perhaps foolhardily, have jumped into the fray. Let's start this one from the very beginning. Why do we have love?

It would seem that anything as powerful as love must serve an important function. Considering love from an evolutionary perspective we can see some good reasons for its origins. First, if we consider why people feel a sense of parental love, the answer seems quite obvious. Strong feelings of parental love goad people into committing the quite sizable amounts of time and resources needed to take care of their children. Humans have an especially long and dependent period of infancy, and if we did not feel very powerful feelings of love toward our children it would be very difficult for them to receive the enormous amount of care they need in order to survive. This behavior can be contrasted with some other species—for example, sea turtles—whose offspring are born self-sufficient and for which we see no evidence of loving parental behaviors. Other species—for example, bears—do show a good deal of protective care from the mother; however, the father is nowhere to be seen. This suggests that young bears require care that can be provided by only the mother, and father bears are quite irrelevant for anything other than fertilizing the eggs. Humans, in contrast, require such an extended period of costly protective care and socialization that they fare best when they have two parents devoted to providing resources and socializing them. In the ancestral environment, it was likely that parents who did not feel especially strong love for their children were less likely to have their children survive the tenuous circumstances of a subsistence lifestyle; hence, those parents did not pass on as many surviving genes as did those who felt strong feelings of love for their children.

The reasoning for romantic love is similar. Evolutionary psychologists contend that the originating impetus for romantic love is the long vulnerable period of human childhood (e.g., Fisher, 2004). Because children in the ancestral environment would have been more likely to survive if two parents were around to provide resources and socialization, some strong incentives were needed to keep the parents together so they would both remain to support the children. According to this reasoning, romantic love was selected as the glue that keeps couples together. Those people who did not develop feelings of love for their partners would have been less likely to stay with them and would have ended up having fewer surviving offspring than those who felt strong feelings of love. Again, according to this line of reasoning, it's all about the kids. This is an evolutionary account for how love came to be.

Because we are all part of the same species, to the extent that this evolutionary account is correct, people from all cultures should be capable of feeling romantic love. And this does appear to be the case. One review of ethnographies of 166 cultures found clear evidence of romantic love in 89% of them (Jankowiak & Fischer, 1992). There was not clear evidence for romantic love in the remaining 11% of cultures; however, in all but one of these cases the ethnographies note that sexual affairs occur, but the researchers did not explore the motives behind why the people enter into them. The authors of the review concluded that the lack of evidence for romantic love in those 11% of societies was likely due to ethnographic oversight rather than a genuine absence of love. To the extent that they are correct, romantic love would qualify

FIGURE 11.11 Romantic love. Universally experienced, although it is not universal in that it serves as a foundation for starting a marriage.

as a human universal—at least a functional universal, if not an accessibility universal (see **Figure 11.11**). Furthermore, much research across cultures shows a number of striking similarities in people's feelings of love toward their partners (e.g., Kim & Hatfield, 2004; Neto, Mullet, & Deschamps, 2000; Philbrick & Opolot, 1980). However, there are some notable cultural differences, too (e.g., Desai, McCormick, & Gaeddert, 1989; Murstein, Merighi, & Vyse, 1991; Wong & Goodwin, 2009).

ARRANGED MARRIAGES. Perhaps the most obvious example of how culture shapes people's thinking about romantic love is the existence of arranged versus love marriages. Historically, the majority of marriages around the world have been arranged by families (Skolnick, 1987) rather than by the couples themselves (although the percentage of arranged marriages has recently been dropping in many cultures around the world, such as in China, India, Japan, and Turkey, and among orthodox Jews; Hortacsu, 1999; Sprecher & Chandak, 1992; Xu & Whyte, 1990). Even today within North America, there are many young people in their twenties, particularly those of Indian and Pakistani descent, who are participating in arranged marriages.

There are different kinds of arranged and love marriages around the world. **Table 11.1** summarize the results of Broude and Green's (1983) survey of the mate selection tactics of 186 small-scale societies. The strategy that individuals can choose their own partners without needing to seek approval, which perhaps is the most normative strategy among Westerners today, was evident in only 31% of small-scale societies for men, and only 8% for women. In another study, college students in a number of countries were asked the following question: "If a man (woman) had all the other qualities you desired, would you marry this person if you were not in love with him (her)?" (Levine, Sato, Hashimoto, & Verma, 1995). Whereas approximately half of students from India and Pakistan said that they would marry this person (and another one-quarter said that they were undecided), the vast majority (more than 80%) of Americans, Britons, Australians, and Latin Americans said they would not, and only a small percentage (less than 5%) of people from these countries said they would. Apparently, love is viewed as a necessary feature for a marriage to begin in some cultures, but not others. Interestingly, this identical question was posed to some American college students a little more than a generation ago, in a 1967 survey (the year that the Beatles recorded their hit single "All You Need Is Love"). In that sample, 65% of the men but only 24% of the women said they would not marry someone they did not love (Kephart, 1967). Not only are there pronounced cultural differences in attitudes toward love, but current attitudes in the United States, particularly among women, are very different from what they were a few decades ago. Marrying someone because you have fallen in love with that person is a relatively new idea and is likely somewhat

TABLE 11.1

Mate selection practices among 186 small-scale societies

Practice	Men	Women
Parents choose partner; individual cannot object	13%	21%
Parents choose partner; individual can object	17%	23%
Individual choice and arranged marriages are both acceptable alternatives	18%	17%
Individuals, parents, kin, and others must reach agreement on an appropriate match	3%	3%
Individual selects partner autonomously; parental, kin, and/or community approval necessary or highly desirable	19%	29%
Individual selects partner autonomously; approval by others unnecessary	31%	8%

Source: Based on Broude & Green (1983), pp. 273-274.

uncommon in the context of all the marriages that have occurred throughout human history.

The likelihood that a culture favors arranged over love marriages is not determined randomly. Rather, it appears to relate to the dominant kind of family structure in the culture. Goode (1959) proposed that romantic love would become more important in cultures as the strength of extended family ties became weaker. Powerful feelings of romantic love could be somewhat irrelevant, or even problematic, for marriage in cultures with strong extended family ties. The Western ideal of romantic love, characterized by intense feelings and mutual absorption, could be disruptive in cultures with large kin networks because such feelings can interfere with people's abilities to respect the wishes of their family members (Dion & Dion, 1993). Furthermore, the existence of strong kin relations provides considerable social pressures for a couple to stay together. In the absence of those social pressures, another kind of glue would be necessary to keep the couple together. Romantic love has been proposed to be that critical glue when other kin are not around (Inkeles, 1953). An analysis of data from 117 nonindustrialized societies found clear support for Goode's thesis (Lee & Stone, 1980). Marriages based on love were more likely in cultures with nuclear family structures than they in cultures with extended family systems. The larger the number of important family relationships that one needs to consider, the more problematic it becomes to ignore their concerns and follow the passions of one's heart.

More generally, individualism appears to be related to the likelihood that one emphasizes romantic love in marriages. Some research on romantic love has noted the critical role that *idealization* of one's partner plays in the experience of romantic love. The Irish playwright George Bernard Shaw once cynically commented, "Love is a gross exaggeration of the difference between one person and everybody else." At one level, there seems to be some truth in Shaw's remark. For example, one study investigated dating and married couples' perceptions of their partners (Murray, Holmes, & Griffin, 1996). The study found that those people who idealized their partner the most (i.e., they viewed the individual in the most unrealistically positive terms compared with how they viewed other people, and with how their partners viewed themselves) also loved their partners the most and were more likely still to be together in their relationship several months later.

The researchers' reasoning for why idealization seems to foster successful relationships is that positively distorted views of one's partner should protect one from having to entertain thoughts about the partner's unlovable characteristics. If a person sees her partner behave badly, such as when he gets angry and kicks the dog, leaves dirty laundry on the floor, or grows overweight, and considers these behaviors objectively, she might have a difficult time integrating the cognitions "I love my partner" and "My partner has many unlovable qualities." This dissonance can be avoided quite simply by distorting her views of her partner, so that undesirable behaviors are instead seen to indicate more positive qualities, such as that the partner is "emotional," "carefree," and "knows how to enjoy the good things in life." When partners are viewed in these ways, the relationship can be buffered against any ugly truths that might threaten it, and romantic love can thrive.

However, such idealization would seem to be less emphasized in more collectivistic cultures where individualized personal agency is not as significant a concern (Averill, 1985). If people's behaviors are perceived as less reflective of their dispositions, as they seem to be in collectivistic cultures (see Chapter 9), there should be less motivation to ensure that one's partner's personality is viewed in such rosy terms. Some research supports this hypothesis. In one study, Japanese and Canadian college students were asked to evaluate the quality of their romantic relationships compared with what they thought most other people's romantic relationships were like (Endo, Heine, & Lehman, 2000). As shown in **Figure 11.12**, people in both countries showed some evidence for idealization, in that they viewed their own romantic relationships as significantly more positive than most other people's romantic relationships. However, the magnitude of this idealization (i.e., the gap between their evaluations of their own romantic relationships and their evaluation of most other people's romantic relationships) was significantly greater among European-Canadians than it was among Japanese, whereas Asian-Canadians fell in between. Hence, idealization of

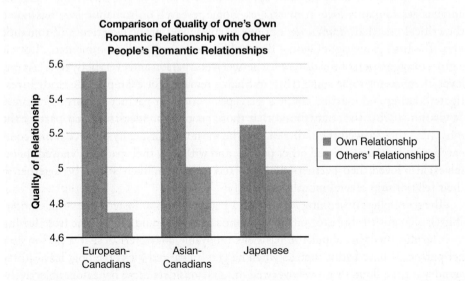

FIGURE 11.12 European-Canadians perceive the quality of their own romantic relationships to be far superior to that of other people. A similar bias holds for Asian-Canadians and Japanese, but it is much smaller.

one's romantic relationships appears to be more pronounced among people from more individualistic cultures. It is possible (although it has not yet been explored) that idealization does not predict relationship longevity among people from collectivistic cultures as well as it does among people from individualistic cultures.

I have found that the issue of arranged marriage is the topic my students seem to view as the most surprising to them. Indeed, many of my students devote a huge amount of their energy and time to trying to find love, precisely because they hold the widely shared belief that love provides the foundation of a marriage. Trying to imagine, in contrast, that one could instead just marry whomever their parents suggested seems to strike many of my students (particularly those of Western descent) as outright unfathomable. They often ask, "How could you have a marriage without love?"

This question reveals a number of assumptions that many Westerners have about love. First is the belief that you will only love someone you have chosen for yourself. However, even though many arranged marriages start out with no feelings of love between the couple, typically the husband and wife come to feel strong feelings of love toward each other. An Indian colleague of mine who had been in a successful arranged marriage for some time explained it to my perplexed Western mind thus: Getting a husband is not all that different from getting a new puppy. When you first receive a new puppy, you have not yet developed feelings of love for it. However, you expect that you will come to love that puppy, and invariably, with time, you do. Likewise, someone in an arranged marriage does not warily approach the new partner as though he or she were a suspicious stranger in a dark alley. Rather, the individual approaches that person as his or her new spouse with the expectation of eventually falling in love. And, with time, they usually do.

A second assumption about love is that it is ultimately an individualistic choice. Being a unique person, I could only come to love someone that I could connect with in a unique and special way. With this view, it seems essential that individuals choose their partners, because only they know their own idiosyncrasies well enough to identify a person they will love. In cultures where arranged marriages are common, however, the typical view is that marriages are the intersection of two families. With this view of marriage, it follows that the families would be in a better position to evaluate the likely success of a marriage than the lone individuals involved. People who enter arranged marriages thus usually trust their families to make the right decision for them, taking into account all the parties involved and making a choice based on what seems to be best for everyone in the long term. Often, then, people do not view their families as preventing them from making the best decision about whom they should marry—rather, they often trust that their families are the only ones who are positioned to make the best decision (see Chapter 8 for more discussion on different attitudes toward making choices).

A third assumption commonly made about love is that a marriage that does not have love at the foundation is bound to be miserable. This does not seem unreasonable given that so many Western marriages do go through times of misery and often end up in divorce and that those times of misery seem to coincide with declines in feelings of love. However, a look at cultures with arranged marriages does not seem to support this assumption. First, in some cultures, people view arranged marriages as being more likely to succeed than love marriages. For example, a survey among adults living in various urban centers in India found that 74% of men and women believed that arranged marriages were more likely to succeed than love marriages (Kishwar, 1994). Furthermore, there appears to be a striking positive correlation between the amount that a culture emphasizes love as the basis of marriage and its divorce rate—an ironic fact that suggests the more we insist on maintaining love in a marriage the less successful we seem to be at doing it (Dion & Dion, 1993). Perhaps there is some truth to the cynical pronouncement by the 17th century British scholar, Robert Burton, that marriage is the last and best cure of romantic love.

Much evidence also suggests that those in arranged marriages are at least as satisfied with their marriages as those in love marriages. For example, Turkish couples (Hortacsu, 1999) and Israeli couples (Shachar, 1991) in arranged marriages have been found to be as much in love with their partners as couples in love marriages. Members of the Unification Church, known colloquially as the "Moonies," underwent an unusual form of arranged marriage in that the Reverend Sun Myung Moon chose the partners each member married at a mass ceremony of more than 1,000 couples at a time. A study that followed these couples in the United States 3 years after they were married found no differences in the marital satisfaction or the marital dissolution of the Moonie marriages compared with rates for the general public (Galanter, 1986). Similarly, men in Japanese arranged marriages were found to be more satisfied than those in love marriages, and men in Chinese arranged marriages were as satisfied as those in love marriages. However, women in Japanese and Chinese arranged marriages were found to be less satisfied in arranged than love marriages (Blood, 1967; Xu & Whyte, 1990), suggesting that the costs of arranged marriages are borne largely by women in those cultures.

"The Bolsons are pleased to announce that their daughter, Naomi, is going to take another shot at marriage."

One extensive study compared marital satisfaction and the time spent in the marriage between Indian couples who were in either arranged or love marriages (Gupta & Singh, 1982). As shown in **Figure 11.13**, although in the initial years of marriage those in love marriages professed more love than those in arranged marriages, over time it was those in arranged marriages who reported having the most love. This pattern held true for both men and women (for similar findings see Kumar & Dhyani, 1996; Yelsma & Athappilly, 1988). Ironically, it was the marriages that started off with less love that ended up with more love. Perhaps some words from a Japanese colleague of mine, who has been in a successful arranged marriage for more than 30 years, can help make sense of these seemingly paradoxical findings. As he described to me, when he first married his wife they had no love for each other—they were strangers. Now, however, they have some love for each other. "Some love" seems like quite a bit in comparison with "no love." In contrast, he pointed out that those who have love marriages typically start out their relationships having a lot of love for each other. However, years later, it is not surprising if many of them report having less love than they had during their steamy courtship period. "Some love" doesn't seem so great compared to the "lot of love" that they had for each other earlier. As such, feelings of love might sometimes grow for those in arranged marriages and decline for those in love marriages because people have different standards of comparison. Of course, it is important to remember in all of this that individuals have vastly different experiences, and the fact that some arranged marriages work out well does not mean that those same benefits would be experienced by everyone across all contexts.

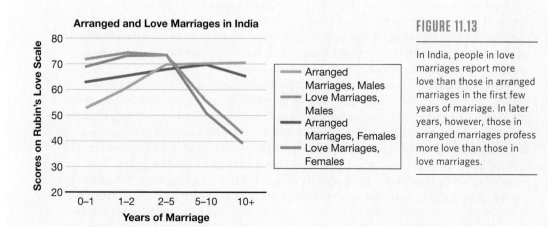

Arranged and Love Marriages in India

Scores on Rubin's Love Scale

Years of Marriage

Legend:
- Arranged Marriages, Males
- Love Marriages, Males
- Arranged Marriages, Females
- Love Marriages, Females

FIGURE 11.13

In India, people in love marriages report more love than those in arranged marriages in the first few years of marriage. In later years, however, those in arranged marriages profess more love than those in love marriages.

In sum, arranged marriages have traditionally been very common in the world, although they are currently declining in popularity. That they are declining does suggest that they are not currently perceived by people in cultures where they occur to be as desirable as they used to be, although in many cultures the evidence of their success rate is quite good. Perhaps the declining rate of arranged marriages reflects changing norms in what people expect out of their relationships.

SUMMARY

Many physical features that people find attractive in others are common across a number of cultures. People in all cultures seem to be attracted to clear complexions, bilateral symmetry, and average features. However, there is considerable cultural variation in what is perceived to be an attractive body, particularly, an attractive female body. The current Western ideal of thinness was not prevalent in the West even a generation ago, and in many cultures heavier bodies are preferred.

It is likely that people universally are attracted to those with whom they interact a lot. However, the well-researched finding that people are attracted to others who are similar to themselves does not generalize to the same degree in all cultures.

Although cultures vary in many ways with respect to relationships, there appear to be four universal basic elements by which relationships can be understood. All relationships appear to consist of one or more of the following elements: communal sharing, authority ranking, equality matching, and market pricing. These basic elements can be combined to form the universe of possible human relations. However, even though these four basic elements are common everywhere, different cultures emphasize some more than others.

There are important cultural differences in how people conceive of friends and enemies. In low-relational-mobility contexts, people view relationships as existing naturally, often without any effort by the individuals to pursue that relationship, and even when the basis of the relationship is not positive. In contrast, in high-relational-mobility contexts, such as in much of Western cultures, people appear to view some kinds of relationships as not existing unless people decide to make the effort to pursue them. These efforts seem to hinge on whether people think the relationship will be rewarding in some way. As evidence of this reasoning, West Africans view friendships as entailing costs because obligations are an important part of friendships; as a result, they are more cautious toward friends in general than are people from Western cultures. Moreover, West Africans are more likely than Westerners to view enemies as a natural part of their relationships. People who move frequently also tend to view relationships differently, as compared to people who maintain stable residences.

The experience of romantic love appears to be found in all cultures, yet it plays a different role in marriages across cultures. In many current and historical cultures, marriages are arranged, and the relationship begins without much in the way of romantic love. In contrast, the norm in many other cultures is that members of a couple should love each other before they consider getting married. Cultures that have extended family systems are more likely to rely on arranged marriage systems than cultures with more nuclear family structures.

THINK ABOUT IT

1. What beauty standards do you think are the most different across cultures?
2. How does the mere exposure effect relate to the propinquity effect?
3. Which of Fiske's elementary forms of relationships are involved in your relationship with your best friend?
4. Why is the similarity-attraction effect weaker in low-relational-mobility contexts?
5. Why does physical attractiveness seem to be associated with less well-being in Ghana and in the rural United States compared with the urban United States?
6. Given what you have read about relational mobility, in what contexts do you think people would invest larger portions of their income on cosmetics and clothes to make them look more attractive? Why?
7. If you accepted a lifetime job in a small town, how do you think your attitudes toward relationships would change from what they are now?
8. From an evolutionary respective, why do humans have romantic love? Why don't salmon seem to have love?
9. What do you think are the pros and cons of arranged marriages compared to love marriages?
10. Why do you think arranged marriages have been on the decline in most parts of the world?

KEY TERMS

Propinquity Effect, 451
Mere Exposure Effect, 452
Similarity-Attraction
    Effect, 453

Communal Sharing, 455
Authority Ranking, 455
Equality Matching, 456
Market Pricing, 456

High Relational Mobility, 460
Low Relational Mobility, 461
Simpático, 467

The Jewish religion places emphasis on following religious practices, whereas the Christian religion places emphasis on private beliefs. As a result, Christians are more likely than Jewish people to view bad thoughts as a moral problem.

MORALITY, RELIGION, AND JUSTICE

The first few months of 2006 were extremely volatile, as the world witnessed a widespread series of enraged demonstrations. Throughout the Muslim world in the Middle East, Africa, and Asia and among Muslim groups in North America, the South Pacific, and Europe, people were furiously, and sometimes violently, expressing their rage. The demonstrations left dozens of people killed, and a number of embassies were burned to the ground. Flags were torched on a daily basis, and there were repeated calls for the violent deaths of the offenders. What was the source of all this widespread outrage? Cartoons. A few months earlier, a Danish newspaper had published cartoons that depicted the Muslim prophet Muhammad. This publication violated a deeply held belief among Muslims that the prophet should never be portrayed. All the worse, many of the cartoons showed the prophet in deliberately offensive ways, such as with a bomb in his turban. Later, citing the importance of freedom of expression, newspapers from many countries around the world reprinted the cartoons, which resulted in even more anger and further fanned the flames of outrage. And 9 years later, the issue was still at the center of a violent conflict. In early 2015 the headquarters of *Charlie Hebdo*, a satirical news magazine in Paris, was attacked and a dozen people were murdered in apparent payback for offensive cartoons of Muhammad that the magazine published. The political stability of much of the world has been threatened by these cartoons.

The issue of whether it was inappropriate to publish caricatures of Muhammad deeply polarized the world. People on each side of the conflict were angry and rather mystified at the reactions of those on the other side. Many Westerners were puzzled over why the cartoons sparked such outrage. Many understood that the cartoons could be seen as offensive to some, but, as many Western commentators argued, such kinds of offense are the price that people pay to live in a society that treasures the value of freedom of expression. The editor of the Danish newspaper justified his decision to publish the cartoons by noting that Christian images are satirized quite frequently—for example, a much-publicized Danish painting showed Jesus with an erection. So why not Muhammad?

On the other hand, many Muslims view the issue of caricaturizing Muhammad in largely sacred terms. They say that some behaviors are viewed as so deeply offensive that they should never be tolerated, even if they might limit freedom of expression. Many Muslims do not believe that freedom trumps all other values (**Figure 12.1**). Indeed, the sign of one Muslim protestor captured the angry feelings shared by many: "Freedom go to Hell!" The publication of the cartoons was viewed by many Muslims to be an attack on the Muslim faith and a gesture to further aggravate already strained relations between the cultures. Later in this chapter we'll make sense of why some Muslims and some Christians saw the publication of the Muhammad cartoons in such different terms.

FIGURE 12.1 Although freedom is a deeply cherished value in much of the world, there are contexts in which some think it should be subjugated by other values, such as preserving that which is sacred.

The cartoon controversy, and the growing tensions in recent years between some people of Christian and Muslim faiths, underscores the central role of culture in world affairs. The conflict reflects what Samuel Huntington had in mind when he argued in his 1996 book *The Clash of Civilizations* that the fundamental source of conflict in the new world would not be primarily ideological or economic but rather cultural and religious.

Huntington's thesis has been controversial, in part because a common perception of many people, particularly academics, is that the world is quickly becoming secularized. That is, as the world develops and progresses, and science continues to make one discovery after another, religious explanations of phenomena are becoming supplanted by rational and scientific explanations. This view, known as **secularization theory**, holds that religion is on the decline and that people around the world are discovering new secular and rational ways to make sense of their lives. The 19th-century German philosopher Friedrich Nietzsche was an early proponent of this view and famously claimed, "God is dead."

There is no doubt that science has made enormous progress since Nietzsche's time and that many prefer scientific explanations over religious accounts.

However, this trend of exploding scientific discovery, together with a move toward a more educated populace across the world, is not living up to Nietzsche's predictions. God is not dead, at least not in the minds of the majority of the world. Although religiosity has been dropping in places like Scandinavia and East Asia (Norenzayan, 2013), in much of the world it remains a significant force. In the United States, despite having the world's largest economy and being home of the greatest number of scientific advances over the past century, religion has not been on the wane. Approximately 94% of Americans report believing in God (Greeley, 1991), and there are many signs that religiosity has increased over the past decades in the United States (e.g., Greeley & Hout, 1999). Many of the religions of the world, especially Islam and Christianity, are growing at breakneck speed (Jenkins, 2002). If anything, religion may even be growing in importance across the planet (Berger, 1999).

Herein lies a problem in which cultural psychology is caught right in the middle. Religiosity appears to be on the upswing in many parts of the world, and people from different cultures and religions are coming into contact with each other more than ever before. However, there has been growing hostility between the different faiths. The terrorist attacks of September 11, 2001, forced everyone to confront the pronounced and important cross-cultural variation that exists in what is perceived to be a good way of living one's life. Osama bin Laden and many other Islamic extremists have viewed countries with industrialized Christian cultures, particularly the United States, as lands of depraved infidels, where people have lost their way. Likewise, many fundamentalist Christians have viewed much in Islam as inherently immoral. The Reverend Franklin Graham, for example, called Islam a "very evil and wicked religion." How can people from different cultural and religious backgrounds view what is right and wrong in such different ways? The consequences of cultural differences in perceptions of morality underlie many of the past and, surely, future conflicts around the world.

"You picked the wrong religion, period. I'm not going to argue about it."

This chapter explores how moral reasoning and perceptions of justice are both similar and different across cultures. Whereas some moral violations are quite universally recognized as problematic, the perception of others varies considerably (e.g., Abarbanell & Hauser, 2010), addressing a central theme of this book regarding the tension between universal and culturally variable aspects of mental processes. Understanding another culture's basis for deciding what is right and wrong is an inherently challenging task. Perhaps in no other domain of psychological research are the challenges of conceptualizing cultural differences more daunting. How do we evaluate what is right and wrong in other cultures if our moral standards were acquired through socialization in our own culture? Are our moral standards limited to our own cultural context, or do moral principles transcend culture? Given the inherent difficulties in addressing these questions, I think this is a good occasion to take a step back and think about how we can learn to understand cultural variation more generally. In the next section I discuss ethnocentrism and the challenge that it presents for considering cultural differences in morality.

Ethnocentrism and Interpreting Cultural Variability

As discussed in Chapter 1, ethnocentrism is a difficult barrier to overcome in trying to understand the ways of other cultures. Typically, ethnocentrism leads people to assume that their own culture's way of life is in some ways better or more natural than that of others. Avoiding an ethnocentric perspective is extremely difficult because people are socialized to think in ways consistent with their cultural values and to evaluate practices in terms of how well they fit with a culture's views on what is good or bad. Because of ethnocentrism bias, it is an enormous challenge to consider standards for psychological phenomena that would be universally valid, rather than those favored within one's own culture.

As a demonstration of just how hard it is to step outside one's own cultural framework when evaluating cultural practices, consider how we would investigate the highly controversial question, "Which cultures provide the highest quality of life?" We could use many different quality-of-life standards to rank cultures, and these different standards would yield vastly different rank orderings of nations. For example, we could operationalize the quality of life as meaning the average level of positive emotional experiences among cultural members, as this would indicate people's subjective satisfaction with how their lives are going. A rank ordering of cultures on this variable would yield Puerto Rico and Mexico to be the world's developmental standard of positive emotions (Inglehart, 2004). Alternatively, we could consider longevity as a quality-of-life standard, as this would provide an objective index of the physical health of different cultural groups. This operationalization of quality of life would reveal that Singapore and Japan are the developmental standard (Central Intelligence Agency, 2006b). Or, a case could be made that per capita income is the best indicator of quality of life, in which case Norway and the United States would represent the developmental standard (Central Intelligence Agency, 2006a). Another possibility is to measure

quality of life in terms of how well countries minimize inequality among their citizens; Denmark and Japan would then represent the standard (Human Development Reports, 2005). Or we might opt for the lowest suicide rates as an indicator of a good life, making Egypt and Peru as the countries providing the highest quality of life for their citizens (Schmidtke et al., 1998). Evolutionary biologists discuss success in terms of an organism's "fitness," which reflects its number of surviving offspring. By that standard of quality of life, the Palestinian Territories and the Democratic Republic of Congo would score the highest in the world (Population Reference Bureau, 2006).

We might consider many other variables to reflect quality of life (spiritual satisfaction, education, lowest crime rates, cleanliness of environment, stability of family relations, number of Nobel Prizes), and for each one we would get a different ranking of the world's cultures and thus a different developmental progression. It is possible to rank cultures on any given variable; however, the problem is in choosing the variable that makes sense. People from different cultures won't agree on the yardstick for measuring cultures because they do not agree on what each culture values most (e.g., Schwartz & Sagiv, 1995). In general, cultures tend to value more those characteristics for which their own culture is particularly accomplished. As Malcolm Gladwell (2011) put it, "Who comes out on top, in any ranking system, is really about who is doing the ranking" (p. 75). This problem is inherent in all efforts to evaluate phenomena across cultures; however, given the tight overlap between values and morality, it is most salient when we consider how cultures differ in their ideas of what is right or wrong. The cultural variation in moral reasoning, described next, would seem to behoove one to be slow to pass judgment on other cultures (e.g., Shweder, 2000) and first consider why the various cultural differences exist as they do.

Kohlberg's Stages of Moral Development

The most influential model of moral reasoning in psychology was created by Lawrence Kohlberg (1971; see **Figure 12.2**). He maintained that cognitive abilities underlie moral reasoning and that these abilities progress as individuals develop, mature, and are educated. The ways people conceive of what is right and what is wrong hinge on the stage of moral development they have reached.

Kohlberg proposed a three-level model that could capture the developmental progression of moral reasoning in all cultures of the world (his model further distinguished between more fine-tuned stages, which I don't discuss here). This model has been enormously influential in the study of moral reasoning and has sparked an immense amount of research, both supporting it and challenging it. The levels are briefly summarized here.

FIGURE 12.2 Lawrence Kohlberg.

Level 1: The Preconventional Level

At the lowest level, individuals understand the cultural rules and labels of what is good and bad but interpret these labels in terms of either the physical or hedonistic consequences of their actions. **Preconventional moral reasoning** suggests that people interpret morality based on a calculation of how much better or worse off they would be for acting in a certain way. What determines whether an action is good or bad is whether it satisfies one's own needs, and occasionally the needs of others. Morality at this level is about trying to behave in a way that provides the best overall return.

Level 2: The Conventional Level

At the second level, people are able to identify themselves with a particular group and social order, and they show loyalty toward this group. The social order of the group is actively maintained, supported, and justified by individuals' efforts to live up to the group's standards. **Conventional moral reasoning** is about viewing actions as moral to the extent that they help maintain and facilitate the social order. Actions are seen as morally wrong if they involve violating any rules or laws that the social order has maintained, regardless of what those rules or laws are about. This level dictates that morality is about following the rules, and individuals should not question where those rules come from.

Level 3: The Postconventional Level

At the postconventional level, moral values and principles are seen to exist separately from the authority of the social groups that hold them. **Postconventional moral reasoning** is based on the consideration of abstract ethical principles of what is right and wrong, and moral decisions are reached based on the logical extensions of those principles. Whether others agree with you or whether there are rules that contradict you are independent of whether the action is viewed to be moral. Good behavior is seen as that which is consistent with a set of universal ethical principles that emphasize justice and individual rights.

Cross-Cultural Evidence for Kohlberg's Model

Researchers use Kohlberg's model to determine the levels at which people or cultures make decisions to solve moral dilemmas. Participants are presented with moral dilemmas and are asked to choose the right solution to that dilemma. Researchers are more interested in the reasons participants give to justify their answers than in the answers themselves. Here is an example of the kind of moral dilemma that is presented to participants:

> In Europe, a woman was near death from a special kind of cancer. There was one drug that the doctors thought might save her. It was a form of radium that a druggist in the same town had recently discovered. The drug was expensive to make, but the druggist was charging 10 times what the drug cost him to make. He paid $200 for the radium and charged $2,000 for a small dose of the drug. The sick woman's husband, Heinz, went to everyone he knew to borrow the money, but he could only get together about $1,000, which is half of what it cost. He told the druggist that his wife was dying, and asked him to sell it cheaper or let him pay later. But the druggist said, "No, I discovered the drug and I'm going to make money from it." So Heinz got desperate and broke into the man's store to steal the drug for his wife. Should Heinz have done that? Why or why not?

Kohlberg maintained that the three levels in his model represent a *universal* pattern of moral development the world over. His own words best summarize this claim: "almost all individuals in all cultures use the same . . . moral categories, concepts, or principles, and all individuals in all cultures go through the same order or sequence of gross stage development, though they vary in rate and terminal point of development" (1971, p. 176). The model is proposed to be universal because the levels are always seen to follow sequentially. People do not reason at a conventional level before they have reasoned at a preconventional level, and this is argued to be as true of Zambians as it is of Americans. The different levels of the model reflect different abilities and motivations to attend to and conceptualize moral concerns.

One aspect of the model that is *not* proposed to be universal is in the levels that different cultures reach. Kohlberg makes no claim that Americans and Zambians are equally likely to reason at the same level. Likewise, Kohlberg never claims that the full range of moral levels should be evident in all cultures. That is, the model presupposes cultural variation in the extent of people's moral reasoning capacities.

Kohlberg's model has been enormously influential in the study of moral psychology, but how well does this perspective explain moral reasoning across cultures?

Much cross-cultural research has explored the applicability of Kohlberg's model. One review explored the 45 studies that had been conducted up to that point, which had investigated the different levels of moral reasoning in 27 cultural areas from around the world (Snarey, 1985). The results indicated some universality in moral reasoning. In all cultural groups there were adults who reasoned at the conventional levels, and in no cultural groups did the average adult reason at the preconventional level, although many samples of children revealed evidence of preconventional reasoning. This review suggests that Kohlberg's model might be universally applicable in explaining preconventional and conventional moral reasoning around the world. However, evidence of postconventional reasoning—reasoning based on justice and individual rights—was not universally found. Although every urban Western sample contained at least some individuals who showed reasoning based on justice and individual rights, not a single person from the traditional tribal and village folk populations that were studied showed such reasoning.

There are two competing interpretations of these pronounced cultural differences. One is that the traditional societies do not provide the educational experiences necessary for their members to reason about justice and individual rights in postconventional terms. Although it is possible that Westerners do show more sophisticated stages of moral reasoning than most of the world, there is the risk of an ethnocentric bias in defining the developmental standard on the basis of the kind of reasoning observed in Western cultures. A second interpretation is to note that urban Western environments are one kind of environment and tribal environments are another kind of environment, and that people develop a moral framework that best fits their environment. This second interpretation would attribute the lack of reasoning about justice and individual rights among tribal and folk populations to possible other categories of moral reasoning that are missing from Kohlberg's framework.

How might we test which of these two interpretations is most compelling? Some researchers have addressed this question by exploring whether there are other ethical principles aside from justice and individual rights on which people in other cultures base their moral reasoning.

Ethics of Autonomy, Community, and Divinity

Shweder and colleagues (1997) argue that Kohlberg's model of moral reasoning represents just one of three codes of ethics that guide people's moral judgments around the world. They refer to the code of ethics inherent in Kohlberg's model as

SIPRESS

"Why is it we never focus on the things that unite us, like falafel?"

an **ethic of autonomy**. This ethic views morality in terms of individual freedom and rights violations. It emphasizes personal choice, the right to engage in free contracts, and individual liberty. An act is seen as immoral under the ethic of autonomy when it directly hurts another person or infringes on another's rights and freedoms as an individual. For example, an immoral action would be to steal someone's lunch money, because it causes harm to that person. The ethic of autonomy appears to be of critical importance in all cultures, and indeed it's hard to imagine how any culture could function if its members did not view harming each other to be problematic.

A second code of ethics that Shweder proposes is an **ethic of community**, which emphasizes that individuals have duties that conform with their roles in a community or social hierarchy. According to this code, there is an ethical principle to uphold one's interpersonal duties and obligations toward others. Actions are seen as wrong when individuals fail to perform their duties. For example, an immoral action would be a son's failure to attend his parents' wedding anniversary celebration because he doesn't feel like it. Immoral behaviors are perceived as those that involve a failure to live up to the duties and obligations associated with one's roles.

A third code of ethics that Shweder proposed is an **ethic of divinity**, which is concerned with sanctity and the perceived "natural order" of things. This code contains the ethical principle that one is obligated to preserve the standards mandated by a transcendent authority. It involves a belief that God (or gods, depending on one's religion) has created a sacred world, and everyone's obligation is to respect and preserve the sanctity of this world. In this ethic, actions are seen as immoral if they cause impurity or degradation to oneself or others, or if one shows any disrespect for God or God's creations. For example, caricaturizing the prophet Muhammad is a blatant violation of this ethic for many Muslims. Immoral behavior in this ethic is framed in terms of sinning against the sacredness of God.

These three different codes of ethics would be seen as moral codes to the extent that they reflect an understanding of right and wrong that is not based on either one's own subjective preferences (which would indicate that the belief is viewed as a personal choice) or a community's view of what is right and wrong (which would indicate that the belief is seen to be a matter of convention). Although Westerners have a tendency to view the ultimate principles of proper behavior as those that protect individual rights, in much of the world the ethics of community and divinity serve as important moral principles. Because these three ethics are not equally elaborated across all cultural contexts (as we'll see later), they lie at the root of some important cross-cultural grievances. For example, in the case of the cartoon controversy introduced at the beginning of this chapter, it appears that the Muslim protestors were viewing the controversy more from the perspective of the ethic of divinity, and publishing cartoons that deface Muhammad are unacceptable according to this ethic. In contrast, the reasoning of the Western newspaper editors appears to have been based on the ethic of autonomy, in which censoring free speech is intolerable. It is difficult for these two conflicting groups to see eye to eye on this issue, then, because their understanding of what is right and wrong is grounded in different moral frameworks.

Ethic of Community

Much research has been conducted on the important role of the ethic of community in guiding moral reasoning. Carol Gilligan has made the case that interpersonal obligations represent a kind of morality that is distinct from an emphasis on individual rights and that women are more likely to reason this way than men are (e.g., Gilligan, 1977). Although there has been much controversy over whether these gender differences in moral reasoning really exist (e.g., Gilligan & Attanucci, 1988; Walker, 1984), there has been much development of Gilligan's claim for an interpersonal foundation of moral reasoning, one that is more prominent in some non-Western cultures.

GEMEINSCHAFT AND GESELLSCHAFT RELATIONS. The debate about whether interpersonal obligations and justice obligations vary in different cultures can be traced back to the work of the 19th-century German sociologist Ferdinand Tonnies (1887/1957). Tonnies argued that there are two means by which individuals can relate to each other in a group. Some groups are categorized as **Gemeinschaft**, which loosely translates from German as "community." Gemeinschaft groups are characteristic of smaller folk organizations, and within these groups interpersonal relationships play an especially important role. Gemeinschaft relationships bind people together with the social glue of concord—that is, relationships are viewed as real, organic, and ends in themselves. People feel connected to others because they feel a unity of spirit, and these relationships tend not to be thought of in instrumental terms, nor are they often evaluated or negotiated. The relationships are central to an individual's identity, and they reflect an understanding of the self that is consistent with an interdependent self. The integral role of interpersonal relations in Gemeinschaft groups suggests that obligations associated with one's relationships would take on the weight of full moral obligations (Snarey & Keljo, 1991).

In contrast, Tonnies argued that another kind of group can be characterized as **Gesellschaft**, which literally means "association" or "society." Gesellschaft groups, which are more characteristic of modern Western societies, treat relationships as imaginary, instrumental, and a means to an end. The primary focus within these groups is on autonomous individuals who are bound to one another through social convention. That is, groups come up with their own sets of rules, norms, and laws by which individuals need to behave, and these rules arise out of public consensus. Relations in Gesellschaft groups tend to be perceived as relatively impersonal and somewhat contractual, which leads to the necessity of justice obligations to govern disputes between individuals. In Gesellschaft groups, individuals can't be expected always to behave in prosocial ways toward others, because they don't have strong obligations toward them; so formalized rules are necessary to keep people in line. When interpersonal relations are reduced to serving utilitarian means among autonomous individuals, as they largely are in Gesellschaft groups, then a morality of justice should take precedence.

In Gemeinschaft groups, the interpersonal obligations that bind individuals together are not objective or impartial enough to be governed by a system of justice and contracts (Snarey & Keljo, 1991). A good example of a Gemeinschaft group is the nuclear family. For the most part, it seems very unfamily-like for families to create contractual agreements regarding who will do the dishes, to govern disputes by appealing to abstract principles of justice, or to give each family member (including young children) equal rights and power over all family decisions. I realize that among some North American families there has been a growing trend in this direction (take the example of children suing their parents, or parents paying children piecemeal rates for completing various chores), which is evidence that North America has become such a prototype of Gesellschaft relations that even the nuclear family has been affected. Throughout most of the world, these kinds of family arrangements would be viewed as incomprehensible, as many other cultures are more firmly entrenched in a Gemeinschaft tradition.

ETHIC OF COMMUNITY IN INDIA. People the world over have obligations toward others; however, an important question is whether they interpret these as *moral* obligations. When I say "moral" here, I mean something specific, and something that might differ from people's typical understanding of the word. Moral obligations are different from other responsibilities in a couple of important ways. First, moral obligations are viewed as *objective obligations*. That is, people believe that they have an obligation to act in a certain way, even if there is no official rule or law that requires them to do so. If the obligation exists only when a law is present, then the obligation is perceived as a matter of convention and is not an objective obligation.

Second, moral obligations are perceived as *legitimately regulated*. That is, people should be prevented from engaging in a moral violation, or they should be punished if they act in such a way. If people feel that someone should not be prevented from engaging in an act, they are viewing the act as a matter of personal choice and not a moral obligation. Most Westerners, for example, would view pickpocketing as a violation of a moral obligation because stealing from another is perceived as wrong, regardless of what rules or laws exist, and would hold that pickpockets should be prevented from stealing. In contrast, most Westerners would view failing to attend a friend's graduation ceremony as a matter of personal choice rather than as a violation of a moral obligation. Westerners might expect people to attend their friend's ceremonies, but they generally don't think they should be punished for not attending. As another example, most Westerners would view a 17-year-old who bought a beer from a bar as committing a conventional violation, not a moral one, as they could imagine that in some cultural contexts this action would not be breaking a law. Violations are considered to be moral ones only if they are objective obligations that can be legitimately regulated.

The moral force of interpersonal obligations has been demonstrated in a number of studies (e.g., Miller, Bersoff, & Harwood, 1990). Many studies of moral reasoning provide people with dilemmas in which neither option seems ideal, but people's moral principles can be discerned by examining the trade-offs that they are willing to make. We can gauge the strength of people's motivations by examining the kinds of things they would give up to preserve them. Imagine, if you will, what you would do if you were in Ben's situation:

> Ben was in Los Angeles on business. When his meetings were over, he went to the train station. Ben planned to travel to San Francisco in order to attend the wedding of his best friend. He needed to catch the very next train if he was to be on time for the ceremony, as he had to deliver the wedding rings.
>
> However, Ben's wallet was stolen in the train station. He lost all of his money as well as his ticket to San Francisco.
>
> Ben approached several officials as well as passengers at the train station and asked them to lend him money to buy a new ticket. But, because he was a stranger, no one was willing to lend him the money he needed. While Ben was sitting on a bench trying to decide what to do next, a well-dressed man sitting next to him walked away for a minute. Looking over at where the man had been sitting, Ben noticed that the man had left his coat unattended. Sticking out of the man's coat pocket was a train ticket to San Francisco. Ben knew that he could take the ticket and use it to travel to San Francisco on the next train. He also saw that the man had more than enough money in his coat pocket to buy another train ticket.

What should Ben do? Should he steal the ticket so he can deliver the wedding rings to his best friend in time for the wedding, or should he not take the ticket and miss the wedding? Imagine that these are the only two possible solutions—there would be no other way for Ben to get to the wedding in time.

This is a tough call, because obviously neither of these solutions is very satisfying. The first solution would require Ben to commit a justice violation, as he would be causing harm to the other innocent passenger. On the other hand, the second solution would require Ben to violate an interpersonal obligation, as his friend is counting on him to deliver the rings on time. Without the rings, the wedding would be ruined. Either way, Ben is committing a violation. We would expect, however, that his decision will indicate which violation he perceives to be more serious. Think about what you would do if you were in Ben's shoes.

Participants were presented with a number of such scenarios that pitted interpersonal and justice obligations against each other. In these scenarios, the extremity of the situation was varied: some involved minor breaches of justice, some moderate breaches, and other extreme breaches of justice obligations. In the example above, for Ben to steal the train ticket was seen as a moderate justice violation. Hindu Indian and American college students were asked to decide what the target in the scenarios should do: Should he protect the interpersonal obligation or should he protect the justice obligation? The results are shown in **Figure 12.3**.

One thing to note about these results is that aside from the Indians in the minor justice breach scenarios, there was a great deal of variability within cultures. Within each culture, many people would choose the justice obligation and many would choose the interpersonal obligation. There is not a widely shared understanding of the best

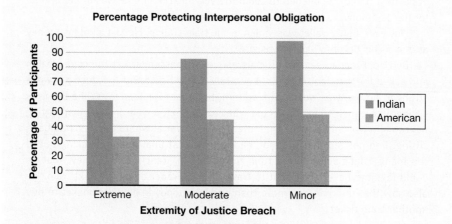

FIGURE 12.3 When interpersonal and justice obligations conflict, Indians tend to prefer protecting interpersonal obligations, whereas Americans tend to prefer protecting justice obligations.

way to resolve these kinds of conflicts. Despite this variation within cultures, there is a clear difference across cultures. Indians are more likely to resolve the conflict by fulfilling their interpersonal obligations than Americans are. Furthermore, other questions in the study revealed that whereas both Indians and Americans viewed the justice breaches in moral terms, Indians were far more likely to view the interpersonal breaches in moral terms (that is, objective obligations that could be legitimately regulated) than Americans. This demonstrates just how seriously Indians take interpersonal obligations, which were perceived as more serious than justice obligations.

The ethic of community thus renders one's social obligations as fully moral obligations. In cultures where this ethic is more strongly embraced, such as in India, the decision of whether to act in ways consistent with one's role obligations is not perceived as a matter of personal choice—it is a moral imperative. Interestingly, the moral basis of acting in ways consistent with one's interpersonal obligations is also associated with different feelings towards those helping actions. Among Americans, when they feel that they have an obligation to help someone out (such as seeing a family member in need) they feel less positive about their helping than when they don't have any specific interpersonal obligations (such as seeing a stranger in need). Indeed, the words *obligation* and *duty* have somewhat negative connotations for Americans; Americans prefer seeing their helping behaviors as a matter of personal choice. In contrast, among Indians, having an interpersonal obligation is associated with more positive feelings toward helping than when there is no such obligation. Obligations and duties are more internalized among Indians, and they derive more pleasure from fulfilling them (Miller, Das, & Chakravarthy, 2013; also see Buchtel, 2009, for similar results with Chinese).

Ethic of Divinity

The third ethic that Shweder proposed was the ethic of divinity. The abstract ethical principle that Shweder argued to be inherent in this moral code was that one is obligated to respect or preserve the sanctity of the natural order of things, as dictated by a transcendent moral authority (such as God). Immoral actions according to this ethic are those that are perceived to violate the natural order of things. What does it mean to violate the natural order of things? To get an idea, consider the following scenario used in a study of violations of the ethic of divinity (Haidt, Koller, & Dias, 1993):

> A man goes to the supermarket once a week and buys a dead chicken. But before cooking the chicken, he has sexual intercourse with it. Then he cooks and eats it.

All right, perhaps I should have warned you that that was coming. I chose that example from the study because it's very effective at making the point. Now that you've read this, I'm guessing that you're most likely thinking this man's behavior is repulsive, bad, and disgusting and that you might even be upset that I asked you to read it. If those are your feelings, you're probably sensing that the natural order of things has been breached. You're experiencing a violation of the ethic of divinity.

However, moral reasoning is not just about having a gut-level reaction that some kinds of behaviors are bad. There are many kinds of actions that people perceive as bad, but not necessarily immoral. Remember that for something to be considered immoral it needs to be viewed as universally wrong and as something that should be prevented. In this particular example, let's assume that the man's behavior was part of a regular ritual in another culture. Would his behavior be wrong then? If you say "No," then you are making the case that this behavior can be understood as a social convention and thus not in full moral terms. Do you think this man should be prevented from doing this again, or punished in any way? Should we make laws against having sex with chickens, or forbid grocers from selling the man any more chickens? If you think "No," then you are interpreting his behavior as a matter of personal choice—a rather unsavory choice, to be sure, but a choice nonetheless.

When this scenario was posed to students at the University of Pennsylvania (who, on average, can be considered to be of high socioeconomic status), only 23% said that the man's behavior would be wrong even if this practice was part of a custom in another culture, and only 27% said that the man should be punished or prevented from doing this again (Haidt et al., 1993). That is, the majority of Penn students did not view the man's behavior as immoral, although the vast majority perceived it to be quite disgusting.

The same question was also posed to high- and low-socioeconomic-status people in two cities in Brazil as well as to low-socioeconomic-status people in Philadelphia. People responded rather differently. Among the Brazilians, about 50% of the high-status participants viewed the practice to be universally wrong, and about 56% felt that the man should be punished. That is, roughly half of the high-status Brazilian participants viewed the behavior in moral terms. For the low-status Brazilians, in contrast, about 87% viewed the behavior as universally wrong, and about 83% felt that the man should be punished. The low-status Americans responded very similarly to the low-status Brazilians, with 87% universalizing their judgments and 80% believing that the man needs to be punished. That is, the majority of the low-status people, regardless of whether they were from Brazil or the United States, viewed the man's behavior as immoral. Other research has also found that people of lower socioeconomic status show more of a concern with the ethic of divinity (Horberg, Oveis, Keltner, & Cohen, 2009).

Why do we find the same behavior viewed as largely not immoral by one group of participants and largely immoral by the other? Other questions the participants were asked shed some light on this question. They were also asked whether the man's behavior was causing harm to anyone or whether they would feel bothered if they saw his behavior. In general, most people did not see the man's behavior as causing anyone much harm, but most people said they would feel bothered if they witnessed this event, and these responses did not differ across the samples. However, these questions did reveal an important cultural difference in terms of how people were concluding whether the behavior was immoral. For the high-status samples, particularly the students from Penn, participants were more likely to view the man's behavior as immoral if they felt that someone was being harmed than if they said they would feel bothered by the event. That is, whether they viewed the man's behavior as immoral hinged largely on whether these participants felt that the behavior caused anyone (usually the man himself, in this instance) any harm. They appeared to operate under the ethic of autonomy principle that moral violations stem from causing harm. In contrast, the low-status participants were more likely to view the man's behavior as immoral if they said they were bothered by the event than if they felt that anyone was being harmed. That is, a moral judgment was largely predicated on whether these participants found the event to be bothersome or disgusting. The low-status participants were not relying much on an ethic of autonomy and instead seemed affected by their emotional reaction to seeing a violation of the perceived natural order.

In sum, when we consider other ethical principles that can guide moral reasoning, it appears that the ethic of autonomy is not the only game in town. Furthermore, the tendency of the low-status participants to base their moral decisions on how bothered they were suggests that the task of reaching moral judgments might not always occur in cold, cognitive terms, in the way that Kohlberg described. Rather, people often come up with moral justifications to rationalize the strong emotions they have when witnessing undesirable behaviors (Haidt, 2001).

Culture Wars

One interesting point about the American participants in the Haidt study discussed above is that the data for the high- and low-status participants were collected just three blocks apart. The college student data were collected on the University of Pennsylvania campus, and the data from the low-socioeconomic-status people were collected from a street corner in an inner-city neighborhood that bordered the campus. Three blocks were all that separated a world of difference in reasoning about what is immoral. This difference underscores something important: There are pronounced differences of opinion on moral issues even within a country, something that has been described as an ongoing "culture war" within the United States (Hunter, 1991).

FIGURE 12.4 The different moral ethics that people embrace underlie many of the ideological differences within countries.

Currently, there is a highly polarized public debate regarding a number of hot-button political issues in the United States (see **Figure 12.4**). Some of the key topics of controversy are abortion, gay marriage, and euthanasia. These debates are often marked by angry protests and repeated arguments that go largely unheeded by the opposing groups. Why don't people come to accept the arguments from the other side and reach a peaceful consensus on these topics? Historically, it was believed that many of the differences of opinion on political issues within the United States were drawn along the lines separating religious denominations, such as Catholics, Jews, and Protestants. Although religious denomination is one important way that cultural worldviews differ within the country (as you'll see in the next section on the morality of thoughts), it is probably not the most relevant difference for making sense of the opposing political alliances that divide the nation today. Hunter (1991) proposed that a culture war exists in the United States and that the battle lines are drawn between those who have an "impulse toward orthodoxy" and those who have an "impulse toward progressivism" (p. 43), regardless of their religious denomination.

Religious adherents who are **orthodox** are committed to the idea of a transcendent authority. This authority is viewed to have existed long before humans and as operating independently of people. Furthermore, this authority is perceived to be more knowledgeable and more powerful than all of human experience. In the orthodox view, this transcendent authority originated a moral code and revealed it to human beings in sacred texts. This moral code is perceived to stand across all times and circumstances and should not be altered to accommodate any societal changes or individual differences. Rather, individuals and society are expected to adapt themselves to this ordained moral code (Jensen, 1997b).

On the other hand, adherents of **progressive** religions emphasize the importance of human agency in understanding and formulating a moral code. Progressivists reject the view that a transcendent authority reveals itself and its will to humans; they believe that humans play an integral role in the formulation of a moral code. Progressivists believe that because social circumstances change, the moral code must change along with them. In this important way, progressivists differ from the orthodox. Note, however, that this is a broad distinction, and an individual's religious impulses and political values do not always fall so neatly into these two types.

Which of Shweder's three moral ethics are typically used by the orthodox and progressivists when they reason about moral issues? Jensen (1997b) reasoned that the ethic of divinity seems to bear a close affinity with orthodox conceptions of morality. Orthodox individuals seek to follow sacred guidelines granted by a transcendent authority as they attempt to come closer to moral and spiritual purity. This emphasis appears to be very much in accordance with the emphasis on striving for purity and avoidance of degradation that characterizes the ethic of divinity. Likewise, the ethic of autonomy has many similarities with progressivists' conceptions of morality. The ethic of autonomy allows individuals to choose what is right and wrong, provided they do not encroach on the rights of others or cause harm. Hence, there are some theoretical parallels in the distinction between progressivists and the orthodox and the ethics of autonomy and divinity. The ethic of community, on the other hand, which defines moral agents in terms of their social groups and views moral obligations as stemming from the individual's memberships in those groups, seems to characterize all religious orientations, regardless of whether one is more orthodox or progressivist. In sum, we might expect that the two camps of the "culture war" that Hunter refers to can be characterized by the ethics they use to make sense of what is right and wrong.

Jensen (1997b) tested this hypothesis by contrasting American Baptists who belonged to either fundamentalist (orthodox) sects or mainline (progressivist) sects. The participants were asked to explain their moral judgments on a variety of politically charged issues, such as suicide and divorce. Jensen examined their responses to see how similar their justifications were to each of the three ethics. For example, participants were asked whether they felt that abortion is wrong, and to explain their answer. Of the orthodox participants, 100% gave at least one reason that was consistent with the ethic of divinity—that is, they spoke of God's exclusive authority to end human life or they referred to the biblical injunction against taking another person's life. Here is a sample reply from an orthodox Baptist to the question of abortion:

> In the Ten Commandments, [God] said that we should not commit murder. . . . I believe in general when a person disobeys God that it has negative repercussions. I think that's why God tells us the things that He does. He knows what's good for us, and if we'd listen to Him, we'd save [ourselves] a lot of trouble.

This participant's responses indicate that people have an obligation to respect God's commands and that people would be better off if they did just that. There is no questioning of what God might have meant about murder, nor whether this commandment might be interpreted differently in the context of abortion in modern, Western societies. In contrast, when the progressivists reasoned about abortion, 90% of them offered at least one reason that was consistent with the ethic of autonomy—that is, they tended to emphasize that individuals had to interpret the scriptures and reach a conclusion for themselves that avoided harming others. Here's a sample reply from a progressivist Baptist:

> There really has to be some sense of rightness and wrongness that has to transcend what God would think, or what the priest would think, or what my mother would think. It's not up to them, it's up to you. . . . I ultimately believe that every individual has to do what they have to do.

Overall, there were pronounced differences in the kinds of reasons that members of the different Baptist sects gave for justifying whether a practice could be seen as morally right or wrong. **Figure 12.5** shows the average number of reasons given by midlife adult participants that were consistent with the three different ethics across all the different political issues (Jensen, 1997a). Progressivists made moral decisions based primarily on the ethic of autonomy (stressing individual rights) and the ethic of community (stressing obligations toward others); the orthodox were more likely to make their judgments based on the ethic of divinity. The most pronounced differences were with respect to the ethic of divinity and the ethic of autonomy. Although the differences between sects were large, people from each sect occasionally offered justifications from each of the three different ethics. Everyone has the potential to reason in these three different ways, although most people tend to favor one ethic over the others. There is a striking moral divide in the ways that people consider political issues, even within the same religion. Subsequent research

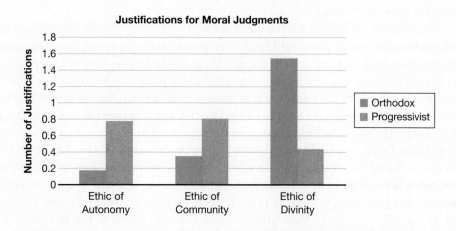

FIGURE 12.5 The justifications of orthodox Baptists tended to reflect the ethic of divinity, whereas the justifications of progressivist Baptists tended to reflect the ethics of autonomy and community.

by Jensen identified this same difference in the use of the three codes of ethics among progressive and orthodox Hindu Indians (Jensen, 1998), which demonstrates that this distinction within cultures is widespread—and is possibly universal. People make judgments about what is right and what is wrong in importantly different ways.

The idea that culture wars exist because people reason about moral issues using different ethics has further been elaborated to explain the moral reasoning of people across the political spectrum (Koleva, Graham, Iyer, Ditto, & Haidt, 2012). Haidt and Graham (2007) expanded on Shweder's three ethics, by identifying five moral intuitions that guide people's moral reasoning. They argued that two separate moral intuitions constituted the ethic of autonomy: specifically, people have intuitions to **avoid harm** and to **protect fairness**. That is, people are sensitive to any behaviors that cause harm to others, and they attend closely to whether resources or rights are distributed in a fair way. Two additional intuitions roughly map onto the ethic of community: People are motivated to **be loyal to their ingroups,** identifying with them, making sacrifices for them, and trusting them more than they trust outgroup members. Also, people tend to **respect hierarchy,** admiring their superiors and believing that subordinates need to act in accordance with the wishes of authority figures. Last, reflecting the ethic of divinity, people are motivated to **achieve purity** and are disgusted at behaviors ruled by the carnal passions (such as lust or gluttony) or by behaviors that suggest contamination of any kind. These five moral intuitions are perceived to be universal concerns for all humans; however, some cultures and some people differ in terms of which of these concerns they emphasize.

To get an idea of how much you are concerned with each of these intuitions, consider how much money you would need to be paid to act in violation of any of them. We can infer that the more money you would need to be paid to violate each of these intuitions, the more strongly you are concerned about protecting each of these values. So, for example, as an assessment of how much you have the intuition to avoid harm, how much money would you need to be paid to stick a pin into the palm of a child you don't know? If you'd be willing to do so for free, you don't have much of an intuition to avoid harm. Protecting fairness can be assessed by the amount you'd need to be paid to say no to a friend's request to help him move into a new apartment, after he had helped you move the month before. Loyalty to ingroups can be assessed by your willingness to burn your country's flag, in private, where no one else would see you. Respect for hierarchy is revealed by your willingness to slap your father in the face (with his permission) as part of a comedy skit. And your intuition to achieve purity could be assessed by your willingness to cook and eat your dog after it dies of natural causes. The more money you'd require to do any of these, the stronger your intuitions for them.

People vary with regards to the strength of their intuitions, and this variation splits down political lines. Americans who identify themselves as strongly liberal tend to have strong intuitions regarding avoiding harm and protecting fairness, but not such strong intuitions for the other three. Americans who identify themselves as strongly conservative, in contrast, tend to have fairly strong intuitions for all five (Graham, Haidt, & Nosek, 2009; **Figure 12.6**). Similar patterns of results have been found by contrasting liberals and conservatives in a wide range of cultures around the world (Graham et al., 2011), suggesting that there is a fairly universal distinction in the moral intuitions of political liberals and conservatives. Moreover, much research shows that Americans who are politically conservative have stronger disgust responses than those who are politically liberal, which is also evidence that more-conservative political beliefs invoke more purity concerns than liberal beliefs (Inbar, Pizarro, & Bloom, 2009).

Although this same set moral foundations may undergird the moral reasoning among people from different cultures, sometimes different foundations are called upon to solve the same problem. For example, in many parts of the world people become vegetarian for moral reasons; however, those reasons can differ across cultures. In North America, vegetarianism is more often associated with liberal political values, which reflect primary concerns with the moral foundations of harm and fairness. In contrast, in India, vegetarianism is more associated with conservative political values, and all five of the moral foundations. Hence, whereas Indian vegetarians embrace more strongly the moral foundations of respecting hierarchy, being loyal to ingroups, and achieving purity compared with omnivores, North American vegetarians don't differ from omnivores on these foundations (Ruby, Heine, Kamble, Cheng, & Waddar, 2013).

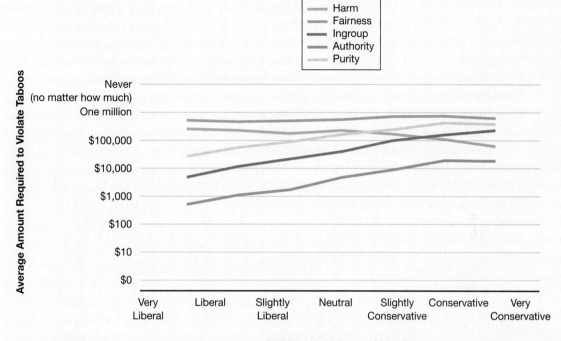

FIGURE 12.6 People who are more politically liberal have stronger moral intuitions for harm avoidance and fairness when compared with their intuition to be loyal to ingroups, to respect authority, and to achieve purity. Political conservatives, in contrast, have strong moral intuitions for all of these.

The Morality of Thoughts

In 1976, while running for the U.S. presidency, Jimmy Carter made a public apology. He confessed that he was guilty of having looked at women with lustful thoughts and of having committed adultery in his heart many times. Carter's confession raises an interesting moral question. Are we morally responsible for the thoughts we entertain? This question addresses the boundaries of our moral worlds—the domains in which we feel it is appropriate to make judgments about what is right and wrong versus the domains in which we feel that such judgments are not relevant. How do our cultural experiences shape where we draw this boundary?

We can contrast Carter's guilty feelings about his lustful fantasies with the apparently unrepentant feelings that Sigmund Freud had about all of the rather nasty thoughts he entertained. Although there is no evidence that Freud engaged in much of the way of immoral behaviors (he was a highly respected citizen in Victorian-era Austria), he certainly considered some provocative thoughts. A view of the rather sordid and wanton ideas that jostled about in Freud's mind is provided by exploring his vast and highly influential writings. Many of Freud's most memorable notions were generated, in part, as he explored his own dreams and introspections. These ideas included his views of the unconscious mind as a cauldron of seething urges, in which boys secretly desire to kill their fathers and have sex with their mothers, girls are distraught in their envy for not having a penis, and the whole of humanity struggles to corral their degenerate motivations to destroy life. If having bad thoughts was a moral issue, then Freud was guilty indeed. However, it is hard to imagine that Freud could have devoted so much thought and effort to exploring his introspections on these unsavory topics if he had felt much guilt for broaching them. Indeed, there is no evidence from his writings that such thoughts bothered him; yet, by all respects, he was an upstanding citizen. Apparently, Freud did not share Carter's view that one's thoughts fall into the domain of moral governance.

Carter and Freud differ from each other in many ways, and one that is relevant to their different moral reasoning is their religious backgrounds. Jimmy Carter was raised as a Southern Baptist, one of the most fundamentalist sects in Protestantism (although he abandoned the sect at the age of 76, interestingly, over a disagreement in moral worldviews). Freud was raised Jewish. Can we see differences in people's views on the morality of thoughts between these two cultural traditions?

Jewish and Christian dogma differ in terms of their holy scriptures. Jewish doctrine is based on the Hebrew Bible and the debates on this doctrine that are included in the Talmud. In contrast, Christian doctrine is based in part on the Hebrew Bible (known to Christians as the Old Testament) but is primarily oriented toward the New Testament, which includes the teachings of Jesus. Exploring these texts reveals some differences relevant to the morality of thoughts. The first place in the Christian Bible that we see clear evidence that thoughts were to be moralized is in the New Testament, where Jesus made the point later echoed by Jimmy Carter, "You have heard that it was said 'you shall not commit adultery': but I say to you, that everyone who looks on a woman to lust for her has committed adultery with her already in his heart" (Matthew 5: 27–28).

In contrast, the Old Testament contains the foundation of the Judeo-Christian moral code in the Ten Commandments. It is interesting that eight of the ten commandments specifically refer to behaviors (e.g., killing is wrong, stealing is wrong), and only two refer to thoughts (e.g., it is wrong to not honor one's parents, it is wrong to covet anything belonging to your neighbor). Even with these last two, however, there is debate as to whether they refer to thoughts or behaviors. Cohen and Rozin (2001) showed that whereas Protestants were more likely to view the commandment to honor one's parents in terms of having respectful thoughts toward them, Jews were more likely to view it in terms of behaviors (e.g., honoring one's parents by taking care of them when they're old). In sum, there is evidence of a transition from a general emphasis on being a good person by *behaving* in moral ways that characterized the Jewish half of the Bible (the Old Testament) to an emphasis on being a good person by *thinking* in moral ways, as stressed in the Christian half of the Bible (the New Testament).

There is also a greater emphasis on faith in Christianity (especially Protestantism) than in Judaism. For example, membership in Judaism is defined by descent; traditionally, one becomes Jewish by being born to a Jewish biological mother. In contrast, membership in Protestant sects is primarily defined by beliefs. For example, one does not become a member of the Baptist church until one publicly accepts the Christian faith and is baptized. The New Testament states "that whosoever believeth in [Jesus] should not perish, but have eternal life" (John 3:15). In contrast to this emphasis on beliefs in Christianity, much of traditional Judaism emphasizes particular practices, such as keeping kosher by avoiding certain foods, such as pork. Jewish faith does not state that it is wrong to *desire* nonkosher foods; what is important is that one does not eat them. In contrast, compared with Judaism, Christianity has fewer practices and instead places more emphasis on one's private communications with God.

Reflecting this differential emphasis in practices and beliefs, a survey asked Jewish and Protestant participants how important practices and beliefs were for being religious; the results revealed that Jewish participants rated practices as more important than beliefs for being religious, whereas Protestants put greater emphasis on beliefs than practices (Cohen, Siegel, & Rozin, 2003).

Would Christians and Jews differ in their views on whether it is wrong for people to have bad thoughts, even if they never act upon the thoughts? In one study, participants read some vignettes that described people who were thinking about immoral behaviors (Cohen & Rozin, 2001). Here is a sample vignette from the study:

> Mr. B. is a 1992 graduate of the University. Since graduation, Mr. B. has worked at an entry-level job in a marketing firm. Mr. B. married his University sweetheart six months after they both had their graduation from University. Mr. B. and his wife do not have any children. One of Mr. B.'s colleagues at work is a very attractive woman. This woman sometimes flirts with Mr. B. and they both know that she would be willing to have a sexual affair with him. For an average of about 20 minutes a day, Mr. B. consciously entertains thoughts about having a sexual affair with his colleague by thinking about where they would have an affair and what it would be like to have an affair with her.

After reading the vignette, participants were asked some questions about Mr. B. One question was what they thought of Mr. B. The Protestant participants reported viewing Mr. B. in significantly more negative terms than the Jewish participants did. Having adulterous thoughts is viewed as more immoral by Protestants than Jews. A second question asked how bad it would be if Mr. B. actually had the sexual affair. Importantly, Jewish participants viewed sexual affairs in at least as negative terms as the Protestant participants did. There was no difference between the religions in how they viewed immoral *behaviors*. Even though there were no religious differences in terms of the perceived immorality of the behaviors, there was a pronounced religious difference in people's reactions to someone thinking about engaging in such behaviors. Apparently, Protestants view one's thoughts to be governed by moral concerns, whereas Jews do not. The moral domain for Jews is focused on what people do, and not what they think about doing.

This religious difference suggests that Protestants and Jews might have different theories about how the mind works. If you can be held morally responsible for your thoughts, it would seem that you must believe these thoughts to be somewhat under your control. It hardly makes sense to morally condemn something that is beyond an individual's control. Not surprisingly, research reveals that Protestants believe people have more control of their thoughts than Jews do (Cohen & Rozin, 2001). Furthermore, one reason to be concerned about someone engaging in immoral thoughts is the possibility that these thoughts might increase the likelihood that the person will engage in the immoral behavior. Indeed, Protestants, more than Jews, have been shown to believe that thoughts lead to behaviors (Cohen & Rozin, 2001). Protestants tend to see thoughts as greasing the path toward behaviors. Not only do the religions differ in their beliefs in the morality of thoughts; they differ in their beliefs about what thoughts do and whether one can control them.

Culture and Fairness

Our discussion on moral intuitions demonstrates that although liberals and conservatives differ somewhat in the kinds of moral intuitions that are of the greatest concern to them, there is relatively little difference between them in the strength of their concerns with the moral intuition of protecting fairness. Treating people fairly seems like a common, if not universal, concern. However, as we'll see, the ways that people judge things to be fair can vary considerably across cultures.

Distributing Resources

One way that we can see how people decide what is fair is by considering the ways that they distribute resources. We can go about assigning rewards (or punishments) to individuals in a number of ways, and these ways speak to people's beliefs about what is fair. For example, your instructor can give out a limited number of good grades to the class. What is the fairest way to distribute them? One way would be to distribute them by the **principle of need,** which dictates that resources are directed toward those who need them the most. If your instructor operated on the principle of need, he or she would give the best grades to those students who were most in need of them. A student, say, who was planning to go to law school as a means to earn the money to support his sick mother would receive a higher grade than a student who was going to be-

"O.K., if you can't see your way to giving me a pay raise, how about giving Parkerson a pay cut?"

come a professional athlete. A second way that grades could be distributed is by the **principle of equality.** This principle dictates that resources should be shared equally among the members of a group. In this case, your instructor could assign everyone in the class the exact same grade, regardless of what each one did in the course. Or your instructor could distribute grades based on the **principle of equity.** This principle states that resources are distributed based on an individual's contributions. The more an individual produces, the more resources he or she receives. The ratio between individuals' inputs (their efforts and abilities in the course) and their outputs (the grades they receive) are held constant. Instructors following this principle would distribute grades based on how many questions the students answered correctly on the exam.

Grades are an unusual resource because they serve the function of indicating how much one has learned, rather than of being a reward in their own right. Because of this, it is likely that instructors everywhere operate exclusively on the principle of equity. However, in the distribution of other kinds of resources, such as salary, the principle of equity is not so universal. The principle of equity does appear to be the dominant form of resource distribution in the West. Most companies in the West compensate their employees by basing their salary largely on what the individual achieves. A pure example of the principle of equity can be seen in companies where salespeople are paid exclusively by commission. The more one sells, the more one earns, and the ratio between one's inputs and outputs is held constant. A social system that rewards individuals on the basis of the equity principle is known as a **meritocracy,** and meritocracies tend to be more common in individualistic societies. Meritocracies have their benefits and costs. They can lead workers to be highly motivated to work hard, because their earnings depend on their efforts, which tends to increase productivity. However, because there usually is only a finite amount of resources that can be distributed among employees, when one worker does especially well, this means that the others are doing relatively worse and will be paid less. Meritocratic systems tend to breed competition among workers, thereby potentially disrupting harmonious relations among them.

In much of the rest of the world (and in industries in the West that have a more collectivistic base through the power of labor unions), the principle of equality is adhered to more. In practical terms, the principle of equality is rarely applied in its strongest form, which would be that every individual receives the exact same level of compensation. Rather, equality tends to be preserved within a certain range of constraints, such as one's age or official credentials. So, for example, all individuals might get the same size raise each year; however, those who have been at the company longer have received more raises and hence are being compensated more. This latter system is known as a **seniority system,** in which time with the company or age is being rewarded. Seniority systems reflect the principle of equality because there is no competition among individuals for compensation. It is determined by the same calculus for everyone. Seniority systems weaken the link between one's inputs and outputs so that individuals might not be motivated to work as hard, although they do promote harmonious relations by decreasing intragroup competition. Interestingly, although it is often assumed that merit-based pay is the way to ensure the greatest amount of effort from one's employees, Japanese workers have traditionally been among the hardest working in the world (e.g., there is a great deal of voluntary overtime and many never take their vacations), and Japanese companies tend to have more seniority-based pay than American organizations (e.g., Ouchi & Jaeger, 1978). The relation between efforts and the principle of equity or equality appears to depend considerably on the cultural context.

The principle of need is manifested in most modern industrialized societies through institutions such as universal health insurance, which gives the sick more benefits than the healthy, or a welfare system, in which those who are needy receive more benefits than those who are not. However, the principle of need also governs people's beliefs in distributing resources in many less formal situations, such as contributing to charities or giving money to beggars.

Which of these three principles of distributing resources do you think is the most fair? Your answer to this reflects your underlying values—values that have likely been shaped by the norms that you have been exposed to in your culture.

Consider the following study that explored how these different principles of resource distribution were embraced across cultures (Berman, Murphy-Berman, & Singh, 1985). The researchers presented Indian and American participants with

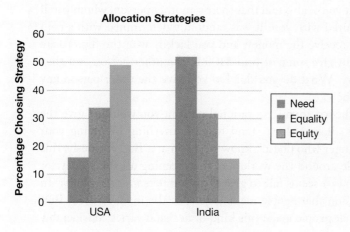

Allocation Strategies

Percentage Choosing Strategy

Need
Equality
Equity

USA   India

FIGURE 12.7

In deciding how to allocate a bonus in a particular scenario, the most popular principle among Americans was to distribute the bonus according to the principle of equity. In contrast, among Indians this was the least popular principle. Rather, Indians favored the principle of need.

a scenario describing how a company had to make a decision about distributing a bonus between two employees. One of the employees was described as having excellent work performance and an adequate economic situation. The other employee had only average work performance but was in a poor financial situation with an illness in the family. The participants needed to decide how to divide up the bonus money. They could choose to give most of the money to the excellent worker, give most of the money to the needy worker, or split the money evenly down the middle. **Figure 12.7** shows the results. The most popular solution for the Americans was to favor the excellent employee (the equity principle), and the least popular one was to favor the needy employee. In stark contrast, the favorite solution of Indians was to give the majority of the money to the needy employee, and the least favorite solution was to reward the excellent employee. A similar study contrasted Japanese and Australian workers and found that Australians preferred an equitable distribution of rewards more positively than did Japanese (Kashima, Siegal, Tanaka, & Isaka, 1988). What is perceived as a fair and just way of distributing resources, then, can vary around the world. Westerners are more likely than those from other cultures to view the equity principle to be the most fair. Indians are most impressed by allocations that take into account the need of the parties involved.

Economic Games and Fairness

The ways that cultures shape what people perceive as a fair way to distribute resources can be seen in another way. Imagine that you're put in the following situation: You have just been given some money, say $100. You're told that you can do anything that you want with the money. But you're also told that there's another person, whom you'll never meet, who has been paired with you. It was randomly determined with a coin flip which one of you would receive the money, and you luckily won the flip. You're told that, if you want, you can give some of your $100 to the other person, but they will never know your identity. What do you do? Do you give the other person any money? And, if so, how much?

According to economic theory, if you're a rational person, you wouldn't give the other person a penny. After all, you don't stand to gain anything by giving your money to an anonymous stranger who doesn't know who you are. But, curiously, this almost never happens. People around the world feel that keeping all the money for themselves is not right, and it just seems fair to give the other person some money. In fact, the most common decision that people make is to split the money 50-50. But, as we'll see, the likelihood that people make this kind of decision varies considerably around the world.

This situation is an economic game called the **dictator game.** The dictator game, as well as some other related and more complex economic games, has been played in more than a dozen different societies around the world. When economists first learned that Western university students played these economic games in apparently "nonrational" ways, giving away money that would not lead to any benefits to them, they came up with an explanation: Humans must have an internalized motivation for fairness that guides their decisions, and it operates even under the unusual situations created when playing economic games that keep their behavior anonymous. Furthermore, economic models were proposed to argue that the reason large-scale societies and markets were possible was that people had these internalized motivations for fairness (e.g., Nowak, Page, & Sigmund, 2000). Their innate desire for fairness allowed people to behave in a trustworthy manner with strangers, which facilitated trade and the development of markets and made it possible for large groups of strangers to live together in relative harmony.

Joe Henrich and colleagues found these ideas interesting but were disturbed by the fact that the models were built on findings based solely on Western university students. As discussed earlier, the psychological tendencies of these WEIRD samples appear unusual, in many ways, and it was possible that people in other cultural contexts might play these economic games differently. To test the generalizability of their findings, Henrich and colleagues launched a series of large-scale international projects involving a network of interdisciplinary researchers to study a number of societies around the world (Henrich et al., 2005; Henrich et al., 2006; Henrich et al., 2010). Most of the societies they selected were small-scale subsistence societies, because people living in these societies have lifestyles that are more similar to the ways that our human ancestors used to live thousands of years ago compared with the lifestyles of people living in modern industrialized societies. Hence, the findings

FIGURE 12.8 Joe Henrich and a Fijian assistant explain how to play an economic game on Yasawa Island in Fiji.

speak to questions regarding the evolution of norms regarding fairness. The researchers taught people in these societies the rules of these economic games, gave them the chance to practice until they demonstrated that they fully understood the games, and then provided people with money equivalent to one day's wage and allowed them to play the games (**Figure 12.8**).

Figure 12.9 shows the offers that were made by people in the different societies for the dictator game (Henrich et al., 2010). The first thing to note is that the dictator game offers made by the American sample were at the tail end of the distribution (a similar pattern was found for other kinds of economic games). The average American response was not representative of how people elsewhere made offers; rather it represents an extreme response, which suggests that it is not a good sample to use for building a model that generalizes to all of humanity. The motivations for fairness were considerably weaker in most of the other societies. How can we understand the cultural variability in people's offers in the dictator game?

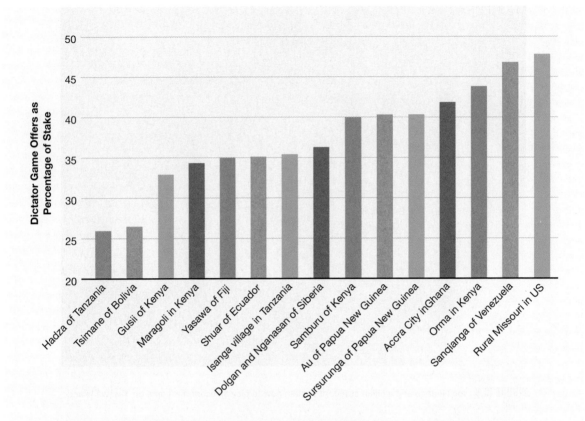

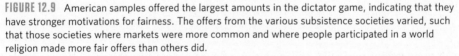

FIGURE 12.9 American samples offered the largest amounts in the dictator game, indicating that they have stronger motivations for fairness. The offers from the various subsistence societies varied, such that those societies where markets were more common and where people participated in a world religion made more fair offers than others did.

The researchers explored the role of a number of variables, including the average wealth of the society, sex, age, family income, household size, and education. Controlling for these factors, they found two variables that predicted which societies made larger (i.e., more fair) offers: market integration and religion. Market integration was operationalized as the percentage of calories consumed in a society that are purchased in a market. This percentage ranged from an amount near zero for the Hadza and the Au to amounts near 100% in the city of Accra and in the United States. The more experience people had in dealing with markets, the stronger their motivations for fairness. Note that this explanation is precisely *opposite* to the one originally offered by economists (e.g., Nowak et al., 2000). That is, rather than markets being the result of people with innate motivations for fairness coming together, the findings suggest that people learned norms to play fair as a result of cultural experiences with markets. Some elements of fairness thus appear to be a product of cultural evolution. The other significant predictor was the percentage of people in a society who participated in a world religion (in this case, Islam or Christianity). In general, larger societies tend to have religions that offer moral guidance (whereas many tribal religions do not), and participating in these religions is associated with people playing an anonymous game more fairly, perhaps because of a belief that their behavior is not anonymous in the eyes of God.

Another economic game that has been used to understand people's motivations for fairness and cooperation is the **public goods game.** Using this game, the economists Fehr and Gächter (2002) gave groups of four Swiss university students the opportunity to contribute some of their money to a common pool. Suppose the participants started out with $10 each. For every dollar that was contributed, the experimenter multiplied it by 1.6 and then redistributed it to all four members (40 cents each). Hence, overall the group would earn the most money if everyone contributed all of his or her money, as in the end each would receive a total of 1.6 times the original contribution (i.e., $16 each, or a total of $64 for the team). However, the game is set up such that participants are tempted to free-ride. The best scenario for a single player would be to refuse to donate any money and have other teammates contribute all of their money, as then that player would take home their original $10 plus the $12 earned from the contributions of his or her teammates. The cheating player would earn $22 but the whole team would take home only $58 total. Individuals can thus potentially profit by free-riding (unless everyone does, and then they'd only receive $10 each), but the best collective outcome is obtained when everyone cooperates. In many ways, this game captures the dynamics that people routinely face in real-life decisions, such as whether to pay their taxes in full, or whether to cut back on their carbon footprint.

Perhaps not surprisingly, Fehr and Gächter found that the teams didn't contribute all that much money, and their contributions got smaller and smaller after each round. The temptations to free-ride were just too great. The researchers then instituted an additional rule by which participants could opt to sacrifice some of their own money to punish another player. So if a player paid one of his or her own dollars, the experimenter would take away $3 from the player who was being punished. And players seemed quite willing to pay their own money in order to punish others. The researchers found that with the addition of this punishment rule, cooperation increased quite dramatically and remained stable across time. They proposed, then, that a key factor that allowed human cooperation to evolve was people's willingness to engage in this kind of **altruistic punishment.** By feeling motivated to punish those who weren't cooperating, people were able to ensure that group members didn't free-ride, which allowed humans to develop norms for cooperation, and for large societies to flourish.

This explanation that punishment led to norms for cooperation was widely embraced. But soon this public goods game was played in many other societies around the world, and the results yielded a curious pattern. On the one hand, everywhere the game was played there were many participants who were willing to engage in altruistic punishment by paying their own money to punish those who were free-riding. However, a distinctive pattern emerged in several other societies. In addition to a tendency for altruistic punishment, in many societies (such as Russia, Saudi Arabia, Greece, and Oman), people showed strong tendencies for what the researchers called **antisocial punishment** (Hermann, Thöni, & Gächter, 2008). That is, people sometimes paid their own money to punish another player, even if that player was cooperating (**Figure 12.10**). The motivations for this antisocial punishment seemed to be largely a function of revenge, in which people would punish a player who had punished them on a previous round. Although this tendency for antisocial punishment tended to be quite negligible in WEIRD societies and was never really noticed before by researchers conducting studies in those countries, motivations for antisocial punishment were strong enough in the societies at the bottom of the figure that it completely removed the cooperation-enhancing effect of the rule that allowed for punishment. It appears that the notion that punishment promotes cooperation holds true only in societies characterized by norms for civic cooperation and high levels of trust (Balliet & Van Lange, 2013).

Antisocial punishment was entirely unexpected by the researchers who first discovered it, but it appears to be quite commonplace in many cultures, and it remains somewhat puzzling. The researchers' data show that societies with weaker norms for civic cooperation and a weaker rule of law engaged in more antisocial punishment in public goods games. Other researchers argue that antisocial punishment can be adaptive in contexts where the rule of law is insufficient, as it's a strategy for establishing status and obtaining the associated benefits when the system can't be relied upon to deliver those (Sylwester, Herrmann, & Bryson, 2013).

In dealing with a system that can't always be trusted to function, people come up with alternative ways to ensure their needs are met. For example, in Brazil, there is a complex sociocultural strategy termed *jetinho,* by which people manipulate or dodge the official rules to achieve things (Ferreira, Fischer, Porto, Pilati, & Milfont, 2012). Moreover, in societies with higher levels of civic cooperation there is a positive correlation between people's sense of civic virtue and their happiness. In contrast, in societies with lower levels of civic cooperation there is no correlation between civic virtue and happiness. That is, the idea that being virtuous is associated with feeling happy does not seem to generalize to contexts where norms for civic cooperation are low (Stavrova, Schlösser, & Fetchenhauer, 2013). There may be costs of being exploited by acting virtuous in contexts where trust and cooperation are weaker.

A real-life example of these weaker norms for civic cooperation can be seen in the game show *Who Wants to Be a Millionaire*. In the show, which was originally created in the UK, contestants are able to use a "lifeline" and can poll the studio audience for help in answering a difficult question. The assumption is that the answer that is

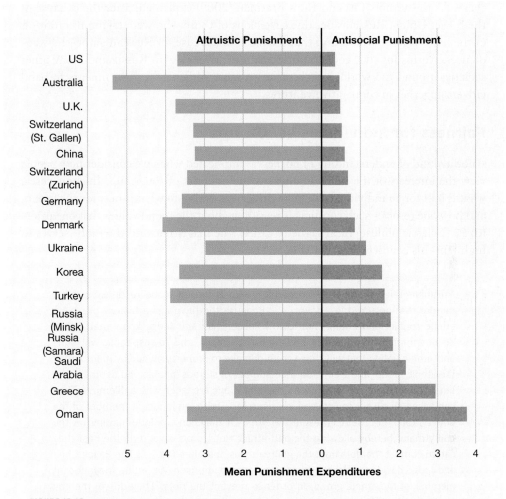

FIGURE 12.10 The left half of this figure indicates the amount that groups paid, on average, to punish those who were not cooperating in the public goods game (altruistic punishment). Overall, there was not a great deal of variability in these motivations across societies. The right half of this figure indicates the amounts that groups paid, on average, to punish those who were cooperating (antisocial punishment). There was far more variability in motivations for antisocial punishment across societies.

most popular among the studio audience is likely to be the correct one. However, when *Who Wants to Be a Millionaire* was introduced in Russia, the contestants quickly found out that they couldn't trust the audiences. Frequently, the audience members would deliberately choose the wrong answers in an apparent effort to mislead the contestants. Not unlike with the public goods game, many members of the Russian audience seemed to be more motivated to sabotage the play of contestants than to help them. As the authors Ori and Rom Brafman (2009) explained, after the collapse of the Soviet Union, Russians became suspicious of those who were trying to profit off of the hard work of others, and that seems to be the case for Russian game-show audiences. Norms for civic cooperation remain relatively low in Russia and many other societies around the world, which makes it more difficult for governments to band citizens together in cooperative ventures.

Fairness for Individuals vs. Groups

Another kind of understanding of fairness is implicated when we consider how people view the interests of the individual versus the interests of the group. In some cases, what is best for an individual can be in direct opposition to what is best for the group, and how one resolves such conflicts is revealing about the moral values that one prioritizes. A classic philosophical vignette called "the magistrate and the mob" serves to highlight this conflict (Smart, 1973):

> An unidentified member of an ethnic group is known to be responsible for a murder that occurred in a town. . . . Because the town has a history of severe ethnic conflict and rioting, the town's Police Chief and Judge know that if they do not immediately identify and punish a culprit, the townspeople will start anti-ethnic rioting that will cause great damage to property owned by members of the ethnic group, and a considerable number of serious injuries and deaths in the ethnic population. . . . The Police Chief and Judge are faced with a dilemma. They can falsely accuse, convict, and imprison Mr. Smith, an innocent member of the ethnic group, in order to prevent the riots. Or they can continue hunting for the guilty man, thereby allowing the anti-ethnic riots to occur, and do the best they can to combat the riots until the guilty man is apprehended. . . . The Police Chief and Judge decide to falsely accuse, convict, and imprison Mr. Smith, the innocent member of the ethnic group, in order to prevent the riots. They do so, thereby preventing the riots and preventing a considerable number of ethnic group deaths and serious injuries.

Most Westerners (and Western philosophers, for that matter) condemn the decision by the Police Chief and Judge. As the philosopher Paul Bloomfield (2004) put it: "Judges ought not find the innocent guilty to prevent riots in the street, period." This reflects a view that individual rights should always be held above all else. However, when this vignette was given to Americans of predominantly European descent and to Chinese living in China, people from the two cultures gave somewhat different answers (Peng, Doris, Nichols, & Stich, in preparation; cited in Doris & Plakias, 2008). Although people from both cultural groups tended to disagree with the Police Chief and Judge's decision, Americans were more likely than the Chinese to view this decision as morally wrong. In addition, the Chinese participants were more likely than the Americans to hold the potential rioters responsible for the scapegoating, suggesting that they attributed more responsibility at the level of the group. The American responses reflect their more-individualistic orientation, with their concern primarily for the rights of the individual. In contrast, the more collectivistic Chinese had relatively more sympathy for the good of the collective. Hence, how one judges the appropriateness of sacrificing an individual for the good of a group varies across cultures. Our moral intuitions regarding what is fair and just are guided by our cultural experiences.

SUMMARY

People do not share the same foundation for their morals around the world, and this is at the root of many disagreements both between and within cultures. There are at least three separate codes of ethics by which people can reason morally, and these vary in their distribution around the world. High-socioeconomic Westerners who belong to progressive sects are likely to base their moral judgments on the ethic of autonomy. With this ethic, they base their judgments of right and wrong on whether individual rights have been protected and justice has been delivered. In India, and likely other cultures in which interdependent concerns are more salient, people are likely to make moral judgments based on the ethic of community. This ethic maintains that people have interpersonal duties toward others that they are morally obligated to uphold. Among lower-socioeconomic Westerners and adherents of orthodox religions, people are more likely to subscribe to the ethic of divinity. Actions that violate the perceived natural order of things and sully God's creations are viewed in moral terms. More generally, people's moral views differ in accordance with their political attitudes. Liberals are primarily concerned with harm and fairness; conservatives are also concerned about ingroup loyalty, authority, and purity.

There is variation in the domains under which people consider whether moral violations have occurred. Protestants appear to view thoughts in moral terms, because they believe that thoughts are relatively controllable and lead to future behaviors. In contrast, Jews tend not to view thoughts in moral terms, because they believe that thoughts are less controllable and are less likely to lead to future behaviors.

What people view as fair also varies across cultures. The principle of equity, in which resources are tied to an individual's contributions, is more favored in the West than it is in India or Japan. In contrast, the principle of need, in which resources go to the needy, is respected more in India. Motivations for fairness are stronger among people who have had much experience with markets and who have been exposed to a world religion. Protecting the rights of the individual over the collective is emphasized more in individualistic than collectivistic cultures.

Cultures also vary in the degree to which they act fairly in economic games. Cultures with more exposure to markets and world religions are more likely to make fair offers in the dictator game, and cultures with weaker norms for civic cooperation are more likely to engage in antisocial punishment in public goods games.

THINK ABOUT IT

1. Why is ethnocentrism a more central issue for the cross-cultural study of morality than for most of the other topics in this book?
2. What moral ethic do you think is most on display in the constitution of your country?
3. Gesellschaft groups have becoming increasingly commonplace around the world. Why do you think that it is? Do you think this pattern will ever be reversed?
4. If you were in Ben's situation in the vignette in the section on the ethic of community, would you take the ticket if that was the only way you could make your friend's wedding? Think about which ethics are most strongly guiding your decision.
5. Think about your feelings about capital punishment, and try to articulate whether you think it is right or wrong. Which of the five moral foundations best characterize your thoughts?
6. As discussed in the text, liberals tend to rely largely on the moral foundations of harm and fairness, whereas conservatives rely more on all five moral foundations. It would seem that a good way to persuade someone who disagreed with you on a moral issue would be to speak to the moral foundations that the person cared about the most. Think about what kind of arguments you could use to speak to the moral foundations of someone who disagreed with you about the morality of abortion.
7. Do you see anything morally dubious in the vignette about Mr. B fantasizing about having an affair with his colleague? Do your feelings about Mr. B match more closely with what the text described for the morality of thoughts of Protestants or of Jews?
8. In what ways do you think a workplace would change if salaries moved more from a meritocracy system to a seniority system?
9. Altruistic punishment seems to be commonplace around the world. Why do you think antisocial punishment is common in some societies?

KEY TERMS

Lunch time in Paris. The French have very different attitudes toward food than Americans, and one of the consequences of this is that French have far lower rates of obesity and heart disease than Americans. This difference in health exists despite French food often being richer and having higher fat content than American food.

13

PHYSICAL HEALTH

About 3.6 million years ago near Laetoli, Tanzania, a trio of early hominids, most likely *Australopithecus afarensis,* walked across a field covered in wet volcanic ash, leaving behind what would later become one of the most significant discoveries in paleoanthropology. Their footprints, which remained preserved in the ash, were subsequently viewed as the earliest direct evidence of bipedality in the hominid line. Unlike the footprints of chimpanzees, in the Laetoli prints the big toes did not protrude directly off to the side, there were no parallel prints made by knuckles to support a quadrupedal gait, and the footprints revealed that the early humans who made them struck with the heel first and then pushed off from their toes in the same way that modern humans do. The shift from being an ape that moved about on all fours to a creature that could walk on its hind legs was a key transition in hominid evolution. Becoming bipedal freed the hands to carry food and make tools, cooled the body by reducing the amount of direct sunlight that struck the body and by exposing the upper body to the wind, and improved the long-distance traveling efficiency of early hominids. The Laetoli footprints provided a window from which to see some of the earliest evidence of behaviors shared with modern humans.

However, these same footprints revealed that the gait of Australopithecines may not have been quite as bipedal as that of modern humans. The early comparisons of the Laetoli footprints with those made by modern humans indicated a few key differences. The Laetoli prints revealed a wider front part of the foot, with the big toe more separated from the second toe and a more pronounced arch (Henrich, Heine, & Norenzayan, 2010b; Stern & Susman, 1983). Although bipedal, the Laetoli Austrolopithecines did not yet appear to be as fully bipedal as modern humans. Their feet still seemed to preserve some key nonhuman characteristics.

However, when one is making conclusions about what the feet of modern humans are like, one needs to consider *whose* feet one is examining. Although the Laetoli footprints indicate a foot that is wider, with a larger gap between the first two toes and a higher arch, than that of most modern humans examined, it is important to note that the individuals who left behind the Laetoli footprints participated in some cultural traditions that differ from those of most modern humans—namely, they didn't wear shoes. And it turns out that this is a critical detail, because habitually wearing shoes changes the shape of one's feet. People who habitually wear shoes tend to have narrower feet, their first two toes are closer together, and they have a lower arch. Indeed, comparisons of the Laetoli footprints with prints left by modern humans who do not wear shoes, such as the Machiguenga (**Figure 13.1**), a foraging tribe from the Peruvian Amazon, show that they were largely indistinguishable (Tuttle, Webb, & Baksh, 1991;

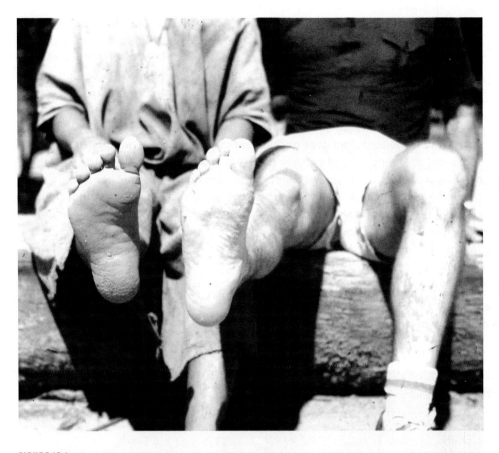

FIGURE 13.1   The left foot belongs to a Machiguengan man who doesn't habitually wear shoes, whereas the right foot belongs to an American man who usually does (from Tuttle, Webb, Weidl, & Baksh, 1990, p. 354).

Tuttle, Webb, Weidl, & Baksh, 1990). Modern humans who do not wear shoes appear to have rather similarly shaped feet to those of the Laetoli Austrolopithecines (although the Laetoli footprints are not clear enough to make a definitive comparison).

Rather remarkably, then, the shape of your feet can also be seen as a cultural product. Wearing shoes changes foot shape (a more extreme example can be seen in the old and now-absent Chinese tradition of foot binding). Likewise, wearing shoes changes the way you run. For most of human evolutionary history, people wore sandals, minimal thin-soled footwear such as moccasins, or nothing on their feet. The modern running shoe with all of its cushioning wasn't invented until the 1970s. Yet people have always run, often for very long distances, without much protective covering on their feet, and rarely reported much damage to their feet. Running has been central enough to human history that some researchers have proposed that humans evolved to be endurance runners (Bramble & Lieberman, 2004), which enabled them to outrun prey over long distances (Carrier, 1984).

Research finds that people run differently in bare feet, such that they are more likely to land on their fore-feet or mid-feet compared with people running with shoes on, who tend to land on their rear-feet (Leiberman et al., 2010), and some anecdotal reports indicate that barefooted running leads to reduced injury rates (Robbins & Hanna, 1987), although this continues to be debated. When children are wearing shoes, they take longer steps than when they are barefoot (Wegener, Hunt, Vanwanseele, Burns, & Smith, 2011). Some cultural groups, such as the Tarahumara of northern Mexico, participate in regular ultra-long-distance kick-ball races across canyons, while barefoot or wearing only minimal sandals, that may last as long as 48 hours and go more than 100 miles (Balke & Snow, 1965; **Figure 13.2**). Over several decades, there have been many reports of seemingly

FIGURE 13.2   These Tarahumara runners are participating in a long-distance kickball race.

superhuman endurance feats by the Tarahumara (e.g., Bennett & Zingg, 1935; Lumholtz, 1894), and some Tarahumara have won international ultramarathons (see McDougall, 2009).

Just as we may draw incorrect conclusions about the nature of feet and running by looking only at people with one set of cultural experiences (i.e., those who wear padded shoes), we may also draw incorrect conclusions about the nature of throwing. In the United States, and in many other cultures where people often play sports that involve a lot of throwing (e.g., baseball, football, and team handball), people (especially boys, who are more likely to have played the sports) have honed their ability to deliver a powerful overhand throw with a complex unfurling of the body. But not all cultures have sporting traditions that emphasize throwing. Brazilians, who have demonstrated great athleticism in a number of sports, especially soccer, have practiced throwing so little that "throwing like a Brazilian" has become an expression (Downey, 2010). Germans too have less-developed skills at throwing compared with Americans (Ehl, Roberton, & Langendorger, 2005). Having experience with throwing leads to the development of more muscles on the dominant arm, as well as thicker bones (see Downey, 2010, for a review).

The notion that cultural experiences can affect the ways that people run and throw reveals something important. Cultural experiences do not just shape the ways that people think; these experiences can also affect people's bodies and health. The inclusion of a chapter on physical health in a psychology text-book may strike you as somewhat odd. Traditionally, physical health has been viewed largely as a biological issue, and as such, many would assume that it lies outside the realm of either cultural influences or psychology. However, the burgeoning field of health psychology has made it clear that psychological variables are inextricably linked with physical health, and as we have seen, culture influences a wide range of psychological variables. Furthermore, a rapidly expanding number of research programs have been documenting that many aspects of human health and biology are indeed influenced by cultural experiences, and some of these in rather profound ways. In this chapter we explore how cultural experiences can affect both human biology and various aspects of health.

Biological Variability of Humans

To the extent that human biology varies across cultures, there are largely two distinct categories of explanation for this variation. One is that humans in different parts of the world were subject to different selection pressures over many generations, which resulted in the human genome diverging across different populations. In other words, there are *innate* biological differences across cultures. The second category of explanation is that people living in different cultures have experiences within their own lifetimes that have an impact on their biology. That is, there are *acquired* biological differences. Let's consider both of these in turn.

Genetic Variation Across Populations

Everyone in the world is genetically unique, having his or her own collection of genetic variants that is not quite identical to anyone else's (with the exception of those born of monozygotic multiple births, who share the same variants with their identical siblings). Despite their uniqueness, individuals do share many genetic variants in common with other people, and in particular, they share even more variants in common with people who have the same ancestral origins. This is because there have been forces from genetic drift and particular selection pressures from geographical and cultural factors that, over many generations, have affected the frequency of particular genetic variants in different regions of the world. Humans, like other species, evolve in response to selection pressures from their environment, and they continue to evolve today. Because the selection pressures vary across geographical and cultural environments, humans have been evolving some particular traits that differ across regions of the world (Hawks, Wang, Cochran, Harpending, & Moyzis, 2007; Laland, Odling-Smee, & Myles, 2010).

However, note that genetic variability in humans is considerably less than in many other species, given how recently modern humans emerged as a species. Modern humans (*Homo sapiens*) first emerged approximately 200,000 years ago, and they all lived in Africa until approximately 50,000–60,000 years ago when some of them migrated elsewhere. The genetic evidence suggests that a relatively small population of *Homo sapiens* quickly expanded in Africa before some humans left that continent, and as a result of this quick expansion, there's far less genetic variability across the different races of humans than there is across different populations of chimpanzees. Moreover, there's more genetic variability among Africans (who have had up to 200,000 years to accumulate genetic changes) than between Africans and people of other cultural backgrounds (who have had only up to 60,000 years to accumulate changes; for a review, see Boyd & Silk, 2006). In sum, compared with other species, humans are less genetically distinct from each other, but different populations of humans do differ from each other in many of their genes.

The most salient example of genetic variability of humans across different populations is that of skin color. People come in different colors, with skin tones ranging from a dark brown among aboriginal Australians, Melanesians, and people from equatorial Africa to a very light yellowish pink among some northern Europeans. Why is there this variation? The most compelling explanation lies in the body's ability to synthesize vitamin D, which is necessary for the intestines to absorb calcium and phosphorus from food to use for bone growth and repair. However, vitamin D is not synthesized in the body unless shortwave ultraviolet radiation (UVR) penetrates the skin layer and catalyzes its production. So the skin must allow enough UVR to pass through to synthesize the vitamin D. On the other hand, too much UVR can cause the breakdown of folic acid, which can cause anemia or birth defects, or can cause skin cancer. Humans first emerged in Africa, where UVR levels are high, so they evolved to have enough melanin in their skin to allow sufficient UVR to penetrate to synthesize vitamin D, but not enough to break down folic acid. However, when humans moved to places where UVR levels are lower, they needed to absorb relatively more UVR; thus, those with less melanin in their skin had a survival advantage over their darker-skinned relatives, and their skin color evolved accordingly (**Figure 13.3**).

Analyses of the amount of UVR that reaches the earth's surface in different parts of the globe correlate strongly with skin color (Jablonski & Chaplin, 2000). Although there are a number of exceptions in which people's skin color diverges from what would be predicted by the amount of UVR that is present, these exceptions tend to support the link between UVR and vitamin D synthesis. For example, the Inuit of Greenland have far darker skin than what would be predicted by the little amount of UVR that reaches the earth there. However, the Inuit have come across a cultural solution to their insufficient UVR: They eat a diet that is especially rich in fish and sea mammal blubber, which are high in vitamin D, and thus they do not

FIGURE 13.3 Skin color varies dramatically around the world. Lighter skin emerged as an adaptation to absorb sufficient ultraviolet radiation in higher latitudes.

require as much catalysis from the sun. Conversely, some people in the Philippines, Vietnam, and Cambodia have lighter skin than would be predicted, but in these cases the populations have migrated from higher latitudes only in recent millennia, so they apparently have not yet evolved appropriately darker skin (Diamond, 2005). Furthermore, the relatively pale skin of Europeans and East Asians appears to have emerged through different genetic routes, suggesting that pale skin has evolved independently for these two populations (Voight, Kudaravalli, Wen, & Pritchard, 2006; Williamson et al., 2007).

Skin color is an example of an adaptive response to climatic differences among populations, and these kinds of adaptations represent one large domain of genetic differences across populations. Differences in climate exert a strong selective force, such that those individuals who are better adapted to the local climate will produce more surviving offspring. For example, evidence suggests that people in different regions of the world have different genetic variants associated with heat stress (Williamson et al., 2007). Altitude also provides another strong selective force—people who live high up on the Tibetan Plateau, at altitudes that approximate the highest points of the contiguous United States, have access to only about 60% of the oxygen that exists at sea level. At this altitude, many people would develop pronounced altitude sickness. However, ethnic Tibetans have evolved genetic variants that allow them to thrive despite the low levels of oxygen (Yi et al., 2010).

Another strong selective force on human evolution has been the presence of certain kinds of local pathogens, such that those individuals who are more genetically resistant to the pathogens are more likely to survive and reproduce (Wang, Kodama, Baldi, & Moyzis, 2006). As an example, in Chapter 3 we discussed how the Spaniards had better genetic resistance to smallpox than did the Incans (because they had lived alongside smallpox-carrying livestock for thousands of years), which is a big factor in explaining why the Spaniards had such a relatively easy time conquering the Incans. As another example, in regions of the world where HIV infection is especially high, it is expected that major genetic resistance against the virus could evolve in as little as 50 years (Cromer, Wolinsky, & McLean, 2010).

Cultural Influences on the Genotype

Genetic adaptations to the local climate, altitude, and pathogens are cases in which geographical factors have shaped the genotype. There are also instances of cultural factors shaping the genotype. For example, most adults in the world who drink milk develop the symptoms of lactose intolerance because they have insufficient lactase enzyme in their intestines to digest this sugar. This state, known as *lactase nonpersistence* because lactase does not persist from childhood through adulthood, was present in the ancestral population of humans before they left Africa. Sometime after, some populations, particularly those in northern Europe, developed a mutation for *lactase persistence* (Hollox, 2005). Recent genetic analyses reveal that lactase persistence has developed in areas precisely where cows have been domesticated for the longest periods, as evidenced by the highest genetic diversity among the cattle populations (Beja-Pereira et al., 2003; see **Figure 13.4**). Dairy farming has been shown to predate the selection of lactase persistence (Holden & Mace, 1997), and thus this genetic change has occurred sometime in the last 10,000 years, since people began to domesticate cattle. A parallel genetic mutation emerged among African cultural groups that raised cattle, distinct from the one common in Europe (Tishkoff et al., 2007), suggesting that the selective pressures to be able to digest lactose into adulthood were strong enough to emerge at least twice independently. In sum, the cultural practice of dairy farming, which brought with it various nutritional advantages, led to the selection of lactase persistence among cattle-raising populations.

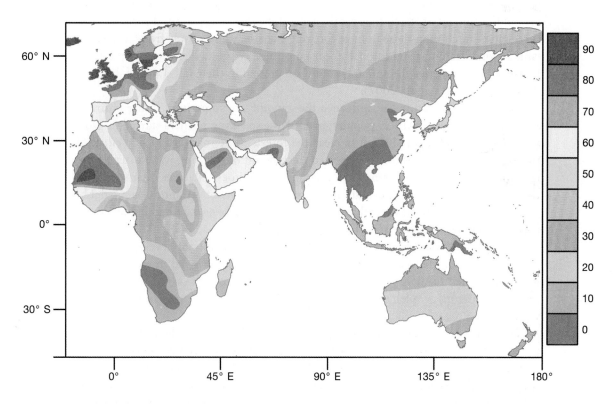

FIGURE 13.4 The ability to digest milk into adulthood is associated with persistence of the enzyme lactase. This map shows where people are most likely to have lactase persistence (the legend indicates the percent who have lactase persistence).

This is an example of the cultural horse pulling the genetic cart. Thus, humans are in a situation, likely unique in the history of the animal kingdom, where they have become so dependent on cultural information to survive that culture has become a selective force on their biological nature. Humans are said to be a product of **culture-gene co-evolution**, as they have both evolved biological predispositions to depend on cultural information, and this cultural information enhances their fitness as it continues to evolve. Moreover, as their culture continues to evolve it places new selective pressures on the genome, which evolves accordingly (Henrich, in press).

There is growing evidence of culture-gene co-evolution and on the strong selective role that culture is playing on the human genome (for reviews, see Hawks et al., 2007; Laland, Odling-Smee, & Myles, 2010). A common domain in which we see evidence for this selection is cultural differences in dietary practices, such as milk consumption. Different cultures vary in what they regularly eat, and long-term, persistent changes in dietary practices have been accompanied by genetic evolution that maximizes the effectiveness of the nutrition that people derive from their diets. For example, humans vary in the amount of starch they eat (in general, people in agricultural societies consume more starch than those in most foraging societies), and people from cultures in which a lot of starch has traditionally been consumed are more likely to have a genetic mutation that increases the amount of amylase protein in their saliva, which helps to digest starch (Perry et al., 2007).

The ways that culture can influence the genome are sometimes rather indirect. For example, in West Africa, populations of Kwa-speaking farmers started to grow yam crops, which required them to clear the forests. One inadvertent side effect of this cultural practice was that it increased the amount of standing water after a rain, creating a better habitat for malaria-carrying mosquitoes. Malaria then spread in these regions and led to the evolution of a particular genetic variant for hemoglobin that is associated with sickle-cell anemia, which has the benefit of making one more resistant to developing malaria (Durham, 1991; Livingstone, 1958). Adjacent populations that did not share the same agricultural practices did not develop this same genetic mutation. Hence, the cultural practice of yam farming led to more pools of water, which led to more malaria-carrying mosquitoes, which served as a selective force for changing people's genetic resistance. The effects of culture can spread quite widely.

Given that there is systematic human genetic variation around the world, and that genes play a role in psychological processes, could genetic differences across populations account for the kinds of psychological differences discussed in this textbook? On the one hand, for most of the studies that we've reviewed, the experimental designs have been essentially correlational. For example, Japanese have been demonstrated to differ in various ways of thinking from Americans, but it's possible that some of those differences are a product of the differences in genes between these two groups rather than of the differences in their cultural experiences. Genes were not identified in any of these studies; however, many of the studies we've discussed have identified findings for which immigrants and their children show a different pattern of responses when compared with people who live in their heritage culture (e.g., Heine & Lehman, 2004; Norenzayan et al., 2002). These studies are important because immigrants are genetically similar to people from their heritage culture yet participate in cultural practices from their host culture, so they are an ideal sample to detect whether cultural experiences play a role in the differences in psychological processes between populations.

Thus far, every cross-cultural study that I know of that includes immigrant samples provides evidence for cultural factors contributing to population differences. Likewise, other studies find effects after manipulating cultural variables, such as priming culture (e.g., Hong, Morris, Chiu, & Benet-Martinez, 2000; Ross, Xun, & Wilson, 2002) or situational sampling (e.g., Kitayama, Markus, Matsumoto, & Norasakkunkit, 1997; Morling, Kitayama, & Miyamoto, 2002). These kinds of studies provide evidence for the role of cultural experiences accounting for the observed differences. Yet, not all of the cross-cultural studies in this book have included such kinds of experimental designs, so the role of genes underlying the psychological differences across cultures remains a theoretical possibility in those studies.

A number of large-scale international research projects (e.g., Hinds et al., 2005; International HapMap Consortium, 2005) have been mapping the frequencies of different gene variants and have identified several that have been associated with psychological variables that differ in their frequencies around the world. For example, alleles associated with at least three different genes predict enhanced social sensitivity (namely, 5-HTTLPR, A118G, and MAOA), and each of these alleles is more common in Asian samples than in European samples (there isn't sufficient data from other regions of the world). Some researchers have proposed that these findings suggest a genetic foundation underlying collectivism (e.g., Chiao & Blizinsky, 2010; Way & Lieberman, 2010)—that is, they suggest that either collectivism emerged as a strategy among people with innate tendencies toward social sensitivity or socially sensitive people living in collectivistic cultures thrived more and had more surviving offspring. This is an intriguing hypothesis, and as these international genetic sequencing studies continue to progress, it's possible that the future may present solid genetic evidence that the human genome plays a role in many of the cultural differences described in this text. However, it's important to note that the relations between genes and psychological outcomes are highly complex and are resistant to simple explanations. For one, each of the three genes linked to social sensitivity are expressed differently depending on people's experiences, they each are only weakly correlated with social sensitivity, and most of the gene association studies have thus far only been conducted in the West.

This last point—that the findings are based on Western data—is critical, because published studies that have explored the relations between genes and psychological variables across cultures commonly find *opposite* effects of the genes across cultures. For example, a genetic variant that is associated with increased emotional-support seeking in times of distress for European-Americans is associated with *decreased* emotional-support seeking among Koreans (Kim et al., 2010a); a variant that is associated with increased attention to foreground objects among European-Americans shows the opposite effect among Koreans (Kim et al., 2010b); a variant that leads to better responses to antidepressants among Caucasians leads to worse responses among Japanese and Koreans (Kim et al., 2000; Smeraldi et al., 1998; Yoshida et al., 2002); and a variant associated with decreased emotional suppression among European-Americans predicted *increased* emotional suppression among Koreans (Kim et al., 2011). Interestingly, those studies that included a sample of Korean-Americans, who are genetically more similar to Koreans but culturally more similar to European-Americans, showed a pattern of results that were more similar to those of European-Americans, demonstrating that cultural experiences can actually shape how genes are expressed in the body (also see Sasaki, Kim, & Xu, 2011). That is, even if gene frequencies may vary across cultures, this does not mean that the associated psychological traits will also vary across cultures in the same way.

My own view on this controversial topic is that although it is theoretically possible that some psychological differences across cultures might be related to population-level genetic differences, the available evidence thus far is not nearly consistent enough to support such a conjecture. This is a rapidly growing topic of research that depends on newly emerging technologies, and over the next decade or so we will have access to far more data that will let us evaluate the extent to which genes underlie cultural differences in psychological processes.

Acquired Physical Variation Across Cultures

As we saw in the case of foot shapes, evidence suggests striking physical variations among people across the world that exist independently of genetics. Take the example of the Moken, a tribe of sea nomads in Southeast Asia who spend seven or eight months a year living on small boats in the archipelagos off of Burma, Thailand, and Malaysia. They depend on diving to spear fish and to retrieve clams, sea cucumbers, lobsters, and other food from the ocean floor. The challenge in this endeavor is that, as any swimmer knows, underwater vision tends to be blurry. Being able to focus underwater would greatly increase one's chances of bringing home a tasty meal. Moken children have more than twice the underwater visual acuity of European children (Gislen et al., 2003), and they accomplish this visual acuity through controlled accommodation that is followed by maximal pupil constriction—a process similar to what enables seals to see clearly underwater (Gislen & Gislen, 2004). This ability is likely not a genetic adaptation. Research shows that it is acquired through practice and that European children can also be trained to develop the same kind of underwater visual acuity as the Moken (Gislen, Warrant, & Kroger, 2005). The difference is that the Moken develop this ability without explicit training and by regularly participating in cultural practices of diving for food.

OBESITY AND DIET. One striking way that people from different cultures vary is in their weight. For example, if we compare cultures using the standard definition of obesity as having a body mass index (BMI) score of at least 30, we can see tremendous variability in obesity rates around the world, ranging from approximately 1.5% of Chinese women to 55% of Samoan women (World Health Organization, 2005). Although there is good evidence that genetic factors are predictors for body weight, and it is possible that certain weight-relevant genes are more common in one culture than in another, culture clearly plays an important role in cross-national differences in body weight. Obesity rates have risen dramatically across the world during the past few decades, particularly in the United States and the United Kingdom (**Figure 13.5**; Organisation for Economic Co-operation and Development [OECD], 2004). This fact cannot be explained by genetic accounts, because these countries have not experienced

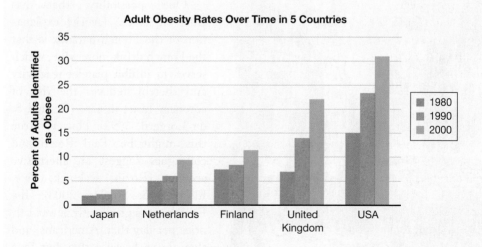

FIGURE 13.5 Over the past few decades, people in many parts of the world have been getting heavier.

an influx into of people carrying overweight genes. Rather, it is more likely that cultural changes over time have given rise to this increase. Some often-discussed key candidates for the obesity epidemic are a greater reliance on high-calorie foods such as fast food and soda, larger portion sizes, a less-active lifestyle as people engage in more sedentary activities such as surfing the Web and playing computer games, and a more suburban lifestyle that involves more driving and less exercise.

Even within the West, there are large discrepancies between nations in obesity rates. For example, the rate of obesity in the United States is about five times the rate in France. This fact is perhaps all the more surprising if you consider the kinds of food that go into the typical French diet. Compared with American cuisine, French cuisine characteristically is rich in delicious yet fat- and sugar-heavy products such as cream, butter, cheese, foie gras, pastries, and chocolate. Reflecting the high amount of fats in their diets, the French tend to have higher blood cholesterol levels than Americans (Renaud & de Lorgeril, 1992). However, despite the greater prevalence of fat in much of French cuisine, the French have a longer lifespan, are thinner, and have lower heart disease rates than Americans (Richard, 1987). This combination of a diet rich in fats yet lower rates of heart disease has puzzled researchers for decades and has been termed the **French paradox**.

One possibility that has emerged as the favorite explanation of the French paradox is that the French drink more wine, which serves to inhibit platelet reactivity and thereby reduces the risk of coronary heart disease (Renaud & de Lorgeril, 1992). However true this might be, Paul Rozin and colleagues suggest an alternative account (Rozin, Kabnick, Pete, Fischler, & Shields, 2003): The French eat significantly fewer calories per day than Americans, and they do so because they live in a different cultural environment that affects the size of their portions and their attitudes toward food. Rozin and colleagues reasoned that the

THE SECRET SHAME OF PARIS

PREDAWN ROUNDUP OF FAT FRENCHWOMEN

amount of food people eat is largely determined by what is put in front of them or by the size of individual portions of food that are sold in stores. So, for example, if the question is how much yogurt a person will eat, the answer is likely determined by the size of the yogurt container. People do not tend to eat, say, one and a half individual-serving containers of yogurt—rather, they tend to eat however much yogurt is in a single container.

Rozin and colleagues explored this question by going to supermarkets in France and the United States and measuring the portion sizes. Yogurt containers in the United States are about 80% bigger than they are in France, and a variety of other foods sold in individual servings, such as chocolate bars, soft drinks, and lasagna, are also larger. Even fruit is larger in the United States than it is in France! Also, food that is served in international chain restaurants varies in portion size. A medium order of french fries at McDonald's in the United States contains about 70% more fries than an order in France. Chicken McNuggets are the same size in both countries, suggesting that this product is shipped internationally; however, a grilled chicken sandwich is bigger in the United States than in France. Rozin and colleagues suggest that this is because the grilled chicken is made from a distinct part of the chicken and that chickens are also bigger in the United States than they are in France! Furthermore, Rozin and colleagues found that the quantities of ingredients specified in cookbooks are also larger in the United States than in France. Americans consume more calories than the French precisely because the cultural norms for portion size are larger for Americans. Rozin and colleagues argue that this excess caloric consumption is likely one key factor behind the higher obesity rates and coronary heart disease rates in the United States.

In many ways, the large portion sizes in the United States and elsewhere are the product of a fairly recent cultural evolution. Take the example of coffee. In 1971 Starbucks started selling Italian-style coffee products to Americans. Recognizing at the time that Americans prefer large servings, they created a larger 12-ounce cup (called tall) which people could choose if the standard 8-ounce Italian size (called short) wasn't sufficient. Soon, however, in response to consumer demand, Starbucks created an even larger 16-ounce size. Because the English word "tall" was already taken, they went with an Italian word and called this size *grande*. But over time this wasn't big enough to satisfy people's desires either, so they created an even larger 20-ounce size, which some clever marketing whiz called *venti* (Italian for "twenty"). Alas, this too didn't prove large enough, and in 2011 Starbucks created a 31-ounce size for their cold drinks called *trenti* (Italian for "thirty"). Could the Starbucks *quaranta* ("forty") be next?

Sadly for our own health, Starbucks has been the norm rather than the exception. Portion sizes have been increasing for virtually all kinds of food in the United States, with portions at fast food chains now being two to five times larger than when they were first introduced (Young & Nestle, 2007), and Americans are estimated to be consuming approximately 200–300 more calories a day than they did in the 1970s (Centers for Disease Control and Prevention, 2004). The increasing rates of obesity shown in Figure 13.5 do not seem as puzzling any more. Cultural changes are affecting our health.

However, portion sizes do not tell the whole story about the French paradox. Rozin and colleagues also draw attention to a number of important ways that French and American attitudes differ toward food. One key difference is that the French view eating as a more leisurely and enjoyable activity than Americans do (Rozin, Fischler, Imada, Sarubin, & Wrzesniewski, 1999). For example, the French tend to spend more time eating their food than Americans do. When they are at McDonald's, the French spend approximately 50% longer eating than Americans do (Rozin, Kabnick, et al., 2003), despite the fact that they're consuming fewer fries, drinking smaller soft drinks, and eating smaller grilled chicken sandwiches. People are expected to savor their food in France. One way this is evident is in people's reaction to the following question: "If you were vacationing and had to choose between the following hotels including meals, which one would you pick? A luxury hotel with average food or an average hotel with excellent food?" Approximately 80% of French chose the hotel with the good food, compared with only 40% of Americans (Rozin et al., 1999).

Americans seem to have conflicted attitudes toward food, especially among women. Rozin and colleagues (1999) showed that Americans make more effort to consume products that appear to have been altered to make them healthier—for example, being made with less salt, fat, or sugar—compared with the French. For example, whereas about 80% of American females report eating products from which fat has been removed (such as low-fat yogurt) a few times a week, only about 20% of French males do. Despite these efforts to eat food that is apparently healthier, however, only about 35% of Americans claim to be healthy eaters, in contrast to about 75% of French. When asked to list whatever words come to mind when one thinks of the word "food," one of the top responses among American females was "fattening," a word that did not appear on the French lists of frequent responses (Rozin, Kurzer, & Cohen, 2002). Relatedly, and tellingly, a survey of American college students from various regions across the United States revealed that 14% of American women reported feeling too *embarrassed* to ever buy a chocolate bar (Rozin, Bauer, & Catanese, 2003).

In a comprehensive survey of attitudes toward food among French, Americans, Japanese, and Belgians, Rozin and colleagues found that women have more negative attitudes toward food than men do, and that American women have the most negative attitudes of all (Rozin et al., 1999). The average responses of the participants in each culture and sex are expressed in **Figure 13.6** using something known as Chernoff figures (Chernoff, 1973). In these figures, each element of the face (i.e., the curve of the mouth, the slant of the eyebrows, the distance between the eyes, the shape of the

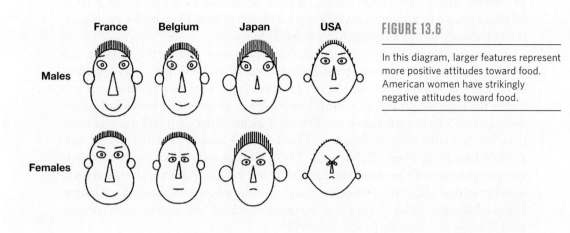

FIGURE 13.6

In this diagram, larger features represent more positive attitudes toward food. American women have strikingly negative attitudes toward food.

head, and so on) is tied to the response to a particular question about food. The more the average participant's response to that item reflects a negative attitude, the more the facial feature reveals a small and unhappy face. To summarize the results, males in all cultures have fairly positive attitudes toward food, especially among the French and Belgians. Females have much less positive attitudes toward food, with American women being especially negative.

CULTURE AND HEIGHT. It is likely not too surprising to have read that culturally shared dietary habits can influence the average weight of people in a culture. However, what is less obvious is that culturally shared dietary habits can have a striking impact on the average *height* of people in a culture. If you travel to the Netherlands today, one characteristic of the people there will likely strike you: They're tall. On average, the Dutch are the tallest people on the planet.

Typically, people tend to think of genetic factors being responsible for height, and genes are usually the best way of making sense of, say, why people on the school basketball team are taller on average than people on the debating team—basketball players tend to have taller parents than debaters do. Genes play a key role in explaining individual differences in height within a particular culture. However, genes are less useful for explaining height differences between cultures and across historical periods (Malcolm, 1974). For example, although Dutch men today average 6'1", slightly more than 3 inches taller than the average American man who stands just under 5'10", in 1865, American men averaged 5'8", which was approximately 3 inches taller than the average Dutch man at the time (the data for men are far more available, because most of these data come from military records, although similar patterns are evident for women; Floud, 1994; Shay, 1994). These rather dramatic changes in the average height of people in a country make it more difficult to look to genes for an answer. Instead, dietary factors are more likely to be responsible.

In the late 19th century, on average, Americans were among the tallest in the world, reflecting their relative advantage in income (their GNP per capita was third highest in the world). For example, at that time, American men stood at approximately the same height as Australians, 1 inch taller than Britons, 2 inches taller than Norwegians, 3 inches taller than the French, 4 inches taller than Italians, and more than 7 inches taller than the Japanese (Floud, 1994; Floud & Harris, 1997; Steckel, 1994; Whitwell, de Souza, & Nicholas, 1997). During this period, the Netherlands was going through an economic slump. The Dutch economy did not start to recover until the second half of the 19th century, and then the average height of Dutch people increased accordingly as their average incomes increased, and continued to increase until this day (Drukker & Tassenaar, 1997).

The reasoning for this link between wealth and height is that wealth brings with it a healthier diet, especially around the ages when people tend to go through growth spurts, such as in infancy and in adolescence (Steckel, 1983). During periods of greater wealth, people are able to get more vitamins and nutrients at those critical growth periods. Another example of this can be seen on the Korean peninsula, where South Korean children are about 5 inches taller than their North Korean counterparts (Schwekendiek, 2009); likewise, Japanese immigrants to California in the 1950s were about 5 inches taller than their compatriots in Japan (Greulich, 1957). Furthermore, specific aspects of diets in cultures appears to affect height; dairy consumption in particular has been linked to height (Wiley, 2005). Moreover, the average heights in countries have not grown steadily across time but rather have fluctuated, coinciding with broad societal changes that affected diet. For example, the average height of Europeans tended to shrink during the Industrial Revolution as people began to move into the cities, populations swelled, and average caloric intake dropped in many places (Komlos, 1998). In sum, height is closely tied to diet, especially at the ages of key growth spurts in the lifespan.

What remains somewhat of a puzzle, however, is that, on average, Americans have largely stopped growing taller, whereas people in much of the rest of the world have continued growing as their incomes have improved (African-American women have actually been getting shorter; Komlos, 2010). In most other industrialized countries today, but not in the United States, people tend to be taller than their parents. One theory is that the eating habits of American teenagers, which include a lot of fast food, are depriving them of some crucial growth-related nutrients, resulting in the American growth spurt shifting from its vertical axis to a horizontal one. Another explanation is that the greater income inequality in the United States, compared with that of the taller Dutch and other tall northern Europeans, means that there are more poor people who do not get appropriate diets, thereby pulling down the national height average (see Bilger, 2004). One explanation, which appears compelling on the surface, does not appear to be responsible—that is, America receives more immigrants from places where people have historically been shorter (such as Mexico and East Asia). However, this cannot be the key factor in the findings discussed earlier, because most of the contemporary American data are based on those who are native-born and speak English at home, and the ethnic backgrounds of the samples are examined separately. The lack of a vertical growth spurt among Americans remains a puzzle.

In sum, physical characteristics of people around the world, such as their ability to focus their eyes underwater, the shape of their feet, and their weight and height, vary greatly, and they do so largely because of their participation in different cultural worlds. These examples provide some striking evidence that culture is not something that simply lies outside of people. In many ways, cultural participation manifests itself physically inside people as well. The boundary of where biology ends and culture begins is not so clear-cut.

Culture and Sleep

Sleep is a biological necessity that serves such essential physiological functions as allowing for physical rest and repair (Adam & Oswald, 1977), consolidating memories (Diekelmann & Born, 2010), and clearing out metabolites from the brain (Xie et al., 2013), although many of the specific functions of sleep remain poorly understood and continue to be debated. Sleep, of some kind, is found in almost all mammal species (Siegel, 2008). However, despite its obvious physiological basis, pronounced cultural variation occurs in the ways people around the world do sleep.

One way that culture affect sleep behavior was discussed in Chapter 5—in most cultures of the world, children co-sleep with their parents whereas in the West it is more common for children to sleep separately. Another way that we can see how culture shapes sleep is to consider how norms vary for the time that people sleep. You have probably heard something to the effect that people function best on a certain number of hours of sleep, say 8 hours, and what this means is that people view it to be healthiest if someone goes to bed at night and stays there sleeping for a full 8 hours straight. However, this notion that people sleep for a single long period through the night is not universal. Consider this passage from the early English ballad, *Old Robin of Portingale*: "And at the wakening of your first sleepe/ You shall have a hott drinke made. And at the wakening of your next sleepe/ Your sorrowes will have a slake." This is referencing an idea commonly found in medieval European literature that people's nightly sleep was separated into two distinct periods, because before the time of electric lighting, people would go to bed sometime after sunset, wake up in the middle of the night for an hour or so, and then return to sleep later (Crook, 2008; Ekirch, 2005; see **Figure 13.7**). Similar patterns have been identified among some subsistence societies today, where two sleeps are punctuated by a period in the middle of the night, when people get up to tend to the fire, maybe have a snack, converse quietly, play music, or have sex. For most of human history, the typical way of sleeping was likely to have these two sleeps with a period of wakefulness in between (Worthman & Melby, 2002). Research with American adults also finds that if people are kept in a room that goes dark for 14 hours each day, they will also revert to a pattern of two sleeps separated by a period of increasing wakefulness in the middle of the night (Wehr et al., 1993).

Moreover, the sheer amount of sleep that people get varies significantly across cultures. For example, Japanese and Korean adults report sleeping about an hour less

FIGURE 13.7 The painting "Midnight," by Henry Fuseli, painted in 1765, shows the time between the "two sleeps" that were common before the advent of electrical lighting.

per day than French adults do (OECD, 2009). Moreover, these cultural differences are not just evident among adults: a systematic study of infants and toddlers in 17 countries around the world found that Japanese infants sleep about 1.5 hours less than North American infants (Mindell et al., 2010). In general, infants from Asian countries were found to sleep much less than infants from Western countries (**Figure 13.8**). And it's not the case that North American infants are sleeping more than the rest of the word; another study found that Dutch infants slept about 1.3 hours more than American infants (Super, Blom, Harkness, Ranade, & Londhe, 2014), indicating that people in countries that occupy the extreme ends of this distribution (Japan and the Netherlands) have pronounced differences in the amount that they sleep.

One challenge with studying sleep, and it's the main reason that sleep remains one of the most poorly understood aspects of human life, is that sleep is difficult to measure directly and unobtrusively; people typically sleep in the privacy of their own homes, away from the watchful eye of the sleep researcher. As a result, the vast majority of published cross-cultural sleep studies rely on people's self-report of sleep for either themselves or their infant children. A limitation of this method is that self-reports might reflect more about what people think about how they should be sleeping as opposed to how much they are actually sleeping.

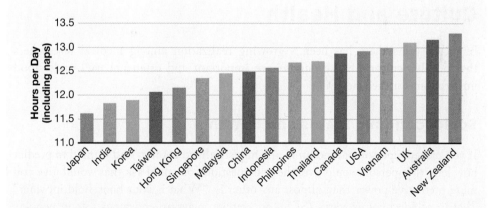

FIGURE 13.8 This shows the amount of sleep, including naps, that parents report that their infants and toddlers get each day around the world. Even among young children, the amount of sleep they get each day varies substantially across cultures (From Mindell et al., 2010).

My colleagues and I recently sought to get more direct physiological measures of sleep by having Japanese, European-Canadian, and Asian-Canadian university students wear a watch for one week at a time that objectively provided biometric measurements of their sleep quality over that time (Cheung, Takemura, & Heine, 2014). A number of interesting findings emerged. First, similar to the pattern observed with infants, Japanese university students slept about 1.2 hours less than the two Canadian samples, who did not differ at all. That Asian-Canadians slept similarly to European-Canadians suggests that sleep is affected more by local cultural norms than by their heritage cultural norms. Despite sleeping less than Canadians, however, Japanese were not any more efficient in their sleep—they did not wake up fewer times over the course of the night, or take less time to fall asleep—the Japanese were just getting by on substantially less sleep than the Canadians. The Japanese students also indicated that their ideal amount of sleep was also about an hour less than that reported by Canadians. Moreover, even though they were sleeping more than the Japanese, the Canadians curiously described themselves as feeling more tired during the day. And Canadians reported that they more strongly held the belief that their health was dependent on getting a sufficient amount of sleep compared with Japanese (also see Benedict, 1946, for similar findings). The reasons that sleep varies as much as it does across cultures remain unclear, but at least these data reveal that culture can shape something as fundamental, and biologically-constrained, as sleep.

Culture and Health

In recent years there has been a growing realization among medical researchers that people's cultural backgrounds have important and often not well understood implications for their health.

Socioeconomic Status and Health

If you picked a person at random in any industrialized country and wanted to predict how long that person would live, the one question you could ask that would give you more predictive power than almost any other is, "What is your household income?" That is, socioeconomic status (SES), on average, plays an enormous role in people's health—a role that until a few decades ago was all but invisible to health researchers. Through a variety of paths, many of which are still not clearly understood, SES impacts health in dramatic and often surprising ways.

Consider a classic study that examined the mortality of civil servants in England across a 10-year period (Marmot, Shipley, & Rose, 1984). The civil servants belonged to one of four hierarchically ranked employment categories. The researchers found that, compared with the top administrators, members of the executive class were 60% more likely to die over that 10-year period, the clerical staff were 120% more likely to die, and the unskilled laborers were 170% more likely to die. That is, there was a clear relation between employment category and mortality, such that those with the highest SES tended to live the longest. These are very large differences (indeed, they are larger than the difference in life expectancy between smokers and nonsmokers; Marmot, 2004), and they have been replicated in many industrialized nations, including Denmark and Norway (Lynge, 1984), Finland (Koskenvuo, Kaprio, Kesaniemi, & Sarna, 1978), France (Leclerc, Lert, & Goldberg, 1984), Japan (Kagamimori, Iibuchi, & Fox, 1983), and New Zealand (Pearce, Davis, Smith, & Foster, 1985).

Take the case of the United States. **Figure 13.9** shows the age-adjusted mortality rate for Americans of varying income levels (Wilkinson, 1994). This figure reveals that with almost every increase in income, mortality rates are lower, and these differences emerge even among those whose incomes are at the highest levels. These kinds of findings were initially met with much resistance and were originally suspected to be the result of various kinds of statistical artifacts, which have since largely been ruled out. Decades of research have now consistently revealed that SES has a very strong relation with health outcomes. If there ever was a good argument

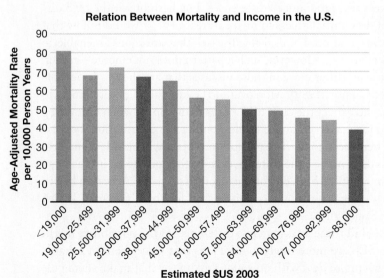

Relation Between Mortality and Income in the U.S.

Estimated $US 2003

FIGURE 13.9

This shows the mortality rate, adjusted for years, of people at different income levels in the United States. On average, the larger one's income, the longer one will live, and this relation holds rather similarly from the poorest through to the richest income groups.

to get a university degree and pursue a high-paying career, it's that you'll likely live longer.

Status differences in health are not limited to industrialized societies. For example, consider the health of three West African ethnic groups that co-reside in northeast Burkina Faso: the Fulani, Mossi, and Rimaibe. This region is endemic with malaria, which is a major cause of death there. The Mossi and Rimaibe have been living in this region for thousands of years and have developed much genetic resistance to malaria over this time. The Fulani, in contrast, moved to this region in the early 19th century as part of the Islamic invasion of sub-Saharan Africa. Unlike the Mossi and Rimaibe, they have not developed much genetic resistance to malaria (Modiano et al., 2001). However, despite being more genetically vulnerable to developing malaria, the Fulani are far *less* likely than the Mossi and Rimaibe to actually develop malaria (Modiano et al., 1996). An apparent reason for this is that the Fulani are the dominant ethnic group in this area. When they first arrived, they conquered, enslaved, and decultured the other ethnic groups in the area, including the Mossi and Rimaibe (see Gordon, 2000). The higher status that they have as conquerors appears to provide them with enough health benefits to more than make up for their greater genetic vulnerability to malaria (Wallace & Wallace, 2002).

Why SES is related to health has proved itself to be a complex problem, with no obvious single answer. One part of the relation is quite direct. Your health may be seriously compromised if you don't have enough money to pay for adequate health care. However, this explanation only goes so far in explaining the findings. Indeed, in the British civil servant study, all of the workers had the same access to state-provided health care, yet there were still pronounced differences. Furthermore, if the SES differences were a result of differential access to medical treatment, it would follow that the differences should be more pronounced for diseases that are more amenable to treatment than those that are not. However, such a pattern does not emerge—rather, if anything, the social classes differ more in those diseases that are the *least* amenable to treatment (Bunker & Gomby, 1989). Moreover, if the key variable were access to medical services, you would expect the class differences to disappear when examining the differences between income levels at the highest end of the distribution, because there should be little difference among these groups in terms of what kinds of medical services people can afford. However, the differences in health tend to be just as large among adjacent SES groups at the high end of the income spectrum. Access to health services, although surely relevant, is not the main reason for the differential health outcomes across the SES spectrum.

So what might be behind these striking class differences? One possibility might be that people lower in SES are more likely to have jobs that place them in hazardous situations, such as having to deal with poisonous toxins, or that make them vulnerable to workplace accidents. However, this explanation cannot explain findings such as those from the British civil servant study, because all of those people had office jobs, yet SES still predicted their health outcomes. Another explanation is that poorer people are more likely to participate in cultural contexts that are more encouraging of unhealthy habits, such as smoking, eating fast food, or living a sedentary lifestyle. These behaviors are surely relevant to health, and there is evidence that people in lower SES groups are more likely to smoke and eat a poorer diet and are less likely to exercise (e.g., Crespo, Ainsworth, Keteyian, Heath, & Smit, 1999; Kaplan & Keil, 1993). However, even when the different levels of these behaviors among the SES groups are controlled for, there still remains a clear relation between SES and health (e.g., Kaplan, 1985; Marmot et al., 1984; Siegrist & Marmot, 2004).

The strong relation between SES and health remains an enormous puzzle that is occupying researchers from many fields around the globe. A number of variables are likely behind this relation. A growing body of evidence has pointed to psychosocial variables that underlie the relation between SES and health (e.g., Chen, 2004; Marmot, 2004). For example, research has revealed that personality characteristics such as hostility and pessimism are associated with increased risk for illnesses. The experiences of growing up in a lower-SES neighborhood, where school achievement tends to be relatively worse than in higher-SES neighborhoods (thereby precluding future employment opportunities), and where people are more likely to witness delinquent and criminally dangerous behaviors (e.g., Chase-Lansdale & Gordon, 1996; Leventhal & Brooks-Gunn, 2000; Sampson & Groves, 1989), would seem to predispose people toward having an overall sense of mistrust and cynicism, leading lower SES individuals to be more hostile and less optimistic about their futures compared with higher-SES individuals. This explanation can address some of the heightened health risks among the poorer classes; however, it is less able to account for the health differences that are observed among the wealthiest groups.

Another psychological variable relevant to health is the availability of cognitive resources to make sound decisions. Research finds that the very experience of poverty appears to lead to cognitive deficits that can undermine decision making, which can have harmful health outcomes (Butterworth, Cherbuin, Sachdev, & Anstey, 2012; Mani, Mullainathan, Shafir, & Zhao, 2013). Poverty leads people to become more risk adverse, and to focus on the near future, which can interfere with people making long-term plans to improve their situation (Haushofer & Fehr, 2014). Moreover, poverty creates a great deal of stress, as poor people are preoccupied with the difficult tradeoffs that they must manage while they juggle expenses and cope with a sporadic and limited income. For example, one study investigated sugar cane farmers in Southern India. This population is noteworthy as their income is seasonal—before the harvest time they are often struggling trying to make ends meet, and then right after the harvest they have sufficient finances again. These farmers scored better on cognitive tests after their harvest, when money was sufficient, than before the harvest, when they were preoccupied with thoughts about taking care of their bills. Similar results were found with American adults who were experimentally led to imagine different kinds of financial hardship (Mani et al., 2013). Poor people are less likely to adhere to medical treatment regimens, which is likely influenced by the same kinds of distraction and cognitive overloads that the experience of poverty engenders (Karter et al., 2004; Katz & Hofer, 1994; Neal et al., 2001).

A key psychological variable involved in mediating the role between SES and health outcomes is stress (Marmot, 2004; Sapolsky, 2005). When people are facing severe chronic stressors in their lives, their risk for illness often increases. There appear to be two primary mechanisms involved: Chronically stressed people are more likely to engage in health-compromising behaviors such as smoking and drinking in order to cope with the difficulties in their lives, and stress directly weakens the immune system's ability to fight off infections and manage other threats (Miller & Cohen, 2005; Segerstrom & Miller, 2004). In general, the less stress a person experiences, the better off is his or her health. And in many ways, stress often derives from psychological interpretations of events. For example, you would likely feel far less stressed discussing your university experiences with a friend than with someone who was interviewing you for a job that you desperately want, even though you might be talking about the same topic.

Higher feelings of stress, as evident by physiological measures, are commonly identified among those of lower SES backgrounds (Chen & Matthews, 2001; Hajat et al., 2010). One reason is that people of lower SES backgrounds are more often vigilant to threat when compared with their wealthier compatriots (Gallo & Matthews, 2003; Kraus, Horberg, Goetz, & Keltner, 2011; Kraus et al., 2012). Someone who is worried about threatening events is more likely to have higher blood pressure and to be at risk for coronary heart disease (Phillips & Klein, 2010). Moreover, stress is more likely to be experienced when a person is feeling a lack of control (e.g., Bugental & Cortez, 1988). Low feelings of control have been shown to be related to a number of negative health outcomes. For example, people who feel that they do not have much control in their jobs tend to have a higher risk of heart disease (e.g., Marmot, Bosma, Hemingway, Brunner, & Stansfeld, 1997), and low levels of control more generally are associated with poor physical functioning and an increased likelihood of illness (e.g., Feldman & Steptoe, 2004; Seeman & Seeman, 1983).

One dramatic demonstration of the link between control and health can be seen in a classic study by Langer and Rodin (Langer & Rodin, 1976; Rodin & Langer, 1977). Residents of a nursing home were divided into two conditions. Those in one condition received an intervention that allowed them to have control over a number of minor life events (e.g., deciding when a plant should be watered, deciding when visitors would come). In contrast, those in the other condition did not receive any such control intervention. As the months went by, those who had been provided with opportunities for control ended up requiring fewer medications, were rated as being in better health, and ultimately, on average, lived longer than those in the no-intervention group.

Control is relevant for making sense of the link between SES and health because people in higher social positions report feeling more in control than those in lower positions (Johnson & Krueger, 2005; Kraus, Piff, & Keltner, 2009; Marmot, Kogevinas, & Elston, 1987), and these differences have been shown to relate to health outcomes (Berkman & Breslow, 1983). For example, one study found that although, in general, lower-SES people had worse health outcomes, those with lower SES who felt that they had much control in their lives had levels of health and well-being that were comparable with those in higher income groups (Lachman & Weaver, 1998). Chen (2007) found that providing low-SES adolescents with some sense of control in a stressful situation led them to show less physiological reactivity (an indication of vulnerability to illness) than those who were not provided with feelings of control. In contrast, high-SES adolescents were unaffected by the manipulation that gave them feelings of control, suggesting that they already experienced sufficient control over their lives. Perhaps the best-supported explanation, then, for why low-SES people tend to have worse health outcomes than high-SES ones is that they feel less control in more aspects of their lives.

Stress and feelings of a lack of control tend to be more pronounced among those who occupy a subordinate position and are subject to the demands of those who are able to make decisions for them. This is not just true of humans. For example, research with various primate populations has revealed that those individuals who are subordinate in a hierarchy experience greater stress hormone levels when they belong to a social system in which the hierarchy is maintained through intimidation rather than through direct physical attacks, when the hierarchy is stable, when subordinate individuals are unable to easily avoid dominant individuals, and when they have low availability of social support (for a review, see Sapolsky, 2005). The societal features that result in the greatest degree of stress among subordinates in various primate populations are remarkably similar to the situation in which many low-SES people find themselves in modernized industrialized societies.

Importantly, it is not only objective SES that is so critical to people's experiences—rather, subjective SES is at least as predictive of health outcomes (Adler, Epel, Castellazzo, & Ickovics, 2000). That is, *feeling* poor can matter as much as actually *being* poor. This suggests that the experience of relative deprivation, of knowing that others are doing better than you, might lead to stress and its associated negative health consequences. One source of evidence in support of this idea is that across cultures there is little relation between absolute level of income and health above a minimum threshold of income. For example, if you look at the life expectancy at birth of various countries around the world alongside the GDP per capita of those countries (adjusted for purchasing power), you can see a striking

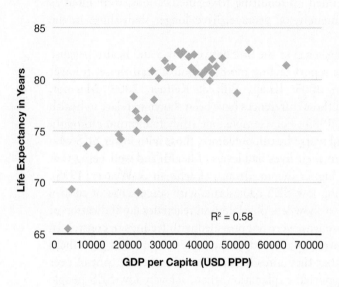

FIGURE 13.10

Each dot represents a country. There is a clear relation between GDP and life expectancy, until the average GDP per capita reaches approximately $30,000. Beyond that point, there is virtually no relation.

curvilinear relation (**Figure 13.10**). Up to a GDP per capita figure of approximately $30,000 per year, there is a clear relation between the absolute wealth of a nation and the average life expectancy of its citizens (OECD Health Statistics, 2013). Apparently, different amounts of average income of nations at lower income levels can make a dramatic difference in people's health outcomes, most likely due to whether these countries can provide basic medical services. Above the per capita GDP $30,000, however, the curve largely flattens out, suggesting very little relation between absolute wealth and life expectancy. Many of the countries in the flat part of the curve have average incomes that are lower than that of the lower-SES Americans shown in Figure 13.9, yet people of those countries do not appear to be much worse off in terms of health outcomes compared with those from wealthier countries. In contrast, poorer Americans are doing far worse than wealthier Americans. The relation between income and health, above this cutoff of around $30,000, is thus largely a relation between health and one's income *relative* to those around them.

Cross-national comparisons reveal some striking evidence for the health problems associated with relative deprivation. For example, Indians living in the poor province of Kerala have far lower absolute incomes than poor African-Americans in the United States. However, people in Kerala outlive African-Americans by a substantial degree (Sen, 1999). The Keralians are poor in absolute terms, but they likely feel less poor because nearly everyone around them is poor. In contrast, poor

Americans often earn an income that is not that poor by international standards; however, they are poor compared to their fellow Americans, and their health suffers accordingly.

In support of the role of relative deprivation in negative health outcomes, it has been shown that in countries in which there is relatively less income inequality, life expectancies tend to be longer. Among industrialized nations, the correlation between a country's GINI coefficient (which reveals the extent of income inequality in the country) and the average life expectancy of its citizens at birth is $r = -.81$, a remarkably strong negative relation (Wilkinson, 1994). For example, Japan has the longest average life expectancy in the world, and it also has one of the most egalitarian income distributions of any major industrialized nation (Marmot & Davey Smith, 1989). Further evidence for the role of income inequality is that the relation between health and social class is weaker in countries with more equal income distributions, such as Sweden and Norway, than in countries with a greater spread, such as the United States or the United Kingdom (Lundberg, 1991; Vagero & Lundberg, 1989). The reasoning is that if there are pronounced differences in status across individuals, then feelings of relative deprivation should be that much greater, leading to more stress and illness, than if the differences in status are less evident. Many other social ills—such as homicide rates, the prevalence of mental illness, illegal drug use, obesity, high school dropout rates, societal distrust, teenage birth rates, and lower status for women—are also associated with a nation's level of income inequality (Wilkinson & Pickett, 2009).

Ethnicity and Health

Socioeconomic status is implicated in people's health outcomes in another way. Disadvantaged minorities around the world also tend to be of lower SES, and they often experience worse health outcomes than those of majority members. In particular, African-Americans in the United States suffer from relatively worse health outcomes. For example, looking at the 15 leading causes of death in the United States, African-Americans have higher death rates than that of European-Americans for 12 of them (see **Table 13.1**). Given that, on average, African-Americans tend to be of much lower SES than European-Americans, many of the reasons for their higher mortality can likely be explained by the SES difference.

However, other factors appear to be involved in the poor health outcomes of many African-Americans than just SES. That is, even when African-Americans and European-Americans of the same SES are compared, there are still some categories of health problems that are more pronounced for African-Americans. In particular, infant mortality rates among African-Americans are about double that of European-Americans (National Center for Health Statistics, 1993), and these differences also hold for those African-Americans who are highly educated (e.g., Pamuk,

TABLE 13.1

Relative prevalence of causes of death among three U.S. ethnic groups

Causes of Death	African-Americans vs. European-Americans	Hispanics vs. European-Americans
1. Heart disease	African-Americans higher	European-Americans higher
2. Cancer	African-Americans higher	European-Americans higher
3. Stroke	African-Americans higher	European-Americans higher
4. Respiratory diseases	European-Americans higher	European-Americans higher
5. Accidents	African-Americans higher	European-Americans higher
6. Diabetes	African-Americans higher	Hispanics higher
7. Flu and pneumonia	African-Americans higher	European-Americans higher
8. Alzheimer's disease	European-Americans higher	European-Americans higher
9. Kidney diseases	African-Americans higher	No difference
10. Septicemia	African-Americans higher	European-Americans higher
11. Suicide	European-Americans higher	European-Americans higher
12. Cirrhosis of the liver	African-Americans higher	Hispanics higher
13. Homicide	African-Americans higher	Hispanics higher
14. Hypertension	African-Americans higher	Hispanics higher
15. Pneumonitis	African-Americans higher	European-Americans higher

Source: National Center for Health Statistics (2003); Williams (2005).

Makuk, Heck, & Reuben, 1998). Likewise, hypertension is particularly high among African-American men, and unlike other health outcomes, hypertension rates are slightly higher for African-American men with college degrees than they are for African-American men with less education (although the opposite pattern holds for African-American women and for European-American men and women; Diez-Roux, Northridge, Morabia, Bassett, & Shea, 1999; Hypertension Detection and Follow-Up Program Cooperative Group, 1977; Pamuk et al., 1998). What can explain these differential outcomes if not SES?

Health differences between African-Americans and European-Americans have been noted for some time, and historically there was a tendency to assume that the differences were due to genetic differences between the races (Wise, 1993). In general, many people often assume, without considering the relevant evidence, that psychological or health differences between African-Americans and European-Americans are due to underlying genetic differences between the races, given the salience of the differences in skin color (see critique by Non, Gravlee, & Mulligan, 2012). However, cultural experiences that differ between these two groups may also be relevant. For example, consider the aforementioned ethnic difference in hypertension rates. The higher rate of hypertension among African-Americans has led some to search for African "hypertension genes." However, a comparison of hypertension rates of Americans and West Africans in Africa (from which most African-Americans are descended) reveals that West Africans have similar hypertension rates as those of European-Americans, and it is only African-Americans that score especially high compared with these other groups (Akinkugbe, 1985; Rotimi et al., 1996). One international epidemiological survey found that Nigerians have lower hypertension rates than European-Americans, whereas Germans and Finns have higher hypertension rates than African-Americans (Cooper et al., 2005). Furthermore, the relevant genetic markers of hypertension do not vary between Africans and African-Americans, greatly weakening a genetic account for the high hypertension rates among African-Americans (Rotimi et al., 1996).

Given that hypertension is clearly linked to stress, it would seem that a more parsimonious explanation is that there is something about being African-American in the United States, with the resultant discrimination and experienced racism, that leads to the stress causing hypertension (Non et al., 2012; Williams, 2003). Indeed, perceptions of discrimination and education are positively correlated among African-Americans (Forman, Williams, & Jackson, 1997), which might help explain why hypertension rates are higher among higher-SES African-American males than among lower-SES African-American males (also see Gravlee, Dressler, & Bernard, 2005). Research further reveals that those African-Americans who most strongly aspire to achieve in the face of discrimination are most at risk for hypertension and other health vulnerabilities (Brody et al., 2013; James, 1994). Similar arguments about the role of experienced racism in health outcomes have been made to account for the ethnic differences in infant mortality (e.g., David & Collins, 1991; Samuels, 1986) and the negative health outcomes among African-Americans more generally (Williams, Yu, Jackson, & Anderson, 1997). In sum, being the target of racism and discrimination appears to be directly related to the average poorer health outcomes of African-Americans.

On the other hand, not all disadvantaged minorities suffer adverse health outcomes. Latinos in the United States, for example, do not tend to suffer much from adverse health outcomes. For the most part, their health outcomes on a variety of measures are quite similar to those of European-Americans, and in a number of cases the outcomes are unexpectedly positive. As shown in Table 13.1, compared to European-Americans, Latinos tend to have *lower* mortality rates for 10 of the 15 leading causes of death (National Center for Health Statistics, 2003; Williams, 2005; also see Markides & Coreil, 1986). This ethnic difference is all the more puzzling, because Latinos tend to be of lower SES than European-Americans and hence should be expected to suffer worse health outcomes. The surprisingly healthy outcomes of Latinos across a variety of conditions has been labeled the **epidemiological paradox** (Karno & Edgerton, 1969).

This paradox is not easily explained away. A number of artifactual accounts proposed to be behind this paradox have largely been discounted. For example, one theory, known as the "healthy migrant hypothesis," proposes that only the healthiest Latinos were able to endure and survive the often taxing and potentially dangerous move to the United States (e.g., Sorlie, Backlund, Johnson, & Rogot, 1993). Hence, the mortality rates in the United States only capture the healthiest subset of Latinos. An alternative account, known as the "salmon bias," proposes that many Latino immigrants return to their home countries when they are old or ill, and thus their deaths are not included in the U.S. data (e.g., Pablos-Mendez, 1994). However, neither of these hypotheses appears to be well supported by the evidence (e.g., Abraido-Lanza, Dohrenwend, Ng-Mak, & Turner, 1999). Moreover, it should be noted that the epidemiological paradox does not apply equally to all groups of Latinos. Puerto Ricans, for example, do not show some of the same unexplained health benefits as Mexicans (e.g., Fuentes-Afflick & Lurie, 1997), and there do not appear to be clear explanations for this.

One explanation for why some groups of Latinos have such unexpected health benefits is that they engage in some more healthful behaviors than non-Latinos. For example, Latinos tend to be less likely to drink and smoke than non-Latinos (although they also tend to exercise less; Perez-Stable, Marin, & Marin, 1994). Furthermore, the longer they have lived in the United States, the more likely they are to engage in unhealthy behaviors, as they come to drink more, smoke more, and are more likely to become obese (Abraido-Lanza et al., 2005). Parallel findings of decreasing mental health alongside acculturation have also been found for Latinos (Alegria et al., 2008). Furthermore, some cultural factors that are more pronounced among Latinos, such as the high value placed on child-bearing (Poma, 1983) and the good deal of emotional support provided by the community (Anderson, Lewis, Giachello, Aday, & Chiu, 1981) also appear to provide an important health buffer. Perhaps Latinos derive health benefits from cultural scripts such as *simpatia* and their unusually high levels of positive affect (e.g., Diener, 2001), as we discussed in Chapter 10. Other studies have shown that positive affect yields significant health benefits (Ostir, Ottenbacher, & Markides, 2004). Although these variables appear to be able to explain part of the reason that Latinos have such healthy outcomes, much of the paradox still remains unresolved and will continue to occupy researchers for some time.

Medicine and Culture

I still recall the first time I caught a cold in Japan, when I was living there with a host family. It was an especially vicious cold, and I was feeling absolutely miserable laid up in bed. My *obaachan,* my host grandmother, ever attentive to my well-being, seemed especially concerned about the bad shape I was in. So she came to my room with some food to make me feel better—a plate of boiled octopus. She insisted that when you are sick you need to get as many nutrients as possible and that boiled octopus is an especially rich source of the nutrients that my sick body so clearly lacked. At the time I had zero appetite, I was feeling nauseous, and I was in a pretty lousy mood. In fact, at that point, there were few things I could imagine wanting to eat less than a plate of boiled octopus. Just looking at it was difficult enough. *Obaachan* could not seem to understand how I could be so ignorant about taking care of my own health. Who would refuse a plate of boiled octopus when they're sick? At the same time, I've always clung to the belief, one that is equally culture-bound, that when I'm sick, a bowl of chicken soup will make me feel better.

Truth be told, neither *obaachan* nor myself really knew all that much about treating illnesses. Neither of us had any training in medicine, and our understanding about illnesses and their treatments was, for the most part, derived from folk theories passed down by our own parents and grandparents. This book has focused on how culture shapes the psychological experiences of people around the world, and the respective cultures of *obaachan* and me have shaped how we understood illnesses and their treatments. However, culture also shapes the psychological experiences of doctors, and therefore it shapes how doctors think about your health. Although there is a great deal of agreement among doctors around the world regarding the causes of various illnesses, their symptoms, and their recommended treatments, there is also a surprising degree of cultural variation. If you visit a doctor in another country, you may come to realize just how much medicine does vary across cultures. In some extreme cases, the kinds of standard procedures in one culture would be seen as medical malpractice in another (for a review, see Payer, 1996).

The medical profession is one of the oldest in the world, and virtually all cultures have people who specialize in treating people's health. Traditionally, medical practices derived from local practices, in particular religious beliefs, as well as by trial and error. Various shamans and healers derived techniques, rituals, and medicines from their own experiences and from knowledge that was passed down across generations (see Clements, 1932; Murdock, 1980). Traditional views of medicine depart greatly from that of modern medical science. An analysis of the theories of the cause of illness across 186 non-Western societies revealed a great degree of variability (Murdock, 1980). Whereas modern medicine views many illnesses as emerging out of the deterioration of organ systems, stress, or infections, none of the 186 societies viewed organ deterioration to be an important cause of illness. Only 3 of the 186 (Ingalik, Javanese, and Siamese) viewed stress to be an important cause of illness, and only 1 (Japanese) viewed infection to be a major cause of illness. In contrast, in traditional non-Western societies, beliefs in supernatural causes of illness are quite widespread. These range from theories that aggressive spirits such as ghosts cause disease (which is the most widespread theory of disease) to accounts of witchcraft, sorcery, mystical retributions, and sinful violations of taboos.

For example, among the Azande of West Africa, the primary cause of illness is attributed to witchcraft (Evans-Pritchard, 1976). Some Zande are believed to be witches, and the source of their witchcraft is believed to be a small organ in their bodies, which can be inherited from their parents. They do not perform any rites, use any potions, or cast any spells—rather, witches conduct their witchcraft entirely through their minds. When a Zande develops a slowly progressing illness, it is believed to be the result of a witch who is consuming the soul of its victim's organs, a little bit at a time. In contrast, when a Zande develops a sudden and acute illness, it is believed to be the result of a sorcerer casting a spell on them. The Azande belief system is not unusual in the context of traditional cultures around the world, and although the specific theories underlying illness vary considerably across societies, in traditional societies the vast majority of theories are supernatural in nature.

In modern times, medicine has come to rely on the scientific method, whereby controlled experiments between different procedures and medicines are conducted and the results are shared across the international medical community. Supernatural beliefs tend to play a far less significant role in most practitioners of modern medicine; however, it is still not uncommon for laypeople to view illnesses as developing from supernatural causes, primarily on religious grounds or on the belief that taboos have been broken or that spirits are threatening them. In general, though, modern medicine is grounded in scientific procedures.

The central role of science in modern medicine would suggest a great deal of universality in doctors' understanding of disease throughout the world. However, doctors tend to be trained within the cultures they grew up in, and within which their patients live. Hence, a lot of medical training does occur

"Don't forget to take a handful of our complimentary antibiotics on your way out."

within the context of particular cultural meaning systems, even when the training is about internationally recognized practices (see Angel & Thoits, 1987).

One way that cultures differ is in the metaphors they use to indicate a healthy body. In traditional Chinese medicine, for example, a healthy body is one in which the dialectical forces of yin and yang are in balance. Any imbalances are believed to ultimately lead to illness. For example, a person who has a condition known as "liver fire" will have symptoms such as headaches, flushed face, and anger, and this illness is believed to be caused by having too much yang and not enough yin. Such an imbalance could be corrected by acupuncture, herbal remedies, exercise, diet, and lifestyle. The metaphor of balancing opposing forces and energies is what guides traditional Chinese medical thought.

Perhaps it is not too surprising that traditional Chinese medicine differs as much as it does from modern Western medicine, given all of the discussion in this book about the ways that psychological experiences (such as holistic thinking styles) differ between people from Eastern and Western cultures. However, considerable differences are found even among doctors of Western cultures in their understanding of medicine.

For example, there are rather striking differences between medical practices of French and American doctors, as described by the medical journalist Lynn Payer (1996). In France, the metaphor of the body that guides doctors is the *terrain*, which is a word that doesn't translate well into English but is perhaps best captured by words such as "constitution" or "resistance." Somewhat similar to Chinese medicine, this view emphasizes how a sense of balance is key to health, in that balance stimulates the immune system. This emphasis on balance shifts drug consumption away from antibiotics and toward various tonics and vitamins that are believed to strengthen the immune system. Long rests and spa visits are also viewed as an important part of a lifestyle that rejuvenates the *terrain*. Similarly, hospital stays are relatively long in France (about double the length in the United States for the same procedures) to provide ample time for recuperation.

The French were traditionally more likely than Americans to see encounters with dirt and germs as something that is not threatening but rather as having beneficial effects—something that can strengthen the *terrain* and guard one against developing future illnesses. Accordingly, French practices with regard to germs have differed from American ones, such as with respect to how frequently one should bathe. These ideas have persisted across time. In the 17th century, French medical opinion stated that bodily secretions offered a layer of protection, so it was considered unhealthy to bathe frequently (Ashenburg, 2007). More recently, a 1976 article in *Le Monde* stated that the French hospital patient had a right to a *monthly* bath and to weekly foot-washings. French dermatologists recommend that people, even those with oily hair, not wash their hair more than once a week, because doing so causes a greater amount of oil to be secreted (Aron-Brunetiere, 1974), and to this day French shampoo their hair with less frequency than any other European nation (Euromonitor International, 2014). French attitudes toward bathing result in per capita consumption of soap in France that was about half of that in England (Payer, 1996). Some striking examples through history include Louis XIV, who is reported to have bathed only twice in his life, both times being prescribed by his doctors. Rather, the norm in his day was for people to clean themselves by changing their clothes, often several times a day. In a romantic letter to his wife, Josephine, Napoleon, upon preparing to return from a long battle, wrote, "Don't bathe, I'm coming home," reflecting the view that the body in its natural state, rather than one scrubbed clean and coated with deodorants, is more attractive. However, medical norms do change across time, and in recent years France has come to attack germs more vigorously through antibiotic prescriptions than other European countries do (Goossens, Ferech, Stichele, & Elseviers, 2005).

In contrast, Payer argues that the metaphor embraced by American doctors is that the body is like a machine that needs to be tended regularly to ensure that it is running well. When there are problems with the body, it is often treated in ways that you might expect to see a machine repaired. American medicine is known as the most aggressive in the world—surgical procedures are used far more in the United States than in other countries (e.g., cesarean sections, coronary bypass surgery, mastectomies, hysterecomies), and malfunctioning parts are removed, replaced, or physically altered (see Vayda, Mindell, & Rutkow, 1982). Whereas American doctors are more likely than doctors from European countries to use surgery rather than drugs, when drugs are prescribed in the United States, they are prescribed at higher dosages than in virtually any other country. In contrast, it is relatively rare for American doctors to prescribe rest and relaxation as curative agents.

And when the machine has started to malfunction and a cause is sought, American doctors are more likely than those from European countries to search for an external cause, such as bacteria or a virus. American doctors prescribe more antibiotics than doctors from elsewhere, and Americans tend to have a greater concern about cleanliness and to avoid contact with germs (e.g., not sitting directly on public toilet seats or kissing family members with colds) more than people from European countries. The belief is that the body is healthy in its default state, unless it runs afoul of an offending germ or external threat.

A recent study demonstrates the degree to which a doctor's understanding of medicine is influenced by cultural experiences (Leeman, Fischler, & Rozin, 2011). The researchers interviewed laypeople and physicians in five countries: France, Germany, Italy, the United Kingdom, and the United States. People were asked 25 questions about their beliefs regarding the relation between diet and health. For example, they were asked how much they agreed with statements about food-related hygiene, eating in moderation, and the healthiness of vitamins and certain products such as fish, meats, and grains. Their answers to all 25 questions were compared on the basis of the respondents' occupation (doctor versus layperson) and country of origin. For 22 of the 25 items there were significant cultural differences—that is, doctors and laypeople from some countries had different views than those from other countries. In contrast, for only 3 of the 25 items was there a significant difference between doctors and laypeople. For the vast majority of items, doctors and laypeople tended to have similar answers to the questions.

Furthermore, when the overall pattern of responses between doctors and laypeople in the five countries were compared using a multidimensional scaling analysis, a striking pattern emerged. **Figure 13.11** shows the correlations between doctors and laypeople in terms of how they responded to the 25 items. Doctors tended to agree more with laypeople from their own country than they did with doctors from other countries. That is, at least for these particular questions, the country where one was raised had a bigger impact on how one viewed the relations between various aspects of diet and health than whether one received formal medical training. However, there is surely far more convergence among doctors from different countries regarding how to diagnose and treat specific diseases than there is in their attitudes toward what constitutes a healthy lifestyle.

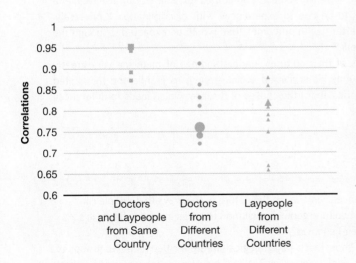

FIGURE 13.11

Distribution of correlations across 25 items between pairs of groups. A middle-sized symbol indicates two scores at the same value, and a large symbol indicates three scores at the same value. Overall, the correlations were strongest between doctors and laypeople from the same country.

SUMMARY

Human biology and physical health are affected by culture. Instances of genetic variation across human populations have health consequences. Some of these are the result of geography, such as fair-skinned people being more at risk for skin cancer in low latitudes, or Tibetans living at high altitude being better at coping with lower oxygen levels. Others are the result of culture, such as the case of people whose ancestors were cattle farmers for many generations being more likely to have lactase persistence. Further, people's biology can vary across cultures with respect to acquired characteristics. For example, the Moken learn how to focus their eyes underwater, wearing shoes changes the shape of one's feet, and body weight and height are related to certain dietary habits.

Health outcomes vary dramatically across socioeconomic status (SES), with people of lower SES being more vulnerable to a wide array of ailments and diseases than people of higher SES. These differences appear to have much to do with people's feelings of psychological control over their lives. Some cultural features interact with SES to affect health outcomes. African-Americans tend to have worse health outcomes for a variety of diseases, and some of these outcomes appear to be due to experiences with discrimination. Conversely, Latino-Americans tend to have better health outcomes than would be expected, although the reasons for this are not all that clear.

Because doctors are products of their cultures, understandings of medicine vary greatly across cultures. Even between highly industrialized societies such as France and the United States, doctors differ in their theories about the causes of disease, which leads to differences in the ways that they treat disease.

THINK ABOUT IT

1. How is it that cultural experiences can change the nature of the ways that people run?
2. What does it mean to say that culture-gene co-evolution involves aspects of people's cultures coming to change their genomes?
3. What kind of evidence would show that a psychological difference between two groups of people is due to differences in gene frequencies? What kind of evidence would show that a difference between two groups is due to differences in cultural experiences?
4. Why do you think portion sizes have increased so much in the United States over the past 50 years but not to the same degree in France?

5. The observed cultural differences in the amount of sleep around the world are quite pronounced but remain largely unexplained. Why do you think Japanese people sleep so much less than North Americans and some Europeans?
6. How is a feeling of a lack of control related to the association between socioeconomic status and health outcomes?
7. What is the epidemiological paradox?
8. Why do doctors around the world have somewhat different beliefs about what constitutes a healthy lifestyle?

KEY TERMS

Culture-Gene Co-Evolution, 528   French Paradox, 532   Epidemiological Paradox, 550

When Chinese suffer from depression, they are more likely than Westerners to be concerned about physical, somatic symptoms, and are less likely to be worrying about psychological symptoms.

14

MENTAL HEALTH

A t the age of 14, Keisuke appeared to be a normal, mentally healthy teen-age Japanese boy. Then one day he went into the family kitchen, closed the door behind him, and did something rather unusual. He refused to leave. Three years later he still had not left the kitchen, nor during that time had he allowed anyone else in. His mother left meals for him at the door three times a day, and he made use of the toilet that was adjacent to the kitchen. The kitchen was filled with garbage, because Keisuke hadn't taken any out since he first moved in there. At first his family cooked on a makeshift stove and ordered a lot of take-out food, but once they realized Keisuke was not going to be leaving, they ended up building another kitchen in the house. It is possible that Keisuke is still living alone in the kitchen today.

As unusual as Keisuke's lifestyle may seem, perhaps the most remarkable fact about his story is how common it is. Keisuke suffers from a condition known as *hikikomori,* which translates loosely as "pull away" or social withdrawal (**Figure 14.1**). It has been defined as a condition in which people have spent at least 6 months in an asocial state, not participating in education or employment, having no intimate relationships with anyone outside of the immediate family,

FIGURE 14.1   The bedroom of a self-incarcerated *hikikomori* sufferer.

with onset before the late 20s, and for which other psychiatric disorders cannot explain the primary symptom of withdrawal (Saito, 1998). It typically first appears among Japanese students (especially boys) at junior high or high school age when they decide that they no longer want to go to school (sometimes in response to a bullying incident) or to have much social interaction with anyone. The typical response is to shut oneself off from the outside world and spend one's days reading books, playing video games, or watching television. Many have endured this self-imposed incarceration for decades. *Hikikomori* sufferers often get to the point where they take out their frustration by physically attacking their parents. Although the condition was rare in earlier decades, today researchers estimate that upward of 1 million Japanese suffer from it, although the magnitude of this number has been disputed because the available data are not especially reliable (Furlong, 2008). This disorder has become a social epidemic with tragic consequences for the families involved (see Jones, 2006, for a discussion).

Although there have been occasional cases of *hikikomori*-like behaviors throughout Japanese history, including the Japanese Shinto origin myth in which the sun goddess, Amaterasu, shut herself in a cave to protest her brother's drunken rampage, only since the 1980s has it become common enough to be recognized as a social problem. The relative homogeneity of Japanese culture provides quite clear role expectations, such that if one feels unable to meet those expectations, he or she may feel under great pressure to fit in (Zielenziger, 2006). A number of sociocultural changes in Japan have been proposed to account for the rapid rise in *hikikomori* cases: a decreasing valuation of work due to the relative economic comfort of Japan, the spread of more lenient and overprotective parenting norms, the decline in birth rate that has allowed children to have their own bedrooms, and a restructuring of the labor market that has eroded the security and predictability of career opportunities (Furlong, 2008; Ogino, 2004; Teo, 2010). It appears most commonly among eldest sons, for whom there exists much family pressure to carry on the family name (Kawanishi, 2004). The condition has become so widespread in Japan that a number of therapeutic interventions are being developed; one of the most common of these is to utilize workers who call themselves *rentaru oneesan* (rental sisters), who strive to create a surrogate sibling relationship with their clients in order to slowly build their trust and entice them out of the house.

There are a number of ways that we can think of *hikikomori* as being particular to Japanese culture in the late 20th and early 21st centuries. First, the hypothesized causes of the disorder are less likely to be present elsewhere. Also, the reactions of parents to *hikikomori* sufferers might emerge differently across cultures. For example, one American psychologist who has researched *hikikomori* argues that if his child behaved like Keisuke, the first thing he would do would be to break down the kitchen door and deal with the child directly (Rees, 2002). Most Japanese parents would not think to take such a direct approach, and the most renowned Japanese expert on *hikikomori,* Tamaki Saito, maintains that such a direct approach would only make matters worse, likely driving the sufferer into violence or suicide. Cultures vary in the ways that parents deal with their children and, in particular, how they deal with a child who is behaving inappropriately. Furthermore, the kinds of symptoms that go along with *hikikomori* do not match any other set of symptoms published in the *DSM-V* (the diagnostic manual of the American Psychiatric Association, which is used in much of the Western world). Indeed, those with *hikikomori,* when considered by the criteria in the *DSM-V,* do not fit into a single category at all and are diagnosed with a wide range of conditions, including social phobia, obsessive-compulsive disorder, depression, and schizophrenia (Sakai, Ishikawa, Takizawa, Sato, & Sakano, 2004). Although there are significant numbers of people with *hikikomori*-like symptoms in South Korea and Taiwan, and the occasional case study with parallels is found in Western countries, no other culture has a prevalence nearly as high as in Japan. *Hikikomori,* for all intents and purposes, appears to be largely a unique Japanese form of psychopathology in its presentation and its prevalence.

This raises an important question: What does it mean to say that a psychological disorder is far more prevalent in one culture than in another? At the very least, cultural differences in such disorders demonstrate that we cannot simply conceive of those disorders as automatically and uniformly unfolding from a set of innate biological causes. Human biology is highly similar everywhere, yet psychological disorders present themselves in a variety of strikingly different ways around the world. These cultural differences tell us that, in some ways, culture is implicated in the expression and experience of psychopathology.

This should perhaps not be too surprising, given what you have read in earlier chapters. In many ways, the minds of people from different cultures do appear to operate in some distinct ways. And if normal psychological functioning differs across cultures in the various ways that we have discussed, it follows that departures from what is normal would likely also differ across cultures as well. This suggests that the criteria for what constitutes mental health and what constitutes problematic abnormalities will vary significantly across cultures (for reviews, see Kleinman, 1988; Lopez & Guarnaccia, 2000).

This chapter investigates how culture shapes people's mental health and delves into how culture shapes clinical and psychiatric conditions. Reflecting a central theme of this text, we will explore whether mental disorders are particular to certain cultures or are universally prevalent. Last, we will consider how culture plays a role in the treatment of mental illnesses.

What Is a Psychological Disorder?

The question of what constitutes a psychological disorder is one that has always challenged psychiatrists and clinical psychologists. Disorders are usually defined as behaviors that are rare and cause some kind of impairment to the individual, although there are many exceptions to this general pattern. Alcohol abuse, for example, is considered a disorder, but it might not seem that rare if you attended a frat party. On the other hand, 20th-century pianist Glenn Gould's musical talents were indeed rare, and his obsession with music greatly interfered with his social life, but at the same time they made him one of the most famous pianists of his time. It's not clear whether his musical talents and obsessions should be described as parts of a disorder.

Although the question of what conditions could be labeled as disorders is often challenging, the question becomes even more difficult when behaviors are considered problematic in one culture but not in another. For example, consider **dhat syndrome,** a disorder that is frequently observed in a number of South Asian cultures (see Obeyesekere, 1985). *Dhat* syndrome is characterized by a belief among young men that they are leaking semen, which causes them to be morbidly anxious, because semen is largely viewed by them to be a source of vitality. The religious scriptures of the Hindus state, "Forty meals produce one drop of blood, 40 drops of blood give rise to one drop of bone marrow, and 40 drops of marrow form one drop of semen" (Akhtar, 1988). According to this view, semen is a very precious commodity, and an excessive loss of it is feared to result in serious illness. *Dhat* syndrome is often associated with crippling feelings of guilt and anxiety about having indulged in certain disapproved sexual acts (such as masturbation) that have apparently resulted in its victims having sprung a more enduring leak.

What would happen if one tried to study *dhat* syndrome in North America? Well, because North Americans tend not to view semen as a precious resource, a key source of vitality, or a bulwark against disease, they likely wouldn't be all that anxious about losing it. Furthermore, because norms regarding what is appropriate sexual behavior differ in South Asia and North America, most North American males would likely not feel much guilt at the thought of engaging in acts that caused them to lose semen. Without the set of culturally shared beliefs regarding semen, sexual activity, and health that are prevalent among South Asians, the entire category of *dhat* syndrome would likely be rather meaningless to most North Americans and to North American psychiatrists. To be diagnosed with the disorder of *dhat* syndrome, one must have a particular set of beliefs that would cause one to be concerned about losing semen in the first place, and such kinds of beliefs are derived from participating in particular cultural contexts. Without the necessary cultural participation, it is highly unlikely that one could experience *dhat* syndrome as a disorder in the way that many South Asians do (see Kleinman, 1988, for further discussion).

Although it may be evident with the instance of *dhat* syndrome that it would be quite fruitless to try to apply an unfamiliar South Asian diagnostic category within North America, what may be less obvious is that the reverse of this situation is how much cross-cultural psychiatry has been conducted (Kleinman, 1988). That is, because the field of psychiatry was largely developed in the West, the disorders that are observed in the West, such as depression, social anxiety, and schizophrenia, are often viewed as the basic categories of diagnosis. When psychiatry is exported to other cultures, there is a tendency to evaluate the psychopathologies that are found in other cultures in terms of how well they fit into those basic categories that were developed in the West. It is possible that in some cases the Western categories of diagnosis do indeed reflect universal categories of mental illnesses, just as there are many universal categories of physical illness, such as diabetes, cancer, or influenza. However, it is also possible that in some cases the disorders reflect culturally specific ways of thinking that are not really meaningful in other cultures. This distinction between universal categories of mental illness and culture-bound syndromes is not always straightforward, because the symptoms of some disorders might also vary across cultures, even though the underlying causes of the problems are the same.

Let's now consider the question of how specific psychopathologies vary or are similar across cultures. We'll begin by exploring some conditions that appear to be culture-bound, and then we'll consider some conditions that appear to be more universal.

Culture-Bound Syndromes

Culture-bound syndromes are those that appear to be greatly influenced by cultural factors and hence occur far less frequently, or are manifested in highly divergent ways, in other cultures. The cases of *hikikomori* and *dhat* are examples of culture-bound syndromes, in that in many other cultures the symptoms that characterize them are largely absent or do not cluster together, do not occur in the same kinds of circumstances, or do not appear at anywhere near the frequency that they do in the places where they have been primarily identified. As such, to gain a good understanding of *hikikomori* or *dhat*, it is important to consider the cultural values and understandings that go along with them. Many culture-bound syndromes have been identified; in the following sections I provide a brief discussion of some of them.

Eating Disorders

Eating disorders are some of the more common psychological disorders in North American college student populations, particularly among women. Take the case of **bulimia nervosa,** a disorder that is often characterized by binge eating and induced vomiting. Estimations for prevalence rates among female university students at American universities have reached as high as 19% (Halmi, Falk, & Schwartz, 1981), although studies using more stringent criteria estimate that the prevalence is more in the range of 5% to 7% (Heatherton, Nichols, Mahamedi, & Keel, 1995). Episodes of binge eating are even more common, with approximately one quarter of female college students having reported past or current periods of regular binge eating (Heatherton et al., 1995). The reported rates were so high at one time that there was talk in the media of eating disorders having reached epidemic proportions (e.g., Brody, 1982), although subsequent research suggests that those fears were largely overblown (Bushnell, Wells, Hornblow, Oakley-Browne, & Joyce, 1990).

How common are eating disorders across cultures? The two most common clinical manifestations of eating disorders are anorexia nervosa and bulimia nervosa. The symptoms of these two conditions are relatively homogenous, both within and across cultures. To be diagnosed with **anorexia nervosa,** one must refuse to maintain a normal body weight, be intensely fearful of gaining weight or becoming fat, deny the seriousness of one's low body weight, and, for postmenarcheal females, miss three consecutive menstrual cycles. To be diagnosed with bulimia nervosa, one must experience recurrent episodes of binge eating (in which one eats an unusually large amount within a 2-hour period while feeling a lack of control over this eating), along with recurrent inappropriate behaviors to prevent weight gain (e.g., self-induced vomiting, misuse of laxatives, excessive exercise), which happens at least twice a week for three months; must have one's self-evaluation be unduly influenced by one's body weight; and must not be concurrently diagnosed with anorexia nervosa.

One commonly held view is that both anorexia and especially bulimia are culture-bound syndromes (e.g., Gordon, 1990). Some evidence for this can be seen in the fact that the rates for both disorders have increased quite dramatically over the past 50 years (Keel & Klump, 2003). For example, in Denmark the incidence of anorexia nervosa and bulimia nervosa each increased by more than a factor of four from the 1970s to the late 1980s (Pagsberg & Wang, 1994). The ages at which people develop eating disorders have gotten significantly younger over recent years, such that it is not uncommon to find 9-year-olds who refuse to eat (Rosen, 2003). Although researchers have yet to specify precisely what is causing such dramatic increases across time, it seems likely that changing cultural norms are at least partly responsible. For example, contestants in the Miss America pageant and *Playboy* centerfolds have become thinner over the course of the past half century (Garner, Garfinkel, Schwartz, & Thompson, 1980; Sypeck, Gray, & Ahrens, 2004; Sypeck et al., 2006), and the number of articles published in women's magazines on methods for weight loss have also increased (Wiseman, Gray, Mosimann, & Ahrens, 1992). Hence, a likely factor in the increase in eating disorders is that women have been receiving more cultural messages that attractive bodies are thin ones.

Furthermore, there is evidence that bulimia and anorexia (for which the evidence is more mixed) are more prevalent in some societies, particularly those with Western cultural influences, than in others. First, looking at bulimia, there is a striking absence of documented cases in much of the world, particularly in Africa and in the Indian subcontinent, and the few documented cases that emerge in other regions of the world, such as in the Middle East and in Southeast and East Asia, appear to be in places where there is more Western influence. In particular, in areas where starvation is a real threat to people's lives, it does seem hard to imagine how people could seek to binge and purge. Furthermore, analyses of the historical literature reveal little evidence in past times of the kinds of behaviors symptomatic of bulimia (Keel & Klump, 2003). By all accounts, it appears that bulimia is a culture-bound syndrome that is largely confined to modern cultures with Western influence (see **Figure 14.2**).

FIGURE 14.2 This billboard denouncing the use of anorexic fashion models appeared in Milan during Italian fashion week. Eating disorders are more common in places that have experienced more Western cultural influence.

The picture for anorexia is somewhat more complex. As noted earlier, rates of anorexia have increased over recent decades. Furthermore, there are a number of studies in which researchers have been unable to find cases of anorexia in some cultures. For example, Mumford, Whitehouse, and Choudry (1992) found no evidence of anorexia in one large sample of Pakistani schoolgirls. There are also far fewer incidences of anorexia in China compared with the West (Lee, 1989; Zhang et al., 1992). However, a number of other studies have found clear evidence of anorexia in diverse cultural contexts with relatively little Western influence, such as in the Caribbean island of Curacao (Hock, van Harten, van Hoeken, & Susser, 1998), Nigeria (Nwaefuna, 1981), Iran (Nobakht & Dezhkam, 2000), and South Korea (Lee et al., 1987). Complicating the picture even more, in some cultures, such as in Hong Kong, those patients who are diagnosed with anorexia often don't show any fear of fatness, which is a key symptom of anorexia in the West. Rather, the Hong Kong anorexics are more likely to report that they have stopped eating because of a lack appetite or because they feel bloated (Lee, Ho, & Hsu, 1993).

Furthermore, Keel and Klump (2003) reviewed the historical literature regarding self-starvation. There have been many instances of people voluntarily starving themselves while in the presence of food. For example, 261 Catholic saints were ordained in the Italian peninsula since the 12th century. For those about which there is adequate information, about half of the saints refused food and became greatly emaciated because of a belief that this reflected divine intervention—a condition that has been termed "holy anorexia" (Bell, 1985). Similar observations of religiously motivated self-starvation were also evident in the 17th and 18th centuries among teenage girls throughout Europe who modeled themselves after ascetic medieval saints (Bemporad, 1996). Although the motivations behind such acts of self-starvation do not seem to be about weight concerns as they largely do today, one speculative account is that people with temperaments that predisposed them to anorexic symptoms were especially attracted to ascetic lifestyles. That is, the same kind of inherited predisposition toward self-starvation might manifest itself through motivations for religious asceticism in some contexts and motivations to avoid weight gain in others.

Hence, on the one hand we see rates of anorexia increasing globally, and there is less reliable evidence for anorexia in some cultures than in the West, suggesting that there are clear cultural influences on the disorder. On the other hand, there are clear instances of anorexia around the world, and there are many historical examples of people starving themselves. Unlike bulimia nervosa, which has all the hallmarks of a culture-bound syndrome, there is evidence that some of the symptoms of anorexia are universal, although they are still influenced a great deal by culture. In particular, excessive concern about one's weight may be especially susceptible to cultural influences, which suggests that anorexia may well be an existential universal, in that it is present everywhere, although the frequency varies considerably across cultures. Anorexia does not meet the standards for a functional universal, however, because in some contexts a similar motivation (i.e., self-starvation) is associated with different ends (avoiding becoming overweight *vs.* being spiritually ascetic).

Koro

One clinical syndrome that has been identified in a variety of countries in South and East Asia, particularly in southern China, is termed **koro,** which, in the Malay language means "head of a turtle." This aptly named disease is most common among men, in whom it manifests as a morbid fear that one's penis is shrinking into one's body. This event is believed to have harmful consequences, including death, and causes tremendous anxiety and terror among those afflicted. It is far less common among women, in whom it tends to manifest as a similar fear that one's nipples are shrinking into one's body. There have been occasions of *koro* epidemics (see Sinha, 2011). In 1967 in Singapore, for example, there was an epidemic of swine flu, which led to the widespread inoculation of pigs. Later, rumors spread that one would develop *koro* after eating inoculated pig meat, and soon hospitals were inundated with several hundred people presenting *koro* symptoms (Ngui, 1969). Somewhat similar kinds of genital-shrinking epidemics have also been reported in West Africa, although there's debate about whether the similarities are close enough for those to also be considered cases of *koro* (Dzokoto & Adams, 2005).

    Koro meets the criteria for a culture-bound syndrome, because its symptomology is nearly absent in most cultures (Tseng, 2001), although it is not clear what cultural factors affect its prevalence. One interpretation is that it's grounded in a classical Chinese medicine account of how an imbalance of yin and yang can cause the genitals to retract (Buckle, Chuah, Fones, & Wong, 2007). However, some American men who have had bad experiences while high on marijuana have reported *koro*-like symptoms (3 men out of a survey of 70 who reported having negative marijuana-induced experiences), in which they too had the fear of their penises shrinking into their bodies. The experiences were so frightening that all of those men reported cutting back on their marijuana use after the incidents (Earleywine, 2001). This, and a number of other rare incidents reported around the world, suggest that some components of *koro* may be universally accessible; however, they only seem to manifest as a clinical syndrome within certain cultures where people have an awareness of the existence of the disorder.

Amok

Amok has been identified in a number of Southeast Asian cultures as "an acute outburst of unrestrained violence, associated with (indiscriminate) homicidal attacks, preceded by a period of brooding and ending with exhaustion and amnesia" (Yap, 1951). Running *amok* primarily occurs among males and is thought to be instigated by stress, a lack of sleep, and alcohol consumption. One theory of the relation between *amok* behavior and Malay culture, where it is most commonly found, is that cultural traditions, especially in rural parts of Malay, exist for people to be passive and nonconfrontational (Carr, 1978). The suggestion is that some who are unable to find culturally sanctioned means to express their frustration ultimately explode in an uncontrolled fit of anger and unresolved tensions.

Running *amok* still occurs in several Southeast Asian countries, and the rate increased in the latter half of the 20th century (Teoh, 1972). It has been common enough in Malaysia that police stations there all have a special two-pronged weapon, depicted in **Figure 14.3**, that allows police to capture *amok* runners by pinning them against a wall. Most people who run *amok* end up being killed in the act, and the few survivors that have been caught have had a divergent set of symptoms leading them to be diagnosed with a variety of other mental disorders, including schizophrenia, endogenous depression, and epilepsy (Schmidt, Hill, & Guthrie, 1977).

Much of the symptomology and cultural meaning associated with *amok* appears to be specific to certain Southeast Asian cultures; however, there are similar phenomena,

FIGURE 14.3 This drawing shows a Malaysian man running *amok* while a group chases him in an effort to subdue him. The forklike object at the far right is a special weapon that was used to catch people who ran *amok*.

such as the mass killings that occasionally occur at schools, offices, and neighbor-hoods in the United States and other Western cultures. One difference is that the Western mass killings tend to be more premeditated, and it is unclear whether these similar behaviors are indicative of a common underlying disorder.

Hysteria

Given that cultures change over time, it's possible that culture-bound disorders might differentiate historical periods as well. One of the most common psychological disor-ders that was diagnosed throughout Europe in the mid-19th century was *hysteria,* in which women exhibited symptoms such as fainting, insomnia, sudden paralysis, tempo-rary blindness, loss of appetite for food or sex, and a general "tendency to cause trouble" (Maines, 1998). The disorder, sometimes referred to as "the great neurosis" (Micale, 1995), was made famous by Jean-Martin Charcot and Sigmund Freud and was the key psychopathology underlying the launch of the psychoanalytic tradition. However, diag-noses of hysteria decreased dramatically in the early 20th century (see Tseng, 2001), and today, hysteria is no longer a diagnostic category and does not appear in the *DSM-V.*

One explanation for the drop in prevalence is that patients with hysteria-like symptoms are being diagnosed with other disorders, such as somatoform disorders, disassociation disorders, and schizophrenia (Ovsiew, 2006). Another explanation is that hysteria's prevalence in the 19th century was a response to the repressive social norms of Victorian Europe (e.g., Drinka, 1984) and that the great amount of atten-tion it received at the time led people to express their distress via symptoms they were familiar with (Shorter, 1987). There is controversy as to whether hysteria can better be understood as a culture-bound disorder or as the reflection of changing classification systems of psychiatry, but it is at least an example of a pathology that appears to vary in prevalence across cultures and time.

Other Culture-Bound Disorders

A whole menagerie of rather bizarre clinical syndromes have been identified in spe-cific cultures that are largely absent in the Western world (for a thorough review, see Tseng, 2001). For example, **frigophobia** (primarily identified in China) is a morbid fear of catching a cold, which leads people to dress themselves in heavy coats and scarves, even in summer (Chang, Rin, & Chen, 1975; see **Figure 14.4**). *Susto* is a condition pe-culiar to Latin America in which people feel that a frightening experience has caused their soul to get dislodged from their bodies, leading to a wide range of physical and psychological symptoms (Rubel, O'Nell, & Collado, 1985). **Voodoo death,** which is largely found in Africa, is a condition in which people are convinced that a curse has been put on them or that they have broken a taboo, which results in a severe fear re-action that sometimes leads to their own deaths (Hughes, 1996).

Latah, which has been identified primarily among people of various Southeast Asian cultures but also in Siberia and among the Ainu in Japan, is a condition in which people fall into a transient dissociated state after some kind of startling event, such as being tickled or thinking that they have seen a snake. The person usually exhibits some kind of unusual behavior, such as barking like a dog, shouting sexually charged statements, or acting in culturally inappropriate ways, after which the person retains no memory of the outburst (Suwanlert, 1988). ***Malgri*** is a syndrome of territorial anxiety that has been identified among various Australian aboriginal groups. When afflicted individuals enter the sea or a new territory without engaging in the appropriate ceremonial procedures, they believe that they are invaded by a totemic spirit that makes them physically sick, tired, and drowsy (Cawte, 1976). ***Agonias*** is an anxiety disorder identified among Portugese and Azoreans in which people report a wide array of different symptoms, including a burning sensation, a loss of breath, hysterical blindness, sleeping, and eating disorders (James, 2002).

Kufungisisa, which translates to "thinking too much" in Shona, a language spoken in Zimbabwe, is a condition associated with anxiety

FIGURE 14.4 People who suffer from frigophobia have a deep fear of catching a cold and will wear many layers of clothing, even in summer, to ensure their body is warm.

and somatic problems that are thought to stem from mental exhaustion. People believe that their mind has been damaged by excessive thinking and can thus no longer properly function, and they experience panic attacks and irritability. Variants of this condition are found in a number of cultures in Africa, in the Caribbean, and among Native Americans, and East Asians. (Patel, Simunyu, & Gwanzura, 1995; Prince, 1960; Wen, 1995). ***Ataques de nervios*** is a condition most identified with Puerto Ricans, in which emotionally charged settings, such as funerals or family conflicts, lead to such symptoms as palpitations, numbness, and a sense of heat rising to the head (Guarniccia, Canino, Rubio-Stipec, & Bravo, 1993).

These various disorders, which do not map clearly onto any syndromes commonly identified in the West, along with other, less-studied ones from various small-scale societies (for a review, see Littlewood & Lipsedge, 1987), further attest to the diverse ways that cultural context shapes psychological experiences, both normal and abnormal.

Universal Syndromes

Whereas culture-bound syndromes make it salient that culturally derived meanings play a fundamental role in the development of psychopathologies, universal syndromes highlight the biological foundation of mental illness. However, even though the following syndromes are universally observed, you'll see that the manifestation of these syndromes also can vary quite dramatically across cultures.

Depression

Depression is one of the most commonly identified psychological disorders in the West. It is also perhaps the most familiar disorder, as everyone has experienced occasions when they experience some of the symptoms of depression, such as sadness, feelings of futility, and a loss of energy. For most people, such feelings are relatively fleeting and are typically confined to the aftermath of a tragedy or personal disappointment. For others, however, these feelings can last for long periods and become extremely debilitating. If they are severe enough, a person might be diagnosed as having a *major depressive disorder (MDD)*.

The most widely accepted definition of a MDD is that provided by the *DSM-V*. To receive such a diagnosis, a person must show evidence of at least five of the following nine symptoms, including at least one of the first two, for two weeks or more: (1) depressed mood, (2) an inability to feel pleasure, (3) change in weight or appetite, (4) sleep problems, (5) psychomotor change, (6) fatigue or loss of energy, (7) feelings of worthlessness or guilt, (8) poor concentration or indecisiveness, and (9) suicidality. A person must also meet a number of additional criteria.

The prevalence of MDD varies depending on the specific criteria that are applied in making the diagnosis, and recent surveys have found that lifetime prevalence rates (meaning that a person has been diagnosed with a MDD at least once in his or her life) range from about 4.9% to 17.1% of the population in the United States (Kessler et al., 1994; Robins & Regier, 1991). Less stringent criteria have found that as many as 44% of Americans are depressed at any given point in time (Flaherty, Gavira, & Val, 1982). In sum, the prevalence of depression varies depending on the application of the diagnostic criteria. However, it appears to be a very common psychopathology.

In contrast, depression is less commonly diagnosed in some other cultures, particularly in China. For example, epidemiological surveys have found that the rates of depression in China on average are about one-fifth of those found in the United States (Kessler et al., 1994). As an extreme example, in 1993 one survey of psychopathology cases in seven regions of China found that out of 19,223 people surveyed, only 16 fulfilled the criteria for a lifetime depressive disorder (Zhang, Shen, & Li, 1998, cited in Parker, Gladstone, & Chee, 2001)—a rate hundreds of times lower than that found in North America. Furthermore, throughout Chinese medical history, there has been far less acknowledgement of any disorders that resemble depression than there has been in the West (for a review, see Ryder, 2004). As common as depression is in North America, it has been, and continues to be, far more rare in China.

China is not the only place where depression rates are relatively lower than they are in the West, and some cultures have rates that are considerably higher (e.g., in one survey, Nigeria had a rate four times that of the United States; Ingram, Scott, & Siegle, 1999). However, international studies of depression have found cases that fit the *DSM-V*-based definition of MDD in every culture that has been explored. This evidence provides support for the universality of MDD as a diagnostic category. However, given the striking variability in the prevalence of depression across cultures, there has been much debate about what can be inferred from international applications of the diagnostic criteria of the *DSM-V* (see Kleinman, 1988).

Likewise, a conceptually similar mental illness—bipolar disorder—is also characterized by the presence of depressive episodes. However, unlike with depression, people with bipolar disorder sometimes experience manic episodes. During these episodes people become hyperactive and may experience extreme euphoria and optimism to the point of impairing their judgment. Cross-cultural studies find that, as in the case of depression, lifetime prevalence rates of bipolar disorder vary around the world, with the rates being highest in English-speaking countries such as the United States and New Zealand, and the lowest being found in South Asia and East Asia (Merikangas et al., 2011). However, there appears to be greater cross-cultural variability in prevalence rates for depression than for bipolar disorder (Weissman et al., 1996). The cross-cultural differences in bipolar disorder are not as well understood as the differences in depression.

The question of the universality of depression is further complicated by another important set of issues. Not all depressed individuals show the same kinds of symptoms. For example, depressed European-Americans often show a flattening of their affect, such that they hardly respond to emotion-eliciting stimuli; however, depressed Asian-Americans show exaggerated emotional responses to the same stimuli (Chentsova-Dutton et al., 2007; Chentsova-Dutton, Tsai, & Gotlib, 2010). Such cultural differences for symptoms can be highly pronounced. Some of the key symptoms for depression are psychological (e.g., depressed mood and feelings of guilt), whereas some are primarily physiological (e.g., fatigue, sleep problems; see **Figure 14.5**). Interestingly, there appear to be reliable cultural differences in the extent to which people emphasize psychological versus physiological symptoms of depression. In general, people are said to be experiencing **somatization** to the extent that they are experiencing symptoms primarily in their bodies. In contrast, a word that is rarely used by psychiatrists (perhaps reflecting what is viewed as normative in the West) is **psychologization** (Ryder et al., 2008), which reflects the extent to which people are experiencing symptoms primarily in their minds.

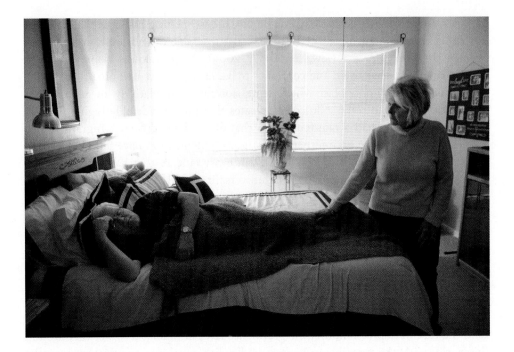

FIGURE 14.5 Depression includes both somatic and psychological symptoms. In general, somatic symptoms are a bigger part of the disorder among Chinese than they are among Westerners.

The anthropologist and psychiatrist Arthur Kleinman conducted a landmark study in a psychiatric hospital in Hunan province in China. There he assessed 100 patients who had been diagnosed as having **neurasthenia**. Neurasthenia is a psychiatric condition that was first described by American neurologist George Miller Beard (1869) as a nervous syndrome of more than 50 symptoms. It was described as "an exhaustion of the nervous system," with symptoms of poor appetite, headaches, insomnia, weakness in the back, hysteria, and an inability to concentrate. It was so commonly diagnosed among Americans in the 19th century and up through World War I that it was known as "the American disease." The diagnosis faded out over the 20th century as the symptoms of neurasthenia (e.g., the exhaustion, headaches, insomnia) began to be seen as less important than the underlying actual psychopathology, and neurasthenia was completely dropped from the *DSM* more than a quarter of a century ago. It is no longer recognized by North American psychiatrists or clinicians as a coherent diagnostic category.

Kleinman (1982) examined the neurasthenia patients, and after extensive interviews with each of them, concluded that 87% of the patients could be described as suffering from some form of clinical depression. The chief complaints of these patients were primarily somatic: headaches (90%), insomnia (78%), dizziness (73%), and various physical pains (49%). In only 9% of the patients was depressed mood offered as a chief complaint. Furthermore, studies have shown that Chinese who fit the diagnostic criteria of neurasthenia, but do not fit those for depression, still respond well to antidepressant medications (e.g., Zhang, 1989).

Other studies have confirmed that somatization is more common among Chinese presentations of depression than among Westerners (e.g., Chang, 1985; Parker, Cheah, & Roy, 2001). For example, one study compared psychiatric outpatients in China and Canada by employing three different assessment procedures: unstructured clinical interviews (which allowed patients to choose what to report), structured clinical interviews (in which patients were asked specifically whether they did or didn't have certain symptoms), and questionnaires (which allowed patients a greater sense of privacy and anonymity in responding to structured questions; Ryder et al., 2008). The findings indicated that Chinese patients experienced more somatic symptoms than psychological symptoms and that Canadian patients reported more psychological symptoms than somatic ones, for all three of the assessment methods. What these studies suggest is that, although among Westerners diagnosed with depression the key symptoms that patients identify and clinicians attend to are psychological, among Chinese diagnosed with the same condition the key symptoms that patients often identify and clinicians attend to are physical. The same condition—depression—appears to manifest itself more so in terms of mood-related concerns among Westerners and more so in terms of headache and sleep-related concerns among Chinese (also see Zhou et al., 2011).

There has been much debate about what causes these cultural differences in the presentation of depression. One possibility is that the differences are due to the social stigma associated with having a mental illness. That is, in Chinese contexts there might be greater social costs in acknowledging a psychological disorder than a physiological one when compared with those in Western contexts. Much evidence suggests that there is indeed such a cultural difference in the stigma associated with mental illness (Lin & Lin, 1981; Ryder, Bean, & Dion, 2000). This possibility would suggest that the experience of depression is identical across cultures, but social stigma results in the Chinese being less willing than Westerners to *discuss* their psychological difficulties. Cultural differences in stigma are surely relevant to the cultural differences in somatization of depression. However, findings that the cultural differences in somatization and psychologization are at least as pronounced in terms of patients' private responses to specific probes in questionnaires regarding their condition as they are in patients' public, spontaneous descriptions of their condition, suggests that there is more to the cultural difference in somatization than merely stigma (Ryder et al., 2008).

A second possibility for the causes of cultural differences in symptom presentation is that the symptoms experienced by people across different cultures may be the same but that people from some cultures tend to focus on, and hence *notice,* different symptoms more than those from other cultures. For example, Westerners might attend more to their psychological symptoms because these are somehow more meaningful and salient to them than to the Chinese, even though the symptoms they are experiencing might be identical. Some findings discussed in Chapter 10 that Westerners appear to be more sensitive than East Asians to their own emotional experiences are consistent with this reasoning (e.g., Matsumoto, Kudoh, Scherer, & Wallbott, 1988; Mesquita & Karasawa, 2002). Furthermore, findings that Chinese psychiatric patients attend less to their emotional states than Westerners do, and that this cultural difference statistically predicts cultural differences in somatization, are also consistent with this account (Ryder et al., 2008).

The different symptoms that depressed Chinese and Western patients report call our attention to a real challenge in psychiatric and clinical diagnoses: What can be said about the nature of a disorder, such as depression, if it can apparently manifest itself in different ways? If the reported experiences are different across cultures, how do we know that people are suffering from the same disease? One strategy is to identify a core set of symptoms of depression that are present in all cultures and exclude the symptoms that are not universally present. However, the cost of this approach is that if we focus only on what is universal, we may well miss out on some culturally specific symptoms that carry a great deal of meaning in some cultures but not in others. For example, depressed mood does not appear to be a core symptom of depression among Chinese, yet, for Westerners, depression is largely about depressed mood.

Applying a universal template for depression does reveal incidents of depression in all cultures, but it does raise a difficult question about the experiences of those who do not fit such a template. That there are fewer people who match the template in some cultures than in others suggests that the template itself contains some culturally specific information and might reflect the cultural biases of the researchers (Kleinman, 1988). The universal features of depression are informative; however, the culturally specific features tell us much as well.

Social Anxiety Disorder

One of the most common anxiety disorders is **social anxiety disorder** (previously known as *social phobia*)—specifically, the fear that one is in danger of acting in an inept and unacceptable manner, and that such poor performance will result in disastrous social consequences (Clark & Wells, 1995). We all suffer some social fears on occasion, as we find ourselves in situations where we realize, often quite rationally, that we stand to look foolish and perhaps lose the favor of others. For people with social anxiety disorder, however, these fears become excessive and can lead them to avoid social anxiety-eliciting situations altogether, thereby impairing their lives. Social anxiety is well documented around the world, reflecting the universal concerns that people share as a social species. It can be problematic if one doesn't fit in with others, and it follows that people have anxieties centered around the key challenges in their lives.

It would seem that social anxiety concerns should be especially prevalent in cultural contexts where there is more emphasis placed on the value of fitting in with others. For example, many East Asian cultures put a premium on saving face and maintaining social harmony. If social concerns are of greater importance in East Asian cultures than they are in North America, we might expect East Asians to evince more concerns and anxieties about the possibility of committing an embarrassing faux pas.

There is much evidence that social anxiety concerns are more pronounced among East Asians. For example, Asian-Americans will acknowledge having more social anxiety symptoms on questionnaires than do European-Americans do (Hsu & Alden, 2007; Okazaki, 1997; Okazaki, Liu, Longworth, & Minn, 2002). Some symptoms of social anxiety, such as being shy, are also perceived less negatively in Asian contexts than in Western ones, perhaps because they are culturally normative. For example, Chinese children who were evaluated as shy were viewed more positively by their peers and teachers, whereas Western children who were viewed as shy were more likely to be rejected by their peers (Chen, Rubin, & Li, 1995). Moreover, among both East Asians and Westerners, interdependence has been found to be associated with heightened social anxiety, while independence is associated with lower social anxiety, highlighting the association between concerns for social harmony and the experience of social anxiety (Hong & Woody, 2007; Norasakkunkit & Kalick, 2002).

The links between interdependence, independence, and social anxiety raise the possibility that people might view social anxiety disorder as less of a problem in Asia than they do in the West. That is, if it's so common to be concerned about one's interpersonal relations, people might be less likely to be troubled by having these anxieties or to find them impairing. Indeed, although East Asians tend to score higher than Westerners on measures of social anxiety, epidemiological surveys find far *less* evidence of people who meet the clinical criteria of social anxiety disorder in East Asia than in the West. For example, epidemiological studies conducted in East Asia find lifetime prevalence rates of social anxiety disorder of approximately 0.5% (Hwu, Yeh, & Chang, 1989; Lee et al., 1987), which contrasts with estimates of at least 7% in North America and Europe (Wittchen & Fehm, 2003).

How can we resolve the paradox that Asian-Americans report more evidence of social anxiety symptoms than European-Americans but that East Asians are less likely to be diagnosed with full-blown social anxiety disorder than Americans? One possibility might be that the norms for social behavior differ between East Asia and the West. In general, Western social norms entail more direct communication, extraversion, and self-promotion than East Asian norms (e.g., Kurman & Sriram, 2002; McCrae, 2002; Searle & Ward, 1990). People who have grown up learning East Asian social norms but later find themselves in a Western social context might feel more anxious because there is a discrepancy between the East Asian social norms that they were raised with and the Western social norms that they are currently living in. On the other hand, East Asians who live in East Asia wouldn't have this same kind of discrepancy between their upbringing and their current culture, so they wouldn't feel the same kind of performance anxiety in social situations. Some evidence in support of this cultural discrepancy hypothesis is that Asian-Canadians report more social anxiety symptoms than do either East Asians living in Asia or European-Canadians (Hsu et al., 2012).

At the same time, when people's social anxieties do become problematic, there is evidence that the symptoms are presented differently across cultures. There is a disorder that was identified by a Japanese psychiatrist in the early 20th century (Morita, 1917) that is termed ***taijin kyoufushou* (TKS).** This term translates loosely as a phobia of confronting others. It is similar to social anxiety disorder in that it is a fear specifically elicited by social situations, and people diagnosed with TKS and those diagnosed with social anxiety disorder both respond favorably to the same antidepressant medication (i.e., fluvoxamine; Stein, 2009). However, the symptoms of TKS are quite distinct from social anxiety disorder. People with social anxiety disorder tend to be preoccupied with anxieties about how they will make fools out of themselves in social situations and how everyone will publicly discover their faults. In contrast, TKS involves a number of physical symptoms, many of which are psychosomatic, such as extensive blushing, heightened body odor, sweating, and a penetrating gaze (for a thorough review of TKS, see Cousins, 1990).

The typical criteria for a diagnosis of the "offensive type" of TKS (which is a diagnostic category) is that the individual is not only preoccupied with these symptoms but is also certain that these symptoms will offend and create a great deal of unease in others. In fact, the major preoccupation of people with the offensive type of TKS is how uncomfortable and tense *others* will feel around them, because of the imagined repulsiveness of their physical faults. This orientation toward others is predicted by holistic thinking styles, interdependent views of self (Norasakkunkit, Kitayama, & Uchida, 2012), and an intolerance of uncertainty (Zhou et al., 2014). People with the offensive type of severe TKS avoid social situations primarily for fear of disturbing others (Miyamoto & Onizawa, 1985). This focus on the discomfort in others has led TKS to be labeled as the "altruistic phobia" (Kasahara, 1986). It is distinct enough from social anxiety disorder, and it is rare enough outside of East Asia (it has more recently been identified in Korea and mainland China; Tseng, 2001), that it has often been considered a "culture-bound" syndrome, similar to ones such as *dhat, koro,* and *amok.*

In sum, social anxiety disorder represents a universal syndrome that is identified everywhere around the world. In East Asian contexts, however, many of the symptoms of social anxiety are more common than they are in the West—common enough, perhaps, that social anxiety could be thought of there as a somewhat normal rather than an abnormal condition. The manifestation of clinically problematic concerns about one's social functioning does appear to vary across cultures, with Western social anxiety disorder having a very different set of symptoms than Japanese TKS.

Suicide

Suicide is one of the most tragic consequences of mental illness. Yet it perhaps represents the facet of mental illness that is most easily compared across cultures, because the outcome of the behavior is well defined and official data are regularly kept around the world. Unlike, say, depression or anorexia, for which there is some dispute about the cross-cultural generalizability of the diagnostic criteria, there is much consensus globally about what suicide is, although the behavior may be motivated by a wide range of conditions.

Although suicide is recognized quite similarly across cultures, its frequency varies enormously. For example, in Lithuania the suicide rate in 1994 was 81.9 men and 13.4 women per 100,000 people. This rate is several hundred times higher than that of Egypt, where in the same year the rate was only 0.1 men and 0.0 women per 100,000 people (Schmidtke et al., 1998). This is a far greater degree of variation than that observed for most other mental disorders. Suicide is a more significant part of some cultures than others, and it is virtually absent in Egypt and in some other Muslim cultures, where religion is especially prohibitive toward suicide.

Furthermore, people in different cultures tend to commit suicide at different points in their lives. **Figure 14.6** shows the suicide rates for different age groups for a few

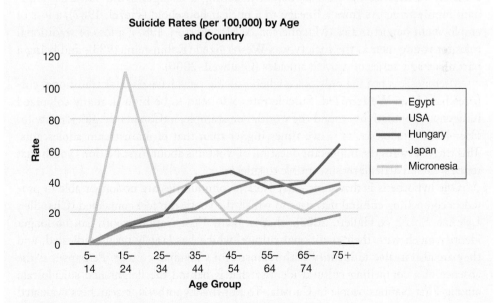

FIGURE 14.6 Suicide rates vary considerably in different countries.

different cultures. In all of the cultures, with the possible exception of Egypt, an increase is seen in the suicide rates among the elderly. Aside from Egypt and Micronesia, the suicide rates for adolescents are also quite similar across cultures. However the rates for other age groups vary considerably (World Health Orgnization, 2004).

Figure 14.6 reveals that Micronesia is a striking outlier, which warrants some discussion. Micronesia did not always have a high suicide rate; in the 1960s, for example, it was less than half of that of the United States (Rubinstein, 1992). However, in the 1970s the island nation documented a dramatic increase in suicides. The pattern of the suicides was strikingly similar across most cases. The vast majority occurred among adolescent males living at home, and, typically, these males had no outward signs of any psychological disorder or of substance abuse. The suicides tended to be sparked by arguments with their peers or families, often about seemingly trivial matters. For example, suicide notes indicated that one adolescent boy killed himself because his parents refused to give him some extra money for beer, and another killed himself because an older brother chastised him for making too much noise (Gladwell, 2000). The method of suicide was also almost always the same, and the highest rates of suicides appeared to be largely limited to certain populations (men between the ages of 15 and 24) on Truk and Marshall Islands, and only in the suburban regions of those islands.

The striking similarity in this unique pattern of suicides, and in the restricted geography of them, suggests that these ritual behaviors have become part of the local cultural environment. It is still not clear what caused this cultural change, but a variety of theories have been offered, including a change in the culture's dominant family structure from a lineage to a nuclear household (Hezel, 1987), a loss of employment opportunities (Macpherson & Macpherson, 1987), a loss of traditional roles for young men as the society was Westernized (Rubinstein, 1983), and being a part of a tragic series of copycat suicides (Gladwell, 2000).

Micronesia is not the only place where suicide rates have risen as traditional cultures have been Westernized. Suicide rates also tend to be high in many colonized indigenous populations around the world. For example, in Canada the suicide rate for First Nations adolescents is five times higher than that of mainstream adolescents. This tragedy raises the important question of what it is about First Nations youth that renders them particularly susceptible to suicide.

One hypothesis is that some First Nation communities are no longer able to provide a compelling cultural narrative to which the youth can feel connected (Chandler, Lalonde, Sokol, & Hallett, 2003). That is, many First Nations youth can no longer identify much with their traditional culture, which has largely been eradicated, and they are also unable to identify with mainstream Canadian culture. Perhaps it is the absence of a compelling cultural identity that is behind the heightened suicide rate among First Nations people in Canada. To test this hypothesis, researchers evaluated the degree to which each First Nations community's current cultural environment was connected to that same culture's past and future. This study revealed the degree to which the community possessed associated cultural facets with which young people could identify. Controlling for other relevant variables (socioeconomic status, population density, geographical location), the researchers showed a clear relation between the community's suicide rate and various indicators of the community's connection to its traditional cultural past (e.g., whether the community had its own political bodies, cultural facilities, self-governed education system, and traditional community law enforcement, and whether it was negotiating a claim to traditional lands). Specifically, the more connections with traditional culture that were present in a community, the lower the community's suicide rate. Indeed, the suicide rates of those from communities with the most links to the traditional past were no higher than that of mainstream Canadians.

The higher suicide rates among First Nations communities with few ties to their cultural heritage, and the unique case of suicides among Micronesian adolescents, demonstrates that people's motivations for suicide can vary considerably across cultures. In the West, suicide is most often seen as stemming from depression, substance abuse, health problems, economic misfortune, and other tragic life events. Although suicides around the world often share such motivating circumstances, in some cultures there appear to be other motivations that are less familiar to the West. Japan is an example of a culture in which suicide plays an unusually significant role. The most famous single incident of suicide in Japan is documented in the true legend of the Chuushingura, better known in the West as the "Forty-Seven Ronin" (**Figure 14.7**).

FIGURE 14.7 A scene from the Chuushingura, when Takumi no Kami committed ritual suicide.

In 1701, upon being humiliated by a high official of the emperor, a feudal lord named Takumi no Kami committed a form of ritual suicide known as *seppuku,* whereby he killed himself by thrusting a sword into his own belly. His 47 retainers then decided to avenge his death by arranging an elaborate plot to assassinate the high official who was responsible for the humiliation. Following the assassination, all 47 retainers then themselves committed *seppuku* to preserve the honor of their families.

This idea of committing suicide to accept responsibility and preserve one's honor can still be observed in modern Japan. In 1998, Katsutoshi Miwata, the baseball scout for the Orix Blue Wave who was credited with discovering Ichiro Suzuki of the Seattle Mariners and New York Yankees, was trying to persuade a top high school pitcher, Nagisa Arakaki, to join the Blue Wave. When Arakaki refused because he wanted to play for another team, Miwata responded by committing suicide, apparently to take responsibility for his failure to recruit the pitcher. Another famous instance involved Juzo Itami, who at the time of his suicide in 1997 was Japan's most internationally renowned movie director and who had directed the cult classic *Tampopo.* A tabloid had informed him that they were going to report that he was having an affair with his assistant. Itami responded to the report by killing himself, which, according to his suicide note, was the only way that he could "prove his innocence." Again, these are instances of motivations for suicide that are less familiar among Westerners, and they reflect the different cultural meanings that suicide has in Japan.

In sum, suicidal tendencies are universal in that they are observed everywhere. However, cultural influences on suicide are clearly evident in that suicide prevalence rates vary tremendously, and the motivations behind suicide also differ across cultures.

Schizophrenia

One of the most debilitating and prevalent mental disorders is schizophrenia (see **Figure 14.8**). To receive a diagnosis of schizophrenia, one must have two or more of the following symptoms, each present for a significant amount of time during a one-month period: delusions, hallucinations, disorganized speech, grossly disorganized

FIGURE 14.8 People suffering from schizophrenia often experience hallucinations, as did the mathematician, John Nash, as portrayed in the movie "A Beautiful Mind."

or catatonic behavior, and negative symptoms (e.g., flattening of mood or a loss of speech; American Psychiatric Association, 2013).

Schizophrenia has been a primary concern for psychiatrists throughout history, and an enormous amount of research has explored it. We know that genetic factors clearly affect one's likelihood of developing schizophrenia. Although only about 1% of the population develops schizophrenia, for those with a cousin with the disorder (with whom they share approximately 12.5% of their genes), the likelihood increases to 2%. Those with a schizophrenic sibling (who shares 50% of their genes) have a 9% chance of developing it, and those with a schizophrenic identical twin (who shares 100% of their genes) have a 48% probability of developing schizophrenia themselves (Gottesman, 1991). Furthermore, there is evidence that certain experiences in the womb can affect the likelihood that those with genetic predispositions will develop schizophrenia (e.g., Cannon, 1998), and there are clear neuroanatomical differences that can be identified between schizophrenic and normal people (e.g., Cannon et al., 1998). Despite the clearly identified relevant genes and perinatal experiences, much is still not known about the causes of schizophrenia. After all, even though identical twins share the same genes, the same mother's womb, and similar family experiences, persons with an identical twin with schizophrenia still have a better than 50% chance of not developing schizophrenia themselves.

Given the clear biological foundation of schizophrenia, it should not be surprising to learn that schizophrenia emerges quite regularly across cultures. Two large multinational epidemiological studies of schizophrenia conducted at a dozen study centers around the world revealed that the annual incidence rates of schizophrenia ranged from 1.5 to 4.2 per 10,000 when a broad definition of schizophrenia was used, and the range of incidence was only 0.7 to 1.4 per 10,000 when a strict definition was applied (Jablensky et al., 1991; World Health Organization, 1973). All of the centers had high scores of specific symptoms, such as lack of insight, predelusional signs, flatness of affect, and auditory hallucinations. Furthermore, longitudinal studies have found that although many other disorders appear to be on the increase in some cultures, rates of schizophrenia remained constant over the period (Lin, Rin, Yeh, Hsu, & Chu, 1969). The uniformity of the symptoms and the narrowness of the range of prevalence speak to the cultural similarity of the manifestation of this disorder.

However, even within a condition with such an obvious biological foundation as schizophrenia, there is some striking evidence for cultural variability. First, it is important to note that the development of a set of universal criteria of what constitutes schizophrenia resulted in the exclusion of the majority of psychotic patients at each of the centers that was studied because they did not meet the specific criteria for schizophrenia. In a way, then, the similarity of the symptoms of those diagnoses with schizophrenia around the world is in part an artifact of the method that was applied: Anyone who experienced different symptoms was simply not included in the study (Kleinman, 1988). Also, considerable variation occurred in the subtypes of schizophrenia that were identified across cultures. *Paranoid schizophrenia* (characterized by delusional visions) was the most commonly observed subtype in most locations, although the proportions varied considerably across locations. For example, 75% of schizophrenics in the United Kingdom received a diagnosis of paranoid schizophrenia compared with only 15% of those in India (World Health Organization, 1973). Although *catatonic schizophrenia* (characterized by a near absence of motor activity and an insensitivity to external stimuli) was rarely observed in the West (only 1%–3% of cases in the United States and the United Kingdom), it was seen in more than 20% in India. Catatonic schizophrenia and paranoid schizophrenia are dramatically different manifestations of the disease, yet the proportions of these subtypes varied widely across the cultures studied.

Likewise, some of the symptoms of schizophrenia vary across population; a key symptom of schizophrenia is the experience of hallucinations, yet there are marked differences in the likelihood that diagnosed schizophrenics report hallucinations across cultures (Bauer et al., 2011). This cultural difference is not surprising, as there are vast cultural differences in the rate of hallucinations among the normal population as well, and hallucinations take on quite different meanings across cultures too (e.g., communicating with ancestors, speaking with God; Larøi et al., 2014). In general, WEIRD samples are quite noteworthy in their relative lack of hallucinations, and in their fear of them.

The most striking finding regarding cultural variation that emerged from these studies was that the course of schizophrenia was *better* for patients in the less-developed societies than in the more industrially advanced ones (Leff, Sartorius, Jablensky, Korten, & Ernberg, 1992). This finding is all the more remarkable given that schizophrenia rates are higher in lower social classes than they are in higher ones (e.g., Hollingshead & Redlich, 1958) and that health outcomes tend to be worse for lower classes more generally. This tendency for schizophrenics to fare better in less-developed societies has led to a number of different explanations. For example, people in less-developed societies tend to have a more fatalistic attitude and less of a primary sense of control, which may lead them to be less blameworthy toward people with schizophrenia (Barrowclough & Hooley, 2003). Also, experiences of hallucinations and beliefs in possession by spirits are far more common in many less-developed societies, so persons who claim to feel as though they're hearing voices or are possessed may be viewed as less problematic (Evans, 1992; Luhrmann, Padmavati, Tharoor, & Osei, 2015). Further, the stronger sense of community felt in many less-developed societies means that those suffering with schizophrenia are less likely to be left on their own and thus are less likely to end up being homeless. Thus far, explanations for cultural differences in the course of schizophrenia remain largely speculative (also see Watters, 2010).

In sum, there is much cross-cultural consistency of schizophrenia around the world—in many ways, schizophrenia emerges as one of the most universally similar psychopathologies across cultures, which fits with the biological bases of the disease that have been identified thus far. However, it is telling that even in the case of a disease with such a clear biological foundation as schizophrenia, it can present itself in such different ways across cultures, and that the course of the disease also varies significantly. This cultural variation in a universal psychopathology underscores the critical role that culture plays in mental health.

Mental Health Treatment

If the experience of mental illness can vary across cultures, we should expect that the treatment of those illnesses would also vary. Cultural expectations and norms can shape the ways that people understand and react to most aspects of mental health treatment. For example, traditional and contemporary forms of psychotherapy that are practiced in the West—in which clients seek out professional help when they have concerns, reflect upon themselves as individuals, explore their inner selves, and verbally disclose their private feelings and emotions to a therapist whom they have likely just met—are very much bound up in several of the Western cultural ideas that have been discussed thus far in this book. These practices would seem to run against the beliefs and understandings of people from many non-Western societies, such as the ideas that there may be stigma associated with acknowledging the existence of mental disorders that can potentially be harmful both to oneself and one's family, that people are embedded in networks of relationships, that it is important for people to attend a great deal to others and their expectations, that emotions and private feelings are not something to be dwelled upon, that a deep understanding of something may be based on what is *not* said (or cannot be said), that people should not unnecessarily disclose their troubles to others, and that one should keep some distance from outgroup members. Because much of the success of mental health treatment revolves around the relationship and information exchange between the client and the therapist, and because the nature of that relationship and the kinds of information that are exchanged are likely shaped by cultural expectations, culture affects the success of treatment.

"I wish I'd started therapy at your age."

One example of the different understandings that people from different cultures may have toward dealing with mental health treatment can be seen in cross-cultural research on social support (Kim, Sherman, & Taylor, 2008). Receiving sufficient social support has been shown to play a key role in coping with psychological distress (Fleming, Baum, Gisriel, & Gatchel, 1982) and is associated with various physical health benefits (for a review, see Cohen & Wills, 1985), both within and across cultures (e.g., Morling, Kitayama, & Miyamoto, 2003). But people seek and provide social support differently across cultures (e.g., Miller et al., 2014). For example, European-Americans are far more likely than East Asians or Asian-Americans to actively seek social support from others, such as to tell a friend about their problems (e.g., Taylor et al., 2004). At first, this may sound surprising, given all that we've learned about the differences between people with independent and interdependent selves. It appears that this cultural difference in social support seeking exists largely because East Asians are more concerned about how seeking social support will disrupt their relationships with others (Kim, Sherman, Ko, & Taylor, 2006). East Asians do depend on social support from close others; however, they are more likely than Westerners to rely on *implicit* social support—that is, they gain emotional comfort by reminding themselves of the close relationships they have. Studies have found that European-Americans show less of a physical stress reaction when they are given the opportunity to seek social support such as asking someone for advice and help, but Asian-Americans show less of a stress response when they think about their close relationships (Taylor, Welch, Kim, & Sherman, 2007). Likewise, European-Americans show more direct evidence of health benefits when they perceive that they have much social support, whereas those same health benefits do not increase alongside perceived support for Asian-Americans (Chiang, Saphire-Bernstein, Kim, Sherman, & Taylor, 2013). Moreover, Asian-Americans find unsolicited social support to reduce their stress more than solicited social support, which reflects their concerns with the social costs of seeking support from others; Euro-Americans, on the other hand, find social support to be equally helpful in reducing stress, regardless of whether they have asked for it or not (Mojaverian & Kim, 2013).

In addition, the kinds of explicit support that people offer their friends varies across cultures–North Americans typically offer more emotion-focused support (such as offering encouraging or comforting words) than problem-focused support (providing specific advice). In contrast, East Asians tend to offer relatively more problem-focused support than emotion-focused support (Chen, Kim, Mojverian, & Morling, 2012). Russians, too, are more likely than North Americans to offer problem-focused support (Chentsova-Dutton, 2012). This cultural difference in tendencies to actively seek social support may help explain why East Asians, in general, are less likely than Westerners to seek mental health treatment from professionals (e.g., Sue, Fujino, Hu, Takeuchi, & Zane, 1991).

The origins of Western psychotherapy are typically traced back to Western Europe and, in particular, to Sigmund Freud, who launched the field of psychoanalysis in the late 19th century. Freud proposed that many of the psychological difficulties people experience are rooted in conflicts and fears that exist at an unconscious level. These can best be treated, Freud argued, by having people explore their memories and traumatic experiences by discussing them in depth in individual sessions, while the therapist plays a key role in helping the clients to interpret their memories and experiences.

When psychoanalysis was introduced in the United States in the 20th century, it was modified somewhat by Carl Rogers, who emphasized a client-centered approach in which the therapist aids the client in his or her self-discovery. Since then, numerous kinds of psychotherapeutic approaches have been developed, with the most common being cognitive behavioral therapy, in which people's thoughts may be restructured by therapists aiding the clients in identifying their dysfunctional cognitive biases or in which their negative reactions to certain situations are alleviated through controlled exposures. In addition, biological modes of explaining and treating mental disorders have become more dominant in psychiatry over the past few decades. However, the commonality across these diverse Western perspectives of mental illness is that the underlying evaluation of people and their conditions hinges on the client's ability to engage in a psychological discourse that is grounded in shared cultural meanings (see Kirmayer, 2007).

In contrast, various approaches to mental illness have emerged in other cultures. One study explored the indigenous healing practices that were commonly used in 16 societies in Africa, Asia, South America, the Middle East, and the Caribbean (Lee, Oh, & Mountcastle, 1992). The researchers found two indigenous models of healing common across these cultures. First, the family was found to play the most important role in resolving mental health problems. Families were seen to share the problems with the individuals and were the key source of guidance, especially from elder members of the family. Moreover, families were often viewed as suffering from whatever stigma may be associated with the mental illnesses. For example, in Saudi Arabia there is much perceived stigma and shame attached to mental illnesses, so families may shelter a disturbed individual from the outside world until the problem becomes unmanageable, at which point they may seek help from the extended family and from the community. The second model of healing in non-Western societies was a focus on spiritualism and religion. Mental illnesses are often perceived as being rooted in an underlying spiritual problem, and treatment is often left to traditional healers, such as shamans and sorcerers.

An example of this spiritual conception of mental illness can be seen in the Yoruba of West Africa. In Yoruba thought, the person is viewed as the union of the *ara* (body), *emi* (mind/soul), and *ori* ("inner head"), each of which come into existence by specific gods (Adeofe, 2004). The *emi*, however, does not have any personal characteristics, and the individual's unique qualities come from the *ori*, which is viewed as a diety. When the Yoruba want to understand someone's mental afflictions, they use divination to understand what has gone wrong with the individual's relationships with the gods (Kirmayer, 2007).

Such different kinds of attitudes toward mental health treatment are not just evident in traditional societies; differences also exist between Western and Japanese psychotherapies. Two therapies that emerged from Japan are noteworthy in their contrasts with Western ones: Morita and Naikan therapies. Reflecting the desire for secondary control among Japanese that was discussed in Chapter 8, the main tenet of Morita therapy is for clients to come to accept the circumstances in their lives as they are (Lebra, 1976). Primarily targeted at those dealing with various kinds of anxieties and depressive symptoms, Morita therapy involves activities such as periods of isolated bed rest, light manual activities (e.g., sweeping), heavy manual labor (e.g., chopping wood), reading of Moritist literature, and life training, all combined with meditation and sessions with the therapist (see Weisz, Rothbaum, & Blackburn, 1984). The goal of Morita therapy is not to change the client's symptoms but to change the person's perspective on the symptoms and to come to see them as a natural part of who they are. People are cured when they learn to live productively in spite of their symptoms (Reynolds, 1980).

In contrast, Naikan therapy seeks to provide clients with insight into their past. In particular, it encourages people to appreciate how indebted they are to the kindnesses of significant others. The therapy has been used to treat people struggling with addiction, depression, and especially sociopathy (the therapy has been used in a majority of Japanese prisons). Clients are led through a guided introspection to reflect upon the kindnesses that they have received from their close relationships (especially their mothers when they were young children) and to consider how little they had offered in return for these kindnesses. The goal of the therapy is to have clients reinterpret their past, which they recognize cannot be changed. However, when they have revisited their past through a prism of gratitude and guilt toward others, it can be restructured to give new meaning to their lives (Reynolds, 1980).

The existence of culturally divergent conceptions of the self, together with culturally specific presentations of mental disorders, highlights how crucial it is for mental health treatments to be a good match with the culture. Psychotherapies that have emerged out of a particular culture, with a particular set of cultural understandings of the self and mental health, very well might not work as effectively when applied to other cultural contexts. In his 2010 book *Crazy Like Us: The Globalization of the American Psyche,* Ethan Watters argues that applying Western mental health treatments around the world has not only resulted in less effective treatments of mental illnesses outside of the West but may have inadvertently led to the spread of some conditions to places where they previously did not exist. For example, he argues that anorexia didn't exist in the same form in Hong Kong prior to the relatively recent importation of the concept, which encouraged both psychiatrists and clients to interpret some related symptoms in this light, and that posttraumatic stress disorder wasn't much of a problem in Sri Lanka following the 2004 tsunami until enough local people had met with well-meaning Western aid workers who insisted that they must be suffering from it (but see Jobson, Moradi, Rahimi-Movaghar, Conway, & Dalgleish, 2014, for some evidence of common symptoms of PTSD across cultures). As the social historian Edward Shorter (1987) put it, each culture provides a "symptom pool" of recognized and discussed symptoms that leads people to express their inner conflicts in a familiar language. Providing people with different conceptions of mental illness may lead them to express their own psychological difficulties in symptoms that are consistent with those conceptions.

Given this cultural diversity in both the kinds of presentations of mental illnesses and in people's understanding of mental illness and treatments, one might assume that therapists would be most effective if, when possible, they could be matched up with clients who share their same cultural background, because the clients can express their views in their own language, will feel that the therapists understand them better, and will be more likely to continue with their treatment (Sue, 1998). However, the therapeutic benefits of this cultural matching of therapists and clients appear to be quite modest (see Maramba & Nagayama Hall, 2002; Shin et al., 2005), can serve to ghettoize therapists from different backgrounds (Ryder & Dere, 2010), and in many situations can be impossible to achieve. Frequently, therapists working in multicultural settings will encounter clients with different cultural understandings of mental illness and treatments, as well as different symptoms; what should a therapist do when encountering clients from other cultural backgrounds?

Therapists who work with clients from different cultural backgrounds should strive to achieve **cultural competence.** Cultural competence entails a number of different aspects (see Sue, 2006). First, it is necessary for therapists to recognize their own cultural influences, so that they can consciously deal with their own defenses, interpretations, and projections that will be relevant when they are interacting with clients from other cultural backgrounds (Sodowsky, Kuo-Jackson, & Loya, 1997). Second, therapists should develop knowledge about the cultural background of their client, and the kinds of expectations that the client likely has for the counseling relationship, so that they can interact with their client in the most effective way. Third, the therapist should develop the appropriate skills to be able to intervene in the therapy sessions in a way that is culturally sensitive and relevant.

At the same time, it is important for the therapist to be flexible about when it appears appropriate to generalize from the client's culture to the mainstream culture, and when it appears more appropriate to individualize the client (Kirmayer & Ban, 2013). After all, each person cannot be reduced to the typical member of their culture, and everyone responds to their cultures differently. Further, in many multicultural therapeutic settings, the clients are exposed to more than one culture, and it is important for therapists to be mindful of how their clients are integrating their diverse cultural experiences together with their own idiosyncratic tendencies.

Perhaps the current state-of-the-art method for therapists working in multicultural settings is the cultural consultation service (Kirmayer, Grolean, Guzder, Blake, & Jarvis, 2003). This entails a group of psychiatrists, psychologists, social workers, psychiatric nurses, medical anthropologists, and trainees from various disciplines who meet regularly to discuss cases that are referred to them by therapists who feel they need expert advice when dealing with multicultural clients. The group brings in interpreters, consultants, and culture brokers from various disciplines to speak on particular cases when their expertise is needed. The group frequently identifies a number of issues relevant to the therapy that lie outside the expertise of many therapists, such as information regarding particular kinds of family systems, identity issues peculiar to certain cultures, migration stresses, and the impact of exposure to torture or war. In the vast majority of cases, therapists have reported that such consultation had been useful in helping them manage their clients. The downside, as you might have inferred, is that such a cultural consultation service can be prohibitively expensive.

SUMMARY

Just as normal psychological processes vary across cultures, so do abnormal ones. The extent of cultural shaping of psychological disorders is most evident in culture-bound disorders, which are disorders that are largely limited to certain cultures. Many of these disorders, such as *koro, dhat,* or *hikikomori,* appear quite foreign to Westerners, and they do not fit in any of the more familiar diagnostic categories used by Western psychiatrists.

Some universally identifiable psychopathologies, such as depression, social anxiety, suicide, and schizophrenia, are also presented in culturally variable ways. Most noteworthy are the findings that symptoms of depression are more likely to be somatized within some cultures (e.g., China), whereas they are more likely to be psychologized in others (e.g., North America). Social anxiety is also universally present; however, it is more common in East Asia—so common, in fact, that it appears to be viewed as more normative there than in the West. When serious anxiety disorders present in Japan, they are more likely to do so with the symptoms of *taijin kyoufushou*, which includes a very different set of symptoms than social anxiety disorder. Suicides vary a great deal in their frequency across cultures and in the motivations that give rise to them. Schizophrenia perhaps is the most cross-culturally similar disorder; however, there is cultural variation in the subtypes of schizophrenia that are most common and in the course of the disease.

Given these cultural differences in the presentation of different mental illnesses, it follows that the treatment of mental illnesses also varies across cultures. To be effective at treating mental illnesses of people from different cultures, therapists should strive to develop cultural competence.

THINK ABOUT IT

1. Why isn't *hikikomori* found as commonly in the West as it is in Japan?
2. In what ways can we say that *dhat* syndrome is a culture-bound syndrome?
3. If depression in China is associated with more somatized symptoms in comparison with depression in the West, how can we say that the two kinds of depression reflect the same underlying condition?
4. What is the role of stigma in interpreting cultural differences in the prevalence of different clinical disorders?
5. What is different between social anxiety disorder and *taijin kyoufushou*?
6. Why do you think people with schizophrenia tend to fare better in less-developed societies when compared with modern industrialized societies?
7. What aspects of psychoanalysis reflect its Western cultural origins?
8. How is social support perceived differently between East Asians and Westerners?
9. What kinds of considerations should a Western clinician take into account when treating a client from an unfamiliar cultural background who is presenting an unfamiliar collection of symptoms?

KEY TERMS

Hikikomori, 560

Dhat Syndrome, 563

Culture-Bound Syndromes, 564

Bulimia Nervosa, 564

Anorexia Nervosa, 565

Koro, 568

Amok, 568

Frigophobia, 570

Susto, 570

Voodoo Death, 570

Latah, 571

Malgri, 571

Agonias, 571

Kufungisisa, 571

Ataques De Nervios, 571

Somatization, 573

Psychologization, 573

Neurasthenia, 574

Social Anxiety Disorder, 576

Taijin Kyoufushou, 578

Cultural Competence, 589

GLOSSARY

accessibility universal The first and highest level of universality, which states that a given cognitive tool exists across cultures, is used to solve the same problem across cultures, and is accessible to the same degree across cultures.

acculturation The process by which people migrate to and learn a culture that is different from their original (or heritage) culture.

achieve purity A moral intuition that people should be disgusted by contamination or behaviors governed by the carnal passions.

acquiescence bias A tendency to agree with most statements one encounters.

agonias An anxiety disorder that can include a wide array of symptoms such as a burning sensation, a loss of breath, hysterical blindness, sleeping disorders, and eating disorders.

agreeableness A personality trait that indicates how warm or pleasant an individual is; part of the *Five Factor model of personality*.

altruistic punishment A person's tendency to incur a cost to punish someone who isn't cooperating with the group.

amok A phenomenon found in Southeast Asia whereby an individual has an acute outburst of indiscriminate violence followed by amnesia and exhaustion.

analytic thinking A type of thinking characterized by a focus on objects and their attributes.

anorexia nervosa An eating disorder characterized by a refusal to maintain a normal (high enough) body weight; an intense fear of gaining weight; denial of the seriousness of one's low body weight; and, for postmenarcheal females, missing three consecutive menstrual cycles.

antisocial punishment A person's tendency to incur a cost to punish someone who is cooperating with the group.

assimilation strategy An acculturation strategy that involves an attempt to fit in and fully participate in the *host culture* while making little or no effort to maintain the traditions of one's *heritage culture*.

associative reasoning Making decisions of categorization based on how similar the events appear to each other.

ataques de nervios A condition in which emotionally charged incidents bring on symptoms such as palpitations, numbness, and a sense of heat rising to the head.

authoritarian parenting Parenting style that places high demands on children, with strict rules, low levels of warmth, and little open dialogue.

authoritative parenting Child-centered parenting, in which parents try to understand their children's feelings but encourage them to be independent while maintaining controls on their behaviors.

authority ranking A type of relational structure in which people are linearly ordered along a hierarchical social dimension in which higher ranking people have prestige and privileges while those ranking lower do not.

autokinetic effect An effect caused by the involuntary saccades of the eyes, which, in the dark, create the illusion of movement.

autonomy ideal A moral principle that young children should sleep alone so they can learn to be self-reliant and take care of themselves.

avoid harm A moral intuition to avoid behaviors that cause harm to others.

back-translation A method of translating research materials from one language to another whereby a translator translates materials from Language A to Language B and then a different translator translates the materials back from Language B to Language A. The original and twice-translated versions in Language A are then compared so that any discrepancies between them can be resolved.

bask in the reflected glory Emphasizing one's connection to successful others in order to feel better about oneself.

between-group manipulation A type of experimental manipulation in which different groups of participants receive different levels of the independent variable(s).

bicultural identity integration The extent to which one's two cultural identities are compatible or in opposition to each other.

blending The tendency for bicultural people to manifest psychological tendencies in between those of their two cultures.

bulimia nervosa An eating disorder characterized by recurrent episodes of binge eating along with recurrent inappropriate behaviors to prevent weight gain (e.g. induced vomiting), which happen at least twice a week for 3 months; a self-evaluation unduly influenced by one's body weight; and no concurrent diagnosis of *anorexia nervosa*.

calling In religious belief, the God-given purpose an individual is meant to fulfill during his or her life.

categorical perception Perceiving stimuli as belonging to separate and discrete categories, even though the stimuli may gradually differ from each other along a continuum.

co-sleeping Children sharing the same bed with their caretakers.

cognitive dissonance The distressing feeling that accompanies the awareness that one is acting inconsistently.

collectivistic cultures Cultures with many practices, institutions, and customs encouraging individuals to place relatively more emphasis on collective goals than individual ones.

color-blind approach Looking beyond individuals' ethnicities or race in an effort to focus on their common human nature.

communal sharing A type of relational structure in which the members of a group emphasize their common identity, and each have the same rights and privileges.

compensatory self-enhancement The means of compensating for doing poorly on a particular activity by focusing on how good one is at something unrelated to that activity.

conscientiousness A personality trait that indicates how responsible and dependable an individual is; part of the *Five Factor model of personality*.

contemporary legends Fictional stories told in modern societies as though they are true.

conventional moral reasoning Moral reasoning in which rightness is determined by whether the behaviors fit with the group's rules, laws, or conventions.

cultural competence This entails a recognition of one's own cultural influences, knowledge about the cultural background of one's client, and skills to intervene in therapy sessions in relevant and culturally sensitive ways.

cultural distance The difference between two cultures in their overall ways of life.

cultural fit The degree to which an individual's personality is compatible with the dominant cultural values of his or her *host culture*.

cultural priming A method that makes ideas associated with particular cultural meaning systems more accessible to participants.

cultural worlds Worlds that contain cultural ideas that have accumulated over time.

culture of honor A culture in which people (especially men) strive to protect their reputation through aggression.

culture-bound syndromes Groups of symptoms that appear to be greatly influenced by cultural factors, and hence occur far less frequently in some cultures than others, or manifest in highly divergent ways across cultures.

culture-gene co-evolution The idea that among humans, culture and genes evolve in tandem. Humans have evolved genetically to be better able to learn cultural information, and as their culture evolves it increases their fitness. Moreover, humans have become so dependent on culture that their culture has become a selective force on their genes.

culture shock The feeling of being anxious, helpless, irritable, and generally homesick due to a move to a new culture.

dependent variable In an experiment, the variable or measure affected by manipulation of the *independent variable*.

deprivation effect A tendency for people to value something more when it is lacking in their culture.

***dhat* syndrome** A culture-bound syndrome, most common in South Asia, in which men develop morbid anxiety around concerns that they are losing semen.

dictator game An economic game in which a pair of people are randomly divided into the roles of a proposer, who determines how much of his or her money to give to the other participant, and a receiver, who receives the money from the proposer.

discounting Reducing the perceived importance of the domain in which one has performed poorly.

display rules The culturally specific rules that govern which facial expressions are appropriate in a given situation and how intensely they should be exhibited.

dispositional attributions Explaining people's behavior in terms of their inner qualities, such as personality traits.

distal causes Initial differences that lead to effects over long periods of time and often through indirect relations.

downward social comparison An individual's comparison of his or her performance with the performance of someone who is doing worse.

dynamic social impact theory A theory suggesting that individuals influence each other through their interactions, which gives rise to clusters of like-minded people separated by geography.

emulative learning A type of social learning focused on the environmental events involved with a model's behavior, such as how the use of one object could potentially affect changes in the state of the environment.

encephalization quotient The ratio of an animal's brain weight to the brain weight predicted for a comparable animal of the same body size.

entity theory of self A view of the self in which a person's abilities and traits are largely innate features that the individual cannot change.

entity theory of the world A view of the world as something that is fixed and beyond an individual's control to change.

epidemiological paradox The surprisingly healthy outcomes of Latinos despite their having lower-than-average socioeconomic status.

equality matching A type of relational structure based on the idea of balance and reciprocity in which people keep track of what is exchanged, and they are motivated to pay back what has been exchanged in equivalent turns.

essentialized gender A gender identity that is believed to reflect an underlying and unchanging nature.

ethic of autonomy A system of values that views morality in terms of individual freedoms and rights violations with an emphasis on personal choice, the right to engage in free contracts, and individual liberty.

ethic of community A system of values that emphasizes that individuals have duties pertaining to their roles in a community or social hierarchy.

ethic of divinity A system of values that emphasizes sanctity and the perceived "natural order" of things.

ethnocentrism The tendency to judge people from other cultures by comparing them to the standards of one's own culture.

evoked culture The notion that all people, regardless of where they are from, have certain biologically encoded behavioral repertoires that are potentially accessible to them, and that these repertoires are engaged when the appropriate situational conditions arise.

existential universal The third level of universality, which states that a given cognitive tool exists across cultures, although the tool is not necessarily used to solve the same problems across cultures, nor is it equally accessible across cultures.

external attributions Interpreting the cause of an action as something outside of oneself.

extraversion A personality trait that indicates how active or dominant an individual is; part of the *Five Factor model of personality*.

face The amount of social value others give an individual if they live up to the standards associated with their position.

facial feedback hypothesis The notion that facial expressions influence emotional experience.

female chastity anxiety The anxiety that unmarried post-pubescent women are vulnerable to shameful sexual activity.

field dependence The tendency to view objects as bound to their backgrounds.

field independence The tendency to separate objects from their backgrounds.

Five Factor model of personality A model of five core traits underlying human personality, including the traits of openness to experience, conscientiousness, extraversion, agreeableness, and neuroticism.

frame-switching The tendency for bicultural people to switch between different cultural selves.

French paradox The fact that despite eating a cuisine that's rich in fat, French people have low obesity rates and relatively long lifespans.

frigophobia A morbid fear of catching a cold, which leads people to dress themselves in heavy coats and scarves even in summer.

functional universal The second level of universality, which states that a given cognitive tool exists across cultures and is used to solve the same problem across cultures, but is more accessible to people from some cultures than others.

fundamental attribution error A tendency to ignore situational information while focusing on dispositional information when making judgments about people's behaviors.

Gemeinschaft A type of group that emphasizes interpersonal relationships as core parts of individuals' identities and views such relationships as ends in themselves.

general psychology Richard Shweder's term for the overarching perspective of the field of psychology of assuming that the mind operates under a set of natural and universal laws that exist independently of the context that the individual is in and of the content of what they are thinking about.

generalizability The degree to which research findings about the particular samples studied can be applied to larger or broader populations.

Gesellschaft A type of group that emphasizes individual members' autonomy and views relationships as instrumental and as means to other ends.

heritage culture A culture identified as a person's culture of origin.

high-context culture Cultures in which there is much consensual information shared among individuals, so that much can be understood without it needing to be explicitly stated.

high relational mobility A context where people have many opportunities to form new relationships and do not feel overly bound by existing relationships.

hikikomori A culture-bound syndrome, largely limited to Japan, in which people, most often adolescent boys, impose a self-incarceration and withdraw from all social interaction for an extended period of time.

holistic thinking A type of thinking characterized by an orientation to the context as a whole.

host culture A culture identified as the new culture when people move from one culture to another.

ideal affect The kinds of emotions that people want to experience, and thus they structure their lives in order to increase their experience of them.

identity denial How a minority group individual's cultural identity may be called into question because he or she does not seem to match the prototype of the culture.

imitative learning A type of social learning in which the learner internalizes aspects of the model's goals and behavioral strategies.

immigrants People who move to a new culture and intend to stay permanently.

incest avoidance A moral principle that post-pubescent family members of the opposite sex should not sleep in the same room together.

incremental theory of self A view of the self in which a person's abilities and traits are malleable and can be improved.

incremental theory of the world A view of the world as flexible and responsive to an individual's efforts to change it.

independent variable In an experiment, the variable or condition that the experimenter manipulates in order to examine its effect on the *dependent variable*.

independent view of self A model of the self in which identity is thought to come from inner attributes that reflect a unique essence of the individual and that remain stable across situations and across the lifespan.

individualistic cultures Cultures with many practices and customs encouraging individuals to prioritize their own personal goals ahead of collective goals and to emphasize the ways in which they are distinct from others.

integration strategy An acculturation strategy that involves attempts to fit in and fully participate in the host culture while at the same time striving to maintain the traditions of one's *heritage culture*.

integrative complexity A willingness and ability to acknowledge and consider different viewpoints on the same issue.

interdependent view of self A model of the self in which individuals are perceived not as separate and distinct entities but as participants in a larger social unit where identity is contingent upon key relationships with ingroup members.

internal attribution Interpreting that an event is caused by characteristics of the person involved.

James-Lange theory of emotions A theory that maintains that emotions are primarily perceptions of physiological responses to stimuli.

koro A culture-bound syndrome, largely found in South and East Asia, in which men become morbidly anxious that their penis is retracting into their body.

kufungisisa An anxiety and somatic disorder in Zimbabwe believed to be caused by excessive thinking. Variants of this disorder are found in several other cultures of the world.

latah A condition in which an individual falls into a transient dissociated state in which he or she exhibits unusual behavior after some kind of startling event.

learned helplessness The feeling of being unable to control or avoid unpleasant events, which causes stress and potentially depression.

linguistic relativity hypothesis *See Whorfian hypothesis*

low-context culture Cultures in which there is relatively less consensual information shared among individuals, so that people need to rely heavily on explicit communication.

low relational mobility A context where people have few opportunities to form new relationships and are guided by commitments and obligations to existing relationships.

loyalty to ingroups A moral intuition that people should put the interests of their ingroup ahead of those of their outgroup.

malgri A syndrome of territorial anxiety in which an individual grows physically sick, tired, and drowsy when entering the sea or a new territory without engaging in the appropriate ceremonial procedures.

marginalization strategy An acculturation strategy that involves little or no effort to participate in the *host culture* or to maintain the traditions of the *heritage culture*.

market pricing A type of relational structure concerned with proportionality and ratios; members of a party calculate the ratios of the goods that are exchanged so that the transaction is equivalent in value for both parties.

mere exposure effect An effect which states that the more people are exposed to a stimulus the more they are attracted to it.

meritocracy A social system that rewards individuals based on their own contributions, according to the *principle of equity*.

methodological equivalence In cross-cultural research, the concern with making sure participants from different cultures understand the research questions or situations in equivalent ways.

migrants People who move from a heritage culture (their original culture) to a host culture (their new culture), including those who intend to stay temporarily and those who intend to move permanently.

minimally counterintuitive ideas Ideas that violate our expectations enough to be considered surprising and unusual but not too outlandish.

Müller-Lyer illusion A visual illusion in which a line with ends that angle away from the line appears longer than a line with ends that angle toward the line.

multicultural approach Attending to and respecting the distinctive aspects of different cultural groups.

naive dialecticism A perspective in which events and objects in the world are perceived as interconnected and fluid. Such a view leads to the acceptance of contradictions between two opposing beliefs.

natural selection The evolutionary process that occurs when three particular conditions are present: (1) individual members of a species vary on certain traits; (2) those varying traits are associated with different survival rates; and (3) those traits have a hereditary basis.

neocortex ratio The ratio of the volume of the neocortex to the volume of the rest of the brain, which is used as a proxy measure of intelligence.

neurasthenia A psychiatric condition characterized as a nervous syndrome consisting of over 50 symptoms, including poor appetite, headaches, insomnia, weakness in the back, hysteria, and an inability to concentrate.

neuroticism A personality trait that indicates how emotionally unstable and unpredictable an individual is; part of the *Five Factor model of personality*.

nonuniversal The fourth, and lowest, level of universality, which states that a given cognitive tool does not exist in all cultures and can be considered a cultural invention.

noun bias The tendency in young children to have a vocabulary with more nouns relative to the number of verbs and other relational words.

objective self-awareness A state of mind in which individuals consider how they appear to others and are conscious of being evaluated.

Occam's razor The principle that any theory should make as few assumptions as possible; it maintains that, all else held equal, the simpler theory is more likely to be correct.

openness to experience A personality trait that reflects a person's intelligence and curiosity about the world; part of the *Five Factor model of personality*.

orthodox A term describing religious adherents committed to the idea of a transcendent authority that operates independently of people and is more knowledgeable and powerful than all of human experience.

permissive parenting Being very responsive, warm, and involved with one's children, but placing few limits and controls on their behaviors.

pluralistic ignorance The tendency for people to collectively misinterpret the thoughts that underlie other people's behaviors.

postconventional moral reasoning Moral reasoning in which rightness is determined by whether the behavior meets abstract ethical principles of justice and individual rights.

power The capability of a study to accurately detect an effect (e.g., a cross-cultural difference) to the extent that one exists; a reflection of how well-designed a study is.

preconventional moral reasoning Moral reasoning in which rightness is determined by the physical or hedonistic consequences of the behavior.

predestination A belief about the afterlife holding that prior to birth, it has already been determined whether one is among the "elect" who will spend eternity in heaven, or among those who will burn in hell forever.

prestige bias A tendency to imitate prestigious others more than less-prestigious others—that is, those who have the respect and attention of others.

prevention orientation A concern with correcting one's weaknesses and avoiding others' negative judgments.

primary control The control experienced when people strive to shape existing realities to fit their perceptions.

principle of equality The principle that resources should be shared equally among the members of a group.

principle of equity The principle that resources should be distributed based on an individual's contributions.

principle of need The principle that resources should be directed toward those who need them the most.

progressive A term describing religious adherents who emphasize the importance of human agency in understanding and formulating a moral code.

promotion orientation A concern with advancing oneself and aspiring for gains.

propinquity effect An effect which states that people are more likely to befriend people they interact with frequently.

protect fairness A moral intuition to attend to whether resources or rights are distributed fairly.

protection of the vulnerable A moral principle that young children who are needy and vulnerable should not be left alone at night.

proximal causes Causes that have direct and immediate relations with their effects.

psychologization When symptoms of an illness are primarily experienced psychologically rather than physically.

public goods game An economic game in which a group of people have the option to contribute some of their money to a common pool, after which the experimenter multiplies the money in the pool and then redistributes it to all the members of the group.

ratchet effect The process by which cultural information becomes more complex and often more useful over time because an initial idea can be learned from others and then modified and improved by the learners.

reference-group effect A tendency for people to evaluate themselves by comparing themselves with others from their own culture.

respect for hierarchy A moral principle that post-pubescent boys are conferred social status by allowing them to not have to sleep with parents or young children.

response bias Factors that distort the accuracy of a person's responses to surveys.

ritualized displays Facial expressions that are expressed in some cultures but not in others as a function of cultural display rules.

rule-based reasoning Making decisions of categorization based on whether the categories follow a fixed rule.

Russian cultural-historical school A school of thought which argued that people interact with their environment through the "tools" or human-made ideas that have been passed down to them through history.

saccades Type of eye movement in which the gaze shifts quickly from one fixation point to another.

sacred couple A moral principle that married couples should be given their own sleeping space for emotional intimacy and sexual privacy.

secondary control The control experienced when people attempt to align themselves with existing realities, leaving their circumstances unchanged but exerting control over the circumstances' psychological impact.

secularization theory A view that religion is on the decline, and that people around the world are turning to secular and rational ways of understanding their lives.

self-enhancement The motivation to view oneself positively.

self-esteem The positivity of individuals' overall evaluation of themselves.

self-improvement The process of seeking out one's potential weaknesses and working on correcting them.

self-serving bias A tendency for people to view themselves in unrealistically positive terms.

seniority system A system that rewards individuals based on older age or a longer time spent with a company.

sensitive period A period of time in an organisms development that allows for the relatively easy acquisition of a particular set of skills.

separation strategy An acculturation strategy that involves efforts to maintain the traditions of the heritage culture while making little or no effort to participate in the host culture.

similarity-attraction effect An effect which states that people tend to be attracted to those who are most like themselves.

simpático A relational style common in many Latin-American cultures in which people emphasize maintaining harmonious relationships and making expressive displays of graciousness, hospitality, and personal harmony.

situation sampling A method used for comparing cultures with psychological measures. Situations are generated by participants in more than one culture, and then those situations are presented to different groups of participants from multiple cultures. This method allows us to see both (a) whether situations common in one culture influence people differently than situations common in another culture, and (b) whether people in one culture respond to the same situations differently than those from another culture.

situational attributions Explaining people's behavior in terms of contextual variables.

social anxiety disorder A fear that one is in danger of acting in an inept and unacceptable manner, and that such behavior will bring disastrous social consequences.

social brain hypothesis The theory that cognitive demands inherent in social living led to the evolution of large primate brains.

socially desirable responding A response bias in which people's responses are distorted by their motivation to be evaluated positively by others.

sojourners People who move to a new culture and intend to stay there only temporarily.

somatization When symptoms of an illness are primarily experienced physically rather than psychologically.

stereotype threat The fear that one might act in a way that will inadvertently confirm a negative stereotype about one's group.

subjective self-awareness A state of mind in which individuals consider themselves from the perspective of the subject and demonstrate little awareness of themselves as individuals.

subjective well-being The feeling of how satisfied one is with one's life.

susto A condition in which an individual feels that a frightening experience has dislodged the soul from his or her body, leading to a wide range of physical and psychological symptoms.

taijin kyoufushou **(TKS)** A disorder similar to *social anxiety disorder* in that it involves fear elicited by social situations, but it is also characterized by physical symptoms, including extensive blushing, body odor, sweating, and a penetrating gaze.

theory of mind A human ability to understand that others have minds that are different from one's own, and thus that other people have their own distinct perspectives and intentions.

transmitted culture The notion that people learn about particular cultural practices through social learning or by modeling the behavior of others who live near them.

two-factor theory of emotions A theory that maintains that emotions are primarily our interpretations of physiological responses to stimuli.

unpackaging Identifying the underlying variables that give rise to different cultural differences.

upward social comparison An individual's comparison of his or her performance with someone who is doing better.

voodoo death A condition in which an individual is convinced that he or she has been cursed or has broken a taboo, which results in a severe level of fear that sometimes leads to death.

WEIRD societies Western, Educated, Industrialized, Rich and Democratic societies—a shorthand for the kinds of societies that the psychological database is largely based on.

Whorfian hypothesis Strong form: The words that are available to people determine how they think. Weak form: The words that are available to people influence how they think.

within-group manipulation A type of experimental manipulation in which each participant receives more than one level of the *independent variable(s)*.

REFERENCES

Abarbanell, L., & Hauser, M. D. (2010). Mayan morality: An exploration of permissible harms. *Cognition. 115,* 207–224.

Abel, T. M., & Hsu, F. I. (1949). Some aspects of personality of Chinese as revealed by the Rorschach Test. *Journal of Projective Techniques, 13,* 285–301.

Abraido-Lanza, A. F., Chao, M. T., & Florez, K. R. (2005). Do healthy behaviors decline with greater acculturation? Implications for the Latino mortality paradox. *Social Science and Medicine, 61,* 1243–1255.

Abraido-Lanza, A. F., Dohrenwend, B. P., Ng-Mak, D. S., & Turner, J. B. (1999). The Latino mortality paradox: A test of the "salmon bias" and healthy migrant hypotheses. *American Journal of Public Health, 89,* 1543–1548.

Abramson, L. Y., Seligman, M. E. P., & Teasdale, J. D. (1978). Learned helplessness in humans: Critique and reformulation. *Journal of Abnormal Psychology, 87,* 49–74.

Abu-Lughod, L. (1986). *Veiled sentiments.* Berkeley, CA: University of California Press.

Adam, K., & Oswald, I. (1977). Sleep is for tissue restoration. *Journal of the Royal College of Physicians of London, 11,* 387–394.

Adams, G. (2005). The cultural grounding of personal relationship: Enemyship in West African worlds. *Journal of Personality and Social Psychology, 88,* 948–968.

Adams, G., Anderson, S. L., & Adonu, J. K. (2004). The cultural grounding of closeness and intimacy. In D. Mashek & A. Aron (Eds.), *The handbook of closeness and intimacy* (pp. 321–339). Mahwah, NJ: Erlbaum.

Adams, G., & Plaut, V. C. (2003). The cultural grounding of personal relationship: Friendship in North American and West African worlds. *Personal Relationships, 10,* 333–348.

Adams, R. B., Rule, N. O., Franklin, R. G., Wang, E., Stevenson, M. T., Yoshikawa, S., et al. (2010). Cross-cultural reading the mind in the eyes: An fMRI investigation. *Journal of Cognitive Neuroscience, 22,* 97–108.

Adeofe, L. (2004). Personal identity in African metaphysics. In L. M. Brown (Ed.), *African philosophy: New and traditional perspectives* (pp. 69–83). New York, NY: Oxford University Press.

Adler, N. E., Epel, E. S., Castellazzo, G., & Ickovics, J. R. (2000). Relationship of subjective and objective social status with psychological and physiological functioning: Preliminary data in healthy, White women. *Health Psychology, 19,* 586–592.

Agiobu-Kemmer, I. (1984). Cognitive aspects of infant development. In H. V. Curran (Ed.), *Nigerian children: Developmental perspectives* (pp. 74–117). London: Routledge Kegan Paul.

Aiello, L. C., & Wheeler, P. (1995). The expensive-tissue hypothesis: The brain and the digestive system in human and primate evolution. *Current Anthropology, 36,* 199–221.

Akhtar, S. (1988). Four culture-bound psychiatric syndromes in India. *International Journal of Social Psychiatry, 34,* 70–74.

Akinkugbe, O. O. (1985). World epidemiology of hypertension in Blacks. In W. Hall, E. Saunders, & N. Shulman (Eds.), *Hypertension in blacks: Epidemiology, pathophysiology, and treatment* (pp. 3–15). Chicago, IL: Year Book.

Alegria, M., Canino, G., Shrout, P. E., Woo, M., Duan, N., Vila, D., & Meng, X.-L. (2008). Prevalence of mental illness in immigrant and non-immigrant U.S. Latino groups. *American Journal of Psychiatry, 165,* 359–369.

Alesina, A., Giuliano, P., & Nunn, N. (2011). The origins of gender roles: Women and the plough. Working paper, Harvard University.

Allan, G. A. (1979). *A sociology of friendship and kinship.* London: Allen & Unwin.

Allen, M. L., Elliott, M. N., Fugligni, A. J., Morales, L. S., Hambarsoomian, K., & Schuster, M. A. (2008). The relationship between Spanish language use and substance use behaviors among Latino youth: A social network approach. *Journal of Adolescent Health, 43,* 372–379.

Allik, J., & McCrae, R. R. (2004). Toward a geography of personality traits: Patterns of profiles across 36 cultures. *Journal of Cross-Cultural Psychology, 35,* 13–28.

Allport, G. W., & Odbert, H. S. (1936). Trait-names: A psycho-lexical study. *Psychological Monographs: General and Applied, 47,* 171–220. (1, Whole No. 211).

Alogna, V. K., et al. (2014). Registered Replication Report: Schooler and Engstler-Schooler (1990). *Perspectives on Psychological Science, 9,* 556–578.

Altrocchi, J., & Altrocchi, L. (1995). Polyfaceted psychological acculturation in Cook Islanders. *Journal of Cross-Cultural Psychology, 26,* 426–440.

Alvergne, A., Jokela, M., & Lummaa, V. (2010). Personality and reproductive success in a high-fertility human population. *Proceedings of the National Academy of Sciences, 107,* 11745–11750.

Amabile, T. M. (1983). The social psychology of creativity: A componential conceptualization. *Journal of Personality and Social Psychology, 45,* 357–376.

American Psychiatric Association (APA). (2013). *Diagnostic and statistical manual of mental disorders* (5th Ed.). Washington, DC: American Psychiatric Publishing.

Anderson, C. A. (1989). Temperature and aggression: Ubiquitous effects of heat on occurrence of human violence. *Psychological Bulletin, 106,* 74–96.

Anderson, E. (1999). *Code of the street: Decency, violence, and the moral life of the inner city.* New York, NY: Norton.

Anderson, J. C., & Linden, W. (2006, April). *The influence of culture on cardiovascular response to anger.* Citation poster session presented at the annual meeting of the American Psychosomatic Society, Denver, CO.

Anderson, R., Lewis, S. Z., Giachello, A. L., Aday, L. A., & Chiu, G. (1981). Access to medical care among the Hispanic population of the Southwestern United States. *Journal of Health and Social Behavior, 22,* 78–89.

Anderson, S. L., Adams, G., & Plaut, V. C. (2008). The cultural grounding of personal relationship: The importance of attractiveness in everyday life. *Journal of Personality and Social Psychology, 95,* 352–368.

Angel, R., & Thoits, P. (1987). The impact of culture on the cognitive structure of illness. *Culture, Medicine, and Psychiatry, 11,* 465–494.

Apfelbaum, E. P., Norton, M, I., & Sommers, S. R. (2012). Racial color blindness: Emergence, practice, and implications. *Current Directions in Psychological Science, 21,* 205–209.

Apfelbaum, E. P., Pauker, K., Sommers, S. R., & Ambady, N. (2010). In blind pursuit of racial equality. *Psychological Science, 21,* 1587–1592.

Apicella, C. L., Azevedo, E. M., Christakis, N. A., & Fowler, J. H. (2014). Evolutionary origins of the endowment effect: Evidence from hunter-gatherers. *American Economic Review, 104,* 1793–1805.

Apicella, C. L., Little, A. C., & Marlowe, F. W. (2007). Facial averageness and attractiveness in an isolate population of hunter-gatherers. *Perception, 36,* 1813–1820.

Arends-Toth, J., & Van de Vijver, F. (2003). Multiculturalism and acculturation: Views of Dutch and Turkish-Dutch. *European Journal of Social Psychology, 33,* 249–266.

Arendt, H. (1964). *Eichmann in Jerusalem.* New York, NY: Penguin Books.

Argyle, M., Shimoda, K., & Little, B. (1978). Variance due to persons and situations in England and Japan. *British Journal of Social and Clinical Psychology, 17,* 335–337.

Armes, K., & Ward, C. (1989). Cross-cultural transitions and sojourner adjustment in Singapore. *Journal of Social Psychology, 12,* 273–275.

Arnett, J. J. (2000). Emerging adulthood: A theory of development from the late teens through the twenties. *American Psychologist, 55,* 469–480.

Arnett, J. J. (2008). The neglected 95%: Why American psychology needs to become less American. *The American Psychologist, 63*(7), 602–614.

Aron-Brunetiere, R. (1974). *La Beaute et la medecine.* Paris: Stock.

Asch, S. E. (1956). Studies of independence and conformity: A minority of one against a unanimous majority. *Psychological Monographs, 70* (Whole No. 416).

Asch, S. E. (1959). A perspective on social psychology. In S. Koch (Ed.), *Psychology: A study of a science. Vol. 3.* New York, NY: McGraw-Hill.

Asch, S. E. (1962). *Social psychology.* New York, NY: Prentice-Hall.

Ashenburg, K. (2007). *The dirt on clean. An unsanitized history.* Toronto, Ontario: Vintage Canada.

Atran, S., & Norenzayan, A. (2004). Religion's evolutionary landscape: Counterintuition, commitment, compassion, communion. *Behavioral and Brain Sciences, 27,* 713–770.

Auld, J. R., Agrawal, A. A., & Relyea, R. A. (2010). Re-evaluating the costs and limits of adaptive phenotypic plasticity. *Proceedings of the Royal Society B: Biological Sciences, 277,* 503–511.

Averill, J. R. (1985). The social construction of emotion: With special reference to love. In K. J. Gergen & K. E. Davis (Eds.), *The social construction of the person* (pp. 89–109). New York, NY: Springer-Verlag.

Avis, J., & Harris, P. L. (1991). Belief-desire reasoning among Baka children: Evidence for a universal conception of mind. *Child Development, 62,* 460–467.

Azuma, H. (1986). Why study child development in Japan? In H. Stevenson, H. Azuma, & K. Hakuta (Eds.), *Child development and education in Japan* (pp. 3–12). New York, NY: Freeman.

Babiker, I. E., Cox, J. L., & Miller, P. M. C. (1980). The measurement of culture distance and its relationship to medical consultation, symptomatology, and examination performance of overseas students at Edinburgh University. *Social Psychiatry, 15,* 109–116.

Bachman, J. G., & O'Malley, P. M. (1984). Black-White differences in self-esteem: Are they affected by response styles? *American Journal of Sociology, 90,* 624–639.

Bachnik, J. M. (1992). The two "faces" of self and society in Japan. *Ethos, 20,* 3–32.

Bagozzi, R., Wong, N., & Yi, Y. (1999). The role of culture and gender in the relationship between positive and negative affect. *Cognition and Emotion, 13,* 641–672.

Baillargeon, R., & DeVos, J. (1991). Object permanence in young infants: Further evidence. *Child Development, 62,* 1227–1246.

Baillet, D., & Van Lange, P. A. M. (2013). Trust, punishment, and cooperation across 18 societies: A meta-analysis. *Perspectives on Psychological Science, 8,* 363–379.

Bakan, D. (1966). *The duality of human existence.* Chicago, IL: Rand McNally.

Balcetis, E., Dunning, D., Miller, R. L. (2008). Do collectivists know themselves better than individualists? Cross-cultural studies of the holier than thou phenomenon. *Journal of Personality and Social Psychology, 95,* 1252–1267.

Balke, B., & Snow, C. (1965). Anthropological and physiological observations on Tarahumara endurance runners. *American Journal of Physical Anthropology, 23,* 293–302.

Baltzell, E. D. (1979). *Puritan Boston and Quaker Philadelphia.* New York, NY: Free Press.

Barber, B. R. (1995). *Jihad vs. McWorld: Terrorism's challenge to democracy.* New York, NY: Ballantine Books.

Bargh, J. A., Chen, M., & Burrows, L. (1996). Automaticity of social behavior: Direct effects of trait construct and stereotype activation on action. *Journal of Personality and Social Psychology, 71,* 230–244.

Baron-Cohen, S. (2003). *The essential difference: Male and female brains and the truth about autism.* New York, NY: Basic Books.

Baron-Cohen, S., Wheelwright, S., Hill, J., Raste, Y., & Plumb, I. (2001). The "Reading the Mind in the Eyes" Test Revised Version: A study with normal adults and adults with Asperger syndrome or high-functioning autism. *Journal of Child Psychology and Psychiatry, 42,* 241–251.

Barrett, J. L., & Nyhof, M. A. (2001). Spreading non-natural concepts: The role of intuitive conceptual structures in memory and transmission of cultural materials. *Journal of Cognition and Culture, 1,* 69–100.

Barrett, L. F. (2006). Solving the emotion paradox: Categorization and the experience of emotion. *Personality and Social Psychology Review, 10,* 20–46.

Barrett, L. F., Mesquita, B., & Gendron, M. (2011). Context in emotion perception. *Current Directions in Psychological Science, 20,* 286–290.

Barrett, L. F., & Russell, J. A. (1999). Structure of current affect. *Current Directions in Psychological Science, 8,* 10–14.

Barrowclough, C., & Hooley, J. M. (2003). Attributions and expressed emotion: A review. *Clinical Psychology Review, 23,* 849–880.

Bates, M. S., Edwards, W. T., & Anderson, K. O. (1993). Ethnocultural influences on variation in chronic pain perception. *Pain, 52,* 101–112.

Bauer, S. M., et al. (2011). Culture and the prevalence of hallucinations in schizophrenia. *Comprehensive Psychiatry, 52,* 319–325.

Baumeister, R. F. (1987). How the self became a problem: A psychological review of historical research. *Journal of Personality and Social Psychology, 52,* 163–176.

Baumeister, R. F., & Jones, E. E. (1978). When self-presentation is constrained by the target's knowledge: Consistency and compensation. *Journal of Personality and Social Psychology, 36,* 608–618.

Baumrind, D. (1971). Current patterns of parental authority. *Developmental Psychology Monographs, 4* (1, Part 2).

Bayraktaroglu, A. (2001). Advice-giving in Turkish: "Superiority" or "solidarity"? In A. Bayraktaroglu & M. Sifianou (Eds.), *Linguistic politeness across boundaries: The case of Greek and Turkish* (pp. 177–208). Philadelphia, PA: John Benjamins.

Beard, G. M. (1869). *American nervousness.* New York, NY: Putnam's.

Beauvois, J. L., & Dubois, N. (1988). The norm of internality in the explanation of psychological events. *European Journal of Social Psychology, 18,* 299–316.

Bechtoldt, M. N., Choi, H.-S., & Nijstad, B. A. (2012). Individuals in mind, mates by heart: Individualistic self-construal and collective value orientation as predictors of group creativity. *Journal of Experimental Social Psychology, 48,* 838–844.

Bechtoldt, M. N., De Dreu, C. K. W., Nijstad, B. A., & Choi, H. (2010). Motivated Information processing, social tuning, and group creativity. *Journal of Personality and Social Psychology, 99,* 622–637.

Becker, M., et al. (2012). Culture and the distinctiveness motive: Constructing identity in individualistic and collectivistic contexts. *Journal of Personality and Social Psychology, 102,* 833–855.

Becker, S. O., & Woessmann, L. (2009). Was Weber wrong? A human capital theory of Protestant economic history. *Quarterly Journal of Economics, 124,* 531–596.

Beja-Pereira, A., et al. (2003). Gene-culture coevolution between cattle milk protein genes and human lactase genes. *Nature Genetics, 35,* 311–313.

Bell, R. M. (1985). *Holy anorexia.* Chicago, IL: University of Chicago Press.

Bemporad, J. R. (1996). Self-starvation through the ages: Reflections on the pre-history of anorexia nervosa. *International Journal of Eating Disorders, 19,* 217–237.

Bendix, R. (1977). *Max Weber: An intellectual portrait.* Berkeley, CA: University of California Press.

Benedict, R. (1934). *Patterns of culture.* New York, NY: Houghton Mifflin.

Benedict, R. (1946). *The chrysanthemum and the sword.* Boston, MA: Houghton Mifflin.

Benet-Martinez, V., & Waller, N. G. (1995). The Big Seven factor model of personality description: Evidence for its cross-cultural generality in a Spanish sample. *Journal of Personality and Social Psychology, 69,* 701–718.

Benet-Martinez, V., Leu, J., Lee, F., & Morris, M. W. (2002). Negotiating biculturalism: Cultural frame switching in biculturals with oppositional versus compatible cultural identities. *Journal of Cross-Cultural Psychology, 33,* 492–516.

Benet-Martinez, V., & Waller, N. G. (1997). Further evidence for the cross-cultural generality of the Big Seven factor model: Indigenous and imported Spanish personality constructs. *Journal of Personality, 65,* 567–598.

Bennett, W. C., & Zingg, R. M. (1935). The Tarahumara: An Indian tribe of northern Mexico. Chicago, IL: University of Chicago Press.

Berger, J. (2013). *Contagious: Why things catch on.* New York, NY: Simon & Schuster.

Berger, P. L. (1999). *The desecularization of the world: Resurgent religion and world politics.* Grand Rapids, MI: Eerdmans.

Berkman, L. F., & Breslow, L. (1983). *Health and ways of living.* Oxford, UK: Oxford University Press.

Berlin, B., & Kay, P. (1969). *Basic color terms: Their universality and evolution.* Berkeley, CA: University of California Press.

Berman, J. J., Murphy-Berman, V., & Singh, P. (1985). Cross-cultural similarities and differences in perceptions of fairness. *Journal of Cross-Cultural Psychology, 16,* 55–67.

Berry, J. W. (1997). Immigration, acculturation, and adaptation. *Applied psychology: An international review, 46,* 5–68.

Berry, J. W., & Annis, R. C. (1974). Acculturation stress: The role of ecology, culture, and differentiation. *Journal of Cross-Cultural Psychology, 5,* 382–406.

Berry, J. W., & Dasen, P. (1974). *Culture and cognition.* London: Methuen.

Berry, J. W., & Kim, U. (1988). Acculturation and mental health. In P. Dasen, J. W. Berry, & N. Sartorius (Eds.), *Cross-cultural psychology and health: Towards applications* (pp. 207–236). London: Sage.

Berry, J. W., Kim, U., Power, S., Young, M., & Bujaki, M. (1989). Acculturation attitudes in plural societies. *Applied Psychology: An International Review, 38,* 185–206.

Berry, J. W., Phinney, J., Sam, D., & Vedder, P. (2006). *Immigrant youth in cultural transition: Acculturation, identity, and adaptation across national contexts.* Mahwah, NJ: Erlbaum.

Berry, J. W., & Sam, D. (1997). Acculturation and adaptation. In J. W. Berry, M. H. Segall, & C. Kagitcibasi (Eds.), *Handbook of cross-cultural psychology* (Vol. 3, pp. 291–326). Boston, MA: Allyn & Bacon.

Best, J., & Horiuchi, G. T. (1985). The razor blade in the apple: The social construction of urban legends. *Social Problems, 32,* 488–499.

Biernat, M., & Manis, M. (1994). Shifting standards and stereotype-based judgments. *Journal of Personality and Social Psychology, 66,* 5–20.

Bilger, B. (2004, April 5). The height gap: Why Europeans are getting taller and taller—and Americans aren't. *New Yorker,* pp. 38–45.

Biswas-Diener, R., & Diener, E. (2002). Making the best of a bad situation: Satisfaction in the slums of Calcutta. *Social Indicators Research, 55,* 329–352.

Blais, C., Jack, R. E., Scheepers, C., Fiset, D., & Caldara, R. (2008). Culture shapes how we look at faces. *PLoS ONE, 3*(8), e3022.

Blascovich, J., Spencer, S. J., Quinn, D., & Steele, C. M. (2001). African Americans and high blood pressure: The role of stereotype threat. *Psychological Science, 12,* 225–229.

Bleidorn, W., Klimstra, T. A., Denissen, J. J. A., Rentrfrow, P. J., Pottern, J., & Gosling, S. D. (2013). Personality maturation around the world: A cross-cultural examination of social investment theory. *Psychological Science, 24,* 2530–2540.

Block, J. (1995). A contrarian view of the five-factor approach to personality description. *Psychological Bulletin, 117,* 187–215.

Blood, R. O. (1967). *Love match and arranged marriage.* New York, NY: Free Press.

Bloomfield, P. (2004). *Moral reality.* New York, NY: Oxford University Press.

Bochner, S. (1994). Cross-cultural differences in the self-concept: A test of Hofstede's individualism/collectivism distinction. *Journal of Cross-Cultural Psychology, 25,* 273–283.

Boiger, M., Gungor, D., Karasawa, M., & Mesquita, B. (2014). Defending honor, keeping face: Interpersonal affordances of anger and shame in Turkey and Japan. *Cognition and Emotion, 28,* 1255–1269.

Boiger, M., Mesquita, B., Uchida, Y., & Barrett, L. F. (2013). Condoned or condemned: The situational affordance of anger and shame in the United States and Japan. *Personality and Social Psychology Bulletin, 39,* 540–553.

Bond, M. H. (1983). How language variation affects inter-cultural differentiation of values by Hong Kong bilinguals. *Journal of Language and Social Psychology, 2,* 57–76.

Bond, M. H. (1988). Finding universal dimensions of individual variation in multicultural studies of values: The Rokeach and Chinese value surveys. *Journal of Personality and Social Psychology, 55,* 1009–1015.

Bond, M. H., & Cheung, T. (1983). College students' spontaneous self-concept. *Journal of Cross-Cultural Psychology, 14,* 153–171.

Bond, M. H., & Tornatzky, L. G. (1973). Locus of control in students from Japan and the United States: Dimensions and levels of response. *Psychologia, 16,* 209–213.

Bond, R., & Smith, P. B. (1996). Culture and conformity: A meta-analysis of studies using Asch's (1952b, 1956) line judgment task. *Psychological Bulletin, 119,* 111–137.

Bornstein, M. H., Tamis-Lemonda, C., Tal, J., Ludemann, P., Toda, S., Rahn, C., et al. (1992). Functional analysis of the contents of maternal speech to infants of 5 and 13 months in four cultures: Argentina, France, Japan and the United States. *Developmental Psychology, 28,* 593–603.

Boroditsky, L. (2000). Metaphoric structuring: Understanding time through spatial metaphors. *Cognition, 75,* 1–28.

Boroditsky, L., Fuhrman, O., & McCormick, K. (2011). Do English and Mandarin speakers think about time differently? *Cognition, 118,* 123–129.

Boroditsky, L., & Gaby, A. (2010). Remembrances of times East: Absolute spatial representations of time in an Australian Aboriginal community. *Psychological Science, 21,* 1635–1639.

Boserup, E. (1970). *Woman's role in economic development.* London: Allen and Unwin.

Boucher, H. C. (2011). The dialectical self-concept II: Cross-role and within-role consistency, well-being, self-certainty, and authenticity. *Journal of Cross-Cultural Psychology, 42,* 1251–1271.

Bowdler, S. (1982). Prehistoric archaeology in Tasmania. In F. Wedorf & A. E. Close (Eds.), *Advances in world archaeology, Vol. 1* (pp. 1–49). New York, NY: Academic Press.

Boyd, R., Richerson, J. P., & Henrich, J. (2011). *The cultural niche.* Unpublished manuscript, University of California at Los Angeles.

Boyd, R., & Silk, J. B. (2006). *How humans evolved* (4th ed.). New York, NY: Norton.

Boyer, P., & Ramble, C. (2001). Cognitive templates for religious concepts: Cross-cultural evidence for recall of counter-intuitive representations. *Cognitive Science, 25,* 535–564.

Brafman, O., & Brafman, R. (2009). *Sway: The irresistible pull of irrational behavior.* New York, NY: Broadway Books.

Brambilla, M., Riva, P., & Rule, N. O. (2013). Familiarity increases the accuracy of categorizing male sexual orientation. *Personality and Individual Differences, 55,* 193–195.

Bramble, D. M., & Lieberman, D. E. (2004). Endurance running and the evolution of *Homo. Nature, 432,* 345–352.

Bräuer, J., Call, J., & Tomasello, M. (2007). Chimpanzees really know what others can see in a competitive situation. *Animal Cognition, 10,* 439–448.

Brehm, J. (1956). Postdecision changes in the desirability of alternatives. *Journal of Abnormal and Social Psychology, 52,* 384–389.

Brewer, M. B. (1991). The social self: On being the same and different at the same time. *Personality and Social Psychology Bulletin, 17,* 475–482.

Briggs, J. L. (1970). *Never in anger: Portrait of an Eskimo family.* Cambridge, MA: Harvard University Press.

Brislin, R. W. (1970). Back-translation for cross-cultural research. *Journal of Cross-Cultural Psychology, 1,* 185–216.

Brocklehurst, M. (2005, November). *Innovation indicators in the financial times.* Thompson Scientific. Retrieved from http://science.thomsonreuters.com/news/2005-11/8298269

Brody, G. H., Yu, T., Chen, E., Miller, G. E., Kogan, S. M., & Beach, S. R. H. (2013). Is resilience only skin deep? Rural African Americans' socioeconomic status-related risk and competence in preadolescence and psychological adjustment and allostatic load at age 19. *Psychological Science, 24,* 1285–1293.

Brody, J. (1982, July 14). Personal Health. *New York Times.*

Brosschot, J. F., & Thayer, J. F. (1998). Anger inhibition, cardiovascular recovery, and vagal function: A model of the link between hostility and cardiovascular disease. *Annals of Behavior Medicine, 20,* 326–332.

Broude, G. J., & Green, S. J. (1983). Cross-cultural codes on husband-wife relationships. *Ethology, 22,* 273–274.

Brown, D. E. (1991). *Human universals.* Philadelphia, PA: Temple University Press.

Brown, J. D., & Kobayashi, C. (2002). Self-enhancement in Japan and America. *Asian Journal of Social Psychology, 5,* 145–168.

Brown, R. A. (2013). Self-ambivalence and psychological adjustment in cultural context: Focus on Japan. *Journal of Cross-Cultural Psychology, 44,* 1263–1274.

Brown, R. P., Osterman, L. L., Barnes, C. D. (2009). School violence and the culture of honor. *Psychological Science, 20,* 1400–1405.

Bruner, J. (1990). *Acts of meaning.* Cambridge, MA: Harvard University Press.

Buchtel, E. (2014). Cultural sensitivity or cultural stereotyping? Positive and negative effects of a cultural psychology class. *International Journal of Intercultural Relations, 39,* 40–52.

Buchtel, E. E. (2009). *A sense of obligation—Culture and the subjective experience of meeting expectations.* Unpublished doctoral dissertation, University of British Columbia.

Buckle, C., Chuah, Y. M. L., Fones, C. S. L., & Wong, A. H. C. (2007). A conceptual history of *koro. Transcultural Psychiatry, 44,* 27–43.

Bugental, D. B., & Cortez, V. L. (1988). Physiological reactivity to responsive and unresponsive children as moderated by perceived control. *Child Development, 59,* 686–693.

Bunker, J. P., & Gomby, D. S. (1989). Preface: Socioeconomic status and health: An examination of underlying processes. In J. P. Bunker, D. S. Gomby, & B. H. Kerner (Eds.), *Pathways to health.* Menlo Park, CA: The Henry J. Kaiser Family Foundation.

Burish, M. J., Kueh, H. Y., & Wang, S. S. H. (2004). Brain architecture and social complexity in modern and ancient birds. *Brain, Behavior, and Evolution, 63,* 107–125.

Burton, R., & Whiting, J. (1961). The absent father and cross-sex identity. *Merrill-Palmer Quarterly, 7,* 85–95.

Bushnell, J. A., Wells, J. E., Hornblow, A. R., Oakley-Browne, M. A., & Joyce, P. (1990). Prevalence of three bulimia syndromes in the general population. *Psychological Medicine, 20,* 671–680.

Buss, D. M. (1989). Sex differences in human mate preferences: Evolutionary hypotheses tested in 37 cultures. *Behavioral and Brain Sciences, 12,* 1–49.

Butler, E. A., Lee, T. L., & Gross, J. J. (2009). Does expressing your emotions raise or lower your blood pressure? The answer depends on cultural context. *Journal of Cross-Cultural Psychology, 40,* 510–517.

Butler, J. C. (2000). Personality and emotional correlates of right-wing authoritarianism. *Social Behavior and Personality, 28,* 1–14.

Butterworth, B., Reeve, R., & Reynolds, F. (2011). Using mental representations of space when words are unavailable: Studies of enumeration and arithmetic in indigenous Australia. *Journal of Cross-Cultural Psychology, 42,* 630–638.

Butterworth, P., Cherbuin, N., Sachdev, P., & Anstey, K. J. (2012). The association between financial hardship and amygdala and hippocampal volumes: Results from the PATH through life project. *Social Cognitive and Affective Neuroscience, 7,* 548–556.

Byrne, D. (1961). Interpersonal attraction and attitude similarity. *Journal of Abnormal and Social Psychology, 62,* 713–715.

Byrne, D., Clore, G. L., & Worchel, P. (1966). Effect of economic similarity-dissimilarity on interpersonal attraction. *Journal of Personality and Social Psychology, 4,* 220–224.

Cacioppo, J. T., Berntson, G. G., Larsen, H. T., Poehlmann, K. M., & Ito, T. A. (2000). The psychophysiology of emotion. In R. Lewis & J. M. Haviland-Jones (Eds.), *The handbook of emotion* (2nd ed., pp. 173–191). New York, NY: Guilford.

Cai, H., Kwan, V. S. Y., & Sedikides, C. (2012). A sociocultural approach to narcissism: The case of modern China. *European Journal of Personality, 26,* 529–535.

Callaghan, T., Rochat, P., Lillard, A., Claux, M. L., Odden, H., Itakura, S., et al. (2005). Synchrony in the onset of mental-state reasoning: Evidence from five cultures. *Psychological Science, 16,* 378–384.

Cameron, J. E., & Lalonde, R. N. (1994). Self, ethnicity, and social group memberships in two generations of Italian Canadians. *Personality and Social Psychology Bulletin, 20,* 514–520.

Cameron, L., Erkal, N., Gangadharan, L., & Meng, X. (2013). Little emperors: Behavioral impacts of China's One-Child Policy. Science, 339, 953-957.

Campbell, D. T., & Fiske, D. W. (1959). Convergent and discrimination validation by the multitrait multimethod matrix. *Psychological Bulletin, 56,* 81–105.

Campbell, J. D., Trapnell, P., Heine, S. J., Katz, I. M., Lavallee, L. F., & Lehman, D. R. (1996). Self-concept clarity: Measurement, personality correlates, and cultural boundaries. *Journal of Personality and Social Psychology, 70,* 141–156.

Cannon, T. D. (1998). Genetic and perinatal influences in the etiology of schizophrenia: A neurodevelopmental model. In M. F. Lenzenweger & R. H. Dworkin (Eds.), *Origins and development of schizophrenia: Advances in experimental psychopathology* (pp. 67–92). Washington, DC: American Psychological Association.

Cannon, T. D., van Erp, T. G. M., Huttunen, M., Lönnqvist, J., Salonen, O., Valanne, L., et al. (1998). Regional grey matter, white matter, and cerebrospinal fluid distributions in schizophrenic patients, their siblings, and controls. *Archives of General Psychiatry, 55,* 1084–1091.

Cantlon, J. F., Cordes, S., Libertus, M. E., & Brannon, E. M. (2009). Comment on "Log or linear? Distinct intuitions of the number scale in Western and Amazonian indigene cultures." *Science, 323,* 38b.

Cao, J., Galinsky, A. D., & Maddux, W. W. (2014). Does travel broaden the mind? Breadth of foreign experiences increases generalized trust. *Social Psychological and Personality Science, 5,* 517–525.

Carey, S. (1985). *Conceptual change in childhood.* Cambridge, MA: Bradford Books.

Carey, S. (2004). Bootstrapping and the origins of concepts. *Daedalus,* 59–68.

Carnegie, D. (1936). *How to win friends and influence people.* New York, NY: Simon & Schuster.

Carr, J. E. (1978). Ethno-behaviorism and the culture-bound syndromes: The case of amok. *Culture, Medicine, and Psychiatry, 2,* 269–293.

Carrier, D. R. (1984). The energetic paradox of human running and hominid evolution. *Current Anthropology, 25,* 283–295.

Cassidy, C. M. (1991). The good body: When big is better. *Medical Anthropology, 13,* 181–213.

Caudill, W. A., & Schooler, C. (1973). Child behavior and child rearing in Japan and the United States: An interim report. *Journal of Nervous and Mental Disease, 157,* 323–338.

Caudill, W., & Weinstein, H. (1969). Maternal care and infant behavior in Japan and America. *Psychiatry, 32,* 12–43.

Cavalcanti, T. V., Parente, S. L., & Zhao, R. (2007). Religion in macroeconomics: A quantitative analysis of Weber's thesis. *Economic Theory, 32,* 105–123.

Cavalli-Sforza, L. L., & Feldman, M. W. (1981). *Cultural transmission and evolution.* Princeton, NJ: Princeton University Press.

Cawte, J. E. (1976). *Malgri:* A culture-bound syndrome. In W. P. Lebra (Ed.), *Culture-bound syndromes, ethnopsychiatry, and alternate therapies* (pp. 22–31). Honolulu, HI: University Press of Hawaii.

Centers for Disease Control and Prevention (CDC). (2004). Trends in intake of energy and macronutrients—United States, 1971–2000. *Morbidity and Mortality Weekly Report, 53,* 80–82.

Central Intelligence Agency. (2006a). *CIA world factbook rank order—GDP per capita.* Retrieved from www.cia.gov/cia/publications/factbook/rankorder/2004rank.html.

Central Intelligence Agency. (2006b). *CIA world factbook rank order—life expectancy at birth.* Retrieved from www.cia.gov/cia/publications/factbook/rankorder/2102rank.html.

Chandler, M., Lalonde, C., Sokol, B., & Hallett, D. (2003). Personal persistence, identity development and suicide. *Monographs of the Society for Research in Child Development, 68,* 1–129.

Chandra, S. (1973). The effects of group pressure in perception: A cross-cultural conformity study. *International Journal of Psychology, 8,* 37–39.

Chang, W. C. (1985). A cross-cultural study of depressive symptomatology. *Culture, Medicine, and Psychiatry, 9,* 295–317.

Chang, W. C., Chua, W. L., & Toh, Y. (1997). The concept of psychological control in the Asian context. In K. Leung, U. Kim, S. Yamaguchi, & Y. Kashima (Eds.), *Progress in Asian social psychology* (pp. 95–117). Singapore: Wiley.

Chang, Y. H., Rin, H., & Chen, C. C. (1975). Frigophobia: A report of five cases. *Bulletin of the Chinese Society of Neurology and Psychiatry, 1*(2), 9–13 (in Chinese).

Chao, R. K. (1994). Beyond parental control and authoritarian parenting style: Understanding Chinese parenting through the cultural notion of training. *Child Development, 65,* 1111–1119.

Chao, R. K., & Tseng, V. (2002). Parenting of Asians. In M. H. Bornstein (Ed.), *Handbook of parenting: Vol. R: Social conditions and applied parenting* (2nd ed., pp. 59–93). Mahwah, NJ: Erlbaum.

Chase-Landsale, L. P., & Gordon, R. A. (1996). Economic hardship and the development of five- and six-year-olds: Neighborhood and regional perspectives. *Child Development, 67,* 3338–3367.

Chee, M. W., Caplan, D., Soon, C. S., Sriram, N., Tan, E. W. L., Tiel, T., et al. (1999). Processing of visually presented sequences in Mandarin and English studies with fMRI. *Neuron, 23,* 127–137.

Chen, C., Burton, M. L., Greenberger, E., & Dmitrieva, J. (1999). Population migration and the variation of dopamine (DRD4) allele frequencies around the globe. *Evolution and Human Behavior, 20,* 309–324.

Chen, C., Lee, S.-Y., & Stevenson, H. W. (1995). Response style and cross-cultural comparisons of rating scales among East Asian and North American students. *Psychological Science, 6,* 170–175.

Chen, E. (2004). Why socioeconomic status affects the health of children: A psychosocial perspective. *Current Directions in Psychological Science, 13,* 112–115.

Chen, E. (2007). Impact of socioeconomic status on physiological health in adolescents: An experimental manipulation of psychosocial factors. *Psychosomatic Medicine, 69,* 348–355.

Chen, E., & Matthews, K. A. (2001). Cognitive appraisal biases: An approach to understanding the relation between socioeconomic status and cardiovascular reactivity in children. *Annals of Behavioral Medicine, 23,* 101–111.

Chen, J. M., Kim, H. S., Mojaverian, T., & Morling, B. (2012). Culture and social support provision: Who gives what and why. *Personality and Social Psychology Bulletin, 38,* 3–13.

Chen, S. X., & Bond, M. H. (2010). Two languages, two personalities? Examining language effects on the expression of personality in a bilingual context. *Personality and Social Psychology Bulletin, 36,* 1514–1528.

Chen, X., Rubin, K. H., & Li, Z. (1995). Social functioning and adjustment in Chinese children: A longitudinal study. *Developmental Psychology, 31,* 531–539.

Cheney, D. L., & Seyfarth, R. M. (1990). *How monkeys see the world.* Chicago, IL: University of Chicago Press.

Cheng, C., Cheung, S.-F., Chio, J. H.-M., & Chan, M.-P. S. (2013). Cultural meaning of perceived control: A meta-analysis of locus of control and psychological symptoms across 18 cultural regions. *Psychological Bulletin, 139,* 152–188.

Cheng, C.-Y., & Leung, A. K.-Y. (2013). Revisiting the multicultural experience–creativity link. The effects of perceived cultural distance and comparison mindset. *Social Psychological and Personality Science, 4,* 475–482.

Chentsova-Dutton, Y. E. (2012). Butting in vs. being a friend: Cultural differences and similarities in the evaluation of imposed social support. *Journal of Social Psychology, 152,* 493–509.

Chentsova-Dutton, Y., Chu, J. P., Tsai, J. L., Rottenberg, J., Gross, J. J., & Gotlib, I. H. (2007). Depression and emotional reactivity: Variation among Asian Americans of East Asian descent and European Americans. *Journal of Abnormal Psychology, 116,* 776–785.

Chentsova-Dutton, Y. E., Tsai, J. L., & Gotlib, I. H. (2010). Further evidence for the cultural norm hypothesis: Positive emotion in depressed and control European-American and Asian-American women. *Cultural Diversity and Ethnic Minority Psychology, 16,* 284–295.

Chentsova-Dutton, Y. E., & Vaughn, A. (2012). Let me tell you what to do: Cultural differences in advice-giving. *Journal of Cross-Cultural Psychology, 43,* 687–703.

Chernoff, H. (1973). Using faces to represent points in k-dimensional space graphically. *Journal of the American Statistical Association, 68,* 361–368.

Cheryan, S., & Monin, B. (2005). "Where are you *really* from?" Asian Americans and identity denial. *Journal of Personality and Social Psychology, 89,* 717–730.

Cheung, B. Y., Chudek, M., & Heine, S. J. (2011). Evidence for a sensitive period for acculturation: Younger immigrants report acculturating at a faster rate. *Psychological Science, 22,* 147–152.

Cheung, B. Y., Takemura, T., & Heine, S. J. (2014). *Cultural influences on sleep in Japan and Canada.* Unpublished manuscript. University of British Columbia.

Cheung, F. M., Cheung, S. F., Leung, K., Ward, C., & Leong, F. (2003). The English version of the Chinese Personality Assessment Inventory. *Journal of Cross-Cultural Psychology, 34,* 433–452.

Cheung, F. M., Leung, K., Fan, R. M., Song, W., Zhang, J., & Zhang, J. (1996). Development of the Chinese Personality Assessment Inventory. *Journal of Cross-Cultural Psychology, 27,* 181–199.

Chiang, J. J., Saphire-Bernstein, S., Kim, H. S., Sherman, D. K., & Taylor, S. E. (2013). Cultural differences in the link between supportive relationships and proinflammatory cytokines. *Social Psychological and Personality Science, 4,* 511–520.

Chiao, J. Y., & Blizinsky, K. D. (2010). Culture-gene coevolution of individualism-collectivism and the serotonin transporter gene. *Proceedings of the Royal Society B: Biological Sciences, 277,* 529–537.

Chiao, J. Y., Iidaka, T., Gordon, H. L., Noguchi, J., Bar, M., Aminoff, E., et al. (2008). Cultural specificity in amygdala response to fear faces. *Journal of Cognitive Neuroscience, 20,* 2167–2174.

Chiao, J. Y., et al. (2009). Neural basis of individualistic and collectivistic views of self. *Human Brain Mapping, 30,* 2813–2820.

Chirkov, V. (2009). Summary of the criticism and of the potential ways to improve acculturation psychology. *International Journal of Intercultural Relations, 33,* 177–180.

Chiu, C., Dweck, C. S., Tong, J. U., & Fu, J. H. (1997). Implicit theories and conceptions of morality. *Journal of Personality and Social Psychology, 73,* 923–940.

Chiu, L. H. (1972). A cross-cultural comparison of cognitive styles in Chinese and American children. *International Journal of Psychology, 7,* 235–242.

Choi, I., & Choi, Y. (2002). Culture and self-concept flexibility. *Personality and Social Psychology Bulletin, 28,* 1508–1517.

Choi, I., Dalal, R., Kim-Prieto, C., & Park. H. (2003). Culture and judgement of causal relevance. *Journal of Personality and Social Psychology, 84,* 46–59.

Choi, I., & Nisbett, R. E. (1998). Situational salience and cultural differences in the correspondence bias and in the actor-observer bias. *Personality and Social Psychology Bulletin, 24,* 949–960.

Choi, S., & Gopnik, A. (1995). Early acquisition of verbs in Korean: A cross-linguistic study. *Journal of Child Language, 22,* 497–529.

Chomsky, N. (1965). *Aspects of the theory of syntax.* Cambridge, MA: MIT Press.

Christakis, N. A., & Fowler, J. H. (2009). *Connected: How your friends' friends' friends affect everything you feel, think, and do.* New York, NY: Back Bay Books.

Chua, A. (2011). *Battle hymn of the tiger mother.* New York, NY: Penguin Press.

Chua, H. F., Boland, J. E., & Nisbett, R. E. (2005). Cultural variation in eye movements during scene perception. *Proceedings of the National Academy of Science, 102,* 12629–12633.

Chudek, M., Cheung, B. Y., & Heine, S. J. (in press). U.S. immigrants' patterns of acculturation are sensitive to their age, language, and cultural contact but show no evidence of a sensitive window for acculturation. *Journal of Culture and Cognition.*

Chudek, M., Heller, S., Birch, S., & Henrich, J. (2011). *Prestige-biased cultural learning: Bystander's differential attention to potential models influences children's learning.* Unpublished manuscript. University of British Columbia.

Church, A. T. (1982). Sojourner adjustment. *Psychological Bulletin, 91,* 540–572.

Church, A. T., Katigbak, M. S., Del Prado, A. M., Ortiz, F. A., Mastor, K. A., Harumi, Y., et al. (2006). Implicit theories and self-perceptions of traitedness across cultures: Toward integration of cultural and trait psychology perspectives. *Journal of Cross-Cultural Psychology, 37*(6), 694–716.

Church, A. T., Katigbak, M. S., & Reyes, J. A. S. (1998). Further exploration of Filipino personality structure using the lexical approach: Do the Big Five or Big Seven dimensions emerge? *European Journal of Personality, 12,* 249–269.

Church, A. T., Reyes, J. A. S., Katigbak, M. S., & Grimm, S. D. (1997). Filipino personality structure and the Big Five Model: A lexical approach. *Journal of Personality, 65,* 477–528.

Cialdini, R. B., Borden, R. J., Thorne, A., Walker, M. R., Freeman, S., & Sloan, L. R. (1976). Basking in reflected glory: Three (football) field studies. *Journal of Personality and Social Psychology, 34,* 366–375.

Cialdini, R. B., Wosinka, W., Barrett, D. W., Butner, J., & Gornik-Durose, M. (1999). Compliance with a request in two cultures. The differential influence of social proof and commitment/consistency on collectivists and individualists. *Personality and Social Psychology Bulletin, 25,* 1242–1253.

Clancy, P. M. (1986). The acquisition of communicative styles in Japanese. In B. B. Schieffelin & E. Ochs (Eds.), *Language socialization across cultures* (pp. 213–230). Cambridge, UK: Cambridge University Press.

Clark, D. M., & Wells, A. (1995). A cognitive model of social phobia. In R. G. Heimberg, M. Liebowitz, D. A. Hope, & F. Schneier (Eds.), *Social phobia: Diagnosis, assessment, and treatment* (pp. 69–93). New York, NY: Guilford.

Clements, F. E. (1932). Primitive concepts of disease. *University of California Publications in American Archaeology and Ethnology, 32,* 185–253.

Clifford, M. M., & Walster, E. (1973). The effect of physical attractiveness on teacher expectations. *Sociology of Education, 46,* 248–258.

Clutton-Brock, T. H., & Harvey, P. H. (1980). Primates, brains and ecology. *Journal of Zoology (London), 190,* 309–323.

Cogan, J. C., Bhalla, S. K., Sefa-Dedeh, A., & Rothblum, E. D. (1996). A comparison study of United States and African students on perceptions of obesity and thinness. *Journal of Cross-Cultural Psychology, 27,* 98–113.

Cohen, A. B., & Rozin, P. (2001). Religion and the morality of mentality. *Journal of Personality and Social Psychology, 81,* 697–710.

Cohen, A. B., Siegel, J. I., & Rozin, P. (2003). Faith versus practice: Different bases for religiosity judgments by Jews and Protestants.

European Journal of Social Psychology, 33, 287–295.

Cohen, D. (1996). Law, social policy, and violence: The impact of regional cultures. *Journal of Personality and Social Psychology, 70,* 961–978.

Cohen, D. (2001). Cultural variation: Considerations and implications. *Psychological Bulletin, 127,* 451–471.

Cohen, D. (2007). Four questions from a relatively young field. In S. Kitayama & D. Cohen (Eds.), *Handbook of cultural psychology.* New York, NY: Guilford.

Cohen, D., & Gunz, A. (2002). As seen by the other . . . The self from the "outside in" and the "inside out" in the memories and emotional perceptions of Easterners and Westerners. *Psychological Science, 13,* 55–59.

Cohen, D., Kim, E., & Hudson, N. W. (2014). Religion, the forbidden, and sublimation. *Current Directions in Psychological Science, 23,* 208–214.

Cohen, D., & Nisbett, R. E. (1994). Self-protection and the culture of honor: Explaining Southern homicide. *Personality and Social Psychology Bulletin, 20,* 551–567.

Cohen, D., & Nisbett, R. E. (1997). Field experiments examining the culture of honor: The role of institutions in perpetuating norms about violence. *Personality and Social Psychology Bulletin, 23,* 1188–1199.

Cohen, D., Nisbett, R. E., Bowdle, B. F., & Schwarz, N. (1996). Insult, aggression, and the Southern culture of honor: An "experimental ethnography." *Journal of Personality and Social Psychology, 70,* 945–960.

Cohen, D., Vandello, J., Puente, S., & Rantilla, A. (1999). "When you call me that, smile!": How norms for politeness, interaction styles, and aggression work together in southern culture. *Social Psychology Quarterly, 62,* 257–275.

Cohen, G. L., Garcia, J., Apfel, N., & Master, A. (2006). Reducing the racial achievement gap: A social-psychological intervention. *Science, 313,* 1307–1310.

Cohen, S., & Wills, T. A. (1985). Stress, social support, and the buffering hypothesis. *Psychological Bulletin, 98,* 310–357.

Cole, M. (1996). *Cultural psychology: A once and future discipline.* Cambridge, MA: Belknap Press.

Cole, M., & Scribner, M. (1974). *Culture and thought.* New York, NY: Wiley.

Cole, M., Gay, J., Glick, J. A., & Sharp, D. W. (1971). *The cultural context of learning and thinking.* New York, NY: Basic Books.

Collard, M., Shennan, S., & Tehrani, J. J. (2005). Branching versus blending in macroscale cultural evolution: A comparative study. In C. P. Lipo, M. J. O'Brien, S. Shennan, & M. Collard (Eds.), *Mapping our ancestors: Phylogenetic methods in anthropology and prehistory.* Hawthorne, NY: Aldine de Gruyter.

Colzato, L. S., van Beest, I., van den Wildenberg, W. P. M., Scorolli, C., Dorchin, S., Meiran, N., Borghi, A. J., & Hommel, B. (2010). God: Do I have your attention? *Cognition, 117,* 87–94.

Colzato, L., S., van den Wildenberg, W. P., & Hommel, B. (2008). Losing the big picture: How religion controls visual attention. *PLoS ONE, 3*(11), e3679.

Conroy, M., Hess, R. D., Azuma, H., & Kashiwagi, K. (1980). Maternal strategies for regulating children's behavior in Japanese and American families. *Journal of Cross-Cultural Psychology, 11,* 153–172.

Cooper, R. S., Wolf-Maier, K., Luke, A., Adeyemo, A., Banegas, J. R., Forrester, T., et al. (2005). An international comparative study of blood pressure in populations of European vs. African descent. *BMC Medicine, 3,* 2.

Corliss, R. (2001, July 9). Film director: Ang Lee. *Time.*

Corral, I., & Landrine, H. (2008). Acculturation and ethnic-minority health behavior: A test of the operant model. *Health Psychology, 27,* 737–745.

Costa, P. T., Jr., & McCrae, R. R. (1992). *Revised NEO Personality Inventory (NEO-PI-R) and NEO Five-Factor Inventory (NEO-FFI) professional manual.* Odessa, FL: Psychological Assessment Resources.

Cousins, S. D. (1989). Culture and selfhood in Japan and the U.S. *Journal of Personality and Social Psychology, 56,* 124–131.

Cousins, S. D. (1990). *Culture and social phobia in Japan and the United States.* Unpublished doctoral dissertation. University of Michigan.

Crespo, C. J., Ainsworth, B. E., Keteyian, S. J., Heath, G. W., & Smit, E. (1999). Prevalence of physical inactivity and its relation to social class in U.S. adults: Results from the Third National Health and Nutrition Examination Survey, 1988–1994. *Medicine and Science in Sports and Exercise, 31,* 1821.

Cromer, D., Wolinsky, S. M., & McLean, A. R. (2010). How fast could HIV change gene frequencies in the human population? *Proceedings of the Royal Society B, 277,* 1981–1989.

Crook, T. (2008). Norms, forms, and beds: Spatializing sleep in Victorian Britain. *Body and Society, 14*(4), 15–35.

Cross, P. (1977). Not can but will college teaching be improved? *New Directions for Higher Education, 17,* 1–15.

Cross, S. E. (1995). Self-construals, coping, and stress in cross-cultural adaptation. *Journal of Cross-Cultural Psychology, 26,* 673–697.

Csikszentmihalyi, M. (1996). *Creativity.* New York, NY: Harper Collins.

Csikszentmihalyi, M., & Hunter, J. (2003). Happiness in everyday life: The uses of experience sampling. *Journal of Happiness Studies, 4,* 185–199.

Cullum, J. G., & Harton, H. C. (2007). Cultural evolution: Interpersonal influence, issue importance, and the development of shared attitudes in college residence halls. *Personality and Social Psychology Bulletin, 33,* 1327–1339.

Cunningham, M. R. (1986). Measuring the physical in physical attractiveness: Quasi-experiments on the sociobiology of female facial beauty. *Journal of Personality and Social Psychology, 50,* 925–935.

Cunningham, M. R., Barbee, A. P., & Pike, C. L. (1990). What do women want? Facialmetric assessment of multiple motives in the perception of male facial physical attractiveness. *Journal of Personality and Social Psychology, 59,* 61–72.

Cunningham, M. R., Roberts, A. R., Barbee, A. P., Druen, P. B., & Wu, C.-H. (1995). "Their ideas of beauty are, on the whole, the same as ours": Consistency and variability in the cross-cultural perception of female physical attractiveness. *Journal of Personality and Social Psychology, 68,* 261–279.

Curhan, K. B., Sims, T., Markus, H. R., Kitayama, S., Karasawa, M., Kawakami, N., Love, G. D., Coe, C. L., Miyamoto, Y., & Ryff, C. D. (2014). *Psychological Science, 25,* 2277–2280.

Custance, D., Whiten, A., & Fredman, T. (1999). Social learning of an artificial fruit task in capuchin monkeys (Cebus apella). *Journal of Comparative Psychology, 113,* 13–23.

Danziger, S., & Ward, R. (2010). Language changes implicit associations between ethnic groups and evaluation in bilinguals. *Psychological Science, 21,* 799–800.

Darwin, C. (1871). *The descent of man, and selection in relation to sex.* London: John Murray.

Darwin, C. (1872/1965). *The expression of emotions in man and animals.* Chicago, IL: University of Chicago Press.

Dasen, P. R. (2000). Rapid social change and the turmoil of adolescence: A cross-cultural perspective. *International Journal of Group Tensions, 29,* 17–49.

David, R., & Collins, J. (1991). Bad outcomes in Black babies: Race or racism? *Ethnicity and Disease, 1,* 216–244.

Davies, I. R. L. (1997). Colour cognition is more universal than colour language. *Behavioral and Brain Sciences, 20,* 186–187.

Davis, B. E., Moon, R. Y., Sachs, H. C., & Ottolini, M. C. (1998). Effects of sleep position on infant motor development. *Pediatrics, 102,* 1135–1140.

Dawkins, R. (1976). *The selfish gene.* Oxford: Oxford University Press.

de la Fuente, J., Santiago, J., Roman, A., Dumitrache, C., & Casasanto, D. (2014). When you think about it, your past is in front of you: How culture shapes spatial conceptions of time. *Psychological Science, 25,* 1682–1690.

De Leersnyder, J., Mesquita, B., & Kim, H. S. (2011). Where do my emotions belong? A study of immigrants' emotional acculturation. *Personality and Social Psychology Bulletin, 37,* 451–463.

De Leersnyder, J., Mesquita, B., Kim, H., Eom, K., & Choi, H. (2014). Emotional fit with culture: A predictor of individual differences in relational well-being. *Emotion, 14,* 241–245.

De Raad, B., Barelds, D. P., Levert, E., Ostendorf, F., Mlacic, B., et al. (2010). Only three personality factors are fully replicable across languages: A comparison of 14 trait tatunomies. *Journal of Personality and Social Psychology, 98,* 160–173.

de Tocqueville, A. (1835/1969). In J. P. Mayer (Ed.), *Democracy in America* (trans. G. Lawrence). Chicago, IL: University of Chicago Press.

de Waal, F. (2001). *The ape and the sushi master: Cultural reflections of a primatologist.* New York, NY: Basic Books.

Deacon, T. W. (1997). *The symbolic species: The co-evolution of language and the brain.* New York, NY: Norton.

Dean, L. G., Kendal, R. L., Schapiro, S. J., Thierry, B., & Laland, K. N. (2012). Identification of the social and cognitive processes underlying human cumulative culture. *Science, 335,* 1114–1118.

Dean, L. G., Vale, G. L., Laland, K. N., Flynn, E., & Kendal, R. L. (2014). Human cumulative culture: A comparative perspective. *Biological Reviews, 89,* 284–301.

Deecke, V. B., Ford, J. K. B., & Spong, P. (2000). Dialect change in resident killer whales: Implications for vocal learning and cultural transmission. *Animal Behaviour, 60,* 629–638.

Dehaene, S. (1997). *The number sense: How the mind creates mathematics.* Oxford, UK: Oxford University Press.

Dehaene, S., Izard, V., Spelke, E., & Pica, P. (2008). Log or linear? Distinct intuitions of the number scale in Western and Amazonian indigenous cultures. *Science, 320,* 1217–1220.

Del Pilar, J. A., & Udasco, J. O. (2004). Deculturation: Its lack of validity. *Cultural Diversity and Ethnic Minority Psychology, 10,* 169–176.

Derex, M., Beugin, M., Godelle, B., & Raymond, M. (2013). Experimental evidence for the influence of group size on cultural complexity. *Nature, 503,* 389–391.

Desai, S. R., McCormick, N. B., & Gaeddert, W. P. (1989). Malay and American undergraduates' beliefs about love. *Journal of Psychology and Human Sexuality, 2,* 93–116.

Deutscher, G. (2010). *Through the looking glass: Why the world looks different in other languages.* New York, NY: Metropolitan Books.

DeWall, C. N., Pond, R. S., Jr., Campbell, W. K., & Twenge, J. M. (2001). Tuning in to psychological change: Linguistic markers of psychological traits and emotions over time in popular U.S. song lyrics. *Psychology of Aesthetics, Creativity, and the Arts, 5,* 200–207.

Dhawan, N., Roseman, I. J., Naidu, R. K., & Rettek, S. I. (1995). Self-concepts across two cultures:

India and the United States. *Journal of Cross-Cultural Psychology, 26,* 606–621.

Di Blas, L., & Forzi, M. (1998). An alternative taxonomic study of personality-descriptive adjectives in the Italian language. *European Journal of Personality, 12,* 75–101.

Diamond, E. L. (1982). The role of anger and hostility in essential hypertension and coronary heart disease. *Psychological Bulletin, 92,* 410–433.

Diamond, J. (1997). *Guns, germs and steel: The fates of human societies.* New York, NY: Norton.

Diamond, J. (2005). Geography and skin colour. *Nature, 435,* 283–284.

Diekelmann, S., & Born, J. (2010). The memory function of sleep. *Nature Reviews Neuroscience, 11,* 114–126.

Diener, E. (2001, June 14–17). *Culture and subjective well-being—Why some nations and ethnic groups are happier than others.* Invited address presented at Thirteenth Annual Convention of the American Psychological Society, Toronto.

Diener, E., & Biswas-Diener, R. (2002). Will money increase subjective well-being? A literature review and guide to needed research. *Social Indicators Research, 57,* 119–169.

Diener, E., Diener, M., & Diener, C. (1995). Factors predicting the subjective well-being of nations. *Journal of Personality and Social Psychology, 69,* 851–864.

Diener, E., Suh, E. M., Smith, H., & Shao, L. (1995). National differences in reported subjective well-being: Why do they occur? *Social Indicators Research, 34,* 7–32.

Diez-Roux, A. V., Northridge, M. E., Morabia, A., Bassett, M. T., & Shea, S. (1999). Prevalence and social correlates of cardiovascular disease risk factors in Harlem. *American Journal of Public Health, 89,* 302–307.

Dion, K. K., & Dion, K. L. (1993). Individualistic and collectivistic perspectives on gender and the cultural context of love and intimacy. *Journal of Social Issues, 49,* 53–69.

Doris, J., & Plakias, A. (2008). How to argue about disagreement: Evaluative diversity and moral relativism. In W. Sinnott-Armstrong (Ed.), *Moral psychology, Vol. 2: The cognitive science of morality: Intuition and diversity* (pp. 303–331). Cambridge, MA: MIT Press.

Dornbusch, S., Ritter, P., Leiderman, P., Roberts, D., & Fraleigh, M. (1987). The relation of parenting syle to adolescent school performance. *Child Development, 58,* 1244–1257.

Downey, G. (2010). Throwing like a Brazilian: On ineptness and a skill-shaped body. In R. Sands (Ed.), *Anthropology of sport and human movement* (pp. 297–326). Lanham, MD: Lexington Books.

Doyle, K. O., & Doyle, M. R. (2001). Meanings of wealth in European and Chinese fairy tales. *American Behavioral Scientist, 45,* 191–204.

Draganski, B., Gaser, C., Busch, V., Schuierer, G., Bogdahn, U., & May, A. (2004). Changes in grey matter induced by training. *Nature, 427,* 311–312.

Drinka, G. F. (1984). *The birth of neurosis: Myth, malady, and the Victorians.* New York, NY: Simon & Schuster.

Druckerman, P. (2012). *Bringing up Bébé: One American mother discovers the wisdom of French parenting.* New York, NY: Penguin.

Drukker, J. W., & Tassenaar, V. (1997). Paradoxes of modernization and material well-being in the Netherlands during the nineteenth century. In R. H. Steckel & R. Floud (Eds.), *Health and welfare during industrialization* (pp. 331–378). Chicago, IL: University of Chicago Press.

Du Bois, W. E. B. (1903/1989). *The souls of Black folk.* New York, NY: Penguin.

Dunbar, R. (2011). How many "friends" can you really have? *Spectrum, IEEE, 48*(6), 81–83.

Dunbar, R. I. M. (1992). Neocortex size as a constraint on group size in primates. *Journal of Human Evolution, 20,* 469–493.

Dunbar, R. I. M. (1993). The co-evolution of neocortical size, group size and language in humans. *Behavioural and Brain Sciences, 16,* 681–735.

Dunbar, R. I. M. (1996). *Grooming, gossip, and the evolution of language.* London: Faber and Faber.

Dunbar, R. I. M. (1998). The social brain hypothesis. *Evolutionary Anthropology, 6,* 178–190.

Dunbar, R. I. M., Marriott, A., & Duncan, N. D. C. (1997). Human conversational behavior. *Human Nature, 8,* 231–246.

Dunlap-Hinkler, D., Kotabe, M., & Mudambi, R. (2010). A story of breakthrough versus incremental innovation: Corporate entrepreneurship in the global pharmaceutical industry. *Strategic Entrepreneurship Journal, 4,* 106–127.

Dunning, D., Meyerowitz, J. A., & Holzberg, A. D. (1989). Ambiguity and self-evaluation: The role of idiosyncratic trait definition in self-serving assessments of ability. *Journal of Personality and Social Psychology, 57,* 1082–1090.

Durham, W. H. (1991). *Coevolution: Genes, culture and human diversity.* Stanford, CA: Stanford University Press.

Dutton, D. G., & Aron, A. P. (1974). Some evidence for heightened sexual attraction under conditions of high anxiety. *Journal of Personality and Social Psychology, 30,* 510–517.

Duval, S. & Wicklund, R. (1972). *A theory of objective self-awareness.* New York, NY: Academic Press.

Dweck, C. S., & Leggett, E. L. (1988). A social-cognitive approach to motivation and personality. *Psychological Review, 95,* 256–273.

Dzokoto, V. (2010). Different ways of feeling: Emotion and somatic awareness in Ghanaians and Euro-Americans. *Journal of Social, Evolutionary, and Cultural Psychology, 4*(2), 68–78.

Dzokoto, V. A., & Adams, G. (2005). Understanding genital-shrinking epidemics in West Africa: Koro, juju, or mass psychogenic illness? *Culture, Medicine, and Psychiatry, 29,* 53–78.

Earleywine, M. (2001). Cannabis-induced Koro in Americans. *Addiction, 96,* 1663–1666.

Eastwood, M. (2003). *Principles of human nutrition* (2nd ed.). Oxford, UK: Blackwell.

Edgerton, R. B. (1971). *The individual in cultural adaptation: A study of four East African peoples.* Berkeley, CA: University of California Press.

Educational Testing Service. (2014). Test and score data summary for TOEFL iBT Tests, January 2013–December 2013 test data.

Edwards, C. P. (1994, April). *Cultural relativity meets best practice, or anthropology and early education, a promising friendship.* Paper presented at the meetings of the American Educational Research Association, New Orleans, LA.

Efrain, M. G., & Patterson, E. W. J. (1974). Voters vote beautiful: The effect of physical appearance on a national election. *Canadian Journal of Behavioural Science, 6,* 352–356.

Ehl, T., Roberton, M. A., & Langendorfer, S. J. (2005). Does the throwing "gender gap" occur in Germany? *Research Quarterly for Exercise and Sport, 76,* 488–493.

Einstein, A. (1954). *Ideas and opinions.* New York, NY: Crown.

Ekirch, A. R. (2005). *At day's close: Night in times past.* New York, NY: Norton.

Ekman, P. (1972). Universal and cultural differences in facial expression of emotion. In J. R. Cole (Ed.), *Nebraska symposium on motivation* (pp. 207–283). Lincoln: University of Nebraska Press.

Ekman, P. (1973). Universal facial expressions in emotion. *Studia Psychologica, 15,* 140–147.

Ekman, P., & Friesen, W. V. (1969). The repertoire of nonverbal behavior: Categories, origins, usage, and coding. *Semiotica, 1,* 49–98.

Ekman, P., & Friesen, W. V. (1971). Constants across cultures in the face and emotion. *Journal of Personality and Social Psychology, 17,* 124–129.

Ekman, P., Levenson, R. W., & Friesen, W. V. (1983). Autonomic nervous system activity distinguishes among emotions. *Science, 221,* 1208–1210.

Ekman, P., Sorenson, E. R., & Friesen, W. V. (1969). Pan-cultural elements in the facial displays of emotions. *Science, 164,* 86–88.

Elfenbein, H. A., & Ambady, N. (2002). On the universality and cultural specificity of emotion recognition: A meta-analysis. *Psychological Bulletin, 128,* 203–235.

Elias, N. (1939/1994). *The civilizing process.* Oxford: Blackwell.

Elliot, A. J., Chirkov, V. I., Kim, Y., & Sheldon, K. M. (2001). A cross-cultural analysis of avoidance (relative to approach) personal goals. *Psychological Science, 12,* 505–510.

Ellsworth, P. C. (1992). Sense, culture, and sensibility. In S. Kitayama & H. R. Markus (Eds.), *Emotion and Culture: Empirical studies of mutual influence.* (pp. 23–50). Washington: APA.

Endo, Y., Heine, S. J., & Lehman, D. R. (2000). Culture and positive illusions in relationships: How my relationships are better than yours. *Personality and Social Psychology Bulletin, 26,* 1571–1586.

Endo, Y., & Meijer, Z. (2004). Autobiographical memory of success and failure experiences. In Y. Kashima, Y. Endo, E. S. Kashima, C. Leung, & J. McClure (Eds.), *Progress in Asian social psychology* (Vol. 4, pp. 67–84). Seoul, Korea: Kyoyook-Kwahak-Sa Publishing Company.

English, T., & Chen, S. (2007). Culture and self-concept stability: Consistency across and within contexts among Asian Americans and European Americans. *Journal of Personality and Social Psychology, 93*(3), 478–490.

English, T., & Chen, S. (2011). Self-concept consistency and culture: The differential impact of two forms of consistency. *Personality and Social Psychology Bulletin, 37,* 838–849.

Epley, N., & Dunning, D. (2000). Feeling "holier than thou": Are self-serving assessments produced by errors in self- or social prediction? *Journal of Personality and Social Psychology, 79,* 861–875.

Erez, M., & Nouri, R. (2010). Creativity: The influence of cultural, social, and work contexts. *Management and Organization Review, 6,* 351–370.

Euromonitor International. (2014). Global bathing habits. Retrieved from http://www.euromonitor.com/medialibrary/PDF/pdf_globalBathing-Habits-v1.1.pdf

Evans, J. (1992). Schizophrenia: Living with madness here and in Zanzibar. *Occupational Therapy in Health Care, 8,* 53–71.

Evans-Pritchard, E. E. (1976). *Witchcraft, oracles, and magic among the Azande.* Oxford, UK: Clarendon Press.

Everett, D. L. (2005). Cultural constraints on grammar and cognition in Piraha. *Current Anthropology, 46,* 621–646.

Falbo, T., Poston, D. L., Jr., Triscari, R. S., & Zhang, X. (1997). Self-enhancing illusions among Chinese schoolchildren. *Journal of Cross-Cultural Psychology, 28,* 172–191.

Falk, C. F., Dunn, E. W., & Norenzayan, A. (2010). Cultural variation in the importance of expected enjoyment for decision making. *Social Cognition, 28,* 609–629.

Falk, C. F., & Heine, S. J. (in press). What is implicit self-esteem, and does it vary across cultures? *Personality and Social Psychological Review.*

Falk, C. F., Heine, S. J., Takemura, K., Zhang, C. C. X., & Hsu, C. (2015). Are implicit self-esteem measures valid for assessing individual and cultural differences? *Journal of Personality, 83,* 56–68.

Farley, R. (2004, January 12). Bright lights and baloney. St. Petersburg Times Online. Retrieved from www.sptimes.com/2004/10/10/Floridian/Bright_lights_and_bal.shtml.

Fausey, C. M., & Boroditsky, L. (2010). Subtle linguistic cues influence perceived blame and financial liability. *Psychonomic Bulletin & Review, 17,* 644–650.

Feather, N. (1966). Effects of prior success and failure on expectations of success and subsequent performance. *Journal of Personality and Social Psychology, 3,* 287–298.

Fehr, E., & Gächter, S. (2002). Altruistic punishment in humans. *Nature, 415,* 137–140.

Feinman, S. (1981).Why is cross-sex-role behavior more approved for girls than boys? A status characteristic approach. *Sex Roles, 7,* 289–300.

Feldman, P. J., & Steptoe, A. (2004). How neighborhoods and physical functioning are related: The roles of neighborhood socioeconomic status, perceived neighborhood strain, and individual health risk factors. *Annals of Behavioral Medicine, 27,* 91–99.

Ferber, R. (1985). *Solve your child's sleep problems.* New York, NY: Simon & Schuster.

Ferreira, M. C., Fischer, R., Porto, J. B., Pilati, R., & Milfont, T. L. (2012). Unraveling the mystery of Brazilian *Jetinho:* A cultural exploration of social norms. *Personality and Social Psychological Bulletin, 38,* 331–344.

Fessler, D. M. T. (2002). Windfall and socially distributed willpower: The psychocultural dynamics of rotating savings and credit associations in a Bengkulu village. *Ethos, 30,* 25–48.

Festinger, L. (1954). A theory of social comparison processes. *Human Relations, 7,* 117–140.

Festinger, L. (1957). *A theory of cognitive dissonance.* Stanford, CA: Stanford University Press.

Festinger, L., Schacter, S., & Back, K. (1950). *Social pressures in informal groups: A study of human factors in housing.* Stanford, CA: Stanford University Press.

Fiorito, G., & Scotto, P. (1992). Observational learning in *Octopus vulgaris. Science, 256,* 545–547.

Fischer, D. H. (1989). *Albion's seed: Four British folkways in America.* New York, NY: Oxford University Press.

Fisher, H. (2004). *Why we love: The nature and chemistry of romantic love.* New York, NY: Henry Holt.

Fishman, J. A. (1980). The Whorfian hypothesis: Varieties of valuation, confirmation, and disconfirmation: 1. *International Journal of the Sociology of Language, 26*, 25–40.

Fiske, A. P. (1991). *Structures of social life.* New York, NY: Free Press.

Fiske, A. P. (1992). The four elementary forms of sociality: Framework for a unified theory of social relations. *Psychological Review, 99*, 689–723.

Fitch, K. (1998). *Speaking relationally: Culture and interpersonal communication in Colombia.* New York, NY: Guilford Press.

Flaherty, J. A., Gavira, F. M., & Val, E. R. (1982). Diagnostic considerations. In E. R. Val, F. M. Gavira, & J. A. Flaherty (Eds.), *Affective disorders: Psychopathology and treatment.* Chicago, IL: Year Book Medical Publishers.

Fleming, R., Baum, A., Gisriel, M. M., & Gatchel, R. J. (1982). Mediating influences of social support on stress at Three Mile Island. *Journal of Human Stress, 8*, 14–22.

Floud, R. (1994). The heights of Europeans since 1750: A new source for European economic history. In J. Komlos (Ed.), *Stature, living standards, and economic development* (pp. 9–24). Chicago, IL: University of Chicago Press.

Floud, R., & Harris, B. (1997). Health, height, and welfare: Britain, 1700–1980. In R. H. Steckel & R. Floud (Eds.), *Health and welfare during industrialization* (pp. 91–126). Chicago, IL: University of Chicago Press.

Flynn, J. R. (1987). Massive IQ gains in 14 nations: What IQ tests really measure. *Psychological Bulletin, 101*, 171–191.

Flynn, J. R. (1994). IQ gains over time. In R. J. Sternberg (Ed.), *The encyclopedia of human intelligence* (pp. 617–623). New York, NY: Macmillan.

Flynn, J. R. (1999). Searching for justice: The discovery of IQ gains over time. *American Psychologist, 54*, 5–20.

Fodor, J. A. (1983). *The modularity of mind: An essay on faculty psychology.* Cambridge, MA: MIT Press.

Fonseca-Azevedo, K., & Herulano-Houzel, S. (2012). Metabolic constraint imposes tradeoff between body size and number of brain neurons in human evolution. *Proceedings of the National Academy of Sciences, 109*, 18571–18576.

Ford, C. S., & Beach, F. A. (1951). *Patterns of sexual behavior.* New York, NY: Harper & Row.

Forman, T. A., Williams, D. R., & Jackson, J. S. (1997). Race, place, and discrimination. In C. Gardner (Ed.), *Perspectives on social problems* (Vol. 9, pp. 231–261). New York, NY: JAI Press.

Fox, J. A. (1978). *Forecasting crime data: An econometric analysis.* Lanham, MD: Lexington Books.

Frager, R. (1970). Conformity and anti-conformity in Japan. *Journal of Personality and Social Psychology, 15*, 203–210.

Freedman, J. L., & Fraser, S. C. (1966). Compliance without pressure: The foot-in-the-door technique. *Journal of Personality and Social Psychology, 4*, 195–202.

Freeman, D. (1983). *Margaret Mead and Samoa: The making and unmaking of an anthropological myth.* Cambridge, MA: Harvard University Press.

Freeman, J. B., Rule, N. O., Adams, R. B., & Ambady, N. (2009). Culture shapes a mesolimbic response to signals of dominance and subordination that associates with behavior. *NeuroImage, 47*, 353–359.

Friesen, W. V. (1972). *Cultural differences in facial expressions in a social situation: An experimental test of the concept of display rules.* Unpublished doctoral dissertation. University of California, San Francisco.

Frieze, I. H., Olson, J. E., & Russell, J. (1991). Attractiveness and income for men and women in management. *Journal of Applied Social Psychology, 21*, 1039–1057.

Fryberg, S. A., & Markus, H. R. (2003). On being American Indian: Current and possible selves. *Self and Identity, 2*, 325–344.

Fryberg, S. A., Markus, H. R., Oyserman, D., & Stone, J. M. (2008). Of warrior chiefs and Indian princesses: The psychological consequences of American Indian mascots. *Basic and Applied Social Psychology, 30*, 208–218.

Fu, A. S., & Markus, H. R. (2014). My mother and me: Why Tiger Mothers motivate Asian-Americans but not European-Americans. *Personality and Social Psychology Bulletin, 40*, 739–749.

Fuentes-Afflick, E., & Lurie, P. (1997). Low birth weight and Latino ethnicity. *Archives of Pediatric Adolescent Medicine, 151*, 665–674.

Fulmer, C. A., Gelfand, M. J., Kruglanski, A. W., Kim-Prieto, C., Diener, E., Pierro, A., et al. (2010). On "feeling right" in cultural contexts: How person-culture match affects self-esteem and subjective well-being. *Psychological Science, 21,* 1563–1569.

Funder, D. C. (2007). *The personality puzzle* (4th ed.). New York, NY: Norton.

Fung, H. H., Carstensen, L. L., & Lang, F. (2001). Age-related patterns in social networks among European-Americans and African-Americans: Implications for socioemotional selectivity across the life span. *International Journal of Aging and Human Development, 52,* 185–206.

Fung, H. H., Stoeber, F. S., Yeung, D. Y. L., & Lang, F. R. (2008). Cultural specificity of socioemotional selectivity: age differences in social network composition among Germans and Hong Kong Chinese. *Journal of Gerontology, B Psychological Science and Social Science, 63,* 156–164.

Furlong, A. (2008). The Japanese *hikikomori* phenomenon: Acute social withdrawal among young people. *Sociological Review, 56,* 309–325.

Furnham, A. (1990). *The Protestant work ethic: The psychology of work-related beliefs and behaviors.* London: Routledge.

Furnham, A., & Bochner, S. (1982). Social difficulty in a foreign culture: An empirical analysis of culture shock. In S. Bochner (Ed.), *Cultures in contact: Studies in cross-cultural interactions* (pp. 161–198). Elmsford, NY: Pergamon.

Furnham, A., & Bochner, S. (1986). *Culture shock.* London: Methuen.

Furnham, A., Bond, M. H., & Heaven, P. (1993). A comparison of Protestant work ethic beliefs in thirteen nations. *Journal of Social Psychology, 133,* 185–197.

Fuson, K. C. (1988). *Children's counting and concepts of number.* New York, NY: Springer-Verlag.

Fuson, K. C., Stigler, J. W., & Bartsch, K. (1988). Grade placement of addition and subtraction topics in Japan, Mainland China, the Soviet Union, Taiwan, and the United States. *Journal for Research in Mathematics Education, 19,* 449–456.

Gabrenya, W. K., Wang, Y., & Latané, B. (1985). Social loafing on an optimizing task: Cross-cultural differences among Chinese and Americans. *Journal of Cross-Cultural Psychology, 16,* 223–242.

Gaertner, S. L., Mann, J., Murrell, A., & Dovidio, J. F. (1989). Reducing intergroup bias: The benefits of recategorization. *Journal of Personality and Social Psychology, 57,* 239–249.

Galanter, M. (1986). "Moonies" get married: A psychiatric follow-up study of a charismatic religious sect. *American Journal of Psychiatry, 143,* 1245–1249.

Galaty, J. G., & Bonte, P. (Eds). (1991). *Herders, warriors, and traders: Pastoralism in Africa.* Boulder, CO: Westview Press.

Gallo, L. C., & Matthews, K. A. (2003). Understanding the association between socioeconomic status and physical health: Do negative emotions play a role? *Psychological Bulletin, 129,* 10–51.

Gangestad, S. W., Haselton, M. G., & Buss, D. M. (2006). Evolutionary foundations of cultural variation: Evoked culture and mate preference. *Psychological Inquiry,17,* 75–95.

Gangestad, S. W., Thornhill, R., & Yeo, R. A. (1994). Facial attractiveness, developmental stability, and fluctuating asymmetry. *Ethology and Sociobiology, 15,* 73–85.

Gardner, G. H. (1962). Cross-cultural communication. *Journal of Social Psychology, 58,* 241–256.

Gardner, W. L., Gabriel, S., & Dean, K. K. (2004). The individual as "melting pot": The flexibility of bicultural self-construals. *Cahiers de Psychologie Cognitive/Current Psychology of Cognition, 22,* 181–201.

Garner, D. M., Garfinkel, P. E., Schwartz, D., & Thompson, M. (1980). Cultural expectations of thinness in women. *Psychological Reports, 47,* 483–491.

Gastil, R. D. (1989). Violence, crime, and punishment. In C. R. Wilson & W. Ferris (Eds.), *Encyclopedia of Southern culture.* Chapel Hill: University of North Carolina Press.

Gawronski, B., Bodenhausen, G. V., & Becker, A. P. (2007). I like it, because I like myself: Associative self-anchoring and post-decisional change of implicit evaluations. *Journal of Experimental Social Psychology, 43,* 221–232.

Geertz, C. (1973). *The interpretation of cultures.* New York, NY: Basic Books.

Geertz, C. (1975). On the nature of anthropological understanding. *American Scientist, 63,* 4–53.

Geertz, C. (1983). *Local knowledge: Further essays in interpretive anthropology.* New York, NY: Basic Books.

Geertz, H. (1959). The vocabulary of emotion: A study of Javanese socialization processes. *Psychiatry, 22,* 225–237.

Gelfand, M. J., Nishii, L. H., Holcombe, K. M., Dyer, N., Ohbuchi, K., & Fukuno, M. (2001). Cultural influences on cognitive representations of conflict: Interpretations of conflict episodes in the United States and Japan. *Journal of Applied Psychology, 86,* 1059–1074.

Gellantly, A. (1995). Colourful Whorfian ideas: Linguistic and cultural influences on the perception and cognition of colour, and on the investigation of them. *Mind and Language, 10,* 119–125.

Gelman, R., & Gallistel, C. R. (2004). Language and the origin of number concepts. *Science, 306,* 441–443.

Gendron, M., Roberson, D., van der Vyver, J. M., & Barrett, L. F. (2014). Perceptions of emotion from facial expressions are not culturally universal: Evidence from a remote culture. *Emotion, 14,* 251–262.

Gentile, B., Twenge, J. M., Campbell, W. K. (2010). Birth cohort differences in self-esteem, 1988–2008: A cross-temporal meta-analysis. *Review of General Psychology, 14,* 261–268.

Gentner, D. (1982). Why nouns are learned before verbs: Linguistic relativity versus natural partitioning. In S. Kuczaj (Ed.), *Language development: Language, cognition and culture.* Hillsdale, NJ: Erlbaum.

Georgas, J., Berry, J. W., van de Vijver, C., & Poortinga, Y. H. (Eds). (2006). *Families across cultures: A 30-nation psychological study.* New York, NY: Cambridge University Press.

Giddens, A. (1992). Introduction in M. Weber (1904/1992), *The Protestant ethic and the spirit of capitalism.* London: Routledge.

Gillette, J., Gleitman, H., Gleitman, L., & Lederer, A. (1999). Human simulations of vocabulary learning. *Cognition, 73,* 135–176.

Gilligan, C. (1977). In a different voice: Women's conceptions of the self and of morality. *Harvard Educational Review, 47,* 481–517.

Gilligan, C., & Attanucci, J. (1988). Two moral orientations: Gender differences and similarities. *Merrill-Palmer Quarterly, 34,* 223–237.

Gilmore, D. D. (1990). *Manhood in the making.* New Haven, CT: Yale University Press.

Gilovich, G., Keltner, D., & Nisbett, R. (2006). *Social psychology.* New York, NY: Norton.

Giorgi, L., & Marsh, C. (1990). The Protestant work ethic as a cultural phenomenon. *European Journal of Social Psychology, 20,* 499–517.

Gislen, A., & Gislen, L. (2004). On the optical theory of underwater vision in humans. *Journal of the Optical Society of America A, 21,* 2061–2064.

Gislen, A., Dacke, M., Kroger, R. H. H., Abrahamson, M., Nilsson, D. E., & Warrant, E. J. (2003). Superior underwater vision in a human population of sea-gypsies. *Current Biology, 13,* 833–836.

Gislen, A., Warrant, E. J., & Kroger, R. H. H. (2005). *Voluntary accommodation improves underwater vision in humans.* Manuscript available from the authors (anna.gislen@cob.lu.se).

Gladwell, M. (2000). *The tipping point: How little things can make a big difference.* Boston, MA: Little, Brown.

Gladwell, M. (2008). *Outliers.* New York, NY: Little, Brown.

Gladwell, M. (2011, February 14). The order of things: What college rankings really tell us. *The New Yorker,* 68–75.

Gleitman, L. (1990). The structural sources of verb meaning. *Language Acquisition: A Journal of Developmental Linguistics, 1,* 3–55.

Gobster, P. H., & Delgado, A. (1992). Ethnicity and recreation use in Chicago's Lincoln Park: In-park user survey findings. In P. Gobster (Ed.), *Managing urban and high-use recreation settings* (pp. 75–81). General Technical Report NC-163: United States Department of Agriculture.

Godart, F., Maddux, W. W., Shipilov, A., & Galinsky, A. D. (in press). A flair for foreign fashion: Individual professional experiences abroad facilitate the creative innovations of organizations. *Academy of Management Journal.*

Goel, M. S., McCarthy, E. P., Phillips, R. S., & Wee, C. C. (2004). Obesity among U.S. immigrant subgroups by duration of residence. *Journal of the American Medical Association, 292,* 2860–2867.

Goh, J. O., Leshikar E. D., Sutton B. P., Tan J. C., Sim S. K., Hebrank A. C., & Park D. C. (2010). Culture differences in neural processing of faces and houses in the ventral visual cortex. *Social, Cognitive, and Affective Neuroscience, 5,* 227–235.

Goh, J. O., et al. (2007). Age and culture modulate object processing and object-scent binding in the ventral visual area. *Cognitive, Affective, & Behavioral Neuroscience, 7,* 44–52.

Goldin, C. (1998). America's graduation from high school: The evolution and spread of secondary schooling in the twentieth century. *Journal of Economic History, 58,* 345–374.

Goncalo, J. A., & Staw, B. M. (2006). Individualism-collectivism and group creativity. *Organizational Behavior and Human Decision Processes, 100,* 96–109.

Goncalves, B., Perra, N., & Vespignani, A. (2011). Modeling users' activity on Twitter networks: Validation of Dunbar's number. *PLoS ONE 6*(8), e22656.

Good, C., Aronson, J., & Inzlicht, M. (2003). Improving adolescents' standardized test performance: An intervention to reduce the effects of stereotype threat. *Journal of Applied Developmental Psychology, 24,* 645–662.

Goode, W. J. (1959). The theoretical importance of love. *American Sociological Review, 24,* 38–47.

Goodenough, W. H. (1970). *Description and comparison in cultural anthropology.* Chicago, IL: Aldine.

Goody, J. (1977). *The domestication of the savage mind.* Cambridge, UK: Cambridge University Press.

Goossens, H., Ferech, M., Stichele, R. V., & Elseviers, M. (2005). Outpatient antibiotic use in Europe and association with resistance: A cross-national database study. *Lancet, 365,* 579–587.

Gordon, A. (2000). Cultural identity and illness: Fulani views. *Culture, Medicine, and Psychiatry, 24,* 297–330.

Gordon, P. (2004). Numerical cognition without words: Evidence from Amazonia. *Science, 306,* 496–499.

Gordon, R. A. (1990). *Anorexia and bulimia: Anatomy of a social epidemic.* Cambridge, UK: Basil/Blackwell.

Goren-Inbar, N., Alperson, N., Kislev, N. E., Simchoni, O., Melamed, Y., Ben-Nun, A., & Werker, E. (2004). Evidence of hominin control of fire at Gesher Benot Ta'aqov, Israel. *Science, 304,* 725–727.

Gosling, S. D., & John, O. P. (1999). Personality dimensions in nonhuman animals: A cross-species review. *Current Direction in Psychological Science, 8,* 69–75.

Goto, S. G., Ando, Y., Huang, C., Yee, A., & Lewis, R. S. (2010). Cultural differences in the visual processing of meaning: Detecting incongruities between background and foreground objects using the N400. *Social and Cognitive Affective Neuroscience, 5,* 242–253.

Gottesman, I. I. (1991). *Schizophrenia. The origins of madness.* New York, NY: Holt.

Gould, S. J. (1981). *The mismeasure of man.* New York, NY: Norton.

Graham, J., Haidt, J., & Nosek, B. (2009). Liberals and conservatives use different sets of moral foundations. *Journal of Personality and Social Psychology, 96,* 1029–1046.

Graham, J., Nosek, B. A., Haidt, J., Iyer, R., Koleva, S., & Ditto, P. H. (2011). Mapping the moral domain. *Journal of Personality and Social Psychology, 101,* 366–385.

Gravlee, C. C., Dressler, W. W., & Bernard, H. R. (2005). Skin color, social classification, and blood pressure in Southeastern Puerto Rico. *American Journal of Public Health, 95,* 2191–2197.

Greeley, A. M. (1991). *Religion around the world: A preliminary report.* Chicago, IL: National Opinion Research Center.

Greeley, A. M., & Hout, M. (1999). Americans' increasing belief in life after death: Religious competition and acculturation. *American Sociological Review, 64,* 813–835.

Greenfield, P. M. (1997). Culture as process: Empirical methods for cultural psychology. In J. W. Berry, Y. H. Poortinga, & J. Pandey (Eds.), *Handbook of cross-cultural psychology* (Vol. 1, pp. 301–346). Boston, MA: Allyn & Bacon.

Greenfield, P. M. (1998). The cultural evolution of IQ. In U. Neisser (Ed.), *The rising curve: Long-term gains in IQ and related measures* (pp. 81–123). Washington, DC: American Psychological Association.

Greenfield, P. M. (2013). The changing psychology of culture from 1800 through 2000. *Psychological Science, 24,* 1722–1731.

Greulich, W. W. (1957). A comparison of the physical growth and development of American-born and native Japanese children. *American Journal of Physical Anthropology, 15,* 489–515.

Grimm, S. D., & Church, A. T. (1999). A cross-cultural study of response biases in personality measures. *Journal of Research in Personality, 33,* 415–441.

Grossmann, I. (2011). *Russian interdependence and holistic cognition.* Unpublished manuscript. University of Michigan, Ann Arbor.

Grossmann, I., & Kross, E. (2010). The impact of culture on adaptive versus maladaptive self-reflection. *Psychological Science, 21,* 1150–1157.

Grossmann, I., & Varnum, M. E. W. (2011). Social class, culture, and cognition. *Social Psychological and Personality Science, 2,* 81–89.

Grossmann, I., & Varnum, M. (in press). Social structure, infectious diseases, disasters, secularism and cultural change in America. *Psychological Science.*

Grossmann, I., et al. (2012). Aging and wisdom: Culture matters. *Psychological Science, 23,* 1059–1066.

Guarniccia, P. J., Canino, G., Rubio-Stipec, M., & Bravo, M. (1993). The prevalence of *ataques de nervios* in the Puerto Rico Disaster Study: The role of culture in psychiatric epidemiology. *Journal of Nervous and Mental Disease, 181,* 157–165.

Guendelman, M. D., Cheryan, S., & Monin, B. (2011). Fitting in but getting fat: Identity threat and dietary choices among U.S. immigrant groups. *Psychological Science, 22,* 959–967.

Guimond, S., et al. (2013). Diversity policy, social dominance, and intergroup relations: Predicting prejudice in changing social and political contexts. *Journal of Personality and Social Psychology, 104,* 941–958.

Gullahorn, J. T., & Gullahorn, J. E. (1963). An extension of the U-curve hypothesis. *Journal of Social Issues, 19,* 33–47.

Guo, T., Ji, L.-J., Spina, R., & Zhang, Z. (2012). Culture, temporal focus, and values of the past and the future. *Personality and Social Psychology Bulletin, 38,* 1030–1040.

Gupta, U., & Singh, P. (1982). Exploratory study of love and liking and type of marriages. *Indian Journal of Applied Psychology, 19,* 92–97.

Gurven, M., von Rueden, C., Massenkoff, M., Kaplan, H., & Vie, M. L. (2013). How universal is the Big Five? Testing the Five-Factor Model of personality variation among forager-farmers in the Bolivian Amazon. *Journal of Personality and Social Psychology, 104,* 354–370.

Gutchess, A. H., Welsh, R. C., Boduroglu, A., & Park, D. C. (2006). Cultural differences in neural function associated with object processing. *Cognitive, Affective, & Behavioral Neuroscience, 6,* 102–109.

Guthrie, G. M., & Zektick, I. N. (1967). Predicting performance in the Peace Corps. *Journal of Social Psychology, 71,* 1–21.

Haidt, J. (2001). The emotional dog and its rational tail: A social intuitionist approach to moral judgment. *Psychological Review, 108,* 814–834.

Haidt, J. & Graham, J. (2007). When morality opposes justice: Conservatives have moral intuitions that liberals may not recognize. *Social Justice Research, 20,* 98–116.

Haidt, J., & Keltner, D. (1999). Culture and facial expression: Open-ended methods find more expressions and a gradient of recognition. *Cognition and Emotion, 13,* 225–266.

Haidt, J., Koller, S. H., & Dias, M. G. (1993). Affect, culture, and morality, or Is it wrong to eat your dog? *Journal of Personality and Social Psychology, 65,* 613–628.

Haight, W. L. (1999). The pragmatics of caregiver-child pretending at home: Understanding culturally specific socialization practices. In A. Goncu (Ed.), *Children's engagement in the world: Sociocultural perspectives* (pp. 128–147). New York, NY: Cambridge University Press.

Hajat, A., et al. (2010). Socioeconomic and race/ethnic differences in daily salivary cortisol profiles: The multi-ethnic study of atherosclerosis. *Psychoneuroendocrinology, 35,* 932–943.

Hall, E. T. (1976). *Beyond culture.* New York, NY: Anchor Books.

Hall, G. S. (1916). *Adolescence.* New York, NY: Appleton.

Hall, R. E. (2013). The bleaching syndrome: Western civilization vis-à-vis inferiorized people of color. In R. E. Hall (Ed.), *The melanin millennium: Skin color as 21st-century international discourse* (pp. 1–18). New York, NY: Springer Science.

Halmi, K. A., Falk, J. R., & Schwartz, E. (1981). Binge-eating and vomiting: A survey of a college population. *Psychological Medicine, 11,* 697–706.

Hamamura, T. (2012). Are cultures becoming more individualistic? A cross-temporal comparison of individualism-collectivism in the United States and Japan. *Personality and Social Psychology Review, 16,* 3–24.

Hamamura, T., & Heine, S. J. (2008). Self-enhancement, self-improvement, and face among Japanese. In E. C. Chang (Ed.), *Self-criticism and self-enhancement: Theory, research, and clinical implications,* (pp. 105-122). Washington, DC: American Psychological Association.

Hamamura, T., Heine, S. J., & Paulhus, D. L. (2008). Cultural differences in response styles: The role of dialectical thinking. *Personality and Individual Differences, 44,* 932–942.

Hamamura, T., Meijer, Z., Heine, S. J., Kamaya, K., & Hori, I. (2009). Approach-avoidance motivations and information processing: A cross-cultural analysis. *Personality and Social Psychology Bulletin, 35,* 454-462.

Hamilton, D. L., & Gifford, R. K. (1976). Illusory correlation in interpersonal perception: A cognitive basis of stereotypic judgments. *Journal of Experimental Social Psychology, 12,* 392–407.

Hamilton, V. L., & Sanders, J. (1992). *Everyday justice: Responsibility and the individual in Japan and the United States.* New Haven, CT: Yale University Press.

Hampden-Turner, C., & Trompenaars, A. (1993). *The seven cultures of capitalism: Value systems for creating wealth in the United States, Japan, Germany, France, Britain, Sweden, and the Netherlands.* New York, NY: Doubleday.

Han, S., & Shavit, S. (1994). Persuasion and culture: Advertising appeals in individualistic and collectivist societies. *Journal of Experimental Social Psychology, 30,* 326–350.

Hanning, R. W. (1977). *The individual in twelfth-century romance.* New Haven, CT: Yale University Press.

Harber, K. D. & Cohen, D. J. (2005). The emotional broadcaster theory of social sharing. *Journal of Language and Social Psychology, 24,* 382–400.

Harrington, L., & Liu, J. H. (2002). Self-enhancement and attitudes toward high achievers: A bicultural view of the independent and interdependent self. *Journal of Cross-Cultural Psychology, 33,* 37–55.

Hart, D., & Edelstein, W. (1992). The relationship of self-understanding in childhood to social class, community type, and teacher-rated intellectual and social competence. *Journal of Cross-Cultural Psychology, 23,* 353–365.

Hart, D., Lucca-Irizarry, N., & Damon, W. (1986). The development of self-understanding in Puerto Rico and the United States. *Journal of Early Adolescence, 6,* 293–304.

Harton, H. C., & Bourgeois, M. J. (2004). Cultural elements emerge from dynamic social impact. In M. Schaller & C. Crandall (Eds.), *The psychological foundations of culture.* Hillsdale, NJ: Erlbaum.

Harwood, R. L., Miller, J. G., & Irizarry, N. L. (1995). *Culture and attachment: Perceptions of the child in context.* New York, NY: Guilford Press.

Hashimoto, H. (2007, February 28–March 3). *Legal reform in Japan: The establishment of American style law schools.* Paper presented at the 44th Annual Meeting of International Studies Association Conference, Chicago, IL.

Haun, D. B. M., Rapold, C. J., Call, J., Janzen, G., & Levinson, S. C. (2006). Cognitive cladistics and cultural override in Hominid spatial cognition. *Proceedings of the National Academy of Sciences, 103,* 17568–17573.

Haushofer, J., & Fehr, E. (2014). The psychology of poverty. *Science, 344,* 862–867.

Hawks, J., Wang, E. T., Cochran, G. M., Harpending, H. C., & Moyzis, R. K. (2007). Recent acceleration of human adaptive evolution. *Proceedings of the National Academy of Sciences, 104,* 20753–20758.

Hayward, R. D., & Kemmelmeier, M. (2011). Weber revisited: A cross-national analysis of religiosity, religious culture, and economic attitudes. *Journal of Cross-Cultural Psychology, 42,* 1406–1420.

Healy, J. M. (1990). *Endangered minds: Why children don't think and what we can do about it.* New York, NY: Simon & Schuster.

Heaphy, E., Sanchez-Burks, J., & Ashford, S. (2011). *Are non-work role references an organizational taboo? Evidence of cultural boundaries and* *reinforcing mechanisms.* Unpublished manuscript. University of Michigan, Ann Arbor.

Heath, C., Bell, C., & Sternberg, E. (2001). Emotional selection in memes: The case of urban legends. *Journal of Personality and Social Psychology, 81,* 1028–1041.

Heatherton, T. F., Nichols, P. A., Mahamedi, F., & Keel, P. (1995). Body weight, dieting, and eating disorder symptoms among college students, 1982–1992. *American Journal of Psychiatry, 152,* 1623–1629.

Heatherton, T. F., Wyland, C. L., Macrae, C. N., Demos, K. E., Denny, B. T., & Kelley, W. M. (2006). Medial prefrontal activity differentiates self from close others. *Social, Cognitive, and Affective Neuroscience, 1,* 18–25.

Hedden, T., Ketay, S., Aron, A., Markus, H. R., & Gabrieli, J. D. E. (2008). Cultural influences on neural substrates of attentional control. *Psychological Science, 19,* 12–17.

Heine, S. J. (2003). An exploration of cultural variation in self-enhancing and self-improving motivations. *Nebraska Symposium of Motivation.*

Heine, S. J. (2005). Constructing good selves in Japan and North America. In R. M. Sorrentino, D. Cohen, J. M. Olson, & M. P. Zanna (Eds.), *Culture and social behavior: The Tenth Ontario Symposium* (pp. 115–143). Hillsdale, NJ: Erlbaum.

Heine, S. J., & Buchtel, E. E. (2009). Personality: The universal and culturally specific. *Annual Review of Psychology, 60,* 369–394.

Heine, S. J., Buchtel, E., & Norenzayan, A. (2008). What do cross-national comparisons of personality traits tell us? The case of conscientiousness. *Psychological Science, 19,* 309–313.

Heine, S. J., Foster, J. A., & Spina, R. (2009). Do birds of a feather universally flock together? Cultural variation in the similarity-attraction effect. *Asian Journal of Social Psychology, 12,* 247–258.

Heine, S. J., & Hamamura, T. (2007). In search of East Asian self-enhancement. *Personality and Social Psychology Review, 11,* 1–24.

Heine, S. J., Kitayama, S., & Hamamura, T. (2007). Which studies test whether self-enhancement is pancultural? Reply to Sedikides, Gaertner, and Vevea, 2007, JPSP. *Asian Journal of Social Psychology, 10,* 198–200.

Heine, S. J., Kitayama, S., & Lehman, D. R. (2001). Cultural differences in self-evaluation: Japanese readily accept negative self-relevant information. *Journal of Cross-Cultural Psychology, 32,* 434–443.

Heine, S. J., Kitayama, S., Lehman, D. R., Takata, T., Ide, E., Leung, C., & Matsumoto, H. (2001). Divergent consequences of success and failure in Japan and North America: An investigation of self-improving motivations and malleable selves. *Journal of Personality and Social Psychology, 81,* 599–615.

Heine, S. J., & Lehman, D. R. (1997a). The cultural construction of self-enhancement: An examination of group-serving biases. *Journal of Personality and Social Psychology, 72,* 1268–1283.

Heine, S. J., & Lehman, D. R. (1997b). Culture, dissonance, and self-affirmation. *Personality and Social Psychology Bulletin, 23,* 389–400.

Heine, S. J., & Lehman, D. R. (2004). Move the body, change the self: Acculturative effects on the self-concept. In M. Schaller & C. Crandall (Eds.), *Psychological foundations of culture* (pp. 305–331). Mahwah, NJ: Erlbaum.

Heine, S. J., Lehman, D. R., Markus, H. R., & Kitayama, S. (1999). Is there a universal need for positive self-regard? *Psychological Review, 106,* 766–794.

Heine, S. J., Lehman, D. R., Peng, K., & Greenholtz, J. (2002). What's wrong with cross-cultural comparisons of subjective Likert scales? The reference-group problem. *Journal of Personality and Social Psychology, 82,* 903–918.

Heine, S. J., & Renshaw, K. (2002). Interjudge agreement, self-enhancement, and liking: Cross-cultural divergences. *Personality and Social Psychology Bulletin, 28,* 442–451, 578–587.

Heine, S. J., Takemoto, T., Moskalenko, S., Lasaleta, J., & Henrich, J. (2008). Mirrors in the head: Cultural variation in objective self-awareness. *Personality and Social Psychology Bulletin, 34,* 879–887.

Henderson, V., & Dweck, C. S. (1990). Motivation and achievement. In S. S. Feldman & G. R. Elliott (Eds.), *At the threshold: The developing adolescent* (pp. 308–329). Cambridge, MA: Harvard University Press.

Henig, R. M. (2010, August 18). What is it about 20-somethings? *New York Times Magazine.*

Henrich, J. (2004). Demography and cultural evolution: How adaptive cultural processes can produce maladaptive losses: The Tasmanian case. *American Antiquity, 69,* 197–214.

Henrich, J. (2015). *The secret of our success.* Princeton, NJ: Princeton University Press.

Henrich, J., Boyd, R., Bowles, S., Camerer, C., Fehr, E., Gintis, H., et al. (2005). "Economic man" in cross-cultural perspective: Behavioral experiments in 15 small-scale societies. *Behavioral and Brain Sciences, 28,* 795–855.

Henrich, J., Ensminger, J., McElreath, R., Barr, A., Barrett, C., Bolyanatz, A., et al., (2010). Markets, religion, community size, and the evolution of fairness and punishment. *Science, 327,* 1480–1484.

Henrich, J., & Gil-White, F. J. (2001). The evolution of prestige: Freely conferred deference as a mechanism for enhancing the benefits of cultural transmission. *Evolution and Human Behavior, 22,* 165–196.

Henrich, J., Heine, S. J., & Norenzayan, A. (2010a). Beyond WEIRD: Towards a broad-based behavioral science. *Behavioral and Brain Sciences, 33,* 111–135.

Henrich, J., Heine, S. J., & Norenzayan, A. (2010b). The weirdest people in the world. *Behavioral and Brain Sciences, 33,* 61–83.

Henrich, J., McElreath, R., Barr, A., Ensminger, J., Barrett, C., Bolyanatz, A., et al. (2006). Costly punishment across human societies. *Science, 312,* 1767–1770.

Herbig, P. A., & Palumbo, F. A. (1996). Innovation—Japanese style. Industrial *Management & Data Systems, 96,* 11–20.

Herdt, B. (2006). *The Sambia: Ritual, sexuality, and change in Papua New Guinea.* Belmont, CA: Thomson Wadsworth.

Herrmann, B., Thöni, C., & Gächter, S. (2008). Antisocial punishment across societies. *Science, 319,* 1362–1367.

Herrmann, E., Josep, C., Hernàndez-Lloreda, M. V., Hare, B., and Tomasello, M. (2007, September). Humans have evolved specialized skills of social cognition: The cultural intelligence hypothesis. *Science, 7,* 1360–1366.

Hess, R. D., Chang, C., & McDevitt, T. M. (1987). Cultural variations in family beliefs about children's performance in mathematics: Comparisons among People's Republic of China, Chinese-American, and Caucasian-American families. *Journal of Educational Psychology, 79,* 179–188.

Hess, T. M., Auman, C., & Colcombe, S. J. (2003). The impact of stereotype threat on age differences in memory performance. *Journals of Gerontology: Series B: Psychological Sciences & Social Sciences, 58,* 3–11.

Hewlett, B. S. (1992). The parent-infant relationship and social-emotional development among Aka Pygmies. In J. L. Roopmarine & D. B. Carter (Eds.), *Parent-child socialization in diverse cultures* (pp. 223–243). Norwood, NJ: Ablex.

Hezel, F. X. (1987). Truk suicide epidemic and social change. *Human Organization, 46,* 283–291.

Higgins, E. T. (1996). The "self-digest": Self-knowledge serving self-regulatory functions. *Journal of Personality and Social Psychology, 71,* 1062–1083.

Hinds, D. A., Stuve, L. L., Nilsen, G. B., Halperin, E., Eskin, E., Ballinger, D. G., et al. (2005). Whole-genome patterns of common DNA variation in three human populations. *Science, 307,* 1072–1079.

Ho, D. Y. F. (1976). On the concept of face. *American Journal of Sociology, 81,* 867–884.

Hock, H. W., van Harten, P. N., van Hoeken, D., & Susser, E. (1998). Lack of relation between culture and anorexia nervosa—Results of an incidence study on Curacao. *New England Journal of Medicine, 338,* 1231–1232.

Hoff, K. & Pandey, P. (2004). *Belief systems and durable inequalities: An experimental investigation of Indian caste.* Policy Research Working Paper. Washington, DC: World Bank.

Hofstede, G. (1980). *Culture's consequences: International differences in work-related values.* Beverly Hills, CA: Sage.

Hofstede, G. (1983). Dimensions of national cultures in fifty countries and three regions. In J. Deregowski, S. Dzuirawiec, & R. Annis (Eds.), *Expiscations in cross-cultural psychology,* Lisse, Netherlands: Swets and Zeitlinger.

Holden, C., & Mace, R. (1997). Phylogenetic analysis of the evolution of lactose digestion in adults. *Human Biology, 69,* 605–628.

Hollingshead, A. B., & Redlich, R. C. (1958). *Social class and mental illness: A community study.* New York, NY: Wiley.

Holloway, R. A., Waldrip, A. M., & Ickes, W. (2009). Evidence that a simpático self-schema accounts for differences in the self-concepts and social behavior of Latinos versus Whites (and Blacks). *Journal of Personality and Social Psychology, 96,* 1012–1028.

Hollox, E. (2005). Genetics of lactase persistence—fresh lessons in the history of milk drinking. *European Journal of Human Genetics, 13,* 267–269.

Holmberg, A. R. (1969). *Nomads of the long bow: The Siriono of Eastern Bolivia.* New York, NY: American Museum Science Books.

Holmes, T. H., & Rahe, R. H. (1967). The social readjustment rating scale. *Journal of Psychosomatic Research, 11,* 213–218.

Holoien, D. S., & Shelton, J. N. (2012). You deplete me: The cognitive costs of colorblindness on ethnic minorities. *Journal of Experimental Social Psychology, 48,* 562–565.

Hölzel, B. K., Carmody, J., Vangel, M., Congleton, C., Yerramsetti, S. M., Gard, T., & Lazar, S. W. (2011). Mindfulness practice leads to increases in regional brain gray matter density. *Psychiatry Research: Neuroimaging, 191,* 36–43.

Hong, J. J., & Woody, S. R. (2007). Cultural mediators of self-reported social anxiety. *Behaviour Research and Therapy, 45,* 1779–1789.

Hong, Y., Chiu, C., Dweck, C. S., Lin, D. M., & Wan, W. (1999). Implicit theories, attributions, and coping: A meaning system approach. *Journal of Personality and Social Psychology, 77,* 588–599.

Hong, Y., Morris, M. W., Chiu, C., & Benet-Martinez, V. (2000). Multicultural minds: A dynamic constructivist approach to culture and cognition. *American Psychologist, 55,* 705–720.

Hopkins B., & Westra T. (1988). Maternal handling and motor development: an intracultural study. *Genet Soc Gen Psychol Monogr.* 114(3), 377–408.

Horberg, E. J., Oveis, C., Keltner, D., & Cohen, A. B. (2009). Disgust and the moralization of purity. *Journal of Personality and Social Psychology, 97,* 963–976.

Horner, V., & Whiten, A. (2005). Causal knowledge and imitation/emulation switching in chimpanzees (*Pan troglodytes*) and children (*Homo sapiens*). *Animal Cognition, 8,* 164–181.

Hortacsu, N. (1999). The first year of family- and couple-initiated marriages of a Turkish sample: A longitudinal investigation. *International Journal of Psychology, 34,* 29–41.

Hoshino-Browne, E., Zanna, A. S., Spencer, S. J., Zanna, M. P., Kitayama, S., & Lackenbauer, S. (2005). On the cultural guises of cognitive dissonance: The case of Easterners and Westerners. *Journal of Personality and Social Psychology, 89,* 294–310.

Hough, W. (1922). Synoptic series of objects in the United States National Museum illustrating the history of inventions. *Proceedings of the United States National Museum, 60,* art. 9, p. 2, pl. 16.

House, J. S., Landis, K. R., & Umberson, D. (1988). Social relationships and health. *Science, 241,* 540–545.

How "the girl in the window" is doing 9 years after her rescue from horrific neglect. (2014, June 18). Retrieved from www.huffingtonpost.com/2014/06/18/girl-in-the-window-danielle-oprah-lierow_n_5505079.html

Hsiao-Ying, T. (1995). Sojourner adjustment: The case of foreigners in Japan. *Journal of Cross-Cultural Psychology, 26,* 523–536.

Hsu, L. (2010). *Social status in the expression of social anxiety: A cross-national comparison.* Unpublished doctoral dissertation. University of British Columbia.

Hsu, L., & Alden, L. (2007). Social anxiety in Chinese- and European-heritage students: The effect of assessment format and judgments of impairment. *Behavior Therapy, 38,* 120–131.

Hsu, L., Woody, S. R., Lee, H.-J., Peng, Y., Zhou, X., & Ryder, A. G. (2012). Social anxiety among East Asians in North America: East Asian socialization or the challenge of acculturation. *Cultural Diversity and Ethnic Minority Psychology, 18,* 181–191.

Hua, C. (2001). *A society without fathers or husbands: The Na of China.* Cambridge, MA: Zone Books.

Huang, C.-M., & Park, D. (2013). Cultural influences on Facebook photographs. *International Journal of Psychology, 48,* 334–343.

Huang, C.-Y., & Lamb, M. E. (2014). Are Chinese children more compliant? Examination of the cultural difference in observed maternal control and child compliance. *Journal of Cross-Cultural Psychology, 45,* 507–533.

Hughes, C. C. (1996). The culture-bound syndromes and psychiatric diagnosis. In J. E. Mezzich, A. Kleinman, H. Fabrega, Jr., & D. L. Parron (Eds.), *Culture and psychiatric diagnosis: A DSM-IV perspective* (pp. 289–307). Washington, DC: American Psychiatric Press.

Hui, C. H., & Triandis, H. C. (1989). Effects of culture and response format on extreme response style. *Journal of Cross-Cultural Psychology, 20,* 296–309.

Human Development Reports. (2005, September 7). *Human development report 2005.* Retrieved from http://hdr.undp.org/reports/global/2005/pdf/hdr05_HDI.pdf

Humphrey, N. K. (1976). The social function of intellect. In P. P. G. Bateson & R. A. Hinde (Eds.), *Growing points in ethology* (pp. 303–317). Cambridge, UK: University of Cambridge Press.

Hunt, E., & Agnoli, F. (1991). The Whorfian hypothesis: A cognitive psychology perspective. *Psychological Review, 98,* 377–389.

Hunter, J. D. (1991). *Culture wars: The struggle to define America.* New York, NY: Basic Books.

Huntington, S. P. (1996). The clash of civilizations and the remaking of world order. New York, NY: Simon & Schuster.

Huttenlocher, J., & Smiley, P. (1987). Early word meaning: The case of object names. *Cognitive Psychology, 19,* 63–89.

Hwu, H. G,, Yeh, E. K., & Chang, L. Y. (1989). Prevalence of psychiatric disorders in Taiwan defined by the Chinese Diagnostic Interview Schedule. *Acta Psychiatrica Scandinavica, 79,* 136–147.

Hypertension Detection and Follow-Up Program Cooperative Group. (1977). Race, education, and prevalence of hypertension. *American Journal of Epidemiology, 106,* 351–361.

Ickes, W., Wicklund, R., & Ferris, C. (1973). Objective self-awareness and self-esteem. *Journal of Experimental Social Psychology, 9,* 202–219.

Ignatieff, M. (1994). *Blood and belonging: Journeys into the new nationalism.* New York, NY: Farrar, Straus, & Giroux.

Inbar, Y., Pizarro, D. A., & Bloom, P. (2009). Conservatives are more easily disgusted than liberals. *Cognition and Emotion, 23,* 714–725.

Inglehart, R., Basanez, M., & Moreno, A. (1998). *Human values and beliefs: A cross-cultural sourcebook.* Ann Arbor, MI: University of Michigan Press.

Inglehart, R., & Klingemann, H. (2000). Genes, culture, democracy, and happiness. In E. Diener & E. Suh (Eds.), *Culture and subjective well-being* (pp. 165–184). Cambridge, MA: MIT Press.

Inglehart, R. F. (2004). *Human beliefs and values: A cross-cultural sourcebook based on the 1999–2002 values surveys.* Mexico City: Siglo XXI.

Inglehart, R. F., & Baker, W. E. (2000). Modernization, cultural change, and the persistence of traditional values. *American Sociological Review, 65,* 19–51.

Ingram, R. E., Scott, W., & Siegle, G. (1999). Depression: Social and cognitive aspects. In T. Millon, P. H. Blaney, & R. D. Davis (Eds.), *Oxford textbook of psychopathology* (pp. 203–226). New York, NY: Oxford University Press.

Inkeles, A. (1953). Some sociological observations on culture and personality studies. In C. Kluckhohn, H. A. Murray, & D. M. Schneider (Eds.), *Personality in nature, society, and culture* (pp. 577–592). New York, NY: Knopf.

Inoue, S., & Matsuzawa, T. (2007). Working memory of numerals in chimpanzees. *Current Biology, 17,* R1004-R1005.

International HapMap Consortium. (2005). A haplotype map of the human genome. *Nature, 437,* 1299–1320.

Irwin, D. E. (2000). Song variation in an avian ring species. *Evolution, 54,* 998–1010.

Ishii, K., Miyamoto, Y., Rule, N. O., & Toriyama, R. (2014). Physical objects as vehicles of cultural transmission: Maintaining harmony and uniqueness through colored geometric patterns. *Personality and Social Psychology Bulletin, 40,* 175–188.

Ishii, K., Reyes, J. A., & Kitayama, S. (2003). Spontaneous attention to word content versus emotional tone: Differences among three cultures. *Psychological Science, 14,* 39–46.

Iyengar, S. S., & Lepper, M. R. (1999). Rethinking the value of choice: A cultural perspective on intrinsic motivation. *Journal of Personality and Social Psychology, 76,* 349–366.

Iyengar, S. S., & Lepper, M. R. (2000). When choice is demotivating: Can one desire too much of a good thing? *Journal of Personality and Social Psychology, 79,* 995–1006.

Izard, C. E. (1994). Innate and universal facial expressions: Evidence from developmental and cross-cultural research. *Psychological Bulletin, 115,* 288–299.

Jablensky, A., Sartorius, N., Ernberg, G., Anker, M., Korten, A., Cooper, J. E., et al. (1991). *Schizophrenia: Manifestations, incidence and course in different cultures: A World Health Organization ten-country study* (Psychological Medicine, Monograph Supplement No. 20). Cambridge, UK: Cambridge University Press.

Jablonski, N. G., & Chaplin, G. (2000). The evolution of human skin coloration. *Journal of Human Evolution, 39,* 57–106.

Jack, R. E., Caldara, R., & Schyns, P. G. (2011). Internal representations reveal cultural diversity in expectations of facial expressions of emotion. *Journal of Experimental Psychology: General.*

Jack, R. E., Garrod, O. G. B., Yu, H., Caldara, R., & Schyns, P. G. (2012). Facial expressions of emotion are not culturaly universal. *Proceedings of the National Academy of Sciences, 109,* 7241–7244.

Jackson, E. F., Fox, W. S., & Crockett, H. J. (1957). Religion and occupational achievement. *American Sociological Review, 35,* 48–63.

Jacobs, R. C., & Campbell, D. T. (1961). The perpetuation of an arbitrary tradition through several generations of a laboratory microculture. *Journal of Abnormal and Social Psychology, 62,* 649–658.

James, S. (2002). *Agonias:* The social and sacred suffering of Azorean immigrants. *Culture, Medicine, and Psychiatry, 26,* 87–110.

James, S. A. (1994). John Henryism and the health of African-Americans. *Culture, Medicine, and Psychiatry, 18,* 163–182.

James, S. R. (1989). Hominid use of fire in the lower and middle Pleistocene: A review of the evidence. *Current Anthropology, 30,* 1–26.

James, W. (1950/1890). *The principles of psychology.* New York, NY: Dover.

Jankowiak, W. R., & Fischer, E. F. (1992). A cross-cultural perspective on romantic love. *Ethnology, 31,* 149–155.

Jenkins, P. (2002). *The next Christendom: The coming of global Christianity.* New York, NY: Oxford University Press.

Jensen, L. A. (1998). Moral divisions within countries between orthodoxy and progressivism: India and the United States. *Journal for the Scientific Study of Religion, 37,* 90–107.

Ji, L. J. (2005). Culture and lay theories of change. In R. M. Sorrentino, D. Cohen, J. M. Olson, & M. P. Zanna (Eds.), *Culture and social behavior: The tenth Ontario symposium* (pp. 117–136). Hillsdale, NJ: Erlbaum.

Ji, L. J. (2008). The leopard cannot change his spots, or can he? Culture and the development of lay theories of change. *Personality and Social Psychology Bulletin, 34,* 613–622.

Ji, L. J., Nisbett, R. E., & Su, Y. (2001). Culture, change, and prediction. *Psychological Science, 12,* 450–456.

Ji, L. J., Peng, K., & Nisbett, R. E. (2000). Culture, control, and perception of relationships in the environment. *Journal of Personality and Social Psychology, 78,* 943–955.

Ji, L. J., Zhang, Z., & Guo, T. (2008). To buy or to sell: Cultural differences in stock market decisions based on price trends. *Journal of Behavioral Decision Making, 21,* 399–413.

Ji, L. J., Zhang, Z., & Nisbett, R. E. (2004). Is it culture or is it language? Examination of language effects in cross-cultural research on categorization. *Journal of Personality and Social Psychology, 87,* 57–65.

Jobson, L., Moradi, A. R., Rahimi-Movaghar, V., Conway, M. A., & Dalgleish, T. (2014). Culture and the remembering of trauma. *Clinical Psychological Science, 2,* 696–713.

Johns, M., Schmader, T., & Martens, A. (2005). Knowing is half the battle: Teaching stereotype threat as a means of improving women's math performance. *Psychological Science, 16,* 175–179.

Johnson, J., & Newport, E. L. (1989). Critical period effects in second language learning: The influence of maturational state on the acquisition of English as a second language. *Cognitive Psychology, 21,* 60–99.

Johnson, S. (2005). *Everything bad is good for you.* New York, NY: Riverhead Books.

Johnson, W., & Krueger, R. F. (2005). Higher perceived life control decreases genetic variance in physical health: Evidence from a national twin study. *Journal of Personality and Social Psychology, 88,* 165–173.

Jokela, M., Elovainio, M., Kivimäki, M., & Keltikangas-Järvinen, L. (2008). Temperament and migration patterns in Finland. *Psychological Science, 19,* 831–837.

Jones, E. E., & Harris, V. A. (1967). The attribution of attitudes. *Journal of Experimental Social Psychology, 3,* 1–24.

Jones, M. (2006, January 15). Shutting themselves in. *New York Times Magazine.*

Jones, R. (1995). Tasmanian archaeology: Establishing the sequence. *Annual Review of Anthropology, 24,* 423–446.

Jones, R. B., Larkins, C., & Hughes, B. O. (1996). Approach/avoidance responses of domestic chicks to familiar and unfamiliar video images of biologically neutral stimuli. *Applied Animal Behaviour Science, 48,* 81–98.

Joshi, M. S., & Carter, W. (2013, 13 February). Unrealistic optimism: East and West? *Frontiers in Psychology.* doi:10.3389/fpsyg.2013.00006

Kagamimori, S., Iibuchi, Y., & Fox, A. J. (1983). A comparison of socioeconomic differences between Japan and England and Wales. *World Health Statistics Quarterly, 36,* 119–128.

Kagan, J., Kearsley, R. B., & Zelazo, P. R. (1977). The effects of infant day care on psychological development. *Evaluation Quarterly, 1,* 109–142.

Kagitcibasi, C. (1970). Social norms and authoritarianism: A Turkish-American comparison. *Journal of Personality and Social Psychology, 16,* 444–451.

Kagitcibasi, C. (1996). *Family and human development across cultures.* Mahwah, NJ: Erlbaum.

Kalin, R., & Tilby, P. (1978). Development and validation of a sex-role ideology scale. *Psychological Reports, 42,* 731–738.

Kanagawa, C., Cross, S. E., & Markus, H. R. (2001). "Who am I?": The cultural psychology of the conceptual self. *Personality and Social Psychology Bulletin, 27,* 90–103.

Kanazawa, S. (2006). No, it ain't gonna be like that. *Evolutionary Psychology, 4,* 120–128.

Kaplan, G. A. (1985). *Twenty years of health in Alameda County: The human population laboratory analyses.* Paper presented at the annual meeting of the Society for Prospective Medicine, San Francisco, CA.

Kaplan, G. A., & Keil, J. E. (1993). Socioeconomic factors and cardiovascular disease: A review of the literature. *Circulation, 88,* 1973–1998.

Kaplan, R. M. (1978). Is beauty talent? Sex interaction in the attractiveness halo effect. *Sex Roles, 4,* 195–204.

Karasik, L. B., Adolph, K. E., Tamis-LeMonda, C. S., & Bornstein, M. H. (2010). WEIRD walking: Cross-cultural research on motor development. *Behavioral and Brain Sciences, 33,* 35–36.

Karno, M., & Edgerton, R. B. (1969). Perception of mental illness in a Mexican-American community. *Archives of General Psychiatry, 20,* 233–238.

Karter, A. J., et al. (2004). Missed appointments and poor glycemic control: An opportunity to identify high-risk diabetic patients. *Medical Care, 42,* 110–115.

Kasahara, Y. (1986). Fear of eye-to-eye confrontation among neurotic patients in Japan. In T. Lebra & W. P. Lebra (Eds.), *Japanese culture and behavior* (pp. 379–387). Honolulu: University of Hawaii Press.

Kashima, E. S., & Kashima, Y. (1998). Culture and language: The case of cultural dimensions and personal pronoun use. *Journal of Cross-Cultural Psychology. 29,* 461–486.

Kashima, Y., Siegal, M., Tanaka, K., & Isaka, H. (1988). Universalism in lay conceptions of distributive justice: A cross-cultural examination. *International Journal of Psychology, 23,* 51–64.

Kashima, Y., Siegal, M., Tanaka, K., & Kashima, E. S. (1992). Do people believe behaviors are consistent with attitudes? Towards a cultural psychology of attribution processes. *British Journal of Social Psychology, 31,* 111–124.

Kashima, Y., Yamaguchi, S., Kim, U., Choi, S., Gelfand, M., & Yuki, M. (1995). Culture, gender, and self: A perspective from individualism-collectivism research. *Journal of Personality and Social Psychology, 69,* 925–937.

Katz, D., & Schnack, R. L. (1938). *Social psychology.* New York, NY: Wiley.

Katz, S. J., & Hofer, T. P. (1994). Socioeconomic disparities in preventive care persist despite universal coverage: Breast and cervical cancer screening in Ontario and the United States. *Journal of the American Medical Association, 272,* 530–534.

Kawamura, S. (1959). The process of subculture propagation among Japanese macaques. *Primates, 2,* 43–60.

Kawanishi, Y. (2004). Japanese youth: The other half of the crisis. *Asian Affairs, 35,* 22–32.

Keel, P. K., & Klump, K. L. (2003). Are eating disorders culture-bound syndromes? Implications for conceptualizing their etiology. *Psychological Bulletin, 129,* 747–769.

Keller, H. (2007). *Cultures of infancy.* Mahwah, NJ: Erlbaum.

Keller, H., Kartner, J., Borke, J., Yovsi, R., & Kleis, A. (2005). Parenting styles and development of the categorical self: A longitudinal study on mirror self-recognition in Cameroonian Nso and German families. *International Journal of Behavioral Development, 29,* 496–504.

Kelly, R. C. (1980). *Etoro social structure: A study in structural contradiction.* Ann Arbor, MI: University of Michigan Press.

Keltner, D. (1995). Signs of appeasement: Evidence for the distinct display of embarrassment, amusement, and shame. *Journal of Personality and Social Psychology, 68,* 441–454.

Kenrick, D. T., Li, N. P., & Butner, J. (2003). Dynamical evolutionary psychology: Individual decision-rules and emergent social norms. *Psychological Review, 1,* 3–28.

Kephart, W. M. (1967). Some correlates of romantic love. *Journal of Marriage and the Family, 29,* 470–474.

Kesebir, P., & Kesebir, S. (2012). The cultural salience of moral character and virtue declined in twentieth century America. *The Journal of Positive Psychology, 7,* 471–480.

Kessler, R. C., McGonagle, K. A., Zhao, S., Nelson, C. B., Hughes, N., Eshleman, S., et al. (1994). Lifetime and 12–month prevalence of DSM-III-R psychiatric disorders in the United States: Results from the National Comorbidity Survey. *Archives of General Psychiatry, 51,* 8–19.

Kim, E., Zeppenfeld, V., & Cohen, D. (2013). Sublimation, culture, and creativity. *Journal of Personality and Social Psychology, 105,* 639–666.

Kim, H. S. (2002). We talk, therefore we think? A cultural analysis of the effect of talking on thinking. *Journal of Personality and Social Psychology, 83,* 828–842.

Kim, H. S., & Drolet, A. (2003). Choice and self-expression: A cultural analysis of variety seeking. *Journal of Personality and Social Psychology, 85,* 373–382.

Kim, H. S., & Drolet, A. (2009). Express your social self: Cultural differences in choice of brand-name versus generic products. *Personality and Social Psychology Bulletin, 35,* 1555–1566.

Kim, H. S., & Markus, H. R. (1999). Deviance or uniqueness, harmony or conformity? A cultural analysis. *Journal of Personality and Social Psychology, 77,* 785–800.

Kim, H. S., & Sherman, D. K. (2007). "Express yourself": Culture and the effect of self-expression on choice. *Journal of Personality and Social Psychology, 92,* 1–11.

Kim, H. S., Sherman, D. K., Ko, D., & Taylor, S. E. (2006). Pursuit of happiness and pursuit of harmony: Culture, relationships, and social support seeking. *Personality and Social Psychology Bulletin, 32,* 1595–1607.

Kim, H. S., Sherman, D. K., Mojaverian, T., Sasaki, J. Y., Park, J., Suh, E. M., et al. (2011). Gene-culture interaction: Oxytocin receptor polymorphism (OXTR) and emotion regulation. *Social Psychological and Personality Science, 2,* 665–672.

Kim, H. S., Sherman, D. K., Sasaki, J. Y., Xu, J., Chu, T. Q., Ryu, C., et al. (2010a). Culture, distress, and oxytocin receptor polymorphism (OXTR) interact to influence emotional support seeking. *Proceedings of the National Academy of Sciences, 107,* 15717–15721.

Kim, H. S., Sherman, D. K., & Taylor, S. E. (2008). Culture and social support. *American Psychologist, 63,* 518–526.

Kim, H. S., Sherman, D. K., Taylor, S. E., Sasaki, J. Y., Chu, T. Q., Ryu, C., et al. (2010b). Culture, serotonin receptor polymorphism and locus of attention. *Social, Cognitive, and Affective Neuroscience, 5,* 212–218.

Kim, J., & Hatfield, E. (2004). Love types and subjective well-being: A cross cultural study. *Social Behavior and Personality, 32,* 173–182.

Kim, K. H. S., Relkin, N., & Lee, K. (1997). Distinct cortical areas associated with native and second languages. *Nature, 388,* 171–174.

Kim, W. J., Kim, L. I., & Rue, D. S. (1997). Korean American children. In G. Johnson-Powell and J. Yamamoto (Eds.), *Transcultural child development: Psychological assessment and treatment* (pp. 183–207). New York, NY: Wiley.

Kim, Y., Cohen, D., & Au, W. (2010). The jury and abjury of my peers: The self in face and dignity cultures. *Journal of Personality and Social Psychology, 98,* 904–916.

Kim, Y.-H., & Cohen, D. (2010). Information, perspective, and judgments about the self in face and dignity cultures. *Personality and Social Psychology Bulletin, 36,* 537–550.

King, C. R., Staurowsky, E. J., Baca, L., Davis, L. R., & Pewewardy, C. (2002). Of polls and race prejudice: *Sports Illustrated*'s errant "Indian wars." *Journal of Sport & Social Issues, 26,* 381–402.

Kinias, Z., Kim, H. S., Hafenbrack, A. C., & Lee, J. J. (2014). Standing out as a signal to selfishness: Culture and devaluation of non-normative characteristics. *Organizational Behavior and Human Decision Processes, 124,* 190–203.

Kirmayer, L. J. (2007). Psychotherapy and the cultural concept of the person. *Transcultural Psychiatry, 44,* 232–257.

Kirmayer, L. J., & Ban, L. (2013). Cultural psychiatry: Research strategies and future directions. *Advances in Psychosomatic Medicine, 33,* 97–114.

Kirmayer, L. J., Groleau, D., Guzder, J., Blake, C., & Jarvis, E. (2003). Cultural consultation: A model of mental health service for multicultural societies. *Canadian Journal of Psychiatry, 48,* 145–153.

Kishwar, M. (1994). Love and marriage. *Manushi, 80,* 11–19.

Kitayama, S., Duffy, S., Kawamura, T., & Larsen, J. T. (2003). Perceiving an object and its context in different cultures: A cultural look at New Look. *Psychological Science, 14,* 201–206.

Kitayama, S., & Ishii, K. (2002). Word and voice: Spontaneous attention to emotional utterances in two languages. *Cognition and Emotion, 16,* 29–59.

Kitayama, S., Ishii, K., Imada, T., Takemura, K., & Ramaswamy, J. (2006). Voluntary settlement and the spirit of independence: Evidence from Japan's "Northern Frontier." *Journal of Personality and Social Psychology, 91,* 369–384.

Kitayama, S., King, A., Yoon, C., Tompson, S., Huff, S., & Liberzon, I. (2014). The dopamine D4 receptor gene (DRD4) moderates cultural difference in independent versus interdependent social orientation. *Psychological Science, 25,* 1169–1177.

Kitayama, S., Markus, H. R., & Kurokawa, M. (2000). Culture, emotion, and well-being: Good feelings in Japan and the United States. *Cognition and Emotion, 14,* 93–124.

Kitayama, S., Markus, H. R., Matsumoto, H., & Norasakkunkit, V. (1997). Individual and collective processes in the construction of the self: Self-enhancement in the United States and self-criticism in Japan. *Journal of Personality and Social Psychology, 72,* 1245–1267.

Kitayama, S., Mesquita, B., & Karasawa, M. (2006). Emotional basis of independent and interdependent selves: Intensity of experiencing engaging and disengaging emotions in the U.S. and Japan. *Journal of Personality and Social Psychology, 91,* 890–903.

Kitayama, S., Snibbe, A. C., & Markus, H. R. (2004). Is there any "free" choice?: Self and dissonance in two cultures. *Psychological Science, 15,* 527–533.

Kitayama, S., & Uchida, Y. (2003). Explicit self-criticism and implicit self-regard: Evaluating self and friend in two cultures. *Journal of Experimental Social Psychology, 39,* 476–482.

Kleinman, A. (1982). Neurasthenia and depression: A study of somatization and culture in China. *Culture, Medicine, and Psychiatry, 6,* 117–190.

Kleinman, A. (1988). *Rethinking psychiatry: From cultural category to personal experience.* New York, NY: Free Press.

Kline, M. A., & Boyd, R. (2010). Population size predicts technological complexity in Oceania. *Proceedings of the Royal Society, B, 277,* 2559–2564.

Kluckhohn, C. (1949). *Mirror for man: The relation of anthropology to modern life:* New York, NY: McGraw-Hill.

Kluegel, J. R., & Smith, E. R. (1986). *Beliefs about inequality: Americans' views of what is and what ought to be.* Hawthorne, NY: Aldine de Gruyter.

Knapp, R. H. (1944). A psychology of rumor. *Public Opinion Quarterly, 8,* 22–37.

Knowles, E. D., Lowery, B. S., Hogan, C. M., & Chow, R. M. (2009). On the malleability of ideology: Motivated construals of color blindness. *Journal of Personality and Social Psychology, 96,* 857–869.

Kohlberg, L. (1971). From is to ought: How to commit the naturalistic fallacy and get away with it in the study of moral development. In L. Mischel (Ed.), *Cognitive development and epistemology* (pp. 151–284). New York, NY: Academic Press.

Koleva, S. P., Graham, J., Iyer, R., Ditto, P. H., & Haidt, J. (2012). Tracing the threads: How five moral concerns (especially purity) help explain culture war attitudes. *Journal of Research in Personality, 46,* 184–194.

Komlos, J. (1998). Shrinking in a growing economy? The mystery of physical stature during the Industrial Revolution. *Journal of Economic History, 58,* 779–802.

Komlos, J. (2010). The recent decline in the height of African-American women. *Economics & Human Biology, 8,* 58–66.

Koopman, C., Eisenthal, S., & Stoeckle, J. D. (1984). Ethnicity in the reported pain, emotional distress and requests of medical outpatients. *Social Science Medicine, 18,* 487–490.

Koskenvuo, M., Kaprio, J., Kesaniemi, A., & Sarna, S. (1978). Differences in mortality from ischemic heart disease by marital status and social class. *Journal of Chronic Diseases, 33,* 95–106.

Kraus, M. W., Cote, S., & Keltner, D. (2010). Social class, contextualism, and empathic accuracy. *Psychological Science, 21,* 1716–1723.

Kraus, M. W., Horberg, E. J., Goetz, J. L., & Keltner, D. (2011). Social class rank, threat vigilance, and hostile reactivity. *Personality and Social Psychology Bulletin, 37,* 1376–1388.

Kraus, M. W., Piff, P. K., & Keltner, D. (2009). Social class, the sense of control, and social explanation. *Journal of Personality and Social Psychology, 97,* 992–1004.

Kraus, M. W., Piff, P. K., Mendoza-Denton, R., Rheinschmidt, M. L., & Keltner, D. (2012). Social class, solipsism, and contextualism: How the rich are different from the poor. *Psychological Review, 119,* 546–572.

Krutzen, M., Mann, J., Heithaus, M. R., Connor, R. C., Bejder, L., & Sherwin, W. B. (2005). Cultural transmission of tool use in bottlenose dolphins. *Proceedings of the National Academy of Sciences, 102,* 8939–8943.

Kuczynski, L., & Kochanska, G. (1990). Development of children's noncompliance strategies from toddlerhood to age 5. *Developmental Psychology, 26,* 398–408.

Kuhn, M. T., & McPartland, T. (1954). An empirical investigation of self-attitudes. *American Sociological Review, 19,* 68–76.

Kühnen, U., & Oyserman, D. (2002). Thinking about the self influences thinking in general: Cognitive consequences of salient self-concept. *Journal of Experimental Social Psychology, 38,* 492–499.

Kühnen, U., Hannover, B., & Schubert, B. (2001). The semantic-procedural interface model of the self: The role of self-knowledge for context-dependent versus context-independent modes of thinking. *Journal of Personality and Social Psychology, 80,* 397–409.

Kumanyika, S. K., Wilson, J. F., & Guilford-Davenport, M. (1993). Weight-related attitudes and behaviors of black women. *Journal of the American Dietetic Association, 93,* 416–422.

Kumar, P., & Dhyani, J. (1996). Marital adjustment: A study of some related factors. *Indian Journal of Clinical Psychology, 23,* 112–116.

Kunda, Z. (1990). The case for motivated reasoning. *Psychological Bulletin, 108,* 480–498.

Kurman, J. (2001). Self-enhancement: Is it restricted to individualistic cultures? *Personality and Social Psychology Bulletin, 12,* 1705–1716.

Kurman, J. (2003). Why is self-enhancement low in certain collectivist cultures? An investigation of two competing explanations. *Journal of Cross-Cultural Psychology, 34,* 496–510.

Kurman, J., & Sriram, N. (2002). Interrelationships among vertical and horizontal collectivism, modesty, and self-enhancement. *Journal of Cross-Cultural Psychology, 33,* 71–86.

Kurman, J., Yoshihara-Tanaka, C., & Elkoshi, T. (2003). Is self-enhancement negatively related to constructive self-criticism? Self-enhancement in Israel and in Japan. *Journal of Cross-Cultural Psychology, 34,* 24–37.

Kuroda, Y., Hayashi, C., & Suzuki, T. (1986). The role of language in cross-national surveys: American and Japanese respondents. *Applied Stochastic Model and Data Analysis, 2,* 43–59.

Kyei, K. G., & Schreckenbach, H. (1975). *No time to die.* Accra, Ghana: Catholic Press.

Lachlan, R. F., Crooks, L., & Laland, K. N. (1998). Who follows whom? Shoaling preferences and social learning of foraging information in guppies. *Animal Behavior, 56,* 181–190.

Lachman, M. E., & Weaver, S. L. (1998). The sense of control as a moderator of social class differences in health and well-being. *Journal of Personality and Social Psychology, 74,* 763–773.

LaFromboise, T., Coleman, H. L. K., & Gerton, J. (1993). Psychological impact of biculturalism: Evidence and theory. *Psychological Bulletin, 114,* 395–412.

Laland, K. N., Odling-Smee, J., & Myles, S. (2010). How culture shaped the human genome: Bringing genetics and the human sciences together. *Nature Reviews Genetics, 11,* 137–148.

Lalonde, R. N., & Cameron, J. E. (1993). An intergroup perspective on immigrant acculturation with a focus on collective strategies. *International Journal of Psychology, 28,* 57–74.

Lambert, T. A., Kahn, A. S., & Apple, K. J. (2003). Pluralistic ignorance and hooking up. *Journal of Sex Research, 40,* 129–133.

Landes, D. S. (1999). *The wealth and poverty of nations.* New York, NY: Norton.

Landy, D., & Sigall, H. (1974). Beauty is talent: Task evaluation as a function of the performer's physical attractiveness. *Journal of Personality and Social Psychology, 29,* 299–304.

Langer, E. J., & Rodin, J. (1976). The effects of choice and enhanced personal responsibility for the aged: A field experiment in an institutional setting. *Journal of Personality and Social Psychology, 34,* 191–198.

Lao Tzu. (2000). *Tao te ching.* Washington, DC: Counterpoint.

Larøi, F., et al. (2014). Culture and hallucinations: Overview and future directions. *Schizophrenia Bulletin, 40,* S213–S220.

Larson, J. R., Foster-Fishman, P. G., & Keys, C. B. (1994). Discussion of shared and unshared information in decision-making groups.

Journal of Personality and Social Psychology, 67, 446–461.

Latané, B. (1996). Dynamic social impact: The creation of culture by communication. *Journal of Communication, 46,* 13–25.

Lavin, T., Hall, D. G., & Leung, D. (2006). *Culture and the acquisition of nouns and verbs.* Manuscript submitted for publication.

Lavin, T., Hall, D. G., & Waxman, S. R. (2006). Culture and verb learning. In K. Hirsh-Pasek and R. Golinkoff (Eds.), *Action meets word: How children learn verbs* (pp. 525–543). Oxford, England: Oxford University Press.

Layous, K., Lee, H., Choi, I., & Lyubomirsky, S. (2013). Culture matters when designing a successful happiness-increasing activity: A comparison of the United States and South Korea. *Journal of Cross-Cultural Psychology, 44,* 1294–1303.

Le Billon, K. (2012). *French kids eat everything: How our family moved to France, cured picky eating, banned snacking, and discovered 10 simple rules for raising happy, healthy eaters.* New York, NY: William Morrow.

Lebra, T. S. (1976). *Japanese patterns of behavior.* Honolulu: University of Hawaii Press.

Lebra, T. S. (1994). Mother and child in Japanese socialization: A Japan-U.S. comparison. In P. Greenfield & R. Cocking (Eds.), *Cross-cultural roots of minority child development* (pp. 259–274). Hillsdale, NJ: Erlbaum.

Leclerc, A., Lert, F., & Goldberg, M. (1984). Les inegalites sociales devant la mort en Grande-Bretagne et en France. *Social Science and Medicine, 19,* 479–487.

Lederer, R. (1987). Anguished English. New York, NY: Dell.

LeDoux, J. E. (1996). *The emotional brain: The mysterious underpinnings of emotional life.* New York, NY: Simon & Schuster.

Lee, A. Y., Aaker, J. L., & Gardner, W. L. (2000). The pleasures and pains of distinct self-construals: The role of interdependence in regulatory focus. *Journal of Personality and Social Psychology, 78,* 1122–1134.

Lee, C. C., Oh, M. Y., & Mountcastle, A. R. (1992). Indigenous models of helping in nonwestern countries: Implications for multicultural counseling. *Journal of Multicultural Counseling and Development, 20,* 3–10.

Lee, C. K., Kwak, Y. S., Rhee, H., Kim, Y. S., Han, J. H., Choi, J. O., et al. (1987). The nationwide epidemiological study of mental disorders in Korea. *Journal of Korean Medical Science, 2,* 19–34.

Lee, D. W., Miyasato, L. E., & Clayton, N. S. (1998). Neurobiological bases of spatial learning in the natural environment: Neurogenesis and growth in the avian and mammalian hippocampus. *Neuroreport, 9,* R15–R27.

Lee, F., Hallahan, M., & Herzog, T. (1996). Explaining real life events: How culture and domain shape attributions. *Personality and Social Psychology Bulletin, 22,* 732–741.

Lee, G. R., & Stone, L. H. (1980). Mate-selection systems and criteria: Variation according to family structure. *Journal of Marriage and the Family, 42,* 319–326.

Lee, S. (1989). Anorexia nervosa in Hong Kong: Why not more in Chinese? *British Journal of Psychiatry, 154,* 683–688.

Lee, S., Ho, T. P., & Hsu, L. K. G. (1993). Fat phobic and non-fat phobic anorexia nervosa: A comparative study of 70 Chinese patients in Hong Kong. *Psychological Medicine, 23,* 999–1017.

Lee, S. W. S., Oyserman, D., & Bond, M. H. (2010). Am I doing better than you? That depends on whether you ask me in English or Chinese: Self-enhancement effects of language as a cultural mindset prime. *Journal of Experimental Social Psychology, 46,* 785–791.

Leeman, R. F., Fischler, C., & Rozin, P. (2011). Medical doctors' attitudes and beliefs about diet and health are more like those of their lay countrymen (France, Germany, Italy, UK and USA) than those of doctors in other countries. *Appetite, 56,* 558–563.

Lefebvre, L., & Giraldeau, L. A. (1994). Cultural transmission in pigeons is affected by the number of tutors and bystanders present. *Animal Behaviour, 47,* 331–337.

Leff, J., Sartorius, N., Jablensky, A., Korten, A., & Ernberg, G. (1992). The International Pilot Study of Schizophrenia: Five-year follow-up findings. *Psychological Medicine, 22,* 131–145.

Lenneberg, E. H. (1967). *Biological foundations of language.* New York, NY: Wiley.

Lenski, G., & Lenski, J. (1987). *Human societies* (5th ed.). New York, NY: McGraw-Hill.

Leu, J., Wang, J., & Koo, K. (2011). Are positive emotions just as positive across cultures? *Emotion, 4,* 994–999.

Leuers, T. R. S., & Sonoda, N. (1999). Independent self-bias. In T. Sugiman, M. Karasawa, J. H. Liu, & C. Ward (Eds.), *Progress in Asian social psychology, Vol. II: Theoretical and empirical contributions* (pp. 87–104). Seoul, Korea: Kyoyook-Kwahak-Sa Publishing.

Leung, A. K., & Cohen, D. (2011). Within- and between-culture variation: Individual differences and the cultural logics of honor, face, and dignity cultures. *Journal of Personality and Social Psychology, 100,* 507–526.

Leung, A. K., Maddux, W. W., Galinsky, A. D., & Chiu, C. (2008). Multicultural experience enhances creativity: The when and how. *American Psychologist, 63,* 169–181.

Leung, A. K.-Y., & Chiu, C.-Y. (2010). Multicultural experience, idea receptiveness, and creativity. *Journal of Cross-Cultural Psychology, 41,* 723–741.

Leung, K., & Bond, M. H. (2004). Social axioms: A model for social beliefs in multicultural perspective. In M. P. Zanna (Ed.), *Advances in experimental social psychology: Vol. 36* (pp. 119–197). San Diego, CA: Elsevier.

Leung, K., Lau, S., & Lam, W. L. (1998). Parenting styles and achievement. A cross-cultural study. *Merril-Palmer Quarterly, 44,* 157–172.

Levenson, R. W. (1992). Autonomic nervous system differences among emotions. *Psychological Science, 3,* 23–27.

Levenson, R. W., Ekman, P., Heider, K., & Friesen, W. V. (1992). Emotion and autonomic nervous system activity in the Minangkabau of West Sumatra. *Journal of Personality and Social Psychology, 62,* 972–988.

Leventhal, T., & Brooks-Gunn, J. (2000). The neighborhoods they live in: The effects of neighborhood residence on child and adolescent outcomes. *Psychological Bulletin, 126,* 309–337.

Levine, R., Sato, S., Hashimoto, T., & Verma, J. (1995). Love and marriage in eleven cultures. *Journal of Cross-Cultural Psychology, 26,* 554–571.

Levine, R. A. (2001). Culture and personality studies, 1918–1960: Myth and history. *Journal of Personality, 69,* 803–818.

Levine, R. V., & Norenzayan, A. (1999). The pace of life in 31 countries. *Journal of Cross-Cultural Psychology, 30,* 178–205.

Levinson, S. C. (1997). Language and cognition: The cognitive consequences of spatial description in Guugu Yimithirr. *Journal of Linguistic Anthropology, 7,* 98–131.

Lewis, C. C. (1995). *Educating hearts and minds.* New York, NY: Cambridge University Press.

Li, L. M. W., Adams, G., Kurtis, T., & Hamamura, T. (in press). Beware of friends: The cultural psychology of relational mobility and cautious intimacy. *Asian Journal of Social Psychology.*

Li, Y. J., Johnson, K. A., Cohen, A. B., Williams, M. J., Knowles, E. D., & Chen, Z. (2012). Fundamental(ist) attribution error: Protestants are dispositionally focused. *Journal of Personality and Social Psychology, 102,* 281–290.

Lieberman, D. E., Venkadesan, M., Werbel, W. A., Daoud, A. I., D'Andrea, S., Davis, I. S., et al. (2010). Foot strike patterns and collision forces in habitually barefoot versus shod runners. *Nature, 463,* 531–535.

Lin, R. Y., Rin, H., Yeh, E. K., Hsu, C. C., & Chu, H. M. (1969). Mental disorders in Taiwan, fifteen years later: A preliminary report. In W. Caudill & T. Y. Lin (Eds.), *Mental health research in Asia and the Pacific* (pp. 66–91). Honolulu, HI: East-West Center Press.

Lin, T.-Y., & Lin, M. C. (1981). Love, denial and rejection: Responses of Chinese families to mental illness. In A. Kleinman & T.-Y. Lin, *Normal and abnormal behavior in Chinese culture* (pp. 387–401). Boston, MA: D. Reidel.

Lindquist, K. A., Wager, T. D., Kober, H., Bliss-Moreau, E., & Barrett, L. F. (2012). The brain basis of emotion: A meta-analytic review. *Behavioral and Brain Sciences, 35,* 121–202.

Lipset, S. M. (1996). *American exceptionalism: A double-edged sword.* New York, NY: Norton.

Little, A. C., Apicella, C. L., & Marlowe, F. W. (2007). Preferences for symmetry in human faces in two cultures: Data from the UK and the Hadza, an isolated group of hunter-gatherers. *Proceedings of the Royal Society B, 274,* 3113–3117.

Little, A. C., Hockings, K. J., Apicella, C. L., & Sousa, C. (2012). Mixed-ethnicity face shape and attractiveness in humans. *Perception, 41,* 1486–1496.

Littlewood, R., & Lipsedge, M. (1987). The butterfly and the serpent: Culture, psychopathology, and biomedicine. *Culture, Medicine, and Psychiatry, 11,* 289–335.

Livingstone, F. B. (1958). Anthropological implications of sickle-cell distribution in West Africa. *American Anthropologist, 60,* 533–562.

Lockwood, P., & Kunda, Z. (1997). Superstars and me: Predicting the impact of role models on the self. *Journal of Personality and Social Psychology, 73,* 91–103.

Lockwood, P., Marshall, T. C., & Sadler, P. (2005). Promoting success or preventing failure: Cultural differences in motivation by positive and negative role models. *Personality and Social Psychology Bulletin, 31,* 379–392.

Loftus, E. F. (1993). The reality of repressed memories. *American Psychologist, 48,* 518–537.

Lopez, S. R., & Guarnaccia, P. J. J. (2000). Cultural psychopathology: Uncovering the social world of mental illness. *Annual Review of Psychology, 51,* 571–598.

Lord, C., Ross, L., & Lepper, M. (1979). Biased assimilation and attitude polarization: The effects of prior theories on subsequently considered evidence. *Journal of Personality and Social Psychology, 37,* 2098–2109.

Loughnan, S., et al. (2011). Economic inequality is linked to biased self-perception. *Psychological Science, 22,* 1254–1258.

Lovejoy, P. E. (2000). *Transformations in slavery: A history of slavery in Africa* (2nd ed.). Cambridge, England: Cambridge University Press.

Lubman, S. (1998, February 23). Some students must learn to question. *San Jose Mercury News,* A1–A12.

Lucy, J. A., & Shweder, R. A. (1979). Whorf and his critics: Linguistic and nonlinguistic influences on color memory. *American Anthropologist, 81,* 581–605.

Luhrmann, T. M., Padmavati, R., Tharoor, H., & Osei, A. (2015). Differences in voice-hearing experiences of people with psychosis in the USA, India, and Ghana: Interview-based study. *The British Journal of Psychiatry, 206,* 41-44.

Lumholtz, C. (1894). *Unknown Mexico.* New York, NY: Scribner's.

Lundberg, O. (1991). Causal explanations for class inequality in health—an empirical analysis. *Social Science and Medicine, 32,* 385–393.

Luria, A. R. (1928). The problem of the cultural development of the child. *Journal of Genetic Psychology, 35,* 493–506.

Luria, A. R. (1976). *Cognitive development: Its cultural and social foundations.* Cambridge, MA: Harvard University Press.

Luttmer, E. F. P., & Singhal, M. (2011). Culture, context, and the taste for redistribution. *American Economic Policy, 3,* 157–179.

Lutz, C. (1988). *Unnatural emotions.* Chicago, IL: University of Chicago Press.

Lydon, J. E., Jamieson, D. W., & Zanna, M. P. (1988). Interpersonal similarity and the social and intellectual dimension of first impressions. *Social Cognition, 6,* 269–286.

Lynge, E. (1984). Socioeconomic occupational mortality differentials in Europe. *Sozial-und Praventivmedizin, 29,* 265–267.

Lynn, R. (1989). Positive correlation between height, head size, and IQ: A nutrition theory of the secular increases in intelligence. *British Journal of Educational Psychology, 59,* 372–377.

Lyons, D. E., Young, A. G., & Keil, F. C. (2007). The hidden structure of overimitation. *Proceedings of the National Academy of Sciences, USA, 104,* 19751–19756.

Lysgaard, S. (1955). Adjustment in a foreign society: Norwegian Fulbright grantees visiting the United States. *International Social Science Bulletin, 7,* 45–51.

Lyubomirsky, S., King, L., & Diener, E. (2005). The benefits of frequent positive affect: Does happiness lead to success? *Psychological Bulletin, 131,* 803–855.

Ma, V., & Schoeneman, T. J. (1997). Individualism versus collectivism: A comparison of Kenyan and American self-concepts. *Basic and Applied Social Psychology, 19,* 261–273.

Ma, Y., Bang, D., Wang, C., Allen, M., Frith, C., Roepstorff, A., & Han, S. (2012). Sociocultural patterning of neural activity during self-reflection. *Social Cognitive and Affective Neuroscience. 9,* 73–80.

Maass, A., Karasawa, M., Politi, F., & Suga, S. (2006). Do verbs and adjectives play different roles in different cultures? A cross-linguistic analysis of person representation. *Journal of Personality and Social Psychology, 90,* 734–750.

MacKinnon, I. (2009, October 30). Jungle woman Rochom P'ngieng wants to return to the wild. *The Telegraph.*

Macmillan, N. A. (1987). Beyond the categorical/continuous distinction: A psychophysical approach to processing modes. In S. Harnad (Ed.), *Categorical perception: The groundwork of cognition* (pp. 53–85). Cambridge, England: Cambridge University Press.

Macpherson, C., & Macpherson, L. (1987). Towards an explanation of recent trends in suicide in Western Samoa. *Man, 22,* 305–330.

Maddux, W. W., Adam, H., & Galinsky, A. D. (2010). When in Rome . . . Learn why the Romans do what they do: How multicultural learning experiences facilitate creativity. *Personality and Social Psychology Bulletin, 36,* 731–741.

Maddux, W. W., Bivolaru, E., Hafenbrack, A. C., Tadmor, C. T., & Galinsky, A. D. (2014). Expanding opportunities by opening your mind: Multicultural engagement predicts job market success through longitudinal increases in integrative complexity. *Social Psychological and Personality Science, 5,* 608–615.

Maddux, W. W., & Galinsky, A. D. (2009). Cultural borders and mental barriers: The relatioship between living abroad and creativity. *Journal of Personality and Social Psychology, 96,* 1047–1061.

Maddux, W. W., Yang, H., Falk, C., Adam, H., Adair, W., et al. (2010). For whom is parting with possessions more painful? Cultural differences in the endowment effect. *Psychological Science, 21,* 1910–1917.

Maddux, W. W., & Yuki, M. (2006). The "ripple effect": Cultural differences in perceptions of the consequences of events. *Personality and Social Psychology Bulletin, 32,* 669–683.

Maguire, E. A., Gadian, D. G., Johnsrude, I. S., Good, C. D., Ashburner, J., Frckowiak, R. S. J., & Frith, C. D. (2000). Navigation-related structural changes in the hippocampi of taxi drivers. *Proceedings of the National Academy of Sciences, 97,* 4398–4403.

Mahalingam, R. (2003a). Essentialism, culture and beliefs about gender among the Aravanis of Tamil Nadu, India. *Sex Roles, 49,* 489–496.

Mahalingam, R. (2003b). Essentialism, culture, and power: Representations of social class. *Journal of Social Issues, 59,* 733–749.

Mahalingam, R. (2007). Essentialism, power, and the representation of social categories: A folk sociology perspective. *Human Development, 50,* 300–319.

Mahalingam, R., & Rodriguez, J. (2003). Essentialism, power and cultural psychology of gender. *Journal of Cognition and Culture, 3,* 157–174.

Mahler, I. (1974). A comparative study of locus of control. *Psychologia, 17,* 135–139.

Maines, R. P. (1998). *The technology of orgasm: "Hysteria," the vibrator, and women's sexual satisfaction.* Baltimore, MD: Johns Hopkins University Press.

Majid, A., & Burenhult, N. (2014). Odors are expressible in language, as long as you speak the right language. *Cognition, 230,* 266–270.

Major, B., Spencer, S., Schmader, T., Wolfe, C., & Crocker, J. (1998). Coping with negative stereotypes about intellectual performance: The role of psychological disengagement. *Personality and Social Psychology Bulletin, 24,* 34–50.

Ma-Kellams, C., & Blascovich, J. (2012). Inferring the emotions of friends versus strangers: The role of culture and self-construal. *Personality and Social Psychology Bulletin, 38,* 933–945.

Ma-Kellams, C., Blascovich, J., & McCall, C. (2012). Culture and the body: East-West differences in visceral perception. *Journal of Personality and Social Psychology, 102,* 718–728.

Malcolm, L. A. (1974). Ecological factors relating to child growth and nutritional status. In A. F. Roche & R. Falkner (Eds.), *Nutrition and malnutrition: Identification and measurement* (pp. 329–352). New York, NY: Plenum Press.

Malinowski, B. (1922/1965). *Argonauts of the Western Pacific: An account of native enterprise and adventure in the archipelagoes of Melanesian New Guinea.* New York, NY: Dutton.

Mandel, N. (2003). Shifting selves and decision making: The effects of self construal priming on consumer risk taking. *Journal of Consumer Research, 30,* 30–40.

Mandelbaum, D. G. (1951). *Selected writings of Edward Sapir in language, culture, and personality.* Berkeley, CA: University of California Press.

Mani, A., Mullainathan, S., Shafir, E., & Zhao, J. (2013). Poverty impedes cognitive function. *Science, 341,* 976–980.

Mann, A. H. (1977). Psychiatric morbidity and hostility in hypertension. *Psychological Medicine, 7,* 653–659.

Manning, P. (1990). *Slavery and African life.* Cambridge, England: Cambridge University Press.

Maramba, G. G., & Nagayama Hall, G. C. (2002). Meta-analyses of ethnic match as a predictor of dropout, utilization, and level of functioning. *Cultural Diversity and Ethnic Minority Psychology, 8,* 290–297.

Marian, V., & Kaushanskaya, M. (2004). Self-construal and emotion in bicultural bilinguals. *Journal of Memory and Language, 51,* 190–201.

Marin, G., Gamba, R. J., & Marin, G. V. (1992). Extreme response style and acquiescence among Hispanics. *Journal of Cross-Cultural Psychology, 23,* 498–509.

Mark, N. (1998). Birds of a feather sing together: Relation of social positions to musical preferences. *Social Forces, 77,* 253–277.

Markides, K. S., & Coreil, J. (1986). The health of Hispanics in the southwestern United States: An epidemiologic paradox. *Public Health Reports, 101,* 253–265.

Markus, H. R., & Kitayama, S. (1991). Culture and the self: Implications for cognition, emotion, and motivation. *Psychological Review, 98,* 224–253.

Markus, H. R., Uchida, Y., Omoregie, H., Townsend, S. S. M., & Kitayama, S. (2006). Going for the gold: Models of agency in Japanese and American contexts. *Psychological Science, 17,* 103–112.

Marmot, M. G. (2004). *The status syndrome: How social standing affects our health and longevity.* New York, NY: Henry Holt.

Marmot, M. G., Bosma, H., Hemingway, H., Brunner, E., & Stansfeld, S. (1997). Contribution of job control and other risk factors to social variations in coronary heart disease incidence. *Lancet, 350,* 235–239.

Marmot, M. G., & Davey Smith, G. (1989). Why are the Japanese living longer? *British Medical Journal, 299,* 1547–1551.

Marmot, M. G., Kogevinas, M., & Elston, M. A. (1987). Social/economic status and disease. *Annual Review of Public Health, 8,* 111–135.

Marmot, M. G., Shipley, M. J., & Rose, G. (1984). Inequalities in death: Specific explanations of a general pattern? *Lancet, 1984*(1), 1003–1006.

Marmot, M. G., Syme, S. L. (1976). Acculturation and coronary heart disease in Japanese-Americans. *American Journal of Epidemiology, 104*(3), 225–247.

Marsh, A. A., Elfenbein, H. A., & Ambady, N. (2003). Nonverbal "accents": Cultural differences in facial expressions of emotion. *Psychological Science, 14,* 373–376.

Marsh, A. A., Elfenbein, H. A., & Ambady, N. (2007). Separated by a common language: Nonverbal accents and cultural stereotypes about Americans and Australians. *Journal of Cross-Cultural Psychology, 38,* 284–301.

Martin, C. F., Bhui, R., Bossaerts, P., Matsuzawa, T., & Camerer, C. F. (2014). Experienced chimpanzees are more strategic than humans in competitive games. *Scientific Reports, 4,* 5182.

Martin, D., Hutchison, J., Slessor, G., Urquhart, J., Cunningham, S. J., & Smith, K. (2014). The spontaneous formation of stereotypes via cumulative cultural evolution. *Psychological Science, 25,* 1777–1786.

Martin, R. D. (1981). Relative brain size and basal metabolic rate in terrestrial vertebrates. *Nature, 293,* 57–60.

Martin, R. D., Chivers, D. J., MacLarnon, A. M., & Hladik, C. M. (1985). Gastrointestinal allometry in primates and other mammals. In W. L. Jungers (Ed.), *Size and scaling in primate biology* (pp. 61–89). New York, NY: Plenum.

Masson, J. L., & Patwardhan, M. W. (1970). *Aesthetic rapture: The Rasadhyaya of the Natyasastra.* Poona, India: Deccan College.

Mastro, D. E., & Greenberg, B. S. (2000). The portrayal of racial minorities on prime time television. *Journal of Broadcasting and Electronic Media, 44,* 690–703.

Masuda, T., Ellsworth, P. C., Mesquita, B., Leu, J., Tanida, S., & van de Veerdonk, E. (2008). Placing the face in context: Cultural differences in the perception of facial emotion. *Journal of Personality and Social Psychology, 94,* 365–381.

Masuda, T., & Nisbett, R. E. (2001). Attending holistically vs. analytically: Comparing the context sensitivity of Japanese and Americans. *Journal of Personality and Social Psychology, 81,* 922–934.

Masuda, T., & Nisbett, R. E. (2006). Culture and change blindness. *Cognitive Science, 30,* 381–399.

Matsumoto, D., Kudoh, T., Scherer, K., & Wallbott, H. (1988). Antecedents of and reactions to emotions in the United States and Japan. *Journal of Cross-Cultural Psychology, 19,* 267–286.

Matsumoto, D., Yoo, S. H., & Fontaine, J. (2008). Mapping expressive differences around the world. The relationship between emotional display rules and individualism versus collectivism. *Journal of Cross-Cultural Psychology, 39,* 55–74.

Mauss, I. B., & Butler, E. A. (2010). Cultural context moderates the relationship between emotion control values and cardiovascular challenge versus threat responses. *Biological Psychology, 84,* 521–530.

Mauss, I. B., Butler, E. A., Roberts, N. A., & Chu, A. (2010). Emotion control values and responding to an anger provocation in Asian-American and European-American individuals. *Cognition and Emotion, 24,* 1026–1043.

Mayberry, R. I. (1993). First-language acquisition after childhood differs from second-language acquisition: The case of American Sign Language. *Journal of Speech and Hearing Research, 36,* 1258–1270.

Mazur, A. (1985). A biosocial model of status in face-to-face primate groups. *Social Forces, 64,* 377–402.

McAdams, D. P. (1992). The five-factor model of personality: A critical appraisal. *Journal of Personality, 60,* 329–361.

McCauley, R. N., & Henrich, J. (2006). Susceptibility to the Müller-Lyer illusion, theory-neutral observation, and the diachronic penetrability of the visual input system. *Philosophical Psychology, 19,* 1–23.

McClelland, D. (1961). *The achieving society.* Princeton, NJ: Van Nostrand.

McCrae, R. R. (2002). NEO-PI-R data from 36 cultures: Further intercultural comparisons. In R. R. McCrae & J. Allik (Eds.), *The Five-Factor model of personality across cultures* (pp. 105–126). New York, NY: Kluwer.

McCrae, R. R., & Costa, P. T., Jr. (1987). Validation of the five-factor model of personality across instruments and observers. *Journal of Personality and Social Psychology, 52,* 81–90.

McCrae, R. R., Terracciano, A., & 79 members of the Personality Profiles of Cultures Project (2005a). Personality profiles of cultures: Aggregate personality traits. *Journal of Personality and Social Psychology, 89,* 407–425.

McCrae, R. R., Terraciano, A., & 78 members of the Personality Profiles of Cultures Project. (2005b). Universal features of personality traits from the observer's perspective: Data from 50 cultures. *Journal of Personality and Social Psychology, 88,* 547–561.

McCrae, R. R., Yik, M. S. M., Trapnell, P. D., Bond, M. H., & Paulhus, D. L. (1998). Interpreting personality profiles across cultures: Bilingual, acculturation, and peer rating studies of Chinese undergraduates. *Journal of Personality and Social Psychology, 74,* 1041–1055.

McDougall, C. (2009). *Born to run: A hidden tribe, superathletes, and the greatest race the world has never seen.* New York, NY: Vintage Press.

McWhiney, G. (1988). *Cracker culture: Celtic ways in the old South.* Tuscaloosa: University of Alabama Press.

Mead, M. (1928). *Coming of age in Samoa: A psychological study of primitive youth for Western civilization.* New York, NY: Blue Ribbon Books.

Mehler, J., Jusczyk, P., & Lambertz, G. (1988). A precursor of language acquisition in young infants. *Cognition, 29,* 143–178.

Menon, T., Morris, M. W., Chiu, C., & Hong, Y. (1999). Culture and the construal of agency: Attribution to individual versus group dispositions. *Journal of Personality and Social Psychology, 76,* 701–717.

Merikangas, K. R., Jin, R., He, J. P., Kessler, R. C., Lee, S., Sampson, N. A., et al. (2011). Prevalence and correlates of bipolar spectrum disorder in the World Mental Health Survey Initiative. *Archives of General Psychiatry, 68,* 241–251.

Mesoudi, A. (2009). The cultural dynamics of copycat suicide. *PLoS ONE 4*(9), e7252.

Mesoudi, A. (2011). Variable cultural acquisition costs constrain cumulative cultural evolution. *PLoS ONE 6*(3), e18239.

Mesoudi, A., Whiten, A., & Laland, K. N. (2006). Towards a unified science of cultural evolution. *Behavioral and Brain Sciences, 29,* 329–383.

Mesquita, B. (2001). Emotions in collectivist and individualist contexts. *Journal of Personality and Social Psychology, 80,* 68–74.

Mesquita, B., & Frijda, N. H. (1992). Cultural variation in emotion: A review. *Psychological Bulletin, 112,* 179–204.

Mesquita, B., & Karasawa, M. (2002). Different emotional lives. *Cognition and Emotion, 17,* 127–141.

Micale, M. S. (1995). *Approaching hysteria: Disease and its interpretations.* Princeton, NJ: Princeton University Press.

Miller, G. E., & Cohen, S. (2005). Infectious disease and psychoneuroimmunology. In K.Vedhara & M. Irwin (Eds.), *Human psychoneuroimmunology* (pp. 219–242). New York, NY: Oxford University Press.

Miller, J. G., (1984). Culture and the development of everyday social explanation. *Journal of Personality and Social Psychology, 46,* 961–978.

Miller, J. G., Bersoff, D. M., & Harwood, R. L. (1990). Perceptions of social responsibilities in India and the United States: Moral imperatives or personal decisions? *Journal of Personality and Social Psychology, 58,* 33–47.

Miller, J. G., Das, R., & Chakravarthy, S. (2011). Culture and the role of choice in agency. *Journal of Personality and Social Psychology, 101,* 46–61.

Miller, J. G., et al. (2014). Culture and the role of exchange vs. communal norms in friendship. *Journal of Experimental Social Psychology, 53,* 79–93.

Miller, K., & Stigler, J. W. (1987). Counting in Chinese: Cultural variation in a basic cognitive skill. *Cognitive Development, 2,* 279–305.

Miller, K. F., & Paredes, D. R. (1996). On the shoulders of giants: Cultural tools and mathematical development. In R. J. Sternberg & T. Ben-Zeev (Eds.), *The nature of mathematical thinking* (pp. 83–117). Mahwah, NJ: Erlbaum.

Miller, K. F., Smith, C. M., Zhu, J., & Zhang, H. (1995). Preschool origins of cross-national differences in mathematical competence: The role of number naming systems. *Psychological Science, 6,* 56–60.

Miller, P. J., Wang, S., Sandel, T., & Cho, G. E. (2002). Self-esteem as folk theory: A comparison of European American and Taiwanese mothers' beliefs. *Parenting: Science and Practice, 2,* 209–239.

Miller, P. J., Wiley, A. R., Fung H., & Liang, C. H. (1997). Personal storytelling as a medium of socialization in Chinese and American families. *Child Development, 68,* 557–568.

Minami, M. (1994). English and Japanese: A cross-cultural comparison of parental styles of narrative elicitation. *Issues in Applied Linguistics, 5,* 383–407.

Mindell, J. A., Sadeh, A., Wiegand, B., How, T. H., & Goh, D. Y. T. (2010). Cross-cultural differences in infant and toddler sleep. *Sleep Medicine, 11,* 274–280.

Minoura, Y. (1992). A sensitive period for the incorporation of a cultural meaning system: A study of Japanese children growing up in the United States. *Ethos, 20,* 304–339.

Miura, I. T. (1987). Mathematics achievement as a function of language. *Journal of Educational Psychology, 79,* 79–82.

Miyamoto, T., & Onizawa, C. (1985). Taijin kyoufushou to seishin bunretsubyou [Taijin kyoufushou and schizophrenia]. *Seishinka MOOK, 12,* 51–60.

Miyamoto, Y., Knoepfler, C. A., Ishii, K., & Ji, L.-J. (2013). Cultural variation in the focus on goals versus processes of actions. *Personality and Social Psychology Bulletin, 39,* 707–719.

Miyamoto, Y., Nisbett, R. E., & Masuda, T. (2006). Culture and the physical environment: Holistic versus analytic perceptual affordances. *Psychological Science, 17,* 113-119.

Miyamoto, Y., & Ryff, C. (2011). Cultural differences in the dialectical and nondialectical emotional styles and their implications for health. *Cognition and Emotion, 25,* 22–30.

Miyamoto, Y., & Schwarz, N. (2006). When conveying a message may hurt the relationship: Cultural differences in the difficulty of using an answering machine. *Journal of Experimental Social Psychology, 42,* 540–547.

Miyamoto, Y., Uchida, Y., & Ellsworth, P. C. (2010). Culture and mixed emotions: Co-occurrence of positive and negative emotions in Japan and the United States. *Emotion, 10,* 404–415.

Miyamoto, Y., et al. (2013). Negative emotions predict elevated interleukin-6 in the United States but not in Japan. *Brain, behavior, and Immunity, 34,* 79–85.

Modiano, D., et al. (2001). The lower susceptibility to *Plasmodium falciparum* malaria of Fulani of Burkina Faso (west Africa) is associated with low frequencies of classic malaria-resistance genes. *Transactions of the Royal Society of Tropical Medicine and Hygiene, 95,* 149–152.

Modiano, D., Petrarca, V., Sirma, B., Nebie, I., Diallo, D., Esposito, F., et al. (1996). Different response to *Plasmodium falciparum* malaria in West African sympatric ethnic groups. *Proceedings of the National Academy of Science, 93,* 13206–13211.

Mojaverian, T., & Kim, H. S. (2013). Interpreting a helping hand: Cultural variation in the effectiveness of solicited and unsolicited social support. *Personality and Social Psychology Bulletin, 39,* 88–99.

Mok, A., & Morris, M. W. (2010). Asian-Americans' creative styles in Asian and American situations: Assimilative and contrastive responses as a function of bicultural identity integration. *Management and Organization Review, 6,* 371–390.

Montagu, A. (1986). *Touching: The human significance of skin.* New York, NY: Harper & Row.

Morita, S. (1917). The true nature of shinkeishitsu and its treatment. In *Anthology of theses commemorating the 25th anniversary of Professor Kure's appointment to his chair.* Tokyo, Japan: Jikei University.

Morling, B. (2000). "Taking" an aerobics class in the U.S. and "entering" an aerobics class in Japan: Primary and secondary control in a fitness context. *Asian Journal of Social Psychology, 3,* 73–85.

Morling, B., & Evered, S. (2006). Secondary control reviewed and defined. *Psychological Bulletin, 132,* 269–296.

Morling, B., Kitayama, S., & Miyamoto, Y. (2002). Cultural practices emphasize influence in the United States and adjustment in Japan. *Personality and Social Psychology Bulletin, 28,* 311–323.

Morling, B., Kitayama, S., & Miyamoto, Y. (2003). American and Japanese women use different coping strategies during normal pregnancy.

Personality and Social Psychology Bulletin, 29, 1533–1546.

Morris, M., & Peng, K. (1994). Culture and cause: American and Chinese attributions for social and physical events. *Journal of Personality and Social Psychology, 67,* 949–971.

Morris, M. W., & Leung, K. (2010). Creativity East and West: Perspectives and parallels. *Management and Organization Review, 6,* 313–327.

Morrison, K. R., Plaut, V. C., & Ybarra, O. (2010). Predicting whether multiculturalism positively or negatively influences White Americans' intergroup attitudes: The role of ethnic identification. *Personality and Social Psychology Bulletin, 36,* 1648–1661.

Morrow, R. D. (1989). Southeast Asian child-rearing practices: Implications for child and youth care workers. *Child and Youth Quarterly, 18,* 273–287.

Mumford, D. B., Whitehouse, A. M., & Choudry, I. Y. (1992). Survey of eating disorders in English-medium schools in Lahore, Pakistan. *International Journal of Eating Disorders, 11,* 173–184.

Murata, A., Moser, J. S., & Kitayama, S. (2013). Culture shapes electrocortical responses during emotional suppression. *Social Cognitive and Affective Neuroscience, 8,* 595–601.

Murdock, G. P. (1980). *Theories of illness: A world survey.* Pittsburgh, PA: University of Pittsburgh Press.

Murphy, F. C., Nimmo-Smith, I., & Lawrence, A. D. (2003). Functional neuroanatomy of emotion: A meta-analysis. *Cognitive, Affective, and Behavioral Neuroscience, 3,* 207–233.

Murray, S. L., Holmes, J. G., & Griffin, D. W. (1996). The benefits of positive illusions: Idealization and the construction of satisfaction in close relationships. *Journal of Personality and Social Psychology, 70,* 79–98.

Murstein, B. I., Merighi, J. R., & Vyse, S. A. (1991). Love styles in the United States and France: A cross-cultural comparison. *Journal of Social and Clinical Psychology, 10,* 37–46.

Musher-Eizenman, D. R., de Lauzon-Guillain, B., Holub, S. C., Leporc, E., & Charles, M. A. (2009). Child and parent characteristics related to parental feeding practices: A cross-cultural examination in the U.S. and France. *Appetite, 52,* 89–95.

Muthukrishna, M., Shulman, B. W., Vasilescu, V., & Henrich, J. (2014). Sociality influences cultural complexity. *Proceedings of the Royal Society B, 281* (1774).

Na, J., & Kitayama, S. (2011). Spontaneous trait inference is culture-specific: Behavioral and neural evidence. *Psychological Science, 22,* 1025–1032.

Nagell, K., Olguin, K., & Tomasello, M. (1993). Processes of social learning in the tool use of chimpanzees (*Pan troglodytes*) and human children (*Homo sapiens*). *Journal of Comparative Psychology, 107,* 174–186.

National Center for Health Statistics (NCHS). (2003). Health, United States, 2002. Hyattsville, MD: U.S. Public Health Service.

National Conference of Bar Examiners (2010). 2009 Statistics. The Bar Examiner, 79(1).

Neal, R. D., et al. (2001). Missed appointments in general practice: Retrospective data analysis from four practices. *British Journal of General Practice, 51,* 830–832.

Needham, J. (1956). History of scientific thought. *Science and civilisation in China, Vol. 2.* Cambridge, MA: Cambridge University Press.

Neff, L. J., Sargent, R. G., McKeown, R. E., & Jackson, K. L. (1997). Black-White differences in body size perceptions and weight management practices among adolescent females. *Journal of Adolescent Health, 20,* 459–465.

Nel, J. A., Valchev, V. H., Rothmann, S., van de Vijver, F. J. R., Meiring, D., & de Bruin, G. P. (2012). Exploring the personality structure in the 11 languages of South Africa. *Journal of Personality, 80,* 915–948.

Nelson, C. A., Fox, N. A., & Zeanah, C. H. (2013). *Romania's abandoned children: Deprivation, brain development, and the struggle for recovery.* Cambridge, MA: Harvard University Press.

Neto, F., Mullet, E., & Deschamps, J. (2000). Cross-cultural variations in attitudes toward love. *Journal of Cross-Cultural Psychology, 31,* 626–635.

Newcomb, T. M. (1961). *The acquaintance process.* New York, NY: Holt, Rinehart & Winston.

Newport, E. L. (1991). Contrasting concepts of the critical period for language. In S. Carey & R. Gelman, (Eds.), *The epigenesis of mind: Essays on biology and cognition. The Jean Piaget Symposium series* (pp. 111–130). Hillsdale, NJ: Erlbaum.

Newton, M. (2002). *Savage girls and wild boys: A history of feral children.* New York, NY: Picador.

Ng, F. F., Pomerantz, E. M., & Lam, S. (2007). European American and Chinese parents' responses to children's success and failure: Implications for children's responses. *Developmental Psychology, 43,* 1239–1255.

Ngui, P. W. (1969). The *koro* epidemic in Singapore. *Australian New Zealand Journal of Psychiatry, 3,* 263–266.

Nguyen, A. D., & Benet-Martinez, V. (2013). Biculturalism and adjustment: A meta-analysis. *Journal of Cross-Cultural Psychology, 44,* 122–159.

Nielsen, M., & Tomaselli, K. (2010). Overimitation in Kalahari Bushman children and the origins of human cultural cognition. *Psychological Science, 21,* 729–736.

Niiya, Y., Ellsworth, P. C., & Yamaguchi, S. (2006). *Amae* in Japan and the United States: An exploration of a "culturally unique" emotion. *Emotion, 6,* 279–295.

Nisbett, R. E. (1993). Violence and U.S. regional culture. *American Psychologist, 48,* 441–449.

Nisbett, R. E. (2003). *The geography of thought.* New York, NY: Free Press.

Nisbett, R. E., & Cohen, D. (1996). *Culture of honor: The psychology of violence in the South.* Boulder, CO: Westview Press.

Nisbett, R. E., Peng, K., Choi, I., & Norenzayan, A. (2001). Culture and systems of thought: Holistic vs. analytic cognition. *Psychological Review, 108,* 291–310.

Nisbett, R. E., & Wilson, T. D. (1977). Telling more than we can know: Verbal reports on mental processes. *Psychological Review, 84,* 231–259.

Nobakht, M., & Dezhkam, M. (2000). An epidemiological study of eating disorders in Iran. *International Journal of Eating Disorders, 28,* 265–271.

Noell, A. M. (1979). *The history of Noell's Ark gorilla show: The funniest show on Earth, which features the "world's only athletic apes."* Tarpon Springs, FL: Noell's Ark Publisher.

Noels, K. A., Pon, G., & Clement, R. (1996). Language, identity, and adjustment: The role of linguistic self-confidence in the acculturation process. *Journal of Language and Social Psychology, 15,* 246–264.

Nomura, N., Noguchi, Y., Saito, S., & Tezuka, I. (1995). Family characteristics and dynamics in Japan and the United States: A preliminary report from the family environment scale. *International Journal of Intercultural Relations, 19,* 59–86.

Non, A. L., Gravlee, C. C., & Mulligan, C. J. (2012). Education, genetic ancestry, and blood pressure in African Americans and Whites. *American Journal of Public Health, 8,* 1559–1565.

Norasakkunkit, V., & Kalick, M. S. (2002). Culture, ethnicity, and emotional distress measures: The role of self-construal and self-enhancement. *Journal of Cross-Cultural Psychology, 33,* 56–70.

Norasakkunkit, V., Kitayama, S., & Uchida, Y. (2012). Social anxiety and holistic cognition: Self-focused social anxiety in the United States and other-focused social anxiety in Japan. *Journal of Cross-Cultural Psychology, 43,* 742–757.

Norenzayan, A. (2006). Evolution and transmitted culture. *Psychological Inquiry, 17,* 123–128.

Norenzayan, A. (2013). *Big Gods: How religion transformed cooperation and conflict.* Princeton, NJ: Princeton University Press.

Norenzayan, A., Atran, S., Faulkner, J., & Schaller, M. (2006). Memory and mystery: The cultural selection of minimally counterintuitive narratives. *Cognitive Science, 30,* 531–553.

Norenzayan, A., Choi, I., & Nisbett, R. E. (2002). Cultural similarities and differences in social inference: Evidence from behavioral predictions and lay theories of behavior. *Personality and Social Psychology Bulletin, 28,* 109–120.

Norenzayan, A., Choi, I. & Peng, K. (2007) Cognition and perception. In S. Kitayama and D. Cohen (Eds.), *Handbook of Cultural Psychology* (pp. 569–594). New York, NY: Guilford Press.

Norenzayan, A., & Heine, S. J., (2005). Psychological universals: What are they, and how can we know? *Psychological Bulletin, 131,* 763–784.

Norenzayan, A., Smith, E. E., Kim, B. J., & Nisbett, R. E. (2002). Cultural preferences for formal versus intuitive reasoning. *Cognitive Science, 26,* 653–684.

Nouri, R., Erez, M., Rockstuhl, T., & Ang, S. (2008). *Creativity in multicultural teams: The effects of cultural diversity and situational strength on creative performance.* The Academy of Management Annual Meeting, August 8–13, Anaheim, CA.

Nowak, M. A., Page, K. M., & Sigmund, K. (2000). Fairness versus reason in the Ultimatum Game. *Science, 289,* 1773–1775.

Nunez, R. E. (2011). No innate number line in the human brain. *Journal of Cross-Cultural Psychology, 42,* 651–668.

Nunn, N. (2008). The long-term effects of Africa's slave trades. *Quarterly Journal of Economics, 123,* 139–176.

Nunn, N., & Wantchekon, L. (2011). The slave trade and the origins of mistrust in Africa. *American Economic Review, 101,* 3221–3252.

Nwaefuna, A. (1981). Anorexia nervosa in a developing country [Letter to the editor]. *British Journal of Psychiatry, 138,* 270.

Oberg, K. (1960). Cultural shock: Adjustment to new cultural environments, *Practical Anthropology, 7,* 177–182.

Obeyesekere, G. (1985). Depression, Buddhism and the work of culture in Sri Lanka. In A. Kleinman & B. Good (Eds.), *Culture and depression* (pp. 134–152). Berkeley, CA: University of California Press.

Obst, L. (2011, January 5). What awards season tells us about the future of comedy. *The Atlantic.* Retrieved from www.theatlantic.com/culture/archive/2011/01/china-vs-judd-apatow-why-american-comedies-are-dying/68866/

OECD Health Statistics. (2013). World Bank for non-OECD countries. Retrieved from http://dx.doi.org/10.1787/health-data-en

Oettingen, G., Little, T. D., Lindenberger, U., & Baltes, P. B. (1994). Causality, agency, and control beliefs in East versus West Berlin children: A natural experiment on the role of context. *Journal of Personality and Social Psychology, 66,* 579–595.

Oettingen, G., & Seligman, M. E. P. (1990). Pessimism and behavioral signs of depression in East versus West Berlin. *European Journal of Social Psychology, 20,* 207–220.

Ogino, T. (2004). Managing categorization and social withdrawal in Japan: Rehabilitation in a private support group for hikikomorians. *International Journal of Japanese Sociology, 13,* 120–133.

Oishi, S. (2002). The experiencing and remembering of well-being: A cross-cultural analysis. *Personality and Social Psychology Bulletin, 28,* 1398–1406.

Oishi, S. (2010). The psychology of residential mobility: Implications for the self, social relationships, and well-being. *Perspectives on Psychological Science, 5,* 5–21.

Oishi, S., & Diener, E. (2003). Culture and well-being: The cycle of action, evaluation, and decision. *Personality and Social Psychology Bulletin, 29,* 939–949.

Oishi, S., Diener, E., Scollon, C. N., & Biswas-Diener, R. (2004). Cross-situational consistency of affective experiences across cultures. *Journal of Personality and Social Psychology, 86,* 460–472.

Oishi, S., Graham, J., Kesebir, S., & Galinha, I. C. (2013). Concepts of happiness across time and cultures. *Personality and Social Psychology Bulletin, 39,* 559–577.

Oishi, S., Ishii, K., & Lun, J. (2009). Residential mobility and conditionality of group identification. *Journal of Experimental Social Psychology, 45,* 913–919.

Oishi, S., Lun, J., & Sherman, G. D. (2007). Residential mobility, self-concept, and positive affect in social interactions. *Journal of Personality and Social Psychology, 93,* 131–141.

Oishi, S., Miao, F. F., Koo, M., Kisling, J., & Ratliff, K. (2011). Residential mobility breeds familiarity-seeking. *Journal of Personality and Social Psychology, 102,* 149–162.

Oishi, S., & Roth, D. P. (2009). The role of self-reports in culture and personality research: It is too early to give up on self-reports. *Journal of Research in Personality, 43,* 107–109.

Oishi, S., Rothman, A. J., Snyder, M., Zehm, J. K., Hertel, A. W., Gonzales, M. H., et al. (2007). The socioecological model of procommunity action: The benefits of residential stability. *Journal of Personality and Social Psychology, 93,* 831–844.

Okazaki, S. (1997). Sources of ethnic differences between Asian American and White American college students on measures of depression and social anxiety. *Journal of Abnormal Psychology, 106,* 52–60.

Okazaki, S., Liu, J. F., Longworth, S. L., & Minn, J. Y. (2002). Asian American–White American differences in expressions of social anxiety: A replication and extension. *Cultural Diversity and Ethnic Minority Psychology, 8,* 234–247.

O'Keefe, J. & Nadel, L. (1978). *The hippocampus as a cognitive map.* Oxford, England: University of Oxford Press.

Opfer, J. E., & Siegler, R. S. (2003). The development of numerical estimation: Evidence for multiple representations of numerical quantity. *Psychological Science, 14,* 237–243.

Organisation for Economic Co-operation and Development. (2004, February 22). *Health at a glance: OECD indicators 2003*: Chart 8. Increasing obesity rates among the adult population in OECD countries. Retrieved from www.oecd.org/LongAbstract/0,2546, en_2649_201185_16361657_1_1_1,00.html

Organization for Economic Co-operation and Development. (2009). *Society at a Glance 2009.* OECD Social Indicators (Chapter 2). Paris: OECD.

Orwell, G. (1990). *Nineteen eighty-four.* London: Penguin. (Original work published 1848)

Ostir, G. V., Ottenbacher, K. J., & Markides, K. S. (2004). Onset of frailty in older adults and the protective role of positive affect. *Psychology and Aging, 19,* 402–408.

Ouchi, W. G., & Jaeger, A. M. (1978). Type Z organization: Stability in the midst of mobility. *Academy of Management Review, 3,* 305–314.

Ovsiew, F. (2006). Hysteria in neurological practice: The somatoform and dissociative disorders. In D. V. Jeste & J. H. Friedman (Eds.), *Current clinical neurology: Psychiatry for neurologists* (pp. 67–79). Totowa, NJ: Humana Press.

Oxford English Dictionary. (1989). Second edition. Oxford, England: Oxford University Press.

Oyserman, D., Coon, H. M., & Kemmelmeier, M. (2002). Rethinking individualism and collectivism: Evaluation of theoretical assumptions and meta-analyses. *Psychological Bulletin, 128,* 3–72.

Oyserman, D. & Lee, S. W. S. (2008). Does culture influence what and how we think? Effects of priming individualism and collectivism. *Psychology Bulletin, 134,* 311–342.

Pablos-Mendez, A. (1994). Letter to the editor. *Journal of the American Medical Association, 271,* 1237–1238.

Pagsberg, A. K., & Wang, A. R. (1994). Epidemiology of anorexia and bulimia nervosa in Bornholm County, Denmark, 1970–1989. *Acta Psychiatrica Scandinavia, 90,* 259–265.

Pamuk, E., Makuk, D., Heck, K., & Reuben, C. (1998). *Health, United States, 1998, with socioeconomic status and health chartbook.* Hyattsville, MD: National Center for Health Statistics.

Panksepp, J. (1998). *Affective neuroscience: The foundations of human and animal emotions.* New York, NY: Oxford University Press.

Parekh, R., & Beresin, E. V. (2001). Looking for love? Take a cross-cultural walk through the personals. *Academic Psychiatry, 25,* 223–233.

Park, D. C., & Huang, C.-M. (2010). Culture wires the brain: A cognitive neuroscience perspective. *Perspectives in Psychological Science, 5,* 391–400.

Park, H., Rabolt, N. J., & Jeon, K. S. (2008). Purchasing global luxury brands among young Korean customers. *Journal of Fashion Marketing and Management, 12,* 244–259.

Park, H., Twenge, J. M., & Greenfield, P. M. (2014). The great recession: Implications for adolescent values and behavior. *Social Psychological and Personality Science, 5,* 310–318.

Parker, G., Cheah, Y. C., & Roy, K. (2001). Do the Chinese somatize depression? A cross-cultural study. *Social Psychiatry and Psychiatric Epidemiology, 36,* 287–293.

Parker, G., Gladstone, G., & Chee, K. T. (2001). Depression in the planet's largest ethnic group: The Chinese. *American Journal of Psychiatry, 158,* 857–864.

Parker, S. T., & Gibson, K. R. (1977). Object manipulation, tool use and sensorimotor intelligence as feeding adaptations in great apes and cebus monkeys. *Journal of Human Evolution, 6,* 623–641.

Patel, V., Simunyu, E., & Gwanzura, F. (1995). *Kufungisisa* (thinking too much): A Shona idiom for nonpsychotic mental illness. *Central African Journal of Medicine, 4*(7), 209–215.

Payer, L. (1996). *Medicine and culture.* New York, NY: Owl Books.

Pearce, N. E., Davis, P. B., Smith, A. H., & Foster, F. H. (1985). Social class, ethnic group, and male mortality in New Zealand, 1974–78. *Journal of Epidemiology and Community Health, 39,* 9–14.

Peng, K., & Nisbett, R. E. (1999). Culture, dialectics, and reasoning about contradiction. *American Psychologist, 54,* 741–754.

Peng, K., Nisbett, R. E., & Wong, N. Y. C. (1997). Validity problems comparing values across cultures and possible solutions. *Psychological Methods, 2,* 329–344.

Perani, D., Paulesu, E., & Galles, N. S. (1998). The bilingual brain: Proficiency and age of acquisition of the second language. *Brain, 121,* 1841–1852.

Perez-Barberia, F. J., Shultz, S., & Dunbar, R. I. M. (2007). Evidence for co-evolution of sociality and relative brain size in three orders of mammals. *Evolution, 61,* 2811–2821.

Perez-Stable, E. J., Marin, G., & Marin, B. V. (1994). Behavioral risk factors: A comparison of Latinos and non-Latino Whites in San Francisco. *American Journal of Public Health, 84,* 971–976.

Perry, G. H., Dominy, N. J., Claw, K. G., Lee, A. S., Fiegler, H., Redon, R., et al. (2007). Diet and the evolution of human amylase gene copy number variation. *Nature Genetics, 39,* 1256–1260.

Peters, H. J., & Williams, J. M. (2006). Moving cultural background to the foreground: An investigation of self-talk, performance, and persistence following feedback. *Journal of Applied Sport Psychology, 18,* 240–253.

Philbrick, J. L., & Opolot, J. A. (1980). Love style: Comparison of African and American attitudes. *Psychological Reports, 46,* 286.

Phillips, J. E., & Klein, W. M. P. (2010). Socioeconomic status and coronary heart disease risk: The role of social cognitive factors. *Social and Personality Psychology Compass, 4,* 704–727.

Phillips, W., & Boroditsky, L. (2003). Can quirks of grammar affect the way you think? Grammatical gender and object concepts. *Proceedings of the 25th Annual Meeting of the Cognitive Science Society,* 928–933.

Phinney, J. S., & Ong, A. D. (2007). Conceptualization and measurement of ethnic identity: Current status and future directions. *Journal of Counseling Psychology, 54,* 271–281.

Pica, P., Lerner, C., Izard, V., & Dehaene, S. (2004). Exact and approximate arithmetic in an Amazonian indigenous group. *Science, 306,* 499–501.

Piedmont, R. L., Bain, E., McCrae, R. R., & Costa, P. T., Jr., (2002). The applicability of the five-factor model in a sub-Saharan culture. In R. R. McCrae & J. Allik (Eds.), *The five-factor model of personality across cultures* (pp. 55–173). New York, NY: Kluwer Academic/Plenum Publishers.

Pigliucci, M. (2005). Evolution of phenotypic plasticity: where are we going now? *Trends in Ecology & Evolution, 20*(9), 481–486.

Pinker, S. (1994). *The language instinct.* New York, NY: William Morrow.

Plaut, V. C., Adams, G., & Anderson, S. L. (2009). Does attractiveness buy happiness? "It depends on where you're from." *Personal Relationships, 16,* 619–630.

Plaut, V. C., Garnett, F. G., Buffardi, L. E., & Sanchez-Burks, J. (2011). What about me? Perceptions of exlusion and Whites' reactions to multiculturalism. *Journal of Personality and Social Psychology, 101,* 337–353.

Plaut, V. C., Markus, H. R., & Lachman, M. E. (2002). Place matters: Consensual features and regional variation in American well-being and self. *Journal of Personality and Social Psychology, 83,* 160–184.

Plaut, V. C., Thomas, K. M., & Goren, M. J. (2009). Is multiculturalism or color blindness better for minorities? *Psychological Science, 20,* 444–446.

Pollack, N. (1995). Cultural elaborations of obesity: Fattening practices in Pacific societies. *Asia Pacific Journal of Clinical Nutrition, 4,* 357–360.

Pollock, D. C., & Van Reken, R. (2009). *Third culture kids: Growing up among worlds.* Boston, MA: Brealey.

Poma, P. A. (1983). Hispanic cultural influences on medical practice. *Journal of the National Medical Association, 75,* 941–946.

Population Reference Bureau. (2006, August). *2006 World population data sheet.* Retrieved from www.prb.org/pdf06/06WorldDataSheet.pdf

Povinelli, D. J., Perilloux, H. K., Reaux, J. E., & Bierschwale, D. T. (1998). Young and juvenile chimpanzees' (*Pan troglodytes*) reactions to intentional versus accidental and inadvertent actions. *Behavioural Processes, 42,* 205–218.

Prentice, D., & Miller, D. (1996). Pluralistic ignorance and the perpetuation of social norms by unwitting actors. In M. Zanna (Ed.), *Advances in experimental social psychology* (pp. 161–209). San Diego, CA: Academic Press.

Price, D. J. de S. (1963). *Little science, big science.* New York, NY: Columbia University Press.

Prince, R. (1960). The "brain fag" syndrome in Nigerian students. *Journal of Mental Science, 104,* 559–570.

Purdie-Vaughns, V., Steele, C. M., Davies, P. G., Ditlmann, R., & Crosby, J. R. (2008). Social identity contingencies: How diversity cues signal threat or safety for African-Americans in mainstream institutions. *Journal of Personality and Social Psychology, 94,* 615–630.

Putnam, R. D. (2000). *Bowling alone: The collapse and revival of American community.* New York, NY: Simon & Schuster.

Putnam, R. D., Leonardi, R., & Nanetti, R. Y. (1993). *Making democracy work.* Princeton, NJ: Princeton University Press.

Pyszczynski, T., & Greenberg, J. (1983). Determinants of reduction in intended effort as a strategy for coping with anticipated failure. *Journal of Research in Personality, 17,* 412–422.

Qin, L., Pomerantz, E. M., & Wang, Q. (2009). Are gains in decision-making autonomy during early adolescence beneficial for emotional functioning? The case of the United States and China. *Child Development, 80,* 1705–1721.

Quinn, D. M., & Crocker, J. (1999). When ideology hurts: Effects of belief in the Protestant ethic and feeling overweight on the psychological well-being of women. *Journal of Personality and Social Psychology, 77,* 402–414.

Ramirez-Esparza, N., Chung, C. K., Sierra-Otero, G., & Pennebaker, J. W. (2012). Cross-cultural constructions of self-schemas: Americans and Mexicans. *Journal of Cross-Cultural Psychology, 43,* 233–250.

Ramirez-Esparza, N., Mehl, R., Alvarez-Bermudez, J., & Pennebaker, J. W. (2009). Are Mexicans more or less sociable than Americans? Insights from a naturalistic observation study. *Journal of Research in Personality, 43,* 1–7.

Ratner, C. (1989). A sociohistorical critique of naturalistic theories of color perception. *Journal of Mind and Behavior, 10,* 361–373.

Rattan, A., Savani, K., Naidu, N. V. R., & Dweck, C. S. (2012). Can everyone become highly intelligent? Cultural differences in societal consequences of beliefs about universal potential for intelligence. *Journal of Personality and Social Psychology, 103,* 787–803.

Redelmeier, D. A., & Singh, S. M. (2001). Survival in Academy Award-winning actors and actresses. *Annals of Internal Medicine, 134,* 955–962.

Rees, P. (2002, October 20). Japan: The missing million. *BBC News.* Retrieved from http://news.bbc.co.uk/2/hi/programmes/correspondent/2334893.stm

Renaud, S., & de Lorgeril, M. (1992). Wine, alcohol, platelets, and the French paradox for coronary heart disease. *The Lancet, 339,* 1523–1526.

Rendell, L., & Whitehead, H. (2001). Culture in whales and dolphins. *Behavioral and Brain Sciences, 24,* 309–382.

Rensink, R. A., O'Regan, J. K., & Clark, J. J. (1997). To see or not to see: The need for attention to perceive changes in scenes. *Psychological Science, 8,* 368–373.

Rentfrow, P. J., Gosling, S. D., Jokela, M., Stillwell, D. J., Kosinski, M., & Potter, J. (2013). Divided we stand: Three psychological regions of the United States and their political, economic, social, and health correlates. *Journal of Personality and Social Psychology, 105,* 996–1012.

Reykowski, J. (1994). Collectivism and individualism as dimensions of social change. In U. Kim, H. Triandis, C. Kagitcibasi, S.-C. Choi, & G. Yoon (Eds.), *Individualism and collectivism: Theory, method, and applications.* Thousand Oaks, CA: Sage.

Reynolds, D. K. (1980). *The quiet therapies: Japanese pathways to personal growth.* Honolulu: University of Hawaii Press.

Rhee, E., Uleman, J. S., Lee, H. K., & Roman, R. J. (1995). Spontaneous self-descriptions and ethnic identities in individualistic and collectivistic cultures. *Journal of Personality and Social Psychology, 69,* 142–152.

Rhodes, G., Lee, K., Palermo, R., Weiss, M., Yoshikawa, S., Clissa, P., et al. (2005). Attractiveness of own-race, other-race, and mixed-race faces. *Perception, 34,* 319–340.

Rhodes, G., Zebrowitz, L. A., Clark, A., Kalick, S. M., Hightower, A., & McKay, R. (2001). Do facial averageness and symmetry signal health? *Evolution and Human Behavior, 22,* 31–46.

Rice, T. W., & Steele, B. J. (2004). Subjective well-being and culture across time and space. *Journal of Cross-Cultural Psychology, 35,* 633–647.

Richard, J. L. (1987, April). Les facteurs de risqué coronarien: Le paradoxe français. *Archives des Maladies du Coeur et des Vaisseaux, 80,* 17–21.

Richardson, A. (1974). *British immigrants and Australia: A psycho-social inquiry.* Canberra: Australian National University Press.

Richerson, P. J., & Boyd, R. (1998). The evolution of human ultra-sociality. In I. Eibl-Eibisfeldt and F. Salter (Eds.), *Ideology, warfare, and indoctrinability* (pp. 71–95). New York: Berghan Books.

Richerson, P. J., & Boyd, R. (2005). *Not by genes alone: How culture transformed human evolution.* Chicago, IL: University of Chicago Press.

Richeson, J. A., & Nussbaum, R. J. (2004). The impact of multiculturalism versus color-blindness on racial bias. *Journal of Experimental Social Psychology, 40,* 417–423.

Rivers, W. H. R. (1926). *Psychology and ethnology.* London: Kegan Paul, Trench, Trubner.

Robbins, S. E., & Hanna, A. M. (1987). Running-related injury prevention through barefoot adaptations. *Medicine & Science in Sports & Exercise, 19,* 148–156.

Roberson, D., Davidoff, J., Davies, I., & Shapiro, L. (2005). Colour categories in Himba: Evidence for the cultural relativity hypothesis. *Cognitive Psychology, 50,* 378–411.

Roberson, D., Davies, I., & Davidoff, J. (2000). Color categories are not universal: Replications and new evidence from a stone-age culture. *Journal of Experimental Psychology: General, 129,* 369–398.

Roberts, S. C., et al. (2005). MHC-heterozygosity and human facial attractiveness. *Evolution and Human Behavior, 26,* 213–226.

Robins, L. N., & Regier, D. A. (1991). *Psychiatric disorders in America: The Epidemiological Catchment Area study.* New York, NY: Free Press.

Robinson, M. D., & Clore, G. L. (2002). Belief and feeling: Evidence for an accessibility model of emotional self-report. *Psychological Bulletin, 128,* 934–960.

Rodgers, J. S., Peng, K., Wang, L., & Hou, Y. (2004). Dialectical self-esteem and East-West differences in psychological well-being. *Personality and Social Psychology Bulletin, 30,* 1416–1432.

Rodin, J., & Langer, E. J. (1977). Long-term effects of a control-relevant intervention with institutionalized aged. *Journal of Personality and Social Psychology, 35,* 897–902.

Rogoff, B. (1981). Schooling and the development of cognitive skills. In H. C. Triandis & A. Heron (Eds.), *Handbook of cross-cultural psychology* (Vol. 4, pp. 233–294). Rockleigh, NJ: Allyn & Bacon.

Rogoff, B. (2003). *The cultural nature of human development.* Oxford, England: Oxford University Press.

Rohner, R. P., & Pettengill, S. M. (1985). Perceived parental acceptance-rejection and parental control among Korean adolescents. *Child Development, 56,* 524–528.

Rosaldo, M. Z. (1980). *Knowledge and passion: Ilongot notions of self and social life.* Cambridge, England: Cambridge University Press.

Rosch Heider, E. (1972). Universals in color naming and memory. *Journal of Experimental Psychology, 93,* 10–20.

Rosch Heider, E., & Olivier, D. C. (1972). The structure of the color space in naming and memory for two languages. *Cognitive Psychology, 3,* 337–354.

Rosen, B. C. (1998). *Winners and losers of the information revolution: Psychosocial change and its discontents.* Westport, CT: Praeger.

Rosen, D. S. (2003). Eating disorders in children and young adolescents: Etiology, classification, clinical features, and treatment. *Adolescent Medicine, 14,* 49–59.

Rosenberg, M. (1965). *Society and the adolescent self-image.* Princeton, NJ: Princeton University Press.

Rosenthal, D. (Ed.) (2004). *Variety international film guide.* Los Angeles, CA: Silman-James Press.

Ross, C. E., & Mirowsky, J. (1984). Socially desirable response and acquiescence in a cross-cultural survey of mental health. *Journal of Health and Social Behavior, 25,* 189–197.

Ross, M., Xun, W. Q. E., & Wilson, A. E. (2002). Language and the bicultural self. *Personality and Social Psychology Bulletin, 28,* 1040–1050.

Rothbaum, F., Pott, M., Azuma, H., Miyake, K., & Weisz, J. (2000). The development of close relationships in Japan and the U.S.: Paths of symbiotic harmony and generative tension. *Child Development, 71,* 1121–1142.

Rothbaum, F., Weisz, J. R., Pott, M., Miyake, K., & Morelli, G. (2000). Attachment and culture:

Security in the United States and Japan. *American Psychologist, 55,* 1093–1104.

Rothbaum, F., Weisz, J. R., & Snyder, S. S. (1982). Changing the world and changing the self: A two-process model of perceived control. *Journal of Personality and Social Psychology, 42,* 5–37.

Rotimi, C., Puras, A., Cooper, R., McFarlane-Anderson, N., Forrester, T., Ogunbiyi, O., & Ward, L. M. R. (1996). Polymorphisms of renin-angiotensin genes among Nigerians, Jamaicans, and African-Americans. *Hypertension, 27,* 558-563.

Rozin, P., Bauer, R., & Catanese, D. (2003). Food and life: Pleasure and worry, among American college students: Gender differences and regional similarities. *Journal of Personality and Social Psychology, 85,* 132–141.

Rozin, P., Fischler, C., Imada, S., Sarubin, A., & Wrzesniewski, A. (1999). Attitudes to food and the role of food in life in the USA, Japan, Flemish Belgium, and France: Possible implications for the diet-health debate. *Appetite, 33,* 163–180.

Rozin, P., Fischler, C., Shields, C., & Masson, E. (2006). Attitudes towards large numbers of choices in the food domain: A cross-cultural study of five countries in Europe and the USA. *Appetite, 46,* 304–308.

Rozin, P., Kabnick, K., Pete, E., Fischler, C., & Shields, C. (2003). The ecology of eating: Smaller portion sizes in France than in the United States help explain the French Paradox. *Psychological Science, 14,* 450–454.

Rozin, P., Kurzer, N., & Cohen, A. B. (2002). Free associations to "food": The effects of gender, generation, and culture. *Journal of Research in Personality, 36,* 419–441.

Rubel, A. J., O'Nell, C. W., & Collado, R. (1985). The folk illness called *susto.* In R. C. Simons & C. C. Hughes (Eds.), *The culture-bound syndromes* (pp. 333–350). Dordrecht, The Netherlands: Reidel.

Rubinstein, D. H. (1983). Epidemic suicide among Micronesian adolescents. *Social Science and Medicine, 17,* 657–665.

Rubinstein, D. H. (1992). Suicidal behavior in Micronesia. In L. P. Kok & W. S. Tseng (Eds.), *Suicidal behavior in the Asia-Pacific region* (pp. 199–230). Singapore: Singapore University.

Ruby, M. B., Falk, C. F., Heine, S. J., Villa, C., & Silverstein, O. (2012). Not all collectivisms are equal: Opposing preferences for ideal affect between East Asians and Mexicans. *Emotion, 12,* 1206–1209.

Ruby, M. B., Falk, C. F., Silberstein, O., Villa, C., & Heine, S. J. (2011). Ideal affect among Latin Americans, Canadians, and East Asians. Unpublished data, University of British Columbia.

Ruby, M. B., Heine, S. J., Kamble, S., Cheng, T. K., & Waddar, M. (2013). Compassion and contamination: Cultural differences in vegetarianism. *Appetite, 71,* 340–348.

Rudmin, F. W. (2003). Critical history of the acculturation psychology of assimilation, separation, integration, and marginalization. *Review of General Psychology, 7,* 3–37.

Rudy, D., & Grusec, J. E. (2006). Authoritarian parenting in individualist and collectivist groups: Associations with maternal emotion and cognition and children's self-esteem. *Journal of Family Psychology, 20,* 68–78.

Rule, N. O., et al. (2010). Polling the face: Prediction and consensus across cultures. *Journal of Personality and Social Psychology, 98,* 1–15.

Russell, J. A. (1991). Culture and the categorization of emotions. *Psychological Bulletin, 110,* 426–450.

Russell, J. A. (1994). Is there universal recognition of emotion from facial expression? A review of the cross-cultural studies. *Psychological Bulletin, 115,* 102–141.

Ryder, A. G. (2004). *Cross-cultural differences in the presentation of depression: Chinese somatization and Western psychologization.* Unpublished doctoral dissertation. University of British Columbia.

Ryder, A. G., Alden, L. E., & Paulhus, D. L. (2000). Is acculturation unidimensional or bidimensional? A head-to-head comparison in the prediction of personality, self-identity, and adjustment. *Journal of Personality and Social Psychology, 79,* 49–65.

Ryder, A. G., Bean, G., & Dion, K. L. (2000). Caregiver responses to symptoms of first-onset psychosis: A comparative study of Chinese- and Euro-Canadian families. *Transcultural Psychiatry, 37,* 225–236.

Ryder, A. G., & Dere, J. (2010). Canadian diversity and clinical psychology: Defining and transcending "cultural competence." *CAP Monitor, 35,* 1, 6–13.

Ryder, A. G., Yang, J., Zhu, X., Yao, S., Yi, J., Heine, S. J., et al. (2008). The cultural shaping of depression: Somatic symptoms in China, psychological symptoms in North America? *Journal of Abnormal Psychology, 117,* 300–313.

Saad, C. S., Damian, R. I., Benet-Martinez, V., Moons, W. G., & Robins, R. W. (2013). Multiculturalism and creativity: Effects of cultural context, bicultural identity, and ideational fluency. *Social Psychological and Personality Science, 4,* 369–375.

Saito, T. (1998). *Sakaitaki hikikomori: Owarani shishunki* [Social withdrawal: Unfinished puberty]. Tokyo, Japan: PHP-Kenkyujo.

Sakai, M., Ishikawa, S., Takizawa, M., Sato, H., & Sakano, Y. (2004). The state of *hikikomori* from a family's point of view: Statistical survey and the role of psychological intervention. *Japanese Journal of Counseling Science, 37,* 168–179.

Sampson, R. J., & Groves, W. B. (1989). Community structure and crime: Testing social-disorganization theory. *American Journal of Sociology, 94,* 774–780.

Sampson, R. J., Raudenbush, S. W., & Earls, F. (1997). Neighborhoods and violent crime: A multilevel study of collective efficacy. *Science, 277,* 918–924.

Samuels, B. (1986). Infant mortality and low birth weight among minority groups in the United States: A review of the literature. In *Report of the Secretary's Task Force on Black and Minority Health* (Vol. 6, pp. 33–85). Washington, DC: U.S. Department of Health and Human Services.

Sanchez-Burks, J. (2002). Protestant relational ideology and (in)attention to relational work settings. *Journal of Personality and Social Psychology, 83,* 919–929.

Sanchez-Burks, J. (2005). Protestant relational ideology: The cognitive underpinnings and organizational implications of an American anomaly. In B. M. Staw & R. M. Kramer (Eds.), *Research in organizational behavior: An annual series of analytical essays and critical reviews* (Vol. 26, pp. 265–305). New York, NY: Elsevier.

Sanchez-Burks, J., Nisbett, R. E., & Ybarra, O. (2000). Cultural styles, relational schemas and prejudice against outgroups. *Journal of Personality and Social Psychology, 79,* 174–189.

Sapolsky, R. M. (2005). The influence of social hierarchy on primate health. *Science, 308,* 648–652.

Sasaki, J. Y., Kim, H. S., & Xu, J. (2011). Religion and well-being: The moderating role of culture and an oxytocin receptor polymorphism. *Journal of Cross-Cultural Psychology, 42,* 1394–1405.

Saucier, G., & Goldberg, L. R. (1998). What is beyond the Big Five? *Journal of Personality, 66,* 495–524.

Saucier, G., Georgiades S., Tsaousis, I., & Goldberg L. R. (2005) The factor structure of Greek personality adjectives. *Journal of Personality and Social Psychology, 88,* 856–875.

Saunders, B. A. C., & Van Brakel, J. (1997). Are there nontrivial constraints on colour categorization? *Behavioral and Brain Sciences, 20,* 167–178.

Savage-Rumbaugh, E. S., McDonald, K., Sevcik, R. A., Hopkins, W. D., & Rubert, E. (1986). Spontaneous symbol acquisition and communicative use by pygmy chimpanzees (*Pan paniscus*). *Journal of Experimental Psychology: General, 115,* 211–235.

Savani, K., Alvarez, A., Mesquita, B., & Markus, H. R. (2013). Feeling close and doing well: The prevalence and motivational effects of interpersonally engaging emotions in Mexican and European American cultural contexts. *International Journal of Psychology, 48,* 682–694.

Savani, K., & Markus, H. R. (2012). A processing advantage associated with analytic perceptual tendencies: European Americans outperform Asians on multiple object tracking. *Journal of Experimental Social Psychology, 48,* 766–769.

Savani, K., Markus, H. R., & Conner, A. L. (2008). Let your preference be your guide? Preferences and choices are more tightly linked for North Americans than for Indians. *Journal of Personality and Social Psychology, 95,* 861–876.

Savani, K., Markus, H. R., Naidu, N. V. R., Kumar, S., & Berlia, N. (2010). What counts as a choice? U.S. Americans are more likely than Indians to construe actions as choices. *Psychological Science, 21,* 391–398.

Savani, K., Morris, M. W., & Naidu, N. V. R. (2012). Deference in Indians' decision making: Introjected goals or injunctive norms? *Journal of Personality and Social Psychology, 102,* 685–699.

Savani, K., Morris, M. W., Naidu, N. V. R., Kumar, S., & Berlia, N. V. (2011). Cultural conditioning: Understanding interpersonal accommodation in India and the United States in terms of the modal characteristics of interpersonal influence situations. *Journal of Personality and Social Psychology, 100,* 84–102.

Schacter, S. (1951). Deviation, rejection, and communication. *Journal of Abnormal and Social Psychology, 62,* 356–363.

Schacter, S., & Singer, J. E. (1962). Cognitive, social, and psychological determinants of emotional state. *Psychological Review, 69,* 379–399.

Schaller, M., Conway, L. G., III, & Tanchuk, T. L. (2002). Selective pressures on the once and future contents of ethnic stereotypes: Effects of the communicability of traits. *Journal of Personality and Social Psychology, 82,* 861–877.

Schieffelin, E. L. (1979). Mediators as metaphors: Moving a man to tears in Papua New Guinea. In A. L. Becker & A. Yengoyan (Eds.), *The imagination of reality: Essays in Southeast Asian Conference Systems.* Norwood, NJ: Ablex.

Schlegel, A., & Barry, H., III. (1991). *Adolescence: An anthropological inquiry.* New York, NY: Free Press.

Schmader, T., & Johns, M. (2003). Converging evidence that stereotype threat reduces working memory capacity. *Journal of Personality and Social Psychology, 85,* 440–452.

Schmidt, K., Hill, L., & Guthrie, G. (1977). Running *amok. International Journal of Psychiatry, 23,* 264–274.

Schmidtke, A., Weinacker, B., Apter, A., Batt, A., Berman, A., Bille-Brahe, U., et al. (1998). *Suicide rates in the world (update).* Retrieved from www.uni-wuerzburg.de/IASR/suicide-rates.htm

Schmitt, D. P., et al. (2007). The geographic distribution of Big Five personality traits: Patterns and profiles of human self-description across 56 nations. *Journal of Cross-Cultural Psychology, 38,* 173–212.

Schmitt, M. T., & Branscombe, N. R. (2002). The meaning and consequences of perceived discrimination in disadvantaged and privileged social groups. *European Review of Social Psychology, 12,* 167–199.

Schooler, J. W., & Engstler-Schooler, T. Y. (1990). Verbal overshadowing of visual memories: Some things are better left unsaid. *Cognitive Psychology, 22,* 36–71.

Schug, J., Yuki, M., Horikawa, H., & Takemura, K. (2009). Similarity attraction and actually selecting similar others: How cross-societal differences in relational mobility affect interpersonal similarity in Japan and the USA. *Asian Journal of Social Psychology, 12,* 95–103.

Schug, J., Yuki, M., & Maddux, W. (2010). Relational mobility explains between- and within-culture differences in self-disclosure to close friends. *Psychological Science, 21,* 1471–1478.

Schwartz, B. (2004). *The paradox of choice: Why more is less.* New York, NY: HarperCollins.

Schwartz, S. H. (1994). Beyond individualism/collectivism: New cultural dimensions of values. In U. Kim, H. C. Triandis, C. Kagitcibasi, S.-C. Choi, & G. Yoon (Eds.), *Individualism and Collectivism: Theory, Method, and Applications.* (pp. 85–119). Thousand Oaks: Sage.

Schwartz, S. H., & Bilsky, W. (1990). Toward a theory of the universal content and structure of values: Extensions and cross-cultural replications. *Journal of Personality and Social Psychology, 58,* 878–891.

Schwartz, S. H., & Boehnke, K. (2004). Evaluating the structure of human values with confirmatory factor analysis. *Journal of Research in Personality, 38,* 230–255.

Schwartz, S. H., & Sagiv, L. (1995). Identifying culture specifics in the content and structure of values. *Journal of Cross-Cultural Psychology, 26,* 92–116.

Schwartz, S. J., Unger, J. B., Zamboanga, B. L., & Szapocznik, J. (2010). Rethinking the concept of acculturation: Implications for theory and research. *American Psychologist, 65,* 237–251.

Schwekendiek, D. (2009). Height and weight differences between North and South Korea. *Journal of Biosocial Science, 41,* 51–57.

Scribner, S. (1977). Modes of thinking and ways of speaking: Culture and logic reconsidered. In P. N. Johnson-Laird & P. C. Wason (Eds.), *Thinking: Reading in cognitive science* (pp. 483–500). New York, NY: Cambridge University Press.

Scribner, S., & Cole, M. (1973). Cognitive consequences of formal and informal education. *Science, 182,* 553–559.

Scribner, S., & Cole, M. (1981). *The psychology of literacy.* Cambridge, MA: Harvard University Press.

Searle, W., & Ward, C. (1990). The prediction of psychological and socio-cultural adjustment during cross-cultural transitions. *International Journal of Intercultural Relations, 14,* 449–464.

Sears, D. (1986). College sophomores in the laboratory: Influences of a narrow data base on social psychology's view of human nature. *Journal of Personality and Social Psychology, 51,* 515–530.

Seder, J. P., & Oishi, S. (2008, February). *Friend-culture: Predictors of diversity in the social networks of college students.* Poster session presented at the annual meeting of the Society for Personality and Social Psychology, Albuquerque, NM.

Sedikides, C., Gaertner, L., & Toguchi, Y. (2003). Pancultural self-enhancement. *Journal of Personality and Social Psychology, 84,* 60–79.

Seeman, M., & Seeman, T. E. (1983). Health behavior and personal autonomy—A longitudinal study of the sense of control in illness. *Journal of Health and Social Behavior, 24,* 144–160.

Segal, M. W. (1974). Alphabet and attraction: An unobtrusive measure of the effect of propinquity in a field setting. *Journal of Personality and Social Psychology, 30,* 654–657.

Segall, M. H., Campbell, D. T., & Herskovits, M. J. (1963). Cultural differences in the perception of geometric illusions. *Science, 193,* 769–771.

Segerstrom, S. C., & Miller, G. E. (2004). Psychological stress and the immune system: A meta-analytic study of 30 years of inquiry. *Psychological Bulletin, 130,* 601–630.

Seginer, R., Trommsdorff, G., & Essau, C. (1993). Adolescent control beliefs: Cross-cultural variations of primary and secondary orientations. *International Journal of Behavioral Development, 16,* 243–260.

Sen, A. K. (1999). *Development as freedom.* Oxford, UK: Oxford University Press.

Senzaki, S., Masuda, T., Takada, A., & Okada, H. (2014). *The transmission of culturally dominant modes of attention: Parent-child joint description activities in Canada and Japan.* Unpublished manuscript.

Seyfarth, R. M., Cheney, D. L., & Marler, P. (1980). Monkey responses to three different alarm calls: evidence of predator classification and semantic communication, *Science, 210,* 801–803.

Shachar, R. (1991). His and her marital satisfaction: The double standard. *Sex Roles, 25,* 451–467.

Shay, T. (1994). The level of living in Japan, 1885–1938. In J. Komlos (Ed.), *Stature, living standards, and economic development* (pp. 173–204). Chicago, IL: University of Chicago Press.

Shen, C., & Tam, H. P. (2008). The paradoxical relationship between student achievement and self-perception: A cross-national analysis based on three waves of TIMSS data. *Educational Research and Evaluation: An International Journal on Theory and Practice, 14,* 87–100.

Shen, H., Wan, F., & Wyer, R. S. (2011). Cross-cultural differences in the refusal to accept a small gift: The differential influence of reciprocity norms on Asians and North Americans. *Journal of Personality and Social Psychology, 100,* 271–281.

Shih, M., Pittinsky, T. L., & Ambady, N. (1999). Stereotype susceptibility: Identity salience and shifts in quantitative performance. *Psychological Science, 10,* 80–83.

Shin, S. M., Chow, C., Camacho-Gonsalves, T., Levy, R., Allen, I., & Leff, H. (2005). A meta-analytic review of racial-ethnic matching for African American and Caucasian American clients and clinicians. *Journal of Counseling Psychology, 52,* 45–56.

Shorter, E. (1987). The first great increase in anorexia nervosa. *Journal of Social History, 21,* 69–96.

Shweder, R. A. (1990). Cultural psychology: What is it? In J. W. Stigler, R. A. Shweder, & G. Herdt (Eds.), *Cultural psychology: Essays on comparative human development* (pp. 1–43). Cambridge, England: Cambridge University Press.

Shweder, R. A. (1997). The surprise of ethnography. *Ethos, 25,* 152–163.

Shweder, R. A. (2000). Moral maps, "first world" conceits, and the new evangelists. In L. E. Harrison & S. P. Huntington (Eds.), *Culture matters: How values shape human progress* (pp. 158–176). New York, NY: Basic Books.

Shweder, R. A., & Bourne, E. J. (1982). Does the concept of the person vary cross-culturally? In A. J. Marsella & G. M. White (Eds.), *Cultural conceptions of mental health and therapy.* New York, NY: Kluwer.

Shweder, R. A., & Bourne, E. J. (1984). Does the concept of the person vary cross-culturally? In R. A. Shweder & R. A. LeVine (Eds.), *Culture theory: Essays on mind, self and emotion* (pp. 158–199). Cambridge, England: Cambridge University Press.

Shweder, R. A., & Haidt, J. (2000). The cultural psychology of the emotions: Ancient and new. In M. Lewis & J. M. Haviland-Jones (Eds.), *Handbook of emotions* (2nd ed., pp. 397–414). New York, NY: Guilford.

Shweder, R. A., Jensen, L. A., & Goldstein, W. M. (1995). Who sleeps by whom revisited: A method for extracting the moral goods implicit in practice. In Goodnow et al. (Eds.), *Cultural practices as contexts for development: New Directions in Child Development* (pp. 21–39). San Francisco, CA: Jossey Bass.

Shweder, R. A., Much, N. C., Mahapatra, M., & Park, L. (1997). The "big three" of morality (autonomy, community, and divinity), and the "big three" explanations of suffering. In A. Brandt & P. Rozin (Eds.), *Morality and health* (pp. 119–169). New York, NY: Routledge.

Siegel, J. M. (2008). Do all animals sleep? *Trends in Neuroscience, 31,* 208–213.

Siegler, R. S., & Opfer, J. E. (2003). The development of numerical estimation: Evidence for multiple representations of numerical quantity. *Psychological Science, 14,* 237–243.

Siegrist, J., & Marmot, M. (2004). Health inequalities and the psychosocial environment—Two scientific challenges. *Social Science and Medicine, 58,* 1463–1473.

Silventoinen, K., Hammar, N., Hedlund, E., Koskenvuo, M., Ronnemaa, T., & Kaprio, J. (2008). Selective international migration by social position, health behaviour, and personality. *European Journal of Public Health, 18,* 150–155.

Simon, L., Greenberg, J., & Brehm, J. (1995). Trivialization: the forgotten mode of dissonance reduction. *Journal of Personality and Social Psychology, 68,* 247–260.

Simonton, D. K., & Ting, S. (2010). Creativity in Eastern and Western civilizations: The lessons of historiometry. *Management and Organization Review, 6,* 329–350.

Singelis, T. M., Bond, M. H., Lai, S. Y., & Sharkey, W. F. (1999). Unpackaging culture's influence on self-esteem and embarrassability: The role of self-construals. *Journal of Cross-Cultural Psychology, 30,* 315–331.

Sinha, M. (2011). Resurgence of *koro:* Perception of mankind. *Asian Journal of Psychiatry, 4,* 153–154.

Siy, J. O., & Cheryan, S. (2013). When compliments fail to flatter: American individualism and responses to positive stereotypes. *Journal of Personality and Social Psychology, 104,* 87–102.

Skolnick, A. S. (1987). *The intimate environment: Exploring marriage and family.* Boston, MA: Little, Brown.

Slingerland, E. (2003). *Confucius analects: With selections from traditional commentaries.* Indianapolis, IN: Hackett.

Smart, J. J. C. (1973). An outline of a system of utilitarian ethics. In J. J. C. Smart & B. A. O. Williams (Eds.), *Utilitarianism: For and against.* Cambridge, England: Cambridge University Press.

Smeekes, A., Verkuyten, M., & Poppe, E. (2012). How a tolerant past affects the present: Historical tolerance and the acceptance of Muslim expressive rights. *Personality and Social Psychology Bulletin, 38,* 1410–1422.

Smeraldi, E., Zanardi, R., Benedetti, F., di Bella, D., Perez, J., & Catalano, M., et al. (1998). Polymorphism within the promoter of the serotnin transporter gene and antidepressant efficacy of fluvoxamine. *Molecular Psychiatry, 3*(6), 508–511.

Smith, P. B., Trompenaars, F., & Dugan, S. (1995). The Rotter locus of control scale in 43 countries: A test of cultural relativity. *International Journal of Psychology, 30,* 377–400.

Snarey, J. (1985). The cross-cultural universality of social-moral development: A critical review of Kohlbergian research. *Psychological Bulletin, 97,* 202–232.

Snarey, J., & Keljo, K. (1991). In a Gemeinschaft voice: The cross-cultural expansion of moral development theory. In W. M. Kurtines & J. L. Gewitz (Eds.), *Handbook of moral behavior and development* (Vol. 1, pp. 395–424). Hillsdale, NJ: Erlbaum.

Snibbe, A. C., Kitayama, S., Markus, H. R., & Suzuki, T. (2003). "They saw a game": Self and group enhancement in Japan and the U.S. *Journal of Cross-Cultural Psychology, 34,* 581–595.

Snibbe, A. C., & Markus, H. R. (2005). You can't always get what you want: Social class, agency, and choice. *Journal of Personality and Social Psychology, 88,* 703–720.

Sodowsky, G. R., Kuo-Jackson, P. Y., & Loya, G. J. (1997). Outcome of training in the philosophy of assessment: Multicultural counseling competencies. In D. B. Pope-Davis & H. L. K. Coleman (Eds.), *Multicultural counseling competencies: Assessment, education and training, and supervision* (pp. 3–42). Thousand Oaks, CA: Sage.

Sorkhabi, N. (2005). Applicability of Baumrind's parent typology to collective cultures: Analysis of cultural explanations of parent socialization effects. *International Journal of Behavioral Development, 29,* 552–563.

Sorlie, P. D., Backlund, E., Johnson, N. J., & Rogot, E. (1993). Mortality by Hispanic status in the United States. *Journal of the American Medical Association, 270,* 2464–2469.

Spencer-Rodgers, J., Peng, K., Wang, L., & Hou, Y. (2004). Dialectical self-esteem and East-West differences in psychological well-being. *Personality and Social Psychology Bulletin, 30,* 1416–1432.

Sprecher, S., & Chandak, R. (1992). Attitudes about arranged marriages and dating among men and women from India. *Free Inquiry in Creative Sociology, 20,* 1–11.

Sroufe, L. A. (1979). The coherence of individual development: Early care, attachment, and subsequent developmental issues. *American Psychologist, 34,* 834–841.

Statistics Canada. (2001). *Education in Canada 2000* (Cat. No. 81–229–XIB). Ottawa, ON.

Stavrova, O., Schlösser, T., & Fetchenhauer, D. (2013). Are virtuous people happy all around the world? Civic virtue, antisocial punishment, and subjective well-being across cultures. *Personality and Social Psychology Bulletin, 39,* 927–942.

Steckel, R. H. (1983). *Height and per capita income.* NBER Working Paper No. W0880. Retrieved from http://ssrn.com/abstract5233738

Steckel, R. H. (1994). Heights and health in the United States, 1710–1950. In J. Komlos (Ed.), *Stature, living standards, and economic development* (pp. 153–172). Chicago, IL: University of Chicago Press.

Steele, C. M. (1992, April). Race and the schooling of Black Americans. *The Atlantic Monthly,* 68–80.

Steele, C. M., & Aronson, J. (1995). Stereotype threat and the intellectual test performance of African Americans. *Journal of Personality and Social Psychology, 69,* 797–811.

Steele, C. M., Spencer, S. J., & Lynch, M. (1993). Self-image resilience and dissonance: The role of affirmational resources. *Journal of Personality and Social Psychology, 64,* 885–896.

Stein, D. J. (2009). Social anxiety disorder in the West and in the East. *Annals of Clinical Psychiatry, 21,* 109–117.

Steinberg, L., Dornbusch, S., & Brown, B. B. (1992). Ethnic differences in adolescent achievement: An ecological perspective. *American Psychologist, 47,* 723–729.

Steinberg L, Lamborn, S. D., Dornbusch, S. M., & Darling, N. (1992). Impact of parenting practices on adolescent achievement: authoritative parenting, school involvement, and encouragement to succeed. *Child Development, 63*(5),1266–1281.

Stephens, N. M., Fryberg, S. A., Markus, H. R., Johnson, C. S., & Covarrubias, R. (2012). Unseen disadvantage: How American universities' focus on independence undermines the academic performance of first-generation college students. *Journal of Personality and Social Psychology, 102,* 1178–1197.

Stephens, N. M., Markus, H. R., & Townsend, S. S. M. (2007). Choice as an act of meaning: The case of social class. *Journal of Personality and Social Psychology, 93,* 814–830.

Stephens, N. M., Townsend, S. S. M., Markus, H. R., & Phillips, L. T. (2012). A cultural mismatch: Independent cultural norms produce greater increases in cortisol and more negative emotions among first-generation college students. *Journal of Experimental Social Psychology, 48,* 1389–1393.

Stern, J. T., & Susman, R. L. (1983). The locomotor anatomy of *Australopithecus afarensis. American Journal of Physical Anthropology, 60,* 279–317.

Stevenson, H. W. (1982). Influences of schooling on cognitive development. In D. A. Wagner & H. W. Stevenson (Eds.), *Cultural perspectives on child development* (pp. 208–224). San Francisco, CA: Freeman.

Stevenson, H. W. (1992). A long way to being number one: What we have to learn from East Asia. *Federation of Behavioral, Psychological and Cognitive Sciences, Science and Public Policy Seminars,* 1–17.

Stevenson, H. W., & Stigler, J. W. (1992). *The learning gap: Why our schools are failing and what we can learn from Japanese and Chinese education.* New York, NY: Summit Books.

Stewart, J. (2010). *Earth (The Book): A visitor's guide to the human race.* NY: Grand Central Publishing.

Stewart, J. E. (1980). Defendant's attractiveness as a factor in the outcome of criminal trials: An observational study. *Journal of Applied Social Psychology, 10,* 348–361.

Stigler, J. W., Shweder, R. A., & Herdt, G. (1990). *Cultural psychology: Essays on comparative human development.* Cambridge, England: Cambridge University Press.

Stone, J., Lynch, C. I., & Sjomeling, M. (1999). Stereotype threat effects on Black and White athletic performance. *Journal of Personality and Social Psychology, 77,* 1213–1227.

Stouffer, S. A., Suchman, E. A., DeVinney, L. C., Star, S. A., & Williams, R. M., Jr. (1949). *The American soldier: Adjustment during army life.* Princeton, NJ: Princeton University Press.

Strack, F., Martin, L. L., & Stepper, S. (1988). Inhibiting and facilitating conditions of the human smile: A nonobtrusive test of the facial feedback hypothesis. *Journal of Personality and Social Psychology, 54,* 768–777.

Stuürmer, S., Benvow, A. E. F., Siem, B., Barth, M., Bodansky, A. N., & Lotz-Schmitt, K. (2013). Psychological foundations of xenophilia: The role of major personality traits in predicting favorable attitudes towards cross-cultural contact and exploration. *Journal of Personality and Social Psychology, 105,* 832–851.

Su, C., & Hynie, M. (2011). Effects of life stress, social support, and cultural norms on parenting styles among Mainland Chinese, European Canadian, and Chinese Canadian immigrant mothers. *Journal of Cross-Cultural Psychology, 42,* 944–962.

Suarez-Orozco, C., & Suarez-Orozco, M. (1995). *Transformations: Migration, family life, and achievement motivation among Latino adolescents.* Stanford, CA: Stanford University Press.

Suarez-Orozco, C., & Suarez-Orozco, M. (2001). *Children of immigration.* Cambridge, MA: Harvard University Press.

Sue, S. (1998). In search of cultural competence in psychotherapy and counseling. *American Psychologist, 53,* 440–448.

Sue, S. (2006). Cultural competency: From philosophy to research and practice. *Journal of Community Psychology, 34,* 237–245.

Sue, S., Fujino, D. C., Hu, L., Takeuchi, D. T., & Zane, N. W. S. (1991). Community mental health services for ethnic minority groups: A test of the cultural responsiveness hypothesis. *Journal of Consulting and Clinical Psychology, 59,* 533–540.

Suedfeld, P., Tetlock, P. E., & Streufert, S. (1992). Conceptual/integrative complexity. In C. P. Smith (Ed.), *Motivation and personality: Handbook of thematic content analysis* (pp. 393–400). New York, NY: Cambridge University Press.

Suh, E. M. (2002). Culture, identity consistency, and subjective well-being. *Journal of Personality and Social Psychology, 83,* 1378–1391.

Suh, E. M., Diener, E., Oishi, S., & Triandis, H. C. (1998). The shifting basis of life satisfaction judgments across cultures: Emotions versus norms. *Journal of Personality and Social Psychology, 74,* 482–493.

Super, C. M. (1976). Environmental effects on motor development: the case of "African infant precocity." *Developmental Medicine and Child Neurology, 18,* 561–567.

Super, C., M., Blom, M. J. M., Harkness, S., Ranade, N., & Londhe, R. (2014). *Culture and infant sleep: A study in the Netherlands and the U.S.* Unpublished manuscript. University of Connecticut.

Sussman, N. M., & Rosenfeld, H. M. (1982). Influence of culture, language, and sex of conversational distance. *Journal of Personality and Social Psychology, 42,* 66–74.

Suwanlert, S. (1988). A study of *latah* in Thailand. *Journal of the Psychiatric Association of Thailand, 33,* 129–133.

Swami, V., et al. (2010). The attractive female body weight and female body dissatisfaction in 26 countries across 10 world regions: Results of the international body project I. *Personality and Social Psychology Bulletin, 36,* 309–325.

Sylwester, K., Herrmann, B., & Bryson, J. (2013). Homo homini lupus? Explaining antisocial punishment. *Journal of Neuroscience, Psychology, and Economics, 6*(3), 167–188.

Sypeck, M. F., Gray, J. J., & Ahrens, A. H. (2004). No longer just a pretty face: Fashion magazines' depictions of ideal female beauty from 1959 to 1999. *International Journal of Eating Disorders, 36,* 342–347.

Sypeck, M. F., Gray, J. J., Etu, S. F., Ahrens, A. H., Mosimann, J. E., & Wiseman, C. V. (2006). Cultural representations of thinness in women, redux: Playboy magazine's depiction of beauty from 1979 to 1999. *Body Image, 3,* 229–235.

Szirmák, Z., & De Raad, B. (1994). Taxonomy and structure of Hungarian personality traits. *European Journal of Personality, 8,* 95–117.

Tadmor, C. T., Galinsky, A. D., & Maddux, W. W. (2012). Getting the most out of living abroad: Biculturalism and integrative complexity as key drivers of creative and professional success. *Journal of Personality and Social Psychology, 103,* 520–542.

Tadmor, C. T., Satterstrom, P., Jang, S., & Polzer, J. T. (2012). Beyond individual creativity: The superadditive benefits of multicultural experience for collective creativity in culturally diverse teams. *Journal of Cross-Cultural Psychology, 43,* 384–392.

Tafarodi, R. W., & Swann, W. B., Jr. (1996). Individualism-collectivism and global self-esteem: Evidence for a cultural trade-off. *Journal of Cross-Cultural Psychology, 27,* 651–672.

Tajfel, H. (1970). Experiments in intergroup discrimination. *Scientific American, 223,* 96–102.

Tajfel, H. (1974). Social identity and intergroup behaviour. *Social Science Information, 13,* 65–93.

Takata, T. (2003). Self-enhancement and self-criticism in Japanese culture: An experimental analysis. *Journal of Cross-Cultural Psychology, 34,* 542–551.

Takemoto, T. (2010, July 10). Japanese superheroes are collectivists. Symposium presentation at the XX Congress of the International Association for Cross-Cultural Psychology, Melbourne, Australia.

Takemura, K. (2014). Being different leads to being connected: On the adaptive function of uniqueness in "open" societies. *Journal of Cross-Cultural Psychology, 45,* 1579–1583.

Takemura, K., Yuki, M., Kashima, E. S., & Halloran, M. (2004). A cross-cultural comparison of behaviors and independent/interdependent self-views. *Progress in Asian Psychology, 5.*

Talhelm, T., Zhang, X., Oishi, S., Shimin, C., Duan, D., Lan, X., & Kitayama, S. (2014). Large-scale psychological differences within China explained by rice versus wheat agriculture. *Science, 344,* 603–608.

Tamis-LeMonda, C. S., Bornstein, M. H., & Cyphers, L. (1992). Language and play at one year: A comparison of toddlers and mothers in the United States and Japan. *International Journal of Behavioral Development, 15,* 19–42.

Tardif, T. (1996). Nouns are not always learned before verbs: Evidence from Mandarin speakers' early vocabularies. *Developmental Psychology, 32,* 492–504.

Taylor, S. E., & Brown, J. D. (1988). Illusion and well-being: A social psychological perspective on mental health. *Psychological Bulletin, 103,* 193–210.

Taylor, S. E., Sherman, D. K., Kim, H. S., Jarcho, J., Takagi, K., & Dunagan, M. S. (2004). Culture and social support: Who seeks it and why? *Journal of Personality and Social Psychology, 87,* 354–362.

Taylor, S. E., Welch, W. T., Kim, H. S., & Sherman, D. K. (2007). Cultural differences in the impact of social support on psychological and biological stress responses. *Psychological Science, 18,* 831–837.

Teo, A. R. (2010). A new form of social withdrawal in Japan: A review of *hikikomori. International Journal of Social Psychiatry, 56,* 178–185.

Teoh, J.-I. (1972). The changing psychopathology of *amok. Psychiatry, 35,* 345–351.

Terracciano, A., et al. (2005). National character does not reflect mean personality trait levels in 49 cultures. *Science, 310,* 96–100.

Thornhill, R. (1992). Fluctuating asymmetry and the mating system of the Japanese scorpionfly *Panorpa japonica. Animal Behavior, 44,* 867–879.

Thorpe, S. K. S., Crompton, R. H., Gunther, M. M., Ker, R. F., & Alexander, R. M. (1999). Dimensions and moment arms of the hind- and forelimb muscles of common chimpanzees (*Pan troglodytes*). *American Journal of Physical Anthropology, 110,* 179–199.

Ting-Toomey, S. (Ed.). (1994). *The challenge of facework: Cross-cultural and interpersonal issues.* Albany: State University of New York Press.

Tishkoff, S. A., Reed, F. A., Ranciaro, A., Voight, B. F., Babbitt, C. G., Silverman, J. S., et al. (2007). Convergent adaptation of human lactase persistence in Africa and Europe. *Nature Genetics, 39,* 31–40.

Tobin, J. J., Wu, D. Y. H., & Davidson, D. (1989). *Preschool in three cultures.* New Haven, CT: Yale University Press.

Tomasello, M. (1996). Do apes ape? In C. M. Heyes & B. G. Galef (Eds.), *Social learning in animals: The roots of culture* (pp. 319–346). New York, NY: Academic Press.

Tomasello, M. (1999). *The cultural origins of human cognition.* Cambridge, MA: Harvard University Press.

Tomasello, M., Carpenter, M., Call, J., Behne, T., & Moll, H. (2005). Understanding and sharing intentions: The origins of cultural cognition. *Behavioral and Brain Sciences, 28,* 675–735.

Tomasello, M., Kruger, A. C., & Ratner, H. H. (1993). Cultural learning. *Behavioral and Brain Sciences, 16,* 495–552.

Tooby, J., & Cosmides, L. (1992). The psychological foundations of culture. In J. H. Barkow, L. Cosmides, & J. Tooby (Eds.), *The adapted mind: Evolutionary psychology and the generation of culture* (pp. 19–136). New York, NY: Oxford University Press.

Tracy, J. L., & Matsumoto, D. (2008). The spontaneous expression of pride and shame: Evidence for biologically innate nonverbal displays. *Proceedings of the National Academy of Sciences, 105,* 11655–11660.

Tracy, J. L., & Robins, R. W. (2008). The nonverbal expression of pride: Evidence for cross-cultural recognition. *Journal of Personality and Social Psychology, 94,* 516–530.

Trafimow, D., Triandis, H. C., & Goto, S. G. (1991). Some tests of the distinction between the private self and the collective self. *Journal of Personality and Social Psychology, 60,* 649–655.

Triandis, H. C. (1989a). Cross-cultural studies of individualism and collectivism. *Nebraska Symposium of Motivation, 37,* 41–133.

Triandis, H. C. (1989b). The self and social behavior in differing cultural contexts. *Psychological Review, 96,* 506–520.

Triandis H. C. (1994). *Culture and social behavior.* New York: McGraw-Hill

Triandis, H. C. (1996). The psychological measurement of cultural syndromes. *American Psychologist, 51,* 407–415.

Triandis, H. C., Marin, G., Lisansky, J., & Betancourt, H. (1984). *Simpatia* as a cultural script of Hispanics. *Journal of Personality and Social Psychology, 47,* 1363–1375.

Triandis, H. C., McCusker, C., & Hui, C. H. (1990). Multimethod probes of individualism and collectivism. *Journal of Personality and Social Psychology, 59,* 1006–1020.

Trommsdorff, G. (1985). Some comparative aspects of socialization in Japan and Germany. In I. R. Lagunes & Y. H. Poortinga (Eds.), *From a different perspective: Studies of behavior across cultures* (pp. 231–240). Lisse, Netherlands: Swets and Zeitlinger.

Trommsdorff, G. (1995). Parent-adolescent relations in changing societies: A cross-cultural study. In P. Noack, M. Hofer, & J. Youniss (Eds.), *Psychological responses to social change: Human development in changing environments* (pp. 189–218). Berlin, Germany: Walter de Gruyter.

Trommsdorff, G., & Iwawaki, S. (1989). Students' perceptions of socialization and gender role in Japan and Germany. *International Journal of Behavioral Development, 12,* 485–493.

Tropp, L. R., & Wright, S. C. (2003). Evaluations and perceptions of self, ingroup, and outgroup: Comparisons between Mexican-American and European-American children. *Self and Identity, 2,* 203–221.

Tsai, J. L., Chentsova-Dutton, Y., & Freire-Bebeau, L. (2002). Emotional expression and physiology in European Americans and Hmong Americans. *Emotion, 2,* 380–397.

Tsai, J. L., Knutson, B. K., & Fung, H. H. (2006). Cultural variation in affect valuation. *Journal of Personality and Social Psychology, 90,* 288–307.

Tsai, J. L., Louie, J., Chen, E., & Uchida, Y. (2006). Learning what feelings to desire: Socialization of ideal affect through children's storybooks. *Personality and Social Psychology Bulletin, 32,* 1–14.

Tsai, J. L., Miao, F. F., & Seppala, E. (2007). Good feelings in Christianity and Buddhism: Religious differences in ideal affect. *Personality and Social Psychology Bulletin, 33,* 409–421.

Tsai, J. L., Simeonova, D. I., & Watanabe, J. T. (2004). Somatic and social: Chinese Americans talk about emotion. *Personality and Social Psychology Bulletin, 30,* 1226–1238.

Tsai, J. L., Ying, Y., & Lee, P. A. (2000). The meaning of "being Chinese" and "being American": Variation among Chinese American young adults. *Journal of Cross-Cultural Psychology, 31,* 302–332.

Tseng, W. (2001). *Handbook of cultural psychiatry.* New York, NY: Academic Press.

Tucker, D. M., & Williamson, P. A. (1984). Asymmetric neural control systems in human self-regulation. *Psychological Review, 91,* 185–215.

Turner, F. J. (1920). *The frontier in American history.* New York, NY: Henry Holt.

Tuttle, R. H., Webb, D. M., & Baksh, M. (1991). Laetoli toes and *Australopithecus afarensis. Human Evolution, 6,* 193–200.

Tuttle, R. H., Webb, D. M., Weidl, E., & Baksh, M. (1990). Further progress on the Laetoli trails. *Journal of Archaeological Science, 17,* 347–362.

Tweed, R. G., & Lehman, D. R. (2002). Learning considered within a cultural context: Confucian and Socratic approaches. *American Psychologist, 57,* 89–99.

Twenge, J. M., Abebe, E. M., & Campbell, W. K. (2010). Fitting in or standing out: Trends in American parents' choices for children's names, 1880–2007. *Social Psychological and Personality Science, 1,* 19–25.

Twenge, J. M., & Campbell, W. K. (2001). Age and birth cohort differences in self-esteem: A cross-temporal meta-analysis. *Personality and Social Psychology Review, 5,* 321–344.

Twenge, J. M., Campbell, W. K., & Freeman, E. C. (2012). Generational differences in young adults' life goals, concern for others, and civic orientation, 1966, 2009. *Journal of Personality and Social Psychology, 102,* 1045–1062.

Twenge, J. M., Campbell, W. K., & Gentile, B. (2012). Generational increases in agentic self-evaluations among American college students, 1966–2009. *Self and Identity, 11,* 409–427.

Twenge, J. M., Campbell, W. K., & Gentile, B. (2013). Changes in pronoun use in American books and the rise of individualism, 1960–2008. *Journal of Cross-Cultural Psychology, 44,* 406–415.

Twenge, J. M., & Kasser, T. (2013). Generational changes in materialism and work centrality, 1976–2007: Associations with temporal changes in societal insecurity and materialistic role modeling. *Personality and Social Psychology Bulletin, 39,* 883–897.

Uchida, Y., & Kitayama, S. (2009). Happiness and unhappiness in East and West: Themes and variations. *Emotion, 9,* 441–456.

Uchida, Y., Townsend, S. S. M., Markus, H. R., & Bergsieker, H. B. (2009). Emotions as within or between people? Cultural variation in lay theories of emotion expression and inference. *Personality and Social Psychology Bulletin, 35,* 1427–1439.

Uhlmann, E. L., Heaphy, E., Ashford, S. J., Zhu, L., & Sanchez-Burks, J. (2013). Acting professional: An exploration of culturally bounded norms against nonwork role referencing. *Journal of Organizational Behavior, 34,* 866–886.

Uhlmann, E. L., Poehlman, T. A., Tannenbaum, D., & Bargh, J. A. (2011). Implicit Puritanism in American moral cognition. *Journal of Experimental Social Psychology, 47,* 312–320.

Uhlmann, E. L., & Sanchez-Burks, J. (2014). The implicit legacy of American Protestantism. *Journal of Cross-Cultural Psychology, 45,* 992–1006.

U.S. Census Bureau. (2014). Selected social characteristics in the United States: 2012 American Community Survey 1-year estimates. Retrieved from http:factfinder2.census.gov/faces/tableservices/jsf/pages/productview.xhtml?pid=ACS_12_1YR_DP02&prodType=table

Uskul, A. K., Kitayama, S. & Nisbett, R. E. (2008) Ecocultural basis of cognition: Farmers and fishermen are more holistic than herders. *Proceedings of the National Academy of Sciences of the United States of America 105,* 8552–8556.

Vagero, D., & Lundberg, O. (1989). Health inequalities in Britain and Sweden. *Lancet, 1989(2),* 35–36.

Valchev, V. H., van de Vijver, F. J. R., Nel, J. A., Rothmann, S., & Meiring, D. (2013). The use of traits and contextual information in free personality descriptions across ethnocultural groups in South Africa. *Journal of Personality and Social Psychology, 104,* 1077–1091.

Van Boven, L. (2000). Pluralistic ignorance and political correctness: The case of affirmative action. *Political Psychology, 21,* 267–276.

Van de Gaer, E., Grisay, A., Schulz, W., & Gebhardt, E. (2012). The reference group effect: An explanation for the paradoxical relationship between academic achievement and self-confidence across countries. *Journal of Cross-Cultural Psychology, 43,* 1205–1228.

Van Hoom, A., & Maseland, R. (2013). Does a Protestant work ethic exist? Evidence from the well-being effect of unemployment. *Journal of Economic Behavior & Organization, 91,* 1–12.

Vandello, J. (2004, January 30–31). *Fewer women, more violence? Examining geographic sex ratios across the United States.* Paper presented at the 5th Annual Conference of the Society of Personality and Social Psychology, Austin, TX.

Vandello, J. A., & Cohen, D. (1999). Patterns of individualism and collectivism across the United States. *Journal of Personality and Social Psychology, 77,* 279–292.

Vandello, J. A., & Cohen, D. (2003). Male honor and female fidelity: Implicit cultural scripts that perpetuate domestic violence. *Journal of Personality and Social Psychology, 84,* 997–1010.

Varnum, M. E. W., Grossmann, I., Kitayama, S., & Nisbett, R. E. (2010). The origin of cultural differences in cognition: The social orientation hypothesis. *Current Directions in Psychological Science, 19,* 9–13.

Varnum, M. E. W., Na, J., Murata, A., & Kitayama, S. (2012). Social class differences in N400 indicate differences in spontaneous trait inference. *Journal of Experimental Psychology: General, 141,* 518–526.

Vayda, E., Mindell, W. R., & Rutkow, I. M. (1982). A decade of surgery in Canada, England and Wales, and the United States. *Archives of Surgery, 117,* 846–853.

Veenhoven, R. (2014). *World Database of Happiness.* Rotterdam, The Netherlands: Erasmus University. Retrieved from http://worlddatabaseofhappiness.eur.nl

Verkuyten, M. (2005). Ethnic group identification and group evaluation among minority and majority groups. Testing the multiculturalism hypothesis. *Journal of Personality and Social Psychology, 88,* 121–138.

Verkuyten, M., & Masson, K. (1996). Culture and gender differences in the perception of friendship by adolescents. *International Journal of Psychology, 31,* 207–217.

Vohs, K. D., Mead, N. L., & Goode, M. R. (2006). The psychological consequences of money. *Science, 314,* 1154–1156.

Voight, B. F., Kudaravalli, S., Wen, X., & Pritchard, J. K. (2006). A map of recent positive selection in the human genome. *PLOS Biology, 4,* e72.

Voigtländer, N., & Voth, H.-J. (2012). Persecution perpetuated: The medieval origins of anti-Semitic violence in Nazi Germany. *The Quarterly Journal of Economics, 127,* 1339–1392.

Vorauer, J. D., Gagnon, A., & Sasaki, S. J. (2009). Salient intergroup ideology and intergroup interaction. *Psychological Science, 20,* 838–845.

Vouloumanos, A., & Werker, J. F. (2004). Tuned to the signal: The special status of speech for young infants, *Developmental Science, 7,* 270–276.

Vygotsky, L. S. (1929). The problem of the cultural development of the child II. *Journal of Genetic Psychology, 36,* 414–434.

Vygotsky, L. S. (1978). *Mind in society.* Cambridge: Harvard University Press.

Wagman, D. (2008, August 17). Anna Karenina is alive and well [Review of the book *What happened to Anna K.*] *Los Angeles Times.* Retrieved from http://articles.latimes.com/2008/aug/17/entertainment/ca-irina-reyn17

Walker, L. J. (1984). Sex differences in the development of moral reasoning: A critical review. *Child Development, 55,* 677–691.

Wallace, R., & Wallace, R. G. (2002). Immune cognition and vaccine strategy: Beyond genomics. *Microbes and Infection, 4,* 521–527.

Wang, E. T., Kodama, G., Baldi, P., & Moyzis, R. K. (2006). Global landscape of recent inferred Darwinian selection for *Homo sapiens. Proceedings of the National Academy of Sciences, 103,* 135–140.

Wang, H., Masuda, T., Ito, K., & Rashid, M. (2012). How much information? East Asian and North American cultural products and information search performance. *Personality and Social Psychology Bulletin, 38,* 1539–1551.

Wang, Q. (2001). "Did you have fun?" American and Chinese mother-child conversations about shared emotional experiences. *Cognitive Development, 16,* 693–715.

Wang, Q. (2004). The emergence of cultural self-constructs: Autobiographical memory and self-description in European American and Chinese children. *Developmental Psychology, 40,* 3–15.

Wang, Q., & Conway, M. A. (2004). The stories we keep: Autobiographical memory in American and Chinese middle-aged adults. *Journal of Personality, 72,* 911–938.

Wang, Q., Leichtman, M. D., & Davies, K. (2000). Sharing memories and telling stories: American and Chinese mothers and their 3-year-olds. *Memory, 8,* 159–177.

Ward, C. (1996). Acculturation. In D. Landis & R. S. Bhagat (Eds.), *Handbook of intercultural training* (2nd ed., pp. 124–147). Thousand Oaks, CA: Sage.

Ward, C., & Kennedy, A. (1995). Crossing-cultures: The relationship between psychological and sociocultural dimensions of cross-cultural adjustment. In J. Pandey, D. Sinha, & P. S. Bhawuk (Eds.), *Asian contributions to cross-cultural psychology* (pp. 289–306). New Delhi, India: Sage.

Watkins, D., Yau, J., Dahlin, B., & Wondimu, H. (1997). The Twenty Statements Test: Some measurement issues. *Journal of Cross-Cultural Psychology, 28,* 626–633.

Watters, E. (2010). *Crazy like us: The globalization of the American psyche.* New York, NY: Free Press.

Way, B. M., & Lieberman, M. D. (2010). Is there a genetic contribution to cultural differences? Collectivism, individualism, and genetic markers of social sensitivity. *Social, Cognitive, and Affective Neuroscience, 5,* 203–211.

Weber, M. (1904/1992). *The Protestant ethic and the spirit of capitalism.* London: Routledge.

Wegener, C., Hunt, A. E., Vanwanseele, B., Burns, J., & Smith, R. M. (2011). Effect of children's shoes on gait: a systematic review and meta-analysis. *Journal of Foot and Ankle Research, 4,* 3.

Wehr, T. A., et al. (1993). Conservation of photoperiod-responsive mechanisms in humans. *American Journal of Physiology, 265,* R846–R857.

Weininger, E. B., & Lareau, A. (2009). Paradoxical pathways: An ethnographic extension of Kohn's findings on class and childrearing. *Journal of Marriage and Family, 71,* 680–695.

Weintraub, K. J. (1978). *The value of the individual: Self and circumstance in autobiography.* Chicago, IL: University of Chicago Press.

Weiss, M. J. (1994). *Latitudes and attitudes: An atlas of American tastes, trends, politics, and passions.* Boston, MA: Little, Brown.

Weissman, M. M., Bland, R. C. Canino, G. J., Faravelli, C., Greenwald, S., Hwu, H. G., et al. (1996). Cross-national epidemiology of major depression and bipolar disorder. *Journal of the American Medical Association, 276,* 293–299.

Weisz, J. R., Rothbaum, F. M., & Blackburn, T. C. (1984). Standing out and standing in: The psychology of control in America and Japan. *American Psychologist, 39,* 955–969.

Welch, M. (2005, December). They shoot helicopters, don't they? How journalists spread rumors during Katrina. *Reasononline.* Retrieved from www.reason.com/0512/co.mw.they.shtml

Wen, J. K. (1995). Sexual beliefs and problems in contemporary Taiwan. In T.-Y. Lin, W. S. Tseng, & E. K. Yeh (Eds.), *Chinese societies and mental health* (pp. 219–230). Hong Kong: Oxford University Press.

Wenar, C. (1982). On negativism. *Human Development, 25,* 1–23.

Werker, J. F., & Tees, R. C. (1984). Cross-language speech perception: Evidence for perceptual reorganization during the first year of life. *Infant Behavior and Development, 7,* 49–63.

Wertsch, J. V. (1998). *Mind as action.* New York, NY: Oxford University Press.

Westermarck, E. (1922). *The history of human marriage* (Vol. 2, 5th ed.) New York, NY: Allerton.

White, K., & Lehman, D. R. (2005). Culture and social comparison seeking: The role of self-motives. *Personality and Social Psychology Bulletin, 31,* 232–242.

Whiten, A. (1998). Imitation of the sequential structure of actions by chimpanzees. *Journal of Comparative Psychology, 112,* 270–281.

Whiten, A., Goodall, J., McGrew, W. C., Nishida, T., Reynolds, V., Sugiyama, Y., et al. (1999). Cultures in chimpanzees. *Nature, 399,* 682–685.

Whiting, B. B. (1976). Unpackaging variables. In K. F. Riegel & J. A. Meacham (Eds.), *The changing individual in a changing world* (Vol. 1, pp. 303–309). Chicago, IL: Aldine.

Whiting, J. W. M. (1964). The effects of climate on certain cultural practices. In W. H. Goodenough (Ed.), *Explorations in cultural anthropology: Essays in honor of George Peter Murdock* (pp. 511–544). New York, NY: McGraw-Hill.

Whiting, J. W. M., & Whiting, B. B. (1979). Aloofness and intimacy of husbands and wives: A cross-cultural study. *Ethos, 3,* 183–207.

Whiting, R. (1990). *You gotta have wa.* New York, NY: Vintage Departures.

Whitwell, G., de Souza, C., & Nicholas, S. (1997). Height, health, and economic growth in Australia, 1860–1940. In R. H. Steckel & R. Floud (Eds.), *Health and welfare during industrialization* (pp. 379–422). Chicago, IL: University of Chicago Press.

Whorf, B. L. (1956). *Language, thought, and reality.* Cambridge, MA: MIT Press.

Wierzbicka, A. (1986). Human emotions: Universal or culture specific? *American Anthropologist, 88,* 584–594.

Wiley, A. S. (2005). Does milk make children grow? Relationships between milk consumption and height in NHANES 1999–2002. *American Journal of Human Biology, 17,* 425–441.

Wilkinson, R., & Pickett, K. (2009). *The spirit level: why greater equality makes societies stronger.* New York, NY: Bloomsbury Press.

Wilkinson, R. G. (1994). The epidemiological transition: From material scarcity to social disadvantage? *Daedalus, 123,* 61–77.

Williams, D. R. (2003). The health of men: Structured inequalities and opportunities. *American Journal of Public Health, 93,* 724–731.

Williams, D. R. (2005, May 6). *Understanding the relationship between race and health: Patterns, paradoxes, and prospects.* Presentation at the Canadian Institute for Advanced Research. Theme: Successful Societies, Cambridge, MA.

Williams, D. R., Yu, Y., Jackson, J. S., & Anderson, N. B. (1997). Racial differences in physical and mental health: Socio-economic status, stress, and discrimination. *Journal of Health Psychology, 2,* 335–351.

Williams, J., & Best, D. (1990). *Sex and psyche: Gender and self viewed cross-culturally.* Beverly Hills, CA: Sage.

Williams, L., Ricciardelli, L. A., McCabe, M. P. Waqa, G., & Bavadra, K. (2006). Body image attitudes and concerns among indigenous Fijian and European Australian adolescent girls. *Body Image, 3,* 275–287.

Williams, T. P., & Sogon, S. (1984). Group composition and conforming behavior in Japanese students. *Japanese Psychological Research, 26,* 231–234.

Williamson, S. H., Hubisz, M. J., Clark, A. G., Payseur, B. A., Bustamante, C. D., & Nielsen, R. (2007). Localizing recent adaptive evolution in the human genome. *PLOS Genetics, 3,* e90.

Wilson, C. (1994). Paris targets Asia's rich markets. *Asian Business, 30,* 52.

Wilss, W. (1982). *The science of translation: Problems and methods.* Tuebingen: Narr.

Winawer, J., Witthoft, N., Frank, M. C., Wu, L., Wade, A. R., & Boroditsky, L. (2007). Russian blues reveal effects of language on color discrimination. *Proceedings of the National Academy of Sciences, 104,* 7780–7785.

Winkielman, P. & Cacioppo, J. T. (2001). Mind at ease puts a smile on the face: Psychophysiological evidence that processing facilitation elicits positive affect. *Journal of Personality and Social Psychology, 81,* 989–1000.

Wise, P. (1993). Confronting racial disparities in infant mortality: Reconciling science and politics. *American Journal of Preventive Medicine, 9* (supplement), 7–16.

Wiseman, C. V., Gray, J. J., Mosimann, J. E., & Ahrens, A. H. (1992). Cultural expectations of thinness in women: An update. *International Journal of Eating Disorders, 11,* 85–89.

Witkin, H. A. (1969). *Social influences in the development of cognitive style.* New York, NY: Rand McNally.

Witkin, H. A., & Berry, J. W. (1975). Psychological differentiation in cross-cultural perspective. *Journal of Cross-Cultural Psychology, 6,* 4–87.

Wittchen, H. U., & Fehm, L. (2003). Epidemiology and natural course of social fears and social phobia. *Acta Psychiatrica Scandinavica, 108,* 4–18.

Wolsko, C., Park, B., Judd, C. M., and Wittenbrink, B. (2000). Framing interethnic ideology: effects of multicultural and color-blind perspectives on judgments of groups and individuals. *Journal of Personality and Social Psychology, 78*(4), 635–654.

Wong, N. Y., & Ahuvia, A. C. (1998). Personal taste and family face: Luxury consumption in Confucian and Western societies. *Psychology & Marketing, 15,* 423–441.

Wong, R. Y. M., & Hong, Y. (2005). Dynamic influences of culture on cooperation in the Prisoner's Dilemma. *Psychological Science, 16,* 429–434.

Wong, S., & Goodwin, R. (2009). Experiencing marital satisfaction across three cultures: A qualitative study. *Journal of Social and Personal Relationships, 26,* 1011–1028.

Woodard, C. (2011). *American nations.* New York, NY: Penguin.

World Heath Organization. (1973). *The international pilot study of schizophrenia.* Geneva, Switzerland: WHO.

World Health Organization. (2004). *Country reports and charts.* Retrieved from www.who.int/mental_health/prevention/suicide/country_reports/en/index.html

World Health Organization. (2005). *WHO global comparable estimates.* Retrieved from www.who.int/ncd_surveillance/infobase/web/InfoBase Common

Worthman, C. M., & Melby, M. K. (2002). Toward a comparative developmental ecology of human sleep. In M. A. Carskadon (Ed.), *Adolescent sleep patterns* (pp. 69–117). Cambridge, England: Cambridge University Press.

Wrangham, R. (2009). *Catching fire: How cooking made us human.* New York, NY: Basic Books.

Wu, S., & Keysar, B. (2007). Cultural effects on perspective taking. *Psychological Science, 18,* 600–606.

Wundt, W. (1921). *Elements of folk psychology.* London: Allen & Unwin.

Xie, L., et al. (2013). Sleep drives metabolite clearance from the adult brain. *Science, 342,* 372–377.

Xu, X., & Whyte, M. K. (1990). Love matches and arranged marriages: A Chinese replication. *Journal of Marriage and the Family, 52,* 709–722.

Yamada, A., & Singelis, T. M. (1999). Biculturalism and self-construal. *International Journal of Intercultural Relations, 23,* 697–709.

Yamagishi, T., Cook, K. S., & Watabe, M. (1998). Uncertainty, trust, and commitment formation in the United States and Japan. *American Journal of Sociology, 104,* 165–194.

Yamagishi, T., & Yamagishi, M. (1994) Trust and commitment in the United States and Japan. *Motivation and Emotion, 18,* 9–66.

Yamaguchi, S., Gelfand, M., Ohashi, M. M., & Zemba, Y. (2005). The cultural psychology of control: Illusions of personal versus collective control in the United States and Japan. *Journal of Cross-Cultural Psychology, 36,* 750–761.

Yap, P. M. (1951). Mental diseases peculiar to certain cultures: A survey of comparative psychiatry. *Journal of Mental Science, 97,* 313–327.

Yelsma, P., & Athappilly, K. (1988). Marital satisfaction and communication practices: Comparisons among Indian and American couples. *Journal of Comparative Family Studies, 19,* 37–54.

Yeshurun, Y., & Sobel, N. (2010). An odor is not worth a thousand words: From multidimensional odors to unidimensional odor objects. *Annual Review of Psychology, 61,* 219–241.

Yi, X., et al. (2010). Sequencing of 50 human exomes reveals adaptation to high altitude. *Science, 329,* 75–78.

Yik, M. S. M., Russell, J. A., Ahn, C., Fernandez-Dols, J. M., & Suzuki, N. (2002). Relating the five-factor model of personality to a circumplex model of affect: A five language study. In R. R. McCrae & J. Allik (Eds.), *The Five-Factor Model of personality across cultures* (pp. 79–104). New York, NY: Kluwer.

Ying, Y., & Liese, L. H. (1991). Emotional well-being of Taiwan students in the U.S.: An examination of pre- to post-arrival differential. *International Journal of Intercultural Relations, 15,* 345–366.

Yoshida, K., Ito, K., Sato, K., Takahashi, H., Kamata, M., Higuchi, H., et al. (2002). Influence of the serotonin transporter gene-linked polymorphic region on the antidepressant response to fluvoxamine in Japanese depressed patients. *Progress in Neuro-Psychopharmacology and Biological Psychiatry, 26,* 383–386.

Yoshihara, M. (2007). *Musicians from a different shore: Asians and Asian Americans in classical music.* Philadelphia, PA: Temple University Press.

You, J., Fung, H. H., & Isaacowitz, D. M. (2009). Age differences in dispositional optimism. A cross-cultural study. *European Journal of Aging, 6,* 247–252.

Young, L. R., & Nestle, M. (2007). Portion sizes and obesity: Responses of fast-food companies. *Journal of Public Health Policy, 28,* 238–248.

Young, M. J., Morris, M. W., Burrus, J., Krishnan, L., & Regmi, M. P. (2011). Deity and destiny: Patterns of fatalistic thinking in Christian and Hindu cultures. *Journal of Cross-Cultural Psychology, 42,* 1030–1053.

Yuki, M., Maddux, W. W., & Masuda, T. (2007). Are the windows to the soul the same in the East and West? Cultural differences in using the eyes and mouth as cues to recognize emotions in Japan and the United States. *Journal of Experimental Social Psychology, 43,* 303–311.

Yuki, M., Schug, J., Horikawa, H., Takemura, K., Sato, K., Yokota, K., et al. (2007). *Development of a scale to measure perceptions of relational mobility in society (CERSS Working Paper 75).* Sapporo, Japan: Hokkaido University, Center for Experimental Research in Social Sciences.

Zajonc, R. B. (1968). Attitudinal effects of mere exposure. *Journal of Personality and Social Psychology Monograph Supplement, 9*(2, pt. 2), 1–27.

Zajonc, R. B. (2005). *Preferences.* Invited address at the 6th Convention of the Society for Personality and Social Psychology, New Orleans, LA.

Zajonc, R. B., Heingartner, A., & Herman, E. M. (1969). Social enhancement and impairment of performance in the cockroach. *Journal of Personality and Social Psychology, 13,* 83–92.

Zajonc, R. B., Wilson, W. R., & Rajecki, D. W. (1975). Affiliation and social discrimination produced by brief exposure in day old domestic chicks. *Animal Behavior, 23,* 131–138.

Zarate, M. A., Uleman, J. S., & Voils, C. I. (2001). Effects of culture and processing goals on the activation and binding of trait concepts. *Social Cognition, 19,* 295–323.

Zatzick, D. F., & Dimsdale, J. E. (1990). Cultural variation in response to painful stimuli. *Psychosomatic Medicine, 52,* 544–557.

Zax, M., & Takahashi, S. (1967). Cultural influences on response style: Comparisons of Japanese and American college students. *Journal of Social Psychology, 71,* 3–10.

Zborowski, M. (1969). *People in pain.* San Francisco: Jossey-Bass.

Zhang, F. C., Mitchell, J. E., Kuang, L., Wang, M. Y., Yang, D. L., Zheng, J., et al. (1992). The prevalence of anorexia nervosa and bulimia nervosa among freshman medical college students in China. *International Journal of Eating Disorders, 12,* 209–214.

Zhang, M. (1989). The diagnosis and phenomenology of neurasthenia: A Shanghai study. *Culture, Medicine and Psychiatry, 13,* 147–161.

Zhang, R., & Li, L. M. W. (2014). The acculturation of relational mobility: An investigation of Asian Canadians. *Journal of Cross-Cultural Psychology, 45,* 1390–1410.

Zhang, R., & Noels, K. A. (2012). When ethnic identities vary: Cross-situation and within-situation variation, authenticity, and well-being. *Journal of Cross-Cultural Psychology, 44,* 552–573.

Zheng, X., & Berry, J. W. (1991). Psychological adaptation of Chinese sojourners in Canada. *International Journal of Psychology, 26,* 451–470.

Zhou, B., Lacroix, F., Sasaki, J., Peng, Y., Wang, X., & Ryder, A. G. (2014). Unpacking cultural variations in social axiety and the offensive-type of *taijin kyofusho* through the indirect effects of intolerance of uncertainty and self-construals. *Journal of Cross-Cultural Psychology, 45,* 1561–1578.

Zhou, M. (1997). Growing up American: The challenge confronting immigrant children and children of immigrants. *Annual Review of Sociology, 23,* 63–95.

Zhou, M., & Bankston, C. L. (1998). *Growing up American: How Vietnamese children adapt to life in the United States.* New York, NY: Sage.

Zhou, X., Dere, J., Zhu, X., Yao, S., Chentsova-Dutton, Y. E., & Ryder, A. G. (2011). Anxiety symptom presentations in Han Chinese and Euro-Canadian outpatients: Is distress always somatised in China? *Journal of Affective Disorders, 135,* 111–114.

Zhu, Y., Zhang, L., Fan, J., & Han, S. (2007). Neural basis of cultural influence on self-representation. *Neuroimage, 34,* 1310–1316.

Zielenziger, M. (2006). *Shutting out the sun: How Japan created its own lost generation.* New York, NY: Vintage Books.

Zillmann, D. (1978). Attribution and misattribution of excitatory reactions. In J. H. Harvey, W. J. Ickes, & R. F. Kidd (Eds.), *New directions in attribution research* (Vol. 2, pp. 335–370). Hillsdale, NJ: Erlbaum.

Zimmermann, J., & Neyer, F. J. (2013). Do we become a different person when hitting the road? Personality development of sojourners. *Journal of Personality and Social Psychology, 105,* 515–530.

Zola, I. K. (1966). Culture and symptoms: An analysis of patients' presenting complaints. *American Sociological Review, 31,* 615–630.

Zuckerman, M. (1979). Attribution of success and failure revisited, or the motivational bias is alive and well in attribution theory. *Journal of Personality, 47,* 245–287.

CREDITS

Chapter 1

Page 2: © Ariadne Van Zandbergen / Africa Imagery / African Pictures / The Image Works; **p. 12:** Figure from Trey Hedden et al., "Cultural influences on neural substrates of attentional control." *Psychological Science* 19(1), pp. 12–17, copyright © 2008 by the Association for Psychological Science. Reprinted by Permission of SAGE Publications; **p.13** (left): © Photoagency Interpress/Global Look/Corbis; **p.13** (right): Reprinted by permission from Macmillan Publishers Ltd.: Nature, 427, 311–312. Draganski, B., Gaser, C., Busch, V., Schuierer, G., Bogdahn, U., & May, A. (2004). Changes in grey matter induced by training. www.unil.ch/lren; **p.16:** Gilbert Herdt; **p.20:** © 2/Sam Diephuis/Ocean/Corbis; **p.29:** © The New Yorker Collection, 2005, Robert Weber, from cartoonbank.com. All Rights Reserved.

Chapter 2

Page 34: © age fotostock / Alamy; **p.36:** Drawing by Jay Matternes. From The History of Noell's Ark Gorilla Show Book Cover by Anna Mae Noell (1979); **p.38:** Anup Shah/Nature Picture Library; **p.40:** © The New Yorker Collection, 2001, David Sipress, from cartoonbank.com; **p.41:** © Splash News/Corbis; **p.45:** © The New Yorker Collection, 1995, Leo Cullum, from cartoonbank.com. All Rights Reserved.; **p.47:** From Hough, W. (1992). Synoptic series of objects in the United States National Museum Illustrating the History of Inventions, Proceedings of the United States National Museum, 60, art. 9, p.2, pl. 16; **p.48:** Robert Leighton The New Yorker Collection/The Cartoon Bank; **p.59:** Inoue, S., & Matsuzawa, T. (2007). Working memory of numerals in chimpanzees. Current Biology, 17, R1004–R1005; **p.61–62** (from left to right): Steve Heine; Isselee/Dreamstime; Tim Jenner/Dreamstime.

Chapter 3

Page 66: Religious Images/UIG/Getty Images; **p.68:** © The New Yorker Collection, 2002, Peter Steiner, from cartoonbank.com. All Rights Reserved.; **p.69:** © Corbis; **p.71:** © The New Yorker Collection, 1994, Mick Stevens, from cartoonbank. com. All Rights Reserved.; **p. 74:** Figure 10.1–Major Axes of the Continents from *Guns, Germs and Steel: The Fate of Human Societies* by Jared Diamond. Copyright © 1997 by Jared Diamond. Used by permission of W.W. Norton & Company, Inc. and by permission of The Random House Group Limited; **p. 75:** Figure 1 from T. Talhelm et al. "Large-scale psychological differences within China explained by rice versus wheat agriculture." *Science* 344(6184):603–608. May 2014. Copyright © 2014, American Association for the Advancement of Science. Reprinted with permission from AAAS; **p.78** (top): National Geographic/Getty Images; **p.78** (bottom): Malcolm Linton/Liaison/Getty Images; **p.80:** Bettmann/Corbis; **p.84:** Corbis; **p.90:** Illustration by H.J. Ford in The yellow

Association, Inc. Vol 55, No. 7, 709–720; **p.291:** ©Focus Films/Courtesy Everett Collection.

Chapter 8

Page 298: © Tibor Bognar / Alamy; **p. 303:** "Rosenberg Self Esteem Scale" from *Society and the Adolescent Self-Image*, revised edition. Middletown, CT: Wesleyan University Press (1989). Morris Rosenberg. Reprinted with permission of Dr. Florence Rosenberg and the Morris Rosenberg Foundation; **p.304:** Christian Petersen/Getty Images; **p.308:** © The New Yorker Collection, 2002, Barbara Smaller, from cartoonbank.com. All Rights Reserved; **p.309:** Courtesy of Coren L. Apicella; **p.316:** Alamy; **p.330:** © Money Sharma/Demotix/Corbis; **p.333:** Bruce Eric Kaplan/The New Yorker Collection/The Cartoon Bank.

Chapter 9

Page 344: © Penny Tweedie / Alamy; **p.347** (top): Rijksmuseum, Amsterdam, The Netherlands / Bridgeman Images; **p.347** (bottom): © Brooklyn Museum/Corbis; **p.348** (left): Smithsonian Institution/CORBIS; **p.348** (right): Royal Ontario Museum/CORBIS; **p.352:** © Zoonar GmbH / Alamy; **p.358** (both): Drawings courtesy of Takahiko Masuda; **p.367:** © MariaTkach/iStock; **p. 389:** Figure 1 reprinted from *Cognition* 130(2), A. Majid & N. Burenhult, "Odors are expressible in language, as long as you speak the right language," pp. 266–270. Copyright © 2014, with permission from Elsevier; **p.391:** © The New Yorker Collection, 2002, from Pat Byrnes cartoonbank.com. All Rights Reserved; **p.393:** Courtesy of Lera Boroditsky; **p.396:** Peter Gordon, Numerical Cognition Without Words: Evidence from Amazonia. Science 15 October 2004: Vol. 306 no. 5695 pp. 496-499. Reprinted with permission from AAAS.

Chapter 10

Page 400: © ZUMA Press, Inc. / Alamy; **p.402:** Photograph from Rosaldo, M. Z. (1980). Knowledge and Passion: Ilongot notions of self and social life. Cambridge University Press: Cambridge: 1980. p. 161. Reprinted with permission of Cambridge University Press; **p.404:** Bettmann/Corbis; **p.406:** University of Nebraska, Lincoln Psychology Department; **p.411:** Copyright Paul Ekman, www.paulekman.com; **p.412:** Photographs courtesy of Dacher Keltner; **p.413:** Courtesy of Jess Tracy;

p.415: Courtesy of ARC. The "Reading the Mind in the Eyes" Test Revised Version: A Study with Normal Adults, and Adults with Asperger Syndrome or High-functioning Autism Simon Baron-Cohen, Sally Wheelwright, Jacqueline Hill, Yogini Raste andIan Plumb. Journal of Child Psychology and Psychiatry Volume 42, Issue 2, pages 241–251, February 2001; **p.417** (far left): David Crausby / Alamy; **p.417** (left): bluecrayola/Shutterstock; **p.417** (right): Chris Willson / Alamy; **p.417** (far right): Everett Kennedy Brown / epa / Corbis; **p.419:** Photographs courtesy of Dacher Keltner; **p.420** (left): Shutterstock; **p.420** (right): © Chris Strong/Agefotostock; **p.425:** © The New Yorker Collection, 2003, Roz Chast, from the cartoonbank.com. All Rights Reserved; **p.432:** © The New Yorker Collection, 2004, Robert Mankoff, from cartoonbank.com. All Rights Reserved; **p.438** (left): © Jon Burbank / The Image Works; **p.438** (right): Tom Merton/Getty Images.

Chapter 11

Page 442: © Paul Liebhardt/Corbis; **p.444:** Kevin Mazur/WireImage/Getty Images; **p.446** (top left): Kevin R. Morris/CORBIS; **p.446** (top right): Gavin Hellier/JAI/CORBIS; **p.446** (bottom left): Remi Benali/Corbis; **p.446** (bottom center): © Michele and Tom Grimm / Alamy; **p.446** (bottom right): Walter McBride/Retna Ltd./Corbis; **p.448:** Courtesy of Gillian Rhodes. Rhodes et al. (2005). Attractiveness of own-race, other-race, and mixed-race faces. Perception, 34, 319–340; **p.450** (left): Scala / Art Resource, NY; **p.450** (center): Scala/Art Resource, NY; **p.450** (right): © Nina Prommer/Retna Ltd./Corbis; **p.456:** © Catchlight Visual Services / Alamy; **p. 458 text excerpt:** Excerpt from "Beware of Friends" by Kojo Gyinaye Kyei. Originally published in *No Time to Die* (Accra, Ghana: Catholic Press, 1975). Copyright © 1975 by Kojo Gyinaye Kyei and Hannah Schreckenbach. Reprinted by permission of Hannah Schreckenbach; **p.458:** Courtesy of Glenn Adams; **p.460:** AP Photo/The Decatur Daily, Gary Cosby Jr.; **p.466:** © Jon Hicks/Corbis; **p.469:** David Butow/Redux; **p.474:** Mike Twohy The New Yorker Collection/The Cartoon Bank.

Chapter 12

Page 478: © Flirt / Alamy; **p.481:** Luke MacGregor/Reuters /Landov; **p.482:** © The New Yorker

NAME INDEX

SUBJECT INDEX